The Computer Glossary

The Computer Glossary

The Complete Illustrated Dictionary

Ninth Edition

Alan Freedman

AMACOM
American Management Association
New York • Atlanta • Boston • Chicago • Kansas City • San Francisco • Washington, D.C.
Brussels • Toronto • Mexico City

Special discounts on bulk quantities of AMACOM books are available to corporations, professional associations, and other organizations. For details, contact Special Sales Department, AMACOM, a division of American Management Association, 1601 Broadway, New York, NY 10019.
Tel.: 212-903-8316. Fax: 212-903-8083.
Web Site: www.amacombooks. org

This publication is designed to provide accurate and authoritative information in regard to the subject matter covered. It is sold with the understanding that the publisher is not engaged in rendering legal, accounting, or other professional service. If legal advice or other expert assistance is required, the services of a competent professional person should be sought.

Library of Congress Cataloging-in-Publication Data

Freedman, Alan, 1942-
        The computer glossary : the complete illustrated
dictionary / Alan Freedman. — 9th ed.
        p. cm.
        ISBN 0-8144-7094-7 (pbk)
1.   Computers–Dictionaries.   2. Electronic data
processing–Dictionaries.   I. Title.

QA76.15.F733 2000
004'.03–dc21

                                        00-055868

Printing number

10 9 8 7 6 5 4 3 2 1

To my Mother,
Who had the vision to send me to
"Automation School"
in 1960.

Illustrations: Peter Felperin and Alan Freedman
Editorial/Production: Irma Lee Morrison
Copy Editing: Lynn Thompson
Publishing Software: PageMaker 6.5
Fonts: Garamond, Helvetica, Courier

A Note from the Author

The purpose of *The Computer Glossary* is
to provide a meaningful definition of the
most important terms in the computer
industry, whether they be hardware or
software products or concepts. I hope you
find it helpful. If there are entries you feel
should be added to the next book, please
contact me by whatever method is most
convenient for you. Thank you for using the
Glossary.

The Computer Language Company Inc.
5521 State Park Road
Point Pleasant, PA 18950
voice: (215) 297-8082
fax: (215) 297-8424
e-mail: freedman@computerlanguage.com
Web: www.computerlanguage.com

Table of Contents

Acknowledgments

It would be impossible to put this book together without the help of hundreds of engineers and public relations people who work for the hardware and software companies. In addition, many readers have contributed terms, suggestions and comments. To all of you, thank you for your assistance.

There are some people that have made important contributions throughout the history of this book, and I would like to acknowledge each of them (in alphabetical order). Many thanks to Paul T. Bergevin, Pamela J. Brannan, Jagdish Dalal, Gary Dawson, Stephen C. Diascro, Jr., Thom Drewke, James J. Farrell, III, Max Fetzer, Lynn Frankel, Steve Gibson, Peter Hermsen, Margaret A. Herrick, Walter A. Levy, Leonard Mikolajczak, Terry O'Donnell, Joel Orr, Gary Saxer, Mark and Joan Shapiro, Stephen Slade, Jim Stroh, Skip Vaccarello, David Wallace, Irving L. Wieselman, Robert F. Williams, Paul & Jan Witte and most importantly, my wife and partner, Irmalee Morrison. I love you dearly Irmalee!

Computer Words You Gotta Know

Computer and Information Basics
hardware
software
data
computer
computer system

minicomputer
mainframe
program
analog
digital

binary
bit
byte
peripheral
floppy disk

hard disk
laser printer
scanner
monitor
keyboard

pointing device
modem
VGA
resolution
font

operating system
DBMS
bus
chip
PC

Macintosh
LAN
Ethernet
Token Ring
x86

client/server
palmtop
laptop computer
notebook computer
local bus

ISA
PCI
AGP
USB
SIMM

DIMM
motherboard
IDE
SCSI
Zip disk

Windows
DOS

Networking
network administrator
communications protocol
LAN
WAN
OSI

topology
Ethernet
Token Ring
ATM
NetWare

TCP/IP
ISDN
DSL
56 Kbps modem
routable protocol

repeater
bridge
router
gateway
hub

layer 3 switch
online services
Windows
client/server
file server

application server
database server
remote access server
UNIX
Windows

Internet

Internet
World Wide Web
intranet
extranet
browser

URL
push technology
FTP
cookie file
e-commerce

Webmaster
Web server
spamming
RealAudio
IP address

ISP
streaming audio
GIF
JPEG
POP

IMAP
HTML
CGI
Perl
Active Server Page

Mainframes

mainframe
channel
front end processor
TP monitor
DASD

dumb terminal
intelligent terminal
frontware
System/360, System/370, System/390
Parallel Sysplex

Irma
SNA
MVS
OS/390
VM

CICS
IMS
TSO
DB2

Graphics & Multimedia

graphics
graphics accelerator
paint program
drawing program
multimedia

image editing
image processing
bit depth
ray tracing
digitizer tablet

Bezier
spline
bitblt
sound card
digitizer tablet

artifact
virtual reality
MIDI
DVD
CD-ROM

CD-R
GIF
BMP
WMF

JPEG
TIFF

A

abend

(ABnormal END) Also called a "crash" or "bomb," it occurs when the computer is presented with instructions or data it cannot recognize or the program is reaching beyond its protective boundary. It is the result of erroneous software logic or hardware failure. A robust operating system allows the offending program to end and continues, otherwise the computer locks up and the user must reboot.

abort

(1) To exit a function or application without saving any data that has been changed.

(2) To stop a transmission.

absolute

In programming, a mathematical function that always returns a positive number. For example, ABS(25-100) yields 75, not -75.

address space of program

abend

This instruction erroneously points outside of its address space into a foreign region of memory.

machine instructions

absolute address

An explicit identification of a memory location, peripheral device, or location within a device. For example, memory byte 107,443, disk drive 2 and sector 238 are absolute addresses. The computer uses absolute addresses to reference memory and peripherals. See *base address* and *relative address*.

abstract data type

A unique data type that is defined by the programmer. It may refer to an object class in object-oriented programming or to a special data type created in traditional, non-OOP languages.

AC

(Alternating Current) The common form of electricity from power plant to home/office. Its direction is reversed 60 times per second in the U.S.; 50 times in Europe. Contrast with *DC*.

AC-3

(Active Coding-3) Dolby's third digital audio coding technology based on a perceptual coding method. It is more advanced than AC-2 and provides six channels of audio in less space than two-channel stereo CD. AC-3 is used in Dolby Digital.

accelerator

A key combination used to activate a task. See *accelerator board* and *graphics accelerator*.

accelerator board

An add-in board that replaces the existing CPU with a higher performance CPU. See *graphics accelerator*.

acceptance test

A test performed by the end user to determine if the system is working according to the specifications in the contract.

access

To store data on and retrieve data from a disk or other peripheral device. See *access arm, access method* and *Microsoft Access*.

access arm

The mechanical arm that moves the read/write head across the surface of a disk similar to a tone arm on a phonograph. The access arm is directed by instructions in the operating system to move the read/write head to a specific track on the disk. The rotation of the disk positions the read/write head over the required sector.

ACCESS.bus

A serial bus that allows a variety of slow-speed peripherals (mouse, keyboard, etc.) to be daisy chained together using telephone wire. Providing a total bandwidth of 100 Kbps, it never caught on and has been superseded by the much faster USB.

access charge

The charge imposed by a communications service or telephone company for the use of its network.

access code

(1) An identification number and/or password used to gain access into a computer system.

(2) The number used as a prefix to a calling number in order to gain access to a telephone service.

access control

The management of permissions for logging onto a computer or network. See *security*.

access line

The line from a customer site to a telephone company's central office.

access method

A software routine that is part of the operating system or network control program which performs the storing/retrieving or transmitting/receiving of data. It is also responsible for detecting a bad transfer of data caused by hardware or network malfunction and correcting it if possible.

access point

A base station in a wireless LAN. Access points are typically stand-alone devices that plug into an Ethernet hub or server. Like a cellular phone system, users can roam around with their mobile devices and be handed off from one access point to the other. See *wireless LAN*.

access provider

An organization that lets users gain entrance to a network, typically the Internet. It generally refers to a smaller Internet service provider (ISP) rather than a UUNET or MCI, which would be called a "service provider." See *ISP*.

access rights

The privileges that are granted to a user, or perhaps to a program, to read, write and erase files in the computer system. Access rights can be tied to a particular server, to directories within that server or to specific programs and data files.

access server

See *communications server*.

access time

(1) Memory access time is how long it takes for a character in memory to be transferred to or from the CPU. In a personal computer, fast RAM chips have an access time of 70 nanoseconds or less. SDRAM chips have a burst mode that obtains the second and subsequent characters in 10 ns or less.

(2) Disk access time is an average of the time it takes to position the read/write head over the requested track. Fast personal computer hard disks have access times of 18 milliseconds or less. Mainframe disks can be less than one millisecond.

accessibility

The ability to gain access to something. With regard to software, it refers either to programs that aid the visually impaired or to electronic distribution.

accumulator

A hardware register used to hold the results or partial results of arithmetic and logical operations.

ACD

(Automatic Call Distribution) Routing incoming telephone calls to the next available operator.

ACF

(Advanced Communications Function) An official product line name for IBM SNA programs, such as VTAM (ACF/VTAM), NCP (ACF/NCP), etc.

ACK

(ACKnowledgment code) The communications code sent from a receiving station to a transmitting station to indicate that it is ready to accept data. It is also used to acknowlege the error-free receipt of transmitted data. Contrast with *NAK*.

ACM

(Association for Computing Machinery, New York, www.acm.org) A membership organization founded in 1947 dedicated to advancing the arts and sciences of information processing. In addition to awards and publications, ACM also maintains special interest groups (SIGs) in the computer field.

acoustic coupler

A device that connects a terminal or computer to the handset of a telephone. It contains a shaped foam bed that the handset is placed in, and it may also contain the modem.

ACPI

(Advanced Configuration and Power Interface) A power management specification developed by Intel, Toshiba and Microsoft that makes hardware status information available to the operating system. ACPI enables a PC to turn its peripherals on and off for improved power management especially in portables.

Acrobat

Document exchange software from Adobe that allows documents created on one platform to be displayed and printed exactly the same on another. An Acrobat driver works with most applications to convert DOS, Windows, UNIX and Mac documents into the Portable Document Format (PDF), which is displayed on the target machine with a free Acrobat reader.

Active Channel

An information delivery system from Microsoft that provides a platform for "pushing" information to users from Internet content providers as well as from internal intranets. Active Channels, which are supported in Internet Explorer Version 4.0 and Windows 98, are based on Microsoft's Channel Definition Format (CDF). See *Active Desktop*.

Active Desktop

Enhanced functionality on the desktop that is part of Internet Explorer 4.0 and higher and Windows 98. It enables Web pages to be turned into desktop items that are updated automatically. A Web page can also be turned into wallpaper, allowing a workgroup home page to be readily visible on each user's computer with links to related information on the intranet. See *Active Channel*.

Active Directory

An advanced, hierarchical directory service that comes with Windows 2000. It is LDAP compliant and built on the Internet's Domain Naming System (DNS). Workgroups are given domain names, just like Web sites, and any LDAP-compliant client (Windows, Mac, UNIX, etc.) can gain access to it. See *directory service*.

active hub

The central connecting device in a network that regenerates signals. Contrast with *passive hub* and *intelligent hub*. See *hub*.

active matrix

An LCD technology used in flat panel computer displays. It produces a brighter and sharper display with a broader viewing angle than passive matrix screens. Active matrix technology uses a thin film transistor at each pixel and is often designated as a "TFT screen." See *passive matrix* and *LCD*.

Active Server Page

A Web page that contains programming code written in VB Script or Jscript. It was developed by Microsoft starting with Version 3.0 of its Internet Information Server (IIS). When IIS encounters an Active Server page requested by the browser, it executes the embedded program. Active Server Pages are Microsoft's alternative to CGI scripts.

ActiveX

A brand name from Microsoft that has been used very specifically and very broadly. Today, it refers generally to ActiveX controls. For a short time, it was used to brand Microsoft's entire COM object architecture.

ActiveX control

A software module based on Microsoft's Component Object Model (COM) architecture. It enables a program to add functionality by calling ready-made components that blend in and appear as normal parts of the program. They are typically used to add user interface functions, such as 3-D toolbars, a notepad, calculator or even a spreasheet.

actuator

A mechanism that causes a device to be turned on or off, adjusted or moved. For example, the actuator is the component that moves the head assembly on a disk drive or an arm of a robot.

Ada

A high-level programming language developed by the U.S. Department of Defense along with the European Economic Community and other organizations. It was designed for embedded applications and process control, but is also used for logistics applications. Ada is Pascal based and very comprehensive.

Ada was named after Augusta Ada Byron (1815-1852), Countess of Lovelace and daughter of Lord Byron. She was a mathematician and colleague of Charles Babbage, who was developing his Analytical Engine. Her programming notes for the machine survived, giving her the distinction of being the first documented programmer in the world.

ADABAS

A DBMS from Software AG, Reston, VA, for IBM mainframes, VAXes, various UNIX platforms and OS/2 PCs. It is an inverted list DBMS with relational capabilities. A 4GL known as NATURAL plus text retrieval, GIS processing, SQL and distributed database functions are also available. Introduced in 1969, it was one of the first DBMSs.

adapter

A device that allows one system to connect to and work with another. Display adapters and network adapters are really controllers, not adapters. See *host adapter* and *expansion bus*.

adaptive compression

A data compression technique that dynamically adjusts the algorithm used based on the content of the data being compressed.

adaptive equalization

A transmission technique that dynamically adjusts its modulation method based on line quality.

adaptive routing

The ability to dynamically select a new communications path to get around heavy traffic or a node or circuit failure.

ADB

(Apple Desktop Bus) The Macintosh communications port for keyboards, mice, trackballs, graphics tablets and other input devices.

ad banner

See *banner ad*.

ad blocker

Software that eliminates advertising and other annoyances from Web pages. It detects banner ads by size (typically 60 pixels high) and by the URLs of major advertising sites where the images come from. Such utilities may also be able to eliminate cookies, referrers and animated GIFs, which are time consuming to download. See *cookie file, referrer* and *animated GIF*.

A/D converter (ADC)

(Analog to Digital Converter) A device that converts continuously varying analog signals from instruments that monitor such conditions as movement, temperature, sound, etc., into binary code for the computer. It may be contained on a single chip or can be one circuit within a chip. See *modem* and *codec*. Contrast with *D/A converter*.

AD/Cycle

(Application Development/Cycle) SAA-compliant software from IBM that provides a system for managing systems development. It provides a structure for storing information about all phases of an information system including systems analysis and design, database design and programming.

add-drop multiplexor

A device that multiplexes lower-speed electrical and/or optical signals into a high-speed optical channel and vice versa. It is used to connect individual lines to backbone trunks. For example, an ADM might connect to a SONET ring on its high-speed side and to several T1s on its low-speed side.

add-in, add-on

Refers to hardware modules, such as printed circuit boards, that are designed to be plugged into a socket within the computer.

address

(1) The number of a particular memory or peripheral storage location. Like post office boxes, each byte of memory and each disk sector has its own unique address. Programs are compiled into machine language, which references actual addresses in the computer.

(2) As a verb, to manage or work with. For example, "the computer can address 2MB of memory."

addressable cursor

A screen cursor that can be programmed to move to any row or column on the screen.

address bus

An internal channel from the CPU to memory across which the addresses of data (not the data) are transmitted. The number of lines (wires) in the address bus determines the amount of memory that can be directly addressed as each line carries one bit of the address.

address mode

The method by which an instruction references memory. An "indexed" address is modified by the contents of an index register before execution. An "indirect" address points to another address. Ultimately, in order to do any actual processing, the instruction must derive real, or absolute addresses, where the required data is located.

address resolution

Obtaining a physical address that is ultimately needed to perform an operation. All instructions executing at the machine level require a physical memory, storage or network node address when referencing the actual hardware. Machine addresses are derived using table lookups and/or algorithms.

address space

The total amount of memory that can be used by a program. It may also refer to virtual memory, which includes memory and disk. For example, the 386 can address 4GB of physical memory and 64TB of virtual memory.

address translation

Transforming one address into another. For example, assemblers and compilers translate symbolic addresses into machine addresses. Virtual memory systems translate a virtual address into a real address.

ad hoc query

A non-standardized inquiry. An ad hoc query is composed to answer a question when the need arises.

ADO

(Active Data Objects) A programming interface from Microsoft that is designed as "the" Microsoft standard for data access. First used with Internet Information Server, it is expected to become available for all Microsoft programming languages and applications. ADO is a COM object.

Adobe

(Adobe Systems, Inc., Mountain View, CA, www.adobe.com) The leading graphics and desktop publishing software company. Founded in 1982 by Dr. John Warnock, Adobe helped pioneer desktop publishing with its PostScript fonts and applications. See *PostScript*.

Adobe Type Manager

A PostScript font utility for the Mac and Windows from Adobe. It scales Type 1 fonts into screen fonts and prints them on non-PostScript printers. Rather than downloading the font to the printer, it sends a bitmap of the entire page of text to the printer. Built into OS/2 and NeXTstep, it was originally developed to provide WYSIWYG screen fonts for the Mac. See *PostScript*.

ADP

(1) (Automatic Data Processing) Synonymous with data processing (DP), electronic data processing (EDP) and information processing.

(2) (Automatic Data Processing, Inc., Roseland, NJ, www.adp.com) A nationwide computer services organization that specializes in payroll processing.

ADPCM

(Adaptive Differential PCM) An advanced PCM technique that converts analog sound into digital data and vice versa. Instead of coding an absolute measurement at each sample point, it codes the difference between samples. It can dynamically switch the scale to compensate for variations in amplitude and frequency.

ADSL

(Asymmetric DSL) See *DSL*.

AFC

(Application Foundation Classes) A class library from Microsoft that provides an application framework and graphics, graphical user interface (GUI) and multimedia routines for Java programmers. AFC Enterprise Libraries include support for data access, directory services, transactions and distributed objects. AFC is compatible with AWT and runs in Windows and other JVM environments. See *JFC, AWT* and *IFC*.

AFE

(Apple File Exchange) A Macintosh utility that converts data files between Mac and PC formats. It also includes a file translator between IBM's DCA format and MacWrite; however, MacLink Plus Translators can be used for additional capability.

AFIPS

(American Federation of Information Processing Societies Inc.) An organization founded in 1961 dedicated to advancing information processing in the U.S. It was the U.S. representative of IFIP and umbrella for 11 membership societies. It was dissolved in 1990 and superseded by FOCUS.

AFP

(1) (AppleTalk Filing Protocol) A client/server protocol used in AppleTalk communications networks. In order for non-Apple networks to access data in an AppleShare server, their protocols must translate into the AFT language.

(2) (Advanced Function Presentation) A page description language from IBM introduced initially as Advanced Function Printing for mainframes. AFP is implemented on various platforms by Print Services Facility (PSF) software, which generates the native IPDS printer language, and depending on version, PostScript and LaserJet PCL as well.

agent

A software routine that waits in the background and performs an action when a specified event occurs. For example, agents could transmit a summary file on the first day of the month or monitor incoming data and alert the user when a certain transaction has arrived. See *workflow*.

AGP

(Accelerated Graphics Port) A high-speed graphics port from Intel that provides a direct connection between the display adapter and memory. AGP is faster than PCI, and only one AGP slot is provided on AGP-equipped motherboards. The PCI slot that would normally hold the display adapter can be used for another device.

AI

(Artificial Intelligence) Devices and applications that exhibit human intelligence and behavior including robots, expert systems, voice recognition, natural and foreign language processing. It also implies the ability to learn or adapt through experience.

AIFF file

(Audio Interchange File Format) A digital audio file format from Apple that is used on the Macintosh.

air interface

The modulation scheme used in a wireless network. It is the wireless counterpart to the physical layer in the OSI model. FDMA, TDMA and CDMA are examples of air interfaces.

AIT

(Advanced Intelligent Tape) A magnetic tape techology from Sony that uses 8mm cassette-style cartridges that hold up to 50GB (AIT-2). It uses advanced metal evaporated (AME) media and includes a built-in head cleaner and an EEPROM chip that stores tape status and indexing information.

AITP

(Association of Information Technology Professionals, Park Ridge, IL, www.aitp.org) Formerly the Data Processing Management Association (DPMA), it is a membership organization founded in 1951 devoted to providing professional development to individuals in information systems. It originated the CDP examinations which were later administrated by the ICCP. It was renamed AITP in 1996.

AIX

(Advanced Interactive eXecutive) IBM's version of UNIX, which runs on Intel PCs, RS/6000 workstations and 390 mainframes. It is based on AT&T's UNIX System V with Berkeley extensions.

Akamai

(Akamai Technologies, Inc., Cambridge, MA, www.akamai.com) A company that provides Internet content delivery with guaranteed peformance using its own worldwide network. Since most of the content of a Web page is graphics, a Web site customer might host the text itself and offload the graphics to Akamai. Akamai (pronounced "AH ka my") is Hawaiian for intellignet, or "cool."

alarm filtering

In network management, the ability to pinpoint the device that has failed. If one device in a network fails, others may fail as a result and cause alarms. Without alarm filtering, the management console reports all deteriorating devices with equal attention.

A-Law

An ITU standard for converting analog data into digital form using pulse code modulation (PCM). Europe uses A-Law, while North America and Japan use mu-Law (u-Law). See *PCM* and *mu-Law*.

ALGOL

(ALGOrithmic Language) A high-level compiler language that was developed as an international language for the expression of algorithms between people and between people and machines. ALGOL-60 (1960) was simple and widely used in Europe. ALGOL-68 (1968) was more complicated and scarcely used, but was the inspiration for Pascal. The following example changes Fahrenheit to Celsius:

```
 fahrenheit
 begin
  real fahr;
  print ("Enter Fahrenheit ");
  read (fahr);
  print ("Celsius is ", (fahr-32.0) * 5.0/9.0);
 end
finish
```

algorithm

A set of ordered steps for solving a problem, such as a mathematical formula or the instructions in a program.

alias

(1) An alternate name used for a field, file or other item.
(2) A phony signal created under certain conditions when digitizing voice.

aliasing

In computer graphics, the stair-stepped appearance of diagonal lines when there are not enough pixels in the image or on screen to represent them realistically. Also called "stair-stepping" and "jaggies." See *anti-aliasing*.

allocate

To reserve a resource such as memory or disk. See *memory allocation*.

allocation unit

Same as *cluster*.

Alpha

A family of RISC-based, 64-bit CPUs and computer systems from Compaq. Originally developed by Digital, the first model introduced in early 1992 was the 150MHz 21064-AA, considered equivalent to a Cray-1 on a single chip. Subsequent models continued to blaze trails for high-speed microprocessors. Alpha-based servers and workstations run under Digital Unix, OpenVMS and Windows NT.

alpha channel

Eight bits in a 32-bit graphics pixel that is used as a separate layer for representing levels of transparency in an object.

alphageometric, alphamosaic

A very-low-resolution display technique that uses elementary graphics symbols as part of its character set.

alphanumeric

The use of alphabetic letters mixed with numbers and special characters as in name, address, city and state. The text you're reading is alphanumeric.

alpha test

The first test of newly developed hardware or software in a laboratory setting. The next step is beta testing with actual users. See *beta test*.

Altair 8800

A microcomputer kit introduced in 1974 from Micro Instrumentation and Telemetry Systems. It sold for $400 and used an 8080 microprocessor. In 1975, it was packaged with Microsoft's MBASIC. Although computer kits were advertised earlier by others, an estimated 10,000 Altairs were sold, making it the first commercially successful microcomputer.

alternate routing

The ability to use another transmission line if the regular line is busy.

alt key

A keyboard key that is pressed with a letter or digit key to command the computer.

alt newsgroup

(ALTernative newsgroup) An Internet newsgroup that is devoted to a very specific topic, often one that is very controversial. Anybody can create an alt newsgroup without any formal voting from other users. See *newsgroup*.

ALU

(Arithmetic Logic Unit) The high-speed CPU circuit that does calculating and comparing. Numbers are transferred from memory into the ALU for calculation, and the results are sent back into memory. Alphanumeric data is sent from memory into the ALU for comparing.

AM

(Amplitude Modulation) A transmission technique that blends the data signal into a carrier by varying (modulating) the amplitude of the carrier. See *modulate*.

Amazon.com

(Amazon.com, Seattle, WA, www.amazon.com) The largest online shopping site and one of the most controversial e-commerce sites on the Web. Founded by Jeff Bezos in 1995, it had 11 employees by year's end. By 1999, it had more than 1600 employees and 4.5 million customers.

ambient

Surrounding. For example, ambient temperature and humidity are atmospheric conditions that exist at the moment.

AMD

(Advanced Micro Devices, Sunnyvale, CA, www.amd.com) A manufacturer of flash memories, programmable logic devices, embedded processors and x86-compatible CPUs. AMD has become a competitor to Intel and its chips are used in many PCs.

Amdahl

(Amdahl Corporation, Sunnyvale, CA) A computer manufacturer founded in 1970 by Gene Amdahl, chief architect of the IBM System/360. In 1975, Amdahl installed its first IBM-compatible mainframe, the 470/V6. Although not the first to make IBM-compatible mainframes, it succeeded where others failed. Amdahl offers a full range of IBM-compatible mainframes as well as application development software and UNIX servers.

Amiga

A personal computer series from Amiga, Inc., (www.amiga.com), that runs under the AmigaDOS operating system. Amigas were introduced by Commodore in 1985 and have been noted for their advanced multimedia architecture. Video Toaster turned the Amiga into a low-cost, high-quality video editing system.

amp

(AMPere) A unit of electrical current in a circuit. *Volts* measure the force or pressure behind the current. *Watts* are a total measurement of power derived from multiplying amps times volts.

amplitude

The strength or volume of a signal, usually measured in decibels.

AMPS

(Advanced Mobile Phone Service) The analog cellular phone system used in North and South America and more than 35 other countries. It is the cellular equivalent of POTS.

analog

A representation of an object that resembles the original. Analog devices monitor conditions, such as movement, temperature and sound, and convert them into analogous electronic or mechanical patterns. For example, an analog watch represents the planet's rotation with the rotating hands on the watch face. Telephones turn voice vibrations into electrical vibrations of the same shape. Analog implies continuous operation in contrast with digital, which is broken up into numbers.

The world turns...

air waves

sound waves

analog channel

In communications, a channel that carries voice or video in analog form as a varying range of electrical frequencies. Contrast with *digital channel*.

analog computer

A device that processes infinitely varying signals, such as voltage or frequencies. A thermometer is a very elementary analog computer. As the temperature varies, the mercury moves correspondingly. Although some special-purpose analog computers are still made, almost all computers are digital, due to their programming flexibility.

analog monitor

A video monitor that accepts analog signals from the computer (digital to analog conversion is performed in the display adapter). It may accept only a narrow range of display resolutions; for example, only VGA or VGA and Super VGA, or it may accept a wide range of signals including TV. See *multiscan monitor* and *RGB monitor*. Contrast with *digital monitor*.

analysis, analyst

See *systems analysis & design, systems analyst* and *business analyst*.

anchor

In desktop publishing, a format code that keeps a graphic near or next to a text paragraph. If text is added, causing the paragraph to move to a subsequent page, the graphic image is moved along with it.

AND, OR & NOT

The fundamental operations of Boolean logic. AND is true if both inputs are true, OR is true if any input is true, and NOT is an inverter; the output is always the opposite. See *Boolean search* and *gate*.

angstrom

A unit of measurement equal to approximately 1/250 millionth of an inch (.1 nanometer). It is used to measure the tiny elements in a chip.

animated GIF

A moving picture in GIF format, which is made up of a series of frames. When displayed, they provide a short animated sequence.

animated graphics

Moving diagrams or cartoons. Often found in computer-based courseware, animated graphics take up far less disk space than video images.

anisotropic

Refers to properties, such as transmission speed, that vary depending on the direction of measurement. Contrast with *isotropic*.

anode

In electronics, a positively charged receiver of electrons that flow from the negatively charged *cathode*.

anomaly

Abnormality or deviation. When the computer does something that cannot be explained, the incident is often called an anomaly.

anonymous FTP

An FTP site on the Internet that contains files that can be downloaded by anyone. The anonymous FTP directory is isolated from the rest of the system and will generally not accept uploads from users.

anonymous post, anonymous remailer

An anonymous post is a message that cannot be traced to the person that created it. An anonymous remailer is an organization that forwards e-mail anonymously stripping out the sender's name and e-mail address. Remailers are used by people that wish to express an opinion to newsgroups or to individuals without fear of excessive responses or retaliation.

ANSI

(American National Standards Institute, New York, www.ansi.org) A membership organization founded in 1918 that coordinates the development of U.S. voluntary national standards in both the private and public sectors. It is the U.S. member body to ISO and IEC. Information technology standards pertain to programming languages, EDI, telecommunications and properties of storage media.

ANSI character set

The ANSI-standard character set that defines 256 characters. The first 128 are ASCII, and the second 128 contain math and foreign language symbols, which are different than those on the PC. See *extended ASCII*.

ANSI terminal

A display terminal that follows commands in the ANSI standard terminal language. Uses escape sequences to control the cursor, clear the screen and set colors, for example. Communications programs often support the ANSI terminal.

anti-aliasing

In computer graphics, a category of techniques that is used to smooth the jagged appearance of diagonal lines. For example, the pixels that surround the edges of the line are filled in with varying shades of gray or color in order to blend the sharp edge into the background. See *dithering*.

antivirus

A program that detects and removes a virus.

AOL

(America OnLine) The the country's largest online service. AOL provides Internet access, conferencing, news, e-mail, education and support forums. Specialized software for Windows and Mac provide navigation through the system.

Apache

(A "patchy" server) A widely-used public domain, UNIX-based Web server from the Apache Group (www.apache.org). It is based on NCSA's HTTPd server. The name came from a body of existing code and many "patch files."

API

(Application Program Interface) A language and message format used by an application program to communicate with another program that provides services for it. APIs are usually implemented by writing function calls. Examples of APIs are the calls made by an application program to such programs as an operating system, messaging system or database management system (DBMS). See *interface*.

APL

(A Programming Language) A high-level, scientific language noted for its brevity and matrix generation capabilities. Developed by Kenneth Iverson in the mid 1960s, it is often used to develop mathematical models. More popular in Europe, APL uses unique character symbols and requires a special font to display and print them.

APM

(Advanced Power Management) An API from Intel and Microsoft for battery-powered computers that lets programs communicate power requirements to slow down and speed up components.

APPC

(Advanced Program-to-Program Communications) A high-level communications protocol from IBM that allows a program to interact with another program. It supports client/server and distributed computing by providing a common programming interface across all IBM platforms for communications over a variety of transport protocols. It provides commands for managing a session, sending and receiving data and transaction security and integrity (two-phase commit).

Apple

(Apple Computer, Inc., Cupertino, CA, www.apple.com) A manufacturer of personal computers and the industry's most fabled story. Founded in a garage by Steve Wozniak and Steve Jobs in 1976 and guided by Mike Markkula, Apple blazed the trails for the personal computer industry.

From its Apple II series to the Macintosh to today's new PowerMacs, Apple has always provided a unique alternative to personal computing. The Macintosh's graphical user interface, which was introduced in 1984, set the standard for ease of use that is unmatched.

Apple II

The personal computer family from Apple that pioneered the microcomputer revolution and was widely used in schools and home. It used the 8-bit 6502 microprocessor running at 1MHz, an 8-bit bus and ran Apple's DOS or ProDOS operating system.

Apple key

The original name of the Command key.

Apple menu

The menu at the top left side of a Macintosh screen that is always available to provide access to desk accessories.

AppleScript

A system-level scripting language used for automating routine tasks. It is part of the System 7 Pro operating system.

AppleShare

Software from Apple that turns a Macintosh into a file server. It works in conjunction with the Mac operating system and can coexist with other Macintosh applications in a non-dedicated mode.

AppleSoft BASIC

Apple's version of BASIC that came with Apple II models. It was installed in firmware and always available.

applet

A small application, such as a utility program or limited-function spreadsheet or word processor. Java programs that are run from the browser are called applets.

AppleTalk

Apple's local area network architecture introduced in 1985. It supports Apple's proprietary LocalTalk access method as well as Ethernet and Token Ring. The AppleTalk network manager and the LocalTalk access method are built into all Macintoshes and LaserWriters.

application

(1) A specific use of the computer, such as for payroll, inventory and billing.

(2) Same as *application program* and *software package*.

application developer

An individual that develops a business application and usually performs the duties of a systems analyst and application programmer.

application development system

A programming language and associated utility programs that allow for the creation, development and running of application programs. DBMSs are often full application development systems, which include a programming language, query language, report writer and the capability to interactively create and manage database files.

application framework

(1) The building blocks of an application.

(2) A class library that provides the foundation for programming an object-oriented application.

application generator

Software that generates application programs from descriptions of the problem rather than by traditional programming. It is at a higher level than a high-level programming language. One statement or descriptive line may generate a huge routine or an entire program. However, application generators always have limits as to what they can be used for.

application integration

(1) Translating data and commands from the format of one application into the format of another. It is essentially data and command conversion on an on-going basis between two or more incompatible systems.

(2) Redesigning disparate information systems into one system that uses a common set of data structures and rules.

application layer

In communications, the interaction at the user or application program level. It is the highest layer within the protocol hierarchy. See *OSI*.

application package

A software package that is created for a specific purpose or industry.

application partitioning

Separating an application into components that run on clients and multiple servers in a client/server environment. Programming languages and development systems that support this architecture, known as "three-tier client/server," may allow the program to be developed as a whole and then separated into pieces later.

application processor

A computer that processes data in contrast with one that performs control functions, such as a front end processor or database machine.

application program

Any data entry, update, query or report program that processes data for the user. It includes the generic productivity software (spreadsheets, word processors, database programs, etc.) as well as custom and packaged programs for payroll, billing, inventory and other accounting purposes. Contrast with *system program*.

application programmer

An individual who writes application programs in a user organization. Most programmers are application programmers. Contrast with *systems programmer*.

application server

(1) A computer in a client/server environment that performs the business logic (the data processing). In a two-tier client/server environment, the user's machine performs the business logic, which connects to the database server (DBMS). The bulk of client/server architecture is two-tier. In a three-tier client/server environment, an independent application server performs the business logic. This was the original definition of the term application server. Increasingly, the term refers to the Web-based usage in definition #2 below. See *file server*.

(2) A computer in an intranet/Internet environment that performs the data processing necessary to deliver up-to-date information as well as process information for Web clients. The application server sits along with or between the Web server and the databases and legacy applications, providing the middleware glue to enable a browser-based application to link to multiple sources of information. See *Web server*.

application sharing

A data conferencing capability that lets two or more users interactively work on the same application at the same time.

application suite

A set of applications designed to work together. In the Windows environment, the application suite is the successor to the integrated package, except that the individual applications are stand alone and can be purchased separately.

APPN

(Advanced Peer-to-Peer Networking) Extensions to IBM's SNA communications that provide necessary enhancements for routing data in a mainframe/LAN environment. It includes improved administration, intermediate node routing and dynamic network services. APPN makes use of LU 6.2 protocols and is implemented in an SNA Node Type 2.1.

arbitration

A set of rules for allocating machine resources, such as memory or peripheral devices, to more than one user or program.

ARC, ARC+Plus

(1) PC compression programs from System Enhancement Associates, Inc., Clifton, NJ. ARC was one of the first compression utilities to become popular in the early 1980s. ARC+Plus provides enhanced features and speed.

(2) The ARC extension was previously used by PKWARE Inc. in its PKARC program.

Archie

(ARCHIvE) An internet utility used for searching file names. Archie servers periodically update catalogs of local files that are available to the public, and Archie lets users search those catalogs.

architecture

See *computer architecture, network architecture* and *software architecture.*

archive

(1) To copy data onto a different disk or tape for backup. Archived files are often compressed to maximize storage media.

(2) To save data onto the disk.

areal density

The bits per square inch of disk surface (BPI x TPI).

argument (arg)

In programming, a value that is passed between programs, subroutines or functions. Arguments are independent items, or variables, that contain data or codes. When an argument is used to customize a program for a user, it is typically called a "parameter."

arithmetic expression

(1) One or more characters or symbols associated with arithmetic, such as $1 + 2 = 3$ or $8 / 6$.

(2) In programming, a non-text expression.

arithmetic operators

The symbols for add, subtract, multiply and divide (+, -, *, /). See *precedence.*

arithmetic overflow

The result from an arithmetic calculation that exceeds the space designated to hold it.

arithmetic underflow

The result from an arithmetic calculation that is too small to be expressed properly. For example, in floating point, a negative exponent can be generated that is too large (too small a number) to be stored in its allotted space.

ARM chips

A family of RISC-based microprocessors and microcontrollers from ARM, Inc., Los Gatos, CA, (www.arm.com). ARM chips are noted for their small die size and low power requirements. They are widely used in PDAs and other hand-held devices, including games and phones, as well as a wide variety of consumer products. The StrongARM chips are high-speed versions that were originally developed with Digital.

ARP

(Address Resolution Protocol) A low-level TCP/IP protocol used to obtain a node's physical address when only its logical IP address is known. An ARP request is broadcast onto the network, and the node with that IP address sends back its hardware address.

ARPANET

(Advanced Research Projects Agency NETwork) The research network funded by DARPA (originally ARPA) and built by BBN, Inc., in 1969. It pioneered packet switching technology and was the original backbone and testbed for the Internet. In 1983, the military part of ARPANET was split off into MILNET.

ARQ

(Automatic Repeat Request) A method of handling communications errors in which the receiving station requests retransmission if an error occurs.

array

An ordered arrangement of data elements. A vector is a one dimensional array, a matrix is a two-dimensional array. Most programming languages have the ability to store and manipulate arrays in one or more dimensions. Multi-dimensional arrays are used extensively in scientific simulation and mathematical processing; however, an array can be as simple as a pricing table held in memory for instant access by an order entry program. See *subscript*.

Price list in one-dimensional array						
Item	Amount	Item	Amount	Item	Amount	etc.
0001	016.43	0002	005.44	0003	110.00	0004

array processor

A computer, or extension to its arithmetic unit, that is capable of performing simultaneous computations on elements of an array of data in some number of dimensions. Common uses include analysis of fluid dynamics and rotation of 3-D objects, as well as data retrieval, in which elements in a database are scanned simultaneously. See *vector processor* and *math coprocessor*.

Sales figures in two-dimensional array					
	Jan	Feb	Mar	Apr	etc.
Product A	24484	09880	45884	83304	
Product B	67300	12372	37461		
Product C	20011	10029			
etc.					

artifact

Some distortion of an image or sound caused by a limitation or malfunction in the graphics hardware or software.

artificial intelligence

See *AI*. Remember... look up the acronym first!

artificial language

A language that has been predefined before it is ever used. Contrast with *natural language*.

AS/400

(Application System/400) A family of minicomputers from IBM introduced in 1988, superseding the System/36 and System/38 lines. The AS/400 uses the OS/400 operating system and is IBM's business-oriented, midrange computer line, which has been very successful.

ASCII

(American Standard Code for Information Interchange) Pronounced "ask-ee." A binary code for text as well as communications and printer control. It is used for most communications and is in the built-in character code in most minicomputers and all personal computers.

ASCII is a 7-bit code providing 128 character combinations, the first 32 of which are control characters. Since the common storage unit is an 8-bit byte (256 combinations) and ASCII uses only 7 bits, the extra bit is used differently depending on the computer. For example, the PC uses the additional values for foreign language and graphics symbols (see ASCII chart below). In the Macintosh, the additional values can be user-defined.

```
                 Standard ASCII            │   Extended ASCII
         The first 32 characters are       │        (DOS)
                control codes.

 0  Null               │33 !│ 81 Q│128 Ç│174 «│220 ▄
 1  Start of heading   │34 "│ 82 R│129 ü│175 »│221 █
 2  Start of text      │35 #│ 83 S│130 é│176 ░│222 █
 3  End of text        │36 $│ 84 T│131 â│177 ▒│223 ▀
 4  End of transmit    │37 %│ 85 U│132 ä│178 ▓│224 α
 5  Enquiry            │38 &│ 86 V│133 à│179 ││225 β
 6  Acknowledge        │39 '│ 87 W│134 å│180 ┤│226 Γ
 7  Audible bell       │40 (│ 88 X│135 ç│181 ╡│227 π
 8  Backspace          │41 )│ 89 Y│136 ê│182 ╢│228 Σ
 9  Horizontal tab     │42 *│ 90 Z│137 ë│183 ╖│229 σ
10  Line feed          │43 +│ 91 [│138 è│184 ╕│230 μ
11  Vertical tab       │44 ,│ 92 \│139 ï│185 ╣│231 τ
12  Form feed          │45 -│ 93 ]│140 î│186 ║│232 Φ
13  Carriage return    │46 .│ 94 ^│141 ì│187 ╗│233 θ
14  Shift out          │47 /│ 95 _│142 Ä│188 ╝│234 Ω
15  Shift in           │48 0│ 96 `│143 Å│189 ╜│235 δ
16  Data link escape   │49 1│ 97 a│144 É│190 ╛│236 ∞
17  Device control 1   │50 2│ 98 b│145 æ│191 ┐│237 ø
18  Device control 2   │51 3│ 99 c│146 Æ│192 └│238 ∈
19  Device control 3   │52 4│100 d│147 ô│193 ┴│239 ∩
20  Device control 4   │53 5│101 e│148 ö│194 ┬│240 ≡
21  Neg. acknowledge   │54 6│102 f│149 ò│195 ├│241 ±
22  Synchronous idle   │55 7│103 g│150 û│196 ─│242 ≥
23  End trans. block   │56 8│104 h│151 ù│197 ┼│243 ≤
24  Cancel             │57 9│105 i│152 ÿ│198 ╞│244 ⌠
25  End of medium      │58 :│106 j│153 Ö│199 ╟│245 ⌡
26  Substitution       │59 ;│107 k│154 Ü│200 ╚│246 ÷
27  Escape             │60 <│108 l│155 ¢│201 ╔│247 ≈
28  File separator     │61 =│109 m│156 £│202 ╩│248 °
29  Group separator    │62 >│110 n│157 ¥│203 ╦│249 ·
30  Record separator   │63 ?│111 o│158 ₧│204 ╠│250 ·
31  Unit separator     │64 @│112 p│159 ƒ│205 ═│251 √
32  Blank space        │65 A│113 q│160 á│206 ╬│252 ⁿ
                       │66 B│114 r│161 í│207 ╧│253 ²
                       │67 C│115 s│162 ó│208 ╨│254 ■
                       │68 D│116 t│163 ú│209 ╤│255
                       │69 E│117 u│164 ñ│210 ╥│
                       │70 F│118 v│165 Ñ│211 ╙│
                       │71 G│119 w│166 ª│212 ╘│
                       │72 H│120 x│167 º│213 ╒│
                       │73 I│121 y│168 ¿│214 ╓│
                       │74 J│122 z│169 ⌐│215 ╫│
                       │75 K│123 {│170 ¬│216 ╪│
                       │76 L│124 |│171 ½│217 ┘│
                       │77 M│125 }│172 ¼│218 ┌│
                       │78 N│126 ~│173 ¡│219 █│
                       │79 O│127 ⌂│
                       │80 P│
```

ASCII art

Pictures created with normal text characters. This is done by hand or with programs that convert scanned images into ASCII characters.

ASCII file

A file that contains data made up of ASCII characters. It is essentially raw text just like the words you're reading now. Each byte in the file contains one character that conforms to the standard ASCII code. Program source code, DOS batch files, macros and scripts are written as straight text and stored as ASCII files.

ASCII text files become a common denominator between applications that do not import each other's formats. If both applications can import and export ASCII files, you can transfer your files between them. Contrast with *graphics file* and *binary file*.

ASCII protocol

The simplest communications protocol for text. It transmits only ASCII characters and uses ASCII control codes. It implies little or no error checking.

ASCII sort

The sequential order of ASCII data. In ASCII code, lower case characters follow upper case. True ASCII order would put the words DATA, data and SYSTEM into the sequence: DATA, SYSTEM, data.

ASF

(Active Streaming Format) Microsoft's streaming media format, which supports audio, video, slide shows and synchronized events.

ASIC

(Application Specific Integrated Circuit) A custom chip designed for a specific application. It is designed by integrating standard cells from a library. ASIC design is faster than designing a chip from scratch, and design changes can be made more easily.

ASM

(1) (Association for Systems Management) An international membership organization based in Cleveland, OH. Founded in 1947 and disbanded in 1996, it sponsored conferences in all phases of administrative systems and management.

(2) The file extension for assembly language source programs.

ASP

(1) (Application Service Provider) An organization that hosts software applications on its own servers within its own facilities. Customer access the application via private lines or the Internet.

(2) See *Active Server Page*.

(3) (Association of Shareware Professionals, Muskegon, MI, www.asp-shareware.org) A trade organization for shareware founded in 1987. Author members submit products to ASP, which are approved, virus checked and distributed monthly via CD to member vendors. CDs are periodically made available to the public.

(4) (Analog Signal Processing) Processing signals completely within the analog domain. Contrast with *DSP*.

aspect ratio

The ratio of width to height of an object. The aspect ratio of the screen of a standard computer monitor and TV set is 4:3.

ASPI

(Advanced SCSI Programming Interface) An interface specification developed by Adaptec, Inc., Milpitas, CA, that provides a common language between drivers and SCSI host adapters. Drivers written to the ASPI interface can access peripherals that reside on different versions of SCSI host adapter hardware.

assembler

Software that translates assembly language into machine language. Contrast with *compiler*, which is used to translate a high-level language, such as COBOL or C, into assembly language first and then into machine language.

assembly language

A programming language that is one step away from machine language. Each assembly language statement is translated into one machine instruction by the assembler. Programmers must be well versed in the computer's architecture, and, undocumented assembly language programs are difficult to maintain. Assembly language is hardware dependent; there is a different assembly language for each CPU series.

Although often used synonomously, assembly language and machine language are not the same. Assembly language is turned into machine language. For example, the assembly instruction COMPARE A,B is translated into COMPARE the contents of memory bytes 2340-2350 with 4567-4577 (where A and B happen to be located). The physical binary format of the machine instruction is specific to the computer it's running in.

associative storage

Storage that is accessed by comparing the content of the data stored in it rather than by addressing predetermined locations.

asymmetric modem

A full-duplex modem that transmits data in one direction at one speed and simultaneously in the other direction at another speed. Contrast with *ping pong*. See *56 Kbps modem*.

asymmetric multiprocessing

A multiprocessing design in which each CPU is dedicated to a specific function. For example, the operating system runs in one CPU and the user application in another. Contrast with *symmetric multiprocessing*.

asymmetric system

(1) A system in which major components or properties are different.

(2) In video compression, a system that requires more equipment to compress the data than to decompress it.

asynchronous

Refers to events that are not synchronized in time. See *asynchronous transmission*. Contrast with *synchronous*.

asynchronous protocol

A communications protocol that controls an asynchronous transmission, for example, ASCII, TTY, Kermit and Xmodem. Contrast with *synchronous protocol*.

asynchronous transmission

The transmission of data in which each character is a self-contained unit with its own start and stop bits. Intervals between characters may be uneven. It is the common method of transmission between a computer and a modem, although the modem may switch to synchronous transmission to communicate with the other modem. Also called "start/stop transmission." Contrast with *synchronous transmission*.

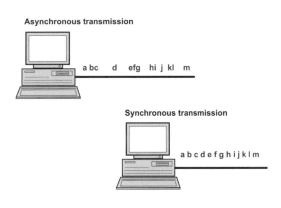

Asynchronous transmission

a bc   d   efg hi j kl m

Synchronous transmission

a b c d e f g h i j k l m

AT

(Advanced Technology) IBM's first 286-based PC, introduced in 1984. It was the most advanced machine in the PC line and featured a new keyboard, 1.2MB floppy and 16-bit data bus. AT-class machines ran much faster than 8088-based XTs.

ATA, ATAPI

(AT Attachment, AT Attachment Packet Interface) The formal names for the IDE interface specifications. The first ATA supported two drives. ATA-2, or Enhanced IDE (EIDE) added support for two more devices, and ATAPI allowed CD-ROMs and tapes to be included. See *IDE* and *LBA*.

Atari

Atari Computer was a manufacturer of video games and computers founded in 1972 by Nolan Bushnell. It became famous for its "Pong" video games and later introduced successful game and home computers. Its ST line competed with the Macintosh during the late 1980s. In 1996, Atari merged with JTS Corporation, manufacturer of hard disks, and in 1998, Hasbro acquired the Atari name and intellectual property rights.

AT bus

Refers to the 16-bit bus introduced with the IBM AT. It was an early term for the ISA bus.

AT command set

A series of machine instructions used to activate features on an intelligent modem. Developed by Hayes Microcomputer Products, Inc., and formally known as the Hayes Standard AT Command Set, it is used entirely or partially by most every modem manufacturer. AT is a mnemonic code for ATtention, which is the prefix that initiates each command to the modem.

ATE

(Automatic Test Equipment) Machines that test electronic systems, primarily chips. See *EDA*.

Athlon

A Pentium III-class CPU chip from AMD. The first models were introduced in 1999 with clock speeds from 500MHz to 650MHz. Using a 200MHz system bus, the Athlon contains the MMX multimedia instructions used in Pentium MMX and Pentium II CPUs along with an enhanced version of AMD's 3DNow 3-D instruction set for faster rendering of games and animation.

ATM

(1) (Asynchronous Transfer Mode) A high-speed cell-switching network technology for LANs and WANs that handles data and realtime voice and video. It combines the high efficiency of packet switching used in data networks, with the guaranteed bandwidth of circuit switching used in voice networks. ATM is widely used as a network backbone in large enterprises, communications carriers and Internet service providers (ISPs). See also *Adobe Type Manager*.

(2) (Automatic Teller Machine) A banking terminal that accepts deposits and dispenses cash. Stand alone or online to a central computer, ATMs are activated by inserting a magnetic card (cash or credit card) that contains the user's account number.

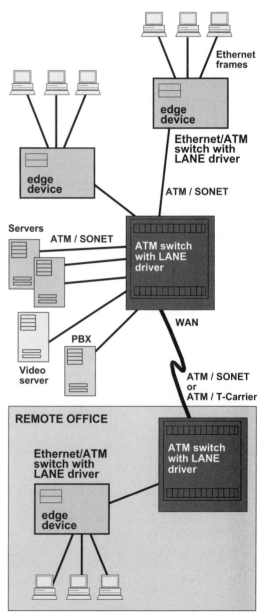

ATM / SONET = ATM cells within SONET frames
ATM / T-Carrier = ATM cells within T1 or T3 frames

atom

In list processing languages, a single element in a list.

atomic

Indivisible. An atomic operation, or atomicity, implies an operation that must be performed entirely or not at all. For example, if machine failure prevents a transaction to be processed to completion, the system will be rolled back to the start of the transaction. See *two-phase commit*.

attached processor

An additional CPU connected to the primary CPU in a multiprocessing environment. It operates as an extension of the primary CPU and shares the system software and peripheral devices.

attenuation

Loss of signal power in a transmission.

attribute

(1) In relational database management, a field within a record. See *file attribute*.

(2) For printers and display screens, a characteristic that changes a font, for example, from normal to boldface or underlined, or from normal to reverse video.

audio

The range of frequencies within human hearing, approximately 20Hz at the low to a high of 20,000Hz.

audio adapter, audio board

Same as *sound card*.

audio codec

A hardware circuit that converts sound into digital code and vice versa using one of several analog to digital conversion methods such as PCM or ADPCM. If the codec is specialized for human voice, it is known as a speech codec, voice codec or vocoder. The term may just refer to the audio compression method, which can be performed in software. See *speech codec*.

audioconferencing

An audio communications session among three or more people that are geographically dispersed. It is provided by a conference function in a PBX or multiline telephone or by the telephone companies. See *videoconferencing* and *data conferencing*.

audio response

See *voice response*.

audio scrubbing

Playing back a section of an audio file by highlighting the particular waveforms. The term was coined in the days of audio tape when moving manually moving the reels back and forth looked like the tape was being scrubbed. See *data scrubbing*.

audiotex

A voice response application that allows users to enter and retrieve information over the telephone. In response to a voice menu, users press the keys or answer questions to select their way down a path of choices. It is used for obtaining the latest financial quotes as well as for ordering products. It is also built into interactive systems that allows databases to be changed. See *VIS*.

audit

An examination of systems, programming and datacenter procedures in order to determine the efficiency of computer operations.

audit software

Specialized programs that perform a variety of audit functions, such as sampling databases and generating confirmation letters to customers. It can highlight exceptions to categories of data and alert the examiner to possible error. Audit software often includes a non-procedural language that lets the auditor describe the computer and data environment without detailed programming.

audit trail

A record of transactions in an information system that provides verification of the activity of the system. The simplest audit trail is the transaction itself. If a person's salary is increased, the change transaction includes the date, amount of raise and name of authorizing manager.

A more elaborate audit trail can be created when the system is being verified for accuracy; for example, samples of processing results can be recorded at various stages. Item counts and hash totals are used to verify that all input has been processed through the system.

AU file

(AUdio file) A digital audio file format from Sun that is used on the Internet. Java programs can play AU files.

AUI

(Attachment Unit Interface) The type of connector used on a network adapter for attaching standard Ethernet cable (thick Ethernet).

authoring program

Software that allows for the development of tutorials, CBT programs and other interactive multimedia presentation.

authorization code

An identification number or password that is used to gain access to a local or remote computer system.

auto

(AUTOmatic) Refers to a wide variety of devices that perform unattended operation.

auto answer

A modem feature that accepts a telephone call and establishes the connection. See *auto dial*.

auto attendant

A voice store and forward system that replaces the human operator and directs callers to the appropriate extensions or voice mailboxes.

auto baud detect

A modem feature that detects the highest speed of the called modem and switches to it.

auto bypass

The ability to bypass a terminal or other device in a network if it fails, allowing the remaining devices to continue functioning.

AutoCAD

A full-featured CAD program from AutoDesk Inc., Sausalito, CA, (www.autodesk.com), that runs on PCs, VAXs, Macs and UNIX workstations. Originally developed for CP/M machines, it was one of the first major CAD programs for personal computers and became an industry standard. There are countless third-party add-on packages for AutoCAD, and many graphics applications import and export AutoCAD's DXF file format.

auto dial

A modem feature that opens the line and dials the telephone number of another computer to establish connection. See *auto answer*.

AUTOEXEC.BAT

(AUTOmatic EXECute BATch) A DOS batch file that executes when the computer is started. It must be stored in the root directory. It is used to load various drivers and TSRs that must reside in memory at all times and to customize DOS for the user's requirements.

autoflow

Wrapping text around a graphic image or from one page to the next.

auto line feed

A feature that moves the cursor or print head to the next line when a CR (carriage return) is sensed. PCs put a LF (line feed) after the CR and do not use this feature. The Mac uses only a CR for end of line and requires it.

auto logon

Performing the complete log-on sequence necessary to gain entry into a computer system without user intervention.

automatic feature negotiation

The ability of a modem to determine and adjust to the speed, error control and data compression method of the modem at the other end of the line.

automation

The replacement of manual operations by computerized methods. Office automation refers to integrating clerical tasks such as typing, filing and appointment scheduling. Factory automation refers to computer-driven assembly lines. See also *COM automation*.

automounting

Making remote files available to a client at the time the file is accessed. Remote directories are associated with a local directory on the client ahead of time, and the mounting takes places the first time a remote file is opened by the client.

auto redial

A modem, fax or telephone feature that redials a busy number several times before giving up.

auto reliable

A modem feature that enables it to send to a modem with or without built-in error detection and compression.

auto resume

A feature that lets you stop working on the computer and take up where you left off at a later date without having to reload applications. Memory contents are stored on disk or kept active by battery and/or AC power.

autosave

Saving data to the disk at periodic intervals without user intervention.

autosizing

The ability of a monitor to maintain the same rectangular image size when changing from one resolution to another.

autostart routine

Instructions built into the computer and activated when it is turned on. The routine performs diagnostic tests, such as checking the computer's memory, and then loads the operating system and passes control to it.

autotrace

A routine that locates outlines of raster graphics images and converts them into vector graphics.

A/UX

Apple's earlier version of UNIX for the Macintosh. It is based on AT&T's UNIX System V with Berkeley extensions.

auxiliary memory

A high-speed memory bank used in mainframes and supercomputers. It is not directly addressable by the CPU, rather it functions like a disk. Data is transferred from auxiliary memory to main memory over a high-bandwidth channel. See *auxiliary storage*.

auxiliary storage

External storage devices, such as disk and tape.

avatar

An image you select or create to represent yourself in a 3-D chat site on the Web. In order to interact with these sites, you need a VRML plug-in. Avatar is a Sanskrit word that means the incarnation of a god on earth. See *VRML*.

AVI

(Audio Video Interleaved) A Windows multimedia video format from Microsoft. It interleaves standard waveform audio and digital video frames (bitmaps) to provide reduced animation at 15 fps at 160x120x8 resolution. Audio is 11,025Hz, 8-bit samples.

avionics

The electronic instrumentation and control equipment used in airplanes and space vehicles.

awk

(Aho Weinberger Kernighan) A UNIX programming utility developed in 1977 by Aho, Weinberger and Kernighan. Due to its unique pattern-matching syntax, it is often used in data retrieval and data transformation. DOS versions are also available.

AWT

(Abstract Windowing Toolkit) A class library from Sun that provides an application framework and graphical user interface (GUI) routines for Java programmers. AWT is included in the Java Foundation Classes (JFC). See *JFC, AFC* and *IFC*.

B

B2B e-commerce

(Business to Business Electronic Commerce) Refers to one business selling to another business via the Web. According to the GarnetGroup, B2B e-commerce is expected to grow from $145 billion in 1999 to more than $7 trillion by 2004, which will represent more than 7% of all sales transactions worldwide. See *e-commerce*.

backbone

In communications, the part of a network that handles the major traffic. It employs the highest-speed transmission paths in the network and may also run the longest distance. Smaller networks are attached to the backbone. A backbone can span a large geographic area or be as small as a backplane in a single cabinet. See *collapsed backbone* and *router*.

backdoor

See *trapdoor*.

back end

The support components of a computer system. It typically refers to the database management system (DBMS), which stores the data. See *front end*.

back-end CASE

CASE tools that generate program code. Contrast with *front-end CASE*.

back end processor

Same as *database machine*.

backhaul

(1) To transmit a telephone call or transmit data beyond its normal destination point and then back again in order to utilize available personnel (operators, agents, etc.) or network equipment that is not located at the destination location.

(2) To transmit data from a remote site to a central site.

background

(1) Non-interactive processing in the computer. See *foreground/background*.

(2) The base, or backdrop, color on screen. For example, in the DOS version of this Glossary, the text color is white on a blue background.

background noise

An extraneous signal that has crept into a line, channel or circuit.

background processing

Processing in which the program is not visibly interacting with the user. Most personal computers use operating systems that run background tasks only when foreground tasks are idle, such as between keystrokes. Advanced multitasking operating systems let background programs be given any priority from low to high.

backlit

An LCD screen that has its own light source from the back of the screen, making the background brighter and characters appear sharper.

BackOffice

A suite of network server software products from Microsoft that includes Windows NT Server, SQL Server, Systems Management Server (SMS), SNA Server and Mail Server.

backplane

An interconnecting device that may or may not have intelligence. It can be as simple as a series of common wires on the bottom or back of a panel or as sophisticated as a microprocessor-driven printed circuit board or electronic device with sockets for plugging in boards or cables. See *bus*.

backside bus

A dedicated channel between the CPU and a level 2 cache. It typically runs at the full speed of the CPU, whereas the frontside bus generally runs slower. See *frontside bus*.

back up
To make a copy of important data onto a different storage medium for safety.

backup
Additional resources or duplicate copies of data on different storage media for emergency purposes. See *full backup, differential backup* and *incremental backup*.

backup & recovery
The combination of manual and machine procedures that can restore lost data in the event of hardware or software failure. Routine backup of databases and logs of computer activity are part of a backup & recovery program. See *checkpoint/restart*.

backup copy
A disk, tape or other machine readable copy of a data or program file. Making backup copies is a discipline most computer users learn the hard way— after a week's work is lost.

backup disk, backup tape
A disk or tape used to hold duplicate copies of important files. Both magnetic and optical disks are used for backup, and a variety of tape technologies are used.

backup power
An additional power source that can be used in the event of power failure. See *UPS*.

Backus-Naur form
Also known as Backus normal form, it was the first metalanguage to define programming languages, developed by John Backus and Peter Naur in 1959.

backward chaining
In AI, a form of reasoning that starts with the conclusion and works backward. The goal is broken into many subgoals or sub-subgoals which can be solved more easily. Known as top-down approach. Contrast with *forward chaining*.

backward compatible
Same as *downward compatible*.

bad sector
A segment of disk storage that cannot be read or written due to a physical problem in the disk. Bad sectors on hard disks are marked by the operating system and bypassed. If data is recorded in a sector that becomes bad, file recovery software, and sometimes special hardware, must be used to restore it.

baloon help
On-screen help displayed in a cartoon-style dialogue box that appears when the pointer (cursor) is placed over the object in question.

balun
(BALanced UNbalanced) A device that connects a balanced line to an unbalanced line; for example, a twisted pair to a coaxial cable. A balanced line is one in which both wires are electrically equal. In an unbalanced line, such as a coax, one line has different properties than the other.

band
(1) The range of frequencies used for transmitting a signal. A band is identified by its lower and upper limits; for example, a 10MHz band in the 100 to 110MHz range.

(2) A contiguous group of tracks that are treated as a unit.

band pass filter
An electronic device that prohibits all but a specific range of frequencies to pass through it.

band printing
Printing a page by creating the output in several rectangular sections, or bands, rather than the entire page. It enables a printer with limited memory to print a full page of text and graphics. Most dot matrix printers and some laser printers benefit from this approach. This is not to be confused with a band printer, which was an early printer that used a metal band of type characters.

bandwidth

The transmission capacity of an electronic line such as a communications network, computer bus or computer channel. It is expressed in bits per second, bytes per second or in Hertz (cycles per second). When expressed in Hertz, the frequency may be a greater number than the actual bits per second, because the bandwidth is the difference between the lowest and highest frequencies transmitted. See *traffic shaping*.

bank

An arrangement of identical hardware components.

bank switching

Engaging and disengaging electronic circuits. Bank switching is used when the design of a system prohibits all circuits from being addressed or activated at the same time, requiring that one unit be turned on while the others are turned off.

banner ad

A graphic image used on a Web site to advertise a product or service. Banner ads (ad banners) are typically 460 pixels wide by 60 pixels high.

BAPCo

(Business Applications Performance Corporation) A nonprofit organization founded in 1991 that develops benchmarks for PC software.

bar chart

A graphical representation of information in the form of bars. See *business graphics*.

bar code

The printed code used for recognition by a scanner. Traditional one-dimensional bar codes use the bar's width as the code, but encode just an ID or account number. Two-dimensional systems, such as PDF 417 from Symbol Technology, hold 1,800 characters in an area the size of a postage stamp. See *UPC*.

barrel distortion

A screen distortion in which the sides bow out. Contrast with *pincushioning*.

base

(1) A starting or reference point.

(2) A component in a bipolar transistor that activates the switch. Same as *gate* in a MOS transistor.

(3) A multiplier in a numbering system. In a decimal system, each digit position is worth 10x the position to its right. In binary, each digit position is worth 2x the position to its right.

base address

The starting address (beginning point) of a program or table. See *base/displacement* and *relative address*.

base alignment

The alignment of a variety of font sizes on a baseline.

LAN Technologies	Bandwidth
Ethernet	10 Mbps (shared)
Switched Ethernet	10 Mbps (node to node)
Fast Ethernet	100 Mbps
Gigabit Ethernet	1000 Mbps
Token Ring	4, 16 Mbps
Fast Token Ring	100, 128 Mbps
FDDI/CDDI	100 Mbps
ATM	25, 45, 155, 622. 2488 Mbps +

To compute actual network throughput, divide bps (bits per sec) by 10 for bytes per second. Then halve the amount to account for overhead. Thus, in a 10 Mbps Ethernet network, there is only 500 thousand bytes per second of usable bandwidth. That means a 10 meg file will take 20 seconds to send. The 10 million bits per second doesn't sound so fast anymore, does it?

WAN Technologies	Bandwidth
UNSWITCHED PRIVATE LINES (point to point)	
T1	24 x 64 Kbps = 1.5 Mbps
T3	672 x 64 Kbps = 44.7 Mbps
Fractional T1	N x 64 Kbps
SWITCHED SERVICES	
Dial-up via modem	9.6, 14.4, 28.8, 33.6, 56 Kbps
ISDN	BRI 64-128 Kbps PRI 1.544 Mbps
Switched 56/64	56 Kbps, 64 Kbps
Packet switched (X.25)	56 Kbps
Frame relay	56 Kbps to 45 Mbps
SMDS	45, 155 Mbps
ATM	25, 45, 155, 622, 2488 Mbps +

baseband

A communications technique in which digital signals are placed onto the transmission line without change in modulation. It is usually limited to a few miles and does not require the complex modems used in broadband transmission. Common baseband LAN techniques are token passing ring (Token Ring) and CSMA/CD (Ethernet).

base/displacement

A machine architecture that runs programs no matter where they reside in memory. Addresses in a machine language program are displacement addresses, which are relative to the beginning of the program. At runtime, the hardware adds the address of the current first byte of the program (base address) to each displacement address and derives an absolute address for execution.

All modern computers use some form of base/displacement or offset mechanism in order to to run multiple programs in memory at the same time.

base font

The default font used for printing if none other is specified.

baseline

The horizontal line to which the bottoms of lowercase characters (without descenders) are aligned. See *typeface*.

baselining tool

A network monitor that analyzes communications usage in order to establish routine traffic patterns.

BASIC

(Beginners All purpose Symbolic Instruction Code) A programming language developed by John Kemeny and Thomas Kurtz in the mid 1960s at Dartmouth College. Originally developed as an interactive, mainframe timesharing language, it has become widely used on small computers.

BASIC is available in both compiler and interpreter form. As an interpreter, the language is conversational and can be debugged a line at a time. BASIC is also used as a quick calculator.

BASIC is considered one of the easiest programming languages to learn. Simple programs can be quickly written on the fly. However, BASIC is not a structured language, such as Pascal, dBASE or C, and it's easy to write spaghetti code that's difficult to decipher later. The following BASIC example converts Fahrenheit to Celsius:

```
10 INPUT "Enter Fahrenheit "; FAHR
20 PRINT "Celsius is ", (FAHR-32) * 5 / 9
```

bastion host

A computer system in a network that is fortified against illegal entry and attack. It acts as a firewall between the outside world and the internal network. See *firewall*.

batch

A group, or collection, of items.

batch data entry

Entering a group of source documents into the computer.

batch file

(1) A file containing data that is processed or transmitted from beginning to end.

(2) A file containing instructions that are executed one after the other. See *BAT file* and *shell script*.

batch file transfer

The consecutive transmission of two or more files.

batch job

Same as *batch program*.

batch operation

Some action performed on a group of items at one time.

batch processing

Processing a group of transactions at one time. Transactions are collected and processed against the master files (master files updated) at the end of the day or some other time period. Contrast with *transaction processing*.

batch program

A non-interactive (non-conversational) program such as a report listing or sort.

batch session

Transmitting or updating an entire file. Implies a non-interactive or non-interruptible operation from beginning to end. Contrast with *interactive session*.

batch stream

A collection of batch processing programs that are scheduled to run in the computer.

batch system

See *batch processing*.

batch terminal

A terminal that is designed for transmitting or receiving blocks of data, such as a card reader or printer.

batch total

The sum of a particular field in a collection of items used as a control total to ensure that all data has been entered into the computer. For example, using account number as a batch total, all account numbers would be summed manually before entry into the computer. After entry, the total is checked with the computer's sum of the numbers. If it does not match, source documents are manually checked against the computer's listing.

BAT file

(BATch file) A file of DOS or OS/2 commands, which are executed one after the other. It has a .BAT extension and is created with a text editor.

batteries

See *lead acid, lithium ion, nickel cadmium, nickel hydride* and *zinc air*.

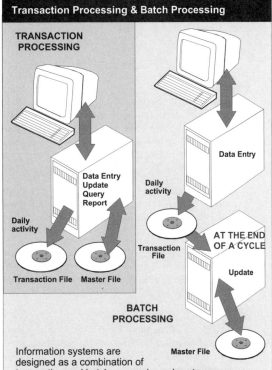

Transaction Processing & Batch Processing

Information systems are designed as a combination of transaction and batch processing subsystems.

The transaction processing is the daily work. Also called online transaction processing (OLTP), it means that the database is updated as soon as a transaction is received: a sales order depletes inventory, a stock sale updates the last close, a pledge adds to the fund raising balance. Transaction processing keeps business records up-to-date the moment transactions are keyed into or transmitted to the system.

Batch processing is updating or searching an entire table from beginning to end. A month-end report is a batch job as is printing payroll checks. There are many jobs that can be more economically processed at the end of a cycle. For example, the electronic transactions for telephone calls are stored in the computer until month end, when they are matched against the customer table for updating with all the other telephone transactions at the same time.

BatteryMark

A Ziff-Davis benchmark that tests battery life on notebook computers running Windows 95/98. It requires a special hardware device to perform the test. See *ZDBOp*.

baud

The signalling rate of a line, which is the number of transitions (voltage or frequency changes) that are made per second. The term has often been erroneously used to specify bits per second. However, only at very low speeds is baud equal to bps; for example, 300 baud is the same as 300 bps. Beyond that, one baud can be made to represent more than one bit. For example, a V.22bis modem generates 1200 bps at 600 baud.

baudot code

Pronounced "baw-doh." One of the first standards for international telegraphy developed in the late 19th century by Emile Baudot. It uses five bits per character.

baud rate

A redundant reference to baud. Baud is a rate.

BBS

(Bulletin Board System) A computer system used as an information source and forum for a particular interest group. They were widely used to distribute shareware and drivers in the U.S. and had their heyday before the Web took off. A BBS functions like a stand-alone Web site without graphics, and each BBS system has its own telephone number to dial into. BBSs are still used throughout the world where there is much less direct Internet access.

bcc:

(Blind Carbon Copy) The field in an e-mail header that names additional recipients for the message. It is similar to carbon copy (cc:), but the names do not appear in the recipient's message. Not all e-mail systems support bcc:, in which case the "hidden" names will appear.

BCD

(Binary Coded Decimal) The storage of numbers in which each decimal digit is converted into binary and is stored in a single character or byte. For example, a 12-digit number would take 12 bytes.

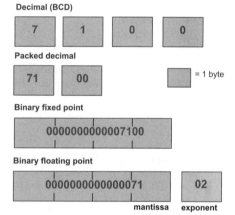

BCS

(The Boston Computer Society) A nonprofit membership organization founded in 1977 by Jonathan Rotenberg and disbanded in 1996. The BCS was one of the first sources for education and technical information about personal computers. At its height in the 1980s, it had more than 30,000 members, although more than 100,000 people were involved at one time or another.

Be

(Be, Inc., Menlo Park, CA, www.be.com) A software company founded in 1990 by Jean Louise Gassee, former head of R&D at Apple, that specializes in operating systems. BeOS is available for x86-based and PowerPC-based desktop computers, and BeIA is designed for Internet appliances. Be originally developed the PowerPC-based BeBox computer, which ran under BeOS and was designed for digital audio, video and 3-D graphics applications.

beaconing

A continuous signalling of error conditions on a LAN.

bead

(1) A small programming subroutine. A sequence of beads that are strung together is known as a "thread."

(2) The insulator surrounding the inner wire of a coaxial cable.

BEA TUXEDO

A TP monitor from BEA Systems, Inc., San Jose, CA, (www.beasys.com), that runs on a variety of UNIX-based computers. Originally developed by AT&T and sold as source code, Novell acquired it, enhanced it and offered it as shrink-wrapped software for various UNIX servers. It was later sold to BEA.

BEA WebLogic

A family of Java-based application servers from BEA Systems, Inc., San Jose, CA, (www.beasys.com). BEA WebLogic Server is the core product that supports the J2EE Java standards. BEA WebLogic Enterprise adds CORBA support and distributed processing. BEA WebLogic Express adds JDBC connectivity and servlet support.

bell character
The control code used to sound an audible bell or tone in order to alert the user (ASCII 7).

Bellcore
See *Telcordia*.

Bell Labs
The research and development center of Lucent Technologies (formerly AT&T). It is one of the most renowned scientific laboratories in the world.

Bell System
AT&T and the Bell Telephone Companies before divestiture. See *RBOC*.

benchmark
A performance test of hardware and/or software. There are various programs that very accurately test the raw power of a single machine, the interaction in a single client/server system (one server/multiple clients) and the transactions per second in a transaction processing system. However, it is next to impossible to benchmark the performance of an entire enterprise network with a great degree of accuracy. See *ZDBOp, BAPCo, Linpack, Dhrystones, Whetstones, Khornerstones* and *SPEC*.

bent pipe architecture
The typical way satellites are used to relay information. Data is transmitted to the satellite, which sends it right back down again like a bent pipe. The only processing performed is to retransmit the signals.

BER
(1) (Basic Encoding Rules) One method for encoding information in the OSI environment. For example, it defines how Boolean data is coded.

(2) (Bit Error Rate) The average number of bits transmitted in error.

Berkeley extensions
See *BSD UNIX*.

Bernoulli Box
An earlier removable disk system for personal computers from Iomega Corporation, Roy, UT, (www.iomega.com). It was introduced in 1983 with a 10MB, 8" floppy disk cartridge. Subsequent 5.25" models provided up to 230MB. The Bernoulli floppy was spun at high speed and bent upward close to the head. Upon power failure, it naturally bent down, following principles of fluid dynamics demonstrated by 18th century Swiss scientist, Daniel Bernoulli.

beta test
A test of hardware or software that is performed by users under normal operating conditions. Unlike the early days of computing, beta versions of applications today are widely distributed to the public. See *alpha test*.

Bezier curve
In computer graphics, a curve that is generated using a mathematical formula which assures continuity with other Bezier curves. It is mathematically simpler, but more difficult to blend than a b-spline curve. Within CAD and drawing programs, Bezier curves are typically reshaped by moving the handles that appear off of the curve.

BFT
(Binary File Transfer) An extension to the fax protocol that allows transmission of raw text instead of an image of the text document. The ability to transfer actual data similar to a common data modem provides a true e-mail capability via fax boards.

BGA
(Ball Grid Array) A popular surface mount chip package that uses a grid of solder balls as its connectors. Available in plastic and ceramic varieties, BGA is noted for its compact size, high lead count and low inductance, which allows lower voltages to be used.

BGP

A routing protocol that is used to span autonomous systems on the Internet. It is a robust, sophisticated and scalable protocol that was developed by the Internet Engineering Task Force (IETF).

bias

The voltage used to control or stabilize an electronic circuit.

bidirectional

The ability to move, transfer or transmit in both directions.

bi-endian

The ability to switch between big endian and little endian ordering.

BIFF

(Binary Interchange File Format) A spreadsheet file format that holds data and charts, introduced with Excel Version 2.2.

big endian

The order of bytes in a word in which the most significant byte is first. Little endian reverses the order. See *bi-endian*.

```
 16 bit number: 5A01h  (23,041 decimal)
    Big endian: 5A01   (Motorola 68xxx)
 Little endian: 015A   (Intel x86)
```

bill of materials

The list of components that make up a system. For example, a bill of materials for a house would include the cement block, lumber, shingles, doors, windows, plumbing, electric, heating and so on. Each subassembly also contains a bill of materials; the heating system is made up of the furnace, ducts, etc. A bill of materials "implosion" links component pieces to a major assembly, while a bill of materials "explosion" breaks apart each assembly or subassembly into its component parts.

bin

(BINary) A popular directory name for storing executable programs, device drivers, etc. (binary files).

binaries

Executable programs in machine language.

binary

Meaning two. The principle behind digital computers. All input to the computer is converted into binary numbers made up of the two digits 0 and 1 (bits). For example, when you press the "A" key on your personal computer, the keyboard generates and transmits the number 01000001 to the computer's memory as a series of pulses. The 1 bits are transmitted as high voltage; the 0 bits are transmitted as low.

Bits are stored as charged and uncharged cells in memory, as positively and negatively charged spots on disk and tape and as pits and no pits on optical media. See *BCD* for illustration.

binary code

A coding system made up of binary digits. See *BCD* and *character code*.

binary compatible

Refers to any data, hardware or software structure (data file, machine code, instruction set, etc.) in binary form that is 100% identical to another. It most often refers to executable programs.

binary field

A field that contains binary numbers. It may refer to the storage of binary numbers for calculation purposes, or to a field that is capable of holding any information, including data, text, graphics images, voice and video.

binary file

(1) An executable program in machine language ready to run.

(2) A file that contains binary numbers.

The Computer Glossary

binary format

(1) Numbers stored in pure binary form in contrast with *BCD* form. See *binary numbers*.

(2) Information stored in a binary coded form, such as data, text, images, voice and video. See *binary file* and *binary field*.

(3) A file transfer mode that transmits any type of file without loss of data.

binary notation

The use of binary numbers to represent values.

binary numbers

Numbers stored in pure binary form. Within one byte (8 bits), the values 0 to 255 can be held. Two contiguous bytes (16 bits) can hold values from 0 to 65,535.

binary search

A technique for quickly locating an item in a sequential list. The desired key is compared to the data in the middle of the list. The half that contains the data is then compared in the middle, and so on, either until the key is located or a small enough group is isolated to be sequentially searched.

binary synchronous

See *bisync*.

binary tree

A data structure in which each node contains one parent and no more than two children.

binary values

The following table shows the maximum number of numeric combinations in a binary structure with all bits set to zero equivalent to one combination. For example, in one bit, which can be 0 or 1, there are two possible values.

Bits		Total Values	Largest binary number Decimal equiv.	Binary
1		2	1	1
2		4	3	11
3		8	7	111
4		16	15	1111
5		32	31	1 1111
6		64	63	11 1111
7		128	127	111 1111
8		256	255	1111 1111
9		512	511	1 1111 1111
10	1K	1,024	1,023	11 1111 1111
11	2K	2,048	2,047	111 1111 1111
12	4K	4,096	4,095	1111 1111 1111
13	8K	8,192	8,191	1 1111 1111 1111
14	16K	16,384	16,383	11 1111 1111 1111
15	32K	32,768	32,767	111 1111 1111 1111
16	64K	65,536	65,535	1111 1111 1111 1111
20	1M	1,048,576		
24	16M	16,777,216		
30	1G	1,073,741,824		
40	1T	1,099,511,627,776		

bind

(1) To assign a machine address to a logical or symbolic reference or address.

(2) To assign a type or value to a variable or parameter. See *binding time*.

(3) Bind may be used in place of terms such as link or interface when referencing software that is made to communicate with other software or with hardware. See *linkage editor*.

bindery

A NetWare file used for security and accounting in NetWare 2.x and 3.x. A bindery pertains only to the server it resides in and contains the names and passwords of users and groups of users authorized to log in to that server. See *NDS*.

binding time

(1) In program compilation, the point in time when symbolic references to data are converted into physical machine addresses.

(2) In programming languages, when a variable is assigned its type (integer, string, etc.). Traditional compilers and assemblers provide early binding and assign types at compilation. Object-oriented languages provide late binding and assign types at runtime when the variable receives a value from the keyboard or other source.

BinHex

A utility and encoding format that originated on the Macintosh which is used to convert binary files into 7-bit ASCII for communications over Internet e-mail. Files formatted in BinHex use the .HQX extension. See *MIME* and *UUencode*.

biomechanics

The study of the anatomical principles of movement. Biomechanical applications on the computer employ stick modeling to analyze the movement of athletes as well as racing horses.

bionic

A machine that is patterned after principles found in humans or nature; for example, robots. It also refers to artificial devices implanted into humans replacing or extending normal human functions.

BIOS

A chip in a PC that provides an interface between the operating system and the peripheral hardware. The BIOS supports all the peripheral devices and internal services such as the realtime clock (time and date). The BIOS accepts requests from the drivers as well as the application programs. On startup, it recognizes all attached devices and stores this information for later use. It also tests the machine and loads the operating system.

bipolar

A category of high-speed microelectronic circuit design, which was used to create the first transistor and the first integrated circuit. Bipolar and MOS are the two major categories of chip design, but bipolar has mostly given way to CMOS.

bipolar transmission

A digital transmission technique that alternates between positive and negative signals. The 1s and 0s are determined by varying amplitudes at both polarities while non-data is zero amplitude.

biquinary code

Meaning two-five code. A system for storing decimal digits in a four-bit binary number.

BISDN

(Broadband IDSN) See *ISDN* and *ATM*.

BI software

(Business Intelligence software) Software that enables users to obtain enterprise-wide information more easily. Such products are considered a step up from the typical decision support tools because they more tightly integrate querying, reporting, OLAP, data mining and data warehousing functions.

bisync

(BInary SYNChronous) A major category of synchronous communications protocols used in mainframe networks. Bisync communications require that both sending and receiving devices are synchronized before transmission of data is started. Contrast with *asynchronous* transmission.

bisynchronous

See *bisync*.

bit

(**BI**nary digi**T**) A single digit in a binary number (0 or 1). Within the computer, a bit is physically a transistor or capacitor in a memory cell, a magnetic spot on disk or tape or a high or low voltage pulsing through a circuit. A bit is like a light bulb: on or off.

Groups of bits make up storage units in the computer, called "characters," "bytes," or "words," which are manipulated as a group. The most common is the byte, made up of eight bits and equivalent to one alphanumeric character. See *space/time*.

bitblit

See *bitblt*.

bitblt

(**BIT BL**ock Transfer) In computer graphics, a hardware feature that moves a rectangular block of bits from main memory into display memory. It speeds the display of moving objects (animation, scrolling) on screen.

bit cell

A boundary in which a single bit is recorded on a tape or disk.

bit density

The number of bits that can be stored within a given physical area.

bit depth

The number of bits used to represent an object. It typically refers to the number of colors that can be displayed at one time, which is based on the number of bits used to hold a pixel. Digital video requires at least 16 bits, while 24 bits produces realistic TV-like images.

```
Color bit depth        Total number of colors
 4-bit (nibble)                    16
 8-bit (one byte)                 256
16-bit (two bytes)             65,536
24-bit (three bytes)       16,777,216
32-bit (four bytes)        16,777,216 + alpha channel
```

bit level device

A device, such as a disk drive, that inputs and outputs data bits. Contrast with *pulse level device*.

bit manipulation

Processing individual bits within a byte. Bit-level manipulation is very low-level programming, often done in graphics and systems programming.

bitmap

(1) In computer graphics, an area in memory that represents the video image. For monochrome screens, one bit in the bitmap represents one pixel on screen. For gray scale or color, several bits in the bitmap represent one pixel or group of pixels on screen.

(2) A binary representation in which each bit or set of bits corresponds to some object (image, font, etc.) or condition.

bitmapped font

A set of dot patterns for each letter and digit in a particular typeface (Times Roman, Helvetica, etc.) for a specified type size (10 points, 12 points, etc.). Bitmapped typefaces are either purchased in groups of pre-generated point sizes, or, for a wide supply of fonts, font generators allow the user to create a variety of point sizes. Bitmapped fonts take up disk space for each point size. Contrast with *scalable font*. See *font* and *font generator*.

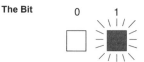

The Bit

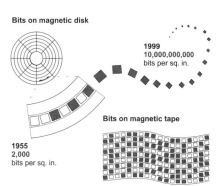

The bit is the smallest element of computer storage. It is a positive or negative magnetic spot on disk and tape and charged cells in memory.

Bits on magnetic disk

1999
10,000,000,000
bits per sq. in.

1955
2,000
bits per sq. in.

Bits on magnetic tape

bitmapped graphics
The raster graphics method for generating images. Contrast with *vector graphics* and *character graphics*.

bit-oriented protocol
A communications protocol that uses individual bits within the byte as control codes, such as IBM's SDLC. Contrast with *byte-oriented protocol*.

bit parallel
The transmission of several bits at the same time, each bit travelling over a different wire in the cable.

bit pattern
A specific layout of binary digits.

bit plane
A segment of memory used to control an object, such as a color, cursor or sprite. Bit planes may be reserved parts of a common memory or independent memory banks each designed for one purpose.

bit rate
The transmission speed of binary coded data. Same as *data rate*.

bit serial
The transmission of one bit after the other on a single line or wire.

bit slice processor
A logic chip that is used as an elementary building block for the computer designer. Bit slice processors usually come in 4-bit increments and are strung together to make larger processors (8 bit, 12 bit, etc.).

bit stream
The transmission of binary signals.

bit stuffing
Adding bits to a transmitted message in order to round out a fixed frame or to break up a pattern of data bits that could be misconstrued for control codes.

bit twiddler
Same as *hacker*.

bit wise
See *bitwise* and *bit manipulation*.

bitwise
Dealing with bits rather than larger structures such as a byte. Bitwise operators are programming commands or statements that work with individual bits. See *bit manipulation*.

BizTalk
An initiative from Microsoft to spearhead XML usage. The "BizTalk Framework" provides a special set of XML tags that provide a common transport envelope for wrapping XML documents for business-to-business and application-to-application interoperability.

black box
(1) A custom-made electronic device, such as a protocol converter or encryption system. Yesterday's black boxes often become today's off-the-shelf products.

(2) (Black Box Corporation, Pittsburgh, PA, www.blackbox.com) An organization that specializes in communications and LAN products. It offers expert services, custom solutions and hard-to-find products.

blank character
A space character that takes up one byte in the computer just like a letter or digit. When you press the space bar on a personal computer keyboard, the ASCII character with a numeric value of 32 is created.

blank squash

The removal of blanks between items of data. For example, in the expression **CITY** + ", " + **STATE**, the data is concatenated with a blank squash resulting in DALLAS, TX rather than DALLAS   TX.

blip

A mark, line or spot on a medium, such as microfilm, that is optically sensed and used for timing or counting purposes.

blitting

Using a bitblt to transfer data.

BLOB

(Binary Large OBject) User-specified data such as an image. A BLOB field in a database holds any binary data.

block

(1) A group of disk or tape records that is stored and transferred as a single unit.

(2) A group of bits or characters that is transmitted as a unit.

(3) A group of text characters that has been marked for moving, copying, saving or other operation.

block device

A peripheral device that transfers a group of bytes (block, sector, etc.) of data at a time such as a disk. Contrast with *character device*.

block diagram

A chart that contains squares and rectangles connected with arrows to depict hardware and software interconnections. For program flow charts, information system flow charts, circuit diagrams and communications networks, more elaborate graphical representations are usually used.

Bluetooth

A wireless personal area network (PAN) technology from the Bluetooth Special Interest Group, (www.bluetooth.com), founded in 1998 by Ericsson, IBM, Intel, Nokia and Toshiba. Bluetooth is an open standard for short-range transmission of digital voice and data between mobile devices (laptops, PDAs, phones) and desktop devices.

BMP file

(Bit MaP file) The raster graphics image format that is native to Windows. It provides for 2, 16, 256 or 16 million colors (1-bit, 4-bit, 8-bit and 24-bit color). BMP files are also called "bump" files.

BNC

(British Naval Connector) A commonly used connector for coaxial cable. The plug looks like a tiny tin can with the lid off and two short pins sticking out on the upper edge on opposite sides. After insertion, the plug is turned, tightening the pins in the socket.

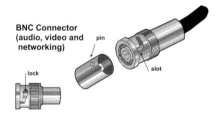

BNC Connector
(audio, video and
networking)

pin

lock

slot

board

See *printed circuit board* and *BBS*.

board level

Electronic components that are mounted on a printed circuit board instead of in a cabinet or finished housing.

BOC

(Bell Operating Company) One of 22 telephone companies that was formerly part of AT&T and now part of one of the seven regional Bell telephone companies.

body type

The typeface and size commonly used for text in paragraph copy. Typically 10 points.

BOF

(Beginning Of File) The status of a file when it is first opened or when an instruction or command has reset the file pointer.

boilerplate

A common phrase or expression used over and over. Boilerplate is stored on disk and copied into the document as needed.

boldface

Characters that are heavier and darker on printed output and brighter than normal on a display screen.

boldface attribute

A code that turns normal characters into boldface characters on a printer or display screen.

boldface font

A set of type characters that are darker and heavier than normal type. In a boldface font, all characters have been designed as bold characters.

bomb

Same as *abend* and *crash*.

BOMP

(Bill Of Materials Processor) One of the first DBMSs used for bill of materials explosion in the early 1960s from IBM. A subsequent version, DBOMP, was used in manufacturing during the 1970s.

Booch

An object-oriented analysis and design method developed by Grady Booch, chief scientist of Rational Software.

Boolean data

Yes/no or true/false data.

Boolean expression

A statement using Boolean operators that expresses a condition which is either true or false.

Boolean logic

The "mathematics of logic," developed by English mathematician George Boole in the mid 19th century. Its rules govern logical functions (true/false). As add, subtract, multiply and divide are the primary operations of arithmetic, AND, OR and NOT are the primary operations of Boolean logic. The AND, OR and NOT operators are commonly used in queries. See *Boolean search*.

Boolean search

A search for specific data. It implies that any condition can be searched for using the Boolean operators AND, OR and NOT. For example, the English language request: "Search for all Spanish and French speaking employees who have MBAs, but don't work in Sales." is expressed in the following dBASE command:

```
list for degree = "MBA" .and. (language = "Spanish" .or. language = "French")
    .and. .not. department = "Sales"
```

boot

Causing the computer to start executing instructions. Personal computers contain built-in instructions in a ROM chip that are automatically executed on startup. These instructions search for the operating system, load it and pass control to it. Starting up a large computer may require more button pushing and keyboard input.

The term comes from "bootstrap," since bootstraps help you get your boots on, booting the computer helps it get its first instructions. See *cold boot, warm boot* and *clean boot*.

bootable disk

A disk that contains the operating system in a form ready to load into the computer. It often refers to a floppy disk that contains the operating system in its boot sectors. If a hard disk personal computer does not find a bootable floppy disk in the primary floppy drive at startup (A: in a PC), it boots from the hard disk.

boot drive
A disk drive that contains the operating system.

boot failure
The inability to locate and/or read the operating system from the designated disk.

BootP
(BOOTstrap Protocol) A low-level TCP/IP protocol used by a diskless workstation or network computer (NC) to boot itself from the network. BootP enables the station to determine its own logical IP address upon startup.

boot record
See *boot sector*.

boot ROM
A memory chip that allows a workstation to be booted from the server or other remote station.

boot sector
An area on disk (usually the first sectors in the first disk partition) reserved for the operating system. On startup, the computer looks in the boot sectors for the operating system, which must be loaded first.

bootstrap
See *boot*.

boot virus
A virus written into the boot sectors of a floppy disk. If the floppy is booted, it infects the system. For example, the Michelangelo virus, which destroys data on March 6th, Michelangelo's birthday, infects a computer if the virus diskette is left in the drive and booted inadvertently when the computer is turned back on.

Borland
See *Inprise/Borland*.

bpi
(Bits Per Inch) The measurement of the number of bits stored in a linear inch of a track on a recording surface, such as on a disk or tape.

BPR
(Business Process Reengineering) See *reengineering*.

bps
(Bits Per Second) The measurement of the speed of data transfer in a communications system.

branch
(1) Same as *GOTO*.

(2) A connection between two blocks in a flowchart or two nodes in a network.

braze
To solder using metals with a very high melting point, such as with an alloy of zinc and copper.

breadboard
A thin plastic board full of holes used to hold components (transistors, chips, etc.) that are wired together. It is used to develop electronic prototypes or one-of-a-kind systems.

break
To temporarily or permanently stop executing, printing or transmitting.

break key
A key that is pressed to stop the execution of the current program or transmission.

breakout box
A device inserted into a multiple-line cable for testing purposes that provides an external connecting point to each wire. A small LED may be attached to each line, which glows when a signal is present.

breakpoint

The location in a program used to temporarily halt the program for testing and debugging.

bricks and mortar

A store (shop, supermarket, department store, etc.) in the real world. Contrast with *clicks and mortar*.

bridge

(1) To cross from one circuit, channel or element over to another.

(2) A device that connects two LAN segments together, which may be of similar or dissimilar types, such as Ethernet and Token Ring. Bridges are inserted into a network to improve performance by keeping traffic contained within smaller segments. Bridges work at the data link layer (OSI layer 2) and are faster than routers which work at the network layer (layer 3). See *transparent bridging, repeater, router, gateway* and *hub*.

bridgeware

Hardware or software that converts data or translates programs from one format into another.

broadband

(1) High-speed transmission at T1 rates (1.544 Mbps) and above.

(2) A technique for transmitting data, voice and video using the same frequency division multiplexing (FDM) technique as cable TV. Modems are required for this method, because the digital data has to be modulated onto the line. Contrast with *baseband*.

broadband wireless

Wireless transmission at high speed. Wireless transmission is slower than wireline speeds, thus, whereas land-based broadband is generally at T1 rates and above, wireless might be considered broadband at 250 Kbps and above.

broadcast

To disseminate information to several recipients simultaneously.

brouter

(Bridging **ROUTER**) A communications device that performs both bridge and routing functions. See *router, gateway* and *hub*.

browse

(1) To view the contents of a file or a group of files. Browser programs generally let you view data by scrolling through the documents or databases. In a database program, the browse mode often lets you edit the data.

(2) To view and edit the class hierarchy of the objects in an object-oriented programming language.

browser

A program that lets you look through a set of data. See *Web browser, microbrowser* and *browse*.

browser cache

Pronounced browser "cash." A temporary storage area in memory or on disk that holds the most recently-downloaded Web pages. See *Web cache* and *cache*.

BSD socket

A communications interface in UNIX first introduced in BSD UNIX. See *UNIX socket*.

BSD UNIX

(Berkeley Software Distribution UNIX) A version of UNIX developed by the Computer Systems Research Group of the University of California at Berkeley from 1979 to 1993. BSD enhancements, known as the "Berkeley Extensions," include networking, virtual memory, task switching and large file names (up to 255 chars.). BSD's UNIX was distributed free, with a charge only for the media.

b-spline

In computer graphics, a curve that is generated using a mathematical formula which assures continuity with other b-splines.

BTAM

(Basic Telecommunications Access Method) IBM communications software used in bisynch, non-SNA mainframe networks. Application programs must interface directly with the BTAM access method.

BTLZ

(British Telecom Lempel Ziv) A data compression algorithm based on the Lempel-Ziv method that can achieve up to 4x the throughput of 2400 and 9600 bps modems.

B-tree

(Balanced-tree) A technique for organizing indexes. In order to keep access time to a minimum, it stores the data keys in a balanced hierarchy that continually realigns itself as items are inserted and deleted. Thus, all nodes always have a similar number of keys.

Btrieve

A file manager from Novell that accompanies its NetWare operating systems. It allows for the creation of indexed files, using the b-tree organization method. Btrieve functions can be called from within many common programming languages. See *Xtrieve*.

bubble

A bit in bubble memory or a symbol in a bubble chart.

bubble chart

A chart that uses bubble-like symbols often used to depict data flow diagrams.

Bubble Jet

Canon's ink jet printer technology.

bubble memory

A solid state semiconductor and magnetic storage device suited for rugged applications. It is about as fast as a slow hard disk and holds its content without power. Bubble memory is conceptually a stationary disk with spinning bits. Only a couple of square inches in size, it contains a thin film magnetic recording layer. Globular-shaped bubbles (bits) are electromagnetically generated in circular strings inside this layer. In order to read or write the bubbles, they are rotated past the equivalent of a read/write head.

bubble sort

A multiple-pass sorting technique that starts by sequencing the first two items, then the second with the third, then the third with the fourth and so on until the end of the set has been reached. The process is repeated until all items are in the correct sequence.

bucket

Another term for a variable. It's just a place to store something.

buffer

A reserved segment of memory used to hold data while it is being processed. In a program, buffers are created to hold some amount of data from each of the files that will be read or written. A buffer may also be a small hardware memory bank used for special purposes.

buffer flush

The transfer of data from memory to disk. Whenever you command your application to save the document you're working on, the program is actually flushing its buffer (writing the contents of one or more reserved areas of memory to the hard disk).

Go Flush Your Cold Buffer!

Try this one out on your colleagues. A cold buffer is a reserved area of memory that contains data, which hasn't been updated for a while. Cold buffers are flushed at periodic intervals. More importantly, this phrase sounds as strange as they get. Better yet, try "go flush your cold buffer into your SCSI DASD" (pronounced scuzzy dazdy). Be sure to say this without cracking a smile, and expect quite a grin from a systems professional. If your friend doesn't understand this phrase, be sure to recommend a good glossary!

buffer pool

An area of memory reserved for buffers.

---

bug

A persistent error in software or hardware. If the bug is in software, it can be corrected by changing the program. If the bug is in hardware, new circuits have to be designed. Although the derivation of bug is generally attributed to the moth that was found squashed between the points of an electromechanical relay in a computer in the 1940s, the term was already in use in the late 1800s. See *software bug*. Contrast with *glitch*.

A Note from the Author

On October 19, 1992, I found my first "real bug." When I fired up my laser printer, it printed blotchy pages. Upon inspection, I found a bug lying belly up in the trough below the corona wire. The printer worked fine after removing it!

bug compatible

A hardware device that contains the same design flaws as the original.

bug inheritance

Software bugs that are brought down from a higher-level class in an object-oriented system.

bulk storage

Storage that is not used for high-speed execution. May refer to auxiliary memory, tape or disk.

bulletin board

See *BBS*.

bump mapping

In computer graphics, a technique for simulating rough textures by creating irregularities in shading.

bundle

To sell hardware and software as a single product or to combine several software packages for sale as a single unit. Contrast with *unbundle*.

bunny suit

The protective clothing worn by an individual in a clean room that keeps human bacteria from infecting the chip-making process. The outfit makes people look like oversized rabbits.

burn in

To test a new electronic system by running it for some length of time. Weak components often fail within the first few hours of use.

burster

A mechanical device that separates continuous paper forms into cut sheets. A burster can be attached to the end of a collator, which separates multipart forms into single parts.

burst mode

A high-speed transmission mode in a communications or computer channel. Under certain conditions, the system sends a burst of data at higher speed. For example, a multiplexor channel may suspend transmitting several streams of data and send one stream at full bandwidth.

bus

A common pathway, or channel, between multiple devices. The ISA and PCI slots in a PC are attached to the bus. A bus is always designed to connect multiple devices, whereas channels such as the serial and parallel ports are used to connect only one. Buses are generally hardware, although software can be designed and linked via a so called "software bus."

The term was coined after a real bus since a bus stops at all bus stops en route. In an electronic bus, the signals go to all stations connected to it. A weak analog perhaps, but the term will live forever.

bus bridge

A device that connects two similar or dissimilar busses together, such as two VMEbuses or a VMEbus and a Futurebus. This is not the same as a communications bridge, which connects networks together. See *bridge*.

bus extender

(1) A board that pushes a printed circuit board out of the way of surrounding boards for testing purposes. It plugs into an expansion slot, and the expansion board plugs into the bus extender.

(2) A device that extends the physical distance of a bus. See *repeater*.

(3) A device that increases the number of expansion slots. It is either an expansion board containing multiple expansion slots, or an expansion board that cables to a separate housing that contains the slots and its own power supply.

business analyst

An individual who analyzes the operations of a department or functional unit with the purpose of developing a general systems solution to the problem that may or may not require automation. The business analyst can provide insights into an operation for an information systems analyst.

business graphics

Numeric data represented in graphic form. While line graphs, bar charts and pie charts are the common forms of business graphics, there are many others. People think in pictures. By transforming numerical data into graphic form, patterns of business activity can be recognized more easily.

business machine

Any office machine, such as a typewriter or calculator, that is used in clerical and accounting functions. The term has traditionally excluded computers and terminals.

BusinessObjects

A query, reporing and analysis tool from Business Objects that runs under Windows and various UNIX clients. It is the leading decision support tool in the business market.

bus mastering

A bus design that allows add-in boards to process independently of the CPU and to be able to access the computer's memory and peripherals on their own.

bus mouse

A mouse that plugs into an expansion board instead of the serial port. This type of mouse was somewhat popular in the 1980s. Its connector looks like a PS/2 connector, but the pin configurations are different and not compatible.

button

(1) A knob, such as on a printer or a mouse, which is pushed with the finger to activate a function.

(2) A simulated button on screen that is "pushed" by clicking it with the mouse.

bypass

In communications, to avoid the local telephone company by using satellites and microwave systems.

byte

The common unit of computer storage from micro to mainframe. It is made up of eight binary digits (bits). A ninth bit may be added in the circuitry as a parity bit for error checking.

A byte holds the equivalent of a single character, such as the letter A, a dollar sign or decimal point. For numbers, a byte can hold a single decimal digit (0 to 9), two numeric digits (packed decimal) or a number from 0 to 255 (binary numbers).

The Byte

A byte is 8 binary digits, or cells.

bytecode

An intermediate language that is executed by a runtime interpreter. Java and Visual Basic source programs are compiled into bytecode, which is then executed by their respective interpreters. See *Java*.

Bytes in memory
In a 64 megabyte memory, there are 67,108,864 of these 8-bit structures.

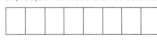

byte-oriented protocol

A communications protocol that uses control codes made up of full bytes. The bisynchronous protocols used by IBM and other vendors are examples. Contrast with *bit-oriented protocol*.

C

A high-level programming language that is widely used. Originally developed at Bell Labs, C and C++, the object-oriented version of C, are used for most commercial software as well as many internal applications. There are C and C++ compilers for every major hardware platform.

C is written as a series of functions that call each other for processing. In fact, the body of every C program is a function named "main." Functions are very flexible, allowing programmers to choose from the standard library that comes with the compiler, to use third party functions from other C suppliers, or to develop their own.

The following C example converts fahrenheit to centigrade:

```
main()    {
float fahr;
printf("Enter Fahrenheit ");
scanf("%f", &fahr);
printf("Celsius is %f\n", (fahr-32)*5/9);
          }
```

C++

An object-oriented version of C created by Bjarne Stroustrup. C++ has become popular because it combines traditional C programming with OOP capability. Smalltalk and other original OOP languages did not provide the familiar structures of conventional languages such as C and Pascal.

C2

The minimum security level defined by the National Computer Security Center. See *NCSC*.

CA

(Computer Associates International, Inc., Islandia, NY,www.cai.com) The world's largest diversified software vendor offering more than 500 applications from micro to mainframe. Founded in 1976 by Charles Wang and three associates, its first product was an IBM mainframe utility.

CAB file

(**CAB**inet file) A file format from Microsoft used to hold compressed files on its distribution disks. The Windows 95/98 Extract program is run at the command line to decompress the files.

cable

A flexible metal or glass wire or group of wires. All cables used in electronics are insulated with a material such as plastic or rubber.

cable categories

The following categories are based on their transmission capacity. The majority of new wiring installations use Category 5 UTP wire in order to be able to run or upgrade to the faster network technologies that will require it. Categories 1 through 5 are based on the EIA/TIA-568 standard.

Category	Cable type	Application
1	UTP	Analog voice
2	UTP	Digital voice, 1 Mbps data
3	UTP, STP	16 Mbps data
4	UTP, STP	20 Mbps data
5	UTP, STP	100 Mbps data
6	Coax	100 Mbps+ data
7	Fiber optic	100 Mbps+ data

cable Internet

Internet access via cable TV. There are two kinds of service. One uses a cable modem to connect to a computer, and the other uses an enhanced cable box that provides Internet access directly at the TV. Both of these differ from WebTV, which requires a phone line.

cable modem

A modem used to connect a computer to a cable TV system that offers Internet access.

cache

Pronounced "cash." A method for improving system performance by creating a secondary memory area closer to the CPU's higher speed. A memory cache, or CPU cache, is a dedicated bank of high-speed memory used to cache data from main memory. A disk cache is a reserved section of main memory used to cache data from the disk. In both cases, a larger block of the program or database is retrieved into the cache than is immediately necessary with the supposition that the next item will be waiting in a higher-speed location when required. See *Web cache* and browser *cache*.

cache server

A dedicated network server or a service within a server that caches Web pages in order to speed up access to information that has already been retrieved by a previous user. See *Web cache*.

caching controller

A disk controller with a built-in cache. See *cache*.

CA-Clipper

An application development system from Computer Associates. Originally a dBASE compiler, it has become a complete stand-alone development environment with many unique features. Clipper was originally developed by Nantucket Corporation.

CAD

(Computer-Aided Design) Using computers to design products. CAD systems are high-speed workstations or personal computers using CAD software and input devices such as graphic tablets and scanners. CAD output is a printed design or electronic input to CAM systems (see *CAD/CAM*).

CAD software is available for generic design or specialized uses, such as architectural, electrical and mechanical design. CAD software may also be highly specialized for creating products such as printed circuits and integrated circuits. See *graphics, CADD*, and *CAE*.

CADAM

A full-featured IBM mainframe CAD application, which includes 3-D capability, solid modeling and numerical control. Originally developed by Lockheed for internal use, it was distributed by IBM starting in the late 1970s. In 1989, IBM purchased the Lockheed subsidiary, CADAM, Inc.

CAD/CAM

(Computer-Aided Design/Computer-Aided Manufacturing) The integration of CAD and CAM. Products designed by CAD are direct input into the CAM system. For example, a device is designed and its electronic image is translated into a numerical control programming language, which generates the instructions for the machine that makes it.

CADD

(Computer-Aided Design and Drafting) CAD systems with additional features for drafting, such as dimensioning and text entry.

CAE

(1) (Computer-Aided Engineering) Software that analyzes designs which have been created in the computer or that have been created elsewhere and entered into the computer. Different kinds of engineering analyses can be performed, such as structural analysis and electronic circuit analysis.

(2) (Common Application Environment) Software development platform that is specified by X/Open.

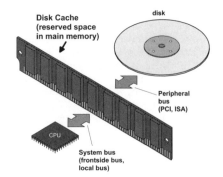

Disk Cache
(reserved space
in main memory)

disk

Peripheral bus
(PCI, ISA)

CPU

System bus
(frontside bus,
local bus)

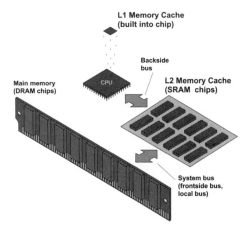

L1 Memory Cache
(built into chip)

Backside
bus

Main memory
(DRAM chips)

CPU

L2 Memory Cache
(SRAM chips)

System bus
(frontside bus,
local bus)

CA-Easytrieve

An application development system for IBM mainframes, DOS and OS/2 from Computer Associates. It includes 4GL query and reporting capabilities and can access many IBM mainframe and PC database formats. Easytrieve was originally developed by Pansophic Systems.

CAI

(1) (Computer-Assisted Instruction) Same as *CBT*.

(2) See *CA*.

CA-IDMS

A full-featured relational DBMS from Computer Associates that runs on minis and mainframes. IDMS (Integrated Data Management System) was developed at GE in the 1960s and marketed by Cullinane, later renamed Cullinet and then acquired by CA in 1989.

CAL

(1) (Computer-Assisted Learning) Same as *CBT*.

(2) (Conversational Algebraic Language) A timesharing language from the University of California.

calculated field

A numeric or date field that derives its data from the calculation of other fields. Data is not entered into a calculated field by the user.

calculator

A machine that provides arithmetic capabilities. It accepts keypad input and displays results on a readout and/or paper tape. Unlike a computer, it cannot handle alphabetic data.

CA-Librarian

A version control system for IBM mainframes from Computer Associates. Librarian's master files can be simultaneously accessed on shared disks by different operating systems. Librarian was originally developed by ADR, Inc.

call

(1) In programming, a statement that references an independent subroutine or program. The call is turned into a branch instruction by the assembler, compiler or interpreter. The routine that is called is responsible for returning to the calling program after it has finished processing.

(2) In communications, the action taken by the transmitting station to establish a connection with the receiving station in a dial-up network.

call center

A company department that handles telephone sales and/or service. Call centers use automatic call distributors (ACDs) to route calls to the appropriate agent or operator.

call control

Also called "call processing," it is the controlling of telephone and PBX functions. It includes connecting, disconnecting and transferring the call, but it does not affect the content of the call. Contrast with *media control*.

call distributor

A PBX feature that routes incoming calls to the next available agent or operator.

CALS

(Computer-Aided Acquisition and Logistics Support) A DOD initiative for electronically capturing military documentation and linking related information.

CAM

(1) (Computer-Aided Manufacturing) The automation of manufacturing systems and techniques, including numerical control, process control, robotics and materials requirements planning (MRP). See *CAD/CAM*.

(2) (Common Access Method) An ANSI standard for SCSI host adapters that supports simultaneous operations on multiple SCSI devices (multitasking I/O). This standard, traditionally unsupported in the PC world, is gradually being implemented in the PC's ROM BIOS under interrupt 4F. See *SCSI*.

candela
A unit of measurement of the intensity of light. An ordinary wax candle generates one candela. See *lumen*.

canned program
A software package that provides a fixed solution to a problem. Canned business applications should be analyzed carefully as they usually cannot be changed much, if at all.

canonical synthesis
The process of designing a model of a database without redundant data items. A canonical model, or schema, is independent of the hardware and software that will process the data.

CA-OpenIngres
A relational database management system (DBMS) from Computer Associates that runs on Windows NT, OS/2, VAXs and most UNIX platforms. CA-OpenIngres is an enhanced version of Ingres, one of the first heavyweight DBMSs and noted for its advanced features. For example, Ingres was the first major DBMS to include triggers and stored procedures.

capacitor
An electronic component that holds a charge. It comes in varying sizes for use in power supplies to the tiny cells in dynamic RAM chips.

CA-Panvalet
A version control system for IBM mainframes from Computer Associates that keeps track of source code, JCL and object modules. Panvalet was originally developed by Pansophic Systems. CA-PAN/LCM is a similar product for PCs, which also provides interfaces to mainframe systems, such as CA-Panvalet and CA-Librarian.

capstan
On magnetic tape drives, a motorized cylinder that traps the tape against a free-wheeling roller and moves it at a regulated speed.

capture buffer
A reserved memory area for holding an incoming transmission.

CA-RAMIS
A fourth-generation retrieval language for IBM mainframes and PCs from Computer Associates. Originally developed by Mathematica, RAMIS was later acquired by Martin Marietta Data Systems, On-Line Software, then CA in 1991. The earliest version of RAMIS was one of the first database packages with a non-procedural language for IBM mainframes.

card
See *printed circuit board, magnetic stripe, punched card* and *HyperCard*.

CardBus
The 32-bit version of the PC Card. See *PC Card*.

card cage
A cabinet or metal frame that holds printed circuit cards.

cardinal number
The number that states how much or how many. In "record 43 has 7 fields," the 7 is cardinal. Contrast with *ordinal number*.

card punch
(1) An early peripheral device that punches holes into cards at 100 to 300 cards per minute.

(2) Same as *keypunch machine*.

card reader
(1) A peripheral device that reads magnetic stripes on the back of a credit card.

(2) An early peripheral device that reads punched cards at 500 to 2,000 cards/minute. The code is detected by light patterns created by the holes in the card.

card services

Software that manages PCMCIA cards. See *PCMCIA*.

CA-Realizer

A Windows development software from Computer Associates that uses a structured superset of BASIC, has its own forms design utilities and includes a runtime module. Realizer was originally developed by Within Technologies.

caret

An up-arrow (^) symbol used to represent a decimal point or the control key. For example, ^Y means Ctrl-Y. It is the shift-6 key on the keyboard.

carpal tunnel syndrome

The compression of the main nerve to the hand due to scarring or swelling of the surrounding soft tissue in the wrist (area formed by carpal bones on top and muscle tendons below). Caused by trauma, arthritis and improper positioning of the wrist, it can result in severe damage to the hands. See *RSI*.

carriage

A printer or typewriter mechanism that holds the platen and controls paper feeding and movement.

carrier

An alternating current that vibrates at a fixed frequency, used to establish a boundary, or envelope, in which a signal is transmitted. Carriers are commonly used in radio transmission (AM, FM, TV, microwave, satellite, etc.) in order to differentiate transmitting stations. For example, an FM station's channel number is actually its carrier frequency. The FM station merges (modulates) its audio broadcast (data signal) onto its carrier and transmits the combined signal over the airwaves. At the receiving end, the FM tuner latches onto the carrier frequency, filters out the audio signal, amplifies it and sends it to the speaker.

Carriers can be used to transmit several signals simultaneously. For example, multiple voice, data and/or video signals can travel over the same line with each residing in its own carrier vibrating at a different frequency.

carrier based

A transmission system that generates a fixed frequency (carrier) to contain the data being transmitted.

carrier detect

A signal that indicates a connection has been made by sensing a carrier frequency on the line. See *RS-232* and *modem*.

carrier frequency

A unique frequency used to "carry" data within its boundaries. It is measured in cycles per second, or Hertz. See *carrier* and *FDM*.

cartridge

A self-contained, removable storage module that contains disks, magnetic tape or memory chips. Cartridges are inserted into slots in the drive, printer or computer. See *font cartridge*.

CAS

(1) (Communications Application Specification) A programming interface from Intel and DCA for activating functions in fax/modems. Introduced in 1988, Intel provides both the boards and the chips. CAS has not been widely used.

(2) (Column Address Strobe) A clock signal in a memory chip used to pinpoint the column of a particular bit in a row-column matrix. See *RAS*.

cascade

A connected series of devices or images. It often implies that the second and subsequent device takes over after the previous one is used up. For example, cascading tapes in a dual-tape backup system means the second tape is written after the first one is full. In a PC, a second IRQ chip is cascaded to the first, doubling the number of interrupts.

cascading style sheet

A style sheet format for HTML documents endorsed by the World Wide Web Consortium. CSS1 (Version 1.0) provides hundreds of layout settings that can be applied to all the subsequent HTML pages that are downloaded. CSS2 (Version 2.0) adds support for XML, oral presentations for the visually impaired, downloadable fonts and other enhancements.

CASE

(Computer Aided Software Engineering or Computer Aided Systems Engineering) Software that is used in any and all phases of developing an information system, including analysis, design and programming. For example, data dictionaries and diagramming tools aid in the analysis and design phases, while application generators speed up the programming phase.

CASE tools provide automated methods for designing and documenting traditional structured programming techniques. The ultimate goal of CASE is to provide a language for describing the overall system that is sufficient to generate all the necessary programs.

case-based reasoning

An AI problem solving technique that catalogs experience into "cases" and matches the current problem to the experience. Such systems are easier to maintain than rule-based expert systems, because changes require adding new cases without the complexity of adding new rules. It is used in many areas including pattern recognition, diagnosis, troubleshooting and planning.

case sensitive

Distinguishing lower case from upper case. In a case sensitive language, "abc" is considered different data than "ABC."

case statement

In programming, a variation of the if-then-else statement that is used when several ifs are required in a row. The following C example tests the variable KEY1 and performs functions based on the results.

```
switch (key1)    {
  case '+':  add();  break;
  case '-':  subtract();  break;
  case '*':  multiply();  break;
  case '/':  divide();  break;
                  }
```

cash memory

See cache.

cassette

A removable storage module that contains a supply reel of magnetic tape and a takeup reel. Data cassettes look like audio cassettes, but are made to higher tolerances.

Castanet

Java-based delivery software for the Internet and intranets from Marimba, Inc., Palo Alto, CA, (www.marimba.com). It automatically pushes application updates and other published content into client machines.

casting

In programming, the conversion of one data type into another.

catalog

A directory of disk files or files used in an application. Also any map, list or directory of storage space used by the computer.

Category 3, 5, etc.

See cable categories.

CA-Telon

An application generator from Computer Associates that generates COBOL and PL/I code for IBM mainframes and COBOL code for AS/400s. Development can be performed on mainframes or PCs. Telon was originally developed by Pansophic Systems.

The Computer Glossary

cathode

In electronics, a device that emits electrons, which flow from the negatively charged cathode to the positively charged anode. See *CRT*.

CATV

(Community Antenna TV) The original name for cable TV, which used a single antenna at the highest location in the community.

CAU

(Controlled Access Unit) An intelligent hub from IBM for Token Ring networks. Failed nodes are identified by the hub and reported via IBM's LAN Network Manager software.

CA-Unicenter

Systems management software from Computer Associates that supports a variety of servers, including Sun, HP, Digital, IBM and NetWare. Unicenter TNG (The Next Generation) manages the global enterprise, including networks, systems, applications and databases regardless of location.

CAV

(Constant Angular Velocity) A disk technique that spins the disk at a constant speed. The number of bits in each track is the same, but their density varies because the inner tracks have smaller circumferences than the outer tracks. Contrast with *CLV*.

CAVE

(Computer Automatic Virtual Environment) A virtual reality system that uses projectors to display images on the walls and ceilings rather than requiring the participant to wear goggles. CAVE is a trademark of the University of Illinois, which developed the CAVE-brand virtual reality system at its Electronic Visualization Laboratory, and made it available to others in 1992. Contrast with *HMD*.

CB

(Citizen's Band) The frequency band for public radio transmission in the 27 MHz range.

CBR

(1) (Computer-Based Reference) Reference materials accessible by computer in order to help people do their jobs quicker. For example, this Glossary on disk!

(2) (Constant Bit Rate) A uniform transmission rate. For example, voice traffic requires a CBR.

CBT

(Computer-Based Training) Using the computer for training and instruction. CBT programs are called "courseware," and provide interactive training sessions for all disciplines. It uses graphics extensively, as well as CD-ROM and videodisc.

CBT courseware is developed with authoring languages, such as Adroit, PILOT and Demo II, which allow for the creation of interactive sessions.

CCA

(1) (Common Cryptographic Architecture) IBM encryption software for MVS and DOS applications.

(2) (Compatible Communications Architecture) A Network Equipment Technology protocol for transmitting asynchronous data over X.25 networks.

CCD

(Charge Coupled Device) An electronic memory that can be charged by light. CCDs can hold a variable charge, which is why they are used in cameras and scanners to record variable shades of light. CCDs are analog, not digital, and are made of a special type of MOS transistor. Analog to digital (ADC) converters quantify the variable charge into a discrete number of colors.

CCFL, CCFT

(Cold Cathode Fluorescent Lamp, Tube) A type of light source for a backlit screen. It weighs more and uses more power than other backlights.

CCIA

(Computer and Communications Industry Association, Washington, DC, www.ccianet.org) A membership organization composed of computer and communications firms. It represents their interests in domestic and foreign trade, and, working with the NIST, keeps members advised of regulatory policy.

CCIS

(Common Channel Interoffice Signaling) A telephone communications technique that transmits voice and control signals over separate channels. Control signals are transmitted over a packet-switched digital network, providing faster connects and disconnects and allowing data, such as calling number, to be included.

CCITT

See *ITU*.

cc:Mail

A messaging system from Lotus that runs on PC LANs. Originally developed by cc:Mail, Inc., Mountain View, CA, Lotus acquired the company in 1991. Mail-enabled applications that are written to the VIM programming interface can use the cc:Mail system.

ccNUMA

(Cache Coherent Non-Uniform Memory Access) A multiprocessing architecture that supports up to several hundred SMP machines all functioning as one. One copy of the operating system is used, and all CPUs share a global memory.

CCP

(Certificate in Computer Programming) The award for successful completion of an examination in computer programming offered by ICCP.

CCS

(1) (Common Communications Support) SAA specifications for communications, which includes data streams (DCA, 3270), application services (DIA, DDM), session services (LU 6.2) and data links (X.25, Token Ring).

(2) (Common Channel Signaling) An integral part of ISDN known as "Signaling System 7," which advances the CCIS method for transmitting control signals. It allows call forwarding, call waiting, etc., to be provided anywhere in the network.

(3) (100 Call Seconds) A unit of measurement equal to 100 seconds of conversation. One hour = 36 CCS.

CD

(Compact Disc) A digital audio disc that contains up to 72 minutes of hi-fi stereo sound. Introduced in 1982, the disc is a plastic platter 4.75" in diameter, with binary code recorded as microscopic pits on one side. Individual selections are playable in any sequence. Other forms of CDs, such as CD-ROMs and CD-I discs, all stem from the audio CD.

Sound waves are sampled 44,056 times per second, and each sample is converted into a 16-bit number. It takes approximately 1.5 million bits of storage for one second of stereo. See also *carrier detect*.

CDA

(Compound Document Architecture) A compound document format from Digital that creates hot links between documents.

CD audio

Same as *CD* and *DAD*.

CDC

See *Control Data*.

CD caddy

A plastic container that holds a CD-ROM disc. The caddy is inserted into the disc drive.

CDDI

(Copper Distributed Data Interface) A version of FDDI that uses unshielded twisted pair (UTP) wires rather than optical fiber. The term is a trademark of Crescendo Communications, Sunnyvale, CA. ANSI's standard for FDDI over UTP is officially TP-PMD (Twisted Pair-Physical Media Dependent).

CDE

(1) (Common Desktop Environment) A graphical user interface for open systems. It is based on Motif with elements from HP, IBM and others. Originally developed by COSE, it is now governed by X/Open.

(2) (Computer Desktop Encyclopedia) The expanded version of this book available in print and on CD-ROM. Visit www.computerlanguage.com.

cdev

(Control Panel DEVice) Customizable settings in the Macintosh Control Panel that pertain to a particular program or device. Cdevs for the mouse, keyboard and startup disk, among others, come with the Mac. Others are provided with software packages and utilities.

CDF

(1) (Central Distribution Frame) A connecting unit (typically a hub) that acts a central distribution point to all the nodes in a zone or domain. See *MDF*.

(2) (Channel Definition Format) Microsoft's push technology for the Internet. CDF channels, which are also known as "Active Channels," are supported in Internet Explorer Version 4.0 and Windows 98.

CD-I

(Compact Disc-Interactive) A compact disc format developed by Philips and Sony that holds data, audio, still video and animated graphics. It provides up to 144 minutes of CD-quality stereo, 9.5 hours of AM-radio-quality stereo or 19 hours of monophonic audio. CD-I discs require a CD-I player and will not play in a CD-ROM player.

CDMA

(Code Division Multiple Access) A method for transmitting simultaneous signals over a shared portion of the spectrum. The foremost application of CDMA is the digital cellular phone technology from QUALCOMM Inc., San Diego, CA, (www.qualcomm.com), that operates in the 800MHz band and 1.9GHz PCS band. CDMA phones are noted for their excellent call quality and long battery life.

CDP

(Certificate in Data Processing) The award for the successful completion of an examination in hardware, software, systems analysis, programming, management and accounting, offered by ICCP.

CDPD

(Cellular Digital Packet Data) A digital wireless transmission system that is deployed as an enhancement to the existing analog cellular network. Based on IBM's CelluPlan II, it provides a packet overlay onto the AMPS network and moves data at 19.2 Kbps over ever-changing unused intervals in the voice channels. See *FDMA*, *TDMA* and *CDMA*.

CD-R, CD recorder

(CD-Recordable) A recordable CD-ROM technology using a disc that can be written only once. The CD-R drives that write the CD-R discs are also called "one-off machines." CD-R discs are used for beta versions and original masters of CD-ROM material as well as a means to distribute a large amount of data to a small number of recipients.

CD-ROM

(Compact Disc Read Only Memory) A compact disc format used to hold text, graphics and hi-fi stereo sound. It's like an audio CD, but uses a different track format for data. The audio CD player cannot play CD-ROMs, but CD-ROM players can play audio CDs and have output jacks for a headphone or speakers.

CD-ROMs hold in excess of 650MB of data, which is equivalent to about 250,000 pages of text or 20,000 medium-resolution images. The first CD-ROM drives transferred data at 150KB per second and speeds continued upward to more than 40 times the original.

CD-ROM changer

A CD-ROM drive that holds a small number of CD-ROMs for individual use on a desktop computer. Although it can swap discs, it typically contains only one drive and can only read one at a time. See *CD-ROM server*.

CD-ROM Extensions

The software required to use a CD-ROM drive on a PC running DOS. It allows the CD-ROM disc to be addressed like a hard or floppy disk and take on the next available drive letter. For example, the hard disk in the computer is C:, and if there are no additional hard disks, then the CD-ROM becomes the D: drive. The CD-ROM Extensions from Microsoft are provided in a file named MSCDEX.EXE.

CD-ROM jukebox

See *CD-ROM changer*.

CD-ROM server

A CD-ROM reader designed for network use and multiple users. It can store large numbers of CD-ROMs and may have several drives for simultaneous reading. See *CD-ROM changer*.

CD-ROM XA

(CD-ROM eXtended Architecture) A CD-ROM enhancement introduced in 1988 by Philips, Sony and Microsoft that lets text and pictures be narrated by allowing concurrent audio and video. CD-ROM XA drives are required for Kodak's Photo CD discs.

CD-RW

(CD-Rewritable) An erasable CD-ROM technology, formerly called "CD-E" for CD-Erasable. CD-RW drives read and write CD-RW disks and also read CD-ROM and CD-R disks. However, CD-RW disks cannot be read by existing CD-ROM drives without modification.

CDV

(1) (Compressed Digital Video) The compression of full-motion video for high-speed, economical transmission.

(2) (CD Video) A small videodisc (5" diameter) that provides five minutes of video with digital sound plus an additional 20 minutes of audio. Most videodisc players can play CDVs along with LDs.

CE

See *Windows CE*.

CEbus

(Consumer Electronic Bus) An EIA standard for a control network for the home using a variety of media, including AC power lines, telephone wire, coaxial cable as well as wireless.

Celeron

A family of lower-cost Pentium II chips from Intel that was introduced in mid 1998. The first models (266 and 300MHz) did not include an external L2 cache and were somewhat sluggish. However, subsequent models added 128KB of cache that runs at the full speed of the CPU like high-end Xeon chips.

cell

(1) An elementary unit of storage for data (bit) or power (battery).

(2) In a spreadsheet, the intersection of a row and column.

cell relay

A transmission technology that uses small fixed-length packets (cells) that can be switched at high speed. It is easier to build a switch that switches fixed-length packets than variable ones. ATM uses a type of cell relay technology.

CELP

(Code Excited Linear Predictive) A speech compression method that achieves high compression ratios along with toll quality audio. LD-CELP (Low-Delay CELP) provides near toll quality audio by using a smaller sample size that is processed faster, resulting in lower delays.

centering cone

A short plastic or metal cone used to align a 5.25" floppy disk to the drive spindle. It is inserted into the diskette's center hole when the drive door is closed.

centimeter

A unit of measurement that is 1/100th of a meter or approximately 4/10ths of an inch (0.39 inch).

centralized processing

Processing performed in one or more computers in a single location. All terminals in the organization are connected to the central computers. Contrast with *distributed processing* and *decentralized processing*.

central office

A local telephone company switching center. There are two types. The first is called an "end office" (EO) or "local exchange" (LE) and connects directly to the outside plant, which is the feeder and distribution system to homes and offices. The end office (often called a Class 5 office) provides customer services such as call waiting and call forwarding. The second type is the "tandem office" (also toll office or tandem/toll office), which is a central office that does not connect directly to the customer. Toll call record generation and accounting used to be handled in the tandem offices. Today, the billing is mostly done in the end offices. See *class 4 switch* and *class 5 switch*.

central processing unit, central processor

See *CPU*.

CENTREX

PBX services provided by a local telephone company. Switching is done in the telephone company's central office. Some services do the switching at the customer's site, but control it in the central office.

Centronics

A standard 36-pin parallel interface for connecting printers and other devices to a computer. It defines the plug, socket and signals used and transfers data asynchronously up to 200 Kbytes/sec. This de facto standard was developed by Centronics Corporation, maker of the first successful dot matrix printers. See *printer cable*.

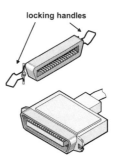

locking handles

A 36-pin Centronics connector is used on PC printers. A 50-pin variation is used for SCSI-1 devices. After insertion, the locking handles on the socket are snapped into the catches on the plug.

Centura

A high-level development system for 32-bit Windows applications from Centura Software Corporation (formerly Gupta Software), Menlo Park, CA. It includes a 4GL, web publishing and three-tier client/server support. It is the 32-bit counterpart of the widely-used 16-bit SQLWindows.

CERDIP

(CERamic DIP) A type of DIP that uses two ceramic layers epoxied together.

CERN

(Conseil Europeen pour la Recherche Nucleaire, Geneva, Switzerland, www.cern.ch) CERN is the European Laboratory for Nuclear Research where the World Wide Web was developed to enhance collaboration on research documents pertaining to particle physics. A complete Web server software package is available at no charge from CERN.

CGA

(Color/Graphics Adapter) IBM's first video display standard for the PC, which provided low-resolution text and graphics. It was superseded by EGA and VGA.

CGI script

(Common Gateway Interface script) A small program written in a language such as Perl, Tcl, C or C++ that functions as the glue between HTML pages and other programs on the Web server. For example, a CGI script would allow search data entered on a Web page to be sent to the database management system (DBMS) for lookup. It would also format the results of that search as an HTML page and send it back to the user. See *JSP* and *Active Server Page*.

CGM

(Computer Graphics Metafile) A standard format for interchanging graphics images. CGM stores images primarily in vector graphics, but also provides a raster format. Earlier GDM and VDM formats have been merged into the CGM standard.

chad

A piece of paper that is punched out on a punched card, paper tape or on the borders of continuous forms. A chadded form is when the holes are cut completely through. A chadless form is when the chads are still attached to one edge of the hole.

chaining

Linking items or records to form a chain. Each link in the chain points to the next item.

challenge/response

An authentication method used to verify the legitimacy of users logging onto the network. When a user logs on, the server uses account information to send a "challenge" number back to the user. The user enters the number into a credit-card sized token card that generates a response which is sent to the server.

change file

A transaction file used to update a master file.

change management

See *version control*.

channel

(1) A high-speed metal or optical fiber pathway between the computer and the control units of the peripheral devices. Channels are used in mainframes and high-end machines. Each channel is an independent unit that can transfer data concurrently with other channels as well as the CPU. For example, in a 10-channel computer, 10 streams of data are being transmitted to and from the CPU at the same time. In contrast, the bus in a personal computer serves as a common, shared channel between all devices. Each device must wait for its turn on the bus.

(2) In communications, any pathway between two computers or terminals. It may refer to the physical medium, such as coaxial cable, or to a specific carrier frequency (subchannel) within a larger channel or wireless medium.

(3) The retail channel made up of distributors and dealers.

channel bank

A multiplexor that merges several low-speed voice or data lines into one high-speed (typically T1) line and vice versa.

channel bonding

Doubling transmission speed by spreading the data over two lines. ISDN modems use channel bonding to split the data stream into two 64 Kbps channels, which use both lines in an ISDN BRI service. Bonded analog modems use two analog telephone lines to double transmission capacity, splitting data into two streams of 33.6 or 56 Kbps. This "dual analog" method often requires the same brand of modem at each end.

channel program

Instructions executed by a peripheral channel. The channel executes the channel program independently of the CPU, allowing concurrent operations to take place in the computer.

chaos

The science that deals with the underlying order of the seemingly random nature of the universe. See *fractals*.

CHAP

(Challenge Handshake Authentication Protocol) An access control protocol that dynamically encrypts the user's ID and password. The logon procedure in the user's machine obtains a key from the CHAP server, which it uses to encrypt the username and password before transmitting it. See *PAP*.

character

A single alphabetic letter, numeric digit, or special symbol such as a decimal point or comma. A character is equivalent to a byte; for example, 50,000 characters take up 50,000 bytes.

character based

Same as *text based*.

character cell

A matrix of dots used to form a single character on a display screen or printer. For example, an 8x16 cell is made up of 16 rows each containing eight dots. Character cells are displayed and printed contiguously; therefore the design of each letter, digit or symbol within the cell must include surrounding blank space.

character code

Same as *data code*.

character data

Alphanumeric data or text. Contrast with *numeric data*.

character device

A peripheral device that transfers data one byte at a time at a time, such as a parallel or serial port. Contrast with *block device*.

character field

A data field that holds alphanumeric characters. Contrast with *numeric field*.

character generator

(1) Circuitry that converts data characters into dot patterns for a display screen.

(2) A device that creates text characters that are superimposed onto video frames.

character graphics

A set of special symbols strung together like letters of the alphabet to create elementary graphics and forms.

characteristic

In logarithms and floating point, the number that indicates where the decimal point is placed.

character mode

Same as *text mode*.

character-oriented protocol

See *byte-oriented protocol*.

character pitch

The measurement of the number of characters per inch. See *cpi*.

character printer

A printer that prints one character at a time, such as a daisy wheel or dot matrix printer. See *printer*.

character recognition

The ability of a machine to recognize printed text. See *OCR* and *MICR*.

character set

(1) A group of unique symbols and codes. For example, the ASCII character set contains 128 characters numbered 0 to 127. The English character set is 26 symbols (A-Z).

(2) See *symbol set*.

character string

A group of alphanumeric characters. Contrast with *numeric data*.

character terminal

A display screen without graphics capability.

chat

A realtime conferencing capability between two or more users on a LAN, BBS or the Internet. The chat is accomplished by typing on the keyboard, not speaking. Each keystroke is transmitted as it is pressed. See *Internet Relay Chat*.

chat mode

An option in a communications program that turns on the chat function.

chat room

An interactive discussion (by keyboard) about a specific topic that is hosted on a BBS, online service or the Internet. See *Internet Relay Chat.*

chat window

A text window used for conferencing between two or more users. See *chat room.*

check bits

A calculated number used for error checking. The number is derived by some formula from the binary value of one or more bytes of data. See *parity checking, checksum* and *CRC.*

check box

A small box that displays an X or checkmark when the associated option is selected.

check digit

A numeric digit used to ensure that account numbers are correctly entered into the computer. Using a formula, a check digit is calculated for each new account number, which then becomes part of the number, often the last digit.

When an account number is entered, the data entry program recalculates the check digit and compares it to the check digit entered. If the digits are not equal, the account number is considered invalid.

checkpoint/restart

A method of recovering from a system failure. A checkpoint is a copy of the computer's memory that is periodically saved on disk along with the current register settings (last instruction executed, etc.). In the event of any failure, the last checkpoint serves as a recovery point.

When the problem has been fixed, the restart program copies the last checkpoint into memory, resets all the hardware registers and starts the computer from that point. Any transactions in memory after the last checkpoint was taken until the failure occurred will be lost.

checksum

A value used to ensure data is transmitted without error. It is created by adding the binary value of each alphanumeric character in a block of data and sending it with the data. At the receiving end, a new checksum is computed and matched against the transmitted checksum. A non-match indicates an error.

Just as a check digit tests the accuracy of a single number, a checksum tests a block of data. Checksums detect single bit errors and some multiple bit errors, but are not as effective as the CRC method.

chicklet keyboard

A keyboard with small, square keys not suitable for touch typing.

child program

A secondary or subprogram called for and loaded into memory by the main program. See *parent program.*

chip

A set of microminiaturized, electronic circuits that are designed for use as processors and memory in computers and countless consumer and industrial products. Chips are the driving force in this industry. Small chips hold from a handful to tens of thousands of transistors. They look like tiny aluminum chips, no more than 1/16" square by 1/30" thick, which is where the term "chip" came from. Large chips, which can be more than a half inch square, hold millions of transistors. It is actually only the top one thousandth of an inch of a chip's surface that holds the circuits. The rest of it is just a base. The terms *chip, integrated circuit* and *microchip* are synonymous. See *logic chip* and *memory chip.*

chip carrier

(1) The package that a chip is mounted in.

(2) A chip package with connectors on all sides. See *leaded chip carrier* and *leadless chip carrier.*

chip on board

A bare chip that is mounted directly on the printed circuit board. After the wires are attached, a "blob" of epoxy or plastic is used to cover the chip and its connections.

chipset

A group of chips designed to work as a unit to perform a function. For example, a modem chipset contains all the primary circuits for transmitting and receiving. A PC chipset contains the system, memory and bus controllers. The chipset, CPU, memory, buses, keyboard circuit and BIOS make up the PC motherboard. Chipsets are typically built on two to four chips, but can be built on one for handheld devices.

chroma key

See *color key*.

chromatic dispersion

The spreading of light rays within an optical fiber, which causes decreased bandwidth.

CICS

(Customer Information Control System) A TP monitor from IBM that provides transaction processing for IBM mainframes. It controls the interaction between applications and users and lets programmers develop screen displays without detailed knowledge of the terminals used. It provides terminal routing, password security, transaction logging for error recovery and activity journals for performance analysis.

CICS commands are written into assembly language, COBOL, PL/I and RPG programs. It implements SNA layers 4, 5 and 6.

CIDR

(Classless Inter-Domain Routing) A method for adding additional Class C IP addresses, which are given to Internet service providers (ISPs) for their customers. Instead of the fixed 7, 14 and 21 bits used in the Class A-B-C network IDs, CIDR uses a variable network ID from 13 to 27 bits. For example, the CIDR address 204.12.01.42/24 indicates that the first 24 bits are used for network ID.

CIF

(1) (Common Intermediate Format) A standard video format used in videoconferencing. CIF formats are defined by their resolution, and standards both above and below the original resolution have been established. The original CIF is also known as Full CIF (FCIF). The bit rates in the chart below are for uncompressed color frames.

CIF Format		Resolution	Bit Rate 30 fps (Mbps)
SQCIF	(Sub Quarter CIF)	128 x 96	4.4
QCIF	(Quarter CIF)	176 x 144	9.1
CIF	(Full CIF, FCIF)	352 x 288	36.5
4CIF	(4 x CIF)	704 x 576	146.0
16CIF	(16 x CIF)	1408 x 1152	583.9

(2) (Cells In Frames) A networking technology developed by Cornell University that allows ATM backbones to be used with Ethernet LANs. CIF utilizes the inherent quality of service in ATM, which allows for realtime voice and video, all the way to the Ethernet end station by placing the ATM cell within the Ethernet frame.

1/4"

RAM I/O Control Unit Clock

ROM

Processor (CPU)

An entire computer on a single chip

CIM

(1) (Computer-Integrated Manufacturing) Integrating office/accounting functions with automated factory systems. Point of sale, billing, machine tool scheduling and supply ordering are part of CIM.

(2) (CompuServe Information Manager) The client program from CompuServe for accessing its services.

cine-oriented

A film-image orientation like that of movie film, which runs parallel to the outer edge of the medium. Contrast with *comic-strip oriented*.

Cinepak

A video compression/decompression algorithm from SuperMac Technologies, Sunnyvale, CA, that is used to compress movie files. It is widely used on the Macintosh and is included in Windows 95/98.

CIO

(Chief Information Officer) The executive officer in charge of all information processing in an organization.

ciphertext

Data that has been coded (enciphered, encrypted, encoded) for security purposes.

CIR

(Committed Information Rate) In a frame relay network, the minimum speed maintained between nodes.

circuit

(1) A set of electronic components that perform a particular function in an electronic system.

(2) Same as *communications channel*.

circuit analyzer

(1) A device that tests the validity of an electronic circuit.

(2) In communications, same as *data line monitor*.

circuit board

Same as *printed circuit board*.

circuit breaker

A protective device that opens a circuit upon sensing a current overload. Unlike a fuse, it can be reset.

circuit card

Same as *printed circuit board*.

circuit cellular

The transmission of data over the cellular network using a voice channel and modem similar to using land-based modems. Contrast with *packet cellular*. See *wireless*.

circuit switching

The temporary connection of two or more communications channels. Users have full use of the circuit until the connection is terminated. Contrast with "message switching," which stores messages and forwards them later, and contrast with "packet switching," which breaks up a message into packets and routes each packet through the most expedient path at that moment.

Circuit switching is used by the telephone company for its voice networks in order to guarantee steady, consistent service for two people engaged in a telephone conversation.

CIS

(1) (CompuServe Information Service) See *CompuServe*.

(2) (Card Information Structure) A data structure on a PCMCIA card that contains information about the card's contents. It allows the card to describe its configuration requirements to its host computer.

CISC

(Complex Instruction Set Computer) Pronounced "sisk." The traditional architecture of a computer which uses microcode to execute very comprehensive instructions. Instructions may be variable in length and use all addressing modes, requiring complex circuitry to decode them. Contrast with *RISC*.

Cisco

(Cisco Systems, Inc., San Jose, CA, www.cisco.com) The leading manufacturer of networking equipment, including routers, bridges, frame switches and ATM switches, dial-up access servers and network management software. Cisco was founded in 1984 by Leonard Bosack and Sandra Lerner, a married couple both employed by Stanford University. Initially targeting universities, Cisco sold its first router in 1986.

Citrix

(Citrix Systems, Inc., Ft. Lauderdale, FL, www.citrix.com) Founded in 1989, it is a company that specializes in multiuser server software. Its Windows NT-based WinFrame server uses Citrix's Intelligent Console Architecture (ICA) to send only screen changes to the client machines. Citrix technology is expected to be built into future versions of Windows NT by Citrix and Microsoft. See *WinFrame*. See also *Cyrix*.

CKO

(Chief Knowledge Officer) The executive officer responsible for exchanging knowledge within an organization. CKOs determine how research storehouses and all other expertise throughout the enterprise can be shared by all departments.

cladding

The plastic or glass sheath that is fused to and surrounds the core of an optical fiber. It keeps the light waves inside the core and adds strength to it. The cladding is covered with a protective outer jacket.

clamping ring

The part of a 5.25" floppy disk drive that presses the disk onto the spindle. It is usually part of the centering cone.

Claris

(Claris Corporation, Santa Clara, CA, www.claris.com) Software subsidiary of Apple that was separated from the corporation in 1988 (although mostly owned by it) and then bought back in 1990.

Claris CAD

A full-featured 2-D CAD program for the Macintosh from Claris Corporation that is noted for its ease of use. It provides an easy-to-learn path into CAD, while offering most features found in CAD programs.

class

In object-oriented programming, a user-defined data type that defines a collection of objects that share the same characteristics. A class member (object) is an "instance" of the class. Concrete classes are designed to be "instantiated." Abstract classes are designed to pass on characteristics through inheritance. See *FCC Class*.

Class 4 switch

AT&T's name for the type of switch used in a telephone tandem office. In the past, Class 4 switches dealt only with high-speed, four-wire T1, T3 and OC-3 connections in contrast to two-wire local lines on Class 5 switches. Today, all switches support four-wire lines.

Class 5 switch

AT&T's name for the type of switch used in a local telephone end office. It provides customer services such as call waiting and call forwarding. In the past, a Class 5 switch implied two-wire ports from the customer and four-wire ports out the back end. Today, all switches support four-wire lines.

Classical IP

An IETF standard for transmitting IP traffic in an ATM network. IP protocols contain IP addresses that have to be converted into ATM addresses, and Classical IP performs this conversion, as long as the destination is within the same subnet. It does not support routing between networks.

class library

A set of ready-made software routines that programmers use for writing object-oriented programs. For example, a class library is commonly available to provide graphical user interface (GUI) functions such as windowing routines, buttons, scroll bars and other elements.

clean boot

Booting the computer without loading anything but the main part of the operating system.

clean room

A room in which the air is highly filtered in order to keep out impurities.

clear memory

To reset all RAM and hardware registers to a zero or blank condition. Rebooting the computer may or may not clear memory, but turning the computer off and on again guarantees that memory is cleared.

CLEC

(Competitive Local Exchange Carrier) An organization offering local telephone services. Although most CLECs are established as a telecommunications service organization, any large company, university or city government has the option of becoming a CLEC and supplying its own staff with dial tone at reduced cost. Contrast with *ILEC*.

click

To select an object by pressing the mouse button when the cursor is pointing to the required menu option or icon.

Click! disk

A low-cost, portable disk drive technology from Iomega Corporation, Roy, UT, (www.iomega.com). It uses floppy-like, 40MB removable cartridges that are half the size of a credit card and were introduced at less than $10 each.

clicks and mortar

Also called "bricks and clicks," it refers to businesses that offer online services via the Web as well as the traditional retail outlets (offline) staffed by people. Coined in 1999 by David Pottruck, co-CEO of the Charles Schwab brokerage firm, it refers to running the two divisions in a cooperative and integrated manner where they both support and benefit from each other. Contrast with *bricks and mortar*. See *e-commerce*.

Iomega's Click! disk is aimed at PDAs and handheld devices such as digital cameras. A Click! cartridge holds 40MB.

clickstream

The trail of mouse clicks made by a user performing a particular operation on the computer. It often refers to linking from one page to another on the World Wide Web.

client

(1) A workstation or personal computer in a client/server environment. See *client/server architecture*.

(2) One end of the spectrum in a request/supply relationship between programs. See *X Window* and *OLE*.

client application

An application running in a workstation or personal computer on a network.

client/server architecture

An architecture in which the client (personal computer or workstation) is the requesting machine and the server is the supplying machine. In this "two-tier" architecture, the client provides the user interface and performs the application processing. The server maintains the databases and processes requests from the client to extract data from or update the database. In "three-tier" client/server architecture, some or all of the application processing is performed in a separate server.

client/server network

(1) A communications network that uses dedicated servers. In this context, the term is used to contrast it with a *peer-to-peer network*, which allows any client to also be a server.

(2) A network that is processing applications designed for client/server architecture.

client/server protocol

A communications protocol that provides a structure for requests between client and server in a network. It refers to OSI layer 7.

clip art

A set of canned images used to illustrate word processing and desktop publishing documents.

clipboard

Reserved memory used to hold data that has been copied from one application in order to be inserted into another.

Clipper

(1) See *CA-Clipper*.

(2) A family of 32-bit RISC microprocessors from Intergraph Corporation, Huntsville, AL, (www.intergraph.com).

(3) An encryption chip endorsed by the U.S. government for general use that would let authorities unscramble the data if needed.

clipping

Cutting off the outer edges or boundaries of a word, signal or image. See *scissoring*.

Two Tier Client/Server

Application Processing

Client

← 50KB

DBMS

Server

Database (10,000 1K records)

Three Tier Client/Server

Application Processing

Client

Application Processing

Server

DBMS

Server

clipping level

A disk's ability to maintain its magnetic properties and hold its content. A high-quality level range is 65-70%; low quality is below 55%.

clock

An internal timing device. Using a quartz crystal, the CPU clock breathes life into the CPU by feeding it a constant flow of pulses. For example, a 200MHz CPU receives 200 million pulses per second. Similarly, in a communications device, the clock synchronizes the data pulses between sender and receiver. A realtime clock keeps track of the time of day, and a timesharing clock interrupts the CPU at regular intervals.

clock/calendar

An internal time clock and month/year calendar that is kept active with a battery. Its output allows software to remind users of appointments, to determine the age of a transaction and to activate tasks at specified times.

clock doubling

Doubling the internal processing speed of a CPU while maintaining the original clock speed for I/O transfers in and out of the chip.

clock pulse

A signal used to synchronize the operations of an electronic system. Clock pulses are continuous, precisely spaced changes in voltage. See *clock speed*.

clock speed

The internal heartbeat of a computer. The clock circuit uses fixed vibrations generated from a quartz crystal to deliver a steady stream of pulses to the CPU. See *MHz*.

clock tripling

Tripling the internal processing speed of a CPU while maintaining the original clock speed for I/O (transfers in/out of the chip).

clone

A device that works like the original. It implies 100% functional compatibility.

closed

With regard to a switch, closed is "on." Open is "off." closed architecture

A system whose technical specifications are not made public. Contrast with *open architecture*.

closed shop

An environment in which only data processing staff is allowed access to the computer. Contrast with *open shop*.

closed system

A system in which specficiations are kept proprietary to prevent third-party hardware or software from being used. Contrast with *open system*.

cluster

The minimum unit of storage on a disk, which is some number of disk sectors based on the drive size and OS version. Windows clusters can be as large as 32KB on 2GB drives. That means a 100-byte file can take up 32KB of space. On Windows 95 and higher PCs, the FAT32 method was added, which brought the cluster size down to 4K.

cluster controller

A control unit that manages several peripheral devices, such as terminals or disk drives.

clustering

Using two or more systems that work together. It generally refers to multiple computer systems that are linked together in order to handle variable workloads or to provide continued operation in the event one fails. Each computer may be a multiprocessor system itself. For example, a cluster of four computers, each with four CPUs, would provide a total of 16 CPUs processing simultaneously.

CLUT

(Color Look Up Table) A hardware or software table that contains color mixing information (intensity of red, green and blue) for each color in a palette or series of palettes.

CLV

(Constant Linear Velocity) A disk technique that spins a disk at different speeds. By varying the speed depending on which track is being accessed, the physical density of bits in each track can be the same, thus allowing the outer tracks to hold more data than the inner tracks.

CLV mechanisms are used in CD-ROM players in order to store larger amounts of data. Contrast with *CAV*.

CMC

(Common Messaging Calls) A programming interface specified by the XAPIA as the standard messaging API for X.400 and other messaging systems. CMC is intended to provide a common API for applications that want to become mail enabled.

CMI

(Computer-Managed Instruction) Using computers to organize and manage an instructional program for students. It helps create test materials, tracks the results and monitors student progress.

CMIP

(Common Management Information Protocol) Pronounced "C-mip." A network monitoring and control standard from ISO. CMOT (CMIP over TCP) is a version that runs on TCP/IP networks, and CMOL (CMIP over LLC) runs on IEEE 802 LANs (Ethernet, Token Ring, etc.).

CMIS

(Common Management Information Services) Pronounced "C-miss." An OSI standard that defines the functions for network monitoring and control.

CMOS

(Complementary MOS) Pronounced "C moss." A type of integrated circuit widely used for processors and memories. It uses PMOS and NMOS transistors in a complementary fashion that results in less power to operate. The term is used loosely to refer to the CMOS RAM in a PC.

CMOS RAM

A small, battery-backed memory bank in a personal computer that is used to hold time, date and system information such as drive types. In a PC, if disk drives are added, removed or changed, the CMOS memory must be updated in order for the operating system to recognize the new devices. Newer PCs can detect new drives automatically, but older systems require manual editing. Pressing a certain key at boot time, such as Del or F1, accesses the CMOS configuration program.

CMS

(1) (Conversational Monitor System) Software that provides interactive communications for IBM's VM operating system. It allows a user or programmer to launch an application from a terminal and interactively work with it. The CMS counterpart in MVS is TSO. Contrast with *RSCS*, which provides batch communications for VM.

(2) (Call Management System) An AT&T call accounting package for its PBXs.

CMYK

(Cyan Magenta Yellow blacK) A color model used for printing. In theory, cyan, magenta and yellow (CMY) can print all colors, but inks are not pure and black comes out muddy. Black ink is required for quality printing. See *RGB*.

CNC

(Computerized Numerical Control) See *numerical control*.

CNE, CNI

(Certified NetWare Engineer, Certified NetWare Instructor) NetWare certification for technical competence.

CO

See *central office*.

coaxial cable

A high-capacity cable used in communications and video, commonly called "co-ax." It contains an insulated solid or stranded wire surrounded by a solid or braided metallic shield, wrapped in a plastic cover. Fire-safe teflon coating is optional.

Although similar in appearance, there are several types of coaxial cable, each designed with a different width and impedance for a particular purpose (TV, baseband, broadband). Coax provides a higher bandwidth than twisted wire pair. See *cable categories*.

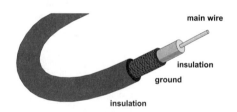

COBOL

(COmmon Business Oriented Language) A high-level business programming language that has been the primary business application language on mainframes and minis. It is a compiled language and was one of the first high-level languages developed. Formally adopted in 1960, it stemmed from the Flowmatic language in the mid 1950s.

COBOL requires more writing than other languages, but winds up more readable as a result. For example, **multiply hourly-rate by hours-worked giving gross-pay** is self-explanatory. COBOL is structured into the following divisions:

Division name	Contains
IDENTIFICATION	Program identification.
ENVIRONMENT	Types of computers used.
DATA	Buffers, constants and work areas.
PROCEDURE	The processing (program logic).

The following COBOL example converts a Fahrenheit number to Celsius. To keep the example simple, it performs the operation on the operator's terminal rather than a user terminal.

```
IDENTIFICATION DIVISION.
PROGRAM-ID.  EXAMPLE.

ENVIRONMENT DIVISION.
CONFIGURATION SECTION.
SOURCE-COMPUTER.    IBM-370.
OBJECT-COMPUTER.    IBM-370.

DATA DIVISION.
WORKING-STORAGE SECTION.
77 FAHR   PICTURE 999.
77 CENT   PICTURE 999.

PROCEDURE DIVISION.
DISPLAY 'Enter Fahrenheit ' UPON CONSOLE.
ACCEPT FAHR FROM CONSOLE.
COMPUTE CENT = (FAHR- 32) * 5 / 9.
DISPLAY 'Celsius is ' CENT UPON CONSOLE.
GOBACK.
```

CobWeb

A Web page that is rarely downloaded because the references to it are obscure or the subject is simply uninteresting.

CODASYL

(**CO**nference on **DA**ta **SY**stems Languages) An organization founded in 1959 by the U.S. Department of Defense. It evolved into a variety of volunteer committees and ultimately disbanded by the mid 1990s. CODASYL was widely known for its definition of COBOL, but it was also involved with the network database model and the data description language (DDL) for defining database schemas.

code

(1) A set of machine symbols that represents data or instructions. See *data code* and *machine language*.

(2) Any representation of one set of data for another. For example, a parts code is an abbreviated name of a product, product type or category. A discount code is a percentage.

(3) To write a program. See *source code* and *line of code*.

(4) To encode for security purposes. See *encryption*.

codec

(1) (**CO**der-**DEC**oder) Hardware or software that converts analog sound, speech or video to digital code (analog to digital) and vice versa (digital to analog). Hardware codecs (chips) are built into devices such as digital telephones and videoconferencing stations. Software codecs are used to record and play audio and video over the Web utilizing the CPU for processing.

(2) (**CO**mpressor/**DEC**ompressor) Hardware or software that compresses digital data into a smaller binary format than the original. It generally refers to software routines that compress/decompress and possibly encrypt/decrypt data. However, the codec as described in definition #1 above is also often called a "compressor/decompressor," because compression is an inherent part of the algorithms that produce the digital code.

code density

The amount of space that an executable program takes up in memory. Code density is important in PDAs and hand-held devices that contain a limited amount of memory.

code generator

See *application generator*.

coder

(1) A junior, or trainee, programmer who writes simple programs or writes the code for a larger program that has been designed by someone else.

(2) Person who assigns special codes to data.

COLD

(Computer Output to LaserDisk) Replacing paper output with optical media. Instead of printing large paper reports, printed output is stored on optical disks and extracted online by users as necessary.

cold boot

Starting the computer by turning power on. Turning power off and then back on again clears memory and many internal settings. Some program failures will lock up the computer and require a cold boot to use the computer again. In other cases, only a warm boot is required. See *boot, warm boot* and *clean boot*.

cold start

Same as *cold boot*.

collaboration products

See *e-mail, groupware, data conferencing* and *videoconferencing*.

collaborative browsing

Synchronizing browser access to the same sites. As one user browses the Web, the other users trail along automatically and link to and view the same pages from their browsers.

collapsed backbone

A network configuration that provides a backbone in a centralized location, to which all subnetworks are attached. It is implemented in a router or switch that uses a high-speed backplane that can handle the simultaneous traffic of all or most all of its ports at full wire speed.

collating sequence

The sequence, or order, of the character set built into a computer. See *ASCII* and *EBCDIC*.

collator

(1) A punched card machine that merges two decks of cards into one or more stacks.

(2) A utility program that merges records from two or more files into one file.

Collapsed Backbone
The collapsed backbone router uses a high-speed backplane to move packets quickly from one port to another. By centralizing the routing in one place, maintenance and troubleshooting is reduced.

co-location

Placing equipment owned by a customer or competitor in an organization's own facility. Telephone companies often allow co-location in order to provide the best interconnection between devices.

Computer distributors and resellers may locate their warehouse within the PC vendor's facility to improve turnaround time to resellers and customers.

color bits

The number of bits associated with each pixel that represent its color. See *bit depth*.

color cycling

In computer graphics, a technique that simulates animation by continuously changing colors rather than moving the objects. Also called "color lookup table animation."

color depth

See *bit depth*.

color key

A technique for superimposing a video image onto another. For example, to float a car on the ocean, the car image is placed onto a blue background. The car and ocean images are scanned together. The ocean is made to appear in the resulting image wherever background (blue) exists in the car image. The ocean is cancelled wherever the car appears (no background).

color map

See *CLUT*.

color model

The method used to represent color for display and printing. See *RGB, CMYK, HSB* and *YUV*.

color palette

Also called a "color lookup table," "lookup table," "index map," "color table" or "color map," it is a commonly-used method for saving file space when creating 8-bit color images. Instead of each pixel containing its own red, green and blue values, which would require 24 bits, each pixel holds an 8-bit value, which is an index number into the color palette. The color palette contains 256 predefined RGB values from 0 to 255.

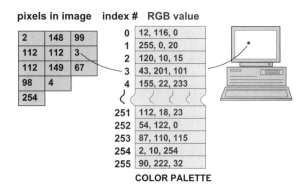

pixels in image	index #	RGB value

				0	12, 116, 0
2	148	99		1	255, 0, 20
112	112	3		2	120, 10, 15
112	149	67		3	43, 201, 101
98	4			4	155, 22, 233
254					
				251	112, 18, 23
				252	54, 122, 0
				253	87, 110, 115
				254	2, 10, 254
				255	90, 222, 32

COLOR PALETTE

color separation

Separating a picture by colors in order to make negatives and plates for color printing. Full color requires four separations: cyan, magenta, yellow and black (CMYK).

color space

A 3-D model of the three attributes of a color, which are hue, value and saturation (chroma).

color space conversion

Changing one color signal into another. It typically refers to converting YUV analog video into digital RGB video. See *YUV*.

column move

Relocating a rectangular block of characters within a text document or a column in a spreadsheet.

COM

(1) (Component Object Model) A component software architecture from Microsoft, which defines a structure for building program routines (objects) that can be called up and executed. Some elements of Windows and many parts of Microsoft's own applications are built as COM objects. VBX, OCX and ActiveX controls are also based on COM. COM capability is built into Windows. COM+ is the latest version. See *OLE, DCOM* and *CORBA*.

(2) (Computer Output Microfilm) Creating microfilm or microfiche from computer output. A COM machine receives print-image output from the computer and creates a film image of each page. Additional graphics (lines, logos, etc.) may be added.

COM1, COM2

The names assigned to serial port #1 and #2 in DOS, Windows and OS/2. The mouse is typically connected to COM1 and the modem to COM2. See *LPT1*.

COM automation

A particular usage of Microsoft's component architecture that lets applications expose their internal functions as COM objects. Called "automation" or "OLE automation," it enables tasks that are normally selected from menus to be automatically executed. For example, a small script could be written to extract data from a database, put it into a spreadsheet, summarize and chart it, all without manual intervention. The script is the automation client, and the database and spreadsheet are the automation servers.

COMDEX

(SOFTBANK COMDEX, Needham, MA, www.comdex.com) A trade show originally created for computer dealers and distributors, although large numbers of end users attend. Shows are held around the world, but COMDEX Fall in Las Vegas, Nevada is the largest with more than 200,000 attendees.

Comdisco

(Comdisco, Inc., Rosemont, IL, www.comdisco.com) A technology services company, originally founded as Computer Discount Company in 1969 by Ken Pontikes. It is the largest independent computer and network equipment leasing company and a leader in network services, asset management and business continuity services.

COM file

(1) (**COM**mand file) An executable DOS or OS/2 program that takes up less than 64K and fits within one segment. It is an exact replica of how it looks in memory. See *EXE file*.

(2) A VMS file containing commands to be executed.

comic-strip oriented

A film-image orientation like a comic strip, which runs perpendicular to the outer edge of the film. Contrast with *cine-oriented*.

comma delimited

A record layout that separates data fields with a comma and usually surrounds character data with quotes, for example:

```
"Pat Smith","5 Main St.","New Hope","PA","18950"
"K. Jones","34 E. 88 Ave.","Syosset","NY","10024"
```

command

Instruction for the computer. See *command-driven, menu-driven* and *function*.

COMMAND.COM

The command processor for DOS and OS/2. COMMAND.COM displays the DOS prompt and executes the internal DOS commands such as Dir and Copy.

command-driven

A program that accepts commands as typed-in phrases. It is usually harder to learn, but may offer more flexibility than a menu-driven program. Once learned, command-driven programs may be faster to use, because the user can state a request succinctly. Contrast with *menu-driven*.

Command key

On Apple keyboards, a key with the outline of an Apple, a propeller, or both. It is pressed along with another key to command the computer.

command language

A special-purpose language that accepts a limited number of commands, such as a query language, job control language (JCL) or command processor.   Contrast with *programming language*, which is a general purpose language.

command line

In a command-driven system, the area on screen that accepts typed-in commands.

command mode

An operating mode that causes the computer or modem to accept commands for execution.

command processor, command interpreter

A system program that accepts a limited number of user commands and converts them into the machine commands required by the operating system or some other control program or application. COMMAND.COM is the command processor that accompanies DOS.

command queuing

The ability to store multiple commands and execute them one at a time.

command set

Same as *instruction set*.

command shell

Same as *command processor*.

comment

A descriptive statement in a source language program that is used for documentation.

...)ut

...lines of code in a program by surrounding them with comment-start and comment-stop

...ial software

Software that is designed and developed for sale to the general public.

Commodore

One of the first personal computer companies. In 1977, Commodore Business Machines of West Chester, Pennsylvania, introduced the PET computer and launched the personal computer industry along with Apple and Radio Shack. Later on, it introduced the Commodore 64 and Commodore 128. These were popular home computers, and over 10 million were sold. In 1985, the Amiga series was introduced, which offered advanced multimedia capabilities that match today's computers. See *Amiga*.

common carrier

A government-regulated organization that provides telecommunications services for public use, such as AT&T, the telephone companies, ITT, MCI and Western Union.

comm port

May refer to any serial communications port or specifically to the serial ports on a PC. See *COM1*.

communications

The electronic transfer of information from one location to another. "Data communications" refers to digital transmission, and "telecommunications" can embrace analog and digital telephony and video as well as data communications. See *communications protocol* and *OSI*.

communications channel

Also called a "circuit" or "line," it is a pathway over which data is transferred between remote devices. It may refer to the entire physical medium, such as a telephone line, optical fiber, coaxial cable or twisted wire pair, or, it may refer to one of several carrier frequencies transmitted simultaneously within the line.

communications controller

A peripheral control unit that connects several communications lines to a computer and performs the actual transmitting and receiving as well as various message coding and decoding activities.

Communications controllers are typically nonprogrammable units designed for specific protocols and communications tasks. Contrast with *front end processor*, which can be programmed for a variety of protocols and network conditions.

communications network

The transmission channels interconnecting all client and server stations as well as all supporting hardware and software.

communications parameters

The basic settings for modem transmission, which include bit rate (14400 bps, 28800 bps, etc.), parity (none, even, odd), number of data bits (7 or 8) and number of stop bits (typically 1).

communications program

Software that manages the transmission of data between computers. In personal computers, it manages transmission to and from the computer's serial port which is typically connected to a modem. Such programs include several file transfer protocols and can also emulate dumb terminals for hookup to minis and mainframes. In a server that shares data with users on the network, the communications programs are the *network operating system* (NOS) and *communications protocols*. In a mini or mainframe, they are the *network control program* and *access methods*.

communications protocol

Hardware and software standards that govern transmission between two stations. On personal computers, communications programs offer a variety of protocols (Zmodem, Ymodem, Kermit, etc.) to transfer files via modem.

On LANs, data link protocols such as Ethernet, Token Ring and FDDI provide the access method (OSI layers 1 and 2) that moves packets from station to station, and higher level protocols, such as NetBIOS, IPX and TCP/IP (OSI layers 3, 4 and 5) control and route the transmission.

The Computer Glossary

communications satellite

A radio relay station in orbit above the earth. See *geosynchronous* and *LEO*.

communications server

See *remote access server, modem server, terminal server* and *communications controller*.

CompactFlash

A flash memory format invented by SanDisk Corporation, Sunnyvale, CA, (www.sandisk.com). At 1.4x1.7" and 3.3mm thick, it is about a third the size of a PC Card. It uses the same PC Card/ATA interface, but has 50 pins instead of 68, and cards support both 3.3 and 5v operation. They can plug into a CompactFlash socket or into a standard Type II PC Card slot with an adapter. Introduced in 1994, CompactFlash has become widely used for handheld digital devices. Second-generation Type II CompactFlash increases thickness from 3 to 5mm allowing for microminiaturized hard disks.

CompactPCI

A combination of the PCI bus contained on a Eurocard form factor. The Eurocard provides more rugged packaging and a more secure plug and socket for embedded systems than the standard PCI card used in desktop computers. It supports hot swapping and provides higher performance (32-bit, 33MHz) than the ISA bus in the PC/104 architecture. CompactPCI also provides modularity as Eurocard comes in several sizes. See *Eurocard*.

compandor

(COMpressor/exPANDOR) A device that improves the signal for AM radio transmission. On outgoing transmission, it raises the amplitude of weak signals and lowers the amplitude of strong signals. On incoming transmission, it restores the signal to its original form.

Compaq

(Compaq Computer Corporation, Houston, TX, www.compaq.com) The leading PC manufacturer founded in 1982 by Rod Canion, Bill Murto and Jim Harris. In 1983, it shipped 53,000 PC-compatible COMPAQ Portables, which resulted in $111 million in revenues and an American business record. Over the years, Compaq has been well respected for its high-quality products.

compare

A fundamental computer capability. By comparing one set of data with another, the computer can locate, analyze, select, reorder and make decisions. After comparing, the computer can indicate whether the data were equal or which set was numerically greater or less than the other.

compatibility mode

A feature of a computer or operating system that allows it to run programs written for a different system. Programs often run slower in compatiblity mode.

compilation

Compiling a program. See *compiler*.

compiler

(1) Software that translates a high-level programming language (COBOL, C, etc.) into machine language. A compiler usually generates assembly language first and then translates the assembly language into machine language. The following example compiles program statements into machine language:

```
Source code    Assembly Language   Machine language
IF COUNT=10    Compare A to B      Compare 3477 2883
 GOTO DONE     If equal go to C    If = go to 23883
  ELSE         Go to D             Go to 23343
 GOTO AGAIN
ENDIF

          Actual machine code
          10010101001010001010100
          10101010010101001001010
          10100101010001010010010
```

(2) Software that converts a high-level language into a lower-level representation. For example, a help compiler converts a text document embedded with appropriate commands into an online help system. A dictionary compiler converts terms and definitions into a dictionary lookup system.

compiler language

See *high-level language* and *compiler*.

compile time

The time it takes to translate a program from source language into machine language. Link editing time may also be included in compile time.

complement

The number derived by subtracting a number from a base number. For example, the tens complement of 8 is 2. In set theory, complement refers to all the objects in one set that are not in another set. Complements are used in digital circuits, because it's faster to subtract by adding complements than by performing true subtraction.

component

One element of a larger system. A hardware component can be a device as small as a transistor or as large as a disk drive as long as it is part of a larger system. Software components are routines or modules within a larger system.

component software

Program modules that are designed to communicate and interoperate with each other at runtime. Components can be large or small. They can be written by different programmers using different development environments and they may or may not be platform independent. Components can run in stand-alone machines, on a LAN or intranet or on the Internet. CORBA, COM and JavaBeans are the primary component software architectures competing today.

COM port

A serial communications port on a PC. See *COM1* and *serial port*.

composite video

The video-only (no audio) part of a TV signal. Used on early personal computers for TV hookup, it mixes red, green, blue and sync signals like a standard TV and is not as crisp as separate red, green and blue cables (RGB).

compound document

A single document that contains a combination of data structures such as text, graphics, spreadsheets, sound and video clips. OLE and OpenDoc are examples of compound document architectures for the desktop. They allow the user to edit each of the data objects by automatically calling in the application that created them.

compression ratio

The measurement of compressed data. For example, a file compressed into 1/4th of its original size can be expressed as 4:1, 25%, 75% or 2 bits per byte. See *data compression*.

compressor

(1) A device that diminishes the range between the strongest and weakest transmission signals. See *compandor*.

(2) A routine or program that compresses data. See *data compression*.

CompTIA

(Computing Technology Industry Association, Lombard, IL, www.comptia.org) Formerly ABCD:The Microcomputer Industry Association, it is a membership organization of resellers, distributors and manufacturers dedicated to business ethics and professionalism, founded in 1982. It sets voluntary guidelines and is involved with many issues including product returns, freight and warranty claims and price protection.

CompuServe

One of the first online services, founded in 1969. It is now part of America Online. It developed the GIF graphics format, which is widely used on the Internet.

compute

To perform mathematical operations or general computer processing.

The Computer Glossary

compute bound

Same as *process bound*.

computer

A general-purpose machine that processes data according to a set of instructions that are stored internally either temporarily or permanently. The computer and all equipment attached to it are called "hardware." The instructions that tell it what to do are called "software." A set of instructions that perform a particular task is called a "program" or "software program."

A computer processes data by retrieving it from the keyboard, disk or communications channel into memory (RAM) and calculating, comparing and copying it. It then outputs the results to the screen, saves them on disk or perhaps transmits them back over a communcations channel.

computer architecture

The design of a computer system. It sets the standard for all devices that connect to it and all the software that runs on it. It is based on the type of programs that will run (business, scientific) and the number of them run concurrently. It includes such components and features as the instruction set, internal bus, caching, RISC vs CISC, memory and storage capacities, virtual memory and fault tolerance.

Computer Associates

See *CA*.

computer cracker

A person who gains illegal entrance into a computer system.

computer designer

A person who designs the electronic structure of a computer.

computer exchange

A commodity exchange through which the public can buy and sell used computers. After a match, the buyer sends a check to the exchange and the seller sends the equipment to the buyer. If the buyer accepts it, the money is sent to the seller less commission. Commissions usually range from 10 to 20%.

```
American Computer Exchange (AmCoEx)
404/250-0050   FAX 404/250-1399
www.amcoex.com

Boston Computer Exchange (BoCoEx)
800/262-6399   FAX 617/542-8849
www.bocoex.com

National Computer Exchange (NaComEx)
212/808-3062   FAX 212/681-9211
www.nacomex.com

United Computer Exchange
800/755-3033   FAX 770/612-1239
www.uce.com
```

computer graphics

See *graphics*.

computer language

A programming language, machine language or the language of the computer industry.

computer literacy

Understanding computers and related systems. It includes a working vocabulary of computer and information system components, the fundamental principles of computer processing and a perspective for how non-technical people interact with technical people.

computer on a chip

A single chip that contains the processor, RAM, ROM, clock and I/O control unit. It is used for myriads of applications from automobiles to toys. See *chip*.

computer power

The effective performance of a computer. It can be expressed in MIPS (millions of instructions per second), clock speed (33Mhz, 66MHz) and in word or bus size, (16-bit, 32-bit). However, as with automobile horsepower, valves and cylinders, such specifications are only guidelines. Real power is whether it gets your job done quickly.

A software package is "powerful" if it has a large number of features.

computer science

The field of computer hardware and software. It includes systems analysis & design, application and system software design and programming and datacenter operations. For young students, the emphasis in typically on learning a programming language or running a personal computer with little attention to information science, the study of information and its uses.

If students were introduced to data administration and DBMS concepts, they would have a better grasp of an organization's typical information requirements.

computer services

Data processing (timesharing, batch processing), software development and consulting services. See *service bureau.*

computer system

The complete computer made up of the CPU, memory and related electronics (main cabinet), all the peripheral devices connected to it and its operating system. Computer systems fall into ranges called "microcomputers" (personal computers), "minicomputers" and "mainframes," roughly small, medium and large.

COMSAT

(COMSAT Corporation, Clarksburg, MD, www.comsat.com) Formerly Communications Satellite Corporation, it is a private company that was created by the U.S. Congress in 1962 that provides satellite communications to major carriers and organizations. In 1965, it launched Early Bird, the first commercial satellite in geosynchronous orbit.

CON

(CONsole) The DOS name for the keyboard and screen.

concatenate

To link structures together. Concatenating files appends one file to another. In speech synthesis, units of speech called "phonemes" (k, sh, ch, etc.) are concatenated to produce meaningful sounds.

concentrator

A device that joins several communications channels together. It is similar to a multiplexor except that it does not spread the signals back out again on the other end. The receiving computer performs that function.

conceptual view

See *view.*

concurrency control

In a DBMS, managing the simultaneous access to a database. It prevents two users from editing the same record at the same time and is also concerned with serializing transactions for backup and recovery.

concurrent operation, concurrent processing

See *multitasking, multiprocessing* and *parallel processing.*

conditional branch

In programming, an instruction that directs the computer to another part of the program based on the results of a compare. In a high-level language, statements such as IF THEN ELSE and CASE, are used to express the compare and conditional branch. In the following (simulated) assembly language example, the second line is the conditional branch.

```
COMPARE FIELDA with FIELDB
GOTO MATCHROUTINE if EQUAL.
```

conditioning

Extra cost options in a private telephone line that improve performance by reducing distortion and amplifying weak signals.

conductor

A material that can carry electrical current. Contrast with *insulator*.

conferencing

See *audioconferencing, videoconferencing* and *data conferencing*.

CONFIG.SYS

A DOS and OS/2 configuration file. It resides in the root directory and is used to load drivers and change settings at startup. Install programs often modify CONFIG.SYS in order to customize the computer for their particular use.

configuration

The makeup of a system. To "configure" is to choose options in order to create a custom system. "Configurability" is a system's ability to be changed or customized.

configuration file

A file that contains information about a specific user, program, computer or file.

configuration management

(1) A system for gathering current configuration information from all nodes in a LAN.

(2) Same as *version control*.

connectionless

In communications, the inclusion of source and destination addresses within each packet so that a direct connection or established session between nodes is not required. Transmission within a local area network (LAN) is typically connectionless. Each data packet sent contains the address of where it is going. Contrast with *connection oriented*.

connection oriented

In communications, requiring a direct connection or established session or circuit between two nodes for transmission. Transmission within a wide area network (WAN) is typically connection oriented. Once established, the circuit, whether physical or virtual, is dedicated to that single transmission until the session is completed. Contrast with *connectionless*.

connection pooling

The ability to open several connections to a database and distribute those connections to the next available request for data. On the Web, connection pooling is performed to improve performance. Otherwise opening a database connection for each user request adds overhead, and maintaining a connection for each user wastes resources.

connectivity

(1) Generally, the term refers to communications networks or the act of communicating between computers and terminals.

(2) Specifically, the term refers to devices such as bridges, routers and gateways that link networks together.

connector

(1) Any plug, socket or wire that links two devices together.

(2) In database management, a link or pointer between two data structures.

(3) In flowcharting, a symbol used to break a sequence and resume the sequence elsewhere. It is often a small circle with a number in it.

connect time

The amount of time a user at a terminal is logged on to a computer system.

console

(1) A terminal used to monitor and control a computer or network.

(2) Any display terminal.

constant

In programming, a fixed value in a program. Minimum and maximum amounts, dates, prices, headlines and error messages are examples.

constant ratio code

A code that always contains the same ratio of 0s to 1s.

consultant

An independent specialist that may act as an advisor or perform detailed systems analysis and design. They often help users create functional specifications from which hardware or software vendors can respond.

contact

A metal strip in a switch or socket that touches a corresponding strip in order to make a connection for current to pass. Contacts may be made of precious metals to avoid corrosion.

contact manager

Software that keeps track of people and related activities. It is similar to a personal information manager (PIM), but is specialized for sales and service reps that make repetitive contact with prospects and customers. The foundation of a contact manager is a name and address database, from which phonecalls, meetings and to-do items are scheduled. The contact manager may also link each record to related e-mail messages and text documents.

contention

A condition that arises when two devices attempt to use a single resource at the same time. See *CSMA/CD*.

contention resolution

Deciding which device gains access to a resource first when more than one wants it at the same time.

context sensitive help

Help screens that provide specific information about the condition or mode the program is in at the time help is sought.

context switching

Switching between active applications. It often refers to a user jumping back and forth between several programs in contrast with repeated task switching performed by the operating system. However, the terms context switching and task switching are used synonymously.

contextual search

To search for records or documents based upon the text contained in any part of the file as opposed to searching on a pre-defined key field.

contiguous

Adjacent or touching. Contrast with *fragmentation*.

continuity check

A test of a line, channel or circuit to determine if the pathway exists from beginning to end and can transmit signals.

continuous carrier

In communications, a carrier frequency that is transmitted even when data is not being sent.

continuous forms

A roll of paper forms with perforations for separation into individual sheets after printing. See *pin feed* and *burster*.

continuous tone

A printing process that produces photographic-like output. In a continuous tone image, pixel patterns (individual dots) are either not visible or are barely visible under a magnifying glass. Various dye sublimation, CYCOLOR and laser technologies can provide up to 256 intensities of color and even blend the inks. See *contone printer, dye sublimation* and *CYCOLOR.*

contone printer

A laser printer that begins to approach continuous tone quality by varying the dot size. However, unlike continuous tone, which can blend inks more thoroughly, contone has a limited number of dot sizes, and dithering is still used to make up shades. See *continuous tone.*

control block

A segment of disk or memory that contains a group of codes used for identification and control purposes.

control break

(1) A change of category used to trigger a subtotal. For example, if data is subtotalled by state, a control break occurs when NJ changes to NM.

(2) (Ctrl-Break) In a DOS PC, the key combination that cancels the running program.

control character

See *control code.*

control code

One or more characters used as a command to control a device. The first 32 characters in the ASCII character set are control codes for communications and printers. There are countless codes used to control electronic devices. See *escape character.*

Control Data

(Control Data Systems, Inc., Arden Hills, MN, www.cdc.dom) Control Data Corporation was one of the first computer companies. Founded in 1957, Bill Norris was its president and guiding force. For more than 30 years, the company was widely respected for its high-speed computers used for government and science. Today, it no longer manufactures hardware, but is involved in systems integration using a variety of computers from other companies. In 1992, it spun off its military involvement into an independent company called Ceridian Corporation, and Control Data Corporation became Control Data Systems.

control field

Same as *key field.*

control key

Abbreviated "ctrl" or "ctl." A key that is pressed with a letter or digit key to command the computer; for example, holding down control and pressing U, turns on underline in some word processors. The caret (shift-6) symbol represents the control key: ^Y means control-Y.

controller

See *control unit (2).*

control network

A network of sensors and actuators used for home automation and industrial control.

Control Panel

A routine that changes the computer's environment settings, such as keyboard and mouse sensitivity, sounds, colors and communications and printer access. It is a desk accessory in the Macintosh and a utility program in Windows.

control program

Software that controls the operation of and has highest priority in a computer. Operating systems, network operating systems and network control programs are examples. Contrast with *application program.*

control unit

(1) Within the processor, the circuitry that locates, analyzes and executes each instruction in the program.

(2) Within the computer, a control unit, or controller, is hardware that performs the physical data transfers between memory and a peripheral device, such as a disk or screen, or a network.

Personal computer control units are contained on a single plug-in expansion board, called a "controller" or "adapter" (disk controller, display adapter, network adapter). In large computers, they may be contained on one or more boards or in a stand-alone cabinet. In single chip computers, a built-in control unit accepts keyboard input and provides serial output to a display.

control variable

In programming, a variable that keeps track of the number of iterations of a process. Its value is incremented or decremented with each iteration, and it is compared to a constant or other variable to test the end of the process or loop.

conventional memory

In a PC, the first 640K of memory. The next 384K is called the "UMA" (upper memory area). The term may also refer to the entire first megabyte (1024K) of RAM, which is the memory that DOS can directly manage without the use of additional memory managers.

conventional programming

Writing a program in a traditional procedural language, such as assembly language or a high-level compiler language (C, Pascal, COBOL, FORTRAN, etc.).

convergence

(1) The intersection of red, green and blue electron beams on one CRT pixel. Poor convergence decreases resolution and muddies white pixels.

(2) See *digital convergence*.

conversational

An interactive dialogue between the user and the computer.

conversion

(1) Data conversion is changing data from one file or database format to another. It may also require code conversion between ASCII and EBCDIC.

(2) Media conversion is changing storage media such as from tape to disk.

(3) Program conversion is changing the programming source language from one dialect to another, or changing application programs to link to a new operating system or DBMS.

(4) Computer system conversion is changing the computer model and peripheral devices.

(5) Information system conversion requires data conversion and either program conversion or the installation of newly purchased or created application programs.

converter

(1) A device that changes one set of codes, modes, sequences or frequencies to a different set. See *A/D converter*.

(2) A device that changes current from 60Hz to 50Hz, and vice versa.

cookie file

A file that contains information (cookies) created by Web sites that is stored on the user's hard disk. It provides a way for the Web site to keep track of a user's patterns and preferences and, with the cooperation of the Web browser, to store them on the user's own hard disk in the COOKIES.TXT file (Netscape) or in separate files in the Favorites folder (Internet Explorer).

cooperative multitasking

See *non-preemtive multitasking*.

cooperative processing

Sharing a job among two or more computers such as a mainframe and a personal computer. It implies splitting the workload for the most efficiency.

coordinate
Belonging to a system of indexing by two or more terms. For example, points on a plane, cells in a spreadsheet and bits in dynamic RAM chips are identified by a pair of coordinates. Points in space are identified by sets of three coordinates.

copper
A reddish-brown metal that is highly conductive and widely used for electrical wire. When a signal "runs over copper," it means that a metal wire is used rather than a glass wire (optical fiber).

copper chip
A chip that uses copper rather than aluminum in the top metalization layers, which interconnect all transistors and components together. Copper provides better performance, because it has less resistance than aluminum.

Coppermine
Intel's code name for Pentium III CPU chips that are the first to use the .18 micron (from .25 micron) manufacturing process. Coppermine chips are not copper chips. Coppermine chips were introduced in late 1999.

coprocessor
A secondary processor used to speed up operations by handling some of the workload of the main CPU. See *math coprocessor* and *graphics coprocessor*.

copy
To make a duplicate of the original. In digital electronics, all copies are identical.

copy buster
A program that bypasses the copy protection scheme in a software program and allows normal, unprotected copies to be made.

copy protection
Resistance to unauthorized copying of software. Copy protection was never a serious issue with mainframes and minicomputers, since vendor support has always been vital in those environments.

The only copy protection system that works is the hardware key, which is used for high-end software, because it is too costly for low-priced products.

CORBA
(Common **ORB** Architecture) A standard from the OMG (Object Management Group) for communicating between distributed objects. CORBA provides a way to execute programs written in any language no matter where they reside in the network or what platform they run on. CORBA allows a program in one location to use a program's services in another.

core
A round magnetic doughnut that represents one bit in a core storage system. A computer's main memory used to be referred to as core.

Corel
(Corel Corporation, Ottawa, Ontario, www.corel.com) Canada's leading software company, founded in 1985 by Dr. Michael Cowpland. For many years, it has been widely known for its award-winning CorelDRAW suite of graphics programs for Windows, Mac and UNIX. Corel offers a variety of business programs, including application suites that include WordPerfect and Quattro Pro. Corel has also embraced the Linux world by offering Linux applications and its own distribution of the OS.

CorelDRAW
A suite of Windows graphics applications from Corel. CorelDRAW was originally a drawing program introduced in 1989, which became popular due to its speed and ease of use. As of CorelDRAW 5, it became a complete suite of applications for image editing, charting and presentations as well as desktop publishing with the inclusion of Corel VENTURA.

Corel VENTURA

A Windows desktop publishing program from Corel. It is a full-featured program suited for producing books and other long documents. It is designed to import data from other graphics and word processing programs and includes several graphics functions from CorelDRAW.

core router

See *edge router*.

co-resident

A program or module that resides in memory along with other programs.

core storage

A non-volatile memory that holds magnetic charges in ferrite cores about 1/16th" diameter. The direction of the flux determines the 0 or 1. Developed in the late 1940s by Jay W. Forrester and Dr. An Wang, it was used extensively in the 1950s and 1960s. Since it holds its content without power, it is still used in specialized applications in the military and in space vehicles.

corona wire

A charged wire in a laser printer that draws the toner off the drum onto the paper. It must be cleaned when the toner cartridge is replaced.

corporate portal

An internal Web site (intranet) that provides proprietary, enterprise-wide information to company employees as well as access to selected public Web sites and vertical-market Web sites (suppliers, vendors, etc.). It is the internal equivalent of the general-purpose portal on the Web. See *portal* and *vertical portal*.

correlation

In statistics, a measure of the strength of the relationship between two variables. It is used to predict the value of one variable given the value of the other. For example, a correlation might relate distance from urban location to gasoline consumption. Expressed on a scale from -1.0 to +1.0, the strongest correlations are at both extremes and provide the best predictions. See *regression analysis*.

corrupted file

A data or program file that has been altered in some manner causing the bits to be rearranged and rendering it unreadable.

corruption

Altering of data or programs due to viruses, hardware or software failure or power failure. See *data recovery*.

counter

(1) In programming, a variable that is used to keep track of anything that must be counted. The programming language determines the number of counters (variables) that are available to a programmer.

(2) In electronics, a circuit that counts pulses and generates an output at a specified time.

country code

A two-character code used to identify a country on the Internet. For example, .ca is the country code for Canada. Most U.S. companies and many companies throughout the world register and use .com domains rather then the their country code.

courseware

Educational software. See *CBT*.

covert channel

A transfer of information that violates a computer's built-in security systems. A covert storage channel refers to depositing information in a memory or storage location that can be accessed by different security clearances. A covert timing channel is the manipulation of a system resource in such a way that it can be detected by another process.

CP

(1) (Copy Protected) See *copy protection*.

(2) (Central Processor) See *processor* and *CPU*.

(3) See *control program*.

CPA

(Computer Press Association, Landing, NJ, www.computerpress.org) An organization founded in 1983 that promotes excellence in computer journalism. Its annual awards honor outstanding journalism in print, broadcast and electronic media.

CPE

(Customer Premises Equipment) Communications equipment that resides on the customer's premises.

CPF

(Control Program Facility) The IBM System/38 operating system that included an integrated relational DBMS.

cpi

(1) (Characters Per Inch) The measurement of the density of characters per inch on tape or paper. A printer's CPI button switches character pitch.

(2) (Counts Per Inch) The measurement of the resolution of a mouse/trackball as flywheel notches per inch (horizontal and vertical flywheels rotate as the ball is moved). Notches are converted to cursor movement.

(3) (CPI) (Common Programming Interface) See *SAA* and *CPI-C*.

CPI-C

(Common Programming Interface for Communications) A general-purpose communications interface under IBM's SAA. Using APPC verbs as its foundation, it provides a common programming interface across IBM platforms. See *APPC*.

CP/M

(Control Program for Microprocessors) A single user operating system for the 8080 and Z80 microprocessors from Digital Research. Created by Gary Kildall, CP/M had its heyday in the early 1980s.

CPM

(Critical Path Method) A project management planning and control technique implemented on computers. The critical path is the series of activities and tasks in the project that have no built-in slack time. Any task in the critical path that takes longer than expected will lengthen the total time of the project.

cps

(Characters Per Second) The measurement of the speed of a serial printer or the speed of a data transfer between hardware devices or over a communications channel. CPS is equivalent to bytes per second.

CPU

(Central Processing Unit) The computing part of the computer. Also called the "processor," it is made up of the control unit and ALU. A personal computer CPU is a single microprocessor chip. A minicomputer CPU is contained on one or more printed circuit boards. A mainframe CPU is made up of several boards.

CPU bound

Same as *process bound*.

CPU cache

See *cache*.

CPU chip

Same as *microprocessor*.

CPU time

The amount of time it takes for the CPU to execute a set of instructions and explicitly excludes the waiting time for input and output.

crash

See *abend* and *head crash*.

crash recovery

The ability to automatically correct a hardware, software or line failure.

crawler

Also known as a spider, ant, robot ("bot") and intelligent agent, a crawler is a program that searches for information on the World Wide Web. It is used to locate new documents and new sites by following hypertext links from server to server and indexing information based on search criteria.

Cray

(Cray Research, Inc., Eagan, MN, www.cray.com) A supercomputer manufacturer founded in 1972 by Seymour Cray. The CRAY-1 shipped in 1976 and could perform 160 million floating point operations per second, a startling number for that time. In 1996, Cray Research was acquired by Silicon Graphics (SGI).

CRC

(Cyclical Redundancy Checking) An error checking technique used to ensure the accuracy of transmitting digital data. The transmitted messages are divided into predetermined lengths which, used as dividends, are divided by a fixed divisor. The remainder of the calculation is appended onto and sent with the message. At the receiving end, the computer recalculates the remainder. If it does not match the transmitted remainder, an error is detected.

crippleware

Demonstration software with built-in limitations; for example, a database package that lets only 50 records be entered.

criteria range

Conditions for selecting records; for example, "Illinois customers with balances over $10,000."

CR/LF

(Carriage Return/Line Feed) The end of line characters used in standard PC text files (ASCII 13 10). In the Mac, only the CR is used; in UNIX, the LF.

crop marks

Printed lines on paper used to cut the form into its intended size.

cross assembler

An assembler that generates machine language for a foreign computer. It is used to develop programs for computers on a chip or microprocessors used in specialized applications, which are either too small or are incapable of handling the development software.

crossbar switch, crosspoint switch

Also known as a NxN switch, it is a switching device that provides for a fixed number of inputs and outputs. For example, a 32x32 switch is able to keep 32 nodes communicating at full speed to 32 other nodes.

cross compiler

A compiler that generates machine language for a foreign computer. See *cross assembler*.

crossfoot

A numerical error checking technique that compares the sum of the columns with the sum of the rows.

crosshatch

A criss-crossed pattern used to fill in sections of a drawing to distinguish them from each other.

crossover cable

Same as *null modem cable*.

cross platform

Refers to developing for and/or running on more than one type of hardware platform.

cross promotion

Advertising a Web site using traditional media such as radio, TV and magazines. Same as "offline advertising" and "cross media."

cross tabulate

To analyze and summarize data. For example, cross tabulation is used to summarize the details in a database file into totals in a spreadsheet.

crosstalk

(1) In communications, interference from an adjacent channel.

(2) (Crosstalk) A family of communications programs for DOS and Windows from DCA, Inc., Alpharetta, GA. Crosstalk was one of the first personal computer communications programs, originating in the CP/M days.

CRT

(Cathode Ray Tube) A vacuum tube used as a display screen in a video terminal or TV. The term often refers to the entire terminal.

Crusoe processor

An x86-based CPU chip from Transmeta Corporation, Santa Clara, CA, (www.transmeta.com), that is designed for Internet appliances and other handheld devices. It consumes significantly less power than mobile x86 chips from Intel, AMD and others because it places more of the processing burden on the software.

crunch

(1) To process data. See *number crunching*.

(2) To compress data. See *data compression*.

cryogenics

Using materials that operate at very cold temperatures. See *superconductor*.

cryptography

The conversion of data into a secret code for transmission over a public network. The original text, or plaintext, is converted into a coded equivalent called "ciphertext" via an encryption algorithm. The ciphertext is decoded (decrypted) at the receiving end and turned back into plaintext.

There are two methods. The traditional one uses a secret key, such as the DES standard. Both sender and receiver use the same key to encrypt and decrypt. This is the fastest method, but transmitting the secret key to the recipient in the first place is not secure. The second method is public-key cryptography, such as RSA, which uses both a private and a public key. See *DES* and *RSA*.

crystal

A solid material containing a uniform arrangement of molecules. See *quartz crystal*.

crystalline

The solid state of a crystal. Contrast with *nematic*.

CSA

(1) (Canadian Standards Association) The Canadian counterpart of U.S. Underwriters Laboratory.

(2) (Client Server Architecture) See *client/server architecture*.

CSMA/CD

(Carrier Sense Multiple Access/Collision Detection) A baseband communications access method. When a device wants to gain access to the network, it checks to see if the network is free. If it is not, it waits a random amount of time before retrying. If the network is free and two devices attempt access at exactly the same time, they both back off to avoid a collision and each wait a random amount of time before retrying.

CSP

(1) (Cross System Product) An IBM application generator that runs in all SAA environments. CSP/ AD (CSP/Application Development) programs provide the interactive development environment and

generate a pseudo code that is interpreted by CSP/AE (CSP/Application Execution) software in the running computer.

(2) (Certified Systems Professional) The award for successful completion of an ICCP examination in systems development.

CSTA

(Computer Supported Telephony Application) An international standard interface between a network server and a telephone switch (PBX) established by the ECMA.

CSU

See *DSU/CSU*.

CSV

(Comma Separated Value) Same as *comma delimited*.

CTI

(Computer Telephone Integration) Combining data with voice systems in order to enhance telephone services. For example, automatic number identification (ANI) allows a caller's records to be retrieved from the database while the call is routed to the appropriate party. Automatic telephone dialing from an address list is an outbound example.

Ctl, Ctrl

See *control key*.

CTO

(Chief Technical Officer) The executive responsible for the technical direction of an organization.

CTOS

An operating system that runs on Unisys' x86-based SuperGen series (formerly the B-series). Originally developed by Convergent Technologies, its message-based approach allows program requests to be directed to any station in the network.

Ctrl-Alt-Del

The key combination that reboots a PC.

CTS

(1) (Clear To Send) The RS-232 signal sent from the receiving station to the transmitting station that indicates it is ready to accept data. Contrast with *RTS*.

(2) See *carpal tunnel syndrome*.

CUA

(Common User Access) SAA specifications for user interfaces, which includes OS/2 PM and character-based formats of 3270 terminals. It is intended to provide a consistent look and feel across platforms and between applications.

CUI

(Character-based User Interface) A user interface that uses the character, or text, mode of the computer and typically refers to typing in commands. Contrast with *GUI*.

Curie point

The temperature (150ø C) at which certain elements are susceptible to magnetism. See *magneto-optic*.

current

The flow of electrons within a wire or circuit, measured in amps.

current directory

The disk directory the system is presently working in. Unless otherwise specified, commands that deal with disk files imply the current directory.

current loop

A serial transmission method originating with teletype machines that transmits 20 milliAmperes of current for a 1 bit and no current for a 0 bit. Today's circuit boards can't handle 20mA current and use optical isolators at the receiving end to detect lower current. Contrast with *RS-232*.

cursive writing

Handwriting.

cursor

(1) A movable symbol on screen that is the contact point between the user and the data. In text systems, it is a blinking rectangle or underline. On graphic systems, it is also called a "pointer," and it changes shape (arrow, square, paintbrush, etc.) when it moves into a different part of the application on screen.

(2) A pen-like or puck-like device used with a digitizer tablet. As the tablet cursor is moved across the tablet, the screen cursor moves correspondingly. See *digitizer tablet*.

cursor keys

The keys that move the cursor on screen, which include the up, down, left and right arrow, home, end, PgUp and PgDn keys. In addition to cursor keys, a mouse or tablet cursor also moves the cursor.

CU-SeeMe

Videoconferencing software for the Internet from White Pine Software Inc., Nashua, NH, (www.wpine.com). CU-SeeMe is available for Windows and Mac and allows point-to-point videoconferencing via modem over the Net.

custom control

The functionality in an application that differs from the stock objects provided in the development system. For example, a custom control is the creation of an animated cursor or a unique style of dialog box or menu, which is not part of the standard system.

customized software

Software designed for an individual customer.

customized toolbar

A toolbar that can be custom configured by the user. Buttons can be added and deleted as required.

cut & paste

To move or copy a block of text or graphics from one document to another.

CUT mode

(Control Unit Terminal mode) A mode that allows a 3270 terminal to have a single session with the mainframe. Micro to mainframe software emulates this mode to communicate with the mainframe. Contrast with *DFT mode*.

cyber

From cybernetics, a prefix attached to everyday words to add a computer, electronic or online connotation.

cybernetics

The comparative study of human and machine processes in order to understand their similarities and differences. It often refers to machines that imitate human behavior. See *AI* and *robot*.

cyberpunk

Relating to futuristic delinquency: hackers breaking into computer banks, survival based on high-tech wits. Stems from science fiction novels such as "Neuromancer" and "Shockwave Rider."

cyberspace

The term coined by William Gibson in his novel "Neuromancer," to refer to a futuristic computer network that people use by plugging their brains into it! The term now refers to the Internet or to the online or digital world in general. See *virtual reality*.

cycle

(1) A single event that is repeated. For example, in a carrier frequency, one cycle is one complete wave.

(2) A set of events that is repeated. For example, in a polling system, all of the attached terminals are tested in one cycle. See *machine cycle* and *memory cycle*.

cycles per second

The number of times an event or set of events is repeated in a second. See *Hertz*.

cycle stealing

A CPU design technique that periodically "grabs" machine cycles from the main processor usually by some peripheral control unit, such as a DMA (direct memory access) device. In this way, processing and peripheral operations can be performed concurrently or with some degree of overlap.

cycle time

The time interval between the start of one cycle and the start of the next cycle.

CYCOLOR

A process for printing photographic-quality images from Cycolor, Inc., Miamisburg, OH, (www.cycolor.com). Originally developed by Mead Imaging, the CYCOLOR process is mostly in the film itself. CYCOLOR DI film contains billions of light-sensitive microcapsules (cyliths), which are variably hardened when exposed to different lights and then pressed between rollers to release the dyes. Several types of CYCOLOR printers are expected in the 2000-2001 timeframe.

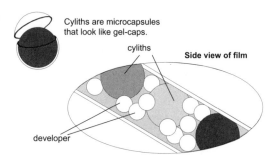

Cyliths are microcapsules that look like gel-caps.

cyliths

Side view of film

developer

cylinder

The aggregate of all tracks that reside in the same location on every disk surface. On multiple-platter disks, the cylinder is the sum total of every track with the same track number on every surface. On a floppy disk, a cylinder comprises the top and corresponding bottom track.

When storing data, the operating system fills an entire cylinder before moving to the next one. The access arm remains stationary until all the tracks in the cylinder have been read or written.

Cyrix

(Cyrix Corporation, Richardson, TX, www.cyrix.com) Founded in 1988, Cyrix was a manufacturer of x86-compatible CPU chips. Its first product was a math coprocessor. In 1992, it introduced a line of 486 CPUs, later followed by the 6x86 Pentium-class and 6x86MX Pentium II-class chips. In 1998, Cyrix was acquired by National Semiconductor and operated as a wholly-owned subsidiary. In 1999, National Semi sold its Cyrix processor business to Via Technologies, Inc., a leader in PC chipset design.

See also *Citrix*.

D

D/A converter (DAC)
(Digital to Analog Converter) A device that converts digital pulses into analog signals. Contrast with *A/D converter*. See *DSP*.

DAD
(1) (Database Action Diagram) Documentation that describes the processing performed on data in a database.

(2) (Digital Audio Disc) Same as *CD*.

daemon
Pronounced "demon." A UNIX program that executes in the background ready to perform an operation when required. It is usually an unattended process initiated at startup. Typical daemons are print spoolers and e-mail handlers or a scheduler that starts up another process at a designated time. The term comes from Greek mythology meaning "guardian spirit." Same as *agent*.

daisy chain
Connected in series, one after the other. Transmitted signals go to the first device, then to the second and so on.

daisy wheel
An earlier print mechanism that used a plastic or metal hub with spokes like an old-fashioned wagon wheel minus the outer rim. At the end of each spoke is the carved image of a type character.

damping
A technique for stabilizing an electronic or mechanical device by eliminating unwanted or excessive oscillations.

DAO
(Data Access Objects) A programming interface for data access from Microsoft. DAO/Jet provides access to the Jet database, and DAO/ODBCDirect provides an interface to ODBC databases via RDO. DAO is a COM object. See *ADO*.

darkened datacenter
Unattended datacenter operation. With printers distributed throughout the enterprise and the use of tape and optical libraries that automatically mount the appropriate disk and tape volume, the datacenter increasingly does not require human intervention.

dark fiber
Unused transmission capacity in a fiber optic trunk.

DARPA
(Defense Advanced Research Projects Agency) See *ARPANET*.

DASD
(Direct Access Storage Device) Pronounced "dazdee." A peripheral device that is directly addressable, such as a disk or drum. The term is used in the mainframe world.

DAT
(1) (Digital Audio Tape) A magnetic tape technology that uses a helical scan read/write head. DAT cassettes contain 4mm-wide tape and look like thick audio cassettes. DAT was Initially a CD-quality audio format, but Sony and HP defined the DDS (Digital Data Storage) format so that DAT could be used by computers. Raw capacities are 2GB for DDS, 4GB for DDS-2, 12GB for DDS-3 and 20GB for DDS-4.

(2) (Dynamic Address Translator) A hardware circuit that converts a virtual memory address into a real address.

data
(1) Technically, raw facts and figures, such as orders and payments, which are processed into information, such as balance due and quantity on hand. However, in common usage, the terms data and information are used synonymously.

The amount of data versus information kept in the computer is a tradeoff. Data can be processed into different forms of information, but it takes time to sort and sum transactions. Up-to-date information can provide instant answers.

A common misconception is that software is also data. Software is executed, or run, by the computer. Data is "processed." Software is "run."

(2) Any form of information whether in paper or electronic form. In electronic form, data refers to files and databases, text documents, images and digitally-encoded voice and video.

(3) The plural form of datum.

data abstraction

In object-oriented programming, creating user-defined data types that contain their own data and processing. These data structures, or objects, are unaware of each other's physical details and know only what services each other performs. This is the basis for polymorphism and information hiding.

data acquisition

(1) The automatic collection of data from sensors and readers in a factory, laboratory, medical or scientific environment.

(2) The gathering of source data for data entry into the computer.

data administration

The analysis, classification and maintenance of an organization's data and data relationships. It includes the development of data models and data dictionaries, which, combined with transaction volume, are the raw materials for database design.

Database administration often falls within the jurisdiction of data administration; however, data administration functions provide the overall management of data as an organizational resource. Database administration is the technical design and management of the database.

data administrator

A person who coordinates activities within the data administration department. Contrast with *database administrator*.

data bank

Any electronic depository of data.

database

(1) A set of interrelated files that is created and managed by a DBMS.

(2) Any electronically-stored collection of data.

DATABASE 2

See *DB2*.

database administrator

A person responsible for the physical design and management of the database and for the evaluation, selection and implementation of the DBMS.

In small organizations, the database administrator and data administrator are one in the same; however, when the two responsibilities are managed separately, the database administrator's function is more technical.

database analyst

See *data administrator* and *database administrator*.

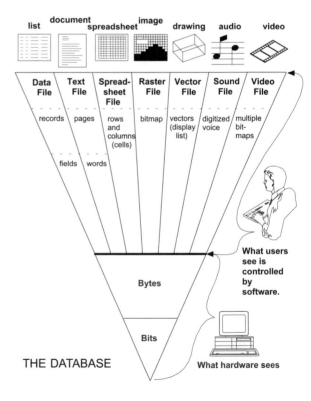

THE DATABASE

database driver

A software routine that accesses a database. It allows an application or compiler to access a particular database format.

database engine

Software that stores and retrieves data in a database. It may be a self-contained entity or part of a comprehensive database management system (DBMS). See *database manager*.

database machine

A specially-designed computer for database access that is coupled to the main computer via high-speed channel. It uses multiple processors to perform fast disk searches.

Contrast with *database server*, which is used in a LAN. The database machine is tightly coupled to the main CPU; the database server is loosely coupled in the network.

database management system

See *DBMS*.

database manager

(1) With personal computers, software that allows a user to manage multiple data files (same as *DBMS*). Contrast with *file manager*, which works with one file at a time.

(2) Software that provides database management capability for traditional programming languages, such as COBOL, BASIC and C, but without the interactive capabilities.

(3) The part of the DBMS that stores and retrieves the data.

database program

A software application that allows for the storage and retrieval of information, which is structured as fields, records and files. Database programs provide a way of creating and manipulating the electronic equivalent of a name and address card that can hold large amounts of information.

database publishing

Using desktop publishing to produce reports of database contents.

database server

A computer in a LAN dedicated to database storage and retrieval. Contrast with *file server*, which stores many kinds of files and programs for shared use.

data bits

The number of bits used to represent one character of data. When transmitting ASCII text via modem, either seven or eight bits may be used. All other forms of data require eight bits.

data bus

An internal pathway across which data is transferred to and from the processor. The expansion slots in personal computers are connected to the data bus.

data carrier

(1) Any medium such as a disk or tape that can hold machine readable data.

(2) A carrier frequency into which data is modulated for transmission in a network.

data cartridge

A removable magnetic tape module driven by a wheel inside the drive that presses against a passive roller in the cartridge. A tension belt is attached to the roller that presses against the supply and takeup reel. See *QIC*.

data cassette

A cassette used to hold computer data. See *cassette*.

datacenter

The department that houses the computer systems and related equipment, including the data library. Data entry and systems programming may also come under its jurisdiction. A control section is usually provided that accepts work from and releases output to user departments.

data code

(1) A coding system used to abbreviate data; for example, codes for regions, classes, products and status.

(2) A digital coding system for data in a computer. Same as *character code*. See *ASCII* and *EBCDIC*.

data collection

Acquiring source documents for the data entry department. It comes under the jurisdiction of the data control or data entry department. See *data acquisition*.

datacom, data communications

See *communications*.

data compression

Encoding data to take up less storage space. Digital data is compressed by finding rpeatable patterns of 0s and 1s. The more patterns that can be found, the more the data can be compressed. Text can generally be compressed to about 40% of its original size and graphics files from 20% to 90%.

data conferencing

Sharing data interactively among several users in different locations. Data conferencing is made up of whiteboards and application sharing. A whiteboard is the electronic equivalent of the chalkboard or flip chart. Application sharing is the same as remote control software, in which multiple participants can interactively work in an application that is loaded on only one user's machine.

data control department

The function responsible for collecting data for input into a computer's batch processing operations as well as the dissemination of the finished reports. The data entry department may be under the jursidiction of the data control department or vice versa.

data definition

(1) In a source language program, the definitions of data structures (variables, arrays, fields, records, etc.).

(2) A description of the record layout in a file system or DBMS.

data dictionary

A database about data and databases. It holds the name, type, range of values, source, and authorization for access for each data element in the organization's files and databases. It also indicates which application programs use that data so that when a change in a data structure is contemplated, a list of affected programs can be generated.

The data dictionary may be a stand-alone system or an integral part of, and used to control, the DBMS. Data integrity and accuracy is better ensured in the latter case.

data dipper

Software in a personal computer that queries a mainframe database.

data division

The part of a COBOL program that defines the data files and record layouts.

data element

The fundamental data structure in a data processing system. Any unit of data defined for processing is a data element; for example, ACCOUNT NUMBER, NAME, ADDRESS and CITY. A data element is defined by size (in characters) and type (alphanumeric, numeric only, true/false, date, etc.). A specific set of values or range of values may also be part of the definition.

Technically, a data element is a logical definition of data, whereas a field is the physical unit of storage in a record. For example, the data element ACCOUNT NUMBER, which exists only once, is stored in the ACCOUNT NUMBER field in the customer record and in the ACCOUNT NUMBER field in the order records.

Data element, data item, field and *variable* all describe the same unit of data and are used interchangeably.

data encryption

See *encryption*, *DES* and *RSA*.

data entry

Entering data into the computer, which includes keyboard entry, scanning and voice recognition. When transactions are entered after the fact (batch data entry), they are just stacks of source documents to the keyboard operator. Deciphering poor handwriting from a source document is a judgment call that is often error prone. In online data entry operations, in which the operator takes information in person or by phone, there's interaction and involvement with the transaction and less chance for error.

data entry department

The part of the datacenter where the data entry terminals and operators are located.

data entry operator

A person who enters data into the computer via keyboard or other reading or scanning device.

data entry program

An application program that accepts data from the keyboard or other input device and stores it in the computer. It may be part of an application that also provides updating, querying and reporting.

The data entry program establishes the data in the database and should test for all possible input errors. See *validity checking, table lookup, check digit* and *intelligent database*.

data error

A condition in which data on a digital medium has been corrupted. The error can be as little as one bit.

data file

A collection of data records. This term may refer specifically to a database file that contains records and fields in contrast to other files such as a word processing document or spreadsheet. Or, it may refer to a file that contains any type of information structure including documents and spreadsheets in contrast to a program file.

data flow

(1) In computers, the path of data from source document to data entry to processing to final reports. Data changes format and sequence (within a file) as it moves from program to program.

(2) In communications, the path taken by a message from origination to destination and includes all nodes through which the data travels.

data flow diagram

A description of data and the manual and machine processing performed on the data.

data fork

The part of a Macintosh file that contains data. For example, in a HyperCard stack, text, graphics and HyperTalk scripts reside in the data fork, while fonts, sounds, control information and external functions reside in the resource fork.

data format

See *file format*.

Data General

(Data General Corporation, Westboro, MA, www.dg.com) One of the first minicomputer companies, founded in 1968 by Edson de Castro. It has introduced a variety of computer series over the years and specializes in UNIX-based servers and RAID systems. In 1999, Data General was acquired by EMC.

data glove

A glove used to report the position of a user's hand and fingers to a computer. See *virtual reality*.

datagram

The unit of data, or packet, transmitted in a TCP/IP network. Each datagram contains source and destination addresses and data. See *TCP/IP* and *UDP*.

data independence

Techniques that allow data to be changed without affecting the applications that process it. There are two kinds of data independence. The first type is data independence for data, which is accomplished in an database management system (DBMS). It allows the database to be structurally changed without affecting most existing programs. Programs access data in a DBMS by field and are concerned with only the data fields they use, not the format of the complete record. Thus, when the record layout is updated (fields added, deleted or changed in size), the only programs that must be changed are those that use those new fields.

The second type is data independence for processing. This means that any data that can possibly be changed should be stored in a database and not "hard wired" into the code of the program. When values change, only the database item is altered, which is a simple task, rather than recompiling programs.

data integrity
The process of preventing accidental erasure or adulteration in a database.

data item
A unit of data stored in a field. See *field*.

data library
The section of the datacenter that houses offline disks and tapes. Data library personnel are responsible for cataloging and maintaining the media.

data line
An individual circuit, or line, that carries data within a computer or communications channel.

data line monitor
In communications, a test instrument that analyzes the signals and timing of a communications line. It either visually displays the patterns or stores the activity for further analysis.

data link
In communications, the physical interconnection between two points (OSI layers 1 and 2). It may also refer to the modems, protocols and all required hardware and software to perform the transmission.

data link escape
A communications control character which indicates that the following character is not data, but a control code.

data link protocol
In communications, the transmission of a unit of data from one node to another (OSI layer 2). It is responsible for ensuring that the bits received are the same as the bits sent. All transmission of data requires a data link function, which may be all that is necessary. For example, Xmodem and Zmodem provide data link capability when transmitting between two personal computers via modem. Ethernet and Token Ring provide data link services over a network.

data management
Refers to several levels of managing data. From bottom to top, they are:

(1) The part of the operating system that manages the physical storage and retrieval of data on a disk or other device. See *access method*.

(2) Software that allows for the creation, storage, retrieval and manipulation of files interactively at a terminal or personal computer. See *file manager* and *DBMS*.

(3) The function that manages data as an organizational resource. See *data administration*.

(4) The management of all data/information in an organization. It includes data administration, the standards for defining data and the way in which people perceive and use it.

data management system
See *DBMS*.

data manipulation
Processing data.

data manipulation language
A language that requests data from a DBMS. It is coded within the application program such as COBOL or C.

data mining

Exploring detailed business transactions. It implies "digging through tons of data" to uncover patterns and relationships contained within the business activity and history. Data mining can be done manually by slicing and dicing the data until a pattern becomes obvious. Or, it can be done with programs that analyze the data automatically. See *OLAP, DSS, EIS, data warehouse* and *slice and dice.*

data model

A description of the principles of organization of a database.

data modeling

The identification of the design principles for a data model.

data modem

A modem used for sending data and not faxes. See *modem* and *fax/modem.*

data module

A sealed, removable storage module containing magnetic disks and their associated access arms and read/write heads.

data name

The name assigned to a field or variable.

data network

A communications network that transmits data. See *communications.*

data packet

One frame in a packet-switched message. Most data communications is based on dividing the transmitted message into variable-length packets. For example, an Ethernet packet can be from 64 to 1518 bytes in length.

data parallel

Same as *SIMD.*

data processing

The capturing, storing, updating and retrieving data and information. It may refer to the industry or to data processing tasks in contrast with other operations, such as word processing.

data processor

(1) A person who works in data processing.

(2) A computer that is processing data, in contrast with a computer performing another task, such as controlling a network.

data projector

A video machine that projects output from a computer onto a remote screen. It is bulkier than a flat LCD panel, but is faster for displaying high-speed animation.

data pump

A circuit that transmits pulses in a digital device. Typically refers to the chipset in a modem that generates the modem's modulation techniques and speeds.

Dataquest

(Dataquest Inc., San Jose, CA, www.dataquest.com) A major market research and analysis firm in the information field. Dataquest offers market intelligence on more than 25 topics and provides conferences, annual subscriptions and custom research. In 1995, Dataquest was acquired by the GartnerGroup.

data rate

(1) The data transfer speed within the computer or between a peripheral and computer.

(2) The data transmission speed in a network.

data recovery

Restoring data that has been physically damaged or corrupted on a disk or tape. Disks and tapes can become corrupted due to viruses, bad software, hardware failure as well as from power failures that occur while the magnetic media is being written.

data representation

How data types are structured; for example, how signs are represented in numerical values or how strings are formatted (enclosed in quotes, terminated with a null, etc.).

data resource management

Same as *data administration*.

data scrubbing

Making data more accurate and consistent; in other words, "cleaning it up". It refers to eliminating duplicate records, correcting misspellings and errors in names and addresses, ensuring consistent descriptions, punctuation, syntax and other content issues. See *audio scrubbing*.

data set

(1) A data file or collection of interrelated data.

(2) The AT&T name for modem.

data sheet

A page or two of detailed information about a product.

data signal

Physical data as it travels over a line or channel (pulses or vibrations of electricity or light).

data sink

A device or part of the computer that receives data.

data source

A device or part of the computer in which data is originated.

data stream

The continuous flow of data from one place to another.

data striping

See *disk striping*.

data structure

The physical layout of data. Data fields, memo fields, fixed length fields, variable length fields, records, word processing documents, spreadsheets, data files, database files and indexes are all examples of data structures.

data switch

A switch box that routes one line to another; for example, to connect two computers to one printer. Manual switches have dials or buttons. Automatic switches test for signals and provide first-come, first-served switching.

data system

Same as *information system*.

data tablet

Same as *digitizer tablet*.

data transfer

The movement of data within the computer system. Typically, data is said to be transferred within the computer, but it is "transmitted" over a communications network. A transfer is actually a copy function since the data is not automatically erased at the source.

data transfer rate

Same as *data rate*.

data transmission

Sending data over a communications network.

data transparency

The ability to easily access and work with data no matter where it is located or what application created it.

data type

A category of data. Typical data types are numeric, alphanumeric (character), dates and logical (true/false). Programming languages allow for the creation of different data types.

When data is assigned a type, it cannot be treated like another type. For example, alphanumeric data cannot be calculated, and digits within numeric data cannot be isolated. Date types must have valid dates.

data warehouse

A database designed to support decision making in an organization. it is batch updated and structured for fast online queries and summaries for managers. Data warehouses can contain enormous amounts of data. See *OLAP, DSS* and *EIS*.

datum

The singular form of data; for example, one datum. It is rarely used, and data, its plural form, is commonly used for both singular and plural.

daughter board

A small printed circuit board that is attached to or plugs into a removable printed circuit board.

dazdee

See *DASD*.

DB

See *database* and *decibel*.

DB2

(DATABASE 2) A relational DBMS from IBM that was originally developed for its mainframes. It is a full-featured SQL language DBMS that has become IBM's major database product. Known for its industrial strength reliability, IBM has made DB/2 available for all its platforms (DB2 for mainframes; DB2/2 for OS/2; DB2/400 for AS/400; DB2/6000 for RS/6000) as well as for the HP 9000, Sun Solaris and Windows NT.

DB-9, DB-15, DB-25...

A category of plugs and sockets with 9, 15, 25, 37 and 50 pins respectively, used to hook up communications and computer devices. The DB refers to the connector, not the purpose of each line.

DB-9 and DB-25 connectors are commonly used for RS-232 interfaces. The DB-25 is also used on the computer end of the parallel printer cable for PCs (the printer end is a Centronics 36-pin connector).

A high-density DB-15 connector is used for the VGA port on a PC, which has 15 pins in the same shell as the DB-9 connector.

DBA

See *database administrator*.

dBASE

A database program for Windows from dBASE Inc., Vestal, NY, (www.dbase2000.com). dBASE was the first comprehensive relational DBMS for personal computers and was originally developed for CP/M machines and later for DOS. It was originally marketed by Ashton-Tate, which was acquired by Borland. dBASE spawned many "Xbase" languages such as CA-Clipper, FoxBASE and FoxPro.

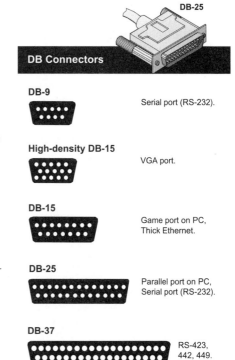

DB Connectors

DB-9
Serial port (RS-232).

High-density DB-15
VGA port.

DB-15
Game port on PC, Thick Ethernet.

DB-25
Parallel port on PC, Serial port (RS-232).

DB-37
RS-423, 442, 449.

DB-50
Dataproducts, Datapoint, etc.

DB/DC

(DataBase/Data Communications) Refers to software that performs database and data communications functions.

DBF file

The dBASE data file extension.

DBLIB

(DataBase LIBrary) The native, low-level programming interface for Sybase and Microsoft SQL Server databases. In the Microsoft world, much of the interaction between applications and databases is programmed using high-level interfaces such as DAO, RDO and ADO.

DBMS

(DataBase Management System) Software that controls the organization, storage, retrieval, security and integrity of data in a database. It accepts requests from the application and instructs the operating system to transfer the appropriate data.

DBMSs may work with traditional programming languages (COBOL, C, etc.) or they may include their own programming language. For example, dBASE and Paradox are database programs with a DBMS, a full programming language and a fourth-generation (4GL) language, making them complete application development systems. 4GL commands let users interactively create database files, edit them, ask questions and print reports without programming. Thousands of applications have been developed in environments such as these.

The following illustration shows the interaction between the DBMS and other system software and applications.

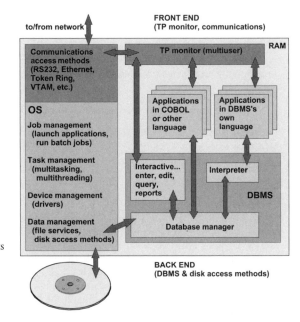

DBS

(Direct Broadcast Satellite) A one-way TV broadcast service direct from a satellite to a small 18" dish antenna. Although DBS service exists in other countries, the first DBS satellite for the United States was launched in December 1993 by Hughes Communications and Hubbard Broadcasting.

DC

(1) (Direct Current) An electrical current that travels in one direction and used within the computer's electronic circuits. Contrast with AC.

(2) (Data Communications) See *DB/DC*.

DCA

(1) (Document Content Architecture) IBM file formats for text documents. DCA/RFT (Revisable-Form Text) is the primary format and can be edited. DCA/FFT (Final-Form Text) has been formatted for a particular output device and cannot be changed. For example, page numbers, headers and footers are placed on every page.

(2) (Digital Communications Associates, Inc., Alpharetta, GA) A manufacturer of communications products that was acquired by Attachmate Corporation, Bellevue, WA.

DCC

(1) (Digital Compact Cassette) A digital tape format that uses a variation of the common analog audio cassette. DCC machines also play analog cassettes.

(2) (Direct Cable Connection) A Windows 95/98 feature that allows PCs to be cabled together for data transfer. DCC actually sets up a network connection between the two machines.

(3) (Digital Content Creation) The development of newsworthy, educational and entertainment material for distribution over the Internet or other digital media.

DCE

(1) (Data Communications Equipment or Data Circuit-terminating Equipment) A device that establishes, maintains and terminates a session on a network. It may also convert signals for transmission. It is typically the modem. Contrast with *DTE*.

(2) (Distributed Computing Environment) A set of programs from OSF used for developing and maintaining client/server applications across heterogeneous platforms in a network.

DCI

(Display Control Interface) An Intel and Microsoft standard for full-motion video in Windows. It improves performance by bypassing the Windows GDI interface and addressing the display adapter directly.

DCOM

(Distributed Component Object Model) Microsoft's technology for distributed objects. DCOM is based on COM, Microsoft's component software architecture, which defines the object interfaces. DCOM defines the remote procedure call which allows those objects to be run remotely over the network. DCOM began shipping with Windows NT 4.0 and is Microsoft's counterpart to CORBA. See *COM, component software* and *CORBA*.

DCS

(1) (Digital Cross-connect System) A network switching and grooming device used by telecom carriers. See *digital cross-connect*.

(2) (Distributed Communications System) A telephone system that puts small switches close to subscribers making local loops shorter and maximizing long lines to the central office.

(3) (Desktop Color Separation) A graphics format for color separation that uses five Encapsulated PostScript (EPS) files, one for each of the CMYK colors, and one master file, which links the other four and contains a preview image.

(4) (Distributed Control System) A process control system that uses disbursed computers throughout the manufacturing line for control.

DCT

(Discrete Cosine Transform) An algorithm, similar to Fast Fourier Transform, that converts data (pixels, waveforms, etc.) into sets of frequencies. The first frequencies in the set are the most meaningful; the latter, the least. For compression, latter frequencies are stripped away based on allowable resolution loss. The DCT method is used in the JPEG and MPEG compression.

DDBMS

(Distributed Database Management System) See *distributed database*.

DDCMP

(Digital Data Communications Message Protocol) Digital's proprietary, synchronous data link protocol used in DECnet.

DDE

(Dynamic Data Exchange) A message protocol in Windows that allows application programs to request and exchange data automatically. A program in one window can query a program in another window.

DDL

(1) (Data Description Language) A language used to define data and their relationships to other data. It is used to create files, databases and data dictionaries.

(2) (Document Description Language) A printer control language from Imagen that runs on the HP LaserJet series.

(3) (Direct Data Link) The ability of a supplier to directly interrogate a customer's inventory database in order to manage scheduling and shipping more efficiently. Pioneered by Ford Motor Co. in 1988, Ford lets suppliers check stock levels in assembly plants throughout North America.

DDM

(Distributed Data Management) Software in an IBM SNA environment that allows users to access data in remote data files within the network. DDM works with IBM's LU 6.2 session to provide peer-to-peer communications and file sharing.

DDP

(Distributed Data Processing) See *distributed processing*.

DDS

(1) (Dataphone Digital Service) An AT&T private line digital service with data rates from 2400 bps to 56Kbps. Private analog lines can be connected to DDS lines.

(2) (Digital Data Service) A private line digital services from non-AT&T carriers.

(3) (Digital Data Storage) A DAT format for data backup. It is a sequential recording method; data must be appended at the end of previous data. See *tape backup*.

deadlock

See *deadly embrace*.

deadly embrace

A stalemate that occurs when two elements in a process are each waiting for the other to respond. For example, in a network, if one user is working on file A and needs file B to continue, but another user is working on file B and needs file A to continue, each one waits for the other. Both are temporarily locked out. The software must be able to deal with this.

deallocate

To release a computer resource that is currently assigned to a program or user, such as memory or a peripheral device.

deblock

To separate records from a block.

debug

To correct a problem in hardware or software. Debugging software is finding the errors in the program logic. Debugging hardware is finding the errors in circuit design.

debugger

Software that helps a programmer debug a program by stopping at certain breakpoints and displaying various programming elements. The programmer can step through source code statements one at a time while the corresponding machine instructions are being executed.

DEC

(Digital Equipment Corporation) The trade name for Digital's products (DECmate, DECnet, etc.). Many people refer to the company as DEC.

decay

The reduction of strength of a signal or charge.

decentralized processing

Computer systems in different locations. Although data may be transmitted between the computers periodically, it implies limited daily communications. Contrast with *distributed processing* and *centralized processing*.

decibel

(dB) The unit that measures loudness or strength of a signal. dBs are a relative measurement derived from an initial reference level and a final observed level. A whisper is about 10 dB, a noisy factory 90 dB, loud thunder 110 dB. 120 dB is painful.

decimal

Meaning 10. The universal numbering system that uses 10 digits. Computers use binary numbers because it is easier to design electronic systems that can maintain two states rather than 10.

decision box

A diamond-shaped symbol that is used to document a decision point in a flowchart. The decision is written in the decision box, and the results of the decision branch off from the points in the box.

decision instruction

In programming, an instruction that compares one set of data with another and branches to a different part of the program depending on the results.

decision support system

See *DSS* and *EIS*.

decision table

A list of decisions and their criteria. Designed as a matrix, it lists criteria (inputs) and the results (outputs) of all possible combinations of the criteria. It can be placed into a program to direct its processing. By changing the decision table, the program is changed accordingly.

decision tree

A graphical representation of all alternatives in a decision making process.

deck

(1) The part of a magnetic tape unit that holds and moves the tape reels.

(2) Set of punched cards.

(3) See *DEC*.

declaration

In programming, an instruction or statement that defines data (fields, variables, arrays, etc.) and resources, but does not create executable code.

DECnet

Digital's communications network, which supports Ethernet-style LANs and baseband and broadband WANs over private and public lines. It interconnects PDPs, VAXs, PCs, Macs and workstations. In DECnet philosophy, a node must be an intelligent machine and not simply a terminal as in other systems.

decoder

A hardware device or software program that converts a coded signal back into its original form.

decollator

A device that separates multiple-part paper forms while removing the carbon paper.

decompiler

A program that converts machine language back into a high-level source language. The resulting code may be very difficult to maintain as variables and routines are named generically: A0001, A0002, etc.

decompress

To restore compressed data back to its original size.

decrement

To subtract a number from another number. Decrementing a counter means to subtract 1 or some other number from its current value.

dedicated channel

A computer channel or communications line that is used for one purpose.

dedicated service

A service that is not shared by other users or organizations.

de facto standard

A widely-used format or language not endorsed by a standards organization.

default

The current setting or action taken by hardware or software if the user has not specified otherwise.

default directory

Same as *current directory*.

default drive

The disk drive used if no other drive is specified.

default font

The typeface and type size used if none other is specified.

default gateway

The router used to forward all traffic that is not addressed to a station within the local subnet.

defragger

Also called an "optimizer program," it is a software utility that defragments a disk.

defragment

To reorganize the disk by putting files into contiguous order. Because the operating system stores new data in whatever free space is available, data files become spread out across the disk if they are updated often. This causes extra read/write head movement to read them back. Periodically, the hard disk should be defragmented to put files back into order.

degausser

A device that removes unwanted magnetism from a monitor or the read/write head in a disk or tape drive.

de jure standard

A format or language endorsed by a standards organization.

delay line

A communications or electronic circuit that has a built-in delay. Acoustic delay lines were used to create the earliest computer memories. For example, the UNIVAC I used tubes of liquid mercury that would slow down the digital pulses long enough (a fraction of a second) to serve as storage.

delete

To remove an item of data from a file or to remove a file from the disk. See *undelete*.

delimiter

A character or combination of characters used to separate one item or set of data from another. For example, in comma delimited records, a comma is used to separate each field of data.

deliverable

The measurable result or output of a process.

Dell

(Dell Computer Corporation, Austin, TX, www.dell.com) A major PC manufacturer founded in 1984 by Michael Dell. Originally selling under the "PCs Limited" brand, Dell was the first to legitimize mail-order PCs by providing quality telephone support.

Delphi

(1) An application development system for Windows from Inprise/Borland, introduced in 1995. It is based on the Object Pascal language.

(2) (Delphi Forums, www.delphi.com) A consumer-oriented Web site that offers self-managed forums on any subject. Delphi was originally an online service that was the first to offer Internet access in 1992.

(3) (Delphi Consulting Group, Boston, MA, www.delphigroup.com) The leading consulting organization in document management and workflow founded in 1987 by Thomas Koulopoulos.

delta modulation

A technique that is used to sample voice waves and convert them into digital code. Delta modulation typically samples the wave 32,000 times per second, but generates only one bit per sample. See *PCM*.

demand paging

Copying a program page from disk into memory when required by the program.

demodulate
To filter out the data signal from the carrier. See *modulate*.

demon
See *daemon*.

demoware
Demonstration software that shows some or all of the features of a commercial product. See *crippleware*.

demultiplex
To reconvert a transmission that contains several intermixed signals back into its original separate signals.

DEN
(Directory Enabled Networks) The management of a network from a central depository of information about users, applications and network resources. Originally an initiative from Microsoft and Cisco, DEN was turned over to the DMTF in 1998. A DEN schema is expected for the CIM model.

denial of service
A condition in which a system can no longer respond to normal requests.

density
See *packing density* and *bit density*.

departmental computing
Processing a department's data with its own computer system. See *distributed processing*.

dependent segment
In database management, data that depends on data in a higher level for its full meaning.

dequeue
Pronounced "d-q." To remove items from a queue in order to process or transmit them.

DES
(Data Encryption Standard) A NIST-standard encryption technique that scrambles data into an unbreakable code for public transmission. It uses a binary number as an encryption key with 72 quadrillion possible combinations. The key, randomly chosen for each session, is used to create the encryption pattern for transmission. See *RSA*.

descending sort
Arranging data from high to low sequence (Z to A, 9 to 0).

descriptor
(1) A word or phrase that identifies a document in an indexed information retrieval system.

(2) A category name used to identify data.

deserialize
To convert a serial stream of bits into parallel streams of bits.

Designer
A full-featured Windows drawing program that is part of the Micrografx Graphics Suite from Micrografx, Inc., Richardson, TX, (www.micrografx.com). Designer is a very sophisticated vector graphics program providing many features of a CAD program, including layers and dimensioning.

desk accessory
In the Macintosh, a program that is always available from the Apple menu no matter what application is running. With System 7, all applications can be turned into desk accessories.

desk checking
Manually testing the logic of a program.

DeskJet
A family of popular desktop ink jet printers for PCs from HP.

desktop
(1) An on-screen representation of a desktop, which is used in the Macintosh, Windows 95/98 and Windows NT.

(2) A buzzword attached to applications traditionally performed on more expensive machines that are now on a personal computer (desktop publishing, desktop mapping, etc.).

desktop accessory
Software that simulates an object normally found on an office desktop, such as a calculator, notepad and appointment calendar. It is typically RAM resident. See *TSR*.

desktop application
See *desktop accessory*.

desktop computer
A computer that is small enough to reside on a desktop. It either refers to personal computers (PCs, Macs, Amigas, PowerPCs, etc.) or to workstations from Sun, IBM, HP, Digital and others.

desktop manager
The part of a GUI that displays the desktop and icons, allows programs to be launched from the icon and files to be visually dragged & dropped, copied and deleted. The desktop manager and window manager make up the GUI, which are all included in the Mac and Windows. In UNIX desktops, the desktop manager is a third-party add-on.

desktop mapping
Using a desktop computer to perform digital mapping functions.

desktop media
The integration of desktop presentations, desktop publishing and multimedia (coined by Apple).

desktop organizer
See *desktop accessory*.

desktop presentations
The creation of presentation materials on a personal computer, which includes charts, graphs and other graphics-oriented information. It implies a wide variety of special effects for both text and graphics that will produce output for use as handouts, overheads and slides as well as sequences that can be viewed on screen. Advanced systems generate animation and control multimedia devices.

desktop publishing
Abbreviated "DTP." Using a personal computer to produce high-quality printed output or camera-ready output for commercial printing. It requires a desktop publishing program, high-speed personal computer, large monitor and a laser printer.

Since DTP has dramatically brought down the cost of high-end page makeup, it is often thought of as "the" way to produce inhouse newsletters and brochures. However, creating quality material takes experience. Desktop publishing is no substitute for a graphics designer who knows which fonts to use and how to lay out the page artistically.

destructive memory
Memory that loses its content when it is read, requiring that the circuitry regenerate the bits after the read operation.

developer's toolkit
A set of software routines and utilities used to help programmers write an application. In graphical interfaces, it provides the tools for creating resources, such as menus, dialog boxes, fonts and icons. It provides the means to link the new application to its operating environment (OS, DBMS, protocol, etc.). See *development system*.

Developer/2000

A client/server application development system for Windows, Mac and Motif from Oracle. Formerly the Cooperative Development Environment, the core programs are Oracle Forms, Oracle Reports and Oracle Graphics. It includes Discoverer/2000, an end user analysis suite made up of Oracle Data Query for reports and queries and Oracle Browser for viewing tables and data dictionaries.

development cycle

See *system development cycle*.

development system

(1) A programming language and related components. It includes the compiler, text editor, debugger, function library and any other supporting programs that enable a programmer to write a program. See *developer's toolkit*.

(2) A computer and related software for developing applications.

development tool

Any hardware or software that assists in the creation of electronic machines or software programs. See *developer's toolkit*.

device

(1) Any electronic or electromechanical machine or component from a transistor to a disk drive. Device always refers to hardware.

(2) In semiconductor design, it is an active component, such as a transistor or diode, in contrast to a passive component, such as a resistor or capacitor.

device address

See *address, I/O address* and *port address*.

device context

A data structure in Windows programming that is used to define the attributes of text and images that are output to the screen or printer. The device context (DC) is maintained by GDI. A DC, which is a handle to the structure, is obtained before output is written and released after the elements have been written. See *GDI*.

device dependent

Refers to programs that address specific hardware features and work with only one type of peripheral device. Contrast with *device independent*. See *machine dependent*.

device driver

See *driver*.

device independent

Refers to programs that work with a variety of peripheral devices. The hardware-specific instructions are in some other program (OS, DBMS, etc.). Contrast with *device dependent*. See *machine independent*.

device level

(1) In circuit design, refers to working with individual transistors rather than complete circuits.

(2) Refers to communicating directly with the hardware at a machine language level.

device name

A name assigned to a hardware device that represents its physical address. For example, LPT1 is a DOS device name for the parallel port.

DFT mode

(Distributed Function Terminal mode) A mode that allows a 3270 terminal to have five concurrent sessions with the mainframe. Contrast with *CUT mode*.

DG

See *Data General*.

DHCP

(Dynamic Host Configuration Protocol) Software that automatically assigns IP addresses to client stations logging onto a TCP/IP network. It eliminates having to manually assign permanent IP addresses. DHCP software typically runs in servers and is also found in network devices such as ISDN routers and modem routers that allow multiple users access to the Internet. Newer DHCP servers dynamically update the DNS servers after making assignments. See *DNS* and *WINS*.

Dhrystones

A benchmark program that tests a general mix of instructions. The results in Dhrystones per second are the number of times the program can be executed in one second. See *Whetstones*.

DIA

(Document Interchange Architecture) An IBM SNA format used to exchange documents from dissimilar machines within an LU 6.2 session. It acts as an envelope to hold the document and does not set any standards for the content of the document, such as layout settings or graphics standards.

diacritical

A small mark added to a letter that changes its pronunciation, such as the French cedilla, which is a small hook placed under the letter "c."

diagnostic board

An expansion board with built-in diagnostic tests that reports results via its own readout. Boards for PCs, such as Landmark's KickStart and UNICORE's POSTcard, have their own POST system and can test a malfunctioning computer that doesn't boot.

diagnostics

(1) Software routines that test hardware components (memory, keyboard, disks, etc.). In personal computers, they are often stored in ROM and activated on startup.

(2) Error messages in a programmer's source code that refer to statements or syntax that the compiler or assembler cannot understand.

diagnostic tracks

The spare tracks on a disk used by the drive or controller for testing purposes.

diagramming program

Software that allows the user to create flow charts, organization charts and other interconnected diagrams. It is similar to a drawing program, but keeps the lines connected to the blocks when the blocks are moved. It may also provide text annotation of the graphic items, allowing an equipment list to be maintained with a network diagram, for example.

dialog box

A small, on-screen window displayed in response to some request. It provides the options currently available to the user.

dial-up adapter

Software that dials up a phone number. For example, for Internet connections in Windows, you should see "TCP/IP-> Dial-Up Adapter" in the Network control panel. This means the TCP/IP (Internet) protocol has been directed to the Dial-Up Adapter. Although "adapter" implies a card plugged into the computer, this is not the case here.

dial-up line

A two-wire line as used in the dial-up telephone network. Contrast with *leased line*.

dial-up network

The switched telephone network regulated by government and administered by common carriers.

diazo film

A film used to make microfilm or microfiche copies. It is exposed to the original film under ultraviolet light and is developed into identical copies. Copy color is typically blue, blue-black or purple.

DIB

(1) (Directory Information Base) Also called "white pages," a database of names in an X.500 system.

(2) (Device Independent Bitmap) An internal data structure in Windows for creating graphics that are not tied to a particular output device. DIBs contain more information than a BMP file so that they can be rendered into any display or printer device. When stored on disk however, they become BMP files. See *BMP file.*

die, dice

The formal term for the square of silicon containing an integrated circuit. The popular term is chip. The plural of die is dice.

dielectric

An insulator (glass, rubber, plastic, etc.). Dielectric materials can be made to hold an electrostatic charge, but current cannot flow through them.

DIF

(1) (Data Interchange Format) A standard file format for spreadsheet and other data structured in row and column form. Originally developed for VisiCalc, DIF is now under Lotus' jurisdiction.

(2) (Display Information Facility) An IBM System/38 program that lets users build custom programs for online access to data.

(3) (Document Interchange Format) A file standard developed by the U.S. Navy in 1982.

(4) (Dual In-line Flatpack) A type of surface mount DIP with pins extending horizontally outward.

differential backup

Backing up only files that have been changed. This is used when only the latest version of a file is required. See *full backup* and *incremental backup.*

differential configuration

The use of wire pairs for each electrical signal for high immunity to noise and crosstalk. Contrast with *single-ended configuration.*

diffusion

A semiconductor manufacturing process that infuses tiny quantities of impurities into a base material, such as silicon, to change its electrical characteristics.

digit

A single character in a numbering system. In decimal, digits are 0 through 9. In binary, digits are 0 and 1.

digital

(1) Traditionally, the use of numbers and comes from digit, or finger. Today, digital is synonymous with computer.

(2) (Digital) See *Digital Equipment.*

digital audio extraction

A feature of most newer CD-ROM drives that allows the digital data from audio CDs to be passed through the computer's bus (IDE, SCSI) just like CD-ROM data. Without this feature, transferring audio CD tracks to the computer requires using the analog output of the drive and converting it back to digital again, resulting in less sound quality. See *ripper* and *MP3.*

digital camera

A video or still camera that records images in digital form. Unlike traditional analog cameras that convert light intensities into infinitely variable signals, digital cameras convert light intensities into discrete numbers for storage on a medium, such as a hard disk or flash disk. As with all digital devices, there is a fixed, maximum resolution and number of colors that can be represented.

digital certificate

The digital equivalent to an ID card in the RSA public key encryption system. Also called "digital IDs," they are issued by certification organizations, such as VeriSign, Inc., Mountain View, CA, (www.verisign.com), after verifying that a public key belongs to a certain owner.

The certificate is actually the owner's public key that has been digitally signed by a certification authority (CA). It is sent along with an encrypted message to verify that the sender is truly the entity identifying itself in the transmission. The recipient uses the widely-publicized public key of the CA to decrypt the sender's public key attached to the message. Then the sender's public key is used to decrypt the actual message. See *digital signature*.

digital channel

A communications path that handles only digital signals. All voice and video signals have to be converted from analog to digital in order to be carried over a digital channel. Contrast with *analog channel*.

digital camera

A video or still camera that records images in digital form. Unlike traditional analog cameras that record infinitely-variable intensities of light, digital cameras record discrete numbers for storage on a flash memory card, floppy disk or hard disk.

digital circuit

An electronic circuit that accepts and processes binary data (on/off) according to the rules of Boolean logic.

digital computer

A computer that accepts and processes data that has been converted into binary numbers. All common computers are digital. Contrast with *analog computer*.

digital convergence

The integration of computers, communications and consumer electronics.

digital cross-connect

A network device used by telecom carriers and large enterprises to switch and multiplex low-speed voice and data signals onto high-speed lines and vice versa. It is typically used to aggregate several T1 lines into a higher-speed electrical or optical line as well as to distributed signals to various destinations.

digital data

Data in digital form. All data in the computer is in digital form.

digital domain

The world of digital. When something is done in the digital domain, it implies that the original data (images, sounds, video, etc.) has been converted into a digital format and is manipulated inside the computer's memory.

digital effects

Special sounds and animations that have been created in the digital domain. Synthetic sounds and reverberation, morphing and transitions between video frames (fades, wipes, dissolves, etc.) are examples.

digital envelope

(1) An encrypted message that uses both secret key and public key cryptography methods. The public key method is used to exchange the secret key, and the secret key is used to encrypt and decrypt the message. See *RSA*.

(2) A frame, or packet, of data that has been encrypted for transmission over a network.

(3) A term occasionally used to describe inserting data into a frame, or packet, for transmission over a network. The envelope metaphor implies a container.

Digital Equipment

A major computer manufacturer, commonly known as DEC or Digital. It was founded in 1957 by Kenneth Olsen, who headed the company until he retired in 1992. Digital pioneered the minicomputer industry with its PDP series and became very successful with its VAX line in the 1980s. Its Alpha architecture is the successor to the VAX. In 1998, Digital was acquired by Compaq.

digital home

A residence that is fully automated. It uses computing devices and home appliances that conform to some common standard for internetworking so that everything can be controlled by computer. The digital home implies network sockets in every room just like AC power receptacles.

digital ID

See *digital certificate.*

digital loop carrier

In telephone communications, a technology that increases the number of channels in the local loop by converting analog signals to digital and multiplexing them back to the end office.

digital mapping

Digitizing geographic information for a geographic information system (GIS).

digital money

Electronic money used on the Internet. The first category is the traditional credit card. Most Web browsers and Internet Service Providers (ISPs) support one of the major security protocols such as Secure Socket Layer (SSL), which provides an encrypted transmission from the user to the Web site.

The second type of digital money is like travelers checks. This digital money is either downloaded as "digital coins" from a participating bank into the user's personal computer or a digital money account is set up within the bank. Either the digital coins or the transactions that debit the account are transmitted to the merchant for payment. All transactions are encrypted for security.

digital monitor

A video monitor that accepts a digital signal from the computer and converts it into analog signals to illuminate the screen. Examples are the earlier MDA, CGA and EGA monitors. Contrast with *analog monitor.*

digital PBX

(digital Private Branch Exchange) A modern PBX that uses digital methods for switching in contrast to older PBXs that use analog methods.

digital radio

The microwave transmission of digital data via line of sight transmitters.

digital recording

See *digital video, nonlinear editing* and *magnetic recording.*

digital signature

An electronic signature that cannot be forged. It is a computed digest of the text that is encrypted with the senders private key and sent along with the text message. The recipient decrypts the signature with the sender's public key and recomputes the digest from the received text. If the digests match, the message is authenticated and proved intact from the sender. See *RSA* and *MAC.*

Signatures and Certificates

A digital signature ensures that the document originated with the person signing it and that it was not tampered with after the signature was applied. However, the sender could still be an impersonator and not the person he or she claims to be. To verify that the message was indeed sent by the person claiming to send it requires a digital certificate (digital ID) which is issued by a certification authority. See *digital certificate.*

digital TV (DTV)

A digital television standard for the U.S. approved by the FCC in 1996 and developed by the Advanced Television Systems Committee (ATSC). In November 1998, digital TV debuted in major U.S. cities. It is expected that digital TV will reach half the U.S. households (top 30 markets) by the end of 2000. Canada, South Korea, Taiwan and Argentina have also adopted the ATSC standard.

digital video

Video recording in digital form. In order to edit video in the computer or to embed video clips into multimedia documents, a video source must originate as digital (digital camera) or be converted to digital.

Frames from analog video cameras and VCRs are converted into digital frames (bitmaps) using frame grabbers or similar devices attached to a personal computer.

Uncompressed digital video signals consume huge amounts of storage, and high-ratio realtime compression schemes such as MPEG are essential for effective use. See *nonlinear video editing* and *HDTV*.

digital wallet

The electronic equivalent of a wallet for e-commerce transactions. A digital wallet (e-wallet) can hold digital money that is purchased similar to travelers checks, a prepaid account like an EZPass system, or it can contain credit card information. The wallet may reside in the user's machine or on the servers of a Web payment service. When stored in the client machine, the wallet may use a digital certificate that identifies the authorized card holder. See *digital money* and *Web payment service*.

digitize

To convert an image or signal into digital code by scanning, tracing on a graphics tablet or using an analog to digital conversion device. 3-D objects can be digitized by a device with a mechanical arm that is moved onto all the corners.

digitizer tablet

A graphics drawing tablet used for sketching new images or tracing old ones. The user makes contact with the tablet with a pen or puck (mistakenly called a mouse) that is either wireless or connected to the tablet by a wire.

dimension

One axis in an array. In programming, a dimension statement defines the array and sets up the number of elements within the dimensions.

dimensioning

In CAD programs, the management and display of the measurements of an object. There are various standards that determine such things as tolerances, sizes of arrowheads and orientation on the paper.

DIMM

(Dual In-line Memory Module) A narrow printed circuit board that holds memory chips. It plugs into a DIMM socket on the motherboard and uses a 168 pin connector. DIMM modules can be added one at a time on a Pentium motherboard.

DIN connector

(Deutsches Institut f•r Normung - German Standards Institute) A plug and socket used to connect a variety of devices; for example, the PC keyboard uses a five-pin DIN. DIN plugs look like an open metal can about a half inch in diameter with pins inside in a circular pattern.

dingbats

A group of typesetting and desktop publishing symbols from International Typeface Corporation that include arrows, pointing hands, stars and circled numbers. They are formally called ITC Zapf Dingbats.

diode

An electronic component that acts primarily as a one-way valve. As a discrete component or built into a chip, it is used in a variety of functions. It is a key element in changing AC into DC. They are used as temperature and light sensors and light emitters (LEDs). In communications, they filter out analog and digital signals from carriers and modulate signals onto carriers. In digital logic, they're used as one-way valves and as switches similar to transistors.

DIP

(Dual In-line Package) A common rectangular chip housing with leads (pins) on both long sides. Tiny wires bond the chip to metal leads that wind their way down into spider-like feet that are inserted into a socket or are soldered onto the board.

DIP switch

(Dual In-line Package switch) A set of tiny toggle switches built into a DIP, which is mounted directly on a circuit board. The tip of a pen or pencil is required to flip the switch on or off. Remember! Open is "off." Closed is "on."

The tip of a pencil is often used to flip a DIP switch.

Direct3D, DirectDraw

See *DirectX*.

direct access

The ability to go directly to a specific storage location without having to go through what's in front of it. Memories (RAMs, ROMs, PROMs, etc.) and disks are the major direct access devices.

direct access method

A technique for finding data on a disk by deriving its storage address from an identifying key in the record, such as account number. Using a formula, the account number is converted into a sector address. This is faster than comparing entries in an index, but it only works well when keys are numerically close: 100, 101, 102.

direct-connect modem

A modem that connects to a telephone line without the use of an acoustic coupler.

Director

A popular multimedia authoring program for Windows and Macintosh from Macromedia. Runtime versions can be run, edited and switched between Windows and Mac platforms. Shockwave is a browser plug-in that lets output from Macromedia's Director, Authorware and Freehand packages be viewed on the Web.

directory

A simulated file drawer on disk. Programs and data for each application are typically kept in a separate directory (spreadsheets, word processing, etc.). Directories create the illusion of compartments, but are actually indexes to the files which may be scattered all over the disk.

directory management

The maintenance and control of directories on a hard disk. Usually refers to menuing software that is easier to use than entering commands.

directory service

A directory of names, profile information and machine addresses of every user and resource on the network. It is used to manage user accounts and network permissions. When sent a user name, it returns the attributes of that individual, which may include a telephone number as well as an e-mail address. Directory services use highly specialized databases that are typically hierarchical in design and provide fast lookups. See *x.500, LDAP, naming service* and *ULS server*.

directory tree

A graphic representation of a hierarchical directory.

DirectX

A set of multimedia programming interfaces from Microsoft for Windows 95/98 and NT that provide low-level access to the hardware for improved performance. DirectDraw and Direct3D provide 2-D and 3-D graphics. DirectSound enables mixing multiple sound sources for sound cards. DirectPlay provides control for multiple users playing the same game via modem, LAN or the Internet. DirectInput provides control for advanced digital input devices for games and virtual reality.

dirty power

A non-uniform AC power (voltage fluctuations, noise and spikes), which comes from the electric utility or from electronic equipment in the office.

disable

To turn off a function. Disabled means turned off, not broken. Contrast with *enable*.

disassembler

Software that converts machine language back into assembly language. Since there is no way to easily determine the human thinking behind the logic of the instructions, the resulting assembly language routines and variables are named and numbered generically (A001, A002, etc.). Disassembled code can be very difficult to maintain.

disc

An alternate spelling for disk. Compact discs and videodiscs are spelled with the "c." Most computer disks are spelled with a "k."

disc fixation

A process that ends the current recording session of a CD-R disc. The disc-at-once method finalizes the session and prevents future data from being appended. Track-at-once allows for more data to be appended, but the disc cannot be read until the final fixation. Multisession allows data to be read and appended at any time.

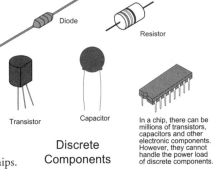

Diode

Resistor

Transistor

Capacitor

Discrete Components

In a chip, there can be millions of transistors, capacitors and other electronic components. However, they cannot handle the power load of discrete components.

discrete

A component or device that is separate and distinct and treated as a singular unit.

discrete component

An elementary electronic device constructed as a single unit. Before integrated circuits (chips), all transistors, resistors and diodes were discrete. They are widely used in amplifiers and other devices that use large amounts of current. They are also still used on circuit boards intermingled with the chips.

discretionary hyphen

A user-designated place in a word for hyphenation. If the word goes over the margin, it will split in that location.

dish

A saucer-shaped antenna that receives, or transmits and receives, signals from a satellite.

disintermediation

The elimination of the middleman. The term has been used to focus on the theoretical advantages of purchasing direct on the Web, such as convenience, cost savings and fast turnaround time.

disk

A direct access storage device. See *floppy disk, hard disk, magnetic disk, optical disk, LaserDisc* and *Video CD*.

disk array

Two or more disk drives combined in a single unit for increased capacity, speed and/or fault tolerant operation. See *RAID*.

disk based

(1) A computer system that uses disks as its storage medium.

(2) An application that retrieves data from the disk as required. Contrast with *memory based*.

disk cache

See *cache*.

disk cartridge

A removable disk module that contains a single hard disk platter or a floppy disk.

disk controller

A circuit that controls transmission to and from the disk drive. In a personal computer, it is an expansion board that plugs into an expansion slot in the bus. See *hard disk*.

disk crash

See *head crash*.

disk drive

A peripheral storage device that holds, spins, reads and writes magnetic or optical disks. It may be a receptacle for disk cartridges, disk packs or floppy disks, or it may contain non-removable disk platters like most personal computer hard disks.

The Computer Glossary

disk dump

A printout of disk contents without report formatting.

disk duplicator

A device that formats and makes identical copies of floppy disks for software distribution. Simple units contain two floppy disks and require manual loading, elaborate units have automatic loading and may also attach the labels.

disk emulator

A solid state replication of a disk drive.

diskette

Same as *floppy disk*.

disk farm

A very large number of hard disks. As more years of computer processing history pile up within the enterprise, databases are reaching staggering proportions. For example, thirty years of sales figures for companies with thousands of products in hundreds of locations result in multiple gigabytes of data. It is not uncommon to need a terabyte disk farm, which would require 250 four-gigabyte drives. See *server farm*.

disk file

A set of instructions or data that is recorded, cataloged and treated as a single unit on a disk. Source language programs, machine language programs, spreadsheets, data files, text documents, graphics files and batch files are examples.

disk format

The storage layout of a disk as determined by its physical medium and as initialized by a format program. For example, a 5.25" 360KB floppy vs a 3.5" 1.44MB floppy or a DOS disk vs a Mac disk. See *low-level format, high-level format* and *file format*.

diskless workstation

A workstation without a disk. Programs and data are retrieved from the network server. The network computer is a diskless workstation.

disk management

The maintenance and control of a hard disk. Refers to a variety of utilities that provide format, copy, diagnostic, directory management and defragmenting functions.

Disk Manager

A driver from Ontrack Data International, Inc., Eden Prarie, MN, that lets older PCs support hard disks greater than 528MB. PCs made before 1994 may have a system BIOS that does not support the larger drives. The Disk Manager diskette and instructions are often bundled with new hard disks.

disk memory

Disk storage. Disks are storage devices, not memory devices, even though some PC vendors and disk drive manufacturers insist on using the term "memory" for disk, which only adds confusion to an already-confusing field.

disk mirroring

The recording of redundant data for fault tolerant operation. Data is written on two partitions of the same disk, on two separate disks within the same system or on two separate computer systems.

disk optimizer

A utility program that defragments a hard disk. See *defragment*.

disk pack

A removable hard disk module used in minis and mainframes that contains two or more platters housed in a dust-free container. For mounting, the bottom of the container is removed. After insertion, the top is removed.

disk partition

A subdivision of a hard disk. The maximum size of a disk partition depends on the operating system used.

disk striping

The spreading data over multiple disk drives to improve performance. Data is interleaved by bytes or by sectors across the drives. For example, with four drives and a controller designed to overlap reads and writes, four sectors could be read in the same time it normally takes to read one. Disk striping does not inherently provide fault tolerance or error checking. It is used in conjunction with various other methods. See *RAID*.

DISOSS

(**DIS**tributed **O**ffice **S**upport **S**ystem) An IBM mainframe centralized document distribution and filing application that runs under MVS. Its counterpart under VM is PROFS. It allows for e-mail and the exchange of documents between a variety of IBM office devices, including word processors and PCs. DISOSS uses the SNADS messaging protocol.

dispatcher

Same as *scheduler*.

dispersed intelligence

Same as *distributed intelligence*.

displacement

Same as *offset*. See *base/displacement*.

display

(1) To show text and graphics on a CRT or flat panel screen.

(2) A screen or monitor.

display adapter

An expansion board that plugs into a desktop computer that converts the images created in the computer to the electronic signals required by the monitor. It determines the maximum resolution, maximum refresh rate and the number of colors that can be sent to the monitor. The monitor must be equally capable of handling its highest resolution and refresh. The VGA card is the common display adapter for the PC.

display attribute

See *attribute*.

display board, display card

See *display adapter*.

Display Data Channel

A VESA standard communications channel between the display adapter and monitor. The Display Data Channel (DDC) requires an additional wire in the cable. The first level implementation provides a unidirectional channel that lets the monitor inform the host of its capabilities. A second bi-directional level allows the host to adjust the monitor.

display device

See *display screen* and *display adapter*.

display element

(1) In graphics, a basic graphic arts component, such as background, foreground, text or graphics image.

(2) In computer graphics, any component of an image.

display entity

In computer graphics, a collection of display elements that can be manipulated as a unit.

display font

Same as *screen font*.

        The Computer Glossary

display frame
In computer graphics, a single frame in a series of animation frames.

display list
In computer graphics, a collection of vectors that make up an image stored in vector graphics format.

display list processor
In computer graphics, an engine that generates graphic geometry (draws lines, circles, etc.) directly from the display list and independently of the CPU.

Display PostScript
The screen counterpart of the PostScript printer language that translates elementary commands in an application to graphics and text elements on screen. It is designed for inclusion in an operating system to provide a standard, device- independent display language.

display screen
A surface area upon which text and graphics are temporarily made to appear for human viewing. It is typically a CRT or flat panel technology.

display terminal
See *video terminal*.

DisplayWrite
An early, full-featured word processing program for PCs from IBM that stemmed from the typewriter-oriented DisplayWriter word processing system first introduced in 1980. DisplayWrite was widely used in organizations that were mostly IBM oriented.

distributed computing
Same as *distributed processing*. See *parallel computing*.

distributed database
A database physically stored in two or more computer systems. Although geographically dispersed, a distributed database system manages and controls the entire database as a single collection of data. If redundant data is stored in separate databases due to performance requirements, updates to one set of data will automatically update the additional sets in a timely manner.

distributed data processing
See *distributed processing*.

distributed file system
Software that keeps track of files stored across multiple networks. It converts file names into physical locations.

distributed function
The distribution of processing functions throughout the organization.

distributed intelligence
The placing processing capability in terminals and other peripheral devices. Intelligent terminals handle screen layouts, data entry validation and other pre-processing steps. Intelligence placed into disk drives and other peripherals relieves the central computer from routine tasks.

distributed logic
See *distributed intelligence*.

distributed objects
Software modules that are designed to work together but reside in multiple computer systems throughout the organization. A program in one machine sends a message to an object in a remote machine to perform some processing. The results are sent back to the calling machine. See *CORBA* and *DCOM*.

distributed processing
A system of computers connected together by a communications network. The term is loosely used to

refer to any computers with communications between them. However, in true distributed processing, each computer system is chosen to handle its local workload, and the network has been designed to support the system as a whole. Contrast with *centralized processing* and *decentralized processing*.

dithering

In computer graphics, the creation of additional colors and shades from an existing palette. In monochrome displays, shades of grays are created by varying the density and patterns of the dots. In color displays, colors and patterns are created by mixing and varying the dots of existing colors.

Dithering is used to create a wide variety of patterns for use as backgrounds, fills and shading, as well as for creating halftones for printing. It is also used in anti-aliasing.

DL/1

(Data Language 1) The database language in IMS.

DLC

(1) (Data Link Control) See *data link* and *OSI*.

(2) (Data Link Control) The protocol used in IBM's Token Ring networks.

(3) (Digital Loop Carrier) See *loop carrier*.

DLL

(Dynamic Link Library) An executable program module that performs some function. DLLs are not launched directly by users. When needed, they are called for by a running application and loaded to perform a specific function. DLLs are generally written so that their routines are shared by more than one application at the same time. See *reentrant code*.

DLP

(Digital Light Processing) A data projection technology from TI that produces clear, readable images on screens in lit rooms. It uses a Digital Micromirror Device (DMD), a chip with more than a million rotating mirrors that cancel or reflect light. Gray scale is achieved by rotating the mirrors very rapidly.

DLSw

(Data Link SWitching) A method for forwarding SNA traffic over all types of wide area networks by encapsulating the data in the TCP/IP protocol. DLSw is employed in the routers and adds overhead. RFC 1490 is a later technology designed to move SNA traffic over frame relay with greater performance.

DLT

(Digital Linear Tape) A magnetic tape technology used for backing up data on medium to large-scale LANs. The tape is 1/2" wide and provides transfer rates faster than most tape technologies, except for 3480/3490 drives. Cartridges provide storage up to 50GB.

DMA

(Direct Memory Access) Specialized circuitry or a dedicated microprocessor that transfers data from memory to memory without using the CPU. On PCs, there are eight DMA channels. Most sound cards are set to use DMA channel 1.

DME

(Distributed Managment Environment) A network monitoring and control protocol defined by the Open Software Foundation (now The Open Group). DME was not widely used.

DMI

(Desktop Managment Interface) A management system for PCs that provides a bi-directional path to interrogate all the hardware and software components within a PC. When PCs are DMI-enabled, their hardware and software configurations can be monitored from a central station in the network.

DMPL

(Digital Microprocessor Plotter Language) A vector graphics file format from Houston Instruments that was developed for plotters. Most plotters support the DMPL or HPGL standards.

DMS

(1) (Document Management System) See *document management*.

(2) (Defense Messaging System) An X.500-compliant messaging system developed by the U.S. Dept. of Defense. It is used by all the branches of the armed forces and federal agencies involved with security.

DMTF

(Desktop Management Task Force) Initiated by Intel in 1992, it created the DMI interface. See *DMI*.

DNA

(1) (Distributed interNet Architecture) Introduced in 1997, it is Microsoft's umbrella term for its enterprise network architecture based on COM and Windows NT 5.0.

(2) (Digital Network Architecture) Introduced in 1978, it is Digital's umbrella term for its enterprise network architecture based on DECnet.

DNS

(Domain Naming System) Software that lets users locate computers on the Internet by domain name. The DNS server maintains a database of domain names (host names) and their corresponding IP addresses. In this hypothetical example, if **www.mycompany.com** were presented to a DNS server, the IP address **204.0.8.51** would be returned. See *WINS*.

docking station

A base station for a laptop that includes a power supply and expansion slots as well as monitor and keyboard connectors. See *port replicator*.

document

(1) Any paper form that has been filled in.

(2) A word processing text file.

(3) In the Macintosh, any text, data or graphics file created in the computer.

documentation

The narrative and graphical description of a system. Documentation for an information system includes:

Operating Procedures

1. Instructions for turning the system on and getting the programs initiated (loaded).

2. Instructions for obtaining source documents for data entry.
3. Instructions for entering data at the terminal, which includes a picture of each screen layout.
4. A description of error messages that can occur and the alternative methods for handling them.
5. A description of the defaults taken in the programs and the instructions for changing them.
6. Instructions for distributing the computer's output and sample pages for each type of report.

System Documentation

1. Data dictionary - Description of the files and databases.
2. System flow chart - Description of the data as it flows from source document to report.
3. Application program documentation - Description of the inputs, processing and outputs for each data entry, query, update and report program in the system.

Technical Documentation

1. File structures and access methods
2. Program flow charts
3. Program source code listings
4. Machine procedures (JCL)

document exchange software

Software that allows document files to be viewed on other computers that do not have the original application that created it. The software comes in two parts. The first component converts the document into a proprietary format for distribution. The second is a viewer program that displays the files. Viewers are generally free.

document handling

A procedure for transporting and handling paper documents for data entry and scanning.

document image management, document image processing

See *document imaging*.

document imaging

The online storage, retrieval and management of electronic images of documents. The main method of capturing images is by scanning paper documents.

Document imaging systems replace large paper-intensive operations. Documents can be shared by all users on a network and document routing can be controlled by the computer (workflow). The systems are often simpler to develop and implement than traditional data processing systems, because users are already familiar with the paper documents that appear on screen.

document management

The capture and management of documents within an organization. The term used to imply the management of documents after there were scanned into the computer. Today, the term has become an umbrella under which document imaging, workflow, text retrieval and multimedia fall.

document management system

Software that manages documents for electronic publishing. It generally supports a large variety of document formats and provides extensive access control and searching capabilities across LANs and WANs. A document management system may support multiple versions of a document. It may also be able to combine text fragments written by different authors. It often includes a workflow component that routes documents to the appropriate users. See *workflow*.

document mark

In micrographics, a small optical blip on each frame on a roll of microfilm that is used to automatically count the frames.

document processing

Processing text documents, which includes indexing methods for text retrieval based on content. See *document imaging*.

docuterm

A word or phrase in a text document that is used to identify the contents of the document.

do loop

A high-level programming language structure that repeats instructions based on the results of a comparison. In a DO WHILE loop, the instructions within the loop are performed if the comparison is true. In a DO UNTIL loop, the instructions are bypassed if the comparison is true. The following DO WHILE loop prints 1 through 10 and stops.

```
counter = 0
do while counter < 10
   counter = counter + 1
   ? counter
enddo
```

domain

(1) In database management, all possible values contained in a particular field for every record.

(2) In communications, all resources under control of a single computer system. In a LAN, a domain is a subnetwork comprised of a group of clients and servers under the control of one security database. Dividing LANs into domains improves performance and security.

(3) In magnetic storage devices, a group of molecules that makes up one bit.

(4) In a hierarchy, a named group that has control over the groups under it, which may be domains themselves.

domain name

The term may refer to any type of domain within the computer field, since there are several types of domains (see above). However, today, it often refers to the address of an Internet site, such as www.computerlanguage.com. See *Internet address* and *InterNIC*.

Is a Name Already Taken?
To find out if a domain name is taken, visit www.networksolutions.com or www.icann.org.

dominant carrier
A telecommunications services provider that has control over a large segment of a particular market.

Domino
See *Lotus Notes*.

dongle
Same as *hardware key*.

door
(1) In a BBS system, a programming interface that lets an online user run an application program in the BBS. In a communications program, the doorway mode passes function, cursor, ctrl and alt keystrokes to the BBS computer in order to use the remote application as if it were on the local machine.

(2) See *drive door*.

dopant
An element diffused into pure silicon in order to alter its electrical characteristics.

doping
Altering the electrical conductivity of a semiconductor material, such as silicon, by chemically combining it with foreign elements. It results in an excess of electrons (n-type) or a lack of electrons (p-type) in the silicon.

DOS
(1) (Disk Operating System) Pronounced "dahss." A generic term for operating system.

(2) (Disk Operating System) A single-user operating system from Microsoft for the PC. It was the first OS for the PC and the base control program for Windows 3.x. Windows 95/98 builds in DOS and Windows NT and 2000 emulate DOS to support DOS applications. See *MS-DOS* and *PC-DOS*.

DOS box
Slang for a DOS session in Windows or OS/2. The "box" is actually an instance of the Intel x86 Virtual 8086 Mode, which simulates an independent, fully functional PC environment.

DOS extender
Software combined with a DOS application that allows it to run in extended memory (beyond 1MB). To gain access to extended memory, it runs the application in Protected Mode.

DOS file
(1) Any computer file created under DOS.

(2) An ASCII text file.

DOS format
The high-level file structure required by DOS. All floppy and hard disks used in DOS and Windows must be low-level formatted and then high-level formatted with the DOS File Allocation Table (FAT).

DOS memory manager
Software that expands DOS' ability to manage more than one megabyte of memory or to manage its first megabyte more effectively.

DOS text file
A file that contains no proprietary coding schemes such as a batch file and source program. It contains only ASCII characters. Text files are read by text editors as well as word processors with "ASCII" or "text" input options.

dot

(1) A tiny round, rectangular or square spot that is one element in a matrix, which is used to display or print a graphics or text image. See *dot matrix*.

(2) A period; for example, V dot 22 is the same as V.22.

dot addressable

The ability to program each individual dot on a video display, dot matrix printer or laser printer.

dot-com company

An organization that offers its services or products exclusively on the Internet. Although a company that makes only Web-based software might be in the dot-com industry, it is generally not considered a dot-com company. Amazon.com, Yahoo and eBay are typical dot-com companies.

dot gain

An increase in size of each dot of ink when printed due to temperature, ink and paper type.

dot matrix

The pattern of dots that form character and graphic images on video screens and printers. Display screens use a matrix (rows and columns) of dots just like TVs. Serial printers use one or two columns of dot hammers that are moved across the paper. Laser printers "paint" dots of light a line at a time onto a light-sensitive photographic drum.

The more dots per square inch, the higher the resolution of the characters and graphics.

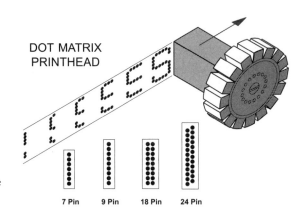

DOT MATRIX PRINTHEAD

7 Pin   9 Pin   18 Pin   24 Pin

dot matrix printer

A printer that forms images out of dots. The common desktop dot matrix printer uses one or two columns of dot hammers that are moved serially across the paper. The more dot hammers used, the higher the resolution of the printed image. 24-pin dot matrix printers produce typewriter-like output.

dot pitch

The distance between a red (or green or blue) dot and the closest red (or green or blue) dot on a color monitor (typically from .28 to .51mm; large presentation monitors may go up to 1.0mm). The smaller the dot pitch, the crisper the image. A .28 dot pitch means dots are 28/100ths of a millimeter apart. A dot pitch of .31 or less provides a sharp image, especially on text. See *slot pitch*.

double buffering

A programming technique that uses two buffers to speed up a computer that can overlap I/O with processing. For example, data in one buffer is being processed while the next set of data is read into the second buffer.

double click

To press the mouse button twice in rapid succession.

double density

Twice the capacity of the prior format.

double precision

Using two computer words instead of one to hold a number used for calculations, thus allowing twice as large a number for more arithmetic precision. Contrast with *single precision*.

double strike

Printing a character twice in order to darken the image.

double word

Twice the length of a single computer word. A double word is typically 32 bits long. See *word*.

down

Refers to a computer that fails to operate due to hardware or software failure. A communications line is down when it is unable to transfer data.

downlink

A communications channel from a satellite to an earth station. Contrast with *uplink*.

download

To receive a file transmitted over a network. In a communications session, download means receive, upload means transmit.

downloadable font

Same as *soft font*.

downsizing

Converting mainframe and mini-based systems to personal computer LANs.

downstream

From the provider to the customer. Upstream is from the customer to the provider.

downtime

The time during which a computer is not functioning due to hardware or system software failure. That's when you truly understand how important it is to have reliable hardware.

downward compatible

Also called "backward compatible." Refers to hardware or software that is compatible with earlier versions. Contrast with *upward compatible*.

DP

See *data processing* and *dot pitch*.

DPCM

(Differential PCM) An audio digitization technique that codes the difference between samples rather than coding an absolute measurement at each sample point. See *ADPCM*.

dpi

(Dots Per Inch) The measurement of printer resolution. A 300 dpi printer means 90,000 dots are printable in one square inch (300x300). 400 dpi generates 160,000 dots; 500 dpi yields 250,000 dots.

DPMA

See *AITP*.

DPMI

(DOS Protected Mode Interface) A programming interface from Microsoft that allows a DOS-extended program to run cooperatively under Windows 3.x.

DPOF

(Digital Print Order Format) A file format for digital film memory cards that stipulates which images are to be printed. At the time of shooting or when reviewing on the camera, it allows the user to specify how many of each image are to be printed.

DPPX

(Distributed Processing Programming EXecutive) An operating system for the 8100, now defunct. DPPX/370 is a version allowing users to migrate to 9370s.

DPSK

(Differential Phase Shift Keying) A common form of phase modulation used in modems. It does not require complex demodulation circuitry and is not susceptible to random phase changes in the transmitted waveform. Contrast with *FSK*.

DQDB

(Distributed Queue Dual Bus) An IEEE 802.6 packet switching network technology for MANs. The first SMDS services offered by the local telephone companies use DQDB.

draft mode

The highest-speed, lowest-quality printing mode.

drag

To move an object on screen in which its complete movement is visible from starting location to destination. The movement may be activated with a stylus, mouse or keyboard keys.

To drag an object with the mouse, point to it. Press the mouse button and hold the button down while moving the mouse. When the object is at its new location, release the mouse button.

drag & drop

A GUI capability that lets you perform operations by moving the icon of an object or function with the mouse into another window or onto another icon. For example, files can be copied or moved by dragging them from one folder to another.

drag lock

The ability to lock onto a screen object so that it can be dragged with the mouse without continuously holding down the mouse (or trackball) button.

drain

The output (receiving) side of the bridge in a field effect transistor. When the gate is charged, current flows from the source to the drain. Same as "collector" in a bipolar transistor.

DRAM

See *dynamic RAM*.

DRAW

(Direct Read After Write) Reading data immediately after it has been written to check for recording errors.

drawing program

A graphics software that allows the user to design and illustrate products and objects. It maintains an image in vector graphics format, which allows all elements of the graphic object to be isolated and manipulated individually.

Drawing programs and CAD programs are similar; however, drawing programs usually provide a large number of special effects for fancy illustrations, while CAD programs provide precise dimensioning and positioning of each graphic element in order that the objects can be transferred to other systems for engineering analysis and manufacturing. Contrast with *paint program*. See *diagramming program*.

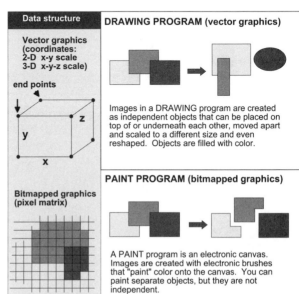

Data structure

Vector graphics (coordinates: 2-D x-y scale 3-D x-y-z scale)

end points

DRAWING PROGRAM (vector graphics)

Images in a DRAWING program are created as independent objects that can be placed on top of or underneath each other, moved apart and scaled to a different size and even reshaped. Objects are filled with color.

Bitmapped graphics (pixel matrix)

PAINT PROGRAM (bitmapped graphics)

A PAINT program is an electronic canvas. Images are created with electronic brushes that "paint" color onto the canvas. You can paint separate objects, but they are not independent.

IMAGE EDITING PROGRAM (bitmapped graphics)

A full-featured image editing program that contains layers enables bitmapped images to be treated independently. They can be placed into or scanned into different layers as if each were a separate canvas. Although bitmap elements cannot be resized as effectively as drawing objects, they can be moved independently within their own layer without affecting the elements in the others. When the final result is obtained, all the layers are "flattened" into one layer.

SCREEN DISPLAY (bitmapped display)

When objects are displayed on screen, they are always turned into a bitmap format no matter whether their underlying structure is vectors or bitmaps.

That's how screens and printers display and print information.

Bitmapped graphics is also known as raster graphics.

DRDA

(Distributed Relational Database Architecture) An SAA-compliant enhancement that allows data to be distributed among DB2 and SQL/DS databases. Users or programs can access data from SAA or non-SAA systems that implement DRDA.

DRDBMS

(Distributed Relational **DBMS**) A relational DBMS that manages distributed databases. See *distributed database*.

DR DOS

A DOS-compatible operating system originally developed by Digital Research. DR DOS inspired Microsoft to improve subsequent versions of MS-DOS.

dribbleware

Software that is publicly displayed and previewed well in advance of its actual release. Dribbleware is one stage beyond vaporware.

drift

Change in frequency or time synchronization of a signal that occurs slowly.

drill down

To move from summary information to the detailed data that created it.

drive

(1) An electromechanical device that spins disks and tapes at a specified speed. Also refers to the entire peripheral unit such as *disk drive* or *tape drive*.

(2) To provide power and signals to a device. For example, "this control unit can drive up to 15 terminals."

drive bay

A cavity for a disk drive in a computer cabinet.

drive door

A panel, gate or lever used to lock a disk in a disk drive. In a 5.25" floppy drive, the drive door is the lever that is turned down over the slot after inserting the disk.

driver

(1) Also called a "device driver," a program routine that links a peripheral device to the operating system. It is written by programmers who understand the detailed knowledge of the device's command language and characteristics and contains the precise machine language necessary to perform the functions requested by the application. When a new hardware device is added to the computer, such as a display adapter, sound card or CD-ROM drive, its driver must be installed in order to run it.

(2) A device that provides signals or electrical current to activate a transmission line or display screen. See *line driver*.

drop in

An extraneous bit on a magnetic medium that was not intentionally written, due to a surface defect or recording malfunction.

drop out

(1) On magnetic media, a bit that has lost its strength due to a surface defect or recording malfunction.

(2) In data transmission, a momentary loss of signal due to system malfunction or excessive noise.

drum

See *magnetic drum*.

drum plotter

A graphics plotter that wraps the paper around a drum. The drum turns to produce one direction of the plot, the pen moves to provide the other.

drum printer

(1) A wide-format ink jet printer. The paper is taped onto a drum for precise alignment.

(2) An old line printer technology that used formed character images around a cylindrical drum as its printing mechanism. When the desired character for the selected position rotated around to the hammer line, the hammer hit the paper from behind and pushed it into the ribbon and onto the character.

drum scanner

A type of scanner used to capture the highest resolution from an image. Photographs and transparencies are taped, clamped or fitted into a clear cylinder (drum) that is spun at speeds exceeding 1,000 rpm during the scanning operation. A light source that focuses on one pixel is beamed onto the drum and moves down the drum a line at a time.

dry plasma etching

A method for inscribing a pattern on a wafer by shooting hot ions through a mask to evaporate the silicon dioxide insulation layer. Dry plasma etching replaces the wet processing method that uses film and acid for developing the pattern.

DS, DS0, DS1, etc.

(Digital Signal) A classification of digital circuits. The DS technically refers to the rate and format of the signal, while the T designation refers to the equipment providing the signals. In practice, "DS" and "T" are used synonymously; for example, DS1 and T1, DS3 and T3.

```
NORTH AMERICA, JAPAN, KOREA, ETC.
          Voice
Service  Channels    Speed
DS0         1          64 Kbps
DS1        24       1.544 Mbps    (T1)
DS1C       48       3.152 Mbps    (T1C)
DS2        96       6.312 Mbps    (T2)
DS3       672      44.736 Mbps    (T3)
DS4      4032     274.176 Mbps    (T4)


          EUROPE (ITU-TSS)
          Voice
Service  Channels   Speed (Mbps)
E1         30          2.048
E2        120          8.448
E3        480         34.368
E4       1920        139.264
E5       7680        565.148


          SONET CIRCUITS
Service           Speed (Mbps)
STS-1    OC1        51.84 (28 DS1s or 1 DS3)
STS-3    OC3       155.52 (3 STS-1s)
STS-3c   OC3c      155.52 (concatenated)
STS-12   OC12      622.08 (12 STS-1s, 4 STS-3s)
STS-12c  OC12c     622.08 (12 STS-1s, 4 STS-3c's)
STS-48   OC48     2488.32 (48 STS-1s, 16 STS-3s)
```

DSA

(1) (Directory Server Agent) An X.500 program that looks up the address of a recipient in a Directory Information Base (DIB), also known as white pages. It accepts requests from the Directory User Agent (DUA) counterpart in the workstation.

(2) (Digital Signature Algorithm) The algorithm used in the Digital Signature Standard (DSS) by the U.S. government. The de facto standard RSA algorithm is more widely used than DSA.

DSL

(Digital Subscriber Line) A technology that increases the digital speed of ordinary telephone lines by a substantial factor over common V.34 (33600 bps) and V.90 (56000 bps) modems. DSL modems offer symmetrical and asymmetrical operation. Asymmetrical versions (ADSL, RADSL, VDSL, etc.) provide higher downstream transmission than upstream, which is suited for Internet usage and video on demand.

Symmetric DSL versions (HDSL, SDSL, IDSL) provide the same speed in both directions. All DSL technologies have distance limitations, typically between two and three miles, between the telephone company's central office and the customer's site.

DSP

(1) (Digital Signal Processor) A special-purpose CPU used for digital signal processing (see below). It provides extra fast instruction sequences, such as shift and add and multiply and add, commonly used in math-intensive signal processing applications.

(2) (Digital Signal Processing) A category of techniques that analyze signals from sources such as sound, weather satellites and earthquake monitors. Signals are converted into digital data and analyzed using various algorithms such as Fast Fourier Transform. DSP chips are used in sound cards for recording and playback, compressing and decompressing and speech synthesis. Other audio uses are in amplifiers that simulate surround sound effects for music and home theater.

DSR

(Data Set Ready) An RS-232 signal sent from the modem to the computer or terminal indicating that it is able to accept data. Contrast with *DTR*.

DSS

(1) (Decision Support System) An information and planning system that provides the ability to interrogate computers on an ad hoc basis, analyze information and predict the impact of decisions before they are made.

DBMSs let you select data and derive information for reporting and analysis. Spreadsheets and modeling programs provide both analysis and "what if?" planning. However, any single application that supports decision making is not a DSS. A DSS is a cohesive and integrated set of programs that share data and information. A DSS might also retrieve industry data from external sources that can be compared and used for historical and statistical purposes.

An integrated DSS directly impacts management's decision-making process and can be a very cost-beneficial computer application. See *EIS* and *OLAP*.

(2) (Digital Signature Standard) A National Security Administration standard for authenticating an electronic message. See *RSA* and *digital signature*.

DSTN

(Dual-scan **STN**) An enhanced STN passive matrix LCD display. The screen is divided into halves, and each half is scanned simultaneously, thereby doubling the number of lines refreshed per second and providing a sharper appearance. DSTN is widely used on laptops. See *STN* and *LCD*.

DSU/CSU

(Digital (or Data) Service Unit/Channel Service Unit) A pair of communications devices that connect an inhouse line to an external digital circuit (T1, DDS, etc.). It is similar to a modem, but connects a digital circuit rather than an analog one.

DSVD

(Digital Simultaneous Voice and Data) An all-digital technology for concurrent voice and data (SVD) transmission over a single analog telephone line. DSVD is endorsed by Intel, Hayes, U.S. Robotics and others and has been submitted to the ITU for possible standardization. DSVD modems became available in the first half of 1995. See *SVD*.

DTE

(Data Terminating Equipment) A communications device that is the source or destination of signals on a network. It is typically a terminal or computer. Contrast with *DCE*.

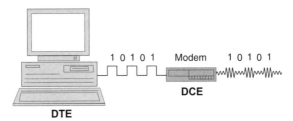

DTMF

(Dual Tone Multi Frequency) The formal name of touch tone (pushbutton) technology found on telephone keypads.

DTP

See *desktop publishing*.

DTR

(Data Terminal Ready) An RS-232 signal sent from the computer or terminal to the modem indicating that it is able to accept data. Contrast with *DSR*.

DTS

(1) (Digital Termination Service) A microwave-based, line-of-sight communications provided directly to the end user.

(2) (DeskTop Server) A motorola 68000-based network server from Banyan.

(3) (Developer Technical Support) The tech-support group for developers at Apple.

DTV

See *digital TV*.

DUA

(Directory User Agent) An X.500 routine that sends a request to the Directory Systems Agent to look up the location of a user on the network.

dual boot

A computer configuration that allows it to be started with either one of two different operating systems. The dual boot feature is contained in one of the operating systems.

dual-scan LCD

A technique used to improve passive matrix color screens. The screen is divided into halves, and each half is scanned simultaneously, doubling the number of lines refreshed per second.

dumb network

A network in which all the processing is at the periphery. The Internet is said to be a "dumb" network, because it serves as a transport between client and server applications that provide the intelligence at both ends.

dumb terminal

A display terminal without processing capability. It is entirely dependent on the main computer for processing. Contrast with *smart terminal* and *intelligent terminal*.

dump

To print the contents of memory, disk or tape without any report formatting. See *memory dump*.

duplex channel

See *full-duplex*.

duplexed system

Two systems that are functionally identical. They both may perform the same functions, or one may be standby, ready to take over if the other fails.

duplicate keys

Identical key data in a file. Primary keys, such as account number cannot be duplicated, since no two customers or employees should be assigned the same number. Secondary keys, such as date, product and city, may be duplicated in the file or database.

DV

(Digital Video) A consumer digital video format endorsed by all major video equipment vendors. Using 1/4" (6.35mm) metal evaporated tape, DV is recorded at 25 Mbps (18.8mm/sec) on three-hour standard cassettes or one-hour MiniDV cassettes (sizes are 125x78x14.6 and 66x48x1.2mm respectively).

DVD

Also known as Digital Videodisc, Digital Versatile Disc and simply DVD, it is a high-capacity movie and storage format. The disc is the same diameter as a CD-ROM, but can be recorded on both sides, each of which holds 4.7GB. Dual-layer versions yield 8.5GB per side.

DVD players are compatible with audio CDs, CD-ROMs, CD-I discs and Video CDs, but not first-generation CD-R disks. DVDs use MPEG-2 compression and provide about 135 minutes of LaserDisc-quality video per side. DVD-ROMs are read-only DVDs, DVD-Rs are write once, and DVD-RAMs are rewritable.

DVD-Audio

The next-generation music format, which was approved by the DVD Forum in early 1999. It provides for 16, 20 and 24-bit samples at a variety of sampling rates from 44.1 to 192KHz, compared to 16 bits and 44.1KHz for CDs.

DVI

(Digital Visual Interface) A digital flat panel interface from the Digital Display Working Group (www.ddwg.org). The DDWG was formed to create a universal standard for attaching a flat panel monitor, and DVI is expected to become widely used. Based on TMDS signaling, the final draft of DVI was introduced in early 1999.

Dvorak keyboard

A keyboard layout designed in the 1930s by August Dvorak, University of Washington, and his brother-in-law, William Dealey. 70% of words are typed on the home row compared to 32% with qwerty, and, more words are typed using both hands.

DVR

(Digital Video Recorder) A consumer video device that digitizes broadcast TV onto a hard disk and plays it back immediately, allowing the viewer to pause at any time and return later. It also records programs for later viewing just like a VCR.

DWDM

See *WDM*.

dweeb

Slang for a very technical person. Dweebs call sales people "slime," because they are interested in technology for profit rather than the art.

DXF

An AutoCAD 2-D graphics file format. Many CAD systems import and export the DXF format for graphics interchange.

dyadic

Two. Refers to two components being used.

dye polymer recording

An optical recording technique that uses dyed plastic layers as the recording medium. A single dye polymer layer is used in some WORM devices. Erasable optical disks use two dyed plastic layers, a top retention layer and a bottom expansion layer. A bit is written by shining a laser through the retention layer onto the expansion layer, which heats the area and forms a bump that expands into the retention layer. The retention layer bumps are the actual bits read by the unit. To erase a bit, another laser (different wavelength) strikes the retention layer and the bump subsides.

dye sublimation

A printer process that produces continuous-tone images like photographic film. Its ribbon contains an equivalent panel of dye for each page to be printed. Color printers have three (CMY) or four (CMYK) consecutive panels for each page, thus the same amount of ribbon is used to print a full-page image as it is to print a tenth of the page. Special dye-receptive paper is used, and ribbon and paper cost more than other printer technologies.

The paper and ribbon are passed together over the printhead, which contains thousands of heating elements that can produce varying amounts of heat. The hotter the element, the more dye is released. By varying the temperature, shades of each color can be overlaid on top of each other. The dyes are transparent and blend into continuous-tone color.

dynamic

Refers to operations performed while the program is running. The expression, "buffers are dynamically created," means that space was created when actually needed, not reserved beforehand.

dynamic address translation

In a virtual memory system, the ability to determine what the real address is at the time of execution.

dynamic binding

Linking a routine or object at runtime based on the conditions at that moment. See *polymorphism*.

dynamic compression

The ability to compress and decompress data in realtime; for example, as it's being written to or read from the disk.

dynamic HTML

(1) A general term for Web pages that are customized for each user; for example, returning values from a search. Contrast with a "static HTML" page that never changes.

(2) Specific enhancements to HTML tags that allow Web pages to function more like regular software. For example, fonts could be changed or images could be selected without having to jump to another page.

dynamic link

The connection established at runtime from one program to another.

dynamic link library

Executable routines available to applications at runtime. They are typically written in reentrant code so they can serve more than one application at the same time. See *DLL*.

dynamic network services

Realtime networking capabilities, such as adaptive routing, automatically reconfiguring the network when a node is added or deleted and the ability to locate any user on the network.

dynamic RAM

The most common type of computer memory, also called "D-RAM" and "DRAM." It usually uses one transistor and a capacitor to represent a bit. The capacitors must be energized hundreds of times per second in order to maintain the charges. Unlike firmware chips (ROMs, PROMs, etc.) both major varieties of RAM (dynamic and static) lose their content when the power is turned off. Contrast with *static RAM*.

dynamic range

A range of signals from the weakest to the strongest.

dynamic SQL

SQL statements interpreted by the SQL database at runtime. Dynamic SQL may be generated by programs or entered interactively by the user. Contrast with *embedded SQL*.

DYNASTY

An application development system for enterprise client/server environments from Dynasty Technologies, Inc., Lisle, IL, (www.dynasty.com). Introduced in 1993, it is a repository-driven system that supports Windows, Mac and Motif clients and NT, OS/2 and major UNIX servers and databases. It provides partitioning for creating three-tier applications. DYNASTY generates C and SQL code.

E

E

See *exponent.*

e-

(Electronic-) The "e-dash" prefix may be attached to anything that has moved from paper to its electronic alternative, such as e-mail, e-cash, etc.

E1

The European counterpart to T1, which transmits at 2.048 Mbits/sec. See *DS* for chart.

EAM

(Electronic Accounting Machine) Same as *tabulating equipment.*

early binding

Assigning types in the compilation phase. See *binding time.*

EAROM

(Electrically Alterable **ROM**) Same as *EEPROM.*

earth station

A transmitting/receiving station for satellite communications. It uses a dish-shaped antenna for microwave transmission.

Easytrieve

See *CA-Easytrieve.*

EBCDIC

(Extended Binary Coded Decimal Interchange Code) Pronounced "eb-suh-dick." The binary code for text as well as communications and printer control from IBM. This code originated with the System/360 and is still used in IBM mainframes and most IBM midrange computers. It is an 8-bit code (256 combinations) that stores one alphanumeric character or two decimal digits in a byte.

EBCDIC and ASCII are the two codes most widely used to represent data characters.

e-beam

See *electron beam.*

e-book

(Electronic-book) A handheld device that is specialized for displaying electronic versions of books. Like its printed counterpart, an e-book lets you set bookmarks and annotate in the margins.

e-business

(Electronic-BUSINESS) Doing business online. The term is often used synonymously with e-commerce, but e-business is more of an umbrella term for having a presence on the Web. An e-business site may be very comprehensive and offer more than just selling its products and services. For example, it may feature a general search facility or the ability to track shipments or have threaded discussions. See *e-commerce.*

e-card

(Electronic-CARD) A digital greeting card or postcard created on the Web and sent to someone via the Web. Most e-card sites are paid for by banner ads which you see while you design your card, while others employ this as a way to attract traffic to the site to sell other products or services.

eCash

A Web payment service from eCash Technologies, Inc., Bothell, WA, (www.ecash.com), that requires an active account from an eCash member bank. Digital coins are stored in the eCash Purse digital wallet on the customer's computer, and coins can be deducted from the wallet when purchasing at eCash-compliant sites. Coins can also be transferred

ECC memory

(Error-Correcting Code memory) A memory system that tests for and corrects errors on the fly. It uses circuitry that generates checksums to correct errors greater than one bit.

ECF

(Enhanced Connectivity Facilities) IBM software that allows DOS PCs to query and download data from mainframes as well as issue mainframe commands. It also allows printer output to be directed from the PC to the mainframe. It uses the SRPI interface and resides in the PC (client) and mainframe (server). Applications issue SRPI commands to request services.

echo cancellation

A high-speed modem technique that isolates and filters out unwanted signals caused by echoes from the main transmitted signal. This permits full-duplex modems to send and receive on the same frequency.

Telephone networks often use echo cancellers in addition to or in place of echo suppressors. Network-based echo cancellation can interfere with modems that do their own, such as V.32, so a method is provided for those modems to disable network echo cancellers.

echo check

In communications, an error checking method that retransmits the data back to the sending device for comparison with the original.

echoplex

A communications protocol that transmits the received data back to the sending station allowing the user to visually inspect what was received.

echo suppressor

A communications technique that turns off reverse transmission in a telephone line, thus effectively making the circuit one way. It is used to reduce the annoying effects of echoes in telephone connections, especially in satellite circuits.

ECL

(Emitter-Coupled Logic) A variety of bipolar transistor that is noted for its extremely fast switching speeds.

ECMA

(European Computer Manufacturers Association, Geneva, Switzerland, www.ecma.ch) An international association founded in 1961 that is dedicated to establishing standards in the information and communications fields. ECMA is a liaison organization to ISO and is involved in JTC1 activities.

e-commerce

(Electronic **COMMERCE**) Doing business online, typically via the Web. It is also called "e-business," "e-tailing" and "I-commerce." Although in most cases e-commerce and e-business are synonymous, e-commerce implies that goods and services can be purchased online, whereas e-business might be used as more of an umbrella term for a total presence on the Web.

ECP

(Enhanced Capabilities Port) See *IEEE 1284*.

EDA

(1) (Electronic Design Automation) Using the computer to design and simulate the performance of electronic circuits on a chip. See *ATE*.

(2) (Enterprise Data Access) Software from Information Builders, Inc., New York, (www.ibi.com), that provides a common interface between a wide variety of SQL programs and SQL databases. It also allows queries on data from different types of databases at the same time.

edge connector

The protruding part of an expansion board that is inserted into an expansion slot. It contains a series of printed lines that go to and come from the circuits on the board.

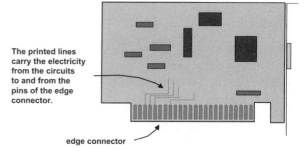

The printed lines carry the electricity from the circuits to and from the pins of the edge connector.

edge connector

edge device

A network device used to convert LAN frames (Ethernet, Token Ring, FDDI) to ATM cells and vice versa. It is typically a switching device with one ATM port and multiple LAN ports. To legacy stations, ports on an edge device look like a router port.

edge router

Also called an "access router," it is a router that sits at the periphery (edge) of a network in contrast with a core router that is in the middle of a network. Edge routers and core routers are relative terms. They are all just routers, but of different size and capacity. One tier's core router is another tier's edge router.

EDI

(Electronic Data Interchange) Electronic communication of transactions between organizations, such as orders, confirmations and invoices. Independent service organizations provide EDI services that enable users to interconnect with another organization's network regardless of type of equipment used. See *X12, Tradacoms* and *EDIFACT*.

EDIFACT

(Electronic Data Interchange For Administration Commerce and Transport) An ISO standard for EDI that is proposed to supersede both X12 and Tradacoms standards to become the worldwide standard.

edit

To make a change to existing data. See *update*.

editable PostScript

A file of PostScript commands that can be edited by a word processor or other program. This allows PostScript documents to be changed without requiring the use of the application that originally created it.

edit mask

A pattern of characters that represent formatting codes through which data is filtered for display or printing. See *picture*.

edit mode

An operational state in a program that allows existing data to be changed.

editor

See *text editor* and *linkage editor*.

edit program

(1) A data entry program that validates user input and stores the newly created records in the file.

(2) A program that allows users to change data that already exists in a file. See *update*.

edit routine

A routine in a program that tests for valid data. See *validity checking*.

EDL

See *nonlinear video editing*.

EDO RAM

(Extended Data Out RAM) A type of dynamic RAM chip that improves the performance of fast page mode memory by about 10%. As a subset of fast page mode, it can be substituted for page mode chips if the memory controller is designed for the faster EDO chips.

EDP

(Electronic Data Processing) The first name used for the computer field.

edutainment

Educational material that is also entertaining.

EEPROM

(Electrically Erasable Programmable Read Only Memory) A memory chip that holds its content without power. It can be erased, either within the computer or externally. It usually requires more voltage for erasure than the common +5 volts used in logic circuits. It functions like non-volatile RAM, but writing to EEPROM is slower than writing to RAM.

EFF

(Electronic Frontier Foundation, Cambridge, MA, www.eff.org) A non-profit civil liberties organization founded in 1990 by Mitchell Kapor and John Perry Barlow. It works in the public interest to protect privacy and provide free access to online information.

EFT

(Electronic Funds Transfer) The transfer of money from one account to another by computer.

EGA

(Enhanced Graphics Adapter) An early IBM video display standard that provided medium-resolution text and graphics. It was superseded by VGA.

EGP

(Exterior Gateway Protocol) A gateway protocol that broadcasts TCP/IP IP addresses to the gateway of another self-contained network.

EIA

(Electronic Industries Association, Washington, DC, www.eia.org) A membership organization founded in 1924 as the Radio Manufacturing Association. It sets standards for consumer products and electronic components. In 1988, it spun off its Information & Telecommunications Technology Group into a separate organization called the TIA.

EIA-232, 422, 423, 449, 485

See *RS-232, RS 422, 423, RS-449* and *RS-485*.

EIA-568

An EIA standard for telecommunications wiring in a commercial building. See *cable categories*.

EIDE

See *IDE*.

Eiffel

An object-oriented programming language developed by Bertrand Meyer, Interactive Software Engineering Inc., Goleta, CA. It runs on DOS, OS/2 and most UNIX platforms. The Eiffel compiler generates C code, which can be modified and recompiled with a C compiler.

EIS

(Executive Information System) An information system that consolidates and summarizes ongoing transactions within the organization. It should provide management with all the information it requires at all times from internal as well as external sources. See *DSS*.

EISA

(Extended **ISA**) Pronounced "ee-suh." A PC bus standard that extended the 16-bit ISA bus (AT bus) to 32 bits and provided bus mastering. ISA cards can plug into an EISA slot. It was announced in 1988 as a 32-bit alternative to the Micro Channel that would preserve investment in existing boards. However, EISA runs at the slow 8MHz speed of the ISA bus in order to accommodate any ISA cards that may be plugged into it. EISA has been superseded by PCI.

EJB

(Enterprise JavaBeans) A component software architecture from Sun that is used to build Java applications that run in the server. It uses a "container" layer that provides common functions such as security and transaction support and delivers a consistent interface to the applications regardless of the type of server. CORBA is the infrastructure for EJBs, and at the wire level, EJBs look like CORBA components. EJBs are the backbone of Sun's J2EE platform, which provides a pure Java environment for developing and running Web-based applications.

electricity

The flow of electrons in a circuit. The speed of electricity is the speed of light (approx. 186,000 miles per second). In a wire, it is slowed due to the resistance in the material.

Its pressure, or force, is measured in "volts" and its flow, or current, is measured in "amperes." The amount of work it produces is measured in "watts" (amps X volts).

electrode
A device that emits or controls the flow of electricity.

electroluminescent (EL)
A flat panel display that provides a sharp, clear image and wide viewing angle. It contains a powdered or thin film phosphor layer sandwiched between an x-axis and a y-axis panel. When an x-y coordinate is charged, the phosphor in that vicinity emits visible light. Phosphors are typically amber, but green is also used.

electrolyte
In a rechargeable battery, the material that allows electricity to flow from one plate to another by conducting ions.

electromagnet
A magnet that is energized by electricity. A coil of wire is wrapped around an iron core. When current flows in the wire, the core generates an energy called "magnetic flux."

electromagnetic radiation
The energy that exists in all things, including humans, which incorporates cosmic rays, gamma rays, x-rays, ultraviolet light, visible light, infrared light and radar.

electromagnetic spectrum
The range of electromagnetic radiation in our known universe, which includes radio waves with large wavelengths to cosmic rays with small wavelengths.

electromechanical
The use of electricity to run moving parts. Disk drives, printers and motors are examples. Electromechanical systems must be designed for the eventual deterioration of moving parts.

electromotive force
The pressure in an electric circuit measured in volts.

electron
An elementary particle that circles the nucleus of an atom. Electrons are considered to be negatively charged.

electron beam
A stream of electrons, or electricity, that is directed towards a receiving object.

electron gun
A device which creates a fine beam of electrons that is focused on a phosphor screen in a CRT.

electronic
The use of electricity in intelligence-bearing devices, such as radios, TVs, instruments, computers and telecommunications. Electricity used as raw power for heat, light and motors is considered electrical, not electronic.

Although coined earlier, "Electronics" magazine (1930) popularized the term. The magazine subheading read "Electron Tubes - Their Radio, Audio, Visio and Industrial Applications." The term was derived from the electron (vacuum) tube.

electronic circuit
See *circuit* and *digital circuit*.

electronic mail
See *e-mail*.

electronic messaging
See *e-mail* and *messaging system*.

electronic printer

A printer that uses electronics to control the printing mechanism, such as a laser printer and certain line printers.

electronic publishing

Providing information in electronic form to readers or subscribers of the service. See *information utility* and *videotex*.

electronic switch

An on/off switch activated by electrical current.

electronic wallet

The electronic equivalent of a checkbook or credit card for making online purchases. It may be software only or a combination of software and smart card.

electron tube

Same as *vacuum tube*.

electrophotographic

The printing technique used in copy machines, laser and LED printers. It uses electrostatic charges, light and dry ink (toner). A selenium-coated, photoconductive drum is positively charged. Using a laser or LEDs, a negative of the image is beamed onto the drum, cancelling the charge and leaving a positively-charged replica of the original image.

A negatively-charged toner is attracted to the positive image on the drum. The toner is then attracted to the paper, which is also positively charged. The final stage is fusing, which uses heat and pressure, pressure alone or light to cause the toner to permanently adhere to the paper.

electrosensitive printer

A dot matrix printer that burns away dots on the outer silver coating of a special black paper.

electrostatic

Stationary electrical charges in which no current flows.

electrostatic plotter, electrostatic printer

A plotter that uses an electrostatic method of printing. Liquid toner models use a postively-charged toner that is attracted to paper which is negatively charged by passing by a line of electrodes (tiny wires or nibs). Models print in in black and white or color, and some handle paper up to six feet wide. Newer units are really large-format laser printers and focus light onto a charged drum using lasers or LEDs.

elegant program

A program that is simple in design, uses the least amount of memory and runs fast.

elevator

Also called a "thumb," it is a square box that slides within a scroll bar. The elevator is dragged up and down to position the text or image on screen.

elevator seeking

A disk access technique that processes multiple requests in a priority based upon which ones are closest to the current position of the read/write head.

ELF

(Extemely Low Frequency) See *low radiation*.

em

In typography, a unit of measure equal to the width of the capital letter M in a particular font.

EMA

(1) (Enterprise Management Architecture) Digital's stategic plan for integrating network, system and application management. It provides the operating environment for managing a multi-vendor network.

(2) (Electronic Messaging Association, Arlington, VA, www.ema.org) A membership organization founded in 1983 devoted to promoting e-mail, voice mail, fax, EDI and other messaging technologies.

EMACS

(Editor MACroS) A UNIX text editor developed at MIT that is used for writing programs. It provides a wide variety of editing features including multiple windows.

e-mail

The transmission of memos and messages over a network. Users can send mail to a single recipient or broadcast it to multiple users. With multitasking workstations, mail can be delivered and announced while the user is working in an application. Otherwise, mail is sent to a simulated mailbox in the network server or host computer, which must be interrogated. See *messaging system* and *EDI*.

E-mail versus Fax

Fax documents are scanned images and are treated like pictures even if they contain only text. E-mail messages are raw ASCII text, which can be edited immediately in any text editor or word processor. In order to send text that will be used by another program, use e-mail. A fax would have to be scanned and turned into text by optical character recognition (OCR), which is error prone.

e-mail attachment

A file that rides along with an e-mail message. The attached file can be of any type.

embedded command

(1) A command inserted within text or other codes.

(2) In word processing, a command within the text that directs the printer to change fonts, print underline, boldface, etc. The command is inserted when the user selects a layout change. Commands are often invisible on screen, but can be revealed if required.

Embedded commands in a document are proprietary to the word processor used. When a document is printed, the text is copied to a temporary file, and the embedded commands are converted into printer commands for the printer. When printing is finished, the temporary file is erased. See *print to disk*.

embedded controller

Controller circuitry built into a device or on the main system board in contrast with a removable card or module.

embedded SQL

SQL statements written into a high-level language source program, such as C or Pascal. In a separate compiling phase, the SQL may be optimized and converted into special function calls. Contrast with *dynamic SQL*.

embedded system

A specialized computer used to control a device such as an automobile, appliance or space vehicle. Operating system and application functions are often combined in the same program.

EMI

(ElectroMagnetic Interference) Electromagnetic waves that eminate from an electrical device. It often refers to both low-frequency waves from electromechanical devices and high-frequency waves (RFI) from chips and other electronic devices. Allowable limits are governed by the FCC.

emitter

The supply of current in a bipolar transistor. Same as source in a MOS transistor.

emoticon

(EMOTional ICON) In e-mail, expressing emotion by typing character combinations. Also called "smileys," the following examples are viewed sideways:

```
:)      original smiley face
:-)     smile
:-(     frown
```

EMS

(1) (Expanded Memory Specification) The first technique that allowed DOS to go beyond its one megabyte memory limit. It allowed access to 32MB of memory by bank switching it through a 64KB

buffer (page frame) in the upper memory area between 640K and 1MB.

(2) (Electronic Message Service) The part of the radio spectrum assigned to electronic messaging over digital satellite circuits.

emulation mode

An operational state of a computer when it is running a foreign program under emulation.

emulator

A device that is built to work like another. A computer can be designed to emulate another model and execute software that was written to run in the other machine. A terminal can be designed to emulate various communications protocols and connect to different networks. The emulator can be hardware, software or both.

en

In typography, a unit of measure equal to one half the width of an em. An en is typically the width of one numeric digit.

enable

To turn on. Contrast with *disable*.

Encapsulated PostScript

See *EPS*.

encapsulation

(1) In object-oriented programming, making the data and processing private within an object, which allows it to be modified without causing problems elsewhere in the program.

(2) In communications, inserting the frame header and data from a higher level protocol into the data frame of a lower level protocol.

encipher

To encode data for security purposes. See *cryptography*.

encode

(1) To assign a code to represent data, such as a parts code.

(2) Same as *encipher* or *encrypt*. See *cryptography*.

encrypt

To encode data for security purposes. See *cryptography*.

encryption

See *cryptography*.

end key

A keyboard key commonly used to move the cursor to the bottom of the screen or file or to the next word or end of line.

endless loop

A series of instructions that are constantly repeated. It can be caused by an error in the program or it can be intentional; for example, a screen demo on continuous replay.

end points

In vector graphics, the two ends of a line (vector). In 2-D graphics, each end point is typically two numbers representing coordinates on x and y axes. In 3-D, each end point is made up of three numbers representing coordinates on x, y and z axes.

engine

(1) A specialized processor, such as a graphics processor. Like any engine, the faster it runs, the quicker the job gets done. See *graphics engine* and *printer engine*.

(2) Software that performs a primary and highly repetitive function such as a database engine, graphics engine or dictionary engine.

(3) Slang for processor.

engineering drawing sizes

```
A - 8 1/2 x 11
B - 11 x 17
C - 17 x 22
D - 22 x 34
E - 34 x 44
```

Enhanced IDE
See *IDE.*

ENIAC
(Electronic Numerical Integrator And Calculator) The first operational electronic digital computer developed for the U.S. Army by John Eckert and John Mauchly at the University of Pennsylvania. Completed in 1946, it was decimal-based, used 18,000 vacuum tubes, took up 1,800 square feet and performed 5,000 additions/second. Today, the equivalent technology is used in a watch.

enquiry character
In communications, a control character that requests a response from the receiving station.

enterprise
The entire organization. See *enterprise networking.*

enterprise data
Centralized data that is shared by many users throughout the organization.

Enterprise JavaBeans
See *EJB.*

enterprise model
A model of how an organization does business. Information systems are designed from this model.

enterprise network
A geographically-dispersed network under the jurisdiction of one organization. It often includes several different types of networks and computer systems from different vendors.

enterprise networking
Managing the network infrastructure in a large enterprise. Much of what goes on has little to do with application development and real data processing of the payroll and orders. Enormous effort is spent planning the integration of disparate networks and systems and managing them, and, planning again for more interfaces as new techniques and methods force vendors to continue to change the ground rules every few years.

entity
In a database, anything about which information can be stored; for example, a person, concept, physical object or event. Typically refers to a record structure.

entity relationship model
In a database, a data model that describes attributes of entities and the relationships among them.

entity type
In a database, a particular kind of file; for example, a customer or product file.

entropy
In data compression, a measure of the amount of non-redundant, non-compressible information in an object.

entry
The input of an item or set of items at a terminal. See *data entry.*

entry point
In programming, the starting point of the instructions in a subroutine.

enumerate

To count or list one by one. An enumerated data type defines a list of all possible values for a variable, and no other value can then be placed into it.

envelope

(1) A range of frequencies for a particular operation.

(2) A group of bits or items that is packaged and treated as a single unit.

environment

A computer configuration that includes the CPU model and system software (operating system, data communications and database systems). It may also include the programming language used. It sets the standards for the applications that run in it.

The term often refers only to the operating system; for example, "This program is running in a UNIX environment."

environment variable

A value entered into DOS, which provides information to an application. For example, it is often used to indicate what directory (folder) to store temporary files in. The DOS Set command is used to store these values.

EOF, EOL, EOM, EOT

(End Of File, End Of Line, End Of Message, End Of Transmission) Status conditions that represent the end of a particular data structure.

EPOC

A 32-bit operating system for handheld devices from Symbian Ltd., London, (www.symbian.com). Used in Psion and other handheld computers, it supports Java applications, e-mail, fax, infrared exchange, data synchronization with PCs and includes a suite of PIM and productivity applications. Symbian was originally a software division in Psion and was spun off to support EPOC as an independent entity.

epoch date

The starting point from which time is measured as the number of days, minutes, etc., from that time.

EPP

(Enhanced Parallel Port) See *IEEE 1284*.

EPROM

(Erasable Programmable **ROM**) A programmable and reusable chip that holds its content until erased under ultraviolet light. EPROMS have a lifespan of a few hundred write cycles. EPROMS are expected to eventually give way to flash memory. An EPROM programmer is a device that writes instructions and data into EPROM chips. Some earlier units were capable of programming both PROMs and EPROMs.

EPS

(Encapsulated PostScript) A PostScript file format used to transfer a graphic image between applications. EPS files contain PostScript code and an optional preview image in TIFF, WMF or PICT format. The preview is used to scale the image on screen. Adobe Illustrator has its own variation of the EPS format. See *PostScript*.

EPSS

(Electronic Performance Support System) A computer system that provides quick assistance and information without requiring prior training to use it. It may incorporate all forms of multimedia delivery as well as AI techniques such as expert systems and natural language recognition.

equalization

In communications, techniques used to reduce distortion and compensate for signal loss (attenuation) over long distances.

equation

An arithmetic expression that equates one set of conditions to another; for example, $A = B + C$. In a programming language, assignment statements take the form of an equation. The above example would assign the sum of B and C to the variable A.

ERA

(Electrically Reconfigurable Array) A programmable logic chip (PLD) technology from Plessey Semiconductor that allows the chip to be reprogrammed electrically.

erase

See *delete*.

erase head

In a magnetic tape drive, the device that erases the tape before a new block of data is recorded.

ergonomics

The science of people-machine relationships. An ergonomically-designed product implies that the device blends smoothly with a person's body or actions.

Erlang

A unit of traffic use that specifies the total capacity or average use of a telephone system. One Erlang is equivalent to the continuous usage of a telephone line. Traffic in Erlangs is the sum of the holding times of all lines divided by the period of measurement.

ERM

See *sales force automation*.

ERP

(Enterprise Resource Planning) An integrated information system that serves all departments within an enterprise. Evolving out of the manufacturing industry, ERP implies the use of packaged software rather than proprietary software written by or for one customer. ERP modules may be able to interface with an organization's own software with varying degrees of effort, and, depending on the software, ERP modules may be alterable via the vendor's proprietary tools as well as proprietary or standard programming languages.

error checking

(1) Testing for accurate transmission of data over a communications network or internally within the computer system. See *parity checking* and *CRC*.

(2) Same as *validity checking*.

error detection & correction

See *error checking* and *validity checking*.

error-free channel

An interface (wire, cable, etc.) between devices that is not subject to external interference; specifically not the dial-up telephone system.

error handling

Routines in a program that respond to errors. The measurement of quality in error handling is based on how the system informs the user of such conditions and what alternatives it provides for dealing with them.

error rate

The measurement of the effectiveness of a communications channel. It is the ratio of the number of erroneous units of data to the total number of units of data transmitted.

ES/3090

A high-end IBM mainframe that incorporates the ESA/370 enhancements.

ES/9000

The IBM System/390 computer line introduced in late 1990 that uses 31-bit addressing with maximum memory capacities from 256MB to 9GB. It's 18 models (Model 120 to Model 960) introduced the widest range of power in a single series at one time with prices ranging from $70K to $23M. Vector processing is optional on high-end water-cooled and certain air-cooled models. See *S/390*.

ESA/370

(Enterprise System Architecture/370) IBM enhancements that increase the performance of high-end 4381 and 3090 mainframes. Introduced in 1988, it increases virtual memory from 2GB to 16TB and adds techniques for managing it more effectively. This architecture is built into System/390 ES/9000 computers.

ESA/390

(Enterprise System Architecture/390) Extensions to ESA/370 for System/390 series. It includes MVS/ESA, VM/ESA and VSE/ESA operating systems.

escape character

A control character often used to precede other characters to control a printer or other device. For example, escape, followed by &l10, sets the LaserJet to landscape mode. In ASCII, escape is decimal 27, hex 1B; in EBCDIC, it is hex 27.

escape key (Esc)

A keyboard key commonly used to exit a mode or routine, or cancel some function.

escape sequence

(1) A machine command that starts with an escape character. Printers are often commanded by escape sequences. See *escape character*.

(2) In a modem, a unique sequence of characters that precedes a command. It allows modem commands (dial, hang up, etc.) to be transmitted with the data. See *TIES*.

ESCON

(Enterprise Systems CONnection) A fiber-optic peripheral channel on an IBM System/390 mainframe. It transfers data up to 17 Mbytes/sec and over very long distances if required (more than five miles). An ESCON Director is a coupling device that provides the actual number of ports.

ESD

(1) (Electronic Software Distribution) Distributing new software and upgrades via the network rather than individual installations on each machine. See *ESL*.

(2) (ElectroStatic Discharge) Sparks (electrons) that jump from an electrically-charged object to an approaching conductive object.

(3) (Entry Systems Division) The IBM division that conceived and developed the original IBM PC.

ESDI

(Enhanced Small Device Interface) A hard disk interface used in PCs that was superseded by IDE and SCSI.

ESDL

(Electronic Software Distribution and Licensing) The combination of ESD and ESL.

ESDS

(Entry Sequence DataSet) A VSAM structure that stores records one after the other without regard to content. Records are retrieved by address. Contrast with *KSDS*.

ESL

(1) A family of client/server development tools for Windows and OS/2 from VMARK Software, Inc., Westboro, MA. It was originally developed by Easel Corporation, which was acquired by VMARK. ESL includes a screen scraper for turning character-based screens into GUI front ends and is often used to develop systems that incorporate the mainframe.

(2) (Electronic Software Licensing) Software that keeps track of the number of active users per application in order to comply with the multiuser licensing contracts that have been purchased.

ESP

(1) (Enhanced-Service Provider) An organization that adds value to basic telephone service by offering such features as call-forwarding, call-detailing and protocol conversion.

(2) (E-tech Speedy Protocol) A proprietary protocol of E-Tech Research used in its modems.

(3) (Electronic Still Photography) Digitizing and transmitting images over a telephone line.

ESS

(1) (Electronic Switching System) A large-scale computer used to switch telephone conversations in a central office.

(2) (Executive Support System) See *EIS*.

Essbase

A leading decision support tool from Hyperion Solutions Corporation, Sunnyvale, CA, (www.hyperion.com), that is optimized for business planning, analysis and management reporting. It provides an OLAP server that runs on Windows NT, OS/2, AS/400 and major UNIX platforms and supports Windows, Mac and UNIX clients.

EtherLoop

(ETHERnet Local LOOP) A transmission technology from Nortel Networks, Brampton, Ontario, (www.nortelnetworks.com) that combines DSL and Ethernet to deliver up to 6 Mbps between the customer and telco central office (CO).

Ethernet

The most widely used LAN technology (Token Ring is next). Ethernet connects up to 1,024 nodes at 10 Mbps over twisted pair, coax and optical fiber. Using the CSMA/CD access method, Ethernet is a shared media LAN. All stations share the total bandwidth within the network segment. See *switched Ethernet*.

10Base5 - 10 Mbps - The First Ethernet

It uses a thick coaxial cable attached to the network nodes via transceivers that tap into the cable and provide a line to a 15-pin plug in the adapter card called an "AUI connector." Also called "thick Ethernet," "ThickWire" and "ThickNet."

10Base2 - 10 Mbps - Thin Coax

An Ethernet standard that uses a thin coaxial cable attached to the network nodes via BNC connectors. It is also called "thin Ethernet," "ThinWire" and "ThinNet."

10BaseT - 10 Mbps - Telephone Wire

All stations use twisted pair to connect in a star configuration to a central hub, also known as a "multiport repeater." 10BaseT is widely used due to the low cost and flexibility of the wire.

100BaseT - 100 Mbps - Fast Ethernet

100BaseTX uses two pairs of Category 5 UTP, 100BaseT4 uses four pairs of Category 3, and 100BaseFX uses multimode optical fibers.

Gigabit Ethernet - 1000 Mbps

The newest Ethernet standard used for network backbones.

EtherTalk

Macintosh software from Apple that accompanies its Ethernet Interface NB Card and adapts the Mac to Ethernet networks.

EULA

(End User License Agreement) The legal agreement between the manufacturer and purchaser of software. It is either printed somewhere on the packaging or displayed on screen at time of installation, the latter being the better method, because it cannot be avoided. The user must click "Accept" or "I Agree" and the license does stipulate the terms of usage, whether the user reads them or not.

Eurocard

A family of European-designed printed circuit boards that uses a 96-pin plug rather than edge connectors. The 3U is a 4x6" board with one plug; the 6U is a 6x12" board with two plugs; the 9U is a 14x18" board with three plugs.

even parity

See *parity checking*.

event driven

An application that responds to input from the user or other application at unregulated times. It's driven by choices that the user makes (select menu, press button, etc.). Contrast with *procedure oriented*.

Exabyte

(Exabyte Corporation, Boulder, CO, www.exabyte.com) The world's largest independent tape drive manufacturer. Its high-capacity 8mm tape drives, introduced in 1987, are sold direct and through OEMs. With acquisitions made in 1993, Exabyte also makes QIC and DAT drives.

Excel

A full-featured spreadsheet for Windows and the Macintosh from Microsoft. It can link many spreadsheets for consolidation and provides a wide variety of business graphics and charts for creating presentation materials.

exception report

A listing of abnormal items or items that fall outside of a specified range.

Exchange

Messaging and groupware software for Windows from Microsoft. The Exchange Server is an Internet-compliant messaging system that runs under Windows NT and can be accessed by Web browsers, the Windows Inbox, Exchange client or Outlook.

executable

A program in machine language that is ready to run in a particular computer environment.

execute

To follow instructions in a program. Same as *run*.

execution time

The time in which a single instruction is executed. It makes up the last half of the instruction cycle.

executive

Refers to an operating system or only to the operating system's kernel.

EXE file

(EXEcutable file) A runnable program in DOS, OS/2 and VMS. In DOS, if a program fits within 64K, it may be a COM file.

exit

(1) To get out of the current mode or quit the program.

(2) In programming, to get out of the loop, routine or function that the computer is currently in.

expanded memory

See *EMS* and *expanded storage*.

expanded storage

Auxiliary memory in IBM mainframes. Data is usually transferred in 4K chunks from expanded storage to central storage (main memory).

expansion board, expansion card

(1) A printed circuit board that plugs into an expansion slot. All the boards (cards) that plug into a personal computer's bus are expansion boards, such as display adapters, disk controllers and sound cards.

(2) See *bus extender*.

expansion bus

An input/output bus typically comprised of a series of slots on the motherboard. Expansion boards are plugged into the bus. ISA, EISA, PCI and VL-bus are examples of expansion buses used in a PC. See also *bus extender*.

expansion slot

A receptacle inside a computer or other electronic system that accepts printed circuit boards. The number of slots determines future expansion. Expansion slots are typically connected to the bus.

expert system

An AI application that uses a knowledge base of human expertise for problem solving. Its success is based on the quality of the data and rules obtained from the human expert. In practice, expert systems perform both below and above that of a human.

expireware

Software with a built-in expiration date, either by date or number of uses.

explode

(1) To break down an assembly into its component pieces. Contrast with *implode*.

(2) To decompress data back to its original form.

Explorer

The file manager in Windows. See also *Microsoft Internet Explorer*.

exponent

The number written above the line and to the right of a number that indicates the power of a number, or how many zeros there are in it. For example 10 to the 3rd power indicates three zeros. The number 467,000 can be stated as 467 x 10 to the 3rd. On a screen or printout, the number is expressed as 467E3. See *floating point*.

exponential growth

Extremely fast growth. On a chart, the line curves up rather than being straight. Contrast with *linear*.

exponential smoothing

A widely-used technique in forecasting trends, seasonality and level change. Works well with data that has a lot of randomness.

export

To convert a data file in the current application program into the format required by another application program.

expression

In programming, a statement that describes data and processing. For example, **VALUE=2*COST** and **PRODUCT="HAT" AND COLOR="GRAY"**.

extended application

A DOS application that runs in extended memory under the control of a DOS extender.

extended ASCII

The second half of the ASCII character set (128 through 255). The symbols are defined by ANSI, by IBM for the PC and by other vendors for proprietary uses. It is non-standard ASCII.

extended maintenance

On-call service that is ordered for periods in addition to the primary period of maintenance.

extended memory

In Intel 286s and up, it is standard memory above one megabyte. Extended memory is used directly by Windows and OS/2 as well as DOS applications that run with DOS extenders. See *PC memory*.

extender

See *bus extender*.

extensible

Capable of being expanded or customized. For example, with extensible programming languages, programmers can add new control structures, statements or data types.

extension

Extensions are file types, or file categories, that are added to the end of DOS and OS/2 file names. The extension is separated from the file name with a dot such as LETTER.DOC. There are more than 500 file extensions in use. Following are some of the more popular. See also *Macintosh extension*.

BAK	Backup	OVR	Overlay module
BAT	DOS, OS/2 batch file	PCX	PC Paintbrush bitmapped image
BIN	Driver, overlay	PIC	Various vector formats:
CFG	Configuration		Lotus 1-2-3,
CHK	DOS Chkdsk chained file		Micrografx Draw,
COM	Executable program		Mac PICT format,
DBF	dBASE database		IBM Storyboard raster graphics
DCA	IBM text	PIF	Windows info. for DOS programs,
DLL	Dynamic link library	PPT	Powerpoint presentation
DOC	Word document	TIF	Bitmapped image
DRV	Driver	TMP	Temporary
EPS	Encapsulated PostScript	TXT	ASCII text
EXE	Executable program	WAV	Windows sound
FON	Font or telephone no.	WK*	Lotus spreadsheet formats
GIF	Bitmapped image	WMF	Windows Metafile
HLP	Help text	XLS	Excel spreadsheet
JPG	Bitmapped image	ZIP	PKZIP compressed
MDB	Access database	$$$	Temporary
OVL	Overlay module		

extent

Contiguous space on a disk reserved for a file or application.

external command

(1) In DOS and OS/2, a function performed by a separate utility program that accompanies the operating system. Contrast with *internal command*.

(2) A user-developed HyperCard command.

external interrupt

An interrupt caused by an external source such as the computer operator, external sensor or monitoring device, or another computer.

external modem

A self-contained modem that is connected via cable to the serial port of a computer. It draws power from a wall outlet. The advantage of an external modem over an internal one is that a series of status lights on the outside of the case may be more helpful if a problem occurs. Contrast with *internal modem*.

external reference

In programming, a call to a program or function that resides in a separate, independent library.

external sort

A sort program that uses disk or tape as temporary workspace. Contrast with *internal sort*.

external storage

Storage outside of the CPU, such as disk and tape.

extranet

A Web site that is made available to external customers or organizations for electronic commerce. Although on the Internet, it generally provides more customer-specific information than a public site. It may require passwords to gain access to the more sensitive information.

e-zine

(Electronic magaZINE) A magazine or newsletter published online. See *Webzine*.

F

f

See *farad*.

F1 key

Function key number one. There are 12 function keys on a PC keyboard. F1 is used for retrieving help in Windows and in most DOS applications.

facilities management

The management of a user's computer installation by an outside organization. All operations including systems, programming and the datacenter can be performed by the facilities management organization on the user's premises.

facsimile

See *fax*.

factorial

The number of sequences that can exist with a set of items, derived by multiplying the number of items by the next lowest number until 1 is reached. For example, three items have six sequences (3x2x1=6): 123, 132, 231, 213, 312 and 321.

fail safe

Same as *fault tolerant*.

fail soft

The ability to fail with minimum destruction. For example, a disk drive can be built to automatically park the heads when power fails. Although it doesn't correct the problem, it minimizes destruction.

fan

A device that uses motor-driven blades to circulate the air in a computer or other electronic system. Today's CPUs run extremely hot, and large computer cabinets use two and three fans to reduce temperature.

fan in, fan out

To direct multiple signals into one receiver and to direct one signal into multiple receivers.

FAQ file

(Frequently Asked Questions file) The most commonly-asked questions about a subject.

farad

A unit of electrical charge that is used to measure the storage capacity of a capacitor. In microelectronics, measurements are usually in microfarads or picofarads.

FastCAD

A full-featured CAD program for DOS or Windows from Evolution Computing, Tempe, AZ, (www.fastcad.com), known for its well-designed user interface. It requires a math coprocessor. Users with less sophisticated requirements can start out with FastCAD's baby brother, EasyCAD.

Fast Ethernet

See *Ethernet*.

Fast Fourier Transform

See *FFT*.

FAT

(File Allocation Table) The part of the DOS, Windows and OS/2 file system that keeps track of where data is stored on disk. When the disk is high-level formatted, the FAT is recorded twice and contains a table with an entry for each disk cluster. The directory list, which contains file name, extension, date, etc., points to the FAT entry where the file starts. See *VFAT* and *FAT32*.

FAT32

The 32-bit version of the file allocation table (FAT) that was added to Windows 95 starting with

OEM Service Release 2 (OSR2) in 1996. FAT32 supports hard disks up to 2TB instead of 2GB. It also reduces cluster waste. On drives up to 8GB, cluster size was reduced from 32K to 4K.

fatal error

A condition that halts processing due to read errors, program bugs or anomalies.

fat binary

A Macintosh executable program that contains machine language in one file for both the Macintosh and PowerMac machines (680x0 and PowerPC CPUs). Software distributed in this format will run native on whichever Mac architecture it is loaded on.

fat client

A client machine in a client/server environment that performs most or all of the application processing with little or none performed in the server. Contrast with *thin client* and *fat server*.

fat pipe

A high-speed communications channel.

fat server

A server in a client/server environment that performs most or all of the application processing with little or none performed in the client. The counterpart to a fat server is a thin client. Contrast with *fat client*. See *client/server architecture*.

fault tolerant

Continous operation in case of failure. A fault tolerant system can be created using two or more computers that duplicate all processing, or having one system stand by if the other fails. It can also be built with redundant processors, control units and peripherals architecturally integrated from the ground up (Tandem, Stratus, etc.).

Fault tolerant operation requires backup power in the event of power failure. It may also imply duplication of systems in disparate locations in the event of natural catastrophe or vandalism.

fax

(FACSimile) Originally called "telecopying," it is the communication of a printed page between remote locations. Fax machines scan a paper form and transmit a coded image over the telephone system. The receiving machine prints a facsimile of the original. A fax machine is made up of a scanner, printer and modem with fax signalling.

Group 3 (203x98 dpi) is still the standard today, but Group 4 machines can transmit a page in just a few seconds and provide up to 400x400 resolution. Group 4 requires 56 to 64 Kbps bandwidth and needs ISDN or Switched 56 circuits. See *fax/modem* and *e-mail*.

fax board

Fax transmission on an expansion board. It uses software that generates fax signals directly from disk files or the screen and transmits a sharper image than a fax machine, which gets its image by scanning. Incoming faxes are printed on the computer's printer.

fax/modem

A combination fax board and data modem available as an external unit or expansion board. It includes a switch that routes the call to the fax or the data modem.

fax server

A computer in a network that provides a bank of fax/modems, allowing users to fax out and remote users to fax in over the next available modem. The fax server may be a dedicated machine or implemented on a file server that is providing other services.

fax switch

A device that tests a phone line for a fax signal and routes the call to the fax machine. When a fax machine dials a number and the line answers, it emits an 1,100Hz tone to identify itself. Some devices handle voice, fax and data modem switching and may require keying in an extension number to switch to the modem.

FC-AL
(Fibre Channel-Arbitrated Loop) A topology for Fiber Channel in which all devices are linked together in a loop. Fibre Channel is also used point-to-point or as a switched topology. See *Fiber Channel*.

FCB
(File Control Block) A method of handling files in DOS 1.0. Older applications that remain compatible with DOS 1.0 may use this method.

FCC
(Federal Communications Commission) The regulatory body for U.S. interstate telecommunications services as well as international service originating in the U.S. It was created under the U.S. Communications Act of 1934, and its board of commissioners is appointed by the President.

FCC Class
An FCC certification of radiation limits on digital devices. Class A certification is for business use. Class B for residential use is more stringent in order to avoid interference with TV and other home reception. See Part 15, Subpart B, of the Federal Register (CFR 47, Parts 0-19).

FCFS
First come, first served.

fci
(Flux Changes per Inch) The measurement of polarity reversals on a magnetic surface. In MFM, each flux change is equal to one bit. In RLL, a flux change generates more than one bit.

F connector
A coaxial cable connector used to connect antennas, TVs and VCRs. It is easily recognized: the plug's inner wire is stripped bare and sticks out of the connector looking very unfinished.

F Connector

FD
(Floppy Disk) For example, FD/HD refers to a floppy disk/hard disk device.

FDDI
(Fiber Distributed Data Interface) An ANSI standard token passing network that uses optical fiber cabling and transmits at 100 Mbits/sec up to two kilometers. FDDI provides network services at the same level as Ethernet and Token Ring (OSI layers 1 and 2).

FDDI is used for MANs and LANs and includes its own Station Management (STM) network management standard. The TP-PMD (CDDI) version runs over copper (UTP), although typically limited to distances up to 100 meters.

FDDI provides an optional "dual counter-rotating ring" topology that contains primary and secondary rings with data flowing in opposite directions. If the line breaks, the ends of the primary and secondary rings are bridged together at the closest node to create a single ring again.

FDISK
A DOS external command used to partition a hard disk, which is necessary before high-level formatting. Fdisk also comes with Windows 95/98.

FDM
(Frequency Division Multiplexing) A method used to transmit multiple signals over a single channel. Each signal (data, voice, etc.) modulates a carrier with a different frequency and all signals travel simultaneously over the channel. Contrast with *TDM*. See *baseband*.

FDMA
(Frequency Division Multiple Access) The technology used in the analog cellular telephone network that divides the spectrum into 30KHz channels. See *TDMA, CDMA* and *CDPD*.

FD:OCA

(Formatted Data:Object Content Architecture) An SAA-compliant (CCS) specification for formatting data in fields.

FDSE

(Full-Duplex Switched Ethernet) An extension to 10BaseT Ethernet that is implemented in a switched Ethernet environment, which has a dedicated line between the station and switch. It is built into the network adapter (NIC) and switch, providing bi-directional transmission that boosts bandwidth from 10 to 20 Mbps.

FDX

See *full-duplex*.

FEA

(Finite Element Analysis) A mathematical technique for analyzing stress, which breaks down a physical structure into substructures, called "finite elements." The finite elements and their interrelationships are converted into equation form and solved mathematically.

Graphics-based FEA software can display the model on screen as it is being built and, after analysis, display the object's reactions under load conditions. Models created in popular CAD packages can often be accepted by FEA software.

feasibility study

The analysis of a problem to determine if it can be solved effectively. The operational (will it work?), economical (costs and benefits) and technical (can it be built?) aspects are part of the study. Results of the study determine whether the solution should be implemented.

feature connector

See *VGA feature connector*.

feature negotiation

See *automatic feature negotiation*.

FEC

(Forward Error Correction) A communications technique that can correct bad data on the receiving end. Before transmission, the data is processed through an algorithm that adds extra bits for error correction. If the transmitted message is received in error, the correction bits are used to repair it.

FED

(Field Emission Display) A flat panel display that is similar to a CRT and provides an image quality equal to or better than a CRT. FEDs are like a thin CRT, using a vacuum-filled chamber and phosphor-coated glass. However, instead of using three cathodes to illuminate the phosphors by scanning the entire screen, FED displays use millions of cone-shaped cathodes that are stationary.

female connector

A receptacle into which the male counterpart of the connector is plugged.

femtosecond

One quadrillionth of a second. See *space/time*.

FEP

See *front end processor*.

ferric oxide

An oxidation of iron used in the coating of magnetic disks and tapes.

ferromagnetic

The capability of a material, such as iron and nickel, to be highly magnetized.

FET

(Field Effect Transistor) A type of transistor used in MOS integrated circuits.

fetch

To locate the next instruction in memory for execution by the CPU.

FF

See *form feed*.

FFT

(Fast Fourier Transform) A class of algorithms used in digital signal processing that break down complex signals into elementary components.

fiber bundle

A set of adjacent optical fibers running in parallel and adhered together. It is used for transmitting light to brighten an area as well as transmitting whole images, but is not used for modern digital communications.

Fiber Channel

See *Fibre Channel*.

fiber loss

The amount of attenuation of signal in an optical fiber transmission.

fiber optic

Communications systems that use optical fibers for transmission. Fiber-optic transmission became widely used in the 1980s when the long-distance carriers created nationwide systems for carrying voice conversations digitally over optical fibers.

Eventually, all transmission systems may become fiber optic-based. Also, in time, the internals of computers may be partially or even fully made of light circuits rather than electrical circuits. See *FDDI, Fibre Channel* and *optical fiber*.

Fibonacci numbers

A series of whole numbers in which each number is the sum of the two preceding ones: 1, 1, 2, 3, 5, 8, 13, etc. It is used to speed up binary searches by dividing the search into the two lower numbers; for example, 13 items would be divided into 5 and 8 items; 8 items would be divided into 5 and 3.

Fibre Channel

A high-speed transmission technology used as a peripheral channel or network backbone. It provides 100 Mbytes/sec in both directions. Fibre Channels can be designed as point-to-point, arbitrated loop (FC-AL) or switched topologies.

fiche

Same as *microfiche*.

FidoNet

The first popular method of providing e-mail and file transfer across multiple BBSs. Although BBS usage has declined dramatically in the U.S., there are still more than 25,000 FidoNet nodes in use around the world, many of which are used to provide an e-mail connection to the Internet.

field

A physical unit of data that is one or more bytes in size. A collection of fields make up a record. A field also defines a unit of data on a source document, screen or report. Examples of fields are NAME, ADDRESS, QUANTITY and AMOUNT DUE.

The field is the common denominator between the user and the computer. When you interactively query and update your database, you reference your data by field name.

A field is a physical unit of storage, whereas a data item refers to the data itself. For example, the data items, Chicago, Dallas and Phoenix are stored in the CITY field.

The terms *field, data element, data item* and *variable* refer to the same unit of data and are often used interchangeably.

field engineer

A person who is responsible for hardware installation, maintentance and repair. Formal training is in electronics, although many people have learned on the job.

field name

An assigned name for a field (NAME, ADDRESS, CITY, STATE, etc.) that will be the same in every record.

field separator

A character used to mark the separation of fields in a record. See *comma delimited* and *tab delimited*.

field service

See *field engineer*.

field squeeze

In a mail merge, a function that eliminates extra blank spaces between words when fixed-length fields are inserted into the document text. See *line squeeze*.

field template

See *picture*.

Fiery engine

A raster image processor (RIP) from Electronics for Imaging, Inc., San Mateo, CA, (www.efi.com), that is noted for its high quality color processing and speed. Since 1991, the Fiery Color Server, which is a combination of hardware and software, has been used to transform digital color copiers into color printers. Toward the end of the 1990s, the Fiery components were added to lower-cost color devices such as laser printers and wide format ink jet printers.

FIF

(Fractal Image Format) A graphics file format from Iterated Systems, Inc., Norcross, GA, that stores fractal images with compression ratios as high as 2,500:1.

FIFO

(First In-First Out) A storage method that retrieves the item stored for the longest time. Contrast with *LIFO*.

fifth-generation computer

A computer designed for AI applications. Appearing after the turn of the century, these systems will represent the next technology leap.

file

A collection of bytes stored as an individual entity. All data on disk is stored as a file with an assigned file name that is unique within the directory it resides in.

To the computer, a file is nothing more than a series of bytes. The structure of a file is known to the software that manipulates it. For example, database files are made up of a series of records. Word processing files, also called "documents," contain a continuous flow of text.

Following are the major types of files stored in a computer system. Except for ASCII text files, all files contain proprietary information contained in a header or interspersed throughout the file.

```
      Type                 Contents
  data file           data records
  document            text
  spreadsheet         rows and columns of cells
  image               rows and columns of bits
  drawing             list of vectors
  audio               sound waves
  MIDI                MIDI instructions
  video               digital video frames
  batch file          text
  source program      text
  object program      machine language
```

file and record locking

A first-come, first-served technique for managing data in a multiuser environment. The first user to access the file or record prevents, or locks out, other users from accessing it. After the file or record is updated, it is unlocked and available.

file attribute

A file access classification that allows a file to be retrieved or erased. Typical attributes are read/write, read only, archive and hidden.

file extension

See *extension*.

file find

A utility that searches all directories for matching file names.

file format

The structure of a file. There are hundreds of proprietary formats for database, word processing and graphics files. See *record layout*.

file layout

Same as *record layout*.

file maintenance

(1) The periodic updating of master files. For example, adding/deleting employees and customers, making address changes and changing product prices. It does not refer to daily transaction processing and batch processing (order processing, billing, etc.).

(2) The periodic reorganization of the disk drives. Data that is continuously updated becomes physically fragmented over the disk space and requires regrouping. An optimizing or defragger program is run (daily, weekly, etc.) that rewrites all files contiguously.

FileMaker

A database management system (DBMS) for the Macintosh and Windows NT from FileMaker, Inc., Santa Clara, CA, (www.filemaker.com), a software subsidiary of Apple. Originally a file manager from Claris Corporation, it has been a popular program for general data management. It provides a variety of statistical functions, fast search capabilities and extensive reporting features.

file manager

(1) Software used to manage files on a disk. It provides functions to delete, copy, move, rename and view files as well as create and manage directories. The file managers in Windows 3.x and Windows 95/98 are File Manager and Explorer.

(2) Software that manages data files. Often erroneously called "database managers," file managers provide the ability to create, enter, change, query and produce reports on one file at a time. They have no relational capabilty and usually don't include a programming language.

file name

A name assigned by the user or programmer that is used to identify a file.

FileNet

A document imaging system from FileNet Corporation, Costa Mesa, CA, (www.filenet.com). Introduced in 1985, FileNet is the most widely-used, high-end workflow automation system. It runs on PCs, Sun and Digital workstations and also offers an RS/6000 document server running UNIX and ORACLE.

file protection

Preventing accidental erasing of data. Physical file protection is provided on the storage medium by turning a switch, moving a lever or covering a notch. On 1/2" tape, a plastic ring in the center of the reel is removed (no ring-no write). In these cases, writing is prohibited even if the software directs the computer to do so.

Logical file protection is provided by the operating system, which can designate a single file as read only. This method allows both regular (read/write) and read only files to be stored on the same disk volume. Files can also be designated as hidden files, which makes them invisible to most software programs.

Protecting Floppies

In order to prevent a 3.5" floppy disk from being erased or written over by the program, make sure you can see through both holes. Looking at the back of the disk with the metal circle in the middle and door at the top, slide the square, plastic window (bottom right) downward uncovering a hole ...rough the disk. Remember... if it's holey, you're protected!

file recovery program
Software that recovers disk files that have been accidentally deleted or damaged.

file server
A high-speed computer in a LAN that stores the programs and data files shared by users on the network. Also called a "network server," it acts like a remote disk drive. See *database server*.

file sharing protocol
A communications protocol that provides a structure for file requests (open, read, write, close, etc.) between stations in a network. If file sharing is strictly between workstation and server, it is also called a "client/server protocol." It refers to layer 7 of the OSI model.

file size
The length of a file in bytes. See "Byte Specifications" in the term *byte*.

file spec
(file **SPEC**ification) A reference to the location of a file on a disk, which includes disk drive, directory name and file name. For example, in DOS and OS/2, **c:\wordstar\books\chapter** is a file spec for the file CHAPTER in the BOOKS subdirectory in the WORDSTAR directory on drive C.

file system
(1) A method for cataloging files in a computer system. See *hierarchical file system*.

(2) A data processing application that manages individual files. Files are related by customized programming. Contrast with *relational database*.

file transfer program
A program that transmits files from one computer to another. Such programs; for example, Travelling Software's LapLink and the Interlink utility that comes with DOS 6, allow the user to control both computers from one machine. See *FTP*.

file transfer protocol
A communications protocol used to transmit files without loss of data. A file transfer protocol can handle all types of files including binary files and ASCII text files. Common examples are Xmodem, Ymodem, Zmodem and Kermit.

file viewer
Software that displays the contents of a file as it would be normally displayed by the application that created it. It is usually capable of displaying a variety of common formats.

fill
(1) In a paint program, to change the color of a bordered area.

(2) In a spreadsheet, to enter common or repetitive values into a group of cells.

fill pattern
(1) A color, shade or pattern used to fill an area of an image.

(2) Signals transmitted by a LAN station when not receiving or transmitting data in order to maintain synchronization.

fill scaling
The ability to change a fill pattern from light to dense. For example, if polka dots were used, the fill pattern could range from thick dots widely separated to very thin dots tightly packed together.

film recorder
A device that takes a 35mm slide picture from a graphics file, which has been created in a CAD, paint or business graphics package. It generates very high resolution, typically 2,000 to 4,000 lines.

It typically works by recreating the image on a built-in CRT that shines through a color wheel onto the film in a standard 35mm camera. Some units provide optional Polaroid camera backs for instant previewing. Film recorders can be connected to personal computers by plugging in a controller board cabled to the recorder.

filter

(1) A process that changes data, such as a sort routine that changes the sequence of items or a conversion routine (import or export filter) that changes one data, text or graphics format into another.

(2) A pattern or mask through which only selected data is passed. For example, certain e-mail systems can be programmed to filter out important messages and alert the user. In dBASE, **set filter to file overdue**, compares all data to the matching conditions stored in OVERDUE.

financial planning language

A language used to create data models and command a financial planning system.

financial planning system

Software that helps the user evaluate alternatives. It allows for the creation of a data model, which is a series of data elements in equation form; for example, **gross profit = gross sales - cost of goods sold**. Different values can be plugged into the elements, and the impact of various options can be assessed (what if?).

A financial planning system is a step above a spreadsheet by providing additional analysis tools; however, increasingly, these capabilities are being built into spreadsheets. For example, sensitivity analysis assigns a range of values to a data element, which causes that data to be highlighted if it ever exceeds that range.

Goal seeking provides automatic calculation. For example, by entering **gross margin = 50%** as well as the minimums and maximums of the various inputs, the program will calculate an optimum mix of inputs to achieve the goal (output).

Finder

The part of early Macintosh operating systems that keeps track of icons, controls the Clipboard and Scrapbook and allows files to be copied. Finder manages one application at a time, while its successor, MultiFinder, manages multiple apps. MultiFinder is now an inherent part of the Mac OS.

fingerprint reader

A scanner used to identify a person's fingerprint for security purposes. After a sample is taken, access to a computer or other system is granted if the fingerprint matches the stored sample. A PIN may also be used with the fingerprint sample.

finite element

See *FEA*.

firewall

A method for keeping a network secure. It can be implemented in a single router that filters out unwanted packets, or it may use a combination of technologies in routers and hosts. Firewalls are widely used to give users access to the Internet in a secure fashion as well as to separate a company's public Web server from its internal network. They are also used to keep internal network segments secure. For example, a research or accounting subnet might be vulnerable to snooping from within.

FireWire

A serial bus developed by Apple and Texas Instruments that allows for the connection of up to 63 devices. FireWire bandwidth is from 100 to 400 Mbits/sec. Also known as the IEEE 1394 standard, FireWire has been initially used to interconnect digital camcorders and other digital video equipment.

firmware

A category of memory chips that hold their content without electrical power and include ROM, PROM, EPROM and EEPROM technologies. Firmware becomes "hard software" when holding program code.

first-generation computer

A computer that used vacuum tubes as switching elements; for example, the UNIVAC I.

fixed disk

A non-removable hard disk such as is found in most personal computers. Programs and data are copied to and from the fixed disk.

fixed-frequency monitor

A monitor that accepts one type of video signal, such as VGA only. Contrast with *multiscan monitor*.

fixed head disk

A direct access storage device, such as a disk or drum, that has a read/write head for each track. Since there is no access arm movement, access times are significantly improved.

fixed length field

A constant field size; for example, a 25-byte name field takes up 25 bytes in each record. It is easier to program, but wastes disk space and restricts file design. Description and comment fields are always a dilemma. Short fields allow only abbreviated remarks, while long fields waste space if lengthy comments are not required in every record. Contrast with *variable length field*.

fixed length record

A data record that contains fixed length fields.

fixed point

A method for storing and calculating numbers in which the decimal point is always in the same location. Contrast with *floating point*.

Fkey

(Function **key**) A Macintosh command sequence using command, shift and option key combinations. For example, Fkey 1 (command-shift 1) ejects the internal floppy.

F keys

See *function keys*.

flag

(1) In communications, a code in the transmitted message which indicates that the following characters are a control code and not data.

(2) In programming, a "yes/no" indicator built into certain hardware or created and controlled by the programmer.

(3) A UNIX command line argument. The symbol is a dash. For example, in the command **head -15 filex**, which prints the first 15 lines of the file FILEX, the **-15** flag modifies the Head command.

flame

Slang for communicating emotionally and/or excessively via electronic mail. See *netiquette*.

Flash

Animation software for Windows and the Mac from Macromedia, Inc., San Francisco, CA, (www.macromedia.com). It is used to develop interactive graphics for Web sites as well as desktop presentations and games. Flash sequences on the Web are displayed by a Web browser plug-in and offline presentations are run by a Flash player that can be included on a floppy or CD-ROM.

flash BIOS

A PC BIOS that is stored in flash memory rather than in a ROM. In order to be upgraded, ROM BIOSs have to be replaced with a newer chip, but flash BIOSs can be updated in place via software. See *BIOS*.

flash disk

A solid state disk made of flash memory. It emulates a standard disk drive in contrast with flash memory cards, which require proprietary software to make them function.

flash memory

A memory chip that holds its content without power. Unlike DRAM and SRAM memory chips, in which a single byte can be written, flash memory must be erased and written in fixed blocks, typically ranging from 512 bytes up to 256KB. Flash memory is widely used as "digital film" in PC Card, CompactFlash, SmartMedia and Memory Stick formats.

flat address space

Memory addressing in which each byte is referenced by a different sequential number starting with 0. Contrast with *segmented address space*.

flatbed plotter

A graphics plotter that draws on sheets of paper that have been placed in a bed. The size of the bed determines the maximum size sheet that can be drawn.

flat file

A stand-alone data file that does not have any pre-defined linkages or pointers to locations of data in other files. The term usually refers to files managed by file managers with no relational capability. In the past, this referred to the very type of file used in relational databases.

flat panel display

A thin display screen that uses any of a number of technologies, such as LCD, plasma, EL and FED, with LCD being the most popular. Traditionally used in laptops, flat panel displays are slowly beginning to replace desktop CRTs. With their low power consumption, low radiation and space-saving footprint, flat panels are expected to eventually become the standard.

flat screen

(1) A display screen in which the CRT viewing surface is flatter than the earlier rounder CRTs. The flat screen provides less distortion at the edges.

(2) See *flat panel display*.

flat shading

In computer graphics, a technique for computing a one-tone shaded surface to simulate simple lighting.

flexible disk

Same as *floppy disk* and *diskette*.

flicker

A fluctuating image on a video screen. See *interlaced*.

flick file

A file format for animation from AutoDesk, Inc. It uses the .FLI file extension.

flip chip

A surface mount chip technology where the chip is packaged in place on the board and then underfilled with an epoxy. A common technique for attachment is to place solder balls on the chip, "flip" the chip over onto the board and melt the solder. Flip chips are also mounted on glass substrates using conductive paste, typically for LCD drivers and smart cards. See *BGA*.

flip-flop

An electronic circuit that alternates between two states. When current is applied, it changes to its opposite state (0 to 1 or 1 to 0). Made of several transistors, it is used in the design of static memories and hardware registers.

Flash Memory Cards

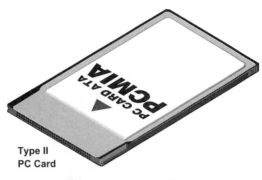

**Type II
PC Card**

CompactFlash

SmartMedia

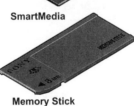

Memory Stick

MultiMediaCard

Flash memory cards have become very popular storage devices.

Type II PC Cards provide auxiliary storage for laptops, but the CompactFlash, SmartMedia and Memory Stick cards are expected to become the digital film of the 21st century.

The MultiMediaCard is designed for the smallest handhelds such as cellular phones and pagers.

floating point

A method for storing and calculating numbers in which the decimal points don't line up as in fixed point numbers. The significant digits are stored as a unit called the "mantissa," and the location of the radix point (decimal point in base 10) is stored in a separate unit called the exponent. Floating point methods are used for calculating a large range of numbers quickly.

Floating point operations can be implemented in hardware (math coprocessor), or they can be done in software. They can also be performed in a separate floating point processor that is connected to the main processor via a channel.

floating point processor

An arithmetic unit designed to perform floating point operations. It may be a coprocessor chip in a personal computer, a CPU designed with built-in floating point capabilities or a separate machine, often called an "array processor," which is connected to the main computer.

floppy disk

A reusable magnetic storage medium. Invented by IBM and introduced in the early 1970s in an 8" square format, floppies have been the primary method for distributing personal computer software up until the mid 1990s when CD-ROMs became a competitive medium.

FLOPS

(FLoating point Operations Per Second) A unit of measurement of floating point calculations. For example, 100 megaflops is 100 million floating point operations per second.

flow chart

A graphical representation of the sequence of operations in an information system or program. Information system flow charts show how data flows from source documents through the computer to final distribution to users. Program flow charts show the sequence of instructions in a single program or subroutine. Different symbols are used to draw each type of flow chart.

flow control

(1) In communications, the management of transmission between two devices. It is concerned with the timing of signals and enables slower-speed devices to communicate with higher-speed ones. There are various techniques, but all are designed to ensure that the receiving station is able to accept the next block of data before the sending station sends it.

(2) In programming, the if-then and loop statements that make up the program's logic.

flush

To empty the contents of a memory buffer onto disk.

flux

The energy field generated by a magnet.

FM

(1) (Frequency Modulation) A transmission technique that blends the data signal into a carrier by varying (modulating) the frequency of the carrier. See *modulate*.

(2) (Frequency Modulation) An earlier magnetic disk encoding method that places clock bits onto the medium along with the data bits. It has been superseded by MFM and RLL.

FM synthesis

A MIDI technique that simulates the sound of musical instruments. It uses operators, typically four of them, which create wave forms or modulate the wave forms. FM synthesis does not create sound as faithfully as wave table synthesis, which uses actual samples of the instruments.

Fn key

(FuNction key) A keyboard key that works like a shift key to activate the second function on a dual-purpose key, typically found on laptops to reduce keyboard size. It is different than the function keys F1, F2, etc.

FOCA

(Font Object Content Architecture) See *MO:DCA*.

FOCUS

(1) A DBMS from Information Builders that runs on more than 35 different platforms. FOCUS has been widely known for its 4GL and report writing capabilities and is the product that built the company. It included a hierarchical database in its first release in 1975 and has evolved to support more than 80 database and file types including Information Builders' own multidimensional database (FOCUS Fusion).

(2) (Federation On Computing in the United States, www.acm.org/focus) The U.S. representative of the International Federation of Information Processing (IFIP). FOCUS was founded in 1991 by the ACM and the IEEE Computing Society (IEEE-CS).

FOIRL

(Fiber Optic Inter Repeater Link) An early IEEE standard for fiber optic Ethernet. FOIRL is limited to .6 miles distance per segment, whereas 10BaseF segments can extend to 1.2 miles. 10BaseF is a more comprehensive standard for complete fiber-based installations.

folder

In a graphical user interface (GUI), a simulated file folder that holds data, applications and other folders. Folders were introduced on the Xerox Star, then popularized on the Macintosh and later adapted to Windows and UNIX. In DOS and Windows 3.1, a folder is known as a directory, and a subfolder (folder within a folder) is a subdirectory.

foldering

Using folders to store and manipulate documents on screen.

Folio

(1) Text management software for PCs from the Folio division of Open Market, Inc., Cambridge, MA, (www.folio.com). It provides storage, retrieval and hypertext capability for text databases. It can import text from over 40 file formats. Folio files are called "Infobases."

(2) (folio) In typography, a printed page number. For example, folio 3 could be the 27th physical page in a book.

font

A set of type characters of a particular typeface design and size. Usually, each typeface (Times Roman, Helvetica, Arial, etc.) is made available in four variations: normal weight, bold, italic and bold italic. Thus, bitmapped fonts, which include pre-defined bitmaps for each point size, four fonts would be required for each point size. For scalable fonts, which allow for any point size to be created on the fly, only four fonts would be required for each typeface.

Fonts are either built into the printer or are available as plug-in cartriges or as soft fonts, which reside in the computer. See *bitmapped font* and *scalable font*.

font cartridge

A set of bitmapped or outline fonts for one or more typefaces contained in a plug-in module for the printer. The fonts are stored in a ROM chip within the cartridge. Contrast with *soft font* and *internal font*.

font compiler

Same as *font generator*.

font editor

Software that allows fonts to be designed and modified.

font family

A set of fonts of the same typeface in assorted sizes, including bold, italic and bold italic variations.

font generator

Software that converts an outline font into a bitmap (dot pattern required for a particular font size). Font generation is not linear, simply expanding a letter to any size. As fonts get bigger, their characteristics must change in order to make them attractive.

Font generation is used to create fonts before they are used in the document. They are then kept on disk for future use. In contrast, font scaling is used to create fonts on the fly as needed. Font generation has for the most part given way to font scaling. See *font scaler*.

font manager
See *font scaler*.

font metric
Typographic information (width, height, kerning) for each character in a font.

font number
An identification number assigned to a font. A program references the font by this number.

font rasterizer
See *font scaler*.

font scaler
Software that converts scalable fonts into bitmaps on the fly as required for display or printing. Examples are TrueType, Adobe Type Manager and Bitstream's Facelift. See *scalable font* and *font generator*.

font style
A typeface variation (normal, bold, italic, bold italic).

font utility
Software that provides functions for managing fonts, including the ability to download, install, design and modify fonts.

font weight
The thickness of characters (light, medium or bold).

foo
A popular name for a temporary file, function or variable, or example of same. Often used in conjunction with "bar," from "fubar" (Fouled Up Beyond All Recognition).

footer
In a document or report, common text that appears at the bottom of every page. It usually contains the page number.

footprint
The amount of geographic space covered by an object. A computer footprint is the desk or floor surface it occupies. A satellite's footprint is the earth area covered by its downlink.

foreground/background
The priority assigned to programs running in a multitasking environment. Foreground programs have highest priority, and background programs have lowest. Online users are given the foreground, and batch processing activities (sorts, updates, etc.) are given the background. If batch activities are given a higher priority, terminal response times may slow down considerably.

In a personal computer, the foreground program is the one the user is currently working with, and the background program might be a print spooler or communications program.

Forest & Trees
A data analysis program for PCs from Trinzic Corporation, Portsmouth, NH, that integrates data from a variety of applications. It provides a control room interface that lets users monitor important business information.

fork
(1) In UNIX, to make a copy of a process for execution.

(2) In the Macintosh, a part of a file. See *data fork* and *resource fork*.

form
(1) A paper form used for printing.

(2) A screen display designed for a particular application.

format
The structure, or layout, of an item. Screen formats are fields on the screen. Report formats are

columns, headers and footers on a page.

Record formats are the fields within a record. File formats are the structure of data files, word processing documents and graphics files (display lists and bitmaps) and all associated codes. See *format program, disk format, DOS Format* and *style sheet.*

format program

Software that initializes a disk. There are two formatting levels. The low-level initializes the disk surface by creating the physical tracks and storing sector identification in them. Low-level format programs are geared to the drive technology used (IDE, SCSI, etc.).

The high-level format lays out the indexes used by the operating system (Mac, DOS, etc.) to keep track of data stored in the sectors. Floppy disk format programs perform both levels on a diskette.

form factor

The physical size of a device.

form feed

Advancing a printer form to the top of the next page. It is done by pressing the printer's form feed (FF) button or by sending the form feed code (ASCII 12) to the printer from the computer.

forms software

Workflow automation software used to create on-screen data entry forms and provide e-mail routing and tracking of the resulting electronic documents.

formula

(1) An arithmetic expression that solves a problem. For example, (**fahrenheit-32**)***5/9** is the formula for converting fahrenheit to centigrade.

(2) In spreadsheets, an algorithm that identifies how the data in a specific number of cells is to be calculated. For example, **+C3*D8** means that the contents of cell C3 are to be multipled by the contents of cell D8 and the results are to be placed where the formula is located.

form view

A screen display showing one item or record arranged like a preprinted form. Contrast with *table view.*

for statement

A high-level programming language structure that repeats a series of instructions a specified number of times. It creates a loop that includes its own control information. The following examples print "Hello" 10 times:

```
    BASIC                  C
for x = 1 to 10     for (x = 0;  x < 10;  x++)
 print "hello"        printf ("hello\n");
next x
```

FORTH

(FOuRTH-generation language) A high-level programming language created by Charles Moore in the late 1960s as a way of providing direct control of the computer. Its syntax resembles LISP, it uses reverse polish notation for calculations, and it is noted for its extensibility.

It is both compiler and interpreter. The source program is compiled first and then executed by its operating system/interpreter. It is used in process control applications that must quickly process data acquired from instruments and sensors. It is also used in arcade game programming as well as robotics and other AI applications. The following polyFORTH example converts Fahrenheit to Celsius:

```
: CONV ( n) 32 - 5 9 * / . ." Celsius
: USER_INPUT  ." Enter Fahrenheit " CONV ;
```

FORTRAN

(FORmula TRANslator) The first high-level programming language and compiler, developed in 1954 by IBM. It was originally designed to express mathematical formulas, and although it is used occasionally for business applications, it is still the most widely used language for scientific, engineering and mathematical problems.

FORTRAN IV is an ANSI standard, but FORTRAN V has various proprietary versions. The following example converts Fahrenheit to Celsius:

```
WRITE(6,*) 'Enter Fahrenheit '
READ(5,*) XFAHR
XCENT = (XFAHR - 32) * 5 / 9
WRITE(6,*) 'Celsius is ',XCENT
STOP
END
```

forum
An information interchange regarding a specific topic or product that is hosted on an online service or BBS. It can include the latest news on the subject, a conferencing capability for questions and answers by participants as well as files for downloading fixes, demos and other related material.

forward chaining
In AI, a form of reasoning that starts with what is known and works toward a solution. Known as bottom-up approach. Contrast with *backward chaining*.

forward compatible
Same as *upward compatible*.

fountain fill
In computer graphics, a painted area that smoothly changes its color or pattern density. A radial fountain fill starts at the center of an area and radiates outward.

fourth-generation computer
A computer made up almost entirely of chips with limited amounts of discrete components. We are currently in the fourth generation.

fourth-generation language
A computer language that is more advanced than traditional high-level programming languages. For example, in dBASE, the command LIST displays all the records in a data file. In second- and third-generation languages, instructions would have to be written to read each record, test for end of file, place each item of data on screen and go back and repeat the operation until there are no more records to process.

First-generation languages are machine languages; second-generation are machine dependent assembly languages; third-generation are high-level programming languages, such as FORTRAN, COBOL, BASIC, Pascal, and C. Although many languages, such as dBASE, are called "fourth-generation languages," they are actually a mix of third and fourth. The dBASE LIST command is a fourth-generation command, but applications programmed in dBASE are third-generation.

Query language and report writers are also fourth-generation languages. Any computer language with English-like commands that doesn't require traditional input-process-output logic falls into this category.

FoxBASE
An earlier Xbase development system for the Macintosh from Microsoft. It was succeeded by FoxPro. Originally developed by Fox Software for DOS, FoxBASE gained a reputation early on for its speed and compatibility with dBASE. See *Visual FoxPro*.

FoxPro
See *Visual FoxPro*.

FPD
See *flat panel display*.

FPGA
(Field Programmable Gate Array) A programmable logic chip with a high density of gates.

FPM RAM
See *page mode memory*.

fps
(Frames Per Second) The measurement of full-motion video performance. See *frame*.

FPU
(Floating Point Unit) A computer circuit that handles floating point operations.

fractals
A technique for describing and greatly compressing images, especially natural objects, such as trees, clouds and rivers. It turns an image into a set of data and an algorithm for expanding it back to the original. The term comes from "fractus," which is Latin for broken or fragmented. It was coined by IBM Fellow and doctor of mathematics Benoit Mandelbrot, who expanded on ideas from earlier mathematicians and discovered similarities in chaotic and random events and shapes.

fractional T1
A service that provides less than full T1 capacity. One or more 64Kbits/sec channels are provided.

FRAD
(Frame Relay Assembler/Dissassembler) A communications device that formats outgoing data into the format required by a frame relay network. It strips the data back out at the other end. It is the frame relay counterpart to the X.25 PAD.

fragmentation
The non-contiguous storage of data on disk. As files are updated, new data is stored in available free space, which may not be contiguous. Fragmented files cause extra head movement, slowing disk accesses. A disk maintenance, or optimizer, program is used to rewrite and reorder all the files.

FRAM
(1) (Ferroelectronic **RAM**) A non-volatile semiconductor memory that retains its content without power for up to 10 years.

(2) (Ferromagnetic **RAM**) A non-volatile memory that records microscopic bits on a magnetic surface.

frame
(1) In computer graphics, one screenful of data or its equivalent storage space.

(2) In communications, a fixed block of data transmitted as a single entity. Also called a "packet."

(3) In desktop publishing, a movable, resizable box that holds a graphic image.

(4) In AI, a data structure that holds a general description of an object, which is derived from basic concepts and experience.

frame buffer
A separate memory component that holds a graphic image. It can have one plane of memory for each bit in the pixel. For example, if eight bits are used per pixel, there are eight memory planes.

frame grabber
A device that accepts standard TV signals and digitizes the current video frame into a bitmap image.

FrameMaker
A desktop publishing program from Adobe that runs on UNIX platforms, Macintosh and Windows. It is noted for its large number of advanced features, including full text and graphics editing capabilities. Optional viewers let documents run on machines without FrameMaker, providing a way to distribute hypertext-based help systems.

frame relay
A high-speed packet switching protocol used for wide area networks (WANs). It is faster than traditional X.25 networks, because it was designed for today's reliable circuits and performs less rigorous error detection. It provides for a granular service up to DS3 rates (45 Mbps) with higher speeds expected. Initially unsuited for realtime voice and video, the FRF.11 standard provides extensions for voice over frame relay.

framework
See *application framework*.

framing bit
Same as *start bit* and *stop bit*.

free-form database

A database system that allows entry of text without regard to length or order. Although it accepts data as does a word processor, it differs by providing better methods for searching, retrieving and organizing the data.

free-form language

A language in which statements can reside anywhere on a line or even cross over lines. It does not imply less syntax structure, just more freedom in placing statements. For example, any number of blank spaces are allowed between symbols. Most high-level programming languages are free-form.

FreeHand

See *Macromedia Freehand.*

Freelance Graphics

A presentation graphics program for Windows from Lotus that is also part of Lotus' SmartSuite set of applications.

Free Software Foundation

(Free Software Foundation, Inc., Boston, MA, www.gnu.org) A non-profit organization founded in 1985 by Richard Stallman, dedicated to eliminating restrictions on copying and modifying programs by promoting the development and use of freely redistributable software. Its GNU computing environment, X Windows and other programs are available for a transaction charge.

freeware

Software distributed without charge. Ownership is retained by the developer who has control over its redistribution, including the ability to change the next release of the freeware to payware. See *shareware* and *public domain software.*

freeze-frame video

Video transmission in which the image is changed once every several seconds rather than 30 or more times per second as in full-motion video.

frequency

The number of oscillations (vibrations) in an alternating current within one second. See *carrier.*

friction feed

A mechanism that allows cut paper forms to be used in a printer. The paper is passed between the platen and a roller that presses tightly against it. Contrast with *tractor feed.*

front end

The head, starting point or input side in a system. For example, it may refer to the graphical interface on a user's workstation where all data is entered or to a communications system, such as a front end processor or TP monitor that accepts incoming transactions and messages. See *back end.*

front-end CASE

CASE tools that aid in systems analysis and design. Contrast with *back-end CASE.*

front end processor

A computer that handles communications processing for a mainframe. It connects to the communications lines on one end and the mainframe on the other. It transmits and receives messages, assembles and disassembles packets and detects and corrects errors. It is sometimes synonymous with a communications controller, although the latter is usually not as flexible.

frontside bus

The primary pathway between the CPU and memory. The speed is derived from the number of parallel lines (16 bit, 32 bit, etc.) and the clock speed (66MHz, 100MHz, etc.). Also known as a "system bus," it is typically faster than the peripheral bus (PCI, ISA, etc.), but slower than the backside bus.

frontware

See *screen scraper.*

FSK

(Frequency Shift Keying) A simple modulation technique that merges binary data into a carrier. It creates only two changes in frequency: one for 0, another for 1.

FSR

(Free System Resource) In Windows, the amount of unused memory in a 64K block (128K for Version 3.1) reserved for managing current applications. Every open window takes some space in this area.

FT-1, FT1

See *fractional T1*.

FTAM

(File Transfer Access and Management) A communications protocol for the transfer of files between systems of different vendors.

FTP

(File Transfer Program & File Transfer Protocol) A set of TCP/IP commands used to log onto a network, list directories and copy files. It can also translate between ASCII and EBCDIC. See *TFTP*.

FUD factor

(Fear Uncertainty Doubt factor) A marketing strategy used by a dominant or privileged organization that restrains competition by not revealing future plans.

full backup

Backing up all files. See *differential backup* and *incremental backup*.

full-duplex

Transmitting and receiving simultaneously. In pure digital networks, this is achieved with two pairs of wires. In analog networks or in digital networks using carriers, it is achieved by dividing the bandwidth of the line into two frequencies, one for sending, one for receiving.

full-duplex Ethernet

See *FDSE*.

full featured

Hardware or software that provides capabilities and functions comparable to the most advanced models or programs of that category.

full-motion video

Video transmission that changes the image 30 frames per second (30 fps). Motion pictures are run at 24 fps. Contrast with *freeze-frame video*.

full path

A path name that includes the drive (if required), starting or root directory, all attached subdirectories and ending with the file or object name. Contrast with *relative path*. See *path*.

full project life cycle

A project from inception to completion.

full-screen mode

Programming capability that allows data to be displayed in any row or column on screen. Contrast with *teletype mode*.

fully populated

A circuit board whose sockets are completely filled with chips.

function

In programming, a self-contained software routine that peforms a job for the program it is written in or for some other program. The function performs the operation and returns control to the instruction following the calling instruction or to the calling program. Programming languages provide a set of standard functions and may allow programmers to define others. For example, the C language is built entirely of functions.

functional decomposition
Breaking down a process into non-redundant operations.

functional specification
The blueprint for the design of an information system. It provides documentation for the database, human and machine procedures, and all the input, processing and output detail for each data entry, query, update and report program in the system.

function call
A request by a program to use a function within the program itself or within another program. The request is made by stating the name of the function followed by any values (parameters, arguments) that may have to be passed to it. Values which are results from the operation performed by the function may be returned back to the calling program.

The function may be written within the program, be part of an external library that is combined with the program when it is compiled or be contained in another program, such as the operating system or DBMS.

function keys
A set of keyboard keys used to command the computer (F1, F2, etc.). F1 is often the help key, but the purpose of any function key is determined by the software currently running.

function library
A collection of program routines. See *function*.

function overloading
In programming, using the same name for two or more functions. The compiler determines which function to use based on the type of function, arguments passed to it and type of values returned.

function prototyping
In programming, formally defining each function in the program with the number and types of parameters passed to it and its return values. The compiler can then flag calls to functions if they do not conform to the prototype.

fuse
(1) A protective device that is designed to melt, or blow, when a specified amount of current is passed through it. PROM chips are created as a series of fuses that are selectively blown in order to create the binary patterns in the chip.

(2) To bond together.

Futurebus+
An IEEE standard multisegment bus that can transfer data at 32, 64, 128 and 256-bits and can address up to 64 bits. Clock speeds range from 25 to 100MHz. At 100MHz and 256 bits, it transfers 3.2 Gbytes/sec.

fuzzy computer
A specially-designed computer that employs fuzzy logic. Using such architectural components as analog circuits and parallel processing, fuzzy computers are designed for AI applications.

fuzzy logic
A mathematical technique for dealing with imprecise data and problems that have many solutions rather than one. Although it is implemented in digital computers which ultimately make only yes-no decisions, fuzzy logic works with ranges of values, solving problems in a way that more resembles human logic.

fuzzy search
An inexact search for data that finds answers that come close to the desired data. It can get results when the exact spelling is not known or help users obtain information that is loosely related to a topic.

G

G

See *giga*.

G3

(1) The third generation of IBM's CMOS-based mainframes (Parallel Enterprise Servers). There were no G1 or G2 designations.

(2) A series of Macintosh desktop machines and PowerBook portables from Apple that use the PowerPC 750 chip. Models were introduced in 1997, running at 233MHz and 266MHz.

G4

(1) The fourth generation of IBM's CMOS-based mainframes (Parallel Enterprise Servers). There were no G1 or G2 designations.

(2) A series of Macintosh desktop machines and PowerBook portables from Apple that use the PowerPC G4 chip. Introduced in 1999, G4 models are the successor to the Macintosh G3 series. The G4 chips include the "Velocity Engine," a vector processor that provides sustained floating point capability up to one gigaflops. See *G3*.

G5

The fifth generation of IBM's CMOS-based mainframes (Parallel Enterprise Servers). Introduced in 1998, G5 doubles the performance of G4 servers, debuts the FICON channel (based on Fibre Channel) and adds hardware-based Triple DES cryptography and numerous internal improvements. Memory was increased to 24GB.

G.7 standards

ITU standards for speech codecs that provides high quality audio at a variety of data rates.

Standard	Method	Kbps
G.711	PCM	64
G.721	ADPCM	32
G.722	ADPCM	64
G.723	ADPCM	20, 40
G.723.1	LD-CELP	5.3, 6.4
G.726	ADPCM	16, 24, 32, 40
G.727	ADPCM	16, 24, 32, 40
G.728	LD-CELP	16
G.729	CELP	8

gain

The amount of increase that an amplifier provides on the output side of the circuit.

GAL

(Generic Array Logic) A programmable logic chip (PLD) technology from Lattice Semiconductor.

gallium arsenide

An alloy of gallium and arsenic compound (GaAs) that is used as the base material for chips. It is several times faster than silicon.

game port

An I/O connector used to attach a joy stick. It is typically a 15-pin socket on the back of a PC. See *serial port*.

gamma correction

An adjustment to the light intensity of a scanner, monitor or printer. It generally refers to the adjustment of the brightness of a display screen in order to compensate for a CRT's irregularity.

gang punch

To punch an identical set of holes into a deck of punched cards.

Gantt chart

A form of floating bar chart usually used in project management to show resources or tasks over time.

gap

(1) The space between blocks of data on magnetic tape.

(2) The space in a read/write head over which magnetic flux (energy) flows causing the underlying magnetic tape or disk surface to become magnetized in the corresponding direction.

gapless

A magnetic tape that is recorded in a continuous stream without interblock gaps.

garbage collection

A routine that searches memory for program segments or data that are no longer active in order to reclaim that space.

gas plasma

See *plasma display*.

gate

(1) An open/closed switch.

(2) A pattern of transistors that makes up an AND, OR or NOT Boolean logic gate. See *gate array*.

(3) In a MOS transistor, the line that triggers the switch.

gate array

A type of chip that contains unconnected logic elements. The finished, customized chip is obtained by adhering the top metal layer of pathways between the elements. This final masking stage is less costly than designing the chip from scratch.

It usually contains only two-input NAND gates, which can be used singularly or connected with other NAND gates to provide all the Boolean operations required for digital logic.

gated

Switched "on" or capable of being switched on and off.

gateway

A computer that performs protocol conversion between different types of networks or applications. For example, a gateway can connect a personal computer LAN to a mainframe network. An electronic mail, or messaging, gateway converts messages between two different messaging protocols. See *bridge*.

Gateway 2000

(Gateway 2000, N. Sioux City, SD, www.gw2k.com) A major PC manufacturer founded in 1985 by Ted Waitt and Mike Hammond. Gateway first sold peripherals to owners of Texas Instrument computers. In 1987, it began to offer complete systems and has continued to drive down the cost of quality PCs by mail. In 1997, it acquired ALR (Advanced Logic Research), a PC company founded in 1984 and noted for its high-end machines.

gauss

A unit of measurement of magnetic energy.

Gaussian distribution

A random distribution of events that is often graphed as a bell-shaped curve. It is used to represent a normal or statistically probable outcome.

Gaussian noise

In communications, a random interference generated by the movement of electricity in the line. Also called "white noise."

Gb, GB

(GigaBit, GigaByte) See *giga* and *space/time*.

Gbps, Gbits/sec

(GigaBits Per Second) Billion bits per second. See *giga* and *space/time*.

GBps, GBytes/sec

(GigaBytes Per Second) Billion bytes per second. See *giga* and *space/time*.

The Computer Glossary

GCR

(1) (Group Code Recording) An encoding method used on magnetic tapes and Apple II and Mac 400K and 800K floppy disks.

(2) (Gray Component Replacement) A method for reducing amount of printing ink used. It substitutes black for the amount of gray contained in a color, thus black ink is used instead of the three CMY inks. See *UCR* and *dot gain*.

GDDM

(Graphical Data Display Manager) Software that generates graphics images in the IBM mainframe environment. It contains routines to generate graphics on terminals, printers and plotters as well as accepting input from scanners. Programmers use it for creating graphics, but users can employ its Interactive Chart Utility (ICU) to create business graphics without programming.

GDI

(Graphics Device Interface) The graphics display system in Microsoft Windows. When an application needs to display or print, it makes a call to a GDI function and sends it the parameters for the object that must be created. GDI in turn "draws" the object by sending commands to the screen and printer drivers, which actually render the images.

geek

See *nerd*.

gender changer

A coupler that reverses the gender of one of the connectors in order that two male connectors or two female connectors can be joined together.

generalized program

Software that serves a changing environment. By allowing variable data to be introduced, the program can solve the same problem for different users or situations. For example, the electronic versions of this Glossary could be programmed to read in a different title and thus be used for any type of dictionary.

General MIDI

A standard set of 128 sounds for MIDI sound cards and devices (synthesizers, sound modules, etc.). By assigning instruments to specific MIDI patch locations, General MIDI provides a standard way of communicating MIDI sound.

MIDI's small storage requirement makes it very desirable as a musical sound source for multimedia applications compared to digitizing actual music. For example, a three-minute MIDI file may take only 20 to 30K, whereas a WAV file (digital audio) could consume up to several megabytes depending on sound quality.

general-purpose computer

Refers to computers that follow instructions, thus virtually all computers from micro to mainframe are general purpose. Even computers in toys, games and single-function devices follow instructions in their built-in program. In contrast, computational devices can be designed from scratch for special purposes (see *ASIC*).

general-purpose controller

A peripheral control unit that can service more than one type of peripheral device; for example, a printer and a communications line.

general-purpose language

A programming language used to solve a wide variety of problems. All common programming languages (FORTRAN, COBOL, BASIC, C, Pascal, etc.) are examples. Contrast with *special-purpose language*.

generator

(1) Software that creates software. See *application generator*.

(2) A device that creates electrical power or synchonization signals.

genlock

(generator **lock**) Circuitry that synchronizes video signals for mixing. In personal computers, a genlock display adapter converts screen output into an NTSC video signal, which it synchronizes with an external video source.

geometry calculations

In 3-D graphics rendering, the transformation from 3-D world coordinates into screen coordinates, the clipping of non-visible parts and lighting.

geostationary, geosynchronous (GEO)

Earth aligned. Refers to communications satellites that are placed 22,282 miles above the equator and travel at the same speed as the earth's rotation, thus appearing stationary.

germanium

The material used in making the first transistors. Although still used in very limited applications, germanium was replaced by silicon years ago.

gesture recognition

The ability to interpret simple hand-written symbols such as check marks and slashes.

Gflops

See *gigaflops*.

ghost

(1) A faint second image that appears close to the primary image on a display or printout. In transmission, it is a result of secondary signals that arrive ahead of or later than the primary signal. On a printout, it is caused by bouncing print elements as the paper passes by.

(2) To display a menu option in a dimmed, fuzzy typeface, indicating it is not selectable at this time.

GHz

(GigaHertZ) One billion cycles per second.

GIF

(Graphics Interchange Format) A popular raster graphics file format developed by CompuServe. It supports 8-bit color (256 colors) and is widely used on the Web, because the files compress well. GIFs include a color table that includes the most representative 256 colors used. Animated GIFs allow a sequence of frames to be repeated. Interlaced GIFs are stored in multiple passes and come into focus in stages as they are being displayed.

giga, gigabit, gigabyte

Billion, billion bits, billion bytes. Also Gb, Gbit and G-bit, or GB, Gbyte and G-byte. See *space/time*.

Gigabit Ethernet

See *Ethernet*.

gigaflops

(GIGA FLoating point OPerations per Second) One billion floating point operations per second.

GIGO

(Garbage In Garbage Out) "Bad input produces bad output." Data entry is critical. All possible tests should be made on data entered into a computer. GIGO also means "Garbage In, Gospel Out."

GIS

(1) (Geographic Information System) A digital mapping system used for exploration, demographics, dispatching and tracking.

(2) (Generalized Information System) An early IBM mainframe query and data manipulation language.

GKS

(Graphical Kernel System) A device-independent graphics language for 2-D, 3-D and raster graphics images. It allows graphics applications to be developed on one system and easily moved to another with minimal or no change. It was the first true standard for graphics applications programmers and has been adopted by both ANSI and ISO.

glare filter
A fine mesh screen that is placed over a CRT screen to reduce glare from overhead and ambient light.

glass house
The large datacenter, which typically contains one or more mainframes and is often constructed with windows to the inside. Glass houses may contain raised floors for underground wiring and are generally very well air conditioned.

glitch
A temporary or random hardware malfunction. It's possible that a bug (permanent error) in a program may cause the hardware to appear as if it had a glitch in it and vice versa. At times it can be extremely difficult to determine whether a problem lies within the hardware or the software.

global
Pertaining to an entire file, database, volume, program or system.

global variable
In programming, a variable that is used by all modules in a program.

glue chip
A support chip that adds functionality to a microprocessor, for example, an I/O processor or extra memory.

GNU
(Gnu's Not UNIX) A project sponsored by the Free Software Foundation that is developing a complete software environment including operating system kernel and utilities, editor, compiler and debugger. Many consultants and organizations provide support for GNU software. See *Linux*.

goal seeking
The ability to calculate a formula backward to obtain a desired input. For example, given the goal **gross margin** = 50% as well as the range of possible inputs, goal seeking attempts to obtain the optimum input.

GOCA
(Graphics Object Content Architecture) See *MO:DCA*.

gooey
See *GUI*.

Gopher
A program that searches for file names and resources on the Internet and presents hierarchical menus to the user. As users select options, they are moved to different Gopher servers on the Internet. Where links have been established, USENET news and other information can be read directly from Gopher. See *Veronica, Archie* and *WAIS*.

GOSIP
(Government Open Systems Interconnection Profile) A U.S. government mandate for compliance with OSI standards after 1990. Since broad adoption of OSI never came to fruition, GOSIP evolved into POSIT (Profiles for Open Systems Internetworking Technologies), which is a set of non-mandatory standards that acknowledge the widespread use of TCP/IP.

GOTO
In a high-level programming language, a statement that directs the computer to go to some other part of the program. Low-level language equivalents are "branch" and "jump."

GOTO-less programming
Writing a program without using GOTO instructions, an important rule in structured programming. A GOTO instruction points to a different part of the program without a guarantee of returning. Instead

of using GOTOs, structures called "subroutines" or "functions" are used, which automatically return to the next instruction after the calling instruction when completed.

Gouraud shading

In computer graphics, a technique developed by Henri Gouraud that computes a shaded surface based on the color and illumination at the corners of polygonal facets.

GPCmark

See *PLB*.

GPF

(General Protection Fault) The name of an abend, or crash, in a Windows application, starting with Version 3.1. When the GPF occurs, an error message is displayed, and the program is generally unable to continue. See *abend*.

GPIB

(General Purpose Interface Bus) An IEEE 488 standard parallel interface used for attaching sensors and programmable instruments to a computer. It uses a 24-pin connector. HP's version is the HPIB.

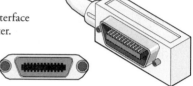

GPIB

GPS

(Global Positioning System) A system for identifying earth locations. By triangulation from three satellites, a hand-held receiving unit can pinpoint where you are on the planet.

GPRS

(General Packet Radio Service) An enhancement to the GSM mobile communications system that supports data packets. GPRS enables continous flows of IP data packets over the system for such applications as Web browsing and file transfer.

GPSS

(General Purpose Simulation System) A programming language for discrete event simulation, which is used to build models of operations such as manufacturing environments, communications systems and traffic patterns. Originally developed by IBM for mainframes, PC versions are available, such as GPSS/PC by Minuteman Software and GPSS/H by Wolverine Software.

grabber hand

A pointer in the shape of a hand that is moved by a mouse to "grab" and relocate objects on screen.

graceful degradation

A system that continues to perform at some reduced level of performance after one of its components fails.

graceful exit

The ability to get out of a problem situation in a program without having to turn the computer off.

grade

The transmission capacity of a line. It refers to a range or class of frequencies that it can handle; for example, telegraph grade, voice grade and broadband.

gradient

A color spread from light to dark to shade an object or give it a sense of depth. It is also used to create a colorful background.

grammar checker

Software that checks the grammar of a sentence. It can check for and highlight incomplete sentences, awkward phrases, wordiness and poor grammar.

grandfather, father, son

A method for storing previous generations of master file data that are continuously updated. The son is the current file, the father is a copy of the file from the previous cycle, and the grandfather is a copy of the file from the cycle before that one.

granularity

The degree of modularity of a system. The more granularity (grains or granules), the more customizable or flexible the system.

graph

A pictorial representation of information. See *business graphics*.

graphical interface

See *GUI*.

graphics

Usually called "computer graphics," it is the creation and management of picture images in the computer. It is defined as "graphics" in this Glossary to keep it next to other "graphics" entries.

A graphics computer system requires a graphics display screen, a graphics input device (tablet, mouse, scanner, camera, etc.), a graphics output device (dot matrix printer, laser printer, plotter, etc.) and a graphics software package; for example, a CAD, drawing or paint program.

Vector Graphics and Raster Graphics

Two methods are used for storing and maintaining pictures in a computer. The first method, called "vector graphics" (also known as object-oriented graphics), maintains the image as a series of points, lines, arcs and other geometric shapes. This method is used for CAD and technical illustrations where the components of a drawing must be separable and individually scalable.

The second method, called "raster graphics" or "bitmapped graphics," resembles television, where the picture image is made up of dots. This method is used when pictures are scanned or photographed into the computer. It is also the format used by paint programs that turn the screen into an electronic canvas.

graphics accelerator

A high-performance display adapter that provides hardware functions for 2-D, 3-D or video operation or all three. When functions are built into the chips on the display adapter, there is less work for the host CPU to do to render the images on screen.

graphics adapter, graphics card

Same as *display adapter*.

graphics based

The display of text and pictures as graphics images; typically bitmapped images. Contrast with *text based*.

graphics coprocessor

Graphics hardware that performs various 2-D and 3-D geometry and rendering functions, offloading the main CPU from performing such tasks. This typically refers to a very high-end graphics subsystem, but may also refer to a graphics accelerator. See *graphics accelerator* and *geometry calculations*.

graphics engine

(1) Hardware that performs graphics processing tasks independently of the computer's CPU. See *graphics accelerator* and *graphics coprocessor*.

(2) Software that accepts commands from an application and builds images and text that are directed to the graphics driver and hardware. Macintosh's QuickDraw and Windows' GDI are examples.

graphics file

A file that contains only graphics data. Contrast with *text file* and *binary file*.

graphics format

The file format used to store a picture as vector graphics or raster graphics. There are more than 100 graphics formats in use worldwide.

graphics interface

See *graphics language* and *GUI*.

graphics language

A high-level language used to create graphics images. The language is translated into images by software or specialized hardware. See *graphics engine*.

graphics mode

A screen display mode that displays graphics. Contrast with *text mode* and *character mode*.

graphics port

(1) A socket on the computer for connecting a graphics monitor.

(2) A Macintosh graphics structure that defines all the characteristics of a graphics window (also called "GrafPort").

graphics primitive

An elementary graphics building block, such as a point, line or arc. In a solid modeling system, a cylinder, cube and sphere are examples of primitives.

graphics processor

Same as *graphics engine*.

graphics tablet

See *digitizer tablet*.

graphics terminal

(1) An I/O device that displays pictures in raster graphics, vector graphics format or both. Images are received via communications or entered with a mouse or light pen. The keyboard may have specialized function keys, wheels or dials.

(2) A terminal or personal computer that displays graphics.

gray scale

A series of shades from white to black. The more shades, or levels, the more realistic an image can be recorded and displayed, especially a scanned photo. Scanners differentiate typically from 16 to 256 gray levels.

Although compression techiques help reduce the size of graphics files, high-resolution gray scale requires huge amounts of storage. At a printer resolution of 300 dpi, each square inch is made up of 90,000 pixels. At 256 levels, it takes one byte per pixel, or 90,000 bytes per square inch of image. See *halftone*.

greek

To display text in a representative form in which the actual letters are not discernible, because the screen resolution isn't high enough to display them properly. Desktop publishing programs let you set which font sizes should be greeked.

green PC

An energy-saving computer or peripheral device. Green computers, printers and monitors go into a low-voltage "suspend mode" if not used after a certain period of time.

grep

(Global Regular Expression and Print) A UNIX pattern matching utility that searches for a string of text and outputs any line that contains the pattern.

ground

An electrically conductive body, such as the earth, which maintains a zero potential (not positively or negatively charged) for connecting to an electrical circuit.

ground current

The current found in a ground line. It may be caused by imbalanced electrical sources; for example, the ground line in a communications channel between two computers deriving power separately.

ground fault

The temporary current in the ground line, caused by a failing electrical component or interference from an external electrical source such as a thunderstorm.

ground loop

An unwanted ground current flowing back and forth between two devices that are grounded at two or more points.

ground noise injection

An intentional insertion of unwanted noise by a power supply into the ground line.

groupware

Software designed to support multiple users that work on related tasks. Groupware is an evolving concept that is more than just multiuser software which allows access to the same data. Groupware provides a mechanism that helps users coordinate and keep track of on-going projects together.

The heart of groupware is a messaging system, because e-mail is used to notify team members, obtain responses and send alerts. Lotus Notes is often considered the father of groupware, because it was the first to popularize a multifunction groupware system and development environment.

GSM

(Global System for Mobile Communications) A digital cellular phone system based on TDMA that is widely deployed in Europe and throughout the world. It is increasingly being used in the U.S. in the PCS band.

guard band

A frequency that insulates one signal from another. In an analog telephone line, the low band is 0-300; the high band is 3300-4000Hz.

GUI

(Graphical User Interface) A graphics-based user interface that incorporates icons, pull-down menus and a mouse. Macintosh, Windows and Motif are examples. See *desktop manager* and *window manager*. Contrast with *CUI*.

GUI accelerator

See *graphics accelerator*.

GVPN

(Global Virtual Private Network) A service from cooperating carriers that provides international digital communications for multinational companies.

GW-BASIC

(Gee Whiz-BASIC) A BASIC interpreter that accompanied MS-DOS in versions prior to 5.0. See *QBasic*.

H

h

(Hexadecimal) A symbol that refers to a hex number. For example, 09h has a numeric value of 9, whereas 0Ah has a value of 10. See *hex*.

H.245

An ITU standard protocol for making an audio and videoconferencing call. It defines flow control, encryption and jitter management as well as the signals for initiating the call, negotiating which features are to be used and terminating the call.

H.261

An ITU standard for compressing an H.320 videoconferencing transmission. The algorithm can be implemented in hardware or software and uses intraframe and interframe compression. It uses one or more 64 Kbps ISDN channels (Px64). H.261 supports CIF and QCIF resolutions. See *CIF*.

H.262

An ITU standard for compressing a videoconferencing transmission. It uses the MPEG-2 compression algorithm.

H.263

An ITU standard for compressing a videoconferencing transmission. It is based on H.261 with enhancements that improve video quality over modems. H.263 supports CIF, QCIF, SQCIF, 4CIF and 16CIF resolutions. See *CIF*.

H.310

An ITU standard for videoconferencing over ATM and Broadband ISDN networks using MPEG compression.

H.320

An ITU standard for videoconferencing over digital lines. Using the H.261 compression method, it allows H.320-compliant videoconferencing room and desktop systems to communicate with each other over ISDN, switched digital and leased lines. A counterpart standard for data conferencing is T.120.

H.321

An ITU standard for videoconferencing over ATM and Broadband ISDN networks.

H.322

An ITU standard for videoconferencing over local area networks (LANs) that can guarantee bandwidth, such as Isochronous Ethernet.

H.323

An ITU standard for videoconferencing over packet-switched networks such as local area networks (LANs) and the Internet. H.323 is expected to be widely supported for Internet telephony.

H.324

An ITU standard for videoconferencing over analog telephone lines (POTS) using modems.

H5

Refers to models of IBM's water-cooled mainframes that use the bipolar chip technology.

hack

Program source code. For example, you might hear a phrase like "nobody has a package to do that, so it must be done through some sort of hack." This means someone has to write programming code to solve the problem, because there is no pre-written routine or program that does it. The purist would say that a hack is writing in languages such as assembly language and C, which are low level and highly detailed. The more liberal hacker would say that writing any programming language counts as hacking.

hacker

A person who writes programs in assembly language or in system-level languages, such as C. Although it may refer to any programmer, it implies very tedious "hacking away" at the bits and bytes. The term has become widely used for people that gain illegal entrance into a computer system. This use of the term is not appreciated by the vast majority of honest hackers. See *hack* and *computer cracker*.

half-duplex

The transmission of data in both directions, but only one direction at a time. Two-way radio was the first to use half-duplex, for example, while one party spoke, the other party listened. Contrast with *full-duplex*.

half height drive

A 5.25" disk drive that takes up half the vertical space of first-generation drives. It is 1 5/8" high by 5.75" wide.

halftone

In printing, the simulation of a continuous-tone image (shaded drawing, photograph) with dots. In photographically-generated halftones, a camera shoots the image through a halftone screen, creating smaller dots for lighter areas and larger dots for darker areas. Digitally-composed printing prints only one size of dot.

In order to simulate varying-size halftone dots in computer printers, dithering is used, which creates clusters of dots in a "halftone cell." The more dots printed in the cell, the darker the gray. As the screen frequency gets higher (more lines per inch), there is less room for dots in the cell, reducing the number of gray levels that can be generated.

In low-resolution printers, there is always a compromise between printer resolution (dpi) and screen frequency (lpi). For example, in a 300 dpi printer, the 8x8 halftone cell required to create 64 grays results in a very coarse 38 lines per inch (300 / 8). However, a high-resolution, 2400 dpi imagesetter can easily handle 256 shades at 150 lpi (2400 / 16).

Hamming code

A communications error correction method that intersperses three check bits at the end of each four data bits. At the receiving station, the check bits are used to detect and correct one-bit errors automatically.

handle

(1) In computer graphics, a tiny, square block on an image that can be grabbed for reshaping.

(2) A temporary name or number assigned to a file, font or other object. For example, an operating system may assign a sequential number to each file that it opens as a way of identifying it.

(3) A nickname used when conferencing like a "CB handle" used by a truck driver.

handler

A software routine that performs a particular task. For example, upon detection of an error, an error handler is called to recover from the error condition.

handoff

Switching a cellular phone transmission from one cell to another as a mobile user moves into a new cellular area. The switch takes place in about a quarter of a second so that the caller is generally unaware of it.

handset

The part of the telephone that contains the speaker and the microphone.

handshaking

Signals transmitted back and forth over a communications network that establish a valid connection between two stations.

hang

To freeze or lock up. When the computer hangs, there is generally no indication of what is causing the problem. The computer could have crashed, or it could be something simple such as no paper in the printer. When a computer crashes however, an error message usually reports the situation.

haptic interface

Communicating with the computer via some tactile method. Haptic devices sense some form of finger, hand, head or body movement.

hard boot

Same as *cold boot*.

hard coded

Software that performs a fixed number of tasks or works with only a fixed number of devices. For example, a program could be written to work with only two types of printers and not allow any other types to be introduced. Hard coded solutions to problems are usually the fastest, but do not allow for future flexibility.

hard copy

Printed output. Contrast with *soft copy*.

hard disk

The primary computer storage medium, which is made of one or more aluminum or glass platters, coated with a ferromagnetic material. Most hard disks are fixed disks, which are permanently sealed in the drive. Removable cartridge disks are gaining in popularity and are increasingly available in more varieties (see *Syquest disk* and *Jaz disk*).

Most desktop hard disks are either IDE or SCSI. The advantage of SCSI is that up to seven or more devices can be attached to the same controller board. Hard disks provide fast retrieval because they rotate constantly at high speed, from 3,000 to 10,000 rpm. They can be turned off at intervals to preserve battery life in laptops.

hard error

(1) A permanent, unrecoverable error such as a disk read error. Contrast with *soft error*.

(2) A group of errors that requires user intervention and includes disk read errors, disk not ready (no disk in drive) and printer not ready (out of paper).

hard hyphen

A hyphen that always prints. Contrast with *soft hyphen*.

hard return

A code inserted into a text document by pressing the enter key. If the hard return does not display as a symbol on screen, it can usually be revealed along with other layout codes in an expanded mode. DOS, Windows and OS/2 insert a CR/LF combo: Carriage Return and Line Feed. Mac uses only a CR, and UNIX only an LF. Contrast with *soft return*.

hard sectored

A sector identification technique that uses a physical mark. For example, hard sectored floppy disks have a hole in the disk that marks the beginning of each sector. Contrast with *soft sectored*.

hard space

A special space character that acts like a letter or digit, used to prevent multiple-word, proper names from breaking between lines.

hardware

Machinery and equipment (CPU, disks, tapes, modem, cables, etc.). In operation, a computer is both hardware and software. One is useless without the other. The hardware design specifies the commands it can follow, and the instructions tell it what to do. See *instruction set*.

Hardware Is "Storage and Transmission"

The more memory and disk storage a computer has, the more work it can do. The faster the memory and disks transmit data and instructions to the CPU, the faster it gets done. A hardware requirement is based on the size of the databases that will be created and the number of users or applications that will be served at the same time. How much? How fast?

Software Is "Logic and Language"

Software deals with the details of an ever-changing business and must process transactions in a logical fashion. Languages are used to program the software. The "logic and language" involved in analysis and programming is generally far more complicated than specifying a storage and transmission requirement.

hardware failure

A malfunction within the electronic circuits or electromechanical components (disks, tapes) of a computer system. Contrast with *software failure*.

hardware interrupt

An interrupt caused by some action of a hardware device, such as the depression of a key or mouse movement. See *interrupt*.

hardware key

A copy protection device supplied with software that plugs into a computer port. The software interrogates the key's serial number during execution to verify its presence. The hardware key acts as a pass-through, but tests for a special code that reads the serial number.

hardware monitor

A device attached to the hardware circuits of a computer that reads electronic signals directly in order to analyze system performance.

pass-through

Hardware Key

hardwired

(1) Electronic circuitry that is designed to perform a specific task. See *hard coded*.

(2) Devices that are closely or tightly coupled. For example, a hardwired terminal is directly connected to a computer without going through a switched network.

harmonic distortion

In communications, frequencies that are generated as multiples of the original frequency due to irregularities in the transmission line.

hash total, hash value

A method for ensuring the accuracy of processed data. It is a total of several fields of data in a file, including fields not normally used in calculations, such as account number. At various stages in the processing, the hash total is recalculated and compared with the original. If any data has been lost or changed, a mismatch signals an error.

HASP

(Houston Automatic Spooling Program) A mainframe spooling program that provides task, job and data management functions.

Hayes compatible

Refers to modems controlled by the Hayes command language. Hayes Microcomputer pioneered the personal computer modem market, but closed its doors in the late 1990s. See *AT command set*.

HD, HDD

See *hard disk*.

HDA

(Head Disk Assembly) The mechanical components of a disk drive (minus the electronics), which includes the actuators, access arms, read/write heads and platters.

HDL

(Hardware Description Language) A language used to describe the functions of an electronic circuit for documentation, simulation or logic synthesis (or all three). Although many proprietary HDLs have been developed, Verilog and VHDL are the major standards. See *Verilog*

HDLC

(High-level Data Link Control) An ISO communications protocol used in X.25 packet switching networks. It provides error correction at the data link layer. SDLC, LAP and LAPB are subsets of HDLC.

HDML

(Handheld Device Markup Language) A specialized version of HTML designed to enable wireless pagers, cellphones and other handheld devices to obtain information from Web pages. It is a subset of WAP with some features that were not included in WAP.

HDR

(High Data Rate) A wireless data technology from QUALCOMM that provides up to a 2.4 Mbps data rate in a standard 1.25MHz CMDA voice channel. HDR can be used to enhance data capabilities in existing cdmaOne networks or in stand-alone data networks.

HDTV

(High Definition TV) A high-resolution TV standard. Japan was the first to develop HDTV and currently broadcasts an 1125-line analog signal picked up on 36" to 50" TV sets that cost about $10,000. Both Japan and Europe's HDTV use traditional analog TV signalling. In 1996, the FCC approved the DTV standard for the U.S., which offers a variety of higher-quality, all-digital signals for TV transmission.

head crash

The physical destruction of a hard disk. Misalignment or contamination with dust can cause the read/write head to collide with the disk's recording surface. The data is destroyed, and both the disk platter and head have to be replaced.

The read/write head touches the surface of a floppy disk, but on a hard disk, it hovers above its surface at a distance that is less than the diameter of a human hair. It has been said that the read/write head flying over the disk surface is like trying to fly a jet plane six inches above the earth's surface.

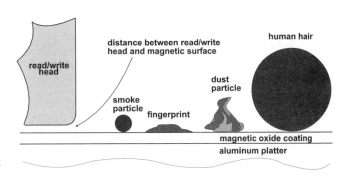

head end

The originating point in a communications system. In cable TV, the head end is where the cable company has its satellite dish and TV antenna for receiving incoming programming. In online services, the head end is the service company's computer system and databases.

header

(1) In data processing, the first record in a file, used for identification. File name, date of last update and other status data are stored in it.

(2) In a document or report, common text printed at the top of every page.

(3) In communications, the first part of the message, which contains controlling data, such as originating and destination stations, message type and priority level.

(4) Any caption or description used as a headline.

header label

A record used for file identification that is recorded at the beginning of the file.

head-per-track disk

A disk drive that has a read/write head positioned over each track, thus eliminating the access arm movement from track to track.

heap

In programming, the free memory currently available to load and run programs.

heat sink

A material that absorbs heat.

helical scan

The diagonal tracking used on videotape and various tape backup systems, (DAT, AIT, DTF, DST, etc.), which increases storage capacity over parallel tracking methods.

help

On-screen instruction regarding the use of a program. On PCs, pressing F1 is the de facto standard for getting help. With graphics-based interfaces (Mac, Windows, etc.), clicking a "?" or HELP button gets help. See *context sensitive help*.

help compiler

Software that translates text and compiler instructions into an online help system.

helper application
An application that adds additional capabilities to the program that is running. See *plug-in*.

Hertz
The frequency of electrical vibrations (cycles) per second. Abbreviated "Hz," one Hz is equal to one cycle per second. In 1883, Heinrich Hertz detected electromagnetic waves.

heterogeneous environment
Equipment from a variety of manufacturers.

heuristic
A method of problem solving using exploration and trial and error methods. Heuristic program design provides a framework for solving the problem in contrast with a fixed set of rules (algorithmic) that cannot vary.

Hewlett-Packard
See *HP*.

hex, hexadecimal
Hexadecimal means 16. The base 16 numbering system is used as a shorthand for representing binary numbers. Every four bits are assigned a hex digit (from 0 to 9 and then A to F).

HFS
(Hierarchical File System) The Macintosh file system that allows files to be placed into folders, and folders to be placed within other folders.

hidden file
A file classification that prevents a file from being accessed. It is usually an operating system file; however, utility programs let users hide files to prevent unauthorized access.

hierarchical
A structure made up of different levels like a company organization chart. The higher levels have control or precedence over the lower levels. Hierarchical structures are a one to many relationship; each item having one or more items below it.

In communications, a hierarchical network refers to a single computer that has control over all the nodes connected to it.

hierarchical communications
A network controlled by a host computer that is responsible for managing all connections. Contrast with *peer-to-peer communications*.

hierarchical file system
A file organization method that stores data in a top-to-bottom organization structure. All access to the data starts at the top and proceeds throughout the levels of the hierarchy.

In DOS and OS/2, the root directory is the starting point. Files can be stored in the root directory, or directories can be created off the root that hold files and subdirectories.

In the Macintosh, the disk window is the starting point. Files can be stored in the disk window, or folders can be created that can hold files and additional folders.

high color
The ability to generate 32,768 colors (15 bits) or 65,536 colors (16-bit). 15-bit color uses five bits for each red, green and blue pixel. The 16th bit may be a color, such as XGA with 5-red, 6-green and 5-blue, or be an overlay bit that selects pixels to display over video input. See *true color*.

high-level format
A set of indexes on the disk that the operating system uses to keep track of the data stored on the disk. See *format program*.

high-level language
A machine-independent programming language, such as FORTRAN, COBOL, BASIC, Pascal and C. It lets the programmer concentrate on the logic of the problem to be solved rather than the intricacies of

the machine architecture such as is required with low-level assembly languages.

There are dramatic differences between high-level languages. Look at the sample code in this Glossary under C, BASIC and COBOL as an example. What is considered high level depends on the era. There were assembly languages thirty years ago that were easier to understand than C.

highlight

To identify an area on screen in order to select, move, delete or change it in some manner.

highlight bar

The currently-highlighted menu item. Choice is made by moving the bar to the desired item and pressing enter or clicking the mouse. The bar is a different color on color screens or reverse video on monochrome screens.

high memory

(1) The uppermost end of memory.

(2) In PCs, the area between 640K and 1M, or the 64K high memory area (HMA) between 1024 and 1088K.

high resolution

A high-quality image on a display screen or printed form. The more dots used per square inch, the higher the quality. To display totally realistic images including the shades of human skin requires about 1,000x1,000 pixels on a 12" diagonal screen. Desktop laser printers print respectable text and graphics at 300 and 600 dpi, but typesetting machines print 1,270 and 2,540 dpi.

high tech

Refers to the latest advancements in computers and electronics as well as to the social and political environment and consequences created by such machines.

HIMEM.SYS

An extended memory manager that is included with DOS and Windows, starting with DOS 5 and Windows 3.0. It allows programs to cooperatively allocate extended memory in 286 and higher PCs. HIMEM.SYS is an XMS driver.

hints

Font instructions that alter space and other features to improve the typeface image at low resolutions. Hints help to make a character uniform and legible especially at small point sizes; for example, they ensure that serifs and accents appear in proper proportion. Hints will have less meaning for printing as common desktop resolutions approach 600 and 800 dpi and more, but rendering typefaces on screens, which have less resolution than printers, will still be valuable.

HIPERLAN

A wireless LAN protocol developed by ETSI that provides a 23.5 Mbps data rate in the 5GHz band. It is similar to Ethernet, but unlike 802.11a, the wireless Ethernet standard at the same rate, HIPERLAN/ 1 provides quality of service (QoS), which lets critical traffic be prioritized. Other

HiPPI

(HIgh Performance Parallel Interface channel) An ANSI-standard high-speed communications channel that uses a 32-bit or 64-bit cable and transmits at 100 or 200 Mbytes/sec. It is used as a point-to-point supercomputer channel or, with a crosspoint switch, as a high-speed LAN.

histogram

A chart displaying horizontal or vertical bars. The length of the bars are in proportion to the values of the data items they represent.

history

A user's input and keystrokes entered within the current session. A history feature keeps track of user commands and/or retrieved items so that they can be quickly reused or reviewed.

HLLAPI

(High Level Language Application Program Interface) An IBM programming interface that allows a PC application to communicate with a mainframe application. The hardware hookup is handled via normal micro to mainframe 3270 emulation. An extended version of the interface (EHLLAPI) has also been defined.

HLS

(Hue Lightness Saturation) A color model that is very closely related to HSV. See *HSV*.

HMA

(High Memory Area) In PCs, the first 64K of extended memory from 1024K to 1088K, which can be accessed by DOS. It is managed by the HIMEM.SYS driver. It was discovered by accident that the first 64K of extended memory, now known as the HMA, could be accessed by DOS, even though it was beyond the traditional one-megabyte barrier.

HMD

(Head Mounted Display) A display system built and worn like goggles that gives the illusion of a floating monitor in front of the user's face. Single-eye units are used to display hands-free instructional material, and dual-eye, or stereoscopic, units are used for virtual reality applications. See also *CAVE*.

hog

A program that uses an excessive amount of computer resources, such as memory or disk, or takes a long time to execute.

Hollerith machine

The first automatic data processing system. It was used to count the 1890 U.S. census. Developed by Herman Hollerith, a statistician who had worked for the Census Bureau, the system used a hand punch to record the data in dollar-bill-sized punched cards and a tabulating machine to count them.

holographic storage

A future technology that records data as holograms, filling up the entire volume of a small optical cylinder. A laser is beamed through a set of LCD shutters that represent the binary pattern to be stored. Another laser is aimed to intersect the first beam at the optical material, which creates the hologram.

home brew

Products that are developed at home by hobbyists.

home button

An icon that represents the beginning of a file or a set of operations.

home computer

In the 1980s, a home computer was the lowest-priced computer of the time, such as an Apple II, Commodore 64 or 128, Tandy Color Computer or Atari ST. Today, the term refers to a PC or Mac.

HomeRF

(HOME Radio Frequency) A wireless personal area network (PAN) technology from the HomeRF Working Group, Portland, OR, (www.homerf.org), founded in 1998 by Compaq, IBM, HP and others. Transmitting in the unlicensed 2.4GHz band, HomeRF uses the Shared Wireless Access Protocol (SWAP) and provides an open standard for short-range transmission of digital voice and data between mobile devices (laptops, PDAs, phones) and desktop devices.

home run

A single wire that begins at a central distribution point (hub, PBX, etc.) and runs to its destination (workstation, telephone, etc.) without connecting to anything else.

hook

In programming, instructions that provide logical breakpoints for future expansion. Hooks may be changed to call some outside routine or function or may be places where additional processing is added.

hop count

The number of gateways and routers in a transmission path. Each hop slows down transmission since the gateway or router must analyze or convert the packet of data before forwarding it to its destination.

hopper

A tray, or chute, that accepts input to a mechanical device, such as a disk duplicator.

horizontal resolution

The number of elements, or dots, on a horizontal line (columns in a matrix). Contrast with *vertical resolution*.

horizontal scan frequency

The number of lines illuminated on a video screen in one second. For example, a resolution of 400 lines refreshed 60 times per second requires a scan rate of 24KHz plus overhead (time to bring the beam back to the beginning of the next line). Same as horizontal sync frequency in TV. Contrast with *vertical scan frequency*.

host

A computer that acts as a source of information or signals. The term can refer to almost any computer, from a centralized mainframe that is host to its terminals, to a server that is host to its clients, to a desktop PC that is host to its peripherals.

host adapter

Also called a "controller," it is a device that connects one or more peripheral units to a computer. It is typically an expansion card that plugs into the bus. IDE and SCSI are examples of peripheral interfaces that call their controllers host adapters. See *host*.

host address

The physical address of a computer in a network. On the Internet, a host address is the IP address of the machine. See *IP address*.

host based

A communications system that is controlled by a large, central computer system.

host mode

A communications mode that allows a computer to answer an incoming telephone call and receive data without human assistance.

hot fix

The capability of being repaired while in operation. For example, many SCSI drives can move the data in sectors that are becoming hard to read to spare sectors on the fly without even the SCSI host adapter being aware of it. In some fault tolerant systems, circuit boards and components can be removed and replaced without turning the system off (also called "hot swapping").

HotJava

A Web browser from Sun that supports the Java programming language, which was also developed by Sun. HotJava executes Java programs embedded directly within Web documents.

hotkey

The key or key combination that causes some function to occur in the computer, no matter what else is currently running. It is commonly used to activate a memory resident (TSR) program.

hot link

A predefined connection between programs so that when information in one database or file is changed, related information in other databases and files are also updated. See *hypertext, compound document* and *OLE*.

hot potato routing

In communications, rerouting a message as soon as it arrives.

hot spot

The exact location of the screen cursor that points to and affects the screen object when the mouse is clicked. It is typically the tip of an arrow or finger pointer or the crosspoint of an X-shaped pointer, but can be elsewhere with other cursor designs.

hot swap

See *hot fix*.

housekeeping

A set of instructions that are executed at the beginning of a program. It sets all counters and flags to their starting values and generally readies the program for execution.

HP

(Hewlett-Packard Company, Palo Alto, CA, www.hp.com) The second largest computer and electronic equipment manufacturer in the U.S. HP was founded in 1939 by William Hewlett and David Packard in a garage behind Packard's California home. First involved with instrumentation and data collection devices, HP branched into business computing in 1972. HP sells over 10,000 different products in the electronics and computer field, and it has gained a worldwide reputation for its rugged and reliable engineering.

In 1999, HP spun off its test and measurement divisions into a new company named Agilent Technologies. The business units involved grossed nearly eight billion in 1998 and employed 45,000 people worldwide. The new company is headquartered at 395 Page Mill Road, the site where Hewlett and Packard constructed their first building in 1943.

HP 3000

A family of business-oriented servers from HP that run under the MPE/iX operating system. Models are available from entry level to mainframe class. Introduced in 1972, the HP3000A was HP's first business computer.

HP 9000

A family of high-performance workstations and servers from HP that are based on HP's PA-RISC architecture and run under the HP/UX operating system. Both workstations and servers are available in a wide range of machines from entry level to supercomputer class.

HPFS

(High Performance File System) The file system, introduced with OS/2 Version 1.2, that handles larger disks (2TB volumes; 2GB files), long file names (256 bytes) and can launch the program by referencing the data as in the Macintosh. It coexists with the existing FAT system.

HPGL

(Hewlett-Packard Graphics Language) A vector graphics file format from HP that was developed as a standard plotter language. Most plotters support the HPGL and DMPL standards.

HPIB

(Hewlett-Packard Interface Bus) HP's version of the IEEE 488 standard GPIB.

HP-UX

HP's version of UNIX that runs on its 9000 family. It is based on SVID and incorporates features from BSD UNIX along with several HP innovations.

HP-VUE

A Motif-based graphical user interface used in HP workstations. Parts of HP-VUE are used in the Common Desktop Environment (CDE).

HSB (HSL, HSV)

(Hue Saturation Brightness) A color model that is similar to the way an artist mixes colors by adding black and white to pure pigments. The pigments are the hues (H), measured in a circle from 0 to 359 degrees (0=red, 60=yellow, 120=green, 180=cyan, 240=blue, 300=magenta). The saturation (S) is the amount of black, and the brightness (B) is the amount of white, each measured from 0 to 100%. HSL and HSV are variations of the color model.

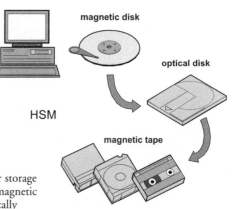

magnetic disk

optical disk

HSM

magnetic tape

HSM

(Hierarchical Storage Management) Moving data to slower storage media when the data is no longer needed for daily use. Since magnetic disks are the most expensive storage medium, data is automatically moved based on age and other criteria. The typical hierarchy is from magnetic disk to optical disk to offline tape. Data on a hard disk is accessed in a fraction of a second. On an optical jukebox, it takes several seconds.

HSSI

(High-Speed Serial Interface) A standard for a serial connection with transmission rates up to 52 Mbps. It is often used to connect to T3 lines.

HTML

(HyperText Markup Language) The document format used on the World Wide Web. Web pages are built with HTML tags, or codes, embedded in the text. HTML defines the page layout, fonts and graphic elements as well as the hypertext links to other documents on the Web. Each link contains the URL, or address, of a Web page residing on the same server or any server worldwide, hence "World Wide" Web.

HTTP

(HyperText Transport Protocol) The communications protocol used to connect to servers on the World Wide Web. Its primary function is to establish a connection with a Web server and transmit HTML pages to the client browser. Addresses of Web sites begin with an **http://** prefix; however, Web browsers default to the HTTP protocol. For example, typing **www.yahoo.com** is the same as typing **http://www.yahoo.com**.

HTTPS

(1) (HyperText Transport Protocol Secure) The protocol for accessing a secure Web server. Using HTTPS in the URL instead of HTTP connects the message to a security protocol. See *security protocol*.

(2) (HyperText Transport Protocol Server) A Web server that runs under Windows NT, developed by the European Microsoft Windows Academic Centre.

hub

A central connecting device in a network that joins communications lines together in a star configuration. Passive hubs are connecting units that add nothing to the data passing through them. Active hubs, also called "multiport repeaters," regenerate the data bits in order to maintain a strong signal, and intelligent hubs provide added functionality.

hue

In computer graphics, a particular shade or tint of a given color.

Huffman coding

A statistical compression method that converts characters into variable length bit strings. Most-frequently-ocurring characters are converted to shortest bit strings; least frequent, the longest. Compression takes two passes. The first pass analyzes a block of data and creates a tree model based on its contents. The second pass compresses the data via the model. Decompression decodes the variable length strings via the tree. See *LZW*.

hybrid computer

A digital computer that processes analog signals which have been converted into digital form. It is used in process control and robotics.

hybrid microcircuit

An electronic circuit composed of different types of integrated circuits and discrete components, mounted on a ceramic base. Used in military and communications applications, it is especially suited for building custom analog circuits including A/D and D/A converters, amplifiers and modulators. See *MCM*.

hybrid network

In communications, a network made up of equipment from multiple vendors.

HyperCard

An application development system from Apple that runs on the Macintosh. Using visual tools, users build "stacks" of "cards" that hold data, text, graphics, sound and video with hypertext links between them. The HyperTalk programming language allows complex applications to be developed.

hypercube

A parallel processing architecture made up of binary multiples of computers (4, 8, 16, etc.). The computers are interconnected so that data travel is kept to a minimum. For example, in two eight-node cubes, each node in one cube would be connected to the counterpart node in the other.

hyperlink

A predefined linkage between one object and another. See *hypertext*.

hypermedia

The use of data, text, graphics, video and voice as elements in a hypertext system. All the various forms of information are linked together so that a user can easily move from one to another.

hypertext

Linking related information. Hypertext is the foundation of the World Wide Web. Links embedded within Web pages are addresses to other Web pages stored locally or in a Web server anywhere in the world.

hyphenation

Breaking words that extend beyond the right margin. Software hyphenates words by matching them against a hyphenation dictionary or by using a built-in set of rules, or both. See *discretionary hyphen*.

hysteresis

The lag between making a change, such as increasing or decreasing power, and the response or effect of that change.

Hz

(HertZ) See *Hertz*.

I

I₂O

(Intelligent I/O) A standard for offloading input and output to an auxiliary processor. The auxiliary processor (I/O processor) manages the data transfer while the CPU does something else. Although I2O is being implemented in small systems, it embodies the principle behind mainframe channels, which can have several hundred data transfers occurring simultaneously.

i860

A RISC-based, 64-bit from Intel that uses a 64-bit data bus, has built-in floating point and 3-D graphics capability and contains over one million transistors. It can be used as a stand-alone CPU or to accelerate performance in existing systems.

IA-64

(Intel Architecture-64) The 64-bit architecture used in Intel's next-generation family of CPU chips. It is designed for fast parallel instruction execution and was designed at the end of the 20th Century, whereas x86 chips (IA-32) hark back to the early 1970s when designs were based on a fraction of the number of transistors that can be built into a chip today. The Itanium is the first chip to use IA-64.

IAB

(Internet Architecture Board) Founded in 1983 as the Internet Activities Board, it is a mostly volunteer organization that provides architectural guidance to and adjudicates conflicts for the Internet Engineering Task Force (IETF). It appoints the IETF Chair and all other Internet Engineering Steering Group (IESG) candidates. It also advises the Internet Society (ISOC) relating to technical and procedural matters.

IAC

(InterApplication Communications) The interprocess communications capability in the Macintosh, starting with System 7.0. IAC messages take place behind the scenes between the Finder and the application and between applications.

IAHC

(Internet Ad Hoc Committee, www.iahc.org) A coalition of participants from the Internet community that was formed to generate new top level domain names. In 1997, it introduced the .firm, .store, .web, .arts, .rec, .info and .nom domains.

IANA

(Internet Assigned Numbers Authority, www.iana.org) The Internet body that was responsible for managing Internet addresses, domain names and protocol parameters. It has been superseded by ICANN (Internet Corporation for Assigned Names and Numbers), which was formed in 1998.

IANA was chartered by the Internet Society (ISOC) and Federal Network Council (FNC) and has been located at and operated by the Information Sciences Institute at the University of Southern California.

IBM

(International Business Machines Corporation, Armonk, NY) The world's largest computer company. It started in New York in 1911 when the Computing-Tabulating-Recording Co. was created by a merger of four companies. In 1914, Thomas J. Watson, Sr., became general manager, and during the next 10 years, turned it into an international enterprise, renamed IBM in 1924. IBM's computer lines are its S/390 mainframes, AS/400 midrange business series, RS/6000 CAD and scientific workstations and servers and its desktop and laptop PCs.

IBM-compatible PC

A personal computer that is compatible with the IBM PC and PS/2 standards. Although this term is still used, it had more validity in the early days when PC makers were trying to copy the IBM PC, and many PCs were not compatible. Today, PCs conform to standards set by Intel.

IBM mainframe

A large computer system made by IBM. IBM mainframes have evolved from the System/360 series, introduced in 1964 to today's S/390 line.

IBM PC

A PC made by IBM. In 1981, IBM introduced the PC and set the standard for the largest computer base in the world to be built upon. First generation PCs had names: XT, AT, etc. Subsequent models starting with the PS/2 used number designations.

iBook

A consumer-based laptop computer from Apple that is the portable counterpart to the iMac desktop machine. It was introduced in July 1999 at Macworld Expo in New York with a 300MHz G3 processor.

IC

See *integrated circuit*.

ICA

(Independent Computing Architecture) The presentation services protocol from Citrix that governs input/output between the client and the server. Originally known as the Intelligent Console Architecture. See *WinFrame* and *Windows Terminal Server*.

ICANN

(Internet Corporation for Assigned Names and Numbers, www.icann.org) A non-profit, international association founded in 1998 and incorporated in the U.S. It is the successor to IANA (Internet Assigned Numbers Authority), which manages Internet addresses, domain names and the parameters associated with Internet protocols (port numbers, router protocols, multicast addresses, etc.). ICANN provides a list of accredited registrars in addition to Network Solutions that accept domain registrations.

ICCP

(Institute for Certification of Computer Professionals, Des Plaines, IL, www.iccp.org). An organization founded in 1973 that offers industry certification and worldwide test centers. The Associate Computer Professional (ACP) exam is open to all, but the Certified Computing Professional (CCP) requires four years of experience, although academic credit may substitute for two.

The CCP combines the former Certified Computer Programmer (CCP), Certified Data Processor (CDP) and Certified Systems Professional (CSP)

ICC profile

(International Color Consortium profile) A color management standard for specifying the attributes of imaging devices such as scanners, digital cameras, monitors and printers so that the color of an image remains true from source to destination. A profile can be embedded within the image itself. For more information, visit the International Color Consortium Web site at www.color.org.

iCOMP

(Intel COmparative Microprocessor Performance) An index of CPU performance from Intel. It tests a mix of 16-bit and 32-bit integer, floating point, graphics and video operations.

icon

A small, pictorial, on-screen representation of an application, data file, system resource or function in a graphical interface (GUI).

ICQ

("I Seek You") A conferencing program for the Internet from Mirabilis, Tel Aviv, Israel, (www.mirabilis.com). It provides interactive chat, e-mail and file transfer and can alert you when someone on your predefined list has also come online. The chat rooms and alerts are managed by the Mirabilis servers. In 1998, Mirabilis and ICQ were acquired by AOL.

IDAPI

(Idependent Database API) A programming interface that provides a common language for applications to access databases on a network. It includes support for non-SQL and non-relational databases. See *ODBC*.

IDC

(International Data Corporation, Framingham, MA, www.idcresearch.com) A major market research, analysis and consulting firm in the information field. Founded in 1964, it provides annual briefings and in-depth reports on all aspects of the industry.

IDE

(1) (Integrated Drive Electronics) A type of hardware interface widely used to connect hard disks, CD-ROMs and tape drives to a PC. IDE incorporates the controller within the drive itself, lowering the cost of the total peripheral system. The drives connect to the computer by attaching to an IDE host adapter that is either on a plug-in card or on the motherboard.

The original IDE host adapter supported two disks. Starting in 1994, second generation Enhanced IDE (EIDE) host adapters provide a second channel for two more disk, tape or CD-ROM drives. Today, most motherboards have EIDE built in and provide two sockets for a total of four devices.

(2) (Integrated Development Environment) A set of programs run from a single user interface. For example, programming languages often include a text editor, compiler and debugger, which are all activated and function from a common menu.

iDEN

(Integrated Digital Enhanced Network) A wireless communications technology from Motorola that provides support for voice, data, short messages (SMS) and dispatch radio (two-way radio) in one phone.

IDL

(Interface Definition Language) A language used to describe the interface to a routine or function. For example, objects in the CORBA distributed object environment are defined by an IDL, which describes the services performed by the object and how the data is to be passed to it.

idle character

In data communications, a character transmitted to keep the line synchronized when there is no data being sent.

idle interrupt

An interrupt generated when a device changes from an operational state to an idle state.

idle time

The duration of time a device is in an idle state, which means that it is operational, but not being used.

IDMS

See *CA-IDMS*.

IEC

(International Electrotechnical Commission) An organization that sets international electrical and electronics standards founded in 1906 and headquartered in Geneva. It is made up of national committees from over 40 countries.

IEEE

(Institute of Electrical and Electronics Engineers, New York, www.ieee.org) A membership organization that includes engineers, scientists and students in electronics and allied fields. Founded in 1963, it has over 300,000 members and is involved with setting standards for computers and communications.

IEEE 1284

An IEEE standard for an enhanced parallel port that is compatible with the parallel port used on PCs. The standard defines the type of cable that must be used in order to increase distances up to 30 feet. It provides transfer rates of 500 Kbytes/sec and 2 Mbytes/sec, compared to 150 Kbytes/sec for the standard port. EPP (Enhanced Parallel Port) mode provides bi-directional to between 600 Kbytes/sec and 1.5 Mbytes/sec. ECP (Enhanced Capabilities Port) uses DMA channels.

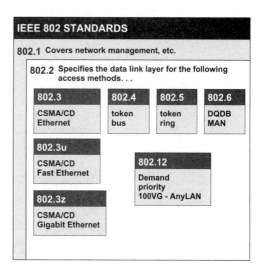

IEEE 488

See *GPIB*.

IEEE 802

The standards from the IEEE for local area networking. Ethernet is covered under 802.3, and Token Ring is covered under 802.5. See illustration on previous page.

IEF

(Information Engineering Facility) CASE software from TI that runs on PCs and MVS mainframes and generates COBOL code for PCs, MVS mainframes, VMS, Tandem, AIX, HP-UX and other UNIX platforms. It is a fully-integrated set of CASE tools.

IETF

(Internet Engineering Task Force, c/o Corporation for National Research Initiatives, Reston, VA, www.ietf.org) Founded in 1986, the IETF is a mostly volunteer organization of working groups dedicated to identifying problems and proposing technical solutions for the Internet. It facilitates transfer of ideas from the Internet Research Task Force (IRTF) to the Internet community and is supported by efforts of the Internet Society (ISOC). The Internet Architecture Board (IAB) provides architectural guidelines for the IETF, and the Internet Engineering Steering Group (IESG) provides overall direction.

IEW

(Information Engineering Workbench) CASE software from Sterling Software, Atlanta, GA (formerly KnowledgeWare), that runs on DOS PCs and generates COBOL, CICS and IMS code for MVS mainframes.

IFC

(Internet Foundation Classes) A class library from Netscape that provides an application framework and graphical user interface (GUI) routines for Java programmers. IFC was later made part of the Java Foundation Classes (JFC). See *JFC, AFC* and *AWT*.

if-then-else

A high-level programming language statement that compares two or more sets of data and tests the results. If the results are true, the THEN instructions are taken; if not, the ELSE instructions are taken. The following is a BASIC example:

```
10   IF ANSWER = "Y"   THEN PRINT "Yes"
20   ELSE PRINT "No"
```

In certain languages, THEN is implied. All statements between IF and ELSE are carried out if the condition is true. All instructions between ELSE and ENDIF are carried out if not true. The following dBASE example produces the same results as above:

```
IF ANSWER = "Y"
    ? "Yes"
  ELSE
    ? "No"
ENDIF
```

IFIP

(International Federation of Information Processing, Geneva, Switzerland) A multinational affiliation of professional groups concerned with information processing, founded in 1960. There is one voting representative from each country, and the U.S. representative is FOCUS. See *FOCUS*.

IFS

(Installable File System) An OS/2 feature that supports multiple file systems. Different systems can be installed (UNIX, CD-ROM, etc.) just like drivers are installed for new peripherals.

IGES

(Initial Graphics Exchange Specification) An ANSI graphics file format that is system independent and also intended for human interpretation. It evolved out of the Air Force's Integrated Computer Automated Manufacturing (ICAM) program in 1979.

The Computer Glossary

IGRP

(Interior Gateway Routing Protocol) A proprietary routing protocol from Cisco that was developed in 1988 to overcome the shortcomings of RIP. IGRP takes bandwidth, latency, reliability and current traffic load into consideration. It is typically used within an autonomous system, such as an Internet domain. Enhanced IGRP (EIGRP) provides enhancements such as the ability to detect a loop in the network.

IIA

(1) (Information Industry Association, Washington, DC, www.infoindustry.org) A trade organization that includes members from all aspects of the information field. Its purpose is to conduct active government relations that safeguard the interests of a healthy, competitive information industry.

(2) (Information Interchange Architecture) IBM formats for exchanging documents between different systems.

IIOP

(Internet Inter-ORB Protocol) The CORBA message protocol used on a TCP/IP network (Internet, intranet, etc.). CORBA is the industry standard for distributed objects, which allows programs (objects) to be run remotely in a network. IIOP links TCP/IP to CORBA's General Inter-ORB protocol (GIOP), which specifies how CORBA's Object Request Brokers (ORBs) communicate with each other.

IIS

See *Microsoft Internet Information Server*.

ILEC

(Incumbent Local Exchange Carrier) A traditional local telephone company such as one of the Regional Bell companies (RBOCs). Contrast with *CLEC*.

illustration program

Same as *drawing program*.

Illustrator

A full-featured drawing program for Windows and Macintosh from Adobe. It provides sophisticated tracing and text manipulation capabilities, as well as color separations. Illustrator is the most widely-used drawing and composition program for the Mac platform.

iMac

A Macintosh computer from Apple introduced in 1998. It is a low-priced, Internet-ready Mac with a new look aimed at the consumer. In was the first computer to come without a floppy disk as standard equipment.

image editing, image enhancement

Changing or improving graphics images either manually using a paint program or by using software routines that alter contrast, smooth lines or filter out unwanted data. See *anti-aliasing*.

image filter

A routine that changes the appearance of an image or part of an image by altering the shades and colors of the pixels in some manner. Filters are used to increase brightness and contrast as well as to add a wide variety of textures, tones and special effects to a picture.

imagemap

A single picture image that is logically separated into areas, each of which is used to select a different option or display a different message when clicked. It is widely used on the Web to provide a navigation bar to link to other topics.

image processing

(1) The analysis of a picture using techniques that can identify shades, colors and relationships that cannot be perceived by the human eye. It is used to solve identification problems, such as in forensic medicine or in creating weather maps from satellite pictures and deals with images in raster graphics format that have been scanned in or captured with digital cameras.

(2) Any image improvement, such as refining a picture in a paint program that has been scanned or entered from a video source.

(3) Same as *imaging*.

imagesetter

A machine that generates output for the printing process, which is either a film-based paper that is photographed or the actual film for making the printing plates. Input comes from the keyboard, or via disk, tape or modem. Earlier machines handled only text and were called "phototypesetters." Most imagesetters today support the PostScript language. See *platesetter*.

imaging

Creating a film or electronic image of any picture or paper form. It is accomplished by scanning or photographing an object and turning it into a matrix of dots (raster graphics), the meaning of which is unknown to the computer, only to the human viewer. Scanned images of text may be encoded into computer data (ASCII or EBCDIC) with page recognition software (OCR). See *micrographics, image processing* and *document imaging*.

imaging model

A set of rules for representing images.

imaging system

See *document imaging, image processing* and *image editing*.

IMAP

(Internet Messaging Access Protocol) A standard mail server expected to be widely used on the Internet. It provides a message store that holds incoming e-mail until users log on and download it. Unlike the POP server, the message headers can be read without downloading all the text and attachments.

impact printer

A printer that uses a printing mechanism that bangs the character image into the ribbon and onto the paper.

impedance

The resistance to the flow of alternating current in a circuit.

implementation

(1) Computer system *implementation* is the installation of new hardware and system software.

(2) Information system *implementation* is the installation of new databases and application programs and the adoption of new manual procedures.

implode

To link component pieces to a major assembly. It may also refer to compressing data using a particular technique. Contrast with *explode*.

import

To convert a file in a foreign format to the format of the program being used.

IMS

(Information Management System) An IBM hierarchical DBMS for mainframes under MVS. It was widely implemented throughout the 1970s and continues to be used. IMS/DC is its transaction processing component (like CICS) that handles the details of communications and SNA networking. IMS/DC is also used to access DB2 databases.

IMT-2000

A framework from the ITU for third generation (3G) wireless phone standards throughout the world that deliver high-speed multimedia data as well as voice.

incident light

In computer graphics, light that strikes an object. The color of the object is based on how the light is absorbed or reflected by the object.

incremental backup

Backing up files that have been changed. However, if a file has been changed for the second or subsequent time since the last full backup, the file doesn't replace the already-backed-up file, rather it is appended to the backup medium. This is used when each revision of a file must be maintained. See *full backup* and *differential backup*.

IND$FILE

An IBM mainframe program that transfers files between the mainframe and a PC functioning as a 3270 terminal.

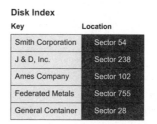

Disk Index

Key	Location
Smith Corporation	Sector 54
J & D, Inc.	Sector 238
Ames Company	Sector 102
Federated Metals	Sector 755
General Container	Sector 28

index

(1) In data management, the most common method for keeping track of data on a disk. Indexes are directory listings maintained by the OS, DBMS or the application.

An index of files contains an entry for each file name and the location of the file. An index of records has an entry for each key field (account no., name, etc.) and the location of the record.

(2) In programming, a method for keeping track of data in a table. See *indexed addressing*.

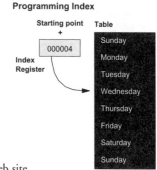

Programming Index

index hole

A small hole punched into a hard sectored floppy disk that serves to mark the start of the sectors on each track.

INDEX.HTML

The default name for a home page in a Web server. The page is appropriately named, because the home page is an index to the entire Web site. When you type in a URL such as www.computerglossary.com, it is the same as entering www.computerglossary.com/index.html.

index mark

A physical hole or notch, or a recorded code or mark, that is used to identify a starting point for each track on a disk.

index register

A high-speed circuit used to hold the current, relative position of an item in a table (array). At execution time, its stored value is added to the instructions that reference it.

indexed addressing

A technique for referencing memory that automatically increments the address with the value stored in an index register. See *subscript (2)*.

indexing

(1) Creating indexes based on key data fields or key words.

(2) Creating timing signals based on detecting a mark, slot or hole in a moving medium.

indirect addressing

An address mode that points to another pointer rather than the actual data. This mode is prohibited in RISC architecture.

inductance

The opposition to the changing flow of current in a circuit, measured in Henrys.

induction

The process of generating an electric current in a circuit from the magnetic influence of an adjacent circuit as in a transformer or capacitor.

industrial strength

Refers to software that is designed for high-volume, multiuser operation. It implies that the software is robust and that there are built-in safeguards against system failures.

inference engine

The processing program in an expert system. It derives a conclusion from the facts and rules contained in the knowledge base using various artificial intelligence techniques.

infix notation

The common way arithmetic operators are used to reference numeric values. For example, **A+B/C** is infix notation. Contrast with *Polish notation* and *reverse Polish notation*.

infopreneur

A person who is in business to gather and disseminate electronic information.

information

The summarization of data. Technically, data are raw facts and figures that are processed into information, such as summaries and totals. But since information can also be raw data for the next job or person, the two terms cannot be precisely defined. Both terms are used synonymously and interchangeably.

As office automation and data processing merge, it may be more helpful to view information the way data is defined and used, namely: data, text, spreadsheets, pictures, voice and video. Data are discretely defined fields. Text is a collection of words. Spreadsheets are data in matrix (row and column) form. Pictures are lists of vectors or frames of bits. Voice is a continuous stream of sound waves. Video is a sequence of frames.

Future databases will routinely integrate all these forms of information.

information appliance

A type of future home or office device that can transmit to or plug into common public or private networks. Envisioned is a "digital highway," like telephone and electrical power networks.

information engineering

An integrated set of methodologies and products used to guide and develop information processing within an organization. It starts with enterprise-wide stategic planning and ends with running applications.

information hiding

Keeping details of a routine private. Programmers only know what input is required and what outputs are expected. See *encapsulation* and *data abstraction*.

information highway

See *information superhighway*.

information industry

(1) Organizations that publish information via online services or through distribution by diskette or CD-ROM.

(2) All computer, communications and electronics-related organizations, including hardware, software and services.

information management

The discipline that analyzes information as an organizational resource. It covers the definitions, uses, value and distribution of all data and information within an organization whether processed by computer or not. It evaluates the kinds of data/information an organization requires in order to function and progress effectively.

Information is complex because business transactions are complex. It must be analyzed and understood before effective computer solutions can be developed. See *data administration*.

information processing

Same as *data processing*.

information resource management

See *Information Systems* and *information management*.

information science

See *information management*.

information superhighway

A proposed high-speed communications system that was touted by the Clinton/Gore administration to enhance education in America in the 21st Century. Its purpose was to help all citizens regardless of their income level. The Internet was originally cited as a model for this superhighway; however, with the explosion of the World Wide Web, the Internet became the information superhighway whether it was ready for it or not.

information system

A business application of the computer. It is made up of the database, application programs, manual and machine procedures and encompasses the computer systems that do the processing.

The database stores the subjects of the business (master files) and its activities (transaction files). The application programs provide the data entry, updating, query and report processing. The manual procedures document how data is obtained for input and how the system's output is distributed. Machine procedures instruct the computer how to perform the batch processing activities, in which the output of one program is automaticaly fed into another program.

RELATIONSHIP BETWEEN SYSTEMS	
structure (is)	**function (does)**

Management System

1. People	Sets organization's goals
2. Machines	and objectives, strategies
	and tactics, plans,
	schedule and controls.

Information System

1. Database	Defines data structures
2. Application	Data entry, updating,
programs	queries and reporting.
3. Procedures	Defines data flow

Computer System

1. CPU	Processes (the 3 C's)
2. Peripherals	Store and retrieve
3. Operating system	Manages computer system

The daily processing is the interactive, realtime processing of the transactions. At the end of the day or other period, the batch processing programs update the master files that have not been updated since the last cycle. Reports are printed for the cycle's activities.

The periodic processing of an information system is the updating of the master files, which adds, deletes and changes the information about customers, employees, vendors and products.

Information Systems

The formal title for a data processing, MIS, or IS department. Other titles are Data Processing, Information Processing, Information Services, Management Information Systems, Management Information Services and Information Technology.

information theory

The study of encoding and transmitting information. From Claude Shannon's 1938 paper, "A Mathematical Theory of Communication," which proposed the use of binary digits for coding information.

information utility

(1) A service bureau that maintains up-to-date databases for public access.

(2) A central source of information for an organization or group.

information warehouse

The collection of all databases in an enterprise across all platforms and departments.

INFORMIX

A relational database management system (DBMS) from Informix Software, Inc., Menlo Park, CA, that runs on most UNIX platforms and NetWare. Development tools include INFORMIX-4GL, a fourth-generation language, and INFORMIX-New Era, a client/server development system for Windows clients that supports INFORMIX and non-INFORMIX databases.

infrared

An invisible band of radiation at the lower end of the electromagnetic spectrum. It starts at the middle of the microwave spectrum and goes up to the beginning of visible light. Infrared transmission requires an unobstructed line of sight between transmitter and receiver. It is used for wireless transmission between computer devices as well as most all hand-held remotes for TVs, video and stereo equipment. Contrast with *ultraviolet*. See *SIR*.

infrastructure

The fundamental structure of a system or organization. The basic, fundamental architecture of any system (electronic, mechanical, social, political, etc.) determines how it functions and how flexible it is to meet future requirements.

Ingres

See *CA-OpenIngres*.

inheritance

In object-oriented programming, the ability of one class of objects to inherit properties from a higher class.

inhouse

An operation that takes place on the user's premises.

INIT

(INITiate) A Macintosh routine that is run when the computer is started or restarted. It is used to load and activate drivers and system routines. Many INITs are memory resident and may conflict with each other like TSRs in the PC environment.

initialize

To start anew, which typically involves clearing all or some part of memory or disk.

ink jet

A printer mechanism that sprays one or more colors of ink onto paper and produces high-quality printing like that of a laser printer.

The continuous stream method produces droplets that are aimed onto the paper by electric field deflectors. The drop-on-demand method uses a set of independently controlled injection chambers.

innoculate

To store characteristics of an executable program in order to detect a possible unknown virus if the file is changed.

i-node

(Identification **NODE**) An individual entry in a directory system that contains the name of and pointer to a file or other object.

Inprise/Borland

(Inprise Corporation, Scotts Valley, CA, www.inprise.com) A software company founded in 1983 by Philippe Kahn as Borland International. Borland was known for its programming languages and development products. In 1998, it changed its name to Inprise, but kept the Borland branding and referred to itself as Inprise/Borland. In 2000, the company merged with Corel.

input

(1) Data that is ready for entry into the computer.

(2) To enter data into the computer.

input area

A reserved segment of memory that is used to accept data from a peripheral device. Same as *buffer*.

input device

A peripheral device that generates input for the computer such as a keyboard, scanner, mouse or digitizer tablet.

input/output

See *I/O*.

input program

Same as *data entry program*.

input queue

A reserved segment of disk or memory that holds messages that have been received or job control statements describing work to be done.

input stream

A collection of job control statements entered in the computer that describe the work to be done.

inquiry program

Same as *query program*.

insert mode

A data entry mode that causes new data typed on the keyboard to be inserted at the current cursor location on screen. Contrast with *overwrite*.

install program

Software that prepares a software package to run in the computer. It copies the files from the distribution diskettes to the hard disk and decompresses them, if required. It may ask you to identify your computer environment in order to link in the drivers for the display, printer and other devices that you have.

installation spec

Documentation from an equipment manufacturer that describes how a product should be properly installed within a physical environment.

instance

In object-oriented programming, a member of a class; for example, "Lassie" is an instance of the class "dog." When an instance is created, the initial values of its instance variables are assigned."

instance variable

In object-oriented programming, the data in an object.

instant print

The ability to use the computer as a typewriter. Each keystroke is transferred to the printer.

instantiate

In object-oriented programming, to create an object of a specific class. See *instance*.

instruction

(1) A statement in a programming language.
(2) A machine instruction.

instruction cycle

The time in which a single instruction is fetched from memory, decoded and executed. The first half of the cycle transfers the instruction from memory to the instruction register and decodes it. The second half executes the instruction.

instruction mix

The blend of instruction types in a program. It often refers to writing generalized benchmarks, which requires that the amount of I/O versus processing versus math instructions, etc., reflects the type of application the benchmark is written for.

instruction register

A high-speed circuit that holds an instruction for decoding and execution.

instruction repertoire

Same as *instruction set*.

instruction set

The repertoire of machine language instructions that a computer can follow (from a handful to several hundred). It is a major architectural component and is either built into the CPU or into microcode. Instructions are generally from one to four bytes long.

instruction time

The time in which an instruction is fetched from memory and stored in the instruction register. It is the first half of the instruction cycle.

insulator
A material that does not conduct electricity. Contrast with *conductor*.

integer
A whole number. In programming, the integer function would yield 123 from 123.898.

integrated
A collection of distinct elements or components that have been built into one unit.

integrated circuit
The formal name for chip.

integrated software package
Software that combines several applications in one program, typically database management, word processing, spreadsheet, business graphics and communications. Such programs (Microsoft Works, AppleWorks, etc.) provide a common user interface for their applications plus the ability to cut and paste data from one to the other.

integrator
In electronics, a device that combines an input with a variable, such as time, and provides an analog output; for example, a watt-hour meter.

integrity
See *data integrity*.

Intel
(Intel Corporation, Santa Clara, CA, www.intel.com) The predominant manufacturer of the CPU chips for the PC world. It was founded in 1968 by Bob Noyce and Gorden Moore in Mountain View, CA. Although known for its x86 family of chips, over the years, Intel has developed a wide variety of chips and board-level products, including the MULTIBUS bus used in industrial applications. Intel started with 12 people and its first year revenues were less than three thousand dollars.

intelligence
Processing capability. Every computer is intelligent!

intelligent controller
A peripheral control unit that uses a built-in microprocessor for controlling its operation.

intelligent database
A database that contains knowledge about the content of its data. A set of validation criteria are stored with each field of data, such as the minimum and maximum values that can be entered or a list of all possible entries.

intelligent form
A data entry application that provides help screens and low levels of AI in aiding the user to enter the correct data.

intelligent hub
A central connecting device in a network that performs a variety of processing functions such as network management, bridging, routing and switching. See *hub*, *passive hub* and *active hub*.

intelligent modem
A modem that responds to commands and can accept new instructions during online transmission. It was originally developed by Hayes.

intelligent paper
Same as *intelligent form*.

intelligent terminal
A terminal with built-in processing capability, but no local disk or tape storage. It may use a general-purpose CPU or may have specialized circuitry as part of a distributed intelligence system. Contrast with *dumb terminal*.

IntelliMouse

A mouse from Microsoft that adds a rubber wheel at the top of the unit between the two buttons. Moving the wheel causes scrolling in applications that are IntelliMouse aware.

IntelliSense

Features in Microsoft applications that help the user by making decisions automatically. By analyzing activity patterns, the software can derive the next step without the user having to explicitly state it. Automatic typo correction and suggesting shortcuts fall under the IntelliSense umbrella.

INTELSAT

(INTELSAT, Washington, DC, www.intelsat.int) An international cooperative of more than 135 member nations. It is the world's largest supplier of commercial satellite services with more than 20 satellites in orbit. It was created in 1964 with 11 countries participating. COMSAT is the U.S. signatory of INTELSAT.

inter

To cross over boundaries; for example, internetwork means from one network to another. Contrast with *intra*.

interactive

Back-and-forth dialog between the user and a computer.

interactive fiction

An adventure game that has been created or modified for the computer. It has multiple story lines, environments and endings, all of which are determined by choices the player makes at various times.

interactive session

Back-and-forth dialogue between user and computer. Contrast with *batch session*.

interactive TV

Two-way communications between the TV viewer and service providers. Although experiments took place throughout the 1980s, interactive TV never took off. With the Internet's momentum and the vast amounts of information and interaction available on it, Internet TV may succeed where interactive TV did not. See *Internet TV* and *digital convergence*.

interactive video

The use of CD-ROM and videodisc controlled by computer for an interactive education or entertainment program. See *CD-ROM* and *videodisc*.

interface

The connection and interaction between hardware, software and the user. Interfacing is a major part of what engineers, programmers and consultants do. Users "talk to" the software. The software "talks to" the hardware and other software. Hardware "talks to" other hardware. All this is interfacing. It has to be designed, developed, tested and redesigned, and with each incarnation, a new specification is born that may become yet one more de facto or regulated standard.

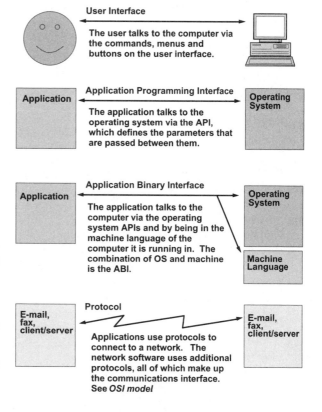

User Interface

The user talks to the computer via the commands, menus and buttons on the user interface.

Application Programming Interface

The application talks to the operating system via the API, which defines the parameters that are passed between them.

Application Binary Interface

The application talks to the computer via the operating system APIs and by being in the machine language of the computer it is running in. The combination of OS and machine is the ABI.

Protocol

Applications use protocols to connect to a network. The network software uses additional protocols, all of which make up the communications interface. See *OSI model*

Interface

interface adapter
In communications, a device that connects the computer or terminal to a network.

interframe coding
In video compression, coding only the differences between frames. See *intraframe coding*.

interlaced
Illuminating a CRT by displaying odd lines and then even lines (every other line first; then filling in the gaps). TV signals are interlaced and generate 60 half frames (30 full frames) per second. Earlier computer displays used to be interlaced at the higest resolution, but today are non-interlaced.

interleave
See *sector interleave* and *memory interleaving*.

interlock
A device that prohibits an action from taking place.

intermediate language
Same as *pseudo language*.

intermediate node routing
Routing a message to non-adjacent nodes; for example, if three computers are connected in series A—B—C, data transmitted from A to C can be routed through B.

intermittent error
An error that occurs sporadically, not consistently. It is the most difficult type of problem to diagnose and repair.

internal bus
A data pathway between closely-connected components, such as between the CPU and memory. See *local bus*.

internal command
In DOS and OS/2, a command, such as Copy, Dir and Rename, which may be used at all times. Internal commands are executed by the command processor programs COMMAND.COM in DOS and CMD.EXE in OS/2. The command processor is always loaded when the operating system is loaded. Contrast with *external command*.

internal font
A set of characters for a particular typeface that is built into a printer. Contrast with *font cartridge* and *soft font*.

internal interrupt
An interrupt that is caused by processing, for example, a request for input or output or an arithmetic overflow error. Contrast with *external interrupt*.

internal modem
A modem that plugs into an expansion slot within the computer. Unlike an external modem, an internal modem does not provide a series of display lights that inform the user of the changing modem states. The user must rely entirely on the communications program. Contrast with *external modem*.

internal sort
Sorting that is accomplished entirely in memory without using disks or tapes for temporary files.

internal storage
Same as *memory*.

internet
(1) A large network made up of a number of smaller networks.

(2) (Internet) "The" Internet is made up of more than 100,000 interconnected networks in over 100 countries, comprised of commercial, academic and government networks. Originally developed for the military, the Internet became widely used for academic and commercial research. Users had access to

unpublished data and journals on a huge variety of subjects. Due to the World Wide Web facility on the Internet, it has become commercialized into a worldwide information highway, providing information on every subject known to humankind.

Internet2

A high-speed network for government, academic and research being developed by more than 100 universities with assistance from private companies and the U.S. government. It is not intended for commercial use or to replace the Internet, but is, in fact, the reincarnation of it. However, whereas the first Internet was designed to primarily exchange text, Internet2 is being developed to exchange realtime, multimedia data at high speed, something today's commercial Internet does not do well. Resulting technological advancements should eventually migrate to the global Internet.

Internet address

There are two kinds of addresses that are widely used on the Internet. One is a person's e-mail address, and the other is the address of a Web site, which is known as its URL. Following is an explanation of Internet e-mail addresses. For more on URLs, see *URL* and *Internet domain names*.

The format for addressing a message to an Internet user is USER NAME @ DOMAIN NAME. For example, the address of the author is **freedman@computerlanguage.com**. There are no spaces between any of the words. FREEDMAN is the user name and COMPUTERLANGUAGE.COM is the domain name. The .COM stands for the commercial top level domain category (see *Internet domain names*).

Internet appliance

A device designed for accessing the Web and/or e-mail. Internet TV services, such as WebTV, are designed for home use, whereas PDAs and specialized handheld devices with wireless connections are geared for remote use. See *Internet TV* and *network computer*.

Internet backbones

A group of communications networks managed by several commercial companies that provide the major high-speed links across the country. ISPs are either connected directly to these backbones or to a larger regional ISP that is connected to one. The backbones themselves are interconnected at various access points known as NAPs.

Internet computer

See *Internet appliance* and *network computer*.

Internet domain names

Following are the top level domains (TLDs) that are widely used. The .edu, .mil and .gov domains are traditionally U.S. domains.

```
.com    commercial
.net    gateway or host
.org    non-profit organization
.edu    educational and research
.gov    government
.mil    military agency
.int    international intergovernmental
```

The **.int** domain name is not widely used. Outside the U.S., the top level domains are typically the country code; for example, **ca** for Canada, **uk** for United Kingdom and **de** for Germany. See *IAHC*.

Internet Explorer

See *Microsoft Internet Explorer*.

Internet fax

Using the Internet to send faxes. Fax servers accept an incoming fax message and route it to a fax server in the same locality as the destination fax machine. The fax server then makes a local telephone call to send the fax.

Internet gateway

A computer system that converts messages back and forth between TCP/IP and other protocols. Internet gateways connect the Internet to all the other communications networks in the world.

Internet PC

See *network computer*.

Internet phone

See *Internet telephony*.

Internet Protocol

See *TCP/IP*.

Internet Relay Chat

Computer conferencing on the Internet. There are hundreds of IRC channels on numerous subjects that are hosted on IRC servers around the world. After joining a channel, your messages are broadcast to everyone listening to that channel. IRC client programs, such as mIRC, provide a graphical interface for all functions, including logging onto popular servers and obtaining a list of active channels. See *MUD*.

Internet Society

(www.isoc.org) An international membership organization dedicated to extending and enhancing the Internet, founded in 1992. It supports Internet bodies such as the IETF and works with governments, organizations and the general public to promote Internet research, information, education and standards. It also helps developing nations design their Internet infrastructure.

Internet Talk Radio

Audio coverage of news events digitized into Internet files at the National Press Building in Washington, DC. ITR files are distributed to FTP sites for users with computers that have sound capabilities.

Internet telephony

Using the Internet for a voice call. It currently does not provide the quality of the dial-up telephone system, because the Internet is designed for data traffic where momentary delays are expected and quite common.

Internet TV

An Internet service for home TV use. It uses a set-top box that connects the TV to a modem and telephone line. The user interface has been specialized for viewing on an interlaced TV screen rather than a computer monitor. WebTV was the first such service to obtain widespread distribution.

Internet utility

Software used to search the Internet. See *Archie, Gopher, Veronica, WAIS* and *Web browser*.

internetwork

To go between one network and another.

interNIC

The domain name registration project that was formed by agreements between Network Solutions, the National Science Foundation, General Atomics and AT&T. Until 1998, InterNIC/Network Solutions was the only domain name registrar. Subsequently, other registrars have been approved by ICANN, and Network Solutions (www.networksolutions.com) still manages the master databases.

interoperable

The ability for one system to communicate or work with another.

interpolate

To estimate values that lie between known values.

interpret

To run a program one line at a time. Each line of source language is translated into machine language and then executed.

interpreter

A high-level programming language translator that translate and runs the program at the same time. It translates one program statement into machine language, executes it, then proceeds to the next statement.
Interpreted programs run slower than their compiler counterparts, because the compiler translates the

entire program before it is run. However, it's convenient to write an interpreted program, since a single line of code can be tested interactively.

Interpreted programs must always be run with the interpreter. For example, in order to run a BASIC or dBASE program, the BASIC or dBASE interpreter must be in the computer.

If a language can be both interpreted and compiled, a program may be developed with the interpreter and compiled for production.

interpretive language

A programming language that requires an interpreter to run it.

interprocess communication

See *IPC*.

interrecord gap

The space generated between blocks of data on tape, created by the starting and stopping of the reel.

interrogate

(1) To search, sum or count records in a file. See *query*.

(2) To test the condition or status of a terminal or computer system.

Create & Modify

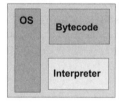
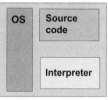
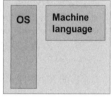

Run

Interpreter

interrupt

A signal that gets the attention of the CPU and is usually generated when I/O is required. For example, hardware interrupts are generated when a key is pressed or when the mouse is moved. Software interrupts are generated by a program requiring disk input or output.

An internal timer may continually interrupt the computer several times per second to keep the time of day current or for timesharing purposes.

When an interrupt occurs, control is transferred to the operating system, which determines the action to be taken. Interrupts are prioritized; the higher the priority, the faster the interrupt will be serviced.

interrupt-driven

A computer or communications network that uses interrupts.

interrupt mask

An internal switch setting that controls whether an interrupt can be processed or not. The mask is a bit that is turned on and off by the program.

interrupt priorities

The sequence of importance assigned to interrupts. If two interrupts occur simultaneously, the interrupt with the highest priority is serviced first.

interrupt vector

In the PC, one of 256 pointers that reside in the first 1KB of memory. Each vector points to a routine in the ROM BIOS or elsewhere in memory, which handles the interrupt.

intersect

In relational database, to match two files and produce a third file with records that are common in both. For example, intersecting an American file and a programmer file would yield American programmers.

intra

Within a boundary; for example, intraoffice refers to operations that take place within the office. Contrast with *inter*.

intraframe coding

Compressing redundant areas within a video frame. See *interframe coding*.

intranet

An inhouse Web site that serves the employees of the enterprise. Although intranet pages may link to the Internet, an intranet is not accessed by the general public. See *extranet*.

inverse multiplexing

Splitting a high-speed channel into several low-speed channels in order to be able to use available transmission facilities. For example, an inverse multiplexor is used to transmit high-speed LAN traffic over leased digital lines (T-carrier), which are made up of several lower-speed channels.

inverse video

Same as *reverse video*.

inverted file, inverted list

In data management, a file that is indexed on many of the attributes of the data itself. For example, in an employee file, an index could be maintained for all secretaries, another for managers. It's faster to search the indexes than every record. Inverted file indexes use lots of disk space; searching is fast, updating is slower.

inverter

(1) A logic gate that converts the input to the opposite state for output. If the input is true, the output is false, and vice versa. An inverter performs the Boolean logic NOT operation.

(2) A circuit that converts DC current into AC current. Contrast with *rectifier*.

invoke

To activate a program, routine, function or process.

I/O

(Input/Output) Transferring data between the CPU and a peripheral device. Every transfer is an output from one device and an input into another.

I/O address

(1) On PCs, a three-digit hexadecimal number (2AB, 2A0, etc.) used to identify and signal a peripheral device (serial port, parallel port, sound card, etc.). Address assignments must be unique, otherwise conflicts will occur. There are usually a small number of selectable addresses on each controller card.

(2) The identifying address of a peripheral device.

I/O area

A reserved segment of memory used to accept data from an input device or to accumulate data for transfer to an output device. See *buffer*.

I/O bound

Refers to an excessive amount of time getting data in and out of the computer in relation to the time it takes for processing it. Faster channels and disk drives improve the performance of I/O bound computers.

IOCA

(Image Object Content Architecture) See *MO:DCA*.

I/O card

See *expansion board* and *PC card*.

The Computer Glossary

I/O channel

See *channel*.

I/O device

Same as *peripheral device*.

I/O interface

See *port* and *expansion slot*.

ion deposition

A printing technology used in high-speed page printers. It is similar to laser printing, except instead of using light to create a charged image on a drum, it uses a printhead that deposits ions. After toner is attracted to the ions on the drum, the paper is pressed directly against the drum fusing toner to paper.

Quality approaches that of a laser printer; however, the ink has not been embedded as deeply, and the paper can smear more easily.

I/O processor

Circuitry specialized for I/O operations. See *front end processor*.

I/O statement

A programming instruction that requests I/O.

IP

(Internet Protocol) The IP part of the TCP/IP protocol, which routes a message across networks. See *TCP/IP* and *datagram*. See also *image processing*.

IP address

(Internet Protocol address) The physical address of a computer attached to a TCP/IP network. Every client and server station must have a unique IP address. Client workstations have either a permanent address or one that is dynamically assigned for each dial-up session (see *DNS*). IP addresses are written as four sets of numbers separated by periods; for example, 204.171.64.2.

IPC

(InterProcess Communication) The exchange of data between one program and another either within the same computer or over a network. It implies a protocol that guarantees a response to a request. Examples are OS/2's Named Pipes, Windows' DDE, Novell's SPX and Macintosh's IAC.

IPDS

(Intelligent Printer Data Stream) The native format built into IBM laser printers, which accepts fonts and formatted raster images. One of its major functions is its communications protocol that negotiates printer transfers from servers in the network that perform the rasterization. IBM used to make only IPDS printers. Today, many of its printers natively support PostScript and PCL (LaserJet) as well. See *PSF* and *AFP*.

IPI

(Intelligent Peripheral Interface) A high-speed hard disk interface used with minis and mainframes that transfers data in the 10 to 25 MBytes/sec range. IPI-2 and IPI-3 refer to differences in the command set that they execute.

IPL

(Initial Program Load) Same as *boot*.

ips

(Inches Per Second) The measurement of the speed of tape passing by a read/write head or paper passing through a pen plotter.

IPSec

(IP SECurity) A security protocol from the IETF that provides authentication and encryption over the Internet. Unlike SSL, which provides services at layer 4 and secures two applications, IPSec works at layer 3 and secures everything in the network. See *IPv6* and *security protocol*.

IP switching

Switching TCP/IP packets at high speed. Ipsilon's IP Switch started the trend by inspecting only the first packet in a flow and setting up a high-speed path through an ATM switch for the remainder of the packets. Various vendors followed suit with other approaches. The goal was to switch IP packets faster than traditional router-based layer 3 forwarding. However, subsequent routers have improved to the point where they can forward packets at even faster speeds while inspecting each and every packet. See *layer 3 switch* and *tag switching.*

IP telephony

The two-way transmission of audio over an IP network. When used in a private intranet or WAN, it is generally known as "voice over IP," or "VoIP." When the public Internet is the transport vehicle, it is referred to as "Internet telephony," however, both terms are used synonymously.

IPv6

(Internet Protocol Version 6) The next generation IP protocol. IPv6 increases the address space from 32 to 128 bits, providing for an unlimited (for all intents and purposes) number of networks and systems. It also supports quality of service (QoS) parameters for realtime audio and video. IPv4 is the current generation (there is no IPv5).

IPX

(Internet Packet EXchange) A NetWare communications protocol used to route messages from one node to another. IPX does not guarantee delivery of a complete message. Either the application has to provide that control or NetWare's SPX protocol must be used. IPX provides services at layers 3 and 4 of the OSI model. See *SPX.*

IR

(1) (Industry Remarketer) Same as *VAR* or *VAD.*

(2) See *infrared.*

Irma

An earlier trade name for a variety of desktop computer to host communications products from Attachmate Corporation, Bellevue, WA, (www.attachmate.com). Irma was not an acronym; it is the lady's name. The Irma board was the first 3270 emulator that turned a PC into a mainframe terminal.

iron oxide

The material used to coat the surfaces of magnetic tapes and lower-capacity disks.

IRQ

(Interrupt ReQuest) A hardware interrupt on a PC. It is a way for a peripheral device to signal the CPU that it is ready to send or receive. Sixteen lines (0-15) accept interrupts from devices such as a mouse or network adapter. IRQs used to be a major headache with PCs until Plug & Play and PCI cards became the norm. Plug & Play assigns IRQs automatically, and PCI cards share IRQs.

IRTF

(Internet Research Task Force) An organization of working groups involved in researching future Internet tecnologies. The IRTF Chair is appointed by the Internet Architecture Board (IAB). When the technologies are deemed ready for development, they are transferred to the Internet Engineering Task Force (IETF).

IS

See *Information Systems.*

IS-IS

(Intermediate System to Intermediate System) An ISO protocol that provides dynamic routing between routers.

ISA

(Industry Standard Architecture) Pronounced "eye-suh." An expansion bus commonly used in PCs. It accepts the plug-in boards that control the display, disks and other peripherals. Originally called the "AT bus," because it was first used in the IBM AT, the ISA bus extended the original PC bus from eight to 16 bits. Today, most Pentium motherboards contain a mix of 16-bit ISA slots and PCI slots.

ISAM

(Indexed Sequential Access Method) A common disk access method that stores data sequentially, while maintaining an index of key fields to all the records in the file for direct access. The sequential order would be the one most commonly used for batch processing and printing (account number, name, etc.).

ISAPI

(Internet Server API) A programming interface on Internet Information Server (IIS), Microsoft's Web server. Using ISAPI function calls, Web pages can invoke programs that are written as DLLs on the server, typically to access data in a database. See *NSAPI*.

ISDN

(Integrated Services Digital Network) An international telecommunications standard for voice, video and data over standard telephone lines at 64 Kbits/sec. ISDN uses circuit-switched bearer channels (B channels) to carry voice and data and uses a separate data channel (D channel) for control signals via a packet-switched network. This out-of-band D channel allows for features such as call forwarding, call waiting and advice of charge.

ISO

(International Standards Organization) An organization that sets international standards, founded in 1946 and headquartered in Geneva. It deals with all fields except electrical and electronics, which is governed by the older International Electrotechnical Commission (IEC), also in Geneva. With regard to information processing, ISO and IEC created JTC1, the Joint Technical Committee for information technology.

It carries out its work through more than 160 technical committees and 2,300 subcommittees and working groups and is made up of standards organizations from more than 75 countries, some of them serving as secretariats for these technical bodies. ANSI is the U.S. member body. Address: ANSI, 1430 Broadway, New York, NY 10018.

ISO 9000

A family of standards and guidelines for quality in the manufacturing and service industries from the International Standards Association.

ISO 9660

The logical format for a CD-ROM which evolved from the High Sierra format. The physical format for a CD-ROM is defined in the Yellow Book.

isochronous

Time dependent. Realtime voice, video and telemetry are examples of isochronous data.

PC BUSES	Bandwidth	
	Bits	**Speed**
ISA	8 16	8-10MHz
EISA	32	8-10MHz
PCI	32 64	33MHz
AGP	32	66MHz
Micro Channel	32	5-20MHz
VL-bus	32	40MHz

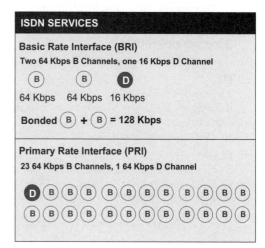

ISDN SERVICES

Basic Rate Interface (BRI)
Two 64 Kbps B Channels, one 16 Kbps D Channel

(B)   (B)   (D)

64 Kbps   64 Kbps   16 Kbps

Bonded (B) + (B) = 128 Kbps

Primary Rate Interface (PRI)
23 64 Kbps B Channels, 1 64 Kbps D Channel

isochronous Ethernet, IsoENET

National Semiconductor's enhancement to Ethernet for handling realtime voice and video. IsoENET adds a 6Mbps synchronous channel, made up of 96 64Kbps ISDN subchannels, to the 10Mbps Ethernet standard.

isometric view

In computer graphics, a rendering of a 3-D object that eliminates the distortion of shape created by true perspective. In isometric views, all lines on each axis are parallel to each other, and the lines do not converge. Such drawings are commonly used in technical illustrations because of their clarity, simplicity and speed of creation.

isotropic

Refers to properties, such as transmission speed, that are the same regardless of the direction that is measured. Contrast with *anisotropic*.

ISP

(Internet Service Provider) An organization that provides Internet access. Small ISPs provide service via modem and ISDN while larger ones also offer private line hookups (T1, fractional T1, etc.). Customers are generally billed a fixed rate per month, but other charges may apply. For a fee, a Web site can be hosted on the ISP's server, allowing the smaller organization to have a presence on the Web with its own domain name.

ISPF

(Interactive System Productivity Facility) IBM mainframe software that executes interactive user interfaces on 3270 terminals. It is created with ISPF's PDF (Program Development Facility) software.

ISV

(Independent Software Vendor) A person or company that develops software.

IT

(Information Technology) Same as *Information Systems*.

ITAA

(Information Technology Association of America, Arlington, VA, www.itaa.org) Formerly the Association of Data Processing Service Organizations (ADAPSO). A membership organization founded in 1960 that defines performance standards, improves management methods and monitors government regulations in the computer services field.

Itanium

See *IA-64*.

iteration

One repetition of a sequence of instructions or events. For example, in a program loop, one iteration is once through the instructions in the loop.

iterative operation

An operation that requires successive executions of instructions or processes.

ITI

(Information Technology Industry Council, Washington, DC, www.itic.org) Formerly the Computer and Business Equipment Manufacturers Association (CBEMA), founded in 1916. ITI is a membership organization composed of approximately 30 large companies. Its mission is to produce market-driven voluntary standards for information technology in the U.S. and abroad.

ITSP

(Internet Telephony Service Provider) An organization, such as an ISP or telephone company (CLEC, LEC, etc.), that supports IP telephony. Using the Internet as the primary backbone, it allows customers to make phone-to-phone calls or PC-to-phone calls. The majority of customers use an ITSP to save money on international calls, and the quality can vary substantially due to the inconsistency of the Internet. The ITSP uses IP gateways to convert between voice and IP packets.

ITU

(International Telecommunications Union, Geneva, Switzerland, www.itu.ch) Formerly the CCITT (Consultative Committee for International Telephony and Telegraphy), it is an international organization founded in 1865 and headquartered in Geneva that sets communications standards. The ITU is comprised of over 150 member countries. The Telecommunications Standards Section (TSS) is one of four organs of the ITU. Any specification with an ITU-T or ITU-TSS designation refers to the TSS organ.

IVR

(Interactive Voice Response) See *voice response*.

IXC

(IntereXchange Carrier) An organization that provides interstate communications services, such as AT&T, MCI and Sprint.

J

J2EE

(Java 2 platform, Enterprise Edition) A platform from Sun for building Web-based enterprise applications. J2EE services are performed in the middle tier between the user's browser and the enterprise's databases and legacy information systems. Its core component is Enterprise JavaBeans (EJBs), followed by JavaServer Pages (JSPs) and Java servlets and a variety of interfaces for linking to the information resources in the enterprise. See *EJB*.

jack

A receptacle into which a plug is inserted.

jacket

A plastic housing that contains a floppy disk. The 5.25" disk is built into a flexible jacket; the 3.25" disk uses a rigid jacket.

JAD

(Joint Application Development) An approach to systems analysis and design introduced by IBM in 1977 that emphasizes teamwork between user and technician. Small groups meet to determine system objectives and the business transactions to be supported. They are run by a neutral facilitator who can move the group toward well-defined goals. Results include a prototype of the proposed system.

jaggies

The stairstepped appearance of diagonal lines on a low-resolution graphics screen.

JAR

(1) (Java ARchive) A file format used to distribute a Java application. It contains all the resources required to install and run a Java program in a single compressed file. JARs are also used to distribute JavaBeans.

(2) A compression program for backup archiving from ARJ Software, Inc., Norwood, MA, (www.arjsoftware.com). JAR is similar to ARJ, but files are not compatible.

Java

A programming language for Internet and intranet applications from the JavaSoft division of Sun. Java was modeled after C++, and Java programs can be called from within HTML documents or launched stand alone. Java was designed to run in small amounts of memory and provides its own memory management.

Java is an interpreted language. Java source code is compiled into "bytecode," which cannot be run by itself. The bytecode must be converted into machine code at runtime. Upon finding a Java applet, the Web browser switches to its Java interpreter (Java Virtual Machine) which translates the byte code into machine code and runs it. This means Java programs are not dependent on any specific hardware and will run in any computer with the Java Virtual Machine.

JavaBeans

A component software architecture from Sun that runs in the Java environment. JavaBeans are independent Java program modules that are called for and executed. They have been used primarily for developing user interfaces at the client side. The server-side counterpart is Enterprise JavaBeans (EJBs). See *EJB* and *component software*.

Java chip

A CPU chip from Sun that executes Java byte codes natively. The microJava 701 is the first implementation of the Java chip, which is based on Sun's picoJava architecture. It executes an extended set of byte codes that enable operating systems written in C and C++ to have low-level access to the CPU in order to control the registers and perform cache management and other OS functions.

JavaOS

A Java operating system from Sun that requires minimal hardware requirements and is intended for network computers and embedded systems. It includes the Java Virtual Machine, which combined with the kernel, are written in the native machine language of the target CPU. Network and graphical user interface components are mostly written in Java.

JavaScript

A popular scripting language that is widely supported in Web browsers and other Web tools. It is easier to use than Java, but not as powerful and deals mainly with the elements on the Web page. On the client, JavaScript is maintained as source code embedded into an HTML document. On the server, it is compiled into bytecode (intermediate language), similar to Java programs.

Java Virtual Machine

A Java interpreter, which is the software that translates Java bytecode into machine language one statement at a time. See *Java*.

Jaz disk

A high-capacity removable hard disk system from Iomega Corporation, Roy, UT, (www.iomega.com). Introduced in 1995, Iomega startled the industry with its breakthrough price of $99 for a 1GB removable disk cartridge.

JBOD

(Just a Bunch Of Disks) A group of hard disks that are not set up as any type of RAID configuration.

JCL

(Job Control Language) A command language for mini and mainframe operating systems that launches applications. It specifies priority, program size and running sequence, as well as the files and databases used.

JDBC

(Java DataBase Connectivity) A programming interface that lets Java applications access a database via the SQL language. JDBC is the Java counterpart of Microsoft's ODBC.

JDK

(Java Development Kit) A Java software development environment from Sun. It includes the JVM, compiler, debugger and other tools for developing Java applets and applications. Each new version of the JDK adds features and enhancements to the language.

JEDEC

(Joint Electronic Device Engineering Council) An international body that sets integrated circuit standards.

JEIDA

(Japanese Electronic Industry Development Association) A Japanese trade and standards organization. JEIDA joined with PCMCIA to standardize the PC card. In 1991, the PC card specifications JEIDA 4.1 and PCMCIA 2.0 are the same.

JES

(Job Entry Subsystem) Software that provides batch communications for IBM's MVS operating system. It accepts data from remote batch terminals, executes them on a priority basis and transmits the results back to the terminals. The JES counterpart in VM is RSCS.

jewel box, jewel case

A plastic container used to package an audio CD or CD-ROM disc.

JFC

(Java Foundation Classes) A class library from Sun that provides an application framework and graphical user interface (GUI) routines for Java programmers. Sun, Netscape, IBM and others contributed to JFC, which combines Sun's Abstract Windowing Toolkit (AWT) and Netscape's Foundation Classes (IFC). See *AFC, IFC* and *AWT*.

JFIF

(JPEG File Interchange Format) The file format for JPEG files. See *JPEG*.

jiff

See *GIF*.

Jini

Pronounced "gee-nee." A Java-based distributed computing environment from Sun in which devices can be plugged into the network and automatically offer their services and make use of other services on the network. Jini creates a "network dialtone" allowing, for example, any PDA or laptop to be plugged in and immediately be able to use printers and other resources.

JIT compiler

(Just-In-Time compiler) A compiler that converts all the source code into machine code just before the program is run. In the case of Java, JIT compilers convert Java's intermediate language (byte code) into native code.

jitter

A flickering transmission signal or display image.

job

A unit of work running in the computer. A job may be a single program or a group of programs that work together.

job class

The descriptive category of a job that is based on the computer resources it requires when running.

job processing

Handling and processing jobs in the computer.

job queue

The lineup of programs ready to be executed.

job scheduling

In a large computer, establishing a job queue to run a sequence of programs over any period of time such as a single shift, a full day, etc.

job stream

A series of related programs that are run in a prescribed order. The output of one program is the input to the next program and so on.

join

In relational database management, to match one file against another based on some condition creating a third file with data from the matching files. For example, a customer file can be joined with an order file creating a file of records for all customers who purchased a particular product. In the following example, a sales file is joined with a product file to derive the product description.

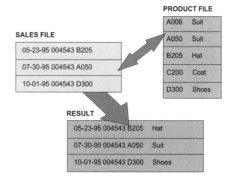

Josephson junction

An ultra-fast switching technology that uses superconductor materials, originally conceived by Brian Josephson. Circuits are immersed in liquid helium to obtain near-absolute zero degrees required for operation. Switching takes place in a few picoseconds. Although Josephson junctions have not materialized for computer circuits, they have been used in medical instruments.

joy stick

A pointing device used to move an object on screen in any direction. It employs a vertical rod mounted on a base with one or two buttons. Joy sticks are used extensively in video games and in some CAD systems.

JPEG

(Joint Photographic Experts Group) An ISO/ITU standard for compressing images using discrete cosine transform. It provides lossy compression (you lose sharpness from the original) and can provide ratios of 100:1 and higher. It depends entirely on the image, but ratios of 10:1 and 20:1 may provide little noticeable loss. The more the loss can be tolerated, the more the image can be compressed. Compression is achieved by dividing the picture into tiny pixel blocks, which are halved over and over until the ratio is achieved.

Jscript

(JavaSCRIPT) Microsoft's implementation of JavaScript. Jscript is built into Internet Explorer. See *VB Script*.

JSP

(JavaServer Page) An extension to the Java servlet technology from Sun that provides a simple programming vehicle for displaying dynamic content on a Web page. The JSP is an HTML page with embedded Java source code that is executed in the Web server or application server. The HTML provides the page layout that will be returned to the Web browser, and the Java provides the processing; for example, to deliver a query to the database and fill in the blank fields with the results. See *servlet*, *Active Server Page* and *CGI script*.

jukebox

A storage device for multiple sets of CD-ROMs, tape cartridges or disk modules.

Julian date

The representation of month and day by a consecutive number starting with Jan. 1. For example, Feb. 1 is Julian 32. Dates are converted into Julian dates for calculation.

jumper

The simplest form of an on/off switch. It is just a tiny, plastic-covered metal block, which is pushed onto two pins to close the circuit.

junction

The point at which two elements make contact. In a transistor, a junction is the point where an N-type material makes contact with a P-type material.

JVM

See *Java Virtual Machine*.

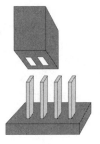

Jumper

K

See *kilo*.

K5, K6

Families of Pentium-class and Pentium II-class CPU chips from AMD. Both types use the standard Socket 7 receptacle for Pentium chips.

Kb, KB

(KiloBit, KiloByte) See *kilo* and *space/time*.

Kbps, Kbits/sec

(KiloBits Per Second) Thousand bits per second. See *kilo* and *space/time*.

KBps, KBytes/sec

(KiloBytes Per Second) Thousand bytes per second. See *kilo* and *space/time*.

Kerberos

A security system developed at MIT that authenticates users. It does not provide authorization to services or databases; it establishes identity at logon, which is used throughout the session.

Kermit

An asynchronous file transfer protocol developed at Columbia University, noted for its accuracy over noisy lines.

kernel

The fundamental part of a program, typically an operating system, that resides in memory at all times and provides the basic services. It is the part of the operating system that is closest to the machine and may activate the hardware directly or interface to another software layer that drives the hardware. See *microkernel*.

kerning

In typography, the spacing of letter combinations, such as WA, MW and TA, where each character overlaps into some of the space of the other for improved appearance.

Kerr effect

A change in rotation of light reflected off a magnetic field. The polarity of a magneto-optic bit causes the laser to shift one degree clockwise or counterclockwise.

key

(1) A keyboard button.

(2) Data that identifies a record. Account number, product code and customer name are typical key fields used to identify a record in a file or database. As an identifier, each key value must be unique in each record. See *sort key*.

(3) A numeric code used by an algorithm to create a code for encrypting data for security purposes.

keyboard buffer

A memory bank or reserved memory area that stores keystrokes until the program can accept them. It lets fast typists continue typing while the program catches up.

keyboard connector

On a PC, there are two types of keyboard connectors. The standard PC uses a 5-pin DIN plug and socket. PS/2s and laptops use a smaller 6-pin mini DIN plug and socket.

keyboard controller

A circuit that monitors keystrokes and generates the required data bits when pressed.

1/2"

PC Keyboard

Keyboard Connector

5/16"

PS/2 (mouse, keyboard)

keyboard enhancer, keyboard macro processor
Same as *macro processor*.

keyboard interrupt
A signal that gets the attention of the CPU each time a key is pressed. See *interrupt*.

keyboard processor
See *keyboard controller*.

keyboard template
A plastic card that fits over the function keys to identify each key's purpose in a particular software program.

key cap
A replaceable, top part of a keyboard key. To identify commonly-used codes, it can be replaced with a custom-printed key cap.

key click
An audible feedback provided when a key is pressed. It may be adjustable by the user.

key command
A key combination (Alt-G, Ctrl-B, Command-M, etc.) used as a command to the computer.

key field
See *key (2)*.

keyframe
In computer graphics animation, a frame that indicates the beginning or end of an object in motion.

key in
To enter data by typing on a keyboard.

keypad
A small keyboard or supplementary keyboard keys; for example, the keys on a calculator or the number/cursor cluster on a computer keyboard.

keypunch
To punch holes in a punched card. It is sometimes used to refer to typing on a computer keyboard.

keypunch department
Same as *data entry department*.

keypunch machine
A punched-card data entry machine. A deck of blank cards is placed into a hopper, and, upon operator command, the machine feeds one card to a punch station. As characters are typed, a series of dies at the punch station punch the appropriate holes in the selected card column.

key system, key telephone system
An inhouse telephone system that is not centrally connected to a PBX. Each telephone has buttons for outside lines that can be dialed directly without having to "dial 9."

key word
(1) A word used in a text search.

(2) A word in a text document that is used in an index to best describe the contents of the document.

(3) A reserved word in a programming or command language.

Khornerstones
A benchmark program that tests CPU, I/O and floating point performance.

KHz
(KiloHertZ) One thousand cycles per second. See *horizontal scan frequency*.

kicks

See *CICS*.

kilo, kilobit, kilobyte

Thousand, thousand bits, thousand bytes. Also Kb, Kbit and K-bit, or KB, Kbyte and K-byte. Kilo or "K" often refers to the precise value 1,024 since computer specifications are usually binary numbers. For example, 64K means 65,536 bytes when referring to memory or storage (64x1024), but a 64K salary means $64,000. The IEEE uses "K" for 1,024, and "k" for 1,000. See *space/time*.

kiosk

A small, self-standing structure such as a newstand or ticket booth. Unattended, multimedia kiosks dispense public information.

kludge

Also spelled "kluge" and pronounced "klooj." A crude, inelegant system, component or program. It may refer to a makeshift, temporary solution to a problem as well as to any product that is poorly designed or that becomes unwieldy over time.

KIOSK

knowledge acquisition

The process of acquiring knowledge from a human expert for an expert system, which must be carefully organized into IF-THEN rules or some other form of knowledge representation.

knowledge base

A database of rules about a subject used in AI applications. See *expert system*.

knowledge based system

An AI application that uses a database of knowledge about a subject. See *expert system*.

knowledge domain

A specific area of expertise of an expert system.

knowledge engineer

A person who translates the knowledge of an expert into the knowledge base of an expert system.

knowledge management

An umbrella term for making more efficient use of the human knowledge that exists within an organization. Knowledge management is the 21st Century equivalent of information management. It is essentialy an industry trying to distinguish itself with specialized groupware and business intelligence (BI) products that offer a wide range of solutions. A major focus is to identify and extract meaningful content from documents, reports and other text and data sources. See *information management, groupware* and *BI software*.

knowledge representation

A method used to code knowledge in an expert system, typically a series of IF-THEN rules (IF this condition occurs, THEN take this action).

KSDS

(Keyed Sequence DataSet) A VSAM structure that uses an index to store records in available free space. Retrieval is by key field or by address. Contrast with *ESDS*.

KSR terminal

(Keyboard Send Receive terminal) Same as *teleprinter*. Contrast with *RO terminal*.

KVM switch

(Keyboard Video Mouse switch) A device used to connect one keyboard, one mouse and one monitor to two or more computers. KVM switches are used to save space on a desktop when two or more computers are routinely used. They are also widely used to control server farms, where it is only necessary to gain access to each machine periodically.

L

L1 cache, L2 cache

An L1 memory cache is the cache built into the CPU chip or packaged within the same module. An L2 cache is external to the chip and is typically made up of SRAM chips on the motherboard. See *cache*.

L2TP

(Layer 2 Tunneling Protocol) A protocol from the IETF for creating virtual private networks (VPNs) over the Internet. It supports non-IP protocols such as AppleTalk and IPX as well as the IPSec security protocol. It is a combination of Microsoft's Point-to-Point Tunneling Protocol and Cisco's Layer 2 Forwarding (L2F) technology. See *VPN, PPTP* and *IPSec*.

label

(1) In data management, a made-up name that is assigned to a file, field or other data structure.

(2) In spreadsheets, descriptive text that is entered into a cell.

(3) In programming, a made-up name used to identify a variable or a subroutine.

(4) In computer operations, a self-sticking form attached to the outside of a disk or tape in order to identify it.

(5) In magnetic tape files, a record used for identification at the beginning or end of the file.

label prefix

In a spreadsheet, a character typed at the beginning of a cell entry. For example, in 1-2-3, a single quote (') identifies what follows as a descriptive label even if it's a number.

LAN

(Local Area Network) A communications network that serves users within a confined geographical area. It is made up of servers, workstations, a network operating system and a communications link.

Servers are high-speed machines that hold programs and data shared by all network users. The workstations, or clients, are the users' personal computers, which perform stand-alone processing and access the network servers as required.

The controlling software in a LAN is the network operating system, such as Windows NT, NetWare or UNIX, which resides on a server. A component part of the software resides in each workstation and allows the application to read and write data from the server as if it were on the local machine.

The physical transfer of data is performed by the access method (Ethernet, Token Ring, etc.) which is implemented in the network adapters that plug into the workstations and servers. The actual communications path is the cable (twisted pair, coax, optical fiber) that interconnects each network adapter. See *MAN, WAN, bridge, router, gateway* and *hub*.

LAN administrator

See *network administrator*.

LAN analyzer

See *network analyzer*.

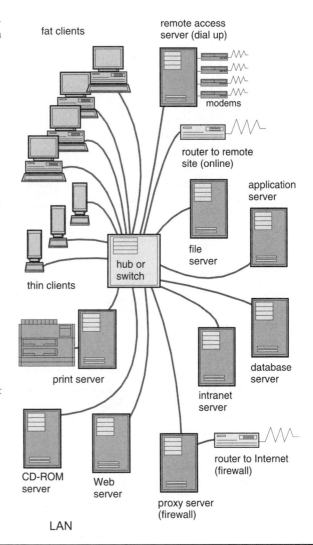

fat clients

remote access server (dial up)

modems

router to remote site (online)

application server

hub or switch

file server

thin clients

database server

intranet server

print server

router to Internet (firewall)

CD-ROM server

Web server

proxy server (firewall)

LAN

landing zone

A safe non-data area on a hard disk used for parking the read/write head.

landscape

A printing orientation that prints data across the wider side of the form. Contrast with *portrait*.

LANE

(**LAN E**mulation) The ability to connect Ethernet and Token Ring networks together via ATM. LANE makes the process transparent, requiring no modification to Ethernet and Token Ring stations. LANE allows common protocols, such as IP, IPX, AppleTalk and DECnet, to ride over an ATM backbone.

LAN emulation

The processing required to support protocols used in legacy LANs connected to an ATM network. Traditional communications protocols were designed for shared media (Ethernet, Token Ring, etc.). Broadcasting reached all nodes automatically. ATM's topology does not lend itself to broadcasting, thus LAN emulation performs lookup functions in software that provide the address resolutions required by protocols such as IP and NetWare's IPX.

language processor

Language translation software. Programming languages, command languages, query languages, natural languages and foreign languages are all translated by software.

LAN Manager

A network operating system from Microsoft that runs as a server application under OS/2. It supports both DOS, Windows and OS/2 clients. LAN Manager was superseded by Windows NT Server, and many parts of LAN Manager are used in NT. See *LAN Server*. See also *network administrator*.

LAN Server

(1) A network operating system from IBM that runs as a server application under OS/2 and supports both DOS, Windows and OS/2 clients. Originally based on LAN Manager when OS/2 was jointly developed by IBM and Microsoft, Version 3.0 runs under IBM's own OS/2 Version 2.0.

(2) A server in a LAN.

LANtastic

A popular peer-to-peer LAN operating system for Windows and DOS from Artisoft, Inc., Tucson, AZ, (www.artisoft.com). Starting with Version 6.0, LANtastic clients can access NetWare, LAN Manager, LAN Server and Windows NT servers.

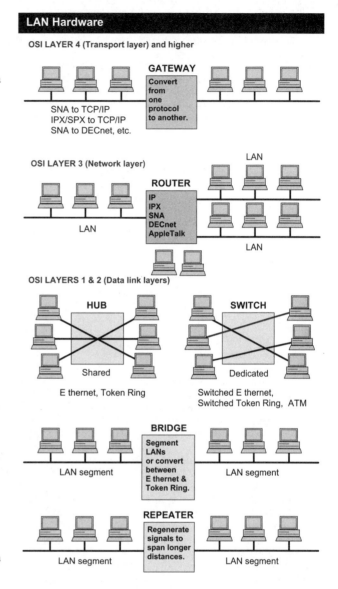

LAN Hardware

OSI LAYER 4 (Transport layer) and higher

GATEWAY — Convert from one protocol to another.

SNA to TCP/IP
IPX/SPX to TCP/IP
SNA to DECnet, etc.

OSI LAYER 3 (Network layer)

ROUTER — IP, IPX, SNA, DECnet, AppleTalk

LAN

OSI LAYERS 1 & 2 (Data link layers)

HUB — Shared — E thernet, Token Ring

SWITCH — Dedicated — Switched E thernet, Switched Token Ring, ATM

BRIDGE — Segment LANs or convert between E thernet & Token Ring.

LAN segment

REPEATER — Regenerate signals to span longer distances.

LAN segment

LAP

(Link Access Procedure) An ITU family of error correction protocols originally derived from the HDLC standard and used on X.25 packet networks. LAP-B, LAP-D, LAP-M and LAP-X are variants.

LapLink

A file transfer program for Windows from LapLink.com, Inc., Bothell, WA, (www.laplink.com), that transfers data between laptops and desktop computers locally or remotely. LapLink.com was formerly Travelling Software, Inc.

laptop computer

A portable computer that has a flat screen and usually weighs less than a dozen pounds. It uses AC power and/or batteries. Most have connectors for an external monitor and keyboard transforming them into desktop computers. See *notebook computer* and *pocket computer*.

laser

(Light Amplification from the Stimulated Emission of Radiation) A device that creates a very uniform light that can be precisely focused. It generates a single wavelength or narrow band of wavelengths and is used in applications such as communications, printing and disk storage. Unlike the transmission of electricity, transmission of light pulses over optical fibers is not affected by nearby electrical interferences. See *LED*.

laser-class printer

A category of computer printers that produces output with the same resolution and color quality of a laser printer. Output from LED, solid ink, dye sublimation and Iris printers is in the same class as laser printers.

LaserDisc

An 8" or 12" optical disk used for full-motion video that uses the LaserVision technology developed by Philips. LaserDisc players can read the CLV format for two hours of recording (one hour per side) as well as the CAV format for a total of one hour. CAV provides direct access capability for interactive training material. The LaserDisc has been obsoleted by DVD. See *Video CD*.

LaserJet

A family of desktop laser printers from HP. Introduced in 1984 at $3,495, the first LaserJet revolutionized the desktop laser printer market, and HP continues to be the leader in the field. LaserJets initially printed at 300 dpi, but resolution was boosted to 600 dpi starting with the LaserJet 4. PCL is the printer command language.

laser printer

A printer that uses the electrophotographic method used in copy machines to print a page at a time. A laser "paints" the dots of light onto a photographic drum or belt. The toner is applied to the drum or belt and then transferred onto the paper. Desktop printers use cut sheets like a copy machine. Large printers may use rolls of paper.

LaserWriter

A family of desktop laser printers from Apple, introduced in 1985. Most models support PostScript and built-in networking.

LAT

(Local Area Transport) A communications protocol from Digital for controlling terminal traffic in a DECnet environment.

LATA

(Local Access and Transport Area) The geographic region set up to differentiate local and long distance telephone calls. Any telephone call between parties within a LATA is handled by the local telephone company.

latch

An electronic circuit that maintains one of two states. See *flip-flop*.

late binding
Linking routines at runtime.

latency
The time between initiating a request for data and the beginning of the actual data transfer. On a disk, latency is the time it takes for the selected sector to come around and be positioned under the read/write head. Channel latency is the time it takes for a computer channel to become unoccupied in order to transfer data.

latent image
An invisible image typically of electrical charges. For example, in a copy machine, a latent image of the page to be copied is created on a plate or drum as an electrical charge.

launch
To cause a program to load and run.

layer
(1) In computer graphics, one of several on-screen "drawing boards" for creating elements within a picture. Layers can be manipulated independently, and the sum of all layers make up the total image.

(2) In communications, a protocol that interacts with other protocols to provide all the necessary transmission services. See *OSI*.

layer 2 switch
A network device that cross connects stations or LAN segments. LAN switches are available for Ethernet, Fast Ethernet, Token Ring and FDDI. A LAN switch is also known as a frame switch. ATM switches are generally considered a category by themselves. See *switched Ethernet*.

layer 3 switch
A high-speed router that forwards traffic at the same speed or near the same speed as a layer 2 switch. See *OSI*.

layer 4 switch
A high-speed router that forwards traffic at the same speed or near the same speed as a layer 2 switch. It is able to make more forwarding decisions than a traditional router since it can analyze layer 4 information. See *OSI*.

layout setting
A value used to format a printed page. Margins, tabs, indents, headers, footers and column widths are examples.

LBA
(Logical Block Addressing) A method used to support IDE hard disks larger than 504MB (528,482,304 bytes) on PCs. The Enhanced IDE standard (ATA-2) specified this method, which provides a cylinder-head-sector translation in the BIOS. LBA is required for compatibility with the FAT32 directory.

LBRV
(Low Bit Rate Voice) A voice sampling technique that analyzes each 15-30 millisecond speech segment independently and converts it into a 30-byte frame.

LCC
See *leaded chip carrier*.

LCD
(Liquid Crystal Display) A display technology that uses rod-shaped molecules (liquid crystals) that flow like liquid and bend light. Unenergized, the crystals direct light through two polarizing filters, allowing a natural background color to show. When energized, they redirect the light to be absorbed in one of the polarizers, causing the dark appearance of crossed polarizers to show. The more the molecules are twisted, the better the contrast and viewing angle.

LCD panel

Also called a "projection panel," it is a data projector that accepts computer output and displays it on a see-through liquid crystal screen that is placed on top of an overhead projector.

LCD printer

An electrophotographic printer that uses a single light source directed by liquid crystal shutters.

LDAP

(Lightweight Directory Access Protocol) A protocol used to access a directory listing. LDAP support is being implemented in Web browsers and e-mail programs, which can query an LDAP-compliant directory. It is expected that LDAP will provide a common method for searching e-mail addresses on the Internet, eventually leading to a global white pages.

lead acid

A rechargeable battery technology widely used in portable gardening tools, but has been used in some portable computers. It uses lead plates and an acid electrolyte. It provides the least amount of charge per pound of the rechargeable technologies. See *nickel cadmium, nickel hydride* and *zinc air*.

leaded chip carrier

A square chip housing with pin connectors on all four sides (provides more I/O paths than a DIP). Contrast with *leadless chip carrier*.

leader

(1) A length of unrecorded tape used to thread the tape onto the tape drive.

(2) A dot or dash used to draw the eye across the printed page, such as in a table of contents.

leading

In typography, the vertical spacing between lines of type (between baselines). The name comes from the early days of typesetting when the space was achieved with thin bars of lead.

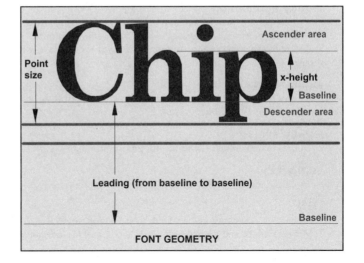

FONT GEOMETRY

leading edge

(1) The edge of a punched card or document that enters the reading station first.

(2) In digital electronics, a pulse as it changes from a 0 to a 1.

(3) In programming, a loop that tests a condition before the loop is entered.

(4) (Leading Edge Products, Inc., Westborough, MA) A PC manufacturer founded in 1980. Its Model M (for Mitsubishi) in 1982 was the first PC-compatible from overseas. Korean Daewoo Corporation supplied it with products since 1984 and acquired it in 1989.

leading zeros

Zeros used to fill a field that do not increase the numerical value of the data. For example, all the zeros in 0000006588 are leading zeros.

leadless chip carrier

A square chip housing with flat contact connectors on all four sides (provides more I/O paths than a DIP). Contrast with *leaded chip carrier*.

leaf

In database management, the last node of a tree.

---

leapfrog test
A storage diagnostic routine that replicates itself throughout the storage medium.

leased line
A private communications channel leased from a common carrier. It can be ordered in pairs, providing a four-wire channel for full-duplex transmission (dial-up system provides only two-wire lines). To improve line quality, it can also be conditioned.

leased line modem
A high-speed modem used in private lines. It may have built-in lower speeds for alternate use in dial-up lines.

LEC
(Local Exchange Carrier) An organization that provides local telephone service, including the RBOCs, large companies such as GTE and hundreds of small, rural telephone companies. A LEC controls the service from its central office (CO) to subscribers within a local geographic area.

LED
(Light Emitting Diode) A display technology that uses a semiconductor diode that emits light when charged. It usually gives off a red glow, although other colors can be generated. It is used in readouts and on/off lights in myriads of electronic appliances. It was the first digital watch display, but was superseded by LCD, which uses less power.

LED printer
An electrophotographic printer that uses a matrix of LEDs as its light source rather than a laser.

legacy application
An application that has been in existence for some time. It often refers to mainframe and ERP applications; however, as users abandoned DOS and Windows 3.1 for Windows 95/98 and NT, they too are called legacy applications. In today's world of the Internet, virtually anything not Web related is often thought of as a legacy app.

legacy LAN
Refers to a LAN topology, such as Ethernet or Token Ring, which has a large installed base or has been in existence for a long time.

legacy system
Refers to a mainframe or minicomputer information system that has been in existence for a long time.

Lempel Ziv
A data compression algorithm that uses an adaptive compression technique.

LEN
(Low Entry Networking) In SNA, peer-to-peer connectivity between adjacent Type 2.1 nodes, such as PCs, workstations and minicomputers. LU 6.2 sessions are supported across LEN connections.

LEO
(Low-Earth Orbit) A communications satellite in orbit 400 to 1600 miles above the earth. Being much closer than 22,282 mile-high geosynchronous satellites (GEOs), LEO signals make the round trip from earth much faster. Thus, low-powered pizza dishes and hand-held devices can be used. LEOs revolve around the globe every couple of hours, and in order to maintain constant communications with the earth, multiple LEOs must be used. Iridium and Globalstar were the first global, LEO-based communications systems that used handheld phones.

letter quality
The print quality of an electric typewriter. Laser printers, ink jet printers and daisy wheel printers provide letter quality printing. 24-pin dot matrix printers provide near letter quality (NLQ), but the characters are not as dark and crisp.

level 1 cache, level 2 cache
See *L1 cache, L2 cache.*

lexicographic sort

Arranging items in alphabetic order like a dictionary. Numbers are located by their alphabetic spelling.

LF

See *line feed*.

LHARC

A popular freeware compression program developed by Haruyasu Yoshizaki that uses a variant of the LZW (LZ77) dictionary method followed by a Huffman coding stage. It runs on PCs, UNIX and other platforms as its source code is also free.

librarian

(1) A person who works in the data library.

(2) See *CA-Librarian*.

library

(1) A collection of programs or data files.

(2) A collection of functions (subroutines) that are linked into the main program when it is compiled.

(3) See *data library*.

library function, library routine

A subroutine that is part of a function library.

library management

See *version control*.

LIFO

(Last In First Out) A queueing method in which the next item to be retrieved is the item most recently placed in the queue. Contrast with *FIFO*.

ligature

Two or more typeface characters that are designed as a single unit (physically touch). Fi, ffi, ae and oe are common ligatures.

light guide

A transmission channel that contains a number of optical fibers packaged together.

light pen

A light-sensitive stylus wired to a video terminal used to draw pictures or select menu options. The user brings the pen to the desired point on screen and presses the pen button to make contact.

Screen pixels are constantly being refreshed. When the user presses the button, allowing the pen to sense light, the pixel being illuminated at that instant identifies the screen location.

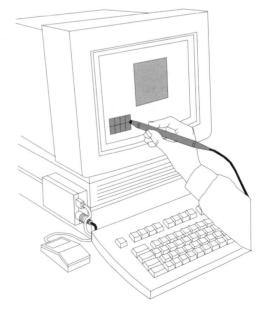

light source

In computer graphics, the implied location of a light source in order to simulate the visual effect of a light on a 3-D object. Some programs can compute multiple light sources.

lightwave

Light in the infrared, visible and ultraviolet ranges, which falls between x-rays and microwaves. Wavelengths are between 10 nanometers and one millimeter.

lightwave system
A device that transmits light pulses over optical fibers at extremely high speeds (Gbits/sec range). Many intercity telephone trunks have been converted to lightwave systems.

lightweight protocol
A communications protocol designed with less complexity in order to reduce overhead. For example, it uses fixed-length headers because they are faster to parse than variable-length headers. To ensure compatibility, it eliminates optional subsets of the standard.

li-ion
See *lithium ion*.

limited distance modem
Same as *short-haul modem*.

Linda
A set of parallel processing functions added to languages, such as C and C++, that allows data to be created and transferred between processes. It was developed by Yale professor David Gelernter, when he was a 23-year old graduate student.

line
(1) In text-based systems, a row of characters.

(2) In graphics-based systems, a row of pixels.

(3) Any communications channel.

line adapter
In communications, a device similar to a modem, that converts a digital signal into a form suitable for transmission over a communications line and vice versa. It provides parallel/serial and serial/parallel conversion, modulation and demodulation.

line analyzer
A device that monitors the transmission of a communications line.

linear
Sequential or having a graph that is a straight line.

linear address space
See *flat address space*.

linear programming
A mathematical technique used to obtain an optimum solution in resource allocation problems, such as production planning.

linear video
Continuous playback of videotape or videodisc. It typically refers to analog video technology.

linear video editing
Editing analog videotape. Before digital editing (nonlinear video editing), video sequences were edited by inserting new frames and reconstructing the balance of the tape by adding the remainder of the frames. Contrast with *nonlinear video editing*.

line driver
In communications, a device that is used to extend the transmission distance between terminals and computers that are connected via private lines. It is used for digital transmission and is required at each end of the line.

line feed
(1) A character code that advances the screen cursor or printer to the next line. The line feed is used as an end of line code in UNIX. In DOS and OS/2 text files, the return/line feed pair (ASCII 13 10) is the standard end of line code.

(2) A printer button that advances paper one line when depressed.

line frequency
The number of times each second that a wave or some repeatable set of signals is transmitted over a line. See *horizontal scan frequency*.

line level
In communications, the signal strength within a transmission channel, measured in decibels or nepers.

line load
(1) In communications, the percentage of time a communications channel is used.

(2) In electronics, the amount of current that is carried in a circuit.

line number
(1) A specific line of programming language source code.

(2) On display screens, a specific row of text or row of dots.

(3) In communications, a specific communications channel.

line of code
A statement in a source program. In assembly language, it usually generates one machine instruction, but in a high-level language, it may generate a series of instructions.

Lines of code are used to measure the complexity of a program. However, comparisons are misleading if the programs are not in the same language or category. For example, 20 lines of code in COBOL might require 200 lines of code in assembly language.

line of sight
An unobstructed view from transmitter to receiver.

line printer
A printer that prints one line at a time. Line printers are usually connected to mainframes and minicomputers.

line squeeze
In a mail merge, the elimination of blank lines when printing names and addresses that contain no data in certain fields, such as title, company and second address line. See *field squeeze*.

```
Without line squeeze      With line squeeze
Pat Smith                 Pat Smith
                          10 South Main
10 South Main             Bearcat, OR 80901
Bearcat, OR 80901
```

link
(1) In communications, a line, channel or circuit over which data is transmitted.

(2) In data management, a pointer embedded within a record that refers to data or the location of data in another record.

(3) In programming, a call to another program or subroutine.

linkage editor (linker)
A utility program that links a compiled or assembled program to a particular environment. It formally unites references between program modules and libraries of subroutines. Its output is a load module, a program ready to run in the computer.

link edit
To use a linkage editor to prepare a program for running.

linked list
In data management, a group of items, each of which points to the next item. It allows for the organization of a sequential set of data in noncontiguous storage locations.

Linpack
A package of FORTRAN programs for numerical linear algebra that is commonly used to create benchmark programs for testing a computer's floating point performance.

Linux

A version of UNIX that runs on x86, Alpha and PowerPC machines. Linux is freeware, and the full distribution of Linux is available on CD-ROM, which includes the complete source code as well as hundreds of tools, applets and utilities. Linus Torvalds created the kernel, and many of the supporting apps and utilities came from the GNU project of the Free Software Foundation. Several companies such as Red Hat, Caldera and VA Linux distribute Linux combined with technical support for a fee.

LIPS

(Logical Inferences Per Second) The unit of measurement of the thinking speed of an AI application. Humans do about 2 LIPS. In the computer, one LIPS equals from 100 to 1,000 instructions.

liquid crystal shutters

A method of directing light onto the drum in an electrophotographic printer. A matrix of liquid crystal dots function as shutters that are opened and closed. See *LCD*.

LISP

(LISt Processing) A high-level programming language used extensively in AI applications as well as in compiler creation. Developed in 1960 by John McCarthy, its syntax and structure is very different than traditional programming languages. For example, there is no syntactic difference between data and instructions.

LISP is available in both interpreter and compiler versions and can be modified and expanded by the programmer. Many varieties have been developed, including versions that perform calculations efficiently. The following Common LISP example converts Fahrenheit to Celsius:

```
(defun convert ()
  (format t "Enter Fahrenheit ")
  (let ((fahr (read)))
   (format t "Celsius is <126>D"
     (truncate (*(-fahr 32)
       (/ 5 9))))))
```

list processing language

A programming language, such as LISP, Prolog and Logo, used to process lists of data (names, words, objects). Although operations such as selecting the next to first, or next to last element, or reversing all elements in a list, can be programmed in any language, list processing languages provide commands to do them. Recursion is also provided, allowing a subroutine to call itself over again in order to repetitively analyze a group of elements.

LISTSERV

Mailing list management software from L-Soft international, Inc., Landover, MD, (www.lsoft.com), that runs on mainframes, VMS, NT and various UNIX machines. LISTSERV scans e-mail messages for the words "subscribe" and "unsubscribe" to automatically update the list. See *mailing list*.

literal

In programming, any part of an instruction that remains unchanged when translated into machine language, such as an output message.

lithium ion

A rechargeable battery technology that provides more than twice the charge per pound as nickel hydride. Although used in camcorders and other devices, Toshiba introduced the first lithium ion notebook in the U.S. in late 1993. Lithium polymer technology may provide twice as much power as lithium ion.

LMDS

(Local Multipoint Distribution Service) A digital wireless transmission system that works in the 28GHz range in the U.S. and 24-40GHz overseas. It requires line of sight between transmitter and receiving antenna, which can be from one to four miles apart depending on weather conditions. LMDS provides bandwidth in the OC-1 to OC-12 range.

load

(1) To copy a program from some source, such as a disk or tape, into memory for execution.

(2) To fill up a disk with data or programs.

(3) To insert a disk or tape into a drive.

(4) In programming, to store data in a register.

(5) In performance measurement, the current use of a system as a percentage of total capacity.

(6) In electronics, the flow of current through a circuit.

load balancing

The fine tuning of a computer system, network or disk subsystem in order to more evenly distribute the data and/or processing across available resouces. For example, in clustering, load balancing might distribute the incoming transactions evenly to all servers, or it might redirect them to the next available server.

loaded line

A telephone line from customer to central office that uses loading coils to reduce distortion.

loader

A program routine that copies a program into memory for execution.

loading coil

A device used in local telephone loops (exceeding 18,000 ft.) that boosts voice-grade transmission. It often adds noise to high-speed data transmission and must be removed for such traffic.

load module

A program in machine language form ready to run in the computer. It is the output of a link editor.

load sharing

Sharing the workload in two or more computers.

local area network

See *LAN*.

local bus

Also called the "system bus," it is the pathway between the CPU, memory and peripheral devices. When the higher-speed VL-bus and PCI bus were introduced, they were called local buses, because they ran at the then-current speed of the local bus. Since then, local buses have gone beyond the speeds of VL-bus and PCI.

local bypass

An interconnection between two facilities without the use of the local telephone company.

local console

A terminal or workstation directly connected to the computer or other device that it is monitoring and controlling.

local loop

A communications line between a customer and the telephone company's central office. See *loop carrier*.

RAM

CPU

bus controller

ISA bus
16 bit

32 or 64 bit
Local bus

bus controller

bus controller

VL bus
32 bit

PCI bus
32 or 64 bit

local memory

The memory used by a single CPU or allocated to a single program or function.

local storage

The disk storage used by a single CPU.

LocalTalk

A LAN access method from Apple that uses twisted pair wires and transmits at 230 Kbps. It runs under AppleTalk and uses a daisy chain topology that can connect up to 32 devices within a distance of 1,000 feet. Third party products allow it to hook up with bus, passive star and active star topologies.

local variable

In programming, a variable used only within the routine or function it is defined in.

lockup

Refers to a computer's inability to respond to user input. See *abend*.

log

A record of computer activity used for statistical purposes as well as backup and recovery.

logic

The sequence of operations performed by hardware or software. Hardware logic is made up of circuits that perform an operations. Software logic (program logic) is the sequence of instructions in a program.
Note: Logic is not the same as logical. See *logical vs physical* and *logical expression*.

logical

(1) A reasonable solution to a problem.

(2) A higher level view of an object; for example, the user's view versus the computer's view. See *logical vs physical*.

logical data group

Data derived from several sources. Same as *view*.

logical drive

An allocated part of a physical drive that is designated and managed as an independent unit.

logical expression

An expression that results in true or false. Same as *Boolean expression*.

logical field

A data field that contains a yes/no, true/false condition.

logical lock

The prevention of user access to data that is provided by marking the file or record through the use of software. Contrast with *physical lock*.

logical operator

One of the Boolean logical operators (AND, OR and NOT).

logical record

A reference to a data record that is independent of its physical location. It may be physically stored in two or more locations.

logical vs physical

High-level versus low-level. Logical implies a higher view than the physical. A message transmitted from Phoenix to Boston logically goes between two cities; however, the physical circuit could be Phoenix to Chicago to Philadelphia to Boston.

logic analyzer

(1) A device that monitors computer performance by timing various segments of the running programs. The total running time and the time spent in selected progam modules is displayed in order to isolate the the least efficient code.

(2) A device used to test and diagnose an electronic system, which includes an oscilloscope for displaying various digital states.

logic array

Same as *gate array* or *PLA*.

logic bomb

A program routine that destroys data; for example, it may reformat the hard disk or insert random bits into data files. It may be brought into a personal computer by downloading a corrupt public-domain program. Once executed, it does its damage right away, whereas a virus keeps on destroying.

logic chip

A processor or controller chip. Contrast with *memory chip*.

logic circuit

A circuit that performs some processing or controlling function. Contrast with *memory*.

logic diagram

A flow chart of hardware circuits or program logic.

logic error

A program bug due to an incorrect sequence of instructions.

logic gate

A collection of transistors and electronic components that make up a Boolean logical operation, such as AND, NAND, OR and NOR. Transistors make up logic gates. Logic gates make up circuits. Circuits make up electronic systems.

logic operation

An operation that analyzes one or more inputs and generates a particular output based on a set of rules. See *AND, OR and NOT* and *Boolean logic*.

logic-seeking printer

A printer that analyzes line content and skips over blank spaces at high speeds.

Logo

A high-level programming language noted for its ease of use and graphics capabilities. It is a recursive language that contains many list processing functions that are in LISP, although Logo's syntax is more understandable for novices.

The following Object Logo example converts Fahrenheit to Celsius:

```
convert
local [fahr]
print "|Enter Fahrenheit |
make "fahr ReadWord
print "|Celsius is |
print (:fahr - 32) * 5 / 9
end
```

log off, log out

To quit, or sign off, a computer system.

log on, log in

To gain access, or sign in, to a computer system. If restricted, it requires users to identify themselves by entering an ID number and/or password. Service bureaus base their charges for the time between logon and logoff.

long card

In PCs, a full-length controller board that plugs into an expansion slot. Contrast with *short card*.

long-haul

In communications, modems or communications devices that are capable of transmitting over long distances.

loop

In programming, a repetition within a program. Whenever a process must be repeated, a loop is set up to handle it. A program has a main loop and a series of minor loops, which are nested within the main loop. Learning how to set up loops is what programming technique is all about.

loopback plug

A diagnostic connector that directs the sending line back into the receiving line for test purposes.

loop carrier

In telephone communications, a system that concentrates a number of analog or digital lines from a remote termination station into the central office. It normally converts analog voice into digital at the remote station; however, it can be adapted to provide ISDN service to a customer.

loosely coupled

Refers to stand-alone computers connected via a network. Loosely coupled computers process on their own and exchange data on demand. Contrast with *tightly coupled*.

lossless compression

Compression techniques that decompress data 100% back to original. Contrast with *lossy compression*.

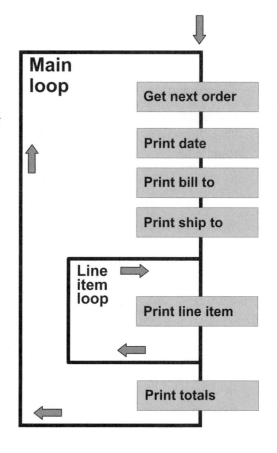

lossy compression

Compression techniques that do not decompress data 100% back to original. Images and audio samples may be able to afford small losses of resolution in order to increase compression. Contrast with *lossless compression*.

lost cluster

Disk records that have lost their identification with a file name. This can happen if a file is not closed properly, which can sometimes occur if the computer is turned off without formally quitting an application.

Lotus

(Lotus Development Corporation, Cambridge, MA, subsidiary of IBM, www.lotus.com) A major software company founded in 1981 by Mitch Kapor. It achieved outstanding success by introducing Lotus 1-2-3, the first spreadsheet for the IBM PC. Over the years, it has developed a variety of applications and has helped set industry standards.

Lotus 1-2-3

A popular spreadsheet from Lotus that runs on a variety of platforms, including DOS, Windows, Mac, Sun, VAX, OS/2, UNIX and IBM mainframes. Its macro language, the first to be widely used in a spreadsheet, has been supplemented with LotusScript, a BASIC-like language that supports Notes manipulation.

Lotus Notes

Messaging and groupware software from Lotus that was introduced in 1989 for OS/2 and later expanded to Windows, Mac, UNIX and NetWare. Notes provides e-mail, document sharing, workflow, group discussions, calendaring and scheduling and also accepts plug-ins for other functions. The unique feature and heart of Notes is its document database. Everything is maintained in a Notes database that can hold mail, group discussions, data fields, text, audio and video. In 1996, Lotus decoupled the Notes client from the server, which was renamed Domino. Domino is Internet compliant and can be accessed by a Web browser.

low frequency

An electromagnetic wave that vibrates in the range from 30 to 300,000 Hertz.

low-level format

The sector identification on a disk that the drive uses to locate sectors for reading and writing. See *format program*.

low-level language

A programming language that is very close to machine language. All assembly languages are low-level languages. Contrast with *high-level language*.

low radiation

Refers to video terminals that emit less VLF (Very Low Frequency) and ELF (Extremely Low Frequency) radiation. This level of radiation cannot be shielded by office partitions. It must be cancelled out from the CRT. Health studies on this are not conclusive and are very controversial. See *MPR II*.

low resolution

A low-grade display or printing quality due to a lower number of dots or lines per inch.

lpi

(Lines Per Inch) The number of lines printed in a vertical inch.

lpm

(Lines Per Minute) The number of lines a printer can print or a scanner can scan in a minute.

LPT1

The logical name assigned to parallel port #1 in DOS and OS/2 (usually connected to a printer). A second parallel device is assigned LPT2. Contrast with *COM1*.

LQ

See *letter quality*.

LRC

(Longitudinal Redundancy Check) An error checking method that generates a parity bit from a specified string of bits on a longitudinal track. In a row and column format, such as on magnetic tape, LRC is often used with VRC, which creates a parity bit for each character.

LS-120

A type of floppy disk that records data magnetically, but uses grooves in the disk to optically align the head over the tracks. The drive supports 120MB floppy disks as well as standard 3.5" floppies.

LSAPI

(Licensing Service API) A programming interface from Microsoft that allows a licensing server to track applications in use for managing multiuser software licenses.

LSL

(Link Support Layer) A common interface for network drivers. It provides a common language between the transport layer and the data link layer and allows different transport protocols to run over one network adapter or one transport protocol to run on different network adapters.

LTO

(Linear Tape Open) A family of open magnetic tape standards developed by HP, IBM and Seagate. LTO was introduced in 1998 with two formats that share common components such as read/write head, track layout and servo technology. The Accelis format uses a dual-hub, cassette-style cartridge with a midpoint load very similar to Magstar MP. The Ultrium format uses a single hub and a wider tape like regular Magstar.

LU

(Logical Unit) In SNA, one end of a communications session. The complete LU to LU session is defined by session type. Common types are:

```
  1   Host to 3770 RJE terminal
  2   Host to 3270 mainframe terminal
  3   Host to 3270 printer
6.2   Program-to-program
  7   Host to 5250 midrange terminal
```

LU 6.2

An SNA protocol that establishes a session between two programs. It allows peer-to-peer communications as well as interaction between programs running in the host with PCs, Macs and midrange computers.

Before LU 6.2, processing was done only in the mainframe. LU 6.2 allows processing to take place at both ends of the communications, necessary for today's distributed computing and client/server environment. See *APPC* and *CPI-C*.

lumen

A unit of measurement of the flow (rate of emission) of light. A wax candle generates 13 lumens; a 100 watt bulb generates 1,200. See *candela*.

luminance

The amount of brightness, measured in lumens, that is given off by a pixel or area on a screen. It is the black/gray/white information in a video signal.

LUN

(Logical Unit Number) The physical number of a device in a daisy change of drives. See *SCSI*.

lurk

To view the interaction in a chat room or online forum without participating by typing in any comments.

Lynx

A text-based Web browser created at the University of Kansas. Though largely supplanted by graphical browsers such as Netscape Navigator and Internet Explorer, Lynx is still popular among people with visual disabilities and those with very slow modem connections.

LZW

(Lempel-Ziv-Welch) A widely-used dictionary compression method that stems from two techniques introduced by Jacob Ziv and Abraham Lempel and enhanced by Unisys researcher Terry Welch. Unisys holds the patent on LZW.

M

M

Formerly known as MUMPS, it is a high-level programming language and integrated database that is widely used in the health-care field. Its extensive string handling capabilities make it suitable for storing vast amounts of free text. It was originally developed in 1966 at Massachusetts General Hospital as the Massachusetts Utility MultiProgramming System.

The MUMPS Development Committee has maintained the language since 1973, and it became an ANSI standard in 1977. The M Technology Association (Silver Spring, MD, www.mtechnology.org) supports the M community through training, meetings and distribution of publications and software. The following M example converts Fahrenheit to Celsius:

```
READ "Enter Fahrenheit ",FAHR
SET CENT=(FAHR-32) * 5/9
WRITE "Celsius is ", CENT
```

MAC

(Message Authentication Code) A number computed from the contents of a text message that is used to authenticate the message. A MAC is like a digital signature, except that a secret key was used in its creation rather than a private key. See *digital signature* and *cryptography*. See also *Macintosh*.

MacAPPC

LU 6.2-compliant software from Apple Computer that allows a Macintosh to be a peer to an IBM APPC application.

MacDFT

Software that provides 3270 emulation for the Macintosh from Apple. It accompanies Apple's TwinAx/Coax board and supports CUT and DFT modes and DFT multiple sessions under SNA.

MacDraw

A Macintosh drawing program from Claris Corporation. It is used for illustrations and elementary CAD work. MacDraw files are a subset of the Claris CAD file format.

Mach

A UNIX-like operating system developed at Carnegie-Mellon University. It is designed with a microkernel architecture that makes it easily portable to different platforms.

machine

Any electronic or electromechanical unit of equipment. A machine is always hardware; however, "engine" refers to hardware or software.

machine address

Same as *absolute address*.

machine code

Same as *machine language*.

machine cycle

The shortest interval in which an elementary operation can take place within the processor. It is made up of some number of clock cycles.

machine dependent

Refers to software that accesses specific hardware features and runs in only one kind of computer. Contrast with *machine independent*. See *device dependent*.

machine independent

Refers to software that runs in a variety of computers. The hardware-specific instructions are in some other program (operating system, DBMS, etc.). Contrast with *machine dependent*. See *device independent*.

machine instruction

An instruction in machine language. Its anatomy is an operation code (op code) followed by operands. The op code is the verb (add, copy, etc.), while the operands are the data to be acted upon (add a to b). There are always machine instructions to INPUT and OUTPUT, to process data by

CALCULATING, COMPARING and COPYING it, and to go to some other part of the program with a GOTO instruction.

machine language

The native language of the computer. In order for a program to run, it must be in the machine language of the computer that is executing it. Although programmers are sometimes able to modify machine language in order to fix a running program, they do not create it. It is created by programs called "assemblers," "compilers" and "interpreters," which convert the programming language into machine language. Machine languages differ substantially. What takes one instruction in one machine can take 10 in another. See *assembly language*.

machine readable

Data in a form that can be read by the computer, which includes disks, tapes and punched cards. Printed fonts that can be scanned and recognized by the computer are also machine readable.

Macintosh

A family of personal computers from Apple. The original Mac with its vertical cabinet was introduced in 1984. The Mac operating system with its graphics-based user interface has provided a measure of consistency and ease of use that is unmatched. The Macintosh family is the largest non-IBM compatible personal computer series in use.

Until 1994, Macs were powered by Motorola's 680x0 family of CPUs. In 1994, Apple introduced the Power Macintoshes (PowerMacs), which use the PowerPC CPUs and provide increased performance. Today, all Macs are PowerPC based. PowerMacs run native PowerMac applications and emulate 680x0 applications. DOS and Windows applications can be run via emulation software from Insignia Solutions or via plug-in boards that contain an x86 CPU.

Macintosh extension

Additional software functions for the Macintosh, which include drivers and other enhancements to the operating system. In System 7, system extensions reside in the Extensions folder. Mac extensions are the counterpart to the CONFIG.SYS file for DOS.

MAC layer

(Media Access Control layer) The protocol sublayer that controls access to the physical transmission medium on a LAN. The MAC layer is implemented in the network adapter (NIC). Common MAC standards are CSMA/CD used in Ethernet and various token passing methods used in Token Ring, FDDI and MAP.

Mac OS X

A UNIX-based operating system for the Mac from Apple. OS X is Apple's next-generation operating system which is based on the Mach 2.5 microkernel, the heart of the NextStep operating system acquired by Apple. The X in OS X is Roman numeral 10, not the letter "x."

macro

(1) A series of menu selections, keystrokes and commands that have been recorded and assigned a name or key combination. When the macro is called or the key combination is pressed, the steps in the macro are executed from beginning to end.

Macros are used to shorten long menu sequences as well as to create miniature programs within an application. Macro languages often include programming controls (IF THEN, GOTO, WHILE, etc.) that automate sequences like any programming language. See *macro recorder*, *batch file* and *shell script*.

(2) In assembly language, a prewritten subroutine that is called for throughout the program. At assembly time, the macro calls are substituted with the actual subroutine or instructions that branch to it. The high-level language equivalent is a function.

macro assembler

An assembler program that lets the programmer create and use macros.

macro instruction

An instruction that defines a macro. In assembly language, MACRO and ENDM are examples that define the beginning and end of a macro. In C, the #DEFINE statement is used.

The Computer Glossary

macro language

(1) Commands used by a macro processor. Same as *script*.

(2) An assembly language that uses macros.

Macromedia Freehand

A full-featured drawing program for Windows and Macintosh from Macromedia, Inc., San Francisco, CA, (www.macromedia.com). It combines a wide range of drawing tools with special effects. FreeHand was first available on the Mac and was originally Aldus Freehand from Aldus Corporation.

macro processor

(1) Software that creates and executes macros from the keyboard.

(2) The part of an assembler that substitutes the macro subroutines for the macro calls.

macro recorder, macro generator

A program routine that converts menu selections and keystrokes into a macro. A user turns on the recorder, calls up a menu, selects a variety of options, turns the recorder off and assigns a key command to the macro. When the key command is pressed, the selections are executed.

macro virus

A virus that is written in a macro language and placed within a document. Viruses have to be "run" in order to do things. When the document is opened and the macro is executed, commands in the macro language do the destruction or the prank. Thankfully, the overwhelming majority of viruses are harmless. Let's pray they stay that way!

MAE

(1) (Macintosh Application Environment) Software from Apple that allows Macintosh programs to run on UNIX workstations under the X Window system. MAE supports AppleTalk and MacTCP, allowing UNIX users to share printers, files and e-mail with other Macintosh users on the network.

(2) (Metropolitan Area Exchange) Originally known as Metropolitan Area Ethernets, MAEs are major network access points (NAPs) in the Internet. See *NAP*.

magnetic card, mag card

(1) See *magnetic stripe*.

(2) Magnetic tape strips used in early data storage devices and word processors.

magnetic coercivity

The amount of energy required to alter the state of a magnet. The higher a magnetic disk's coercivity index, the more data it can store.

magnetic disk

The primary computer storage device. Like tape, it is magnetically recorded and can be re-recorded over and over. Disks are rotating platters with a mechanical arm that moves a read/write head between the outer and inner edges of the platter's surface. It can take as long as one second to find a location on a floppy disk to as short as one millisecond on an ultra-fast hard disk. See *floppy disk* and *hard disk*.

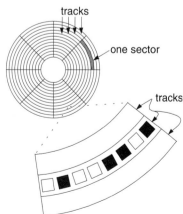

Tracks and Sectors

The disk surface is divided into concentric tracks (circles within circles). The thinner the tracks, the more storage. The data bits are recorded as tiny spots on the tracks. The tinier the spot, the more bits per inch and the greater the storage. Most disks hold the same number of bits on each track, even though the outer tracks are physically longer than the inner ones. Some disks pack the bits as tightly as possible within each track.

Tracks are further divided into sectors, which hold the least amount of data that can be read or written at one time; for example, READ TRACK 7 SECTOR 24. In order to update the disk, one or more sectors are read into the computer, changed and written back to disk. The operating system figures out how to fit data into these fixed spaces. See *hard disk* and *floppy disk*.

magnetic drum
An early high-speed, direct access storage device that used a magnetic-coated cylinder with tracks around its circumference. Each track had its own read/write head.

magnetic field
An invisible energy emitted by a magnet. Same as *flux*.

magnetic ink
A magnetically detectable ink used to print the MICR characters that encode account numbers on bank checks.

magnetic oxide
See *ferric oxide*.

magnetic recording
With regard to computers, the technique used to record, or write, digital data in the form of tiny spots (bits) of negative or positive polarity on tapes and disks. A read/write head discharges electrical impulses onto the moving ferromagnetic surface. Reading is accomplished by sensing the polarity of the bit with the read/write head.

magnetic stripe
A small length of magnetic tape adhered to ledger cards, badges and credit cards. It is read by specialized readers that may be incorporated into accounting machines and terminals. Due to heavy wear, the data on the stripe is in a low-density format that may be duplicated several times.

magnetic tape
A sequential storage medium used for data collection, backup and historical purposes. Like videotape, computer tape is made of flexible plastic with one side coated with a ferromagnetic material. Tapes come in reels, cartridges and cassettes of many sizes and shapes. Although still used, the 1/2" open-reel tape from the earliest days of computers has been mostly superseded by cartridges with enhanced storage capacities.

□ 0 bit ■ 1 bit recording channels (tracks)

Locating a specific record on tape requires reading every record in front of it or searching for markers that identify predefined partitions. Although most tapes are used for archiving rather than routine updating, some drives can allow rewriting in place if the byte count does not change. Otherwise, updating requires copying files from one tape to a scratch tape.

Tape is more economical than disks for archival data. However, if tapes are stored for the duration, they must be periodically recopied or the tightly coiled magnetic surfaces may contaminate each other.

magneto-optic disk, MO disk
A rewritable optical disk that uses a combination of magnetic and optical methods. MO disks use removable cartridges and come in two sizes. The 3.5" disks are single sided and hold 128MB, 230MB or 640MB. The 5.25" disks are double sided and hold 650MB, 1.3GB, 2.6GB or 5.2GB.

magneto-resistance
A high-density magnetic recording method that uses two technologies for the read/write head. The write head is the standard inductive type, but the magneto-resistance read head can read a fainter signal on the disk, thus allowing the bits to be packed more tightly together.

Magstar, Magstar MP
A high-performance magnetic tape technology from IBM. The Magstar is the latest model in the half-inch, single-hub cartridge line that comprises the 3480, 3490 and 3490e. Designated the 3590, the Magstar boosts capacity to 10GB and provides ESCON and SCSI connectivity to IBM mainframes and midrange systems.

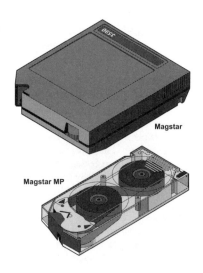

Magstar

Magstar MP

Magstar MP is completely different than the Magstar line. It uses a 5GB cassette-style cartridge rather than a single-hub unit and 8mm tape rather than half inch. The Magstar MP cartridge was especially designed for picking in a robotic library. Instead of at the beginning, the starting point is in the middle of the tape for faster retrieval.

mailbox

A simulated mailbox on disk that holds incoming or outgoing electronic mail and messages.

mail client

An e-mail program that resides in the user's computer and has access to mail servers on the network. See *universal client.*

mail enabled

Refers to an application that has built-in, although typically very limited, mail capabilities. For example, it can send or send and receive a file that it has created over one or more messaging systems. See *messaging API.*

mailing list

An automated e-mail system on the Internet, which is maintained by subject matter. There are more than 10,000 such lists. New users generally subscribe by sending an e-mail with the word "subscribe" in it and subsequently receive all new postings made to the list automatically. Mailing lists are also called "listprocs" and "listservs," the latter coming from the popular LISTSERV package.

mail merge

Printing customized form letters. A common feature of a word processor, it uses a letter and a name and address list. In the letter, Dear A: Thank you for ordering B from our C store..., A, B and C are merge points into which data is inserted from the list. See *field squeeze* and *line squeeze.*

mail protocol

See *messaging protocol* and *messaging system.*

mail server

A computer in a network that provides "post office" facilities. It stores incoming mail for distribution to users and forwards outgoing mail through the appropriate channel. The term may refer to just the software that performs this service, which can reside on a machine with other services. See *messaging system.*

mail system

See *electronic mail* and *messaging system.*

mainframe

A large computer. In the "ancient" mid 1960s, all computers were called mainframes, since the term referred to the main CPU cabinet. Today, it refers to a large computer system.

There are small, medium and large-scale mainframes, handling from a handful to several thousand online terminals and/or desktop PCs. Large-scale mainframes can have gigabytes of main memory and terabytes of disk storage. Large mainframes are made up of many microprocessors that control input and output and monitor conditions for fault tolerance.

main line

See *main loop.*

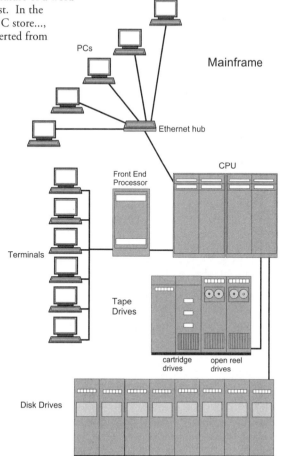

main loop

The primary logic in a program. It contains the instructions that are repeated after each event or transaction has been processed. See *loop*.

main memory

Same as *memory*.

main storage

Same as *memory*.

maintenance

(1) Hardware maintenance is the testing and cleaning of equipment.

(2) Information system maintenance is the routine updating of master files, such as adding and deleting employees and customers and changing credit limits and product prices.

(3) Software, or program, maintenance is the updating of application programs in order to meet changing information requirements, such as adding new functions and changing data formats. It also includes fixing bugs and adapting the software to new hardware devices.

(4) Disk or file maintenance is the periodic reorganizing of disk files that have become fragmented due to continuous updating.

maintenance credits

Monetary credits issued to a customer by the vendor for qualified periods during which the vendor's products are not functioning properly.

maintenance service

A service provided to keep a product in good operating condition.

major key

The primary key used to identify a record, such as account number or name.

make

To compile a multi-module program. The make utility recompiles only those modules that have been updated since the last compilation.

male connector

A plug or socket that contains pins. The female counterpart contains receptacles.

MAN

(Metropolitan Area Network) A communications network that covers a geographic area such as a city or suburb. See *LAN* and *WAN*.

management console

A terminal or workstation used to monitor and control a network.

management science

The study of statistical methods, such as linear programming and simulation, in order to analyze and solve organizational problems. Same as *operations research*.

management support

See *DSS* and *EIS*.

management system

The leadership and control within an organization. It is made up of people interacting with other people and machines that, together, set the goals and objectives, outline the strategies and tactics, and develop the plans, schedules and necessary controls to run an organization.

Manchester Code

A self-clocking data encoding method that divides the time required to define the bit into two cycles. The first cycle is the data value (0 or 1) and the second cylce provides the timing by shifting to the opposite state.

mantissa

The numeric value in a floating point number. See *floating point*.

MAP

(Manufacturing Automation Protocol) A communications protocol introduced by General Motors in 1982. MAP provides common standards for interconnecting computers and programmable machine tools used in factory automation. At the lowest physical level, it uses the IEEE 802.3 token bus protocol.

MAP is often used in conjunction with *TOP*, an office protocol developed by Boeing Computer Services. TOP is used in the front office and MAP is used on the factory floor.

map

(1) A set of data that has a corresponding relationship to another set of data.

(2) A list of data or objects as they are currently stored in memory or disk.

(3) To transfer a set of objects from one place to another. For example, program modules on disk are mapped into memory. A graphic image in memory is mapped onto the video screen. An address is mapped to another address.

(4) To relate one set of objects with another. For example, a logical database structure is mapped to the physical database. A vendor's protocol stack is mapped to the OSI model.

MAPI

(Mail API) A programming interface that enables an application to send and receive mail over the Microsoft Mail messaging system. Simple MAPI is a subset of MAPI that includes a dozen functions for sending and retrieving mail.

MAPPER

(MAintaining, Preparing and Processing Executive Reports) A Unisys mainframe fourth-generation language. In 1980, it was introduced as a high-level report writer and was later turned into a full-featured development system used successfully by non-technical users.

mapping

See *map* and *digital mapping*.

marginal test

A system test that introduces values far above and far below the expected values.

mark

(1) A small blip printed on or notched into various storage media used for timing or counting purposes.

(2) To identify a block of text in order to perform some task on it such as deletion, copying and moving.

(3) To identify an item for future reference.

(4) In digital electronics, a 1 bit. Contrast with *space*.

(5) On magnetic disk, a recorded character used to identify the beginning of a track.

(6) In optical recognition and mark sensing, a pencil line in a preprinted box.

(7) On magnetic tape, a *tape mark* is a special character that is recorded after the last character of data.

mark sensing

Detecting pencil lines in predefined boxes on paper forms. The form is designed with boundaries for each pencil stroke that represents a yes, no, single digit or letter, providing all possible answers to each question. A mark sense reader detects the marks and converts them into digital code.

markup language

A set of labels that are embedded within text to distinguish individual elements or groups of elements for display or identification purposes. The labels are typically known as "tags." Markup languages identify elements within a continuous stream of text rather than more structured data in a database. However, XML is a markup language that turns text streams into the equivalent of database records. SGML is the foundation markup language from which HTML and XML were devised.

mask

(1) A pattern used to transfer a design onto an object. See *photomask*.

(2) A pattern of bits used to accept or reject bit patterns in another set of data. For example, the Boolean AND operation can be used to match a mask of 0s and 1s with a string of data bits. When a 1 occurs in both the mask and the data, the resulting bit will contain a 1 in that position.

Hardware interrupts are often enabled and disabled in this manner with each interrupt assigned a bit position in a mask register.

maskable interrupts

Hardware interrupts that can be enabled and disabled by software.

mask bit

A 1 bit in a mask used to control the corresponding bit found in data.

masked

A state of being disabled or cut off.

MASM

(Macro ASeMbler) An assembly language that allows macros to be defined and used.

massively parallel

A parallel processing architecture that uses hundreds or thousands of processors. See *MPP*.

mass storage

A high-capacity, external storage such as disk or tape.

master

Primary, controlling. See *master-slave communications* and *master file*.

master card

A master record in punched card format.

master clock

A clock that provides the primary source of internal timing for a processor or stand-alone control unit.

master console

The main terminal used by the computer operator or systems programmer to command the computer.

master control program

See *operating system*.

master file

A collection of records pertaining to one of the main subjects of an information system, such as customers, employees, products and vendors. Master files contain descriptive data, such as name and address, as well as summary information, such as amount due and year-to-date sales. Contrast with *transaction file*.

master record

A set of data for an individual subject, such as a customer, employee or vendor. See *master file*.

master-slave communications

Communications in which one side, called the master, initiates and controls the session. The other side (slave) responds to the master's commands.

Mathcad

Mathematical software for Windows and Mac from Mathsoft, Inc., Cambridge, MA, (www.mathsoft.com). It allows complicated mathematical equations to be expressed, performed and displayed.

math coprocessor

A mathematical circuit that performs high-speed floating point operations. It is generally built into the CPU chip. In older PCs, such as the 386 and 486SX, the math coprocessor was an optional and separate chip. The math coprocessor is used primarily in CAD and spreadsheet applications to improve performance. See *array processor* and *vector processor*.

Mathematica

Mathematical software for PCs and Macs from Wolfram Research, Inc., Champaign, IL, (www.wolfram.com). It includes numerical, graphical and symbolic computation capabilities, all linked to the Mathematica programming language. Its use requires a math coprocessor.

mathematical expression

A group of characters or symbols representing a quantity or an operation. See *arithmetic expression*.

mathematical function

A rule for creating a set of new values from an existing set; for example, the function $f(x) = 2x$ creates a set of even numbers (if x is a whole number).

matrix

An array of elements in row and column form. An x-y matrix is a two-dimensional matrix, and an x-y-z matrix is a three-dimensional matrix.

MAU

(Multi-station Access Unit) A central hub in a token ring local area network. See *hub*.

maximize

In a graphical environment, to enlarge a window to full size. Contrast with *minimize*.

Mb, MB

(1) (Mb, lower case "b") (MegaBit) Adherence to "b" and "B" for bit and byte is not always followed. See *mega* and *space/time*.

(2) (MB, upper case "B") (MegaByte or MotherBoard) MB mostly stands for megabyte, but on ads for raw components, it may refer to motherboard.

Mbone

(Multicast backBONE) A collection of sites on the Internet that support the IP multicasting protocol (one-to-many) and allow for live audio and videoconferencing.

Mbps, Mbits/sec

(MegaBits Per Second) One million bits per second. Adherence to "b" and "B" for bit and byte is not always followed. See *mega* and *space/time*.

MBps, MBytes/sec

(MegaBytes Per Second) One million bytes per second. Adherence to "b" and "B" for bit and byte is not always followed. See *mega* and *space/time*.

MCA

See *Micro Channel*.

MCB

(Memory Control Block) An identifier (16-bytes) that DOS places in front of each block of memory it allocates.

MCGA

(Multi Color Graphics Array) An IBM video display standard built into low-end PS/2 models. It was not widely supported.

MCI

(Media Control Interface) A high-level programming interface from IBM/Microsoft for controlling multimedia devices. It includes text commands such as open, play and close for languages such as Visual Basic, as well as functions for languages such as C. See *RIFF* and *AVI*.

MCI decision

An FCC decree in 1969 that granted MCI the right to compete with the Bell System by providing private, intercity telecommunications services.

MCM

(MultiChip Module or MicroChip Module) A chip housing that uses a ceramic base and contains two or more raw chips closely connected with high-density lines. This packaging method saves space and speeds processing due to short leads between chips. MCMs were originally called "microcircuits" or "hybrid microcircuits," since this technique is well suited for mixing analog and digital components together.

MCP

(MultiChip Package) A chip package that contains two or more chips. It is essentially a multichip module (MCM) that uses a laminated, printed-circuit-board-like substrate (MCM-L) rather than ceramic (MCM-C). MCPs are also tested after packaging, whereas the bare die of ceramic-based MCMs were tested before packaging so as not to waste the more costly ceramic substrate if the chips were no good. See *MCM*.

MCU

(1) (MicroController Unit) A control unit on a single chip.

(2) (Multipoint Control Unit) A device that connects multiple sites for audio and video conferencing.

MDA

(Monochrome Display Adapter) The first IBM PC monochrome video display standard for text only. Due to its lack of graphics, MDA cards were often replaced with Hercules cards, which provided both text and graphics.

MDBS IV

A DBMS from Micro Data Base Systems, Inc., Lafayette, IN, that runs on DOS, OS/2, UNIX, MPE and VMS servers. Noted for its performance and maturity (in 1984, MDBS III was the first client/server DBMS), it provides a superset of hierarchical, network and relational storage concepts. M/4 for Windows is a single-user Windows version.

MDF

(Main Distribution Frame) A connecting unit between external and internal lines. It allows for public or private lines coming into the building to connect to internal networks. See *CDF*.

MDI

(Medium Dependent Interface) Refers to an Ethernet port connection. The MDI-X port on an Ethernet hub is used to connect to a workstation (the X stands for crossing the transmit and recieve lines). An MDI port (not crossed) is used to connect to the MDI-X port of another hub.

mechanical mouse

A mouse that uses a rubber ball that rolls against wheels inside the unit. Contrast with *optical mouse*.

media

A material that stores or transmits data, for example, floppy disks, magnetic tape, coaxial cable and twisted pair.

media control

Also called "media processing," in computer telephony it refers to some processing or altering of the call; for example, digitizing the content. Contrast with *call control*.

media conversion

Converting data from one storage medium to another, such as from disk to tape or from one type of disk pack to another.

media failure

A condition of not being able to read from or write to a storage device, such as a disk or tape, due to a defect in the recording surface.

medium frequency

An electromagnetic wave that oscillates in the range from 300,000 to 3,000,000 Hz. See *electromagnetic spectrum*.

meg, mega, megabit, megabyte

Million, million bits, million bytes. Also Mb, Mbit and M-bit, or MB, Mbyte and M-byte. See *space/time*.

megaflops

(mega FLoating point OPerations per Second) One million floating point operations per second.

megahertz

One million cycles per second. See *MHz*.

megapel display

In computer graphics, a display system that handles a million or more pixels. A resolution of 1,000 lines by 1,000 dots requires a million pixels for the full screen image.

membrane keyboard

A dust and dirtproof keyboard constructed of two thin plastic sheets (membranes) that contain flexible printed circuits made of electrically conductive ink. The top membrane is the printed keyboard and a spacer sheet with holes is in the middle. When a user presses a simulated key, the top membrane is pushed through the spacer hole and makes contact with the bottom membrane, completing the circuit.

memo field

A data field that holds a variable amount of text. The text may be stored in a companion file, but it is treated as if it were part of the data record.

memory

The computer's workspace (physically, a collection of RAM chips). It is an important resource, since it determines the size and number of programs that can be run at the same time, as well as the amount of data that can be processed instantly.

Memory is like an electronic checkerboard, with each square holding one byte of data or instruction. Each square has a separate address like a post office box and can be manipulated independently. As a result, the computer can break apart programs into instructions for execution and data records into fields for processing.

Memory Doesn't Usually Remember

Oddly enough, the computer's memory doesn't remember anything when the power is turned off. That's why you have to save your files before you quit your program. Although there are memory chips that do hold their content permanently (ROMs, PROMs, EPROMs, etc.), they're used for internal control purposes and not for the user's data.

Other terms for memory are *RAM, main memory, main storage, primary storage, read/write memory, core* and *core storage*.

memory allocation

Reserving memory for specific purposes. Operating systems generally reserve all the memory they need at startup. Application programs use memory when loaded and may allocate more after being loaded. If there is not enough free memory, they cannot run.

memory bank

A physical section of memory. See *memory interleaving*.

memory based

Programs that hold all data in memory for processing. Almost all spreadsheets are memory based so that a change in data at one end of the spreadsheet can be instantly reflected at the other end.

memory cache

See *cache*.

memory card

A credit-card-sized memory module used as additional storage in laptops and palmtops. It typically uses flash memory. Note that when you add more random access memory (RAM) in a laptop, the plug-in memory cards are not disk substitutes, rather they extend the working storage of the unit and are typically proprietary modules that are vendor dependent. The memory card that functions as a disk is contained on a PC Card (PCMCIA). See *flash memory* and *solid state disk*.

memory cell

One bit of memory. In dynamic RAM memory, a cell is made up of one transistor and one capacitor. In static RAM memory, a cell is made up of about five transistors.

memory chip

A chip that holds programs and data either temporarily (RAM), permanently (ROM, PROM) or permanently until changed (EPROM, EEPROM).

memory cycle

A series of operations that take place to read or write a byte of memory. For destructive memories, it includes the regeneration of the bits.

memory cycle time

The time it takes to perform one memory cycle.

memory dump

A display or printout of the contents of memory. When a program abends, a memory dump can be taken in order to examine the status of the program at the time of the crash. The programmer looks into the buffers to see which data items were being worked on when it failed. Counters, variables, switches and flags are also inspected.

memory effect

See *nickel cadmium* and *nickel hydride*.

memory interleaving

A category of techniques for increasing memory speed. For example, with separate memory banks for odd and even addresses, the next byte of memory can be accessed while the current byte is being refreshed.

memory leak

A condition caused by a program that does not free up the extra memory it allocates. In programming languages, such as C and C++, the programmer must specifically allocate additional chunks of memory to hold data and variables as required. When the routine is exited, the program is supposed to deallocate the memory. A serious memory leak will eventually usurp all the memory, bringing everything to a halt. In other environments, such as Java, the operating system allocates and deallocates memory automatically, which is the way it should work. See *garbage collection*.

memory management

Refers to a variety of methods used to store data and programs in memory, keep track of them and reclaim the memory space when they are no longer needed. In traditional minicomputers and mainframes, it comprises virtual memory, bank switching and memory protection techniques. See *virtual memory*, *memory protection* and *garbage collection*.

memory manager

Software that manages memory in a computer. See *memory management*.

memory map

The location of instructions and data in memory.

memory mapped I/O

A peripheral device that assigns specific memory locations to input and output. For example, in a memory mapped display, each pixel or text character derives its data from a specific memory byte or bytes. The instant this memory is updated by software, the screen is displaying the new data.

memory protection
A technique that prohibits one program from accidentally clobbering another active program. Using various different techniques, a protective boundary is created around the program, and instructions within the program are prohibited from referencing data outside of that boundary.

memory resident
A program that remains in memory at all times. See *TSR*.

Memory Stick
A flash memory card from Sony designed for handheld digital appliances such as cameras and camcorders. Introduced in 1998 with 4 and 8MB capacities, the tiny modules are less than 1x2" and about a tenth of an inch thick (.85 x 1.97 x .11"). Transfer to a PC is made via a PC Card adapter.

MEMS
(MicroElectroMechanical Systems) Semiconductor chips that have a top layer of mechanical devices such as mirrors or fluid sensors. They are used as pressure sensors, chemical sensors and light reflectors and switches.

menu
An on-screen list of available functions that can be performed at this time.

menu-driven
Using menus to command the computer. Contrast with *command-driven*.

menuing software
Software that provides a menu for launching applications and running operating system commands.

Merced
The former name for Intel's Itanium chip, the first to use the IA-64 architecture.

merchant server
A server in a network that handles online purchases and credit card transactions. It implements an electronic commerce protocol that ensures a secure transmission between the clients and cooperating banks. The term may refer to the entire computer system or just the software that provides this service. A merchant server is also called a "commerce server."

merge
See *mail merge* and *concatenate*.

merge purge
To merge two or more lists together and eliminate unwanted items. For example, a new name and address list can be added to an old list while deleting duplicate names or names that meet certain criteria.

mesa
A semiconductor process used in the 1960s for creating the sublayers in a transistor. Its deep etching gave way to the planar process.

mesh network
A net-like communications network in which there are at least two pathways to each node. Since the term network means net-like as well as communications network, the term mesh is used to avoid saying network communications network.

message
(1) In communications, a set of data that is transmitted over a communications line. Just as a program becomes a job when it's running in the computer, data becomes a message when it's transmitted over a network.

(2) In object-oriented programming, communicating between objects, similar to a function call in traditional programming.

message based
An interface that is based on a set of commands. A message-based system is a type of client/server relationship, in which requests are made by a client component, and the results are provided by a server

component. It implies greater flexibility and interoperability in contrast with a hard coded operation, which would have to be modified by reprogramming the source code.

message digest

A condensed text string that has been distilled from the contents of a text message. Its value is derived using a one-way hash function and is used to create a digital signature. See *digital signature*.

message handling

(1) An electronic mail system. See *messaging system*.

(2) In communications, the lower level protocols that transfer data over a network, which assemble and disassemble the data into the appropriate codes for transmission.

message handling system

Same as *messaging system*.

message queue

A storage space in memory or on disk that holds incoming transmissions until the computer can process them.

message switch

A computer system used to switch data between various points. Computers have always been ideal switches due to their input/output and compare capabilities. It inputs the data, compares its destination with a set of stored destinations and routes it accordingly. Note: A message switch is a generic term for a data routing device, but a messaging switch converts mail and messaging protocols.

message transfer agent

Store and forward capability in a messaging system. See *messaging system*.

messaging API

A programming interface that enables an application to send and receive messages and attached files over a messaging system. VIM, MAPI and CMC are examples. Novell's SMF-71, although also called an API, is actually the message format that mail must be placed into for submission to Novell's MHS. There are no functions associated with it.

messaging gateway

A computer system that converts one messaging protocol to another. It provides an interface between two store and forward nodes, or message transfer agents (MTAs).

messaging middleware

Software that provides an interface between applications, allowing them to send data back and forth to each other asynchronously. Data sent by one program can be stored in a queue and then forwarded to the receiving program when it becomes available to process it.

messaging protocol

The rules, formats and functions for exchanging messages between the components of a messaging system. The major industry messaging protocols are the international X.400, SMTP (Internet), IBM's SNADS and Novell's MHS. Widely-used messaging products such as cc:Mail and Microsoft Mail use proprietary messaging protocols.

messaging switch

A messaging hub that provides protocol conversion between several messaging systems. Examples of switches include Soft-Switch's EMX, HP's OpenMail and Digital's MAILbus. A messaging switch differs from a messaging gateway in that it supports more than two protocols and connections as well as providing management and directory integration.

messaging system

Software that provides an electronic mail delivery system. It is comprised of three functional areas, which are either packaged together or are modularized as independent components. (1) The user agent (UA) is the mail program (Eudora, Outlook, etc.) that submits and receives the message, (2) The message transfer agent (MTA) stores and forwards the message. (3) The message store, or MS, holds the mail and allows it to be selectively retrieved and deleted. It also provides a list of its contents.

meta-data

Data that describes other data. Data dictonaries and repositories are examples of meta-data. The term may also refer to any file or database that holds information about another database's structure, attributes, processing or changes. Although the term is widely used without the dash, the word Metadata is a trademark of Metadata Information Partners. See *data dictionary* and *repository*.

metafile

A data file that can store more than one type of information. For example, a Windows Metafile (WMF) can hold pictures in vector graphics and raster graphics formats as well as text. A Computer Graphics Metafile (CGM) allows for both types of graphics.

metalanguage

A language used to describe another language.

metamail

A public-domain UNIX utility that composes and decomposes a MIME message on the Internet.

metaphor

The derivation of metaphor means "to carry over." Thus the "desktop metaphor" as so often described means that the office desktop has been brought over and simulated on computers.

meter

The basic unit of the metric system (39.37 inches). A yard is about 9/10ths of a meter (0.9144 meter).

method

In object-oriented programming, a method is the processing that an object performs. When a message is sent to an object, the method is implemented.

methodology

The specific way of performing an operation that implies precise deliverables at the end of each stage.

metric

Measurement. Although metric generally refers to the decimal-based metric system of weights and measures, software engineers often use the term as simply "measurement." For example, "is there a metric for this process?" See *software metrics*.

Mflops

See *megaflops*.

MHS

(Message Handling Service) A messaging system from Novell that supports multiple operating systems and other messaging protocols. Optional modules support SMTP, SNADS and X.400. It uses the SMF-71 messaging format. Standard MHS runs on a DOS machine attached to the server. Global MHS runs as a NetWare NLM. Under NetWare, MHS runs on top of IPX. See also *messaging system*.

MHz

(MegaHertZ) One million cycles per second. It often references a computer's clock rate, the raw measure of internal speed. For example, a 50MHz 486 computer processes data internally (calculates, compares, etc.) twice as fast as a 25MHz 486. However, disk speed and caching play a major role in the computer's actual performance. See *MIPS*.

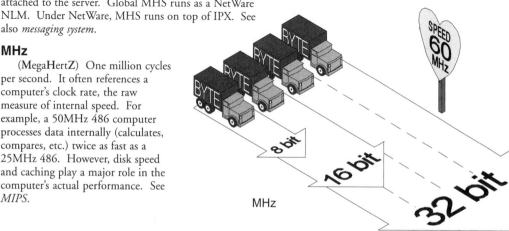

MHz

MIB

(Management Information Base) An SNMP structure that describes the particular device being monitored. See *SNMP*.

mickey

A unit of mouse movement typically set at 1/200th of an inch.

MICR

(Magnetic Ink Character Recognition) The machine recognition of magnetically-charged characters typically found on bank checks and deposit slips. MICR readers detect the characters and convert them into digital data.

micro

(1) A microcomputer or personal computer.

(2) One millionth. See *space/time*.

(3) Microscopic or tiny.

microbrowser

A Web browser designed for small display screens on smart phones and other handheld wireless devices. See *smart phone* and *WAP*.

Micro Channel

Also known as MCA (Micro Channel Architecture), it is a proprietary 32-bit bus introduced by IBM with its PS/2 personal computers. Also used in RS/6000 and ES/9370 models, Micro Channel boards contain built-in ID and have been easier to install than ISA boards. IBM dropped the Micro Channel in 1996 in favor of the PCI bus.

microchip

Same as *chip*.

microchip module

See *MCM*.

microcircuit

A miniaturized, electronic circuit, such as is found on an integrated circuit. See *chip* and *MCM*.

microcode

A permanent memory that holds the elementary circuit operations a computer must perform for each instruction in its instruction set. It acts as a translation layer between the instruction and the electronic level of the computer and enables the computer architect to more easily add new types of machine instructions without having to design electronic circuits. See *microprogramming*.

microcomputer

Same as *personal computer*.

microcontroller

See *MCU*.

microelectronics

The miniaturization of electronic circuits. See *chip*.

microfiche

Pronounced "micro-feesh." A 4x6" sheet of film that holds several hundred miniaturized document pages. See *micrographics*.

microfilm

A continuous film strip that holds several thousand miniaturized document pages. See *micrographics*.

micrographics

The production, handling and use of microfilm and microfiche. Images are created by cameras or by

COM units that accept computer output directly. The documents are magnified for human viewing by readers, some of which can automatically locate a page using indexing techniques.

Microfiche and microfilm have always been an economical alternative for high-volume data and picture storage. However, optical disks are quickly superseding fiche and film for archival storage. See *COLD*.

microimage
In micrographics, any photographic image of information that is too small to be read without magnification.

microinstruction
A microcode instruction. It is the most elementary computer operation that can take place; for example, moving a bit from one register to another. It takes several microinstructions to carry out one machine instruction.

microjacket
In micrographics, two sheets of transparent plastic that are bonded together to create channels into which strips of microfilm are inserted and stored.

microkernel
The hardware-dependent component of an operating system that is designed to be more easily portable to multiple platforms. The rest of the operating system interacts with the microkernel in a message-based relationship and does not have to be rewritten. Only the microkernel has to be reprogrammed to the architecture of the new hardware. See *kernel*.

micromainframe
A personal computer with mainframe or near mainframe speed.

micro manager
A person who manages personal computer operations within an organization and is responsible for the analysis, selection, installation, training and maintenance of personal computer hardware and software.

micromechanics
The microminiaturization of mechanical devices (gears, motors, rotors, etc.) using similar photomasking techniques as in chip making.

micron
One millionth of a meter. Approx. 1/25,000 of an inch. The tiny elements that make up a transistor on a chip are measured in microns. For example, the 486 used 1.0 micron technology, the first Pentiums were .8 micron. Today, the state-of-the-art is .18 micron.

microprocessor
A CPU on a single chip. In order to function as a computer, it requires a power supply, clock and memory. First-generation microprocessors were Intel's 8080, Zilog's Z80, Motorola's 6800 and Rockwell's 6502. The first microprocessor was created by Intel.

microprogram, microprogramming
A microprogram is the same as "microcode." Microprogramming is writing microcode. See *microcode*.

micropublishing, microrepublishing
In micrographics, micropublishing is issuing new or reformatted information on microfilm for sale or distribution. Microrepublishing is issuing microfilm that has been previously or is simultaneously published in hardcopy for sale or distribution.

microsecond
One millionth of a second. See *space/time*.

Microsoft
(Microsoft Corporation, Redmond, WA, www.microsoft.com) The world's largest software company. Microsoft was founded in 1975 by Paul Allen and Bill Gates, two college students who wrote the first BASIC interpreter for the Intel 8080 microprocessor. Microsoft's outstanding success came from its DOS

and Windows operating systems. It is also the leader in Windows applications and programming languages.

Microsoft Access

A DBMS for Windows from Microsoft that directly reads Paradox, dBASE and Btrieve files. Using ODBC, it can access Microsoft and SYBASE SQL Server and Oracle data. Access BASIC is its programming language, and "Wizards" ask you questions to create forms, reports and graphs.

Microsoft C

A C compiler and development system for DOS and Windows applications from Microsoft. It includes the Windows Software Development Kit (SDK). As of Version 7.0, it included C++ capability. See *Visual C++*.

Microsoft Cluster Server

Clustering software from Microsoft for Windows NT. It provides rudimentary load balancing and two-node failover, which allows a second server to take over if the first one fails.

Microsoft Internet Explorer (IE)

Microsoft's Web browser, which was initially provided with Windows 95 and then integrated into Windows 98. It is the leading Web browser on the market.

Microsoft Internet Information Server (IIS)

Web server software from Microsoft that runs under Windows NT. It supports Netscape's SSL security protocol and turns an NT-based PC into a Web site. The Internet Explorer browser is also included.

Microsoft Message Queue Server (MSMQ)

Messaging middleware for Windows NT from Microsoft that allows programs to send messages to other programs. It can be used to queue up transactions in a transaction processing system, for example. MSMQ is optionally used with Microsoft Transaction Server. See *messaging middleware*.

Microsoft Network

An online service from Microsoft that was launched with Windows 95. Originally intended as a general-purpose service similar to America Online (at that time), MSN evolved into an Internet service provider (ISP).

Microsoft Office

The leading suite of applications for Windows from Microsoft. It includes Access, PowerPoint, Word and Excel. The applications have been designed for tight integration and sharing of common functions such as spell checking and graphing. Objects can be dragged and dropped between applications.

Microsoft Transaction Server (MTS)

A TP monitor for Windows NT servers from Microsoft that supports transaction-based applications. It also serves as the infrastructure for a multitier system. It is used in the middle tier between the client and the database server.

Microsoft Word

A full-featured word processing programs for DOS, Windows and Mac from Microsoft. The Windows and Mac versions provide rudimentary desktop publishing capabilities. The earlier DOS version provided both graphics-based and text-based interfaces for working with a document.

Microsoft Works

An integrated software package for Windows and the Macintosh from Microsoft. It provides file management with relational-like capabilities, word processing, spreadsheet, business graphics and communications capabilities in one package.

microspacing

Positioning characters for printing by making very small horizontal and vertical movements. Many dot matrix printers and all laser printers have this ability.

MicroStation

A full-featured 2-D and 3-D CAD program for DOS, Windows, Mac and UNIX workstations from

Bentley Systems, Inc., Exton, PA, (www.bentley.com). Created in 1984, MicroStation is a high-end package that is used worldwide in environments where many designers work on large, complex projects.

micro to mainframe

An interconnection of personal computers to mainframes. See *3270 emulator*.

microwave

An electromagnetic wave that vibrates at 1GHz and above. Microwaves are the transmission frequencies used in communications satellites as well as in line-of-sight systems on earth.

middleware

Software that functions as a conversion or translation layer. It is also a consolidator and integrator. Custom-programmed middleware solutions have been developed for decades to enable one application to communicate with another that either runs on a different platform or comes from a different vendor or both. Today, there is a diverse group of products that offer packaged middleware solutions. See *application integration* and *messaging middleware*.

MIDI

(Musical Instrument Digital Interface) A standard protocol for the interchange of musical information between musical instruments, synthesizers and computers. It defines the codes for a musical event, which includes the start of a note, its pitch, length, volume and musical attributes, such as vibrato. It also defines codes for various button, dial and pedal adjustments used on synthesizers.

MIDI makes an ideal system for storing music on digital media due to its small storage requirement compared with digitizing actual music. Since the advent of General MIDI, a standard for defining MIDI instruments, MIDI has become widely used for musical backgrounds in multimedia applications.

See *General MIDI, MIDI sequencer, MPU-401, wavetable synthesis, FM synthesis* and *sound card*.

MIDI Mapper

A Windows application that converts MIDI sound sequences (MIDI messages) to conform to a particular MIDI sound card or module. The keyboard map is used to assign values to non-standard keyboard keys. The patch map assigns sounds to an instrument number. The channel map assigns input channels to output channels.

MIDI sequencer

A hardware device or software application that allows for the composition, editing and playback of MIDI sound sequences. Media player applications can play MIDI sound files, but creating and modifying MIDI files requires a sequencer.

midrange computer

A medium-sized computer system or server. Midrange computers encompass a very broad range between high-end PCs and mainframes and cost from $25,000 to more than a million dollars. IBM's AS/400s, HP's 3000s and Compaq's Alpha families are examples. Formerly called "minicomputers," which used dumb terminals connected to centralized systems, most midrange computers today function as servers in a client/server configuration.

MIF

(1) (Maker Interchange Format) An alternate file format for a FrameMaker document. A MIF file is ASCII text, which can be created in another program and imported into FrameMaker.

(2) (Managment Information File) A DMI file format that describes a hardware or software component used in a PC. It can contain data, code or both. See *DMI*.

millimeter

One thousandth of a meter, or 1/25th of an inch.

millisecond

One thousandth of a second. See *space/time*.

MIMD

(Multiple Instruction stream Multiple Data stream) A computer architecture that uses multiple processors, each processing its own set of instructions simultaneously and independently of the others. Contrast with *SIMD*.

MIME

(Multipurpose Internet Mail Extensions) A common method for transmitting non-text files via Internet e-mail, which was originally designed for ASCII text. MIME encodes the files using one of two encoding methods and decodes it back to its original format at the receiving end.

MIME type

A file identification derived from the MIME encoding system that identifies the content of a file. In order to define the content of attachments, MIME types are embedded in e-mail messages. Web servers send the MIME type to the requesting browser so that it can launch the appropriate helper application or plug-in.

mini, minicomputer

A medium-scale computer that functions as a multiuser system for up to several hundred users. The minicomputer industry was launched in 1959 after Digital introduced its PDP-1 for $20,000, an unheard-of low price for a computer in those days. Subsequently, a variety of systems became available from HP, Data General, Wang and others. The minicomputer evolved into a centralized system with dumb terminals. The term was also used for high-end, single-user workstations. See *midrange computer*.

MiniDisc

A compact digital audio disc from Sony that comes in read-only and rewritable versions. Introduced in late 1993, the MiniDisc has been popular in Japan. The read-only 2.5" disc stores 140MB compared to 650MB on a CD, but holds the same 74 minutes worth of music.

minimize

In a graphical environment, to hide an application that is currently displayed on screen. The window is removed and represented with an icon on the desktop or taskbar.

MINIX

A version of UNIX for the PC, Mac, Amiga and Atari ST developed by Andrew Tannenbaum and published by Prentice-Hall. It comes with complete source code.

minor key

A secondary key used to identify a record. For example, if transactions are sorted by account number and date, account number is the major key and date is the minor key.

MIP mapping

A texture mapping technique that uses multiple texture maps, or MIP maps. Each MIP map is half the size of the first one, providing several texture maps for various levels of depth.

MIPS

(1) (Million Instructions Per Second) The execution speed of a computer. High-speed personal computers and workstations perform at 200 MIPS and higher. MIPS ratings are not an exact science. Some are best-case mixes while others are averages. In addition, it takes more instructions in one machine to do the same in another (RISC vs CISC, mainframe vs micro).

(2) (MIPS Computer Systems, Inc., Sunnyvale, CA, subsidiary of Silicon Graphics.) A designer of RISC-based microprocessors made under license by various companies. MIPS chips use an "R" and number designation; for example, R4000, R5000, etc.

mirroring

See *disk mirroring*.

mirror site

An alternate site that contains the same information. Many software vendors have mirror sites on the Web due to the high volume of requests they get for drivers and beta copies of programs.

MIS

(Management Information System) An information system that integrates data from all the departments it serves and provides operations and management with the information they require. MIS was "the" buzzword of the 1970s when online systems were implemented in all large organizations. See *DSS* and *Information Systems*.

mission critical

Vital to the operation of an organization. In the past, mission critical information systems were implemented on mainframes and minicomputers. Increasingly, they are being designed for and installed on personal computer networks. See *client/server architecture*.

mixed object

Same as *compound document*.

ML

A symbolic programming language developed in the 1970s at the University of Edinburgh, Scotland. Although similar to LISP, its commands and structures are like Pascal.

mm

(MilliMeter) One thousandth of a meter.

MMDS

(Multichannel Multipoint Distribution Service or Microwave Multipoint Distribution Service) A digital wireless transmission system that works in the 2.2-2.4GHz range. It requires line of sight between transmitter and receiver, which can be 30 or more miles apart. It was designed initially as a one-way service for bringing cable TV to subscribers in remote areas or in locations that are difficult to install cable.

MMU

(Memory Management Unit) A virtual memory circuit that translates logical addresses into physical addresses.

MMX

(MultiMedia EXtensions) Enhancements to Intel's Pentium CPUs that allow software to perform fast multimedia (audio, video) operations that would otherwise require additional hardware. MMX added 57 new instructions, many of which are found in digital signal processing (DSP) chips. In the Pentium III, 70 additional instructions were added, known as the Katmai new instructions (KNI).

mnemonic

Pronounced "nuh-monic." Means memory aid. A name assigned to a machine function. For example, in DOS, COM1 is the mnemonic assigned to serial port #1. Programming languages are almost entirely mnemonics.

MNP

(Microcom Networking Protocol) A family of communications protocols from Microcom, Inc., Norwood, MA, that have become de facto standards for error correction (classes 2 though 4) and data compression (class 5).

MO

See *magneto-optic disk*.

mobile positioning

The ability to pinpoint the location of a caller in a mobile communications system. These location-based services are used for emergency purposes as well as enhanced business services such as location sensitive billing, traffic updates, fleet management and asset and people tracking.

mod

See *modulo*.

modal

Mode oriented. A modal operation switches from one mode to another. Contrast with *non-modal*.

modal bandwidth

The capacity of an optical fiber measured in MHz-km (megahertz over one kilometer). One MHz-km equals approximately .7 to .8 Mbps. Thus, a 100 MHz-km fiber can carry about 70 to 80 Mbps of data.

modal dispersion

A signal distortion in an optical fiber in which the light pulses spread out, and the receiving device cannot detect the beginnings and ends of pulses.

MO:DCA

(Mixed Object:Document Content Architecure) An IBM compound document format for text and graphics elements in a document. Formats for specific objects are specified in OCAs (Object Content Architectures): PTOCA for Presentation and Text that has been formatted for output, GOCA for vector Graphics objects, IOCA for bitmapped Images and FOCA for Fonts.

mode

An operational state that a system has been switched to. It implies at least two possible conditions. There are countless modes for hardware and software.

model

(1) A style or type of hardware device.

(2) A mathematical representation of a device or process used for analysis and planning. See *data model*.

model-based expert system

An expert system based on fundamental knowledge of the design and function of an object. Such systems are used to diagnose equipment problems, for example. Contrast with *rule-based expert system*.

modeling

Simulating a condition or activity by performing a set of equations on a set of data. See *data modeling*.

modem

(MOdulator-DEModulator) A device that adapts a terminal or computer to a telephone line. It converts the computer's digital pulses into audio frequencies (analog) for the telephone system and converts the frequencies back into pulses at the receiving side. The modem also dials the line, answers the call and controls transmission speed, which ranges up to 56,600 bps.

modem eliminator

A device that allows two close computers to be connected without modems. For personal computers, it is the same as a null modem cable. In synchronous systems, it provides active intelligence for synchronization.

modem pool, modem server

A collection of modems and software that let users dial out and remote users dial in on the next available modem. The modem pool may be internal or external to the remote access server. See *remote access server* and *communications server*.

Modula-2

(MODUlar LAnguage-2) An enhanced version of Pascal introduced in 1979 by Swiss professor Nicklaus Wirth, creator of Pascal. It supports separate compilation of modules.

modular programming

Breaking down the design of a program into individual components (modules) that can be programmed and tested independently. It is a requirement for effective development and maintenance of large programs and projects.

modulate

To vary a carrier wave. Modulation blends a data signal (text, voice, etc.) into a carrier for transmission over a network. Major methods are AM (amplitude modulation) - modulate the height of the carrier wave, FM (frequency modulation) - modulate the frequency of the wave, and PM (phase modulation) - modulate the polarity of the wave. Contrast with *demodulate*. See *carrier*.

module

A self-contained hardware or software component that interacts with a larger system. Hardware modules are often made to plug into a main system. Program modules are designed to handle a specific task within a larger program.

modulo

A mathematical operation (modulus arithmetic) in which the result is the remainder of the division. For example, 20 MOD 3 results in 2 (20/3 = 6 with a remainder of 2).

moire

Pronounced "mor-ray." In computer graphics, a visible distortion. It results from a variety of conditions; for example, when scanning halftones at a resolution not consistent with the printed resolution or when superimposing curved patterns on one another. Internal monitor misalignment can also be a cause.

MOLAP

See *OLAP*.

monadic

One. A single item or operation that deals with one item or operand.

monitor

(1) A display screen used to present output from a computer, camera, VCR or other video generator. A monitor's clarity is based on video bandwidth, dot pitch, refresh rate and convergence.

(2) Software that provides utility and control functions such as setting communications parameters. It typically resides in a ROM chip and contains startup and diagnostic routines.

(3) Software that monitors the progress of activities within a computer system.

(4) A device that gathers performance statistics of a running system via direct attachment to the CPU's circuit boards.

monochrome

Also called "mono." The display of one foreground color and one background color; for example, black on white, white on black and green on black. Monochrome screens have been widely used on mini and mainframe terminals. Non-color laptop screens on PCs are often said to be "monochrome VGA" screens, but they are actually gray-scale screens, not monochrome.

monolithic integrated circuit

A common form of chip design, in which the base material (substrate) contains the pathways as well as the active elements that take part in its operation.

monophonic

Sound reproduction using a single channel. Contrast with *stereophonic*.

monospacing

Uniform horizontal spacing, such as 10 characters per inch. Contrast with *proportional spacing*.

Monte Carlo method

A technique that provides approximate solutions to problems expressed mathematically. Using random numbers and trial and error, it repeatedly calculates the equations to arrive at a solution.

mopy

To print several originals. The term comes from Multiple Original Prints plus a "y" to make it rhyme with "copy." As more information is created digitally and printers become faster, it is increasingly easier to print multiple originals than to use a copy machine later. In other words, "don't copy...mopy!"

morphing

Transforming one image into another; for example, a car into a tiger. From metamorphosis. See *tweening*.

morray

See *moire*.

Morse code

A character code represented by dots and dashes, developed by Samuel Morse in the mid-19th century. A dot can be a voltage, carrier wave or light beam of one duration, while a dash is a longer duration. It was used to send telegraph messages before the telephone and was used in World War II for signalling by light.

MOS

(Metal Oxide Semiconductor) Pronounced "moss." One of two major categories of chip design (the other is bipolar). It derives its name from its use of metal, oxide and semiconductor layers. There are several varieties of MOS technologies, including PMOS, NMOS and CMOS.

Mosaic

A Web browser created by the University of Illinois National Center for Supercomputing Applications (NCSA) and released on the Internet in early 1993. Mosaic was "the" application that caused interest in the World Wide Web to explode.

MOSFET

(Metal Oxide Semiconductor Field Effect Transistor) A common type of transistor fabricated as a discrete component or into MOS integrated circuits.

motherboard

The main printed circuit board in an electronic device, which contains sockets that accept additional boards. In a personal computer, the motherboard contains the bus, CPU and coprocessor sockets, memory sockets, keyboard controller and supporting chips.

Chips that control the video display, serial and parallel ports, mouse and disk drives may or may not be present on the motherboard. If not, they are independent controllers that are plugged into an expansion slot on the motherboard.

Motif

The standard graphical user interface on UNIX workstations. Formerly governed by the Open Software Foundation (OSF/Motif), it is now administered by The Open Group.

motion path

In computer graphics, the path to be followed by an animated object.

Motorola

(Motorola, Inc., Schaumburg, IL, www.motorola.com) A leading manufacturer of semiconductor devices and electronic products. Founded in Chicago in 1928 by Paul V. Galvin as the Galvin Manufacturing Corporation, its first product allowed radios to operate from household current instead of batteries. Motorola is known for its huge variety of chips and telecommunications products.

mount

To cause a file on a remote workstation or server to be available for access locally. For example, in NFS (Network File System), a server maintains a list of its directories that are available to clients. When a client mounts a directory on the server, that directory and its subdirectories become part of the client's directory hierarchy. See *automounting*.

mouse

A puck-like object used as a pointing and drawing device. As it is rolled across the desktop, the screen cursor (pointer) moves correspondingly.

mouse pad

A fabric-covered rubber pad roughly 9" square that provides a smooth surface for rolling a mouse.

mouse port

A socket in the computer into which a mouse is plugged.

MOV

(1) (Metal Oxide Varistor) A discrete electronic component used in surge suppresssors that diverts excessive voltage to the ground and/or neutral lines.

(2) An assembly language instruction that moves (copies) data from one location to another.

move

(1) In programming, to copy data from one place in memory to another. At the end of the move, source and destination data are identical.

(2) In word processing and graphics, to relocate text and images to another part of the document or drawing.

MP3

(MPEG Audio Layer 3) An audio compression technology that is part of the MPEG-1 and MPEG-2 specifications. Developed in Germany in 1991 by the Fraunhofer Institute, MP3 uses perceptual audio coding to compress CD-quality sound by a factor of 12, while providing almost the same fidelity. MP3 music files are played via software or a physical player that cables to the PC for transfer.

MP3 has made it feasible to download quality audio from the Web very quickly, causing it to become a worldwide auditioning system for new musicians and labels. Established bands post sample tracks from new albums to encourage CD sales, and new bands post their music on MP3 sites in order to develop an audience.

MPC

(Multimedia PC) An earlier certification from the PC Working Group, Washington, DC, for PCs that met minimum requirements for multimedia applications. In the late 1990s, PCs far surpassed the MPC specs and MPC certification became a moot point.

MPE

(MultiProgramming Executive) A multitasking operating system that runs on the HP 3000 series.

MPEG

(Moving Pictures Experts Group) An ISO/ITU standard for compressing full-motion video. MPEG I provides a standard image of 352x240, 30 fps, 15-bit color and CD-quality sound. MPEG II is an evolving standard for full broadcast-quality video. MPEG I is used in Video CD. See *JPEG*.

MPLS

(MultiProtocol Label Switching) A specification for layer 3 switching from the IETF. Similar to Cisco's tag switching, MPLS uses labels, or tags, that contain forwarding information, which are attached to IP packets by a router that sits at the edge of the network known as a label edge router (LER). The routers in the core of the network, known as label switch routers (LSRs), examine the label more quickly than if they had to look up destination addresses in a routing table.

MPP

(Massively Parallel Processing) An architecture that uses multiple processors. Each CPU contains its own memory and copy of the operating system and application, and each of these sybsystems communicates with the others via a high-speed interconnect. In order to use MPP effectively, an information processing problem must be breakable into pieces that can be solved simultaneously. Contrast with *SMP*.

MPR II

The Swedish government standard for maximum video terminal radiation. The earlier MPR I is less stringent. See *TCO*.

MPU

(MicroProcessor Unit) Same as *microprocessor*.

MPU-401

A MIDI standard from Roland Corporation that has become the de facto interface for connecting a personal computer to a MIDI device.

MQSeries

Messaging middleware from IBM that allows programs to communicate with each other across all IBM platforms, Windows, VMS and a variety of UNIX platforms. Introduced in 1994, it provides a common programming interface (API) that programs are written to. The MQ stands for Message Queue. See *messaging middleware*.

M-R

See *magneto-resistance*.

MRCI

(Microsoft Realtime Compression Interface) The programming interface for Microsoft's DoubleSpace technology used in DOS 6.

ms

(1) (MilliSecond) See *space/time*.

(2) (MS) See *Microsoft*.

MSa/s

(MegaSAmples per Second) A measurement of sampling rate in millions of samples per second.

MSCDEX

(MicroSoft CD-ROM EXtensions) See *CD-ROM Extensions*.

MS-DOS

(MicroSoft-Disk Operating System) A single user operating system for PCs from Microsoft. It is functionaly identical to IBM's PC-DOS version, except that starting with DOS 6, MS-DOS and PC-DOS each provided different sets of auxiliary utility programs. Both MS-DOS and PC-DOS are called DOS. See *DOS*.

MSIE, MSMQ, MSN

See *Microsoft Internet Explorer*, *Microsoft Message Queue Server* and *Microsoft Network*.

MSP

(1) A Microsoft Paint graphics file format.

(2) (Microsoft Solution Provider) A Microsoft certification for qualifying resellers that sell and provide training and support on Microsoft products. A certain number of employees must be Microsoft Certified Professionals.

mSQL

(Mini SQL) A relational DBMS that runs on a variety of UNIX servers as well as Windows and OS/2. Scripting languages such as W3-mSQL (which comes with mSQL), PHP and MsqlPerl are used to access the database from Web pages, and programming languages such as C can be used as well.

MS-Windows

(MicroSoft Windows) See *Windows*.

MTA

(Message Transfer Agent) The store and forward part of a messaging system. See *messaging system*.

MTBF

(Mean Time Between Failure) The average time a component works without failure. It is the number of failures divided by the hours under observation.

MTTR

(Mean Time To Repair) The average time it takes to repair a failed component.

MUD

(MultiUser Dungeon, MultiUser Dimension, MultiUser Dialogue) Interactive games played by several people on the Internet. Originally dungeons and dragon games with demons, elves and magicians, MUDs have been created for science fiction themes, cartoon characters and other types of games. MUDs have also evolved into 3-D virtual reality sites.

mu-Law

A North American standard for converting analog data into digital form using pulse code modulation (PCM). North America and Japan use mu-Law, while Europe uses A-Law. Mu-Law is also written as u-Law, because the correct spelling of the term is with the Greek letter for "m," which looks like a "u." See *PCM* and *A-Law*.

MULTIBUS

An advanced bus architecture from Intel used in industrial, military and aerospace applications. It includes message passing, auto configuration and software interrupts. MULTIBUS I is 16-bits; MULTIBUS II is 32-bits.

multicasting

The ability to transmit a message to multiple recipients at the same time. Multicasting is used in teleconferencing as well as by communications protocols that need to broadcast a request to all nodes on the network.

multichip module

See *MCM*.

multidimensional views

Looking at data in several dimensions; for example, sales by region, sales by sales rep, sales by product category, sales by month, etc. See *OLAP*.

multidrop line

See *multipoint line*.

multifrequency monitor

A monitor that adjusts to all frequencies within a range (multiscan) or to a set of specific frequencies, such as VGA and Super VGA.

multilaunch

To open the same application based in a server simultaneously from two or more clients.

multilayer switch

See *layer 3 switch*.

multiline

A cable, channel or bus that contains two or more transmission paths (wires or optical fibers).

Multidimensional views (pivot table)

By product

By region

By sales rep

Query

Spreadsheets
Database programs
OLAP databases

multimedia

Disseminating information in more than one form. Includes the use of text, audio, graphics, animated graphics and full-motion video. See *MPC*.

Multimedia Extensions

Windows routines that support audio recording and playback, animation playback, joysticks, MIDI, the MCI interface for CD-ROM, videodiscs, videotapes, etc., and the RIFF file format. See *MPC*.

multimedia upgrade kit

The hardware and software necessary to turn a standard PC into a multimedia PC, which includes the CD-ROM drive, sound card and speakers.

multimode fiber

An optical fiber with a core diameter of from 50 to 100 microns. It is the most commonly used optical fiber. Light can enter the core at different angles, making it easier to connect the light source. However, light rays bounce around within the core causing some distortion and providing less bandwidth than single-mode fiber. Contrast with *single-mode fiber*.

Multiple Master

A font technology from Adobe that allows a typeface to be generated in different styles, from condensed to expanded and from light to heavy.

multiplexing

Transmitting multiple signals over a single communications line or computer channel. The two common multiplexing techniques are FDM, which separates signals by modulating the data onto different carrier frequencies, and TDM, which separates signals by interleaving bits one after the other. See *inverse multiplexing*.

multiplexor

In communications, a device that merges several low-speed transmissions into one high-speed transmission and vice versa.

multiplexor channel

A computer channel that transfers data between the CPU and several low-speed peripherals (terminals, printers, etc.) simultaneously. It may have an optional burst mode that allows a high-speed transfer to only one peripheral at a time.

multiplier-accumulator

A general-purpose floating point processor that multiplies and accumulates the results of the multiplication. Newer versions also perform division and square roots.

multipoint line

In communications, a single line that interconnects three or more devices.

multiported memory

A type of memory that provides more than one access path to its contents. It allows the same bank of memory to be read and written simultaneously.

multiprocessing

Simultaneous processing with two or more processors in one computer, or two or more computers processing together. When two or more computers are used, they are tied together with a high-speed channel and share the general workload between them. If one fails, the other takes over.

It is also accomplished in special-purpose computers, such as array processors, which provide concurrent processing on sets of data. Although computers are built with various overlapping features, such as executing instructions while inputting and outputting data, multiprocessing refers specifically to concurrent instruction executions. See *parallel processing, bus mastering* and *fault tolerant*.

multiprogramming

Same as *multitasking*.

multiscan monitor

A monitor that adjusts to all frequencies within a range. See *multifrequency monitor*.

MultiSync monitor

A family of multiscan monitors from NEC Technologies, Inc. NEC popularized the multiscan monitor.

multitasking

Running two or more programs in one computer at the same time. It is controlled by the operating system. The number of programs that can be effectively multitasked depends on the amount of memory available, CPU speed, hard disk capacity and speed, as well as the efficiency of the operating system.

Multitasking is accomplished due to the differences in I/O and processing speed. While one program is waiting for input, instructions in another program are executed. In interactive programs, the delay between keystrokes is used to execute instructions in other programs. In batch processing systems, the milliseconds of delay transferring data to and from a disk are used to execute instructions in other programs.

multithreading

Multitasking within a single program. It is used to process multiple transactions or messages concurrently. It is also required for creating synchronized audio and video applications. Multithreading functions are often written in *reentrant code*.

multi-timbral

The ability to play multiple instrument sounds (patches) simultaneously. See *timbre*.

multiuser

A computer shared by two or more users.

multivariate
The use of multiple variables in a forecasting model.

MUMPS
See *M*.

music CD
Generally refers to an audio CD, otherwise known as "Red Book audio." However, the term could refer to a CD-ROM that contains sound files, such as WAV and MID files.

MUX
(MUltipleXor) See *multiplexor*.

MVIP
(MultiVendor Integration Protocol) A voice bus and switching protocol for PCs originated by a number of companies, including Natural Microsystems of Natick, MA, its major supporter. It provides a second communications bus within the PC that is used to multiplex up to 256 full-duplex voice channels from one voice card to another.

MVS
(Multiple Virtual Storage) Introduced in 1974, the primary operating system used on IBM mainframes (the others are VM and DOS/VSE). MVS is a batch processing-oriented operating system that manages large amounts of memory and disk space. Online operations are provided with CICS, TSO and other system software.

MVS/XA (MVS/eXtended Architecture) was introduced in 1981 with IBM's 370/XA architecture, and MVS/ESA (MVS/Enterprise Systems Architecture) in 1988 with the ESA/370 machines. In 1996, MVS/ESA was packaged with an extensive set of utilities and renamed OS/390. The name MVS is still used to refer to the base control program in OS/390. See *OS/390*.

N

NAK

(Negative AcKnowledgement) A communications code used to indicate that a message was not received, or that a terminal does not wish to transmit. Contrast with *ACK*.

Named Pipes

An IPC facility in LAN Manager that allows data to be exchanged from one application to another either over a network or running within the same computer. The use of the term pipes for interprocess communication was coined in UNIX.

naming service (name resolution)

Software that converts a name into a physical address on a network, providing logical to physical conversion. Names can be user names, computers, printers, services or files. The transmitting station sends a name to the server containing the naming service software, which sends back the actual address of the user or resource. The process is known as name resolution.

A naming service functions as a Yellow Pages for the network, which is precisely what Sun's NIS system was originally called. In AppleTalk, the naming service is embedded within the protocol. In the case of the Internet or other IP network, DNS servers and WIN servers return the IP address for the submitted name. See *DNS, WINS* and *directory service*.

NAND

(Not AND) A Boolean logic operation that is true if any single input is false. Two-input NAND gates are often used as the sole logic element on gate array chips, because all Boolean operations can be created from NAND gates.

nanometer

One billionth of a meter.

nanosecond

One billionth of a second. Used to measure the speed of logic and memory chips, a nanosecond can be visualized by converting it to distance. In one nanosecond, electricity travels about nine inches in a wire.

Even at 186,000 miles per second, electricity is never fast enough for the hardware designer who worries over a few inches of circuit path. The slightest delay is multiplied millions of times, since millions of pulses are sent through a wire in a single second. See *space/time*.

nanotechnology

A future science that builds devices at the atomic and molecular level. For example, a bit might be represented by only one atom some time in the future. Nanotechnology could be used to build anything, not just computers and communications devices.

NAP

(Network Access Point) A junction point where national Internet service providers interconnect with each other. Connection at one or more of these points means "on the Internet." When the Internet went commercial in 1995, there were four official NAPs and seven de facto NAPs. Due to the congestion at these exchanges, large ISPs agree to peer privately and interconnect with each other at many other points throughout the country where equipment at both companies is conveniently located.

NAPLPS

(North American Presentation-Level Protocol Syntax) An ANSI-standard protocol for videotex and teletext. It compresses data for transmission over narrow-bandwidth lines and requires decompression on the receiving end. PRODIGY uses this format for transmitting and displaying some of its graphics.

Napster

A Windows application and music indexing service from Napster, Inc., San Mateo, CA, (www.napster.com), that includes an MP3 player, chat capability and MP3 file sharing. The application works in conjunction with Napster's Web site, which provides an index to MP3 music files residing on other computers currently logged onto the Internet.

narrowband

In communications, a voice grade transmission of 2,400 bps or less, or a sub-voice grade transmission from 50 to 150 bps.

National Cristina Foundation

(National Cristina Foudation, Stamford, CT, www.cristina.org) A not-for-profit public charity that seeks donations of used or excess computers. Founded in 1984 by Yvette Marrin and Bruce McMahan, it was named in honor of McMahan's daughter, Cristina, who has cerebral palsy. Donations are directed to programs that rehabilitate people with disabilities, students at risk of failing and the economically disadvantaged. The foundation has helped hundreds of thousands of individuals in the U.S. and abroad.

native application

An application designed to run in the computer environment (machine language and OS) being referenced. The term is used to contrast a native application with an interpreted one such as a Java application, which is not native to a single platform. The term may also be used to contrast a native application with an emulated application, which was originally written for a different platform.

native language

Same as *machine language.* See *native mode.*

native mode

(1) The normal running mode of a computer, executing programs from its built-in instruction set. Contrast with *emulation mode.*

(2) The highest performance state of a computer, such as the 386 running in Protected Mode.

natural language

English, Spanish, French, German, Japanese, Russian, etc.

natural language query

A query expressed by typing English, French or any other spoken language in a normal manner. For example, "how many sales reps sold more than a million dollars in any eastern state in January?" In order to allow for spoken queries, both a voice recognition system and natural language query software are required. See *voice recognition.*

NAU

(1) (Network Access Unit) An interface card that adapts a computer to a local area network.

(2) (Network Addressable Unit) An SNA component that can be referenced by name and address, which includes the SSCP, LU and PU.

NB card

(NuBus card) See *NuBus.*

NC

See *network computer* and *numerical control.*

NCB

(Network Control Block) A packet structure used by the NetBIOS communications protocol.

NCGA

(National Computer Graphics Association) A Fairfax, Virginia-based organization dedicated to developing and promoting the computer graphics industry. It maintained a clearinghouse for industry information. NCGA closed its doors in 1996.

NCP

(1) (Network Control Program) See *SNA* and *network control program.*

(2) (NetWare Core Protocol) The file sharing protocol used in a NetWare network. It is the internal NetWare language used to communicate between client and server and provides access to files and the NDS and bindery directory services. See *file sharing protocol.*

(3) (Not Copy Protected) Software that can be easily copied.

NCR

(NCR Corporation, Dayton, OH, www.ncr.com) A major manufacturer of computers and financial terminals, founded in 1884 by John Henry Patterson. In 1991, AT&T acquired the company and ran it as a wholly-owned subsidiary, later renaming it AT&T Global Information Systems. The NCR name did remain on ATM and POS terminals as well as microelectronics and business forms. In 1996, AT&T GIS was spun off, renamed NCR, and it became an independent company once again.

NCR paper

(No Carbon Required paper) A multiple-part paper form that does not use carbon paper. The ink is adhered to the reverse side of the previous sheet.

NCSA

(National Center for Supercomputer Applications, Urbana-Champaign, IL, www.ncsa.uiuc.edu) A high-performance computing facility located at the University of Illinois at Urbana-Champaign. Founded in 1985 by a National Science Foundation grant, the NCSA provides supercomputer resources to hundreds of universities and organizations engaged in scientific research.

NCSC

(National Computer Security Center) The arm of the U.S. National Security Agency that defines criteria for trusted computer products. Following are the Trusted Computer Systems Evaluation Criteria (TCSEC), DOD Standard 5200.28, also known as the Orange Book. The Red Book is the networks counterpart.

Level D is a non-secure system. C1 requires group log-on. C2 requires individual user log-on with password and audit mechanism. B1 provides DOD clearances for data (top secret, secret and unclassified). B2 guarantees path between user and security system and assures that system can be tested and clearances cannot be downgraded. B3 uses a viable mathematical model. A1 is highest security and uses a proven model.

n-dimensional

Some number of dimensions.

NDIS

(Network Driver Interface Specification) A network driver interface from Microsoft. See *network driver interface*.

NDS

(NetWare Directory Service) A global naming service in NetWare 4.0 based on X.500 for compatibility with other public directories. The NDS Directory maintains information about all the resources in the network, including users, groups, servers, volumes and printers. NDS replaces the bindery file used in previous versions of NetWare and is backward compatible with it.

negative logic

The use of high voltage for a 0 bit and low voltage for a 1 bit. Contrast with *positive logic*.

nematic

The stage between a crystal and a liquid that has a threadlike nature; for example, a liquid crystal.

nerd

A person considered socially dull. Although intelligent or even genius in work matters, nerds immerse themselves in scientific and technical subjects. A "geek" is another term for a nerdy person. Contrast with *hacker*, a very technical computer person that may or may not be a nerd.

nesting

In programming, the positioning of a loop within a loop. The number of loops that can be nested may be limited by the programming language. See *loop*.

NetBEUI

(NetBIOS Extended User Interface) Pronounced "net-booey." The transport layer for NetBIOS. NetBIOS and NetBEUI were originally part of a single protocol suite that was later separated. NetBIOS sessions can be transported over NetBEUI, TCP/IP and SPX/IPX protocols. See *NetBIOS*.

NetBIOS

The native networking protocol in DOS and Windows networks. Although originally combined with its transport layer protocol (NetBEUI), NetBIOS today provides a programming interface for applications at the session layer (layer 5). NetBIOS can ride over NetBEUI, its native transport, which is not routable, or over TCP/IP and SPX/IPX, which are. See *NetBEUI*.

netcast

See *Webcast*.

netiquette

(NETwork etIQUETTE) Proper manners when conferencing between two or more users on an online service or the Internet. Emily Post may not have told you to curtail your cussing via modem, but netiquette has been established to remind you that profanity is not in good form over the network. Using UPPER CASE TO MAKE A POINT all the time and interjecting emoticons throughout a message is also not good netiquette. See *flame*.

NetMeeting

A set of collaboration and conferencing functions that come with and add groupware capabilities to Internet Explorer. It includes a whiteboard and application sharing, a text chat window as well as audioconferencing and videoconferencing.

NetPC

A Windows-based computer that obtains its software installations from a server in the network. It is Wintel's counter to the network computer (NC), which is designed to lower the costs of software administration. However, unlike the NC which downloads software every time it is used, a NetPC installs Windows the first time it is turned on, and it remains installed on the local hard disk like it does in every Windows PC.

Netscape

(Netscape Communications Corporation, Mountain View, CA, www.netscape.com) Part of America Online (AOL), Netscape specializes in Internet software, including the Netscape Navigator Web browser. Founded in 1994 by James Clark, former patriarch of SGI, and Marc Andreessen, who, along with Eric Bina, created the Mosaic browser at the University of Illinois, Netscape quickly became the number one topic of conversation as Internet and Web fever enveloped the nation in the mid 1990s.

Netscape color palette

A palette of 216 colors that Netscape displays the same on its Windows and Mac browsers. If other colors are used in images, Netscape will dither them, and the results will differ between the platforms.

Netscape Communicator

A suite of Web browsing and groupware tools from Netscape. It includes the Navigator browser, Messenger e-mail client, Collabra threaded discussions, Composer HTML editor and Conference, which provides audio and videoconferencing, whiteboard, text chat and collaborative browsing.

Netscape Navigator

A Web browser for Windows, Macintosh and X Windows from Netscape. It provides secure transmission over the Internet, and Netscape server software provides encryption based on the RSA method. Navigator was once the most popular Web browser, but has lost its lead to Internet Explorer. Netscape Navigator is often referred to as simply "Netscape."

NetShow

Client and server software from Microsoft for streaming audio and video over the Internet. It uses the Active Streaming Format (ASF) and provides utilities for translating common audio, video and image formats into ASF.

NetView

IBM SNA network management software that provides centralized monitoring and control for SNA, non-SNA and non-IBM devices. NetView/PC interconnects NetView with Token Ring LANs, Rolm CBXs and non-IBM modems, while maintaining control in the host.

NetWare

A family of network operating systems from Novell that support DOS, Windows, OS/2 and Mac clients. NetWare is the most widely-used LAN control program. Except for Personal NetWare and previous Lite versions, NetWare is a stand-alone operating system that runs in the server. The latest version is NetWare 5, which was introduced in 1998.

In 1996, NetWare 4.11 was combined with Novell's Web server and related components in a package entitled IntranetWare. The NetWare name was retained for the OS portion. Later, the IntranetWare name was dropped, and NetWare became the brand name again. See *NDS*.

NetWare NFS

Software from Novell that implements the NFS distributed file system on NetWare servers. It allows UNIX and other NFS client machines to access files on the NetWare server.

network

(1) An arrangement of objects that are interconnected. See *LAN*.

(2) In communications, the transmission channels interconnecting all client and server stations as well as all supporting hardware and software.

network accounting

The reporting of network usage. It gathers details about user activity including the number of logons and resources used (disk accesses and space used, CPU time, etc.).

network adapter

A printed circuit board that plugs into a client machine or server and controls the exchange of data over a network. It performs the electronic functions of the access method, or data link protocol, such as Ethernet and Token Ring. The twisted pair, coax or fiber optic transmission medium interconnects all adapters in the network.

network administrator

A person who manages a communications network and is responsible for its efficient operation. Responsibilities include network security, installing new applications, distributing software upgrades, monitoring daily activity, enforcing licensing agreements, developing a storage management program and providing for routine backups.

network analyzer

Software only or a combination of a hardware device and software that monitors traffic on a network. It can also read any unencrypted text that is transmitted over the network.

network architecture

(1) The design of a communications system, which includes the hardware, software, access methods and protocols used. It also defines the method of control; for example, whether computers can act independently or are controlled by other computers monitoring the network.

(2) The access method in a LAN, such as Ethernet and Token Ring.

network card

See *network adapter*.

network cloud

A cloud-like symbol in a network diagram used to reduce an entire communications network into points of entry and exit.

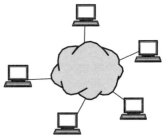

network computer

(1) A computer in the network.

(2) A desktop computer that provides connectivity to intranets and/ or the Internet. It is designed as a "thin client" that downloads all applications from the network server and obtains all of its data from and stores all changes back to the server. The network computer (NC) is similar to a diskless workstation and does not have floppy or hard disk storage. NCs have replaced terminals in some applications but have not as yet gained significant market share.

network control program

Software that manages the traffic between terminals and the host mini or mainframe. It resides in the communications controller or front end processor. In a personal computer LAN, it is called a "network operating system" and resides in the server and manages requests from the workstations. IBM's SNA network control program is called *NCP*.

network database

(1) A database that runs in a network. It implies that the DBMS was designed with a client/server architecture.

(2) A database that holds addresses of other users in the network.

(3) A database organization method that allows for data relationships in a net-like form. A single data element can point to multiple data elements and can itself be pointed to by other data elements. Contrast with *relational database*.

network driver

Software that performs the data link protocol in a network and activates the network adapter.

network driver interface

A software interface between the transport protocol and the data link protocol (network driver). The interface provides a protocol manager that accepts requests from the transport layer and activates the network adapter. Network adapters with compliant network drivers can be freely interchanged.

In PC LANs, the two primary network driver interfaces are Novell's ODI and Microsoft's NDIS. Novell provides an ODI interface utility that allows NDIS and ODI protocols to work in the same computer.

network effect

The resulting increased value of a product because more and more people use it. Telephones, fax machines and computer operating systems are examples. Its success is due to compatibility and conformity, not always superior technology.

network engineer

A person who designs, implements and supports local area and wide area networks within an organization. Network engineers are high-level technical analysts specializing in networks. See *network administrator*.

network layer

Internetworking services provided by the network as defined by layer 3 of the OSI model. See *OSI*.

network management

Monitoring an active communications network in order to diagnose problems and gather statistics for administration and fine tuning. Examples of network management products are IBM's NetView, HP's OpenView, Sun's SunNet Manager and Novell's NMS. Examples of network management protocols are SNMP, CMIP and DME.

network manager

See *network administrator*.

network modem

A modem shared by all users in a network. See *ACS*.

network operating system

A multiuser operating system that manages network resources. It manages multiple requests (inputs) concurrently and provides the security necessary in a multiuser environment. It may be a completely self-contained operating system, such as NetWare, Windows NT or UNIX, or it may require an existing operating system in order to function (LAN Server requires OS/2; LANtastic requires DOS, etc.).

A portion of the network operating system, or NOS, resides in each client machine and each server. It handles requests by clients for data and applications from the server as well as input and output to shared network devices, such as printers, faxes and modems.

network protocol

A communications protocol used by the network. There are many layers of protocols. See *OSI*.

network ready

Software designed to run in a network and be shared by multiple users.

network security

The authorization of access to files and directories in a network. Users are assigned an ID number and password that allows them access to information and programs within their authority. Network security is controlled by the network administrator.

network server

See *file server*.

neural network

A modeling technique based on the observed behavior of biological neurons and used to mimic the performance of a system. It consists of a set of elements that start out connected in a random pattern, and, based upon operational feedback, are molded into the pattern required to generate the required results. It is used in applications such as robotics, forecasting, image processing and pattern recognition.

NeWS

(Network Extensible Windowing Support) A networked windowing system (similar to X Windows) from SunSoft that renders PostScript fonts on screen the way they print on a PostScript printer.

newsgroup

A discussion group on the Internet. It is an on-going collection of messages about a particular subject. See *Usenet*.

Newton

The mobile computing technology used in Apple's MessagePad PDA introduced in 1993. The MessagePad was more commonly known by the Newton name than MessagePad.

NeXT

Founded in 1985 in Redwood City, CA, by Steven Jobs, co-founder of Apple, NeXT Computer created a family of high-resolution workstations running under the UNIX-based NEXTSTEP operating system. In 1993, the hardware was discontinued, and the company became NeXT Software, focusing on OPENSTEP, the object-oriented development environment within NEXTSTEP for x86, Sun and HP machines. In 1996, Apple acquired NeXT and returned Steve Jobs to the company he founded.

new media

(1) The forms of communicating in the digital world, which includes electronic publishing on CD-ROM, DVD, digital television and perhaps, most significantly, the Internet. It implies the use of desktop and portable computers as well as wireless, handheld devices. Most every company in the computer industry is involved with new media in some manner.

(2) The concept that new methods of communicating in the digital world allow smaller groups of people to congregate online and share, sell and swap goods and information. It also allows more people to have a voice in their community and in the world in general.

NFS

(Network File System) A distributed file system from SunSoft that allows data to be shared across a network regardless of machine, operating system, network architecture or protocol. This de facto UNIX standard lets remote files appear as if they were local on a user's machine. The combination of TCP/IP, NFS and NIS comprise the primary networking components of UNIX.

nibble

Half a byte (four bits).

NIC

(Network Interface Card) Same as *network adapter*.

NICAD, nickel cadmium

A rechargeable battery technology that has been widely used. It provides more charge per pound than lead acid, but less than nickel hydride. Its major problem is the memory effect. It "remembers" how full the battery is when it is recharged and does not deliver electricity below that point. Nickel cadmium batteries should be completely drained to maintain the longest charge. Although often used to refer to nickel cadmium, NICAD is a trademark of SAFT America, Inc., Valdosta, GA. See *lead acid, nickel hydride* and *zinc air*.

nickel hydride

A rechargeable battery technology that provides more charge per pound than lead acid and nickel cadmium, but less than zinc air. It does not suffer from the nickel cadmium memory effect. It uses nickel and metal hydride plates with potassium hydroxide as the electrolyte. See *lead acid, nickel cadmium* and *zinc air.*

NIS

(Network Information Services) A naming service from SunSoft that allows resources to be easily added, deleted or relocated. Formerly called Yellow Pages, NIS is a de facto UNIX standard. NIS+ is a redesigned NIS for Solaris 2.0 products. The combination of TCP/IP, NFS and NIS comprise the primary networking components of UNIX.

NIST

(National Institute of Standards & Technology) The standards-defining agency of the U.S. government, formerly called the National Bureau of Standards.

NJE

(Network Job Entry) An IBM mainframe protocol that allows two JES devices to communicate with each other.

NLM

(NetWare Loadable Module) Software that enhances or provides additional functions in a NetWare 3.x server. Support for database engines, workstations, network protocols, fax and print servers are examples. The NetWare 2.x counterpart is a VAP.

NLQ

(Near Letter Quality) The print quality that is almost as sharp as an electric typewriter. The slowest speed of a dot matrix printer often provides NLQ.

NMOS

(N-Channel **MOS**) Pronounced "N moss." A type of microelectronic circuit used for logic and memory chips. NMOS transistors are faster than their PMOS counterpart and more of them can be put on a single chip. It is also used in CMOS design.

NMS

(NetWare Management System) A SNMP-based network management software from Novell for monitoring and controlling NetWare networks.

node

(1) In communications, a network junction or connection point (terminal, client station, server, switch, router, etc.).

(2) In database management, an item of data that can be accessed by two or more routes.

(3) In computer graphics, an endpoint of a graphical element.

noise

An extraneous signal that invades an electrical transmission. It can come from strong electrical or magnetic signals in nearby lines, from poorly fitting electrical contacts, and from power line spikes.

non-blocking

The ability of a signal to reach its destination without interference or delay.

non-document mode

A word processing mode used for creating source language programs, batch files and other text files that contain only text and no proprietary headers and format codes. All text editors output this format.

non-impact printer

A printer that prints without banging a ribbon onto paper, such as a thermal or ink jet printer.

non-interlaced

Illuminating a CRT by displaying lines sequentially from top to bottom. Non-interlaced monitors eliminate annoying flicker found in interlaced monitors, which illuminate half the lines in the screen in the first cycle and the remaining half in the second cycle. Contrast with and see *interlaced* for illustration.

nonlinear
A system in which the output is not a uniform relationship to the input.

nonlinear video editing
Storing video in the computer for editing. It is much easier to edit video in the computer than with earlier analog editing systems. Today's digital nonlinear editing systems provide high-quality post-production editing on a personal computer. However, lossy compression is used to store digital images, and some detail will be lost.

Depending on the purpose for the video presentation, output is either the final video turned back into analog or an edit decision list (EDL) that describes frame sources and time codes in order to quickly convert the original material into the final video in an editing room. For commercial production, the latter allows editing to be done offline rather than in a studio that costs several hundred dollars per hour.

Prior to digital, a system using several analog tape decks was considered a nonlinear video editing system. Contrast with *linear video editing*.

non-modal
Not mode oriented. A non-modal operation moves from one situation to another without apparent mode switching.

non-preemptive multitasking
A multitasking environment in which an application is able to give up control of the CPU to another application only at certain points; for example, when it's ready to accept input from the keyboard. Under this method, one program performing a large number of calculations for example, can dominate the machine and cause other applications to have limited access to the CPU.

Non-preemtive multitasking is also called "cooperative multitasking," because programs must be designed to cooperate with each other in order to work together effectively in this environment.

A non-preemtive multitasking operating system cannot guarantee service to a communications program running in the background. If another application has usurped the CPU, the CPU cannot process the interrupts from the communications program quickly enough to capture the incoming data, and data can be lost. Contrast with *preemptive multitasking*.

non-procedural language
A computer language that does not require traditional programming logic to be stated. For example, a command, such as LIST, might display all the records in a file on screen, separating fields with a blank space. In a procedural language, such as COBOL, all the logic for inputting each record, testing for end of file and formatting the screen has to be explicitly programmed.

Query languages, report writers, interactive database programs, spreadsheets and application generators provide non-procedural languages for user operation. Contrast with and see *procedural language* for an example.

non-routable protocol
A communications protocol that contains only a device address and not a network address. It does not incorporate an addressing scheme for sending data from one network to another. Examples of non-routable protocols are NetBIOS and DEC's LAT protocols. Contrast with *routable protocol*.

non trivial
A favorite word used among programmers for any task that isn't simple.

non-volatile memory
Memory that holds its content without power. Firmware chips (ROMs, PROMs, EPROMs, etc.) are examples. Disks and tapes may be called non-volatile memory, but they are usually considered storage devices.

no-op
(NO OPeration) An instruction that does nothing but hold the place for a future machine instruction.

NOR

(Not **OR**) A Boolean logical operation that is true if all inputs are false, and false if any input is true. An exclusive NOR is true if both inputs are the same.

normalization

In relational database management, a process which breaks down data into record groups for efficient processing. There are six stages. By the third stage (third normal form), data is identified only by the key field in the record. For example, ordering information is identified by order number, customer information, by customer number.

normal wear

Deterioration due to natural forces that act upon a product under average, everyday use.

Norton Utilities

Widely-used utility programs for DOS, Windows and Macintosh from Symantec Corporation, Cupertino, CA, (www.symantec.com). It includes programs to search, edit and undelete files, restore damaged files, defragment the disk and more. Originally from Peter Norton Computing, these programs were the first to popularize disk utilities for the PC.

NOS

See *network operating system*.

NOT

A Boolean logic operation that reverses the input. If a 0 is input, a 1 is output, and vice versa. See *AND, OR & NOT*.

notation

How a system of numbers, phrases, words or quantities is written or expressed. Positional notation is the location and value of digits in a numbering system, such as the decimal or binary system.

notebook computer

A laptop computer that weighs from approximately five to seven pounds. A "subnotebook" is typically under four pounds.

Notes

See *Lotus Notes*.

Novell

(Novell Inc., Provo, UT, www.novell.com) Novell was founded as Novell Data Systems in 1981 by Jack Davis and Geroge Canova and initially manufactured terminals for IBM mainframes. In 1983, Ray Noorda became CEO and president of a restructured Novell, Inc., which would concentrate on the development of its NetWare operating system, which became the most widely used NOS in the PC world.

Novell network

A LAN controlled by one of Novell's NetWare operating systems. See *NetWare*.

no wait state memory

Memory fast enough to meet the demands of the CPU. Idle wait states do not have to be introduced.

NPN

(New Public Network) The IP-based public telephone network that supports voice, video and data. It is being built in the 2000s.

nroff

(Nontypesetting RunOFF) A UNIX utility that formats documents for terminals and dot matrix printers. Using a text editor, troff codes are embedded into the text and the nroff command converts the document into the required output. Complex troff codes are ignored. See *troff*.

NRZ

(Non-Return-to-Zero) A data transmission method in which the 0s and 1s are represented by different polarities, typically positive for 0 and negative for 1. See *NRZI*.

NRZI

(Non-Return-to-Zero Inverted) A magnetic recording and data transmission method in which the polarity of the bit is reversed when a 1 bit is encountered. All subsequent 0s following the 1 are recorded at the same polarity.

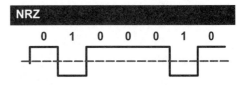

ns

(NanoSecond) See *nanosecond*.

NSAPI

(NetScape API) A programming interface on Netscape's Web Server. Using NSAPI function calls, Web pages can invoke programs on the server, typically to access data in a database. NSAPI is an alternative to using CGI scripts on Netscape Web servers. See *ISAPI*.

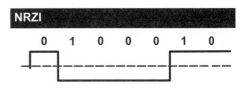

NSTL

(National Software Testing Lab, Philadelphia) An independent organization that evaluates computer hardware and software. It adheres to controlled testing methods to ensure objective results and publishes its findings in Software Digest Ratings Report and PC Digest.

NT

(Windows New Technology) See *Windows*.

NTFS

(NT File System) A file system used in Windows NT which uses the Unicode character set and allows file names up to 255 characters in length. The NTFS is designed to recover on the fly from hard disk crashes. Windows NT supports multiple file systems, and it can run with a DOS FAT, an OS/2 HPFS and a native NTFS, each in a different partition on the hard disk. NT's security features require that the NTFS be used.

NTSC

(National TV Standards Committee) The U.S. TV standard administered by the FCC that is currently 525 lines transmitted at 60 half frames/sec (interlaced). It is a composite of red, green and blue signals for color and includes an FM frequency for audio and an MTS signal for stereo. NTSC reconvenes to change TV standards.

NTT DoCoMo

(NTT Mobile Communications Network, Inc., Japan) Founded in 1991, NTT DoCoMo is a spinoff of Japan's NTT (Nippon Telegraph and Telephone Corporation) which provides wireless services, including cellular, paging, satellite and maritime and in-flight telephone services.

NuBus

A bus architecture (32-bits) originally developed at MIT and defined as a Eurocard (9U). Apple has changed its electrical and physical specs for its Macintosh series. Many Macs have one or more NuBus slots for peripheral expansion.

NUI

(1) (Network User Interface) A user interface for a computer attached to the network. The NUI is designed to work with remote applications and files as easily as local files.

(2) (Notebook User Interface) A term coined by Go Corporation for its PenPoint pen-based interface.

(3) (Network User Identifier) A code used to gain access into local European packed-switched networks.

null

The first character in ASCII and EBCDIC. In hex, it prints as 00; in decimal, it prints as a blank. It is naturally found in binary numbers when a byte contains no 1 bits. It is also used to pad fields and act as a delimiter; for example, in C, it specifies the end of a character string.

null modem cable

An RS-232 cable used to connect two personal computers in close proximity. It connects to both serial ports and crosses the sending wire on one end to the receiving wire on the other.

null pointer

In programming, a reference to zero. May be the response of an unsuccessful search function.

null string

In programming, a character string that contains no data.

NUMA

(Non-Uniform Memory Access) A multiprocessing architecture in which memory is separated into close and distant banks. NUMA is similar to SMP, in which multiple CPUs share a single memory. However, in SMP, all CPUs access a common memory at the same speed. In NUMA, memory on the same processor board as the CPU (local memory) is accessed faster than memory on other processor boards (shared memory), hence the "non-uniform" nomenclature.

number crunching

Refers to computers running mathematical, scientific or CAD applications, which perform large amounts of calculations.

numerical aperture

The amount of light that can be coupled to an optical fiber. The greater the aperture, the easier it is to connect the light source to the fiber.

numerical control

A category of automated machine tools, such as drills and lathes, that operate from instructions in a program. Numerical control (NC) machines are used in manufacturing tasks, such as milling, turning, punching and drilling.

First-generation machines were hardwired to perform specific tasks or programmed in a very low-level machine language. Today, they are controlled by their own microcomputers and programmed in high-level languages, such as APT and COMPACT II, which automatically generate the tool path (physical motions required to perform the operation).

The term was coined in the 1950s when the instructions to the tool were numeric codes. Just like the computer industry, symbolic languages were soon developed, but the original term remained.

numeric data

Refers to quantities and money amounts used in calculations. Contrast with *string* or *character data*.

numeric field

A data field that holds only numbers to be calculated. Contrast with *character field*.

NURB

(Non-Uniform Rational B-spline) A type of B-spline that yields a smoother curve. NURBS require more calculation to generate than B-splines.

NZ

(Non Zero) A value greater or less than 0.

OAI

(Open Application Interface) A computer to telephone interface that lets a computer control and customize PBX and ACD operations.

object

(1) A self-contained module of data and its associated processing. Objects are the software building blocks of object technology. See *object technology* and *object-oriented programming*.

(2) In a compound document, an independent block of data, text or graphics that was created by a separate application.

object bus

The protocol that governs communications between objects in a distributed objects system. For example, DCOM is the object bus for Microsoft's COM-based objects. See *distributed objects, DCOM* and *CORBA*.

object code

Same as *machine language*.

object database

See *object-oriented database*.

object language

(1) A language defined by a metalanguage.

(2) An object-oriented programming language.

(3) Same as *machine language* or *target language*.

object module

The output of an assembler or compiler, which must be linked with other modules before it can be executed.

object-oriented analysis

The examination of a problem by modeling it as a group of interacting objects. An object is defined by its class, data elements and behavior. For example; in an order processing system, an invoice is a class, and printing, viewing and totalling are examples of its behavior. Objects (individual invoices) inherit this behavior and combine it with their own data elements.

object-oriented database

A database that holds abstract data types (objects) and is managed by an object-oriented DBMS. See *object-oriented DBMS*.

object-oriented DBMS

A DBMS that manages objects (abstract data types). An object-oriented DBMS, or ODBMS, is suited for multimedia applications as well as data with complex relationships that are difficult to model and process in a relational DBMS. Because any type of data can be stored, an ODBMS allows for fully integrated databases that hold data, text, pictures, voice and video.

object-oriented design

Transforming an object-oriented model into the specifications required to create the system. Moving from object-oriented analysis to object-oriented design is accomplished by expanding the model into more and more detail.

object-oriented graphics

Same as *vector graphics*.

object-oriented interface

A graphical interface that uses icons and a mouse, such as Mac, Windows and Motif.

object-oriented programming

Abbreviated "OOP," the programming technology that supports the creation and processing of objects.

object-oriented technology

A variety of disciplines that support object-oriented programming, including object-oriented analysis and object-oriented design.

object program

A machine language program ready to run in a particular operating environment. It has been assembled, or compiled, and link edited.

object-relational database

See *universal server*.

object technology

The use of objects as the building blocks for applications. Objects are independent program modules written in object-oriented programming languages. Just as hardware components are routinely designed as modules to plug into and work with each other, objects are software components designed to work together at runtime without any prior linking.

OC

(Optical Carrier) The transmission speeds defined in the SONET specification. OC defines transmission by optical devices, and STS is the electrical equivalent.

```
Service          Speed (Mbps)
OC-1    STS-1        51.84 (28 DS1s or 1 DS3)
OC-3    STS-3       155.52 (3 STS-1s)
OC-3c   STS-3c      155.52 (concatenated)
OC-12   STS-12      622.08 (12 STS-1, 4 STS-3)
OC-12c  STS-12c     622.08 (12 STS-1, 4 STS-3c)
OC-48   STS-48     2488.32 (48 STS-1, 16 STS-3)
OC-192  STS-192    9953.28 (192 STS-1, 64 STS-3)
OC-768  STS-768   38813,12 (768 STS-1, 256 STS-3)
```

OCR

(Optical Character Recognition) Machine recognition of printed characters. OCR systems recognize different OCR fonts, as well as typewriter and computer-printed characters. Advanced OCR systems can recognize hand printing.

octal

A numbering system that uses eight digits. It is used as a shorthand method for representing binary numbers that use six-bit characters. Each three bits (half a character) is converted into a single octal digit. Okta is Greek for 8.

octet

An eight-bit storage unit. In the international community, octet is often used instead of byte.

OCX

(OLE Control EXtension) A component software technology from Microsoft that enables a Windows program to add funtionality by calling ready-made components. Generally called "OLE controls" or "OLE custom controls," they appear to the end user as just another part of the program. OCXs are Microsoft's second-generation component architecture. OCXs have been renamed ActiveX controls. See *VBX* and *ActiveX control*.

ODBC

(Open DataBase Connectivity) A database programming interface from Microsoft that provides a common language for Windows applications to access databases on a network.

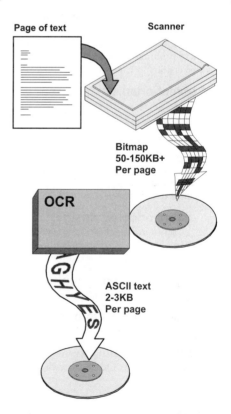

Page of text   Scanner

Bitmap
50-150KB+
Per page

OCR

ASCII text
2-3KB
Per page

ODBC is made up of the function calls programmers write into their applications and the ODBC drivers themselves.

ODBMS
See *object-oriented DBMS*.

odd parity
See *parity checking*.

ODI
(Open Data-Link Interface) A network driver interface from Novell. ODI is based on the LSL interface developed by AT&T for its UNIX System V operating system. See *network driver interface* and *LSL*.

ODMG
(Object Database Management Group, Burnsville, MN, www.odmg.org) An organization founded in 1991 to promote standards for object databases.

Oe, Oersted
Pronounced "ers-ted," the measurement of magnetic resistance. The higher the Oe, the more current required to magnetize it.

OEM
(Original Equipment Manufacturer) A manufacturer that sells equipment to a reseller. Also refers to the reseller itself. OEM customers either add value to the product before reselling it, private label it, or bundle it with their own products. See *VAR*.

off-hook
The state of a telephone line that allows dialing and transmission but prohibits incoming calls from being answered. The term stems from the days when a telephone handset was lifted off of a hook. Contrast with *on-hook*.

office automation
The integration of office information functions, including word processing, data processing, graphics, desktop publishing and e-mail. The backbone of office automation is a local area network (LAN).

Office Vision
Integrated office automation applications from IBM that run in all IBM computer families. It was the first major implementation of SAA and includes e-mail, scheduling, document creation and decision support capabilities.

offline
Not connected to or not installed in the computer. If a terminal, printer or other device is physically connected to the computer, but is not turned on or in ready mode, it is still considered offline. Disks and tapes that have been demounted and stored in the data library are considered offline. Contrast with *online*.

offline browser, offline reader
Software that downloads e-mail and selected data from an online service, allowing the user to browse the captured material after disconnecting. It automates retrieving routine data and saves online fees by shortening the connect time.

offline storage
Disks and tapes that are kept in a data library.

offload
To remove work from one computer and do it on another. See *cooperative processing*.

offset
(1) The distance from a starting point, either the start of a file or the start of a memory address. Its value is added to a base value to derive the actual value. An offset into a file is simply the character

location within that file, usually starting with 0; thus "offset 240" is actually the 241st byte of the file. See *relative address*.

(2) In word processing, the amount of space a document is printed from the left margin.

off-the-shelf

Refers to products that are packaged and available for sale.

ohm

A unit of measurement for electrical resistance. One ohm is the resistance in a circuit when one volt maintains a current of one amp.

OLAP

(OnLine Analytical Processing) Decision support software that allows the user to quickly analyze information that has been summarized into multidimensional views and hierarchies. For example, OLAP tools are used to perform trend analysis on sales and financial information. They can enable users to drill down into masses of sales statistics in order to isolate the products that are the most volatile.

Traditional OLAP products, also known as multidimensional OLAP, or MOLAP, summarize transactions into multidimensional views ahead of time. User queries on these types of databases are extremely fast, because most of the consolidation has already been done.

A relational OLAP, or ROLAP, tool extracts data from a traditional relational database. Using complex SQL statements against relational tables, it is able to create the multidimensional views on the fly.

A database OLAP, or DOLAP, refers to a relational DBMS that is designed to host OLAP structures and perform OLAP calculations.

A Web OLAP, or WOLAP, refers to OLAP data that is accessible from a Web browser.

OLCP

(OnLine Complex Processing) Processing complex queries, long transactions and simultaneous reads and writes to the same record. Contrast with *OLTP*, in which records are updated in a more predictable manner.

OLE

(Object Linking and Embedding) Windows' compound document protocol that allows one document to be embedded within or linked to another. When an embedded object (document, drawing, etc.) is clicked, the application that created it is launched, and the object can be edited. Changes made to the embedded object affect only the document that contains it.

If linked object references an original file outside of the document. Thus, if you make a change to a linked object, all the documents that contain that link are automatically updated the next time you open them.

OLE automation

See *COM automation*.

OLE control

See *OCX* and *ActiveX control*.

OLED

(Organic **LED**) A type of LED that provides a wide viewing angle, uses low power and does not

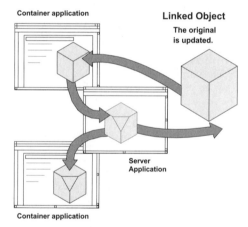

Container application

Linked Object
The original
is updated.

Server Application

Container application

OLE

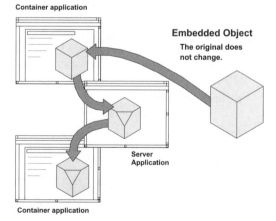

Container application

Embedded Object
The original does
not change.

Server Application

Container application

require a backlight. OLED screens can also be fabricated on plastic, which makes them more flexible and durable if dropped. An OLED is made of thin layers of carbon-based (organic) elements that emit light when energized.

OLTP

(OnLine Transaction Processing) See *transaction processing* and *OLCP*.

OMG

(Object Management Group, Framingham, MA, www.omg.org) An international organization founded in 1989 to endorse technologies as open standards for object-oriented applications. The OMG specifies the Object Management Architecture (OMA), a definition of a standard object model for distributed environments.

OMI

(Open Messaging Interface) A messaging protocol developed by Lotus, now included in VIM.

omnidirectional

In all directions. For example, an omnidirectional antenna can pick up signals in all directions.

OMNIS 7

A client/server development system for creating Windows and Mac applications from Blyth Software, Foster City, CA, (www.blyth.com). It includes its own database manager for local and laptop use and supports a wide variety of databases. OMNIS includes visual programming tools and a 4GL for application development.

ONC

(Open Network Computing) A family of networking products from SunSoft for implementing distributed computing in a multivendor environment. Includes TCP/IP and OSI protocols, NFS distributed file system, NIS naming service and TI-RPC remote procedure call library.

one-off

One at a time. CD-ROM recorders (CD-R drives) are commonly called one-off machines because they write one CD-ROM at a time.

on-hook

The state of a telephone line that can receive an incoming call. Contrast with *off-hook*.

onion diagram

A graphical representation of a system that is made up of concentric circles. The innermost circle is the core, and all outer layers are dependent on the core.

online

(1) A peripheral device (terminal, printer, etc.) that is ready to operate. A printer can be attached and turned on, yet still not online, if the ONLINE or SEL light is out. Pressing the ONLINE button will usually turn it back online.

(2) An online computer system refers to a system with terminals, but does not imply how the system functions. All the following are online systems. Data collection systems accept data from terminals, but do not update master files. Interactive systems imply data entry and updating. Transaction processing systems update necessary files as transactions arrive (orders, financial quotes, etc.). Realtime systems provide an immediate response to a question.

Want to impress your friends?

Although complete overkill, it is not incorrect to say that one has an online, realtime, interactive, transaction processing system. However, don't say this to an experienced systems analyst!

online help

On-screen instruction that is immediately available.

online industry

The collection of service organizations that provide dial-up access to databases, shopping, news, weather, sports, e-mail, etc.

online services

Organizations that provide databases and services via a communications link such as an analog modem, cable modem, ISDN, DSL or T1 line. Before the Internet became popular, services such as America Online, CompuServe and Prodigy were known for the types of databases they offered. Today, most all offer Internet access and distinguish themselves by their software, which provides a main menu for all activities.

on the fly

As needed. Implies little or no degradation in performance to accomplish the task. See *realtime* and *realtime compression*.

OOA, OOD, OODB, OODBMS, OOP

See *object-oriented analysis, object-oriented design, object-oriented database, object-oriented DBMS* and *object-oriented programming*.

op amp

(Operational Amplifier) A device that amplifies analog signals. It uses two inputs; one for power and one for data. It is used in myriads of applications from communications to stereo.

op code

See *operation code*.

open

(1) To identify a disk or tape file for reading and writing. The open procedure "locks on" to an existing file or creates a new one.

(2) With regard to a switch, open is "off."

open architecture

A system in which the specifications are made public in order to encourage third-party vendors to develop add-on products. Much of Apple's early success was due to the Apple II's open architecture. The PC is open architecture.

open computing

See *open systems*.

OpenDoc

A compound document and component software architecture from Apple, IBM, Sun and others that, although highly praised for its technology, never caught on.

open file

A disk or tape file that has been made available to the application for reading and writing by the operating system. All files must be "opened" and "closed."

OpenGL

(OPEN Graphics Language) A 3-D graphics language developed by SGI, which has become a de facto standard endorsed by many vendors. OpenGL can be implemented as an extension to an operating system or a window system and is supported by most UNIX-based workstations, Windows and X Window. Most high-end 3-D accelerators support OpenGL.

Open Group

(The Open Group, Cambridge, MA, www.opengroup.org) Formed in 1966 as the merger of the Open Software Foundation (OSF) and X/Open organizations, The Open Group is dedicated to promoting open standards. The OSF side is responsible for research and development and licensing of source code, while X/Open is responsible for certification and registration.

OPEN LOOK

An X Window-based graphical user interface for UNIX developed by Sun. It was widely used, but gave way to Motif, which became the standard GUI for UNIX.

open pipe

A continuous path from sender to receiver, such as found in a circuit-switching network or leased line. Transmitted data is not broken up into packets.

open shop

A computing environment that allows users to program and run their own programs. Contrast with *closed shop*.

open source

Free source code of a program, which is made available to the development community at large. The rationale is that a broader group of programmers will utlimately produce a more useful and more bug-free product for everyone, especially because more people will be reviewing the code.

In addition to better code, open source software allows an organization to modify the product for its own use rather than hope that the vendor of a proprietary product will implement its suggestions in a subsequent release. Examples of popular open source programs are the Apache Web server, sendmail mail server and Linux operating system.

open system

A vendor-independent system that is designed to interconnect with a variety of products. It implies that standards are determined from a consensus of interested parties rather than one or two vendors. Contrast with *closed system*. See *OSI*.

"Open systems" often refers to UNIX-based computer systems, since UNIX runs on more different kinds of hardware than any other operating environment. See *Open Group*.

OpenView

Network management software from HP. It supports SNMP and CMIP protocols, and third-party products that run under OpenView support SNA and DECnet network management protocols. OpenView is an enterprise-wide network management solution.

OpenVMS

A later version of the VMS operating system from Digital that runs on VAX and Alpha systems.

Opera

A Web browser for Windows, EPOC, BeOs and Linux from Opera Software, Oslo, Norway, (www.opera.com). Developed at Telenor (Norwegian Telecom) in 1994 and commercialized by Opera in 1995, it is noted for its unique features, including its fast rendering of Web pages, built-in zoom and ability to print just a highlighted section of the page.

operand

The part of a machine instruction that references data or a peripheral device. In the instruction, **ADD A to B**, A and B are the operands (nouns), and ADD is the operation code (verb). In the instruction **READ TRACK 9, SECTOR 32**, track and sector are the operands.

operating system

The master control program that runs the computer. It is the first program loaded when the computer is turned on, and its main part, called the "kernel," resides in memory at all times. It may be developed by the vendor of the computer it's running in or by a third party. The operating system sets the standards for the application programs that run in it. All programs must "talk to" the operating system.

The difference between an operating system and a network operating system is its multiuser capability. For example, DOS and Windows are single-user OSs designed for one person at a desktop computer. Windows NT and UNIX are network operating systems, because they are designed to manage multiple user requests at the same time and handle the related security.

An operating system provides the user interface and controls multitasking. It handles the input and output to the disk and all peripheral devices. In a large computer, it handles job scheduling.

operation code

The part of a machine instruction that tells the computer what to do, such as input, add or branch. The operation code is the verb; the operands are the nouns.

operations research

See *management science*.

operator

(1) A person who operates the computer and performs such activities as commanding the operating

system, mounting disks and tapes and placing paper in the printer. Operators may also write the job control language (JCL), which schedules the daily work for the computer. See *datacenter*.

(2) In programming and logic, a symbol used to perform an operation on some value such as an arithmetic + or a Boolean AND.

operator overloading

In programming, the ability to use the same operator to perform different operations. For example, arithmetic operators such as +, -, * and / could be defined to perform differently on certain kinds of data.

OPI

(Open Prepress Interface) An extension to PostScript that provides color separations. It was developed by Aldus Corporation, which was later acquired by Adobe.

optical amplifier

A device that boosts light signals in an optical fiber. Unlike regenerators, which have to convert the light signal to electricity in order to amplify it and then convert it back to light, the optical amplifier amplifies the light signal itself. The rare earth material, erbium, is used for creating the first successful optical amplifiers.

optical cross-connect

A network device used by telecom carriers to switch high-speed optical signals (OC-3, OC-12, OC-48, etc.). It differs from a digital cross-connect in that it deals with mulitple high-speed signals that are switched in their entirety and not multiplexed together.

optical disk

A direct access disk written and read by light. Optical disks are generally slower than magnetic disks, but their storage capacities are greater per square inch. There are a variety of fixed and removable media on the market. See *magneto-optic disk, CD, CD-ROM, CD-R, WORM* and *DVD*.

optical fiber

A thin glass wire designed for light transmission, capable of transmitting billions of bits per second. Unlike electrical pulses, light pulses are not affected by random radiation in the environment.

.9" diameter

High-density polyethylene jacket

Metal armor

Rip cord

Inner sheath

Dielectric strength member

Water-blocking tape

Core tube

Each of the 12 ribbons has 24 fibers

Optical Fiber

optical isolator

A device used with current loop transmission that uses an LED and photoresistor to detect current in the line.

optical mouse

A mouse that uses light to get its bearings. It is rolled over a small desktop pad that contains a reflective grid. The mouse emits a light and senses its reflection as it is moved. Contrast with *mechanical mouse*.

optical reader

An input device that recognizes typewritten or printed characters and bar codes and converts them into their corresponding digital codes.

optical recognition

See *OCR*.

optical switch

An all-optical fiber-optic switching device that maintains the signal as light from input to output. Traditional switches that connect optical fiber lines convert photons from the input side to electrons internally in order to perform the switching process.

optical zoom

The use of lenses to change the focal length of a digital camera. It is the same as a zoom lens on a traditional 35mm analog film cameras. Digital cameras have both optical and digital zoom. The digital zoom is performed in software. Nothing is better than the optical zoom, because it sees the real objects being photographed.

optimizer

Hardware or software that improves performance. See *defragger*.

optoelectronics

Merging light and electronics technologies, such as in optical fiber communications systems.

OR

A Boolean logic operation that is true if any of the inputs is true. An exclusive OR is true if only one of the inputs is true, but not both.

Oracle

(Oracle Corporation, Redwood Shores, CA, www.oracle.com) The world's largest database and application development software vendor founded in 1977 by Larry Ellison. The Oracle database was the first DBMS to incorporate the SQL language and to be ported to a wide variety of platforms. Oracle offers a variety of application development tools and is a major promoter of the network computer.

Oracle8

Oracle's relational database managment system (DBMS). This is the current version of Oracle's flagship product, which includes such features as replication and high availability. Oracle8 runs on more than 80 platforms and includes object-oriented extensions.

Oracle8i

A version of Oracle8 that enables Internet developers to write applications and database procedures in the same language. Introduced in 1999, noteworthy features are increased performance and support for XML and Java. A JVM (Java interpreter) is built into the DBMS so that triggers and stored procedures can be written and executed in Java rather than PL/SQL.

Orange Book

The documentation for the technical specifications of Photo CDs. See also *NCSC*.

ORB

(Object Request Broker) Software that handles the communication of messages from the requesting program (client) to the object as well as any return values from the object back to the calling program. See *CORBA* and *DCOM*. See also *ORB disk*.

ORB disk

A high-capacity removable hard disk system from Castlewood Systems, Inc., Pleasanton, CA, (www.castlewoodsystems.com). Introduced in late 1998 with a capacity of 2.2GB and a 12MB transfer rate, ORB drives use magnetoresistive (MR) read/write head technology.

ordinal number

The number that identifies the sequence of an item, for example, record #34. Contrast with *cardinal number*.

orientation

In typography, the direction of print across a page. See *portrait*.

OS

See *operating system*.

OS/2

A single user, multitasking operating system for PCs from IBM that runs OS/2, DOS and Windows applications. Although OS/2 is highly regarded as a robust operating system, it did not gain widespread market share. Presentation Manager (PM) was the first name for its GUI, which was later renamed Workplace Shell. The Presentation Manager name was retained to refer to the programming interface used to write OS/2 applications.

Version 3.0 was renamed "OS/2 Warp" and came packaged with Internet utilities and other productivity applications.

OS/390

The primary operating system used in IBM mainframes. OS/390 was originally the MVS/ESA operating system renamed and repackaged in 1996 with an extensive set of utilities. See *MVS*.

OS/9

A UNIX-like, realtime operating system from Microware Systems Corporation for Motorola 68000 CPUs. Originally developed for the 6809 chip, a version of OS/9 was created for CD-I players.

OS/9000

A portable version of OS/9, written in C, which runs on 386s and up and 68020s and up.

oscillate

To swing back and forth between the minimum and maximum values. An oscillation is one cycle, typically one complete wave in an alternating frequency.

oscillator

An electronic circuit used to generate high-frequency pulses. See *clock*.

oscilloscope

Test instrument that displays electronic signals (waves and pulses) on a screen. It creates its own time base against which signals can be measured, and display frames can be frozen for visual inspection.

OSD

(1) (On-Screen Display) An on-screen control panel for adjusting monitors and TVs. The OSD is used for contrast, brightness, horizontal and vertical positioning and other monitor adjustments.

(2) (Open Software Description) A data format for describing a software package, module or component. Based on XML, OSD is designed for distributing and updating software via push technology. Initially introduced for Windows, it is expected to be adopted for other platforms.

OSF

(Open Software Foundation) See *Open Group*.

OSI

(Open System Interconnection) An ISO standard for worldwide communications that defines a framework for implementing protocols in layers. OSI never became a universal standard, but it serves as an excellent teaching model. Learning the OSI layers and functions is essential for understanding communications networks.

Control is passed from one layer to the next, starting at the application layer in one station, proceeding to the bottom layer, over the channel to the next station and back up the hierarchy.

Most of this functionality exists in all communications networks; however, some systems often incorporate two or three layers into one.

Application - Layer 7
The top layer defines the language and syntax programs use to communicate with other programs. For example, a program in a client uses commands to request data from a program in the server.

Presentation - Layer 6
Converts one type of data encoding to another; for example, ASCII to EBCDIC or different floating point and binary formats.

Session - Layer 5
Coordinates and manages the dialogue; for example, making sure that the previous request has been fulfilled before the next one is sent. In practice, this layer is often not used or similar services are incorporated into the transport layer.

Transport - Layer 4
Responsible for overall end to end validity and integrity of the transmission. It ensures that the total message sent is the total message received.

Network - Layer 3
In routable protocols, such as IP, IPX and AppleTalk, it establishes the route over the internetwork between the sending and receiving stations.

Data Link - Layer 2
This layer divides the message into frames (Ethernet, Token Ring, etc.) and transmits them from node to node. There is no detection of lost frames.

Physical - Layer 1
This layer is responsible for passing bits onto and receiving them from the connecting medium. It deals only with the electrical and mechanical characteristics of the signals and signalling methods.

OSPF

(Open Shortest Path First) A router protocol that determines the least expensive path for routing a message. OSPF was originally developed to replace the RIP protocol.

OSR2

(OEM Service Release 2) Also known as Win95B, it is a version of Windows 95 released to PC vendors in late 1996 that included a variety of bug fixes as well as support for enhanced power management, FAT32, IDE bus mastering, 32-bit CardBus and Version 1.1 of DMI.

OS X

See *Mac OS X*.

OTPROM

(One Time **PROM**) A PROM chip that can be programmed only once.

outline font

A type of font made from basic outlines of each character. The outlines are scaled into actual characters (bitmaps) before printing. See *scalable font*.

outline processor

Software that allows the user to type in thoughts and organize them into an outline form.

out of band

See *signaling in/out of band*.

output

(1) Any computer-generated information displayed on screen, printed on paper or in machine readable form, such as disk and tape.

(2) To transfer or transmit from the computer to a peripheral device or communications line.

output area

A reserved segment of memory (buffer) used to collect data to be transferred out of the computer.

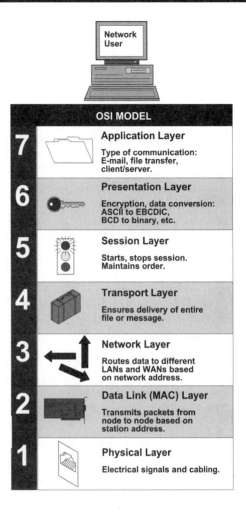

The Computer Glossary

output bound

Excessive overall slowness due to moving data out of the computer to low-speed lines or devices. See *printer buffer*.

output device

Any peripheral that presents output from the computer, such as a screen or printer. Although disks and tapes receive output, they are called "storage devices."

outsourcing

Contracting with outside consultants, software houses or service bureaus to perform systems analysis, programming and datacenter operations. See *facilities management*.

OverDrive

Intel's trade name for its CPU upgrade chips.

overflow error

An error that occurs when calculated data cannot fit within the designated field. The result field is usually left blank or is filled with some symbol to flag the error condition.

overhead

(1) The amount of processing time used by system software, such as the operating system, TP monitor or database manager.

(2) In communications, the additional codes transmitted for control and error checking, which take more time to process.

overlay

(1) A preprinted, precut form placed over a screen, key or tablet for indentification purposes. See *keyboard template*.

(2) A program segment called into memory when required. When a program is larger than the memory capacity of the machine, parts of the program not in constant use can be set up as overlays. Each overlay called in overwrites the existing overlay in memory. Virtual memory provides automatic overlays.

overlay card

A controller that digitizes NTSC signals from a video source for display in the computer.

overloading

In programming, the ability to use the same name for more than one variable or procedure, requiring the compiler to differentiate them based on context.

oversampling

Creating a more accurate digital representation of an analog signal. In order to work with real-world signals in the computer, analog signals are sampled some number of times per second (frequency) and converted into digital code. Using averaging and different algorithms, samples can be generated between existing samples, creating more digital information for complex signals, "smoothing out the curve" so to speak. See *sampling rate*.

overscan

Outside of the normal rectangular viewing area on a display screen. Contrast with *underscan*.

overstrike

(1) To type over an existing character.

(2) A character with a line through it.

overwrite

(1) A data entry mode that writes over existing characters on screen when new characters are typed in. Contrast with *insert mode*.

(2) To record new data on top of existing data such as when a disk record or file is updated.

P

P6

The Intel code name for the Pentium Pro, which is optimized for 32-bit applications. The P6 generation includes the Pentium Pro and Pentium II.

P7

Refers to the IA-64 CPU architecture that supersedes the Pentium line. See *IA-64* and *Itanium*.

PABX

(Private Automatic Branch eXchange) Same as *PBX*.

PACBASE

Integrated CASE software for mainframes and UNIX systems from CGI Systems, Malvern, PA, subsidiary of IBM, (www.cgisystems.com). It supports a wide variety of databases including DB2 and Oracle. PACLAN is the version for PC servers running OS/2 and Windows NT. PACBASE generates COBOL code for the servers. Visual Age for PACBASE is used to create the client side.

pack

(1) To compress data in order to save space. Unpack refers to decompressing data. See *data compression*.

(2) An instruction that converts a decimal number into a packed decimal format. Unpack converts a packed decimal number into decimal.

(3) In database programs, a command that removes records that have been marked for deletion.

packaged software

See *software package*.

packed decimal

A storage mode that places two decimal digits into one byte, each digit occupying four bits. The sign occupies four bits in the least significant byte. See *BCD* for illustration.

packet

A frame or block of data used for transmission in packet switching and other communications methods.

packet cellular

The transmission of data over the cellular network. Data is divided into packets, or frames, for error checking. Contrast with *circuit cellular*. See *CDPD* and *wireless*.

packetized voice

The transmission of realtime voice in a packet switching network.

packet over SONET (POS)

A metropolitan area network (MAN) or wide area network (WAN) transport technology that carries IP packets directly over SONET transmission without any data link facility such as ATM in between.

packet radio

The wireless transmission of data, which is divided into packets, or frames, for error checking.

packet switching

A networking technology that breaks up a message into smaller packets for transmission. It is the most common form of data transmission technology used in LANs, MANs and WANs.

Unlike circuit switching, which requires a constant point-to-point circuit to be established, each packet in a packet switched network contains a destination address. Thus all packets in a single message do not have to travel the same path. They can be dynamically routed over the network as circuits become available or unavailable. The destination computer reassembles the packets back into their proper sequence. Contrast with *circuit switching*.

packing density

The number of bits or tracks per inch of recording surface. Also refers to the number of memory bits or other electronic components on a chip.

pad

(1) To fill a data structure with padding characters.

(2) (PAD) (Packet Assembler/Disassembler) A communications device that formats outgoing data into packets of the required length for transmission in an X.25 packet switching network. It also strips the data out of incoming packets.

padding

Characters used to fill up unused portions of a data structure, such as a field or communications message. A field may be padded with blanks, zeros or nulls.

paddle

An input device that moves the screen cursor in a back-and-forth motion. It has a dial and one or more buttons and is typically used in games to hit balls and steer objects. See *joy stick*.

page

(1) In virtual memory systems, a segment of the program that is transferred into memory.

(2) In videotex systems, a transmitted frame.

(3) In word processing, a printed page.

page break

In printing, a code that marks the end of a page. A "hard" page break, inserted by the user, breaks the page at that location. "Soft" page breaks are created by word processing and report programs based on the current page length setting.

page description language

A device-independent, high-level language for defining printer output. If an application generates output in a page description language, such as PostScript, the output can be printed on any printer that supports it.

page fault

A virtual memory interrupt that reads the required page from disk when the next instruction or item of data is not in memory.

page frame

See *EMS*.

page header

Common text that is printed at the top of every page. It generally includes the page number and headings above each column.

PageMaker

A full-featured desktop publishing program for Windows and Macintosh from Adobe. PageMaker is used to create ads, brochures, newsletters and books of all sizes and kinds. Originally introduced for the Mac in 1985 by Aldus Corporation, it set the standard for desktop publishing.

page makeup

Formatting a printed page, which includes the layout of headers, footers, columns, page numbers, graphics, rules and borders.

PageMill

Web authoring software for Windows and Macintosh from Adobe. It provides a visual environment for creating Web pages. SiteMill is an additional program that works with PageMill for managing the entire site.

page mode memory

The common dynamic RAM chip design. Memory bits are accessed by row and column coordinates. Page mode memory is also called "fast page mode memory" (also FPM memory, FPM RAM, FPM DRAM). The "fast" designation was added back when newer chips ran at 100 nanoseconds and faster.

page printer

A type of printer that prints a page at a time. See *laser printer* and *ion deposition*.

page recognition

Software that recognizes the content of a printed page which has been scanned into the computer. It uses OCR to convert the printed words into computer text and should be able to differentiate text from other elements on the page, such as pictures and captions.

pagination

(1) Page numbering.

(2) Laying out printed pages, which includes setting up and printing columns, rules and borders. Although pagination is used synonymously with *page makeup*, the term often refers to the printing of long manuscripts rather than ads and brochures.

paging

In virtual memory, the transfer of program segments (pages) into and out of memory.

paint

(1) In computer graphics, to "paint" the screen using a tablet stylus or mouse to simulate a paintbrush.

(2) To transfer a dot matrix image as in the phrase "the laser printer paints the image onto a photosensitive drum."

(3) To create a screen form by typing anywhere on screen. To "paint" the screen with text.

paint program

A graphics program that allows the user to simulate painting on screen with the use of a graphics tablet or mouse. Paint programs create raster graphics images.

pair gain

The number of additional wire pairs that may be served by applying a technology such as digital loop carrier to existing telephone lines (wire pairs). See *digital loop carrier*.

PAL

(1) (Paradox Application Language) Paradox's programming language.

(2) (Programmable Array Logic) A programmable logic chip (PLD) technology from Advanced Micro Devices.

(3) (Phase Alternating Line) A European TV standard that uses 625 lines of resolution (100 more than NTSC).

palette

(1) In computer graphics, the total range of colors that can be used for display, although typically only a subset of them can be used at one time. May also refer to the collection of painting tools available to the user.

(2) A set of functions or modes.

Palm

The leading handheld electronic organizer from Palm Computing, Inc., Santa Clara, CA, (www.palm.com). The first Palm was the PalmPilot introduced in April 1996, which sold more than 350,000 units by year end.

palmtop

A computer small enough to hold in one hand and operate with the other. Palmtops may have specialized keyboards or keypads for data entry applications or have small qwerty keyboards.

pan

(1) In computer graphics, to move (while viewing) to a different part of an image without changing magnification.

(2) (PAN) (Personal Area Network) A wireless network that serves a single person or small workgroup. It has a limited range and is used to transfer data between a laptop or PDA and a desktop machine or server as well as to a printer.

(4) (PAN) (Personal Area Network) A transmission technology developed at IBM's Almaden Research Center, San Jose, CA, that lets people transfer information by touch. For example, you could exchange electronic business cards by shaking hands.

Panvalet
See *CA-Panvalet*.

PAP
(Password Authentication Protocol) The most basic access control protocol for logging onto a network. A table of usernames and passwords is stored on a server. When users log on, their usernames and passwords are sent to the server for verification. Contrast with *CHAP*, which encrypts the username and password before transmitting it.

paperless office
Long predicted, the paperless office is still a myth. Although paper usage has been reduced in some organizations, it has increased in others. Today's PCs make it easy to churn out documents.

paper tape
(1) A slow, low-capacity, sequential storage medium used in the first half of the 20th century to hold data as patterns of punched holes.

(2) A paper roll printed by a calculator or cash register.

paradigm
Pronounced "para-dime." A model, example or pattern.

Paradox
A relational database management (DBMS) and application development system for DOS and Windows from Corel. When Paradox was first released under DOS, it was noted for its visual query by example method, which made asking questions much easier than comparable products of the time. Originally developed by Ansa Corporation, it was later acquired by Borland and then Corel.

paragraph
In DOS programming, a 16 byte block. Memory addresses are generated as "segment:offset," where the segment is expressed in paragraphs.

paragraph tag
In desktop publishing, a style sheet assigned to a text paragraph. It defines font, tab, spacing and other settings.

parallel computing
Solving a single problem with multiple computers or computers made up of multiple processors. See *array processor* and *hypercube*.

Parallel Enterprise Server
A family of S/390 mainframes from IBM that are air cooled and use microprocessor-based CMOS technology. Using symmetric multiprocessing (SMP), one Server can hold up to 10 CPUs, and up to 32 Servers can be tied together. The first models of this type were introduced in 1994.

parallel interface
A multiline channel that transfers one or more bytes simultaneously. Personal computers generally connect printers via a Centronics 36-wire parallel interface, which transfers one byte at a time over eight wires, the remaining ones being used for control signals. Large computer parallel interfaces transfer more than one byte at a time. It is faster than a serial interface, because it transfers several bits concurrently. Contrast with *serial interface*. See *Centronics*.

parallelizing
To generate instructions for a parallel processing computer.

parallel port
A socket on a computer used to connect a printer or other peripheral device. It may also be used to attach a portable hard disk, tape backup or CD-ROM. Transferring files between two PCs can be accomplished by cabling the parallel ports of both machines together and using a file transfer program such as LapLink.

On the back of a PC, the parallel port is a 25-pin female DB-25 connector. In a PC, the parallel port circuit is contained on a small expansion card that plugs into an expansion slot. Typically two serial ports, one parallel port and one game port are on the card. These ports are often also included on an IDE host adapter card, which takes up only one expansion slot and provides hard and floppy disk control as well as I/O.

An enhanced parallel port, or EPP, which is present on high-end PCs, dramatically improves the speed of the parallel port and is completely compatible with earlier devices. See *EPP*.

parallel processing
(1) An architecture within a single computer that performs more than one operation at the same time. See *pipeline processing* and *vector processor*.

(2) A multiprocessing architecture made up of multiple CPUs or computer systems. Either one operation is performed on many sets of data (SIMD), or different parts of the job are worked on simultaneously (MIMD). See *hypercube* and *multiprocessing*.

Parallel Sysplex
IBM's umbrella name for its System/390 multiprocessing architecture. It includes a variety of features that allow multiple S/390 computers to be clustered together as a single system with data sharing and workload balancing.

parallel transmission
Transmitting data one or more bytes at a time. Contrast with *serial transmission*.

parameter
(1) Any value passed to a program by the user or by another program in order to customize the program for a particular purpose. A parameter may be anything; for example, a file name, a coordinate, a range of values, a money amount or a code of some kind. Parameters may be required as in parameter-driven software (see below) or they may be optional. Parameters are often entered as a series of values following the program name when the program is loaded.

A DOS switch is a parameter. For example, in the DOS Dir command **dir /p** the DOS switch **/p** (pause after every screenful) is a parameter.

(2) In programming, a value passed to a subroutine or function for processing. Programming today's graphical applications with languages such as C, C++ and Pascal requires knowledge of hundreds, if not thousands, of parameters.

parameter-driven
Software that requires external values expressed at runtime. A parameter-driven program solves a problem that is partially or entirely described by the values (parameters) that are entered at the time the program is loaded. For example, typing **bio 12-11-42** might load a program that calculates biorhythms for someone born on December 11, 1942. In this case 12-11-42 is a required parameter.

parental control software
A special browser or filtering program designed to reject Web sites not suited for children. Such programs may screen pages by word content, site rating or by URL, using an updated database of objectionable sites.

parent-child
In database management, a relationship between two files. The parent file contains required data about a subject, such as employees and customers. The child is the offspring; for example, the child of a customer file may be the order file.

parent program
The main, or primary, program or first program loaded into memory. See *child program*.

PA-RISC
(Precision Architecture-RISC) A proprietary RISC-based CPU architecture from HP that was introduced in 1986. It is the foundation of HP's computer families.

parity bit
An extra bit attached to the byte, character or word used to detect errors in transmission.

parity checking

An error detection technique that tests the integrity of digital data within the computer system or over a network. Parity checking uses an extra ninth bit that holds a 0 or 1 depending on the data content of the byte. Each time a byte is transferred or transmitted, the parity bit is tested.

Even parity systems make the parity bit 1 when there is an even number of 1 bits in the byte. Odd parity systems make it 1 when there is an odd number of 1 bits.

parity drive

A separate disk drive that holds parity bits in a disk array. See *RAID*.

parity error

An error condition that occurs when the parity bit of a character is found to be incorrect.

park

To retract the read/write head on a hard disk to its home location before the unit is physically moved in order to prevent damage. Most modern drives park themselves when the power is turned off.

parse

To analyze a sentence or language statement. Parsing breaks down words into functional units that can be converted into machine language. For example, to parse the dBASE expression

```
sum salary for title = "MANAGER"
SUM must be identified as the primary command, FOR as a conditional search,
TITLE as a field name and MANAGER as the data to be searched.
Parsing breaks down a natural language request, such as "What's the total of all
the managers' salaries" into the commands required by a high-level language,
such as in the example above.
```

parser

A routine that performs parsing operations on a computer or natural language.

partition

A reserved part of disk or memory that is set aside for some purpose.

Pascal

A high-level programming language developed by Swiss professor Niklaus Wirth in the early 1970s and named after the French mathematician, Blaise Pascal. It is noted for its structured programming, which caused it to achieve popularity initially in academic circles. Pascal has had strong influence on subsequent languages, such as Ada, dBASE and PAL.

Pascal is available in both interpreter and compiler form and has unique ways of defining variables. For example, a set of values can be stated for a variable, and if any other value is stored in it, the program generates an error at runtime. A Pascal set is an array-like structure that can hold a varying number of predefined values. Sets can be matched and manipulated providing powerful non-numeric programming capabilities.

The following Turbo Pascal example converts Fahrenheit to Celsius:

```
program convert;
var
fahr, cent : integer;
begin
  write('Enter Fahrenheit ');
  readln(fahr);
  cent := (fahr - 32) * 5 / 9;
  writeln('Celsius is ',cent)
end.
```

passive hub

A central connecting device in a network that joins wires from several stations in a star configuration. It does not provide any processing or regeneration of signals. Contrast with *active hub* and *intelligent hub*. See *hub*.

passive matrix

A common LCD technology used in laptops. See *LCD*.

password

A word or code used to serve as a security measure against unauthorized access to data. It is normally managed by the operating system or DBMS. However, the computer can only verify the legitimacy of the password, not the legitimacy of the user. See *NCSC*.

patch

A temporary or quick fix to a program. Too many patches in a program make it difficult to maintain. It may also refer to changing the actual machine code when it is inconvenient to recompile the source program.

path

(1) In communications, the route between any two nodes. Same as line, channel, link or circuit.

(2) In database management, the route from one set of data to another, for example, from customers to orders.

(3) The route to a file on a disk. In DOS and OS/2, the path for file MYLIFE located in subdirectory STORIES within directory JOE on drive C: looks like:

```
c:\joe\stories\mylife
```

The equivalent UNIX path follows. UNIX knows which drive is used:

```
/joe/stories/mylife
```

The Macintosh also uses a path in certain command sequences; for example, with "hard disk" as the drive, the same path is:

```
hard disk:joe:stories:mylife
```

PAX

(1) (Private Automatic Exchange) An inhouse intercom system.

(2) (Parallel Architecture Extended) A parallel processing environment standard based on Intel's i860 RISC chip, UNIX System V and Alliant Computer's parallel and 3-D graphics technologies.

PBX

(Private Branch eXchange) An inhouse telephone switching system that interconnects telephone extensions to each other, as well as to the outside telephone network. It may include functions such as least cost routing for outside calls, call forwarding, conference calling and call accounting.

Modern PBXs use all-digital methods for switching and can often handle digital terminals and telephones along with analog telephones.

PC

(1) See also *printed circuit board*.

(2) (Personal Computer) Although the term PC is sometimes used to refer to any kind of personal computer (Mac, Amiga, etc.), in this Glossary and in general, PC refers to computers that conform to the PC standard originally developed by IBM.

Today the PC industry is governed by Intel, Microsoft and major PC vendors collectively. The PC is the world's largest computer base.

PC/104

A modular system architecture that uses 3.5" square boards that snap together. PC/104 products are widely used, because this "stack through" bus, which uses the ISA technology, provides a compact and rugged design for building process control and embedded systems.

PC-8

A symbol set that contains the extended ASCII characters of the IBM PC.

PCB, PC board
See *printed circuit board.*

PC bus
The bus architecture used in first-generation IBM PCs and XTs. It refers to the original 8-bit bus, which accepted only 8-bit expansion boards. In 286s and up, it was superseded by the 16-bit AT bus, later known as the ISA bus.

PC Card
A credit-card sized, removable module for portable computers standardized by PCMCIA. PC Cards are also known as "PCMCIA cards." PC Cards are 16-bit devices that are used to attach modems, network adapters, sound cards, radio transceivers, solid state disks and hard disks to a portable computer.

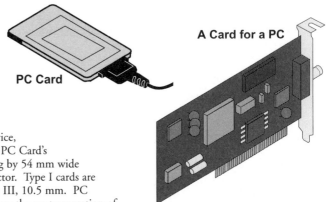

PC Card

A Card for a PC

The PC Card is a "plug and play" device, which is configured automatically by the PC Card's software. All PC Cards are 85.6 mm long by 54 mm wide (3.37" x 2.126") and use a 68-pin connector. Type I cards are 3.3 mm thick, Type II, 5.0 mm and Type III, 10.5 mm. PC Cards are 16-bit devices. CardBus cards are the next generation of PC Cards that add 32-bit capability and faster throughput.

PC CPU models
The brains of the PC is a CPU, or processor, from the Intel 8086 family (x86) of microprocessors or from a company that makes a compatible CPU. IBM also makes its own x86-compatible chips. See *x86.*

PC data buses
The bus in a PC is the common pathway between the CPU and the peripheral devices. Controller boards for the monitor, speakers, network and other peripheral connections plug directly into slots in the bus. See *ISA* and *PCI.*

PC-DOS
The DOS operating system supplied by IBM with its PCs. The heart of PC-DOS and MS-DOS function identically and they are both referred to as DOS. Starting with PC-DOS 6, the accompanying utilities differed from MS-DOS.

PCI
(Peripheral Component Interconnect) An expansion bus commonly used in PCs, Macintoshes and workstations. It was designed primarily by Intel and first appeared on PCs in late 1993. PCI provides a high-speed data path between the CPU and peripheral devices (video, disk, network, etc.). There are typically three or four PCI slots on the motherboard. In a Pentium PC, there is generally a mix of PCI and ISA slots or PCI and EISA slots.

PCjr
(PC junior) IBM's first home computer introduced in 1983. Its original keyboard was unsuitable for typing, but adequate keyboards were later added. It was discontinued in 1985.

PCL
(Printer Control Language) The command language for the HP LaserJet printers. It has become a de facto standard used in many printers and typesetters. PCL Level 5, introduced with the LaserJet III in 1990, also supports Compugraphic's Intellifont scalable fonts. Starting with the LaserJet 5 in 1996, PCL Level 6 streamlines the graphics and font commands, reducing the amount of information that has to be sent to the printer.

PCM

(1) (Pulse Code Modulation) A technique for converting analog signals into digital form that is widely used by the telephone companies in their T1 circuits.
Every minute of the day, millions of telephone conversations, as well as data transmissions via modem, are converted into digital via PCM for transport over high-speed intercity trunks. See *ADPCM, A-Law, mu-Law* and *sampling rate*.

(2) (Plug Compatible Manufacturer) An organization that makes a computer or electronic device that is compatible with an existing machine.

PCMCIA

See *PC Card*.

PC memory

The original PC design was constrained to one megabyte of memory with various operating system functions located in fixed memory positions. This fixed positioning has given rise to the most confusing platform in history. Following are the major memory areas of a PC:

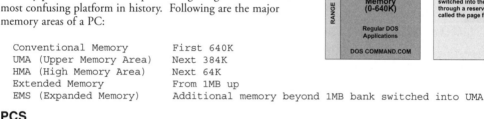

```
Conventional Memory        First 640K
UMA (Upper Memory Area)    Next 384K
HMA (High Memory Area)     Next 64K
Extended Memory            From 1MB up
EMS (Expanded Memory)      Additional memory beyond 1MB bank switched into UMA
```

PCS

(Personal Communications Services) Refers to wireless services that emerged after the U.S. Government auctioned commercial licenses in 1994 and 1995. This radio spectrum in the 1.8-2GHz range is typically used for digital cellular transmission that competes with analog and digital services in the 800Mhz and 900MHz bands.

PCX

A popular raster graphics file format that handles monochrome, 2-bit, 4-bit, 8-bit and 24-bit color and uses RLE to achieve compression ratios of approximately 1.1:1 to 1.5:1. Images with large blocks of solid colors compress best under the RLE method.

PDA

(Personal Digital Assistant) A handheld computer that serves an an organizer, electronic book or note taker and includes features such as pen-based entry and wireless transmission to a cellular service or desktop system.

PDES

(Product Data Exchange Specification) A standard format for exchanging data between advanced CAD and CAM programs. It describes a complete product, including the geometric aspects of the images as well as manufacturing features, tolerance specifications, material properties and finish specifications. See *IGES*.

PDF

See *Acrobat*.

PDIP

(Plastic DIP) A common type of DIP made of plastic.

PDL

See *page description language*.

PDM, PDMS

(Product Data Management, Product Data Management System) An information system used to manage product development from inception to manufacturing and maintenance. It handles all the data necessary at all stages including plans, geometric models, CAD drawings, images, NC programs as well as all related project data, notes and documents. PDMs are developed for workgroups as well as the entire enterprise.

PDP

(Programmed Data Processor) A minicomputer family from Digital that started with the 18-bit PDP-1 in 1959. In 1965, Digital legitimized the minicomputer industry with the PDP-8, which sold for about $20,000. In 1970, the PDP-11 was introduced, which became extremely successful.

PE

(1) (Phase Encoding) An early magnetic encoding method used on 1600bpi tapes in which a 1 is an up transition and a 0 is a down transition in the center of the bit cell.

(2) (Processing Element) One of multiple CPUs in a parallel processing system.

(3) (Professional Engineer) An engineering degree.

peek/poke

Instructions that view and alter a byte of memory by referencing a specific memory address. Peek displays the contents; poke changes it.

peer

In communications, a functional unit that is on the same protocol layer as another.

peer-to-peer communications

Communications in which both sides have equal responsibility for initiating, maintaining and terminating the session. Contrast with *master-slave communications*, in which the host controls everything and determines which users can initiate which sessions. If the host were programmed to allow all users to initiate all sessions, it would look like a peer-to-peer system to the user.

peer-to-peer network

A communications network that allows all workstations and computers in the network to act as servers to all other users on the network. Dedicated file servers may be used, but are not required as in a *client/server network*.

Do not confuse this term with "peer-to-peer communications." A peer-to-peer network implies peer-to-peer communications, but peer-to-peer communications does not imply a peer-to-peer network. Don't you love the extensive thought and analysis that goes into naming things in this business in order to make the terms perfectly clear and understandable!

pel

Same as *pixel*.

pen-based computing

Using a stylus to enter hand writing and marks into a computer. See *gesture recognition*.

Pentium

A family of CPU chips from Intel. The term may also refer to a PC that uses the chip. The first Pentium was introduced in 1993 as the successor to the 486. Although the integer performance of Pentium chips rivals RISC-based CPUs (Alpha, HP-PA, MIPS, SPARC, etc.), their floating point performance is generally slower. Variations of the Pentium were later introduced, including the Pentium Pro, Pentium MMX, Pentium II and Pentium III.

PEP

(Packet Exchange Protocol) A Xerox protocol used internally by NetWare to transport internal Netware NCP commands (NetWare Core Protocols). It uses PEP and IPX for this purpose. Application programs use SPX and IPX.

peripheral

Any hardware device connected to a computer, such as a monitor, keyboard, printer, plotter, disk or tape drive, graphics tablet, scanner, joy stick, paddle and mouse.

peripheral controller

See *control unit (2)*.

peripheral device
See *peripheral*.

Perl
(Practical Extraction Report Language) A programming language written by Larry Wall that combines syntax from several UNIX utilities and languages. Perl is designed to handle a variety of system administrator functions. Because of its comprehensive string handling capabilities, it is widely used on Web servers. Stemming from the UNIX world, Perl has been adapted to other platforms. See also *PURL*.

permanent font
(1) A soft font that is kept in the printer's memory until the printer is turned off.

(2) Same as *internal font*.

permanent memory
Same as *non-volatile memory*.

permutation
One possible combination of items out of a larger set of items. For example, with the set of numbers 1, 2 and 3, there are six possible permutations: **12, 21, 13, 31, 23** and **32**.

persistence
(1) In a CRT, the time a phosphor dot remains illuminated after being energized. Long-persistence phosphors reduce flicker, but generate ghost-like images that linger on screen for a fraction of a second.

(2) In object technology, the storage of an object on a disk or other permanent storage device.

persistent link
See *hot link*.

personal computer
Synonymous with microcomputer, a computer that serves one user in the office or the home. PCs are the largest installed base of personal computers. Macintoshes are second.

personal workstation
Same as *personal computer* or *workstation*.

PGA
(1) (Pin Grid Array) A chip housing with high density of pins (200 pins can fit in 1.5" square). Used for large amounts of I/O, its underside looks like a "bed of nails."

(2) (Programmable Gate Array) A type of gate array that is programmed by the customer.

(3) (Professional Graphics Adapter) An early IBM display standard for PCs (640x480x256) with 3-D processing. It was not widely used.

PGP
(Pretty Good Privacy) Public key cryptography software from Pretty Good Privacy, Inc., San Mateo, CA, (www.pgp.com). It was developed by Phil Zimmermann, founder of the company, and it is based on the RSA cryptographic method. A version for personal, non-business use is available on various BBSs and Internet hosts. See *cryptography*.

phase change recording
An optical recording technology that uses a short, high-intensity laser pulse to create a bit by altering the crystalline structure of the material. The bit either reflects or absorbs light when read. A medium-intensity pulse is used to restore the crystalline structure.

phase encoding
See *PE*.

phase locked
A technique for maintaining synchronization in an electronic circuit. The circuit receives its timing from input signals, but also provides a feedback circuit for synchronization.

phase modulation

A transmission technique that blends a data signal into a carrier by varying (modulating) the phase of the carrier. See *modulate*.

PHIGS

(Programmer's Hierarchical Interactive Graphics Standard) A graphics system and language used to create 2-D and 3-D images. Like the GKS standard, PHIGS is a device independent interface between the application program and the graphics subsystem.

It manages graphics objects in a hierarchical manner so that a complete assembly can be specified with all of its subassemblies. It is a very comprehensive standard requiring high-performance workstations and host processing.

phone connector

(1) A plug and socket for a two or three-wire coaxial cable used to plug microphones and headphones into amplifiers. The plug is a single prong a quarter inch in diameter and 1.25" in length. See *phono connector*.

(2) A plug and socket for a telephone line, typically the RJ-11 modular connector.

phone hawk

Slang for a person who calls up a computer via modem and either copies or destroys data.

phoneme

A speech utterance, such as "k," "ch," and "sh," that is used in synthetic speech systems to compose words for audio output.

Phong shading

In computer graphics, a technique developed by Phong Bui Tuong that computes a shaded surface based on the color and illumination at each pixel. It is more accurate than Gouraud shading, but requires much more extensive computation.

phono connector

Also called an "RCA connector," a plug and socket for a two-wire coaxial cable used to connect audio and video components. The Apple II has a video out phono connector for a TV. The plug is a 1/8" thick prong that sticks out 5/16" from the middle of a cylinder. See *phone connector*.

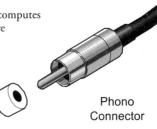

Phono Connector

phosphor

A rare earth material used to coat the inside face of a CRT. When struck by an electron beam, the phosphor emits a visible light for a few milliseconds. In color displays, red, green and blue phosphor dots are grouped as a cluster.

Photo CD

A CD imaging system from Kodak that digitizes 35mm slides or negatives onto a CD-ROM disc. The Photo CD is created by photo finishers that have a Kodak Picture Imaging Workstation. A replica of each image in the form of contact prints is also included. A multisession CD-ROM drive is required to read Photo CD images that were added after the original set. Most new drives provide this capability.

photocomposition

Laying out a printed page using electrophotographic machines, such as phototypesetters and laser printers. See *page makeup* and *pagination*.

photolithography

A lithographic technique used to transfer the design of the circuit paths and electronic elements on a chip onto a wafer's surface. A photomask is created with the design for each layer of the chip. The wafer is coated with a light-sensitive film (photoresist) and is exposed to light shining through the photomask. The light hardens the film, and when the wafer is exposed to an acid bath (wet processing) or hot ions (dry processing), the unhardened areas are etched away.

photomask

An opaque image on a transluscent plate that is used as a light filter to transfer an image from one device to another. See *chip*.

photomicrography

Photographing microscopic images.

photon

A unit of energy. Elementary particle of electromagnetic radiation (light, radio waves, X-rays, etc.).

photonics

The science of building machine circuits that use light instead of electricity.

photooptic memory

A storage device that uses a laser beam to record data onto a photosensitive film.

photorealistic

Having the image quality of a photograph.

photoresist

A film used in photolithography that temporarily holds the pattern of a circuit path or microscopic element of a chip. When exposed to light, it hardens and is resistant to the acid bath that washes away the unexposed areas.

photosensor

A light-sensitive device that is used in optical scanning machinery.

Photoshop

A popular high-end image editor for the Macintosh and Windows from Adobe. The original Mac versions were the first to bring affordable image editing down to the personal computer level in the late 1980s. Since then, Photoshop has become the de facto standard in image editing. Although it contains a large variety of image editing features, one of Photoshop's most powerful capabilities is layers, which allows images to be rearranged under and over each other for placement.

physical

Refers to devices at the electronic, or machine, level. Contrast with *logical*. See *logical vs physical*.

physical address

The actual, machine address of an item or device.

physical format

See *record layout* and *low-level format*.

physical link

(1) An electronic connection between two devices.

(2) In data management, a pointer in an index or record that refers to the physical location of data in another file.

physical lock

Prevention of user access to data provided by a locking on/off switch or file protection mechanism such as on a floppy disk. Contrast with *logical lock*.

PIC

(1) (PICture) A file extension used for graphics formats. Lotus PIC is a vector format for 1-2-3 charts and graphs. Videoshow PIC is a vector format that is a subset of the NAPLPS standard.

(2) (Programmable Interrupt Controller) An Intel 8259A chip that controls interrupts. Starting with the 286-based AT, there are two PICs in a PC, providing a total of 15 usable IRQs. The PIC has been superseded by an Advanced Programmable Interrupt Controller, or 82489DX chip, that is enhanced for multiprocessing. See *IRQ*.

pica

(1) In word processing, a monospaced font that prints 10 characters per inch.

(2) In typography, about 1/6th of an inch (0.166") or 12 points.

Pick System

A multiuser operating environment and database management system (DBMS) from Pick Systems, Inc., Irvine, CA, (www.picksys.com), that runs on x86, PowerPC and UNIX platforms. It has been highly praised for its ease of use, flexibility and advanced features. The DBMS portion of the Pick System is widely used in third-party products. R83 is the original Pick System. R93 and Advanced Pick are later versions. D3 is the DBMS, and D3 Pro Plus is a Linux/DBMS package.

picosecond

One trillionth of a second. Pronounced "pee-co-second."

PICT

(PICTure) A Macintosh graphics file format that stores images in the QuickDraw vector format. When PICT files are converted to the PC, they use the .PCT file extension.

picture

In programming, a pattern that describes the type of data allowed in a field or how it will print. The pattern is made up of a character code for each character in the field; for example, 9999 is a picture for four numeric digits. A picture for a telephone number could be (999) 999-9999. XXX999 represents three alphanumerics followed by three numerics. Pictures are similar but not identical in all programming languages.

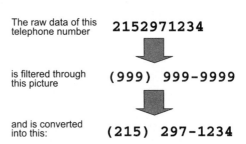

The raw data of this telephone number **2152971234**

is filtered through this picture **(999) 999-9999**

and is converted into this: **(215) 297-1234**

picture element

See *pixel*.

PID

(1) (Process IDentifier) A temporary number assigned by the operating system to a process or service.

(2) (Proportional Integral Derivative) A controller used to regulate a continuous process such as grinding or cooking.

pie chart

A graphical representation of information in which each unit of data is represented as a pie-shaped piece of a circle. See *business graphics*.

piezoelectric

The property of certain crystals that causes them to oscillate when subjected to electrical pressure (voltage).

PIF

(Program Information File) A Windows data file used to hold requirements for DOS applications running under Windows. Windows comes with a variety of PIFs, but users can edit them and new ones can be created with the PIF editor if a DOS application doesn't work properly. An application can be launched by clicking on its PIF.

piggyback board

A small printed circuit board that plugs into another circuit board in order to enhance its capabilities. It does not plug into the motherboard, but would plug into the boards that plug into the motherboard.

PIL

(Publishing Interchange Language) A standard for document interchange that defines the placement of text and graphics objects on the page. It does not address the content of the objects.

PIM

(Personal Information Manager) Software that organizes names and addresses and random notes for fast retrieval. It provides a combination of features such as a telephone list with automatic dialing, calendar, scheduler and tickler. A PIM lets you jot down text for any purpose and retrieve it based on any of the words you typed in. PIMs vary widely, but all of them attempt to provide methods for managing information the way you use it on a daily basis.

pin

(1) The male lead on a connecting plug (serial port, monitor cable, keyboard connector, etc.) or the spiderlike foot on a chip. Each pin is plugged into a socket to complete the circuit.

(2) (PIN) (Personal Identification Number) A personal password used for identification purposes.

pinch roller

A small, freely-turning wheel in a tape drive that pushes the tape against a motor-driven wheel in order to move it.

pin compatible

Refers to a chip or other electronic module that can be plugged into the same socket as the chip or module it is replacing.

pincushioning

A screen distortion in which the sides bow in. Contrast with *barrel distortion*.

pin feed

A method for moving continuous paper forms. Pins at both ends of a rotating platen or tractor engage the forms through pre-punched holes at both sides.

ping

(Packet INternet Groper) An Internet utility used to determine if a particular IP address is online. It sends out a packet and waits for a response.

ping pong

(1) A half-duplex communications method in which data is transmitted in one direction and acknowledgement is returned at the same speed in the other. The line is alternately switched from transmit to receive in each direction. Contrast with *asymmetric modem*.

(2) To go in one direction and then in the other.

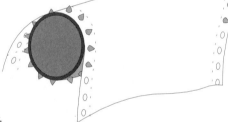

Pin Feed

pinouts

The description and purpose of each pin in a multiline connector.

pipe

A shared space that accepts the output of one program for input into another. In DOS, OS/2 and UNIX, the pipe command is a vertical line (|). For example, in DOS and OS/2, the statement, **dir | sort** directs the output of the directory list to the sort utility.

pipeline processing

A category of techniques that provide simultaneous, or parallel, processing within the computer It refers to overlapping operations by moving data or instructions into a conceptual pipe with all stages of the pipe processing simultaneously. For example, while one instruction is being executed, the computer is decoding the next instruction. In vector processors, several steps in a floating point operation can be processed simultaneously.

piracy

The illegal copying of software for personal or commercial use.

pitch

The number of printed characters per inch. With proportionally spaced characters, the pitch is variable and must be measured as an average. See *dot pitch*.

pixel

(**PIX** [picture] **EL**ement) The smallest element on a video display screen. A screen is broken up into thousands of tiny dots, and a pixel is one or more dots that are treated as a unit. A pixel can be one dot on a monochrome screen, three dots (red, green and blue) on color screens, or clusters of these dots.

PKZIP, PKUNZIP

Popular compression programs for DOS, Windows, OS/2 and UNIX from PKWARE Inc., Brown Deer, WI, (www.pkware.com). "Zipping" compresses files into a .zip archive, and "unzipping" decompresses them.

PLA

(**P**rogrammable **L**ogic **A**rray) A programmable logic chip (PLD) technology from Philips/Signetics.

plaintext

Normal text that has not been encrypted and is readable by text editors and word processors. Contrast with *ciphertext*.

planar

A technique developed by Fairchild Instruments that creates transistor sublayers by forcing chemicals under pressure into exposed areas. Planar superseded the mesa process and was a major step toward creating the chip.

planning system

See *spreadsheet* and *financial planning system*.

plasma display

Also called "gas discharge," it is a flat-screen technology that contains an inert ionized gas sandwiched between x- and y-axis panels. A pixel is selected by charging one x- and one y-wire, causing the gas in that vicinity to glow. Plasma displays were initially monochrome, typically orange, but color displays are increasingly being used for large screens.

platesetter

A machine that generates plates for a printing press. A platesetter is similar in function to an imagesetter, except that instead of producing film from which the plates are made, the plates themselves are made. See *imagesetter*.

platform

A hardware or software architecture. The term originally dealt with only hardware, and it is still used to refer to a CPU model or computer family. For example, the x86, or PC, is the world's largest hardware platform. AS/400 and SPARC are other examples.

Platform also refers to an operating system, in which case the hardware may or may not be implied. For example, when a program is said to "run on the Windows platform," it means that the program has been compiled into the Intel x86 machine language and that it communicates with the Windows operating system. If Windows were to become extremely popular on Alpha hardware, then "it runs on the Windows platform" would be ambiguous. In order to differentiate, one would have to say "Windows for Alpha" or "Windows for Intel."

platter

One of the disks in a disk pack or hard disk drive. Each platter provides a top and bottom recording surface. See *magnetic disk*.

PLB

(**P**icture **L**evel **B**enchmark) A benchmark for measuring graphics performance on workstations. The Benchmark Interface Format (BIF) defines the PLB format, the Benchmark Timing Methodology (BTM) performs the test, and the Benchmark Reporting Format (BRF) generates results in GPCmarks. Image quality is not rated.

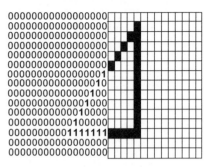

Monochrome Pixels
The simplest pixel representation is a monochrome image in which one bit represents a dark or light pixel (black or white, black or amber, etc.).

PLC

(Programmable Logic Controller) A computer used in process control applications. PLC microprocessors are typically RISC-based and are designed for high-speed, realtime and rugged industrial environments.

PLCC

(Plastic LCC) A widely-used type of leaded chip carrier. See *LCC*.

PLD

(Programmable Logic Device) A logic chip that is programmed at the customer's site. There are a wide variety of PLD techniques; however, most PLDs are compatible with the PAL method from Advanced Micro Devices.

The PLD is not a storage chip like a PROM or EPROM, although fuse-blowing techniques are used. It contains different configurations of AND, OR and NOR gates that are "blown" together. Contrast with *gate array*, which requires a manufacturing process to complete the programming.

PL/I

(Programming Language 1) A high-level IBM programming language introduced in 1964 with the System/360 series. It was designed to combine features of and eventually supplant COBOL and FORTRAN, which never happened. A PL/I program is made up of procedures (modules) that can be compiled independently. There is always a main procedure and zero or more additional ones. Functions, which pass arguments back and forth, are also provided.

PL/M

(Programming Language for Microprocessors) A dialect of PL/I developed by Intel as a high-level language for its microprocessors. PL/M+ is an extended version of PL/M, developed by National Semiconductor for its microprocessors.

plot

To create an image by drawing a series of lines. In programming, a plot statement creates a single vector (line) or a complete circle or box that is made up of several vectors.

plotter

A graphics printer that draws images with ink pens. It requires data in vector graphics format, which makes up an image as a series of point-to-point lines. See *flatbed plotter* and *drum plotter*.

PLP

(Presentation Level Protocol) A North American standard protocol for videotex.

PL/SQL

(Procedural Language/SQL) A programming language from Oracle that is used to write triggers and stored procedures that are executed by the Oracle DBMS. It is also used to add additional processing (sorting and other manipulation) of the data that has been returned by the SQL query. See *Oracle8i*.

plug and play

(1) The ability to add a new component and have it work without having to perform any technical analysis or procedure.

(2) (Plug and Play) Also abbreviated PnP, it is a Microsoft/Intel standard for PC expansion boards starting with Windows 95. It eliminates most of the frustration of configuring the system when adding new peripherals. IRQ and DMA settings and I/O and memory addresses self configure each time the computer is turned on.

plugboard

A board containing a matrix of sockets used to program early tabulating machines and computers. A wire is inserted into one output and one input socket, closing a circuit and activating a function. Complicated programs looked like "mounds of spaghetti."

plug compatible

Hardware that is designed to perform exactly like another vendor's product. A plug compatible CPU runs the same software as the machine it's compatible with. A plug compatible peripheral works the same as the device it's replacing.

plug-in

An auxiliary program that works with a major software package to enhance its capability. For example, plug-ins are widely used in image editing programs such as Photoshop to add a filter for some special effect. Plug-ins are added to Web browsers to enable them to support new types of content (audio, video, etc.). The term is widely used for software, but could also be used to refer to a plug-in module for hardware.

PM

See *preventive maintenance* and *phase modulation*.

PMOS

(Positive channel **MOS**) Pronounced "P moss." A type of microelectronic circuit in which the base material is positively charged. PMOS transistors were used in the first microprocessors and are still used in CMOS. They are also used in low-cost products (calculators, watches, etc.).

PMS

(Pantone Matching System) A color matching system that has a number assigned to over 500 different colors and shades. This standard for the printing industry has been built into many graphics and desktop publishing programs to ensure color accuracy.

PNG

(Portable Network Graphics) A raster graphics file format endorsed by the World Wide Web Consortium. It is expected to eventually replace the GIF format, because there are lingering legal problems with GIFs. CompuServe owns the format, and Unisys owns the compression method. In addition, GIF is a very basic graphics format that is limited to 256 colors (8-bit color).

PNNI

(Private Network-to-Network Interface) A routing protocol used between ATM switches in an ATM network. It lets the switches inform each other about network topology so they can make appropriate forwarding decisions.

PnP

See *Plug and Play*.

pocket computer

A hand-held, calculator-sized computer that runs on batteries. It can be plugged into a personal computer for data transfer.

Pocket Excel, Pocket Word

Versions of Micrsoft applications for the Windows CE operating system.

point

(1) To move the cursor onto a line or image on screen by rolling a mouse across the desk or by pressing the arrow keys.

(2) In typography, a unit equal to 1/72nd of an inch, used to measure the vertical height of a printed character.

point and shoot

To select a menu option or activate a function by moving the cursor onto a line or object and pressing the return key or mouse button.

pointer

(1) In database management, an address embedded within the data that specifies the location of data in another record or file.

(2) In programming, a variable that is used as a reference to the current item in a table (array) or to some other object, such as the current row or column on screen.

(3) An on-screen symbol used to identify menu selections or the current screen location. It is moved by a mouse or other pointing device.

pointing device

An input device used to move the pointer (cursor) on screen. The major pointing devices are the mouse, trackball, pointing stick and touchpad.

point of sale

Capturing data at the time and place of sale. Point of sale systems use personal computers or specialized terminals that are combined with cash registers, optical scanners for reading product tags, and/or magnetic stripe readers for reading credit cards.

Point of sale systems may be online to a central computer for credit checking and inventory updating, or they may be stand-alone machines that store the daily transactions until they can be delivered or transmitted to the main computer for processing.

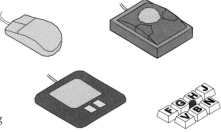

Pointing Device

point-to-multipoint

A communications network that provides a path from one location to multiple locations (from one to many).

point-to-point

A communications network that provides a path from one location to another (point A to point B).

Poisson distribution

A statistical method developed by the 18th century French mathematician S. D. Poisson, which is used for predicting the probable distribution of a series of events. For example, when the average transaction volume in a communications system can be estimated, Poisson distribution is used to determine the probable minimum and maximum number of transactions that can occur within a given time period.

poke

See *peek/poke*.

polarity

(1) The direction of charged particles, which may determine the binary status of a bit.

(2) In micrographics, the change in the light to dark relationship of an image when copies are made. Positive polarity is dark characters on a light background; negative polarity is light characters on a dark background.

polarized

A one-way direction of a signal or the molecules within a material pointing in one direction.

policy management

Enforcing the rules and regulations of the organization that pertain to information and computing. It includes the types of internal and external information that employees have permission to view while on the job as well as the kinds of software they may install on their own desktop machines. See *security*.

Polish notation

A method for expressing a sequence of calculations developed by the Polish logician Jan Lukasiewicz in 1929. For example, A(B+C) would be expressed as
* A + B C. In reverse Polish notation, it would be A B C + *.

polling

A communications technique that determines when a terminal is ready to send data. The computer continually interrogates its connected terminals in a round robin sequence. If a terminal has data to send, it sends back an acknowledgement and the transmission begins. Contrast with *interrupt-driven*, in which the terminal generates a signal when it has data to send.

polling cycle

One round in which each and every terminal connected to the computer or controller has been polled once.

polygon

In computer graphics, a multi-sided object that can be filled with color or moved around as a single entity.

Polygon

Polyline

polyhedron

A six- or more-sided object. A group of connected polygons.

polyline

In computer graphics, a single entity that is made up of a series of connected lines.

polymorphic virus

A virus that changes its binary pattern each time it infects a new file to keep it from being identified. See *stealth virus.*

polymorphism

Meaning many shapes. In object-oriented programming, the ability of a generalized request (message) to produce different results based on the object that it is sent to.

polyphonic

The ability to play back some number of musical notes simultaneously. For example, 16-voice polyphony means a total of 16 notes, or waveforms, can be played concurrently.

POP

(1) (Point of Presence) The point at which a line from a long distance carrier (IXC) connects to the line of the local telephone company or to the user if the local company is not involved. For online services and Internet providers, the POP is the local exchange users dial into via modem.

(2) (Post Office Protocol) A standard mail server commonly used on the Internet, the latest version of which is POP3. It provides a message store that holds incoming e-mail until users log on and download it. POP is a simple system with little selectivity. All pending messages and attachments are downloaded at the same time. POP uses the SMTP messaging protocol. See *IMAP* and *messaging system.*

(3) An instruction that retrieves an item from a stack. See *push/pop.*

POP-1

(Package for Online Programming) The first of a family of programming languages introduced in England in the mid 1960s. It used reverse polish notation. Successors were POP-2, POP-9X, POP-10, POP-11, POPCORN, POP++, POPLOG and POPLER.

populate

To plug in chips or components into a printed circuit board. A fully populated board is one that contains all the devices it can hold.

port

A pathway into and out of the computer or a network device such as a switch or router. For example, the serial and parallel ports on a personal computer are external sockets for plugging in communications lines, modems and printers. Every network adapter has a port (Ethernet, Token Ring, etc.) for connection to the local area network (LAN). Any device that transmits and receives data implies an available port to connect to each line. See *porting* and *port number.*

portable

Refers to software that can be easily moved from one type of machine to another. It implies a product that has a version for several hardware platforms or has built-in capabilities for switching between them. However, a program that can be easily converted from one machine type to another is also considered portable.

portable computer

A personal computer that can be easily transported. Compared to desktop models, it has limited expansion slots and disk capacity.

port address

A physical identification of an I/O port. See *I/O address.*

port aggregation
Using multiple transmission paths between network devices in order to increase transmission speed. Port aggregation between a server and a switch requires multiple network adapters (NICs) in the server or adapters with multiple ports.

portal
A Web "supersite" that provides a variety of services including Web searching, news, white and yellow pages directories, free e-mail, discussion groups, online shopping and links to other sites. Web portals are the Web equivalent of the original online services such as CompuServe and AOL. Although the term was initially used to refer to general purpose sites, it is increasingly being used to refer to vertical market sites.

port expander
A device that connects several lines to one port in the computer. A line is given access to the port either by a hardware switch or through software selection.

porting
Converting software from one language to another in order to run in a different computer environment. "To port" is the verb, but a port is something else. See *port*.

port number
In a TCP/IP-based network such as the Internet, it is a number assigned to an application program running in the computer. The number is used to link the incoming data to the correct service. Well-known ports are standard port numbers used by everyone; for example, port 80 is used for HTTP traffic (Web traffic). See *port*.

portrait
An orientation in which the data is printed across the narrow side of the form.

port replicator
A device used to connect peripherals to a laptop. All the desktop devices are permanently plugged into the port replicator, which quickly connects to the laptop. It is like a docking station without expansion slots.

port switching hub
An intelligent network hub that attaches to multiple LAN segments. Via software, it allows the station ports to be connected to one of the segments. This is a type of virtual LAN, because one LAN segment can be located on different floors or geographic locations.

POS
See *point of sale*.

positive logic
The use of low voltage for a 0 bit and high voltage for a 1 bit. Contrast with *negative logic*.

POSIX
(Portable Operating System Interface for UNIX) An IEEE 1003.1 standard that defines the language interface between application programs and the UNIX operating system. Adherence to the standard ensures compatibility when programs are moved from one UNIX computer to another. POSIX is primarily composed of features from UNIX System V and BSD UNIX.

POST
(1) (Power On Self Test) A series of built-in diagnostics that are performed when the computer is first started. Proprietary codes are generated (POST codes) that indicate test results. See *diagnostic board*.

(2) (post) To send a message to an Internet newsgroup. See *Usenet*.

postfix notation
See *reverse Polish notation*.

postprocessor
Software that provides some final processing to data, such as formatting it for display or printing.

PostScript

A page description language from Adobe that is used extensively on Macs and PCs as well as workstations, minis and mainframes. It is the de facto standard in commercial typesetting and printing houses. Most all accept and may even require PostScript files as electronic input. PostScript fonts come in Type 1 and Type 3 formats. Type 1 fonts are widely used and are made by Adobe and other companies.

pot, potentiometer

A device that controls the amount of current that flows through a circuit, such as a volume switch on a radio.

POTS

(Plain Old Telephone Service) The traditional analog telephone network.

power

(1) See *computer power*.

(2) (POWER) (Performance Optimization With Enhanced RISC) A RISC-based CPU architecture from IBM used in its RS/6000 workstation and parallel computer line. The PowerPC, enhanced by Motorola and Apple, is a single-chip version of the POWER architecture.

power adapter

A transformer that converts AC power from a wall outlet into the DC power required by an electronic device.

PowerBook

Apple's trade name for its portable computers, which are widely used and very popular.

PowerBuilder

A high-level application development system for Windows client/server applications from Powersoft Corporation, Concord, MA, (www.powersoft.com). It uses a programming language called PowerScript that is similar to BASIC. PowerBuilder supports SQL and several databases, including DB2 and Oracle.

power down

To turn off the computer in an orderly manner by making sure all applications have been closed normally and then shutting the power.

power good

A signal transmitted from the power supply to the circuit board indicating that the power is stable. For various power supply definitions, see *power supply*.

PowerMac

A PowerPC-based Macintosh, formally designated the "Power Macintosh." The first models were introduced in 1994 along with more than 100 applications that were ported to the new architecture. Since then, Apple has migrated all of its Macintosh line from the Motorola 680x0 CPU family to the PowerPC RISC chip.

power management

Maximizing battery power by using low-voltage CPUs and slowing down components when they are inactive. See *SMM*.

PowerPC

A family of CPU chips designed by Apple, IBM and Motorola, introduced in 1993. Both IBM and Motorola offer the chips for sale, but IBM owns the architecture. The PowerPC is designed to span a range of computing devices from hand-held machines to supercomputers.

To date, PowerPC chips have been used as the CPUs in Apple's PowerMacs, IBM's RS/6000 and AS/400 models as well as in embedded systems. IBM originally offered the PowerPC as a stand-alone AIX or Windows NT machine, but has since dropped these models.

power platform

Refers to a mature, high-speed computer system.

PowerPoint

A desktop presentation program from Microsoft for the Macintosh and Windows. It was the first desktop presentation program for the Mac and provides the ability to create output for overheads, handouts, speaker notes and film recorders.

PowerShare

Software from Apple that resides in a Macintosh server and provides messaging store and forward, authentication of network users, encryption of messages and other workgroup/enterprise services.

power supply

An electrical system that converts AC current from the wall outlet into the DC currents required by the computer circuitry. In a personal computer, +5, -5, +12 and -12 voltages are generated. The 5 volts are used for the electronic circuitry, and the 12 volts are required for the drives.

power surge

An oversupply of voltage from the power company that can last up to several seconds. Power surges are the most common cause of loss to computers and electronic equipment. See *spike* and *sag*.

PowerTalk

Messaging software from Apple that is included in the Macintosh System 7 Pro operating system. It provides a unified mail box that holds different types of communication including e-mail, fax, voice mail and pager. It provides for RSA digital signatures, which guarantees the authenticity of documents electronically signed by other users.

power up

To turn the computer on in an orderly manner.

power user

A person who is very proficient with personal computers. It implies knowledge of a variety of software packages.

pph

(Pages Per Hour) Measures printing speed.

ppi

(1) (Pixels Per Inch) The measurement of the display or print elements.

(2) (Points Per Inch, Pulses Per Inch) The measurement of mouse movement.

ppm

(Pages Per Minute) The measurement of printing speed.

PPP

(Point-to-Point Protocol) A data link protocol that provides dial-up access over serial lines. It can run on any full-duplex link from POTS to ISDN to high-speed lines (T1, T3, etc.). Developed by the Internet Engineering Task Force in 1991, it has become popular for Internet access as well as a method for carrying higher level protocols.

PPTP

(Point-to-Point Tunneling Protocol) A protocol that encapsulates other protocols for transmission over an IP network. For example, it can be used to send NetWare IPX packets over the Internet. Due to its RSA encryption, PPTP is also used to create a private network (VPN) within the public Internet.

PQFP

(Plastic Quad FlatPack) A surface mount chip housing with flat leads on all four sides.

PRAM

(Parameter RAM) Pronounced "P RAM." A battery-backed part of the Macintosh's memory that holds Control Panel settings and the settings for the hidden desktop file. If the command and option keys are held down at startup, the desktop settings are cleared and a dialog to rebuild the desktop is initiated.

precedence

The order in which an expression is processed. Mathematical precedence is normally:

1. unary + and - signs
2. exponentiation
3. multiplication and division
4. addition and subtraction

In the following two examples:

fahrenheit-32*5/9 and **(fahrenheit-32)*5/9**

the first one is incorrect, because multiplication is evaluated before subtraction. Logical precedence is normally:

1. NOT
2. AND
3. OR

In the dbase query:

```
list for item = "TIE" .and. color = "GRAY" .or. color = "RED"
```

all gray ties and anything red will be selected, since ANDs are evaluated before ORs. Grouping the colors in parentheses yields only gray and red ties as follows:

```
(color="GRAY" .or. color="RED")
```

precision

The number of digits used to express the fractional part of a number. The more digits, the more precision. See *single precision* and *double precision*.

predicate

In programming, a statement that evaluates an expression and provides a true or false answer based on the condition of the data.

preemptive multitasking

A multitasking method that shares processing time with all running programs. Preemptive multitasking creates a true timesharing environment in which all running programs get a recurring slice of time from the CPU. Depending on the operating system, the time slice may be the same for all programs or it may be adjustable to meet the current mix of programs and users. For example, background programs can be given more CPU time no matter how heavy the foreground load and vice versa. Contrast with *non-preemptive multitasking*.

prepress

In typography and printing, the preparation of camera-ready materials up to the actual printing stage, which includes typesetting and page makeup.

preprocessor

Software that performs some preliminary processing on the input before it is processed by the main program.

presentation graphics

Business graphics, charts and diagrams used in a presentation. Presentation graphics software provides predefined backgrounds and sample page layouts to assist in the creation of complete computer-driven slide shows, which in combination with a data projector, are obsoleting the 35mm slide presentation.

preventive maintenance

The routine checking of hardware that is performed by a field engineer on a regularly scheduled basis. See *remedial maintenance*.

PRI
See *ISDN*.

primary index
The index that controls the current processing order of a file. See *secondary index*.

primary storage
The computer's internal memory (RAM). Contrast with *secondary storage*.

primitive
(1) In computer graphics, a graphics element that is used as a building block for creating images, such as a point, line, arc, cone or sphere.

(2) In programming, a fundamental instruction, statement or operation.

(3) In microprogramming, a microinstruction, or elementary machine operation.

print buffer
See *printer buffer*.

print column
A column of data on a printed report that may be subtotalled or totalled. Print columns are the heart of a report writer's description.

printed circuit board
A flat board that holds chips and other electronic components. The board is made of reinforced fiberglass or plastic and interconnects components via copper pathways. The main printed circuit board in a system is called a "system board" or "motherboard," while smaller ones that plug into the slots in the main board are called "boards" or "cards."

The printed circuit board of the 1960s connected discrete components together. The circuit board of the 1990s interconnects chips, each containing hundreds of thousands and millions of elementary components.

The "printed" circuit is really an etched circuit. A copper foil is placed over the glass or plastic base and covered with a photoresist. Light is shined through a negative image of the circuit paths onto the photoresist, hardening the areas that will remain after etching. When passed through an acid bath, the unhardened areas are washed away. A similar process creates the microminiaturized circuits on a chip.

printer
A device that converts computer output into printed images. The most common types of printers are ink jet, dot matrix and laser printers.

printer buffer
A memory device that accepts printer output from one or more computers and transmits it to the printer. It lets the computer dispose of its printer output at full speed without waiting for each page to print. Printer buffers with automatic switching are connected to two or more computers and accept their output on a first-come, first-served basis.

printer cable
A wire that connects a printer to a computer. On a PC, the cable has a 25-pin DB-25 male connector for the computer and a 36-pin Centronics male connector for the printer.

printer driver
Software routine that converts an application program's printing request into the language the printer understands.

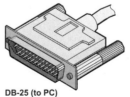
DB-25 (to PC)

Centronics (to printer)

printer engine
The unit within the printer that does the actual printing. For example, in a laser printer, it is the "copy machine" unit, which transfers and fuses the toner onto the paper. It is specified by its resolution and speed.

printer file

(1) A document in print image format ready to be printed.

(2) Same as *printer driver*.

printer font

A font used for printing. Printer and screen resolutions are not the same, thus fonts generated for the printer will not display accurately on screen. Contrast with *screen font*.

print head

A mechanism that deposits ink onto paper in a character printer.

print image

A text or graphics document that has been prepared for the printer. Format codes for the required printer have been embedded in the document at the appropriate places. With text files, headers, footers and page numbers have been created and inserted in every page.

print queue

Disk space that holds output designated for the printer until the printer can receive it.

print screen

The ability to print the current on-screen image. See *screen dump*.

print server

A computer in a network that controls one or more printers. It stores the print-image output from all users of the system and feeds it to the printer one job at a time. This function may be part of the network operating system or an add-on utility.

print spooler

Software that manages printing in the background. When an application is made to print, it quickly generates the output on disk and the spooler feeds the print images to the printer at slower printing speeds. This second step can be run in the background without appreciably interfering with user interaction in the foreground. See *spooling*.

print to disk

To redirect output from the printer to the disk. The resulting file contains text and graphics with all the codes required to direct the printer to print it. The file can be printed later or at a remote location without requiring the word processor, DTP or drawing program that was originally used to create it. This is actually the first stage of a print spooling operation. See *print spooler*.

privacy

The authorized distribution of information (who has a right to know?). Contrast with *security*, which deals with unauthorized access to data.

private file

A file made available only to the user that created it. Contrast with *public file*.

private key

See *cryptography*.

private line

(1) A dedicated line leased from a common carrier.

(2) A line owned and installed by the user.

PRMD

(PRivate Management Domain) An inhouse e-mail service. See *X.400*.

PRML

(Partial Response Maximum Likelihood) A technique used to differentiate a valid signal from noise by measuring the rate of change at various intervals of the rising waveform. Bits generated by a modem or by reading a hard disk have uniform characteristics, whereas random noise does not.

PRN

(PRiNter) The DOS name for the first connected parallel port.

problem-oriented language

A computer language designed to handle a particular class of problem. For example, COBOL was designed for business, FORTRAN for scientific and GPSS for simulation.

procedural language

A programming language that requires programming discipline, such as COBOL, FORTRAN, BASIC, C, Pascal and dBASE. Programmers writing in such languages must develop a proper order of actions in order to solve the problem, based on a knowledge of data processing and programming. Contrast with *non-procedural language*.

The following dBASE example shows procedural and non-procedural language to list a file.

```
Procedural              Non-procedural
use filex               use filex
do while .not. eof      list name, amountdue
  ? name, amountdue
  skip
enddo
```

procedure

(1) Manual *procedures* are human tasks.

(2) Machine *procedures* are lists of routines or programs to be executed, such as described by the job control language (JCL) in a mini or mainframe, or the batch processing language in a personal computer.

(3) In programming, another term for a subroutine or function.

procedure oriented

An application that forces the user to follow a predefined path from step A to step B. Data entry programs are typical examples. Contrast with *event driven*.

process

To manipulate data in the computer. The computer is said to be processing no matter what action is taken upon the data. It may be updated or simply displayed on screen.

In order to evaluate a computer system's performance, the time it takes to process data internally is analyzed separately from the time it takes to get it in and out of the computer. I/O is usually more time consuming than processing.

process bound

An excessive amount of processing causing an imbalance between I/O and processing. Process-bound applications may slow down other users in a multiuser system.

A personal computer is process bound when it is recalculating a spreadsheet, for example.

process color

A color printed from four separate printing plates. Four-color process printing uses cyan, magenta, yellow and black (CMYK) inks to produce full color reproduction. Contrast with *spot color*.

process control

The automated control of a process, such as a manufacturing process or assembly line. It is used extensively in industrial operations, such as oil refining, chemical processing and electrical generation. It uses analog devices to monitor real-world signals and digital computers to do the analysis and controlling. It makes extensive use of analog/digital, digital/analog conversion.

processing

Manipulating data within the computer. The term is used to define a variety of computer functions and methods. See *centralized processing, distributed processing, batch processing, transaction processing* and *multiprocessing*.

processor

(1) Same as *CPU*.

(2) May refer to software. See *language processor* and *word processor*.

processor unit
Same as *computer*.

process printing
See *process color*.

Prodigy
An online information service that provides access to the Internet, e-mail and a variety of databases. Launched in 1988, Prodigy was the first consumer-oriented online service in the U.S. Prodigy was founded as a partnership of IBM and Sears and was acquired by International Wireless in 1996. See *online services*.

production database
A central database containing an organization's master files and daily transaction files.

production system
A computer system used to process an organization's daily work. Contrast with a system used only for development and testing or for ad hoc inquiries and analysis.

productivity software
Refers to word processors, spreadsheets, database management systems, PIMs, schedulers and other software packages that are designed for individual use. Contrast with custom-designed, multiuser information systems that provide the primary data processing in an organization.

PROFS
(**PR**ofessional **OF**fice System) IBM office automation software for the VM mainframe environment. It provides an e-mail facility for text and graphics, a library service for centrally storing text, electronic calendars and appointment scheduling, and it allows document interchange with DISOSS users. PROFS uses IBM's proprietary ZIP messaging protocol.

program
A collection of instructions that tell the computer what to do. A program is called "software," thus "program," "software" and "instructions" are synonymous. A program is written in a programming language and is converted into the computer's machine language by software called assemblers, compilers and interpreters.

A program is made up of:

  1. machine instructions
  2. buffers
  3. constants and counters

Instructions are the directions that the computer will follow (the program's "logic"). Buffers are reserved space, or input/output areas, that accept and hold the data while it's being processed. They can receive any kind of information required by the program.

Constants are fixed values used to compare the data against, such as minimums and maximums and dates. Menu titles and error messages are another example of constants.

Counters, also called "variables," are reserved space for summing money amounts, quantities, virtually any calculations, including those necessary to keep track of internal operations, such as how many times a function should be repeated.

The program calls for data in an input-process-output sequence. After data has been input into one of the program's buffers from a peripheral device (keyboard, disk, etc.), it is processed. The results are then output to a peripheral device (screen, printer, etc.). If data has been updated, it is output back onto the disk.

The application program, which does the actual data processing, does not instruct the computer to do everything. When it is ready for input or needs to output data, it sends a request to the operating system, which performs those services and then turns control back to the application program.

program development
See *system development cycle*.

program generator

See *application generator*.

program logic

A sequence of instructions in a program. There are many logical solutions to a problem. If you give a specification to ten programmers, each one may create program logic that is slightly different than all the rest, but the results can be the same. The solution that runs the fastest is usually the most desired, however.

Program logic is written using three classes of instructions: sequential processing, selection and iteration.

1. Sequential processing is the series of steps that do the actual data processing. Input, output, calculate and move (copy) instructions are used in sequential processing.

2. Selection is the decision making within the program and is performed by comparing two sets of data and branching to a different part of the program based on the results. In assembly languages, the compare and branch instructions are used. In high-level languages, IF THEN ELSE and CASE statements are used.

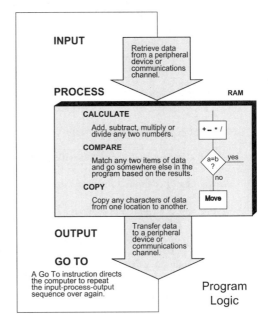

Program Logic

3. Iteration is the repetition of a series of steps and is accomplished with DO LOOPS and FOR LOOPS in high-level languages and GOTOs in assembly languages. See *loop*.

programmable

Capable of following instructions. What sets the computer apart from all other electronic devices is its programmability.

programmable calculator

A limited-function computer capable of working with only numbers and not alphanumeric data.

program maintenance

Updating programs to reflect changes in the organization's business or to adapt to new operating environments. Although maintaining old programs written by ex-employees is often much more difficult than writing new ones, the task is usually given to junior programmers, because the most talented professionals don't want the job.

Program Manager

The control center for Windows 3.x operation. It provides the means to launch applications and manage the desktop. Program Manager may be replaced with another shell, such as Norton's Desktop for Windows, HP's Dashboard, hDC's Power Launcher or Paper Software's SideBar, all of which provide similar functionality with a different user interface.

programmatic interface

Same as *API*.

programmer

A person who designs the logic for and writes the lines of codes of a computer program. See *application programmer* and *systems programmer*.

Programmer's Switch

The physical buttons included with the Macintosh (fkey on the LC) that include a System Reset button and a Debugging button that will invoke MacsBug if present or switch to the built in monitor in ROM.

programmer analyst

A person who analyzes and designs information systems and designs and writes the application programs for the system. In theory, a programmer analyst is both systems analyst and applications programmer. In practice, the title is sometimes simply a reward to a programmer for tenure. Which skill is really dominant is of concern when recruiting people with such titles.

programming

Creating a computer program. The steps are:

1. Developing the program logic to solve the particular problem.

2. Writing the program logic in a specific programming language (coding the program).

3. Assembling or compiling the program to turn it into machine language.

4. Testing and debugging the program.

5. Preparing the necessary documentation.

The logic is generally the most difficult part of programming. However, depending on the programming language, writing the statements may also be laborious. One thing is certain. Documenting the program is considered the most annoying activity by most programmers.

programming interface

See *API*.

programming language

A language used to write instructions for the computer. It lets the programmer express data processing in a symbolic manner without regard to machine-specific details. See *ALGOL, ADA, APL, BASIC, C, C++, COBOL, dBASE, Forth, FORTRAN, Lisp, Logo, MUMPS, Pascal, Prolog, REXX* and *Visual Basic*.

program state

An operating mode of the computer that executes instructions in the application program. Contrast with *supervisor state*.

program statement

A phrase in a high-level programming language. One program statement may result in several machine instructions when the program is compiled.

program step

An elementary instruction, such as a machine language instruction or an assembly language instruction. Contrast with *program statement*.

program-to-program communications

Communications between two programs. Often confused with peer-to-peer communications, it is a set of protocols a program uses to interact with another program. Peer-to-peer establishment is the network's responsibility. You can have program-to-program communications in a master-slave environment without peer-to-peer capability.

progressive scan

Same as *non-interlaced*.

projection panel

See *LCD panel*.

project manager

Software used to monitor the time and materials on a project. All tasks to complete the project are entered into the database, and the program computes the critical path, the series of tasks with the least amount of slack time. Any change in the critical path slows down the entire project.

Prolog

(**PRO**gramming in **LOG**ic) A programming language used for developing AI applications (natural language translation, expert systems, abstract problem solving, etc.). Developed in France in 1973, it is used throughout Europe and Japan and is gaining popularity in the U.S.

PROM

(Programmable Read Only Memory) A permanent memory chip that is programmed, or filled, by the customer rather than by the chip manufacturer. It differs from a ROM, which is programmed at the time of manufacture. PROMs have been mostly superseded by EPROMs, which can be reprogrammed. See *PROM programmer*.

PROM blower, PROM programmer

A device that writes instructions and data into PROM chips. The bits in a new PROM are all 1s (continuous lines). The PROM programmer only creates 0s, by "blowing" the middle out of the 1s. Some earlier units were capable of programming both PROMs and EPROMs.

prompt

A software message that requests action by the user; for example, "Enter employee name." Command-driven systems issue a cryptic symbol when ready to accept a command; for example, the dot (.) in dBASE, the $ or % in UNIX, and the venerable C:\> in DOS.

propagation

The transmission (spreading) from one place to another.

propagation delay

The time it takes to transmit a signal from one place to another.

properties

Attributes that are associated with something. Windows uses the term extensively to refer to the configuration of hardware and the characteristics and features of software and data files. In Windows 3.1, the Properties option in the File menu shows the path of an icon in a Program Group in Program Manager. In Windows 95/98, right clicking on an icon almost always brings up a Properties option that provides details about the file or device.

Property Sheet

A dialog box in Windows 9x that shows the configuration settings of a particular resource. Right clicking icons and menu items displays a Properties option that can be selected.

proportional spacing

Character spacing based on the width of each character. For example, an I takes up less space than an M. In monospacing (fixed), the I and M each take up the same space. See *kerning*.

proprietary software

Software owned by an organization or individual. Contrast with *public domain software*.

Protected Mode

In Intel 286s and up, an operational state that allows the computer to address all of memory. It also prevents an errant program from entering into the memory boundary of another. In a 386 and up, it provides access to 32-bit instructions and sophisticated memory management modes. See *32-bit processing, Real Mode, Virtual 8086 Mode* and *memory protection*.

protocol

Rules governing transmitting and receiving of data. See *communications protocol* and *OSI*.

protocol analyzer

See *network analyzer*.

protocol port

In TCP/IP networks, a number assigned to different types of data in order to distribute incoming traffic to the appropriate program running in the computer. It is not a physical plug or socket, but a logical assignment. See *well-known port*.

protocol stack

The hierarchy of protocols used in a communications network. Network architectures designed in layers, such as TCP/IP, OSI and SNA, are referred to as stacks.

protocol suite

Same as *protocol stack*.

prototyping

(1) Creating a demo of a new system. Prototyping is essential for clarifying information requirements. The design of a system (functional specs) must be finalized before the system can be built. While analytically-oriented people may have a clear picture of requirements, others may not.

Using fourth-generation languages, systems analysts and users can develop the new system together. Databases can be created and manipulated while the user monitors the progress.

Once users see tangible output on screen or on paper, they can figure out what's missing or what the next question might be if this were a production system. If prototyping is carefully done, the end result can be a working system.

Even if the final system is reprogrammed in other languages for standardization or machine efficiency, prototyping has served to provide specifications for a working system rather than a theoretical one.

(2) See *function prototyping*.

proxy cache

Pronounced proxy "cash." A facility in a proxy server that caches incoming Web pages on the hard disk. If the next page requested by a browser is already in the proxy cache, the page is retrieved locally instead of from the Internet. See *Web cache*.

proxy server

A type of firewall. Also called a "proxy" or "application level gateway," it is an application that breaks the connection between sender and receiver. All input is forwarded out a different port, closing a straight path between two networks and preventing a hacker from obtaining internal addresses and details of a private network.

PS/2

The IBM PC series introduced in 1987 that superseded the original PC line. It introduced the 3.5" floppy disk, VGA graphics and Micro Channel bus. The 3.5" disks and VGA are common in all PCs, but Micro Channel has given way to the PCI bus.

PS/2 connector

A 6-pin mini DIN plug and socket used to connect a keyboard and mouse to a computer. The PS/2 port was originally used on IBM's PS/2 models and later adapted to laptops and desktop PCs.

PS/2 mouse

A mouse that uses a PS/2 plug to connect to the computer. If the PC does not have a PS/2 socket, a PS/2 mouse can be plugged into the PC's serial port using a PS/2 to serial port adapter.

pseudo compiler

A compiler that generates a pseudo language, or intermediate language, which must be further compiled or interpreted for execution.

pseudo-duplexing

A communications technique that simulates full-duplex transmission in a half-duplex line by turning the line around very quickly.

pseudo language

An intermediate language generated from a source language, but not directly executable by a CPU. It must be interpreted or compiled into machine language for execution. It facilitates the use of one source language for different types of computers.

PSF

(Print Services Facility) Software from IBM that performs printer rasterization for IBM's AFP and other page description languages. PSF products are available for mainframes, AS/400 and RS/6000 series and output the IPDS format. Various versions also input and output PostScript and PCL (LaserJet).

PSK

See *DPSK*.

PSN

(Packet-Switched Network) A communications network that uses packet switching technology.

PSS

See *EPSS*.

PSTN

(Public Switched Telephone Network) The worldwide voice telephone network. See *NPN*.

PSW

(Program Status Word) A hardware register that maintains the status of the program being executed.

PTOCA

(Presentation Text Object Content Architecture) See *MO:DCA*.

PTT

(Postal, Telegraph & Telephone) The governmental agency responsible for combined postal, telegraph and telephone services in many European countries.

PU

(Physical Unit) In SNA, software responsible for managing the resources of a node, such as data links. A PU supports a connection to the host (SSCP) for gathering network management statistics.

PU 2.1

(Physical Unit 2.1) In SNA, the original term for Node Type 2.1, which is software that provides peer-to-peer communications between intelligent devices (PCs, workstations, minicomputers). Only LU 6.2 sessions are supported between Type 2.1 nodes (PU 2.1).

public domain software

Software in which ownership has been relinquished to the public at large. See *freeware* and *shareware*.

public file

A file made available to all other users connected to the system or network. Contrast with *private file*.

public key

See *cryptography*.

publish & subscribe

To provide a source of information that users can selectively retrieve. The service can be free or paid, and the information is typically provided via e-mail or the Web. See *push technology*.

puck

The mouse-like object used to draw on a digitizer tablet.

pull-down menu

A menu that is displayed from the top of the screen downward when its title is selected. The menu remains displayed while the mouse button is depressed. To select a menu option, the highlight bar is moved (with the mouse) to the appropriate line and the mouse button is let go. The drop-down menu is a variation that keeps the menu open after its title is selected. To select a menu option, the highlight bar is moved to the line and the mouse button is clicked.

pulse level device

A disk drive or other device that inputs and outputs raw voltages. Data coding/decoding is in the controller the device. Contrast with *bit level device*.

punch block

Also called a "quick-connect block," a device that interconnects telephone lines from remote points. The wires are pushed, or punched, down into metal teeth that strip the insulation and make a tight connection.

punched card

An early storage medium made of thin cardboard stock that holds data as patterns of punched holes. Each of the 80 or 96 columns holds one character. The holes are punched by a keypunch machine or card punch peripheral and are fed into the computer by a card reader.

Although still used as turnaround documents, punched cards are practically obsolete. However, from 1890 until the 1970s, they were synonymous with data processing. Concepts were simple: the database was the file cabinet; a record was a card. Processing was performed on individual machines known as sorters, collators, reproducers, calculators and accounting machines.

PURL

(Persistent **URL**) A URL that points to another URL. PURLs are used when document pages are expected to be moved to different locations from time to time. The PURL is maintained as the official URL for that resource, and when that PURL is requested, a PURL server redirects the browser to the actual current URL. See also *Perl*.

push/pop

Instructions that store and retrieve an item on a stack. Push enters an item on the stack, and pop retrieves an item, moving the rest of the items in the stack up one level. See *stack*.

push/pull tractor

A printer tractor that can be switched from pushing paper onto the platen to pulling it from the platen. Single-sheet continuous forms can be pushed, but most multipart forms and labels must be pulled to prevent jamming.

push technology

A data distribution technology in which selected data is automatically delivered into the user's computer at prescribed intervals or based on some event that occurs. Contrast with "pull technology," in which the user specifically asks for something by performing a search or requesting an existing report, video or other data type.

PVC

(Permanent Virtual Circuit) A point-to-point connection that is established ahead of time. All PVCs defined at the time of subscription to a particular service are known as a VPN (virtual private network). Contrast with *SVC*.

PVGA

(Paradise **VGA**) A VGA adapter or VGA chips from the Paradise Division of Western Digital.

Px64

An ITU standard for transmitting audio and video in 64 Kbits/sec ISDN channels (P represents number of channels used). Although video conferencing can be done in only one or two channels, more channels are required for smooth motion.

PXP

(Packet eXchange Protocol) See *PEP*.

Q

Q&A

An integrated file manager and word processor for DOS and Windows from Symantec Corporation, Cupertino, CA, that includes mail merge capability as well as a programming language for customizing data entry forms and reports. Its Intelligent Assistant feature provides a query language that can learn new words from the user.

QAM

(1) (Quadrature Amplitude Modulation) A modulation technique that generates four bits out of one baud. For example, a 600 baud line (600 shifts in the signal per second) can effectively transmit 2,400 bps using this method. Both phase and amplitude are shaped with each baud, resulting in four possible patterns.

(2) (Quality Assessment Measurement) A system used to measure and analyze voice transmission.

QBasic

A BASIC interpreter from Microsoft that comes with DOS starting with DOS 5. It supersedes Microsoft's GW-BASIC and includes REMLINE.BAS, a program that helps convert GW-BASIC programs to QBasic.

QBE

(Query By Example) A method for describing a query originally developed by IBM for mainframes. A replica of an empty record is displayed and the search conditions are typed in under their respective columns (fields).

Q-bus

A bus architecture used in Digital's PDP-11 and MicroVAX series.

QCIF

See *CIF*.

QEMM

(Quarterdeck EMM) A popular DOS and Windows memory manager from Quarterdeck Corporation, Marina del Rey, CA. QEMM was very popular in the DOS-only days.

QIC

(Quarter Inch Cartridge) A magnetic tape technology used for backing up data. QIC tapes come in two form factors: 3.5" Minicartridges and 5.25" Data Cartridges. The Minicartridges use .25"-wide and .315"-wide tape in several drive and cartridge options. Data Cartridges only use .25" tape and are expected to slow in usage in favor of QIC Minicartridge, DAT, 8mm and DLT formats.

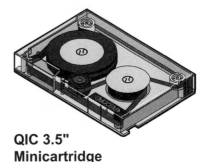

**QIC 3.5"
Minicartridge**

QIC-Wide

(Quarter Inch Cartridge-**Wide**) An extension to the QIC tape from Sony that provides more storage capacity. It increases recording density and uses .315" wide tape rather than .25". It uses the standard QIC Minicartridge with a redesigned housing. QIC-Wide drives support both QIC-Wide and DC2000 formats. Travan drives support QIC-Wide tapes.

QMF

(Query Management Facility) An IBM fourth-generation language for end-user interaction with DB2.

QoS

(Quality Of Service) The ability to define a level of performance in a system. For example, ATM networks specify modes of service that ensure optimum performance for traffic such as realtime voice and video.

quantize

To assign a number to a sample. The larger the number the more the digital sample represents the analog signal. See *sampling*.

quantum computing

A future technology for designing computers based on quantum mechanics, the science of atomic structure and function. It uses the "qubit," or quantum bit, which can hold several values. Although theoretical, it is believed that if such a device were built, it could factor large numbers 10,000 times faster than today's computers.

QuarkXPress

A desktop publishing program for the Macintosh and Windows from Quark, Inc., Denver, CO. Originally developed for and very popular on the Mac, it is noted for its precise typographic control and advanced text and graphics manipulation.

quartz crystal

A slice of quartz ground to a prescribed thickness that vibrates at a steady frequency when stimulated by electricity. The tiny crystal, about 1/20th by 1/5th of an inch, creates the computer's heartbeat.

Quattro Pro

A Windows spreadsheet from Corel that provides advanced graphics and presentation capabilities, including goal seeking, 3-D graphing and the ability to create multi-layered slide shows. It is optionally keystroke compatible with Lotus 1-2-3. Quattro Pro was originally developed by Borland, then purchased by Novell in 1994 and Corel in 1996.

query

To interrogate a database (count, sum and list selected records). Contrast with *report*, which is usually a more elaborate printout with headings and page numbers. The report may also be a selective list of items; hence, the two terms may refer to programs that produce the same results.

query language

A generalized language that allows a user to select records from a database. It uses a command language, menu-driven method or a query by example (QBE) format for expressing the matching condition.

Query languages are usually included in DBMSs, and stand-alone packages are available for interrogating files in non-DBMS applications. See *query program*.

query program

Software that counts, sums and retrieves selected records from a database. It may be part of a large application and be limited to one or two kinds of retrieval, such as pulling up a customer account on screen, or it may refer to a query language that allows any condition to be searched and selected.

queue

Pronounced "Q." A temporary holding place for data. See *message queue* and *print queue*.

Quickdraw

The graphics display system built into the Macintosh. It accepts commands from the application and draws the corresponding objects on the screen. It provides a consistent interface that software developers can work with.

Quicken

A popular personal financial management program for PCs and Macs from Intuit, Menlo Park, CA, (www.intuit.com). It is used to write checks, organize investments and produce a variety of financial reports.

QuickTime

Multimedia extensions to Macintosh's System 7 that add sound and video capabilities. A QuickTime file can contain up to 32 tracks of audio, video, MIDI or other time-based control information. Most major Macintosh DBMSs (database management systems) support QuickTime. Apple also provides a QuickTime for Windows version for Windows-based PCs.

qwerty keyboard

The standard English language typewriter keyboard.

Q, w, e, r, t and y are the letters on the top left, alphabetic row. It was originally designed to slow typing to prevent the keys from jamming. See *Dvorak keyboard*.

R

R/3 (R/2)

An integrated suite of client/server applications from SAP America, Inc., Wayne, PA, (www.sap.com). It is the client/server versions of SAP's R/2 mainframe applications. R/3 includes information systems for manufacturing, distribution, order processing, accounting and human resources. It includes the ABAP/4 Development Workbench.

R3000, R4000, R5000, R8000, R10000

Families of 32-bit and 64-bit RISC processors from MIPS. MIPS licenses the design to other companies.

RACF

(Resource Access Control Facility) IBM mainframe security software introduced in 1976 that verifies user ID and password and controls access to authorized files and resources.

rack, rack mounted

A rack is a standard-sized frame or cabinet into which components are mounted. All sorts of electronic devices and computer equipment are available as rack mounted models.

RAD

(Rapid Application Development) An approach to systems development that includes automated design and development tools (CASE) and joint application development (JAD). Developed by industry guru, James Martin, it focuses on human management and user involvement as much as on technology.

It also emphasizes developing the system incrementally and delivering working pieces every three to four months, rather than waiting until the entire project is completed before implementation.

radio

The transmission of electromagnetic energy (radiation) over the air or through a hollow tube called a "waveguide." Although radio is often thought of as only AM or FM, all airborne transmission is radio, including satellite and line-of-sight microwave.

radio buttons

A series of on-screen buttons that allow only one selection. If a button is currently selected, it will de-select when another button is selected.

radio frequency

See *RF*.

radiosity

A rendering method that simulates light reflecting off one surface and onto another. It provides a more accurate method of rendering light and shadows than ray tracing. See *reflection mapping* and *ray tracing*.

radix

The base value in a numbering system. For example, in the decimal system, the radix is 10.

radix point

The location in a number that separates the integral part from the fractional part. For example, in the decimal system, it is the decimal point.

RAID

(Redundant Array of Independent Disks) A category of disk arrays (two or more drives working together) that provide increased performance and various levels of error recovery and fault tolerance. RAID can be implemented in software using standard disk controllers, or it can be designed into the disk controller itself.

The term used to mean Redundant Arrays of "Inexpensive" Disks. Today, all hard disks are inexpensive by comparison.

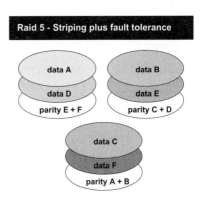

Raid 5 - Striping plus fault tolerance

data A
data D
parity E + F

data B
data E
parity C + D

data C
data F
parity A + B

RAM

(Random Access Memory) A group of memory chips that function as the computer's primary workspace. More RAM in the computer means more applications can be made instantly available to the user. With limited RAM, the computer has to temporarily store parts of active programs and data on the disk to make room for the next function you request. More RAM means more processing workspace and less swapping of instructions and data back and forth from the disk. Most RAM chips are of the dynamic RAM (DRAM) type.

RAMAC

(Random Access Method of Accounting and Control) The first hard disk computer which was introduced by IBM in 1956. All 50 of its 24" platters held a total of five million characters! It was half computer, half tabulator. It had a drum memory for program storage, but its I/O was wired by plugboard.

After 38 years, IBM resurrected the RAMAC name with the introduction of a high-capacity disk storage system in 1994. The differences between the 1956 and 1994 RAMACs are rather dramatic. Areal density rose from 2000 bits per square inch to 260 million increasing total storage capacity from 5MB to 90GB. Access times changed from 600 ms to 9.5 ms.

Rambus DRAM

See *RDRAM*.

RAM cache

See *cache*.

RAM card

(1) A printed circuit board containing memory chips that is plugged into a socket within the computer.

(2) A credit-card-sized module that contains memory chips and battery. See *memory card*.

RAM chip

(Random Access Memory chip) A memory chip. See *dynamic RAM, static RAM, RAM* and *memory*.

RAMDAC

(Random Access Memory Digital to Analog Converter) The VGA controller chip that maintains the color palette and converts data from memory into analog signals for the monitor.

RAM disk

A disk drive simulated in memory. To use it, files are copied from magnetic disk into the RAM disk. Processing is faster, because there's no mechanical disk action, only memory transfers. Updated data files must be copied back to disk before the power is turned off, otherwise the updates are lost. Also known as "e-disk" and "virtual disk."

RAMIS

See *CA-RAMIS*.

RAM refresh

Recharging dynamic RAM chips many times per second in order to keep the bit patterns valid.

RAM resident

Refers to programs that remain in memory in order to interact with other programs or to be instantly popped up when required by the user. See *TSR*.

random access

Same as *direct access*.

random noise

Same as *Gaussian noise*.

random number generator

A program routine that produces a random number. Random numbers are created easily in a computer, since there are many random events that take place; for example, the duration between keystrokes. Only a few milliseconds' difference is enough to seed a random number generation routine with a different number each time. Once seeded, an algorithm computes different numbers throughout the session.

range

(1) In data entry validation, a group of values from a minimum to a maximum.

(2) In spreadsheets, a series of cells that are worked on as a group. It may refer to a row, column or rectangular block defined by one corner and its diagonally opposite corner.

ransom note typography

Using too many fonts in a document. The term comes from the text in a ransom note that is pasted together from words cut out of different magazines and newspapers.

RARP

See *ARP*.

RAS

(1) (Remote Access Service) A function in Windows that provides access to remote computer users via modem. See also *remote access server*.

(2) (Reliability Availability Serviceability) Originally an IBM term, it refers to a computer system's overall reliability, its ability to respond to a failure and its ability to undergo maintenance without shutting it down entirely.

(3) (Row Address Strobe) A clock signal in a memory chip used to pinpoint the row of a particular bit in a row-column matrix. See *CAS*.

raster display

A display terminal that generates dots line by line on the screen. TVs and almost all computer screens use the raster method. Contrast with *vector display*.

raster graphics

In computer graphics, a technique for representing a picture image as a matrix of dots. It is the digital counterpart of the analog method used in TV. However, unlike TV, which uses one standard format (NTSC), there are many raster graphics formats used in the computer, such as GIF, TIF, BMP and PCX. Raster graphics images are also known as bitmapped images. Contrast with *vector graphics*.

raster image processor

See *RIP*. Remember... look up the acronym first!

rasterize

To perform the conversion of vector graphics images, vector fonts or outline fonts into bitmaps for display or printing. Unless output is printed on a plotter, which uses vectors directly, all non-bitmapped images must be rasterized into bitmaps for display or printing. See *font scaler*.

raster scan

Displaying or recording a video image line by line.

raw data

Data that has not been processed.

ray tracing

A rendering method that simulates light reflections, refractions and shadows. It follows a light path from a specific source and computes each pixel in the image to simulate the effect of the light. It is a very process-intensive operation. See *reflection mapping* and *radiosity*.

R:BASE

A relational DBMS for DOS, Windows and OS/2 from Microrim, Inc., Bellevue, WA, (www.microrim.com). It provides a complete programming language as well as an application generator

rAnSOm Note tYpOgraphy

It's great to have all these NEAT fonts.

But sometimes people get carried away!

More than three fonts in an entire page generally become tiresome.

There is elegance in simplicity!

But that is not demonstrated here.

for developing programs. It was the first DBMS to compete with dBASE II in the early 1980s. R:WEB is a runtime version of R:BASE for the Web.

RBOC

(Regional Bell Operating Company) One of the regional telephone companies created by the breakup of AT&T on January 1, 1984.

RC5

The latest in a family of secret key cryptographic methods developed by RSA Data Security, Inc., Redwood City, CA. Algorithms previously developed by RSA were RC2 and RC4, and all use a variable-length key. RC5 is more secure than RC4 but is slower. RSA Data Security is more widely known for its RSA public key method. See *RSA*.

RCA connector

Same as *phono connector*.

RCS

(1) (Remote Computer Service) A remote timesharing service.

(2) (Revision Control System) A UNIX utility that provides version control.

Rdb

(Relational DataBase/VMS) A relational DBMS that runs under OpenVMS on Digital VAX and Alpha systems. Rdb was originally developed by Digital and later acquired by Oracle.

RDBMS

(Relational DataBase Management System) See *relational database*.

RDO

(Remote Data Objects) A programming interface for data access from Microsoft. It is used in Visual Basic to access remote ODBC databases.

RDRAM

(Rambus DRAM) A dynamic RAM chip technology from Rambus, Inc., Mountain View, CA, that transfers data at 600 MBytes/sec (up to 10 times faster than conventional DRAMs). It requires modified motherboards, but eliminates the need for memory caches.

read

To input into the computer from a peripheral device (disk, tape, etc.). Like reading a book or playing an audio tape, reading does not destroy what is read.

A read is both an input and an output (I/O), since data is being output from the peripheral device and input into the computer. Memory is also said to be read when it is accessed to transfer data out to a peripheral device or to somewhere else in memory. Every peripheral or internal transfer of data is a read from somewhere and a write to somewhere else.

read cycle

The operation of reading data from a memory or storage device.

reader

A machine that captures data for the computer, such as an optical character reader, magnetic card reader and punched card reader. A microfiche or microfilm reader is a self-contained machine that reads film and displays its contents.

read error

A failure to read the data on a storage or memory device. Although it is not a routine phenomenon, magnetic and optical recording surfaces can become contaminated with dust or dirt or be physically damaged, and cells in memory chips can malfunction.

When a read error occurs, the program will allow you to bypass it and move on to the next set of data, or it will end, depending on the operating system. However, if the damaged part of a disk contains control information, the rest of the file may be unreadable. In such cases, a recovery program must be used to retrieve the remaining data if there is no backup.

readme file

A text file copied onto software distribution disks that contains last-minute updates or errata that have not been printed in the documentation manual.

read only

(1) Refers to storage media that permanently hold their content; for example, ROM and CD-ROM.

(2) A file which can be read, but not updated or erased. See *file attribute*.

read-only attribute

A file attribute that, when turned on, indicates that a file can only be read, but not updated or erased.

readout

(1) A small display device that typically shows only a few digits or a couple of lines of data.

(2) Any display screen or panel.

read/write

(1) Refers to a device that can both input and output or transmit and receive.

(2) Refers to a file that can be updated and erased.

read/write channel

Same as *I/O channel*.

read/write head

A device that reads (senses) and writes (records) data on a magnetic disk or tape. For writing, the surface of the disk or tape is moved past the read/write head. By discharging electrical impulses at the appropriate times, bits are recorded as tiny, magnetized spots of positive or negative polarity.

For reading, the surface is moved past the read/write head, and the bits that are present induce an electrical current across the gap.

read/write memory

Same as *RAM*.

real address

Same as *absolute address*.

RealAudio

The most popular streaming audio technology for the Internet and intranets from RealNetworks Inc., Seattle, WA, (www.real.com). A browser equipped with a RealAudio plug-in enables news, sports and other programs transmitted from RealAudio servers to be heard on the user's computer.

RealMedia

A streaming media technology for the Internet from RealNetworks Inc., Seattle, WA, (www.real.com). Using the Realtime Streaming Protocol (RTSP), it is designed to handle any type of media, including MIDI, text and animation, and allow multiple streams to be synchronized simultaneously; for example, sending images intermixed with audio.

Real Mode

An operational state in Intel 286s and up in which the computer functions as an 8086/8088. It is limited to one megabyte of memory. See *Protected Mode* and *Virtual 8086 Mode*.

RealPC

A DOS emulator for the Macintosh from FWB Software, San Francisco, CA, (www.fwb.com). Known earlier as SoftPC, it was originally developed by Insignia Solutions. RealPC is used to run DOS games and other DOS application on the Mac.

real storage

Real physical memory in a virtual memory system.

realtime

An immediate response. It refers to process control and embedded systems; for example, space flight computers must respond instantly to changing conditions. It also refers to fast transaction processing systems as well as any electronic operation fast enough to keep up with its real-world counterpart (animating complex images, transmitting live video, etc.).

realtime clock

An electronic circuit that maintains the time of day. It may also provide timing signals for timesharing operations.

realtime compression

The ability to compress and decompress data without any noticeable loss in speed compared to non-compressed data. PC products such as Stacker and SuperStor let you create a separate compressed drive on your hard disk. All data written to that drive is compressed and decompressed when read back. Realtime compression is included with DOS 6.

realtime conferencing

A "live" teleconferencing session that uses communications equipment fast enough to keep up with the speech and movements of all participants. See *teleconferencing*.

realtime image

A graphics image that can be animated on screen at the same speed as the real-world object.

realtime information system

A computer system that responds to transactions by immediately updating the appropriate master files and/or generating a response in a time frame fast enough to keep an operation moving at its required speed. See *transaction processing*.

realtime operating system

A master control program that can provide immediate response to input signals and transactions.

realtime system

A computer system that responds to input signals fast enough to keep an operation moving at its required speed.

realtime video

The ability to transmit video live without missing any frames. It requires very high transmission capacity. See *ATM*.

RealVideo

A streaming video technology for the Internet and intranets from RealNetworks, Inc., Seattle, WA, (www.real.com). A browser equipped with a RealPlayer or RealVideo plug-in enables video broadcasts from RealVideo servers (RealServers) to be viewed on screen.

reasonable test

A type of test that determines if a value falls within a range considered normal or logical. It can be made on electronic signals to detect extraneous noise as well as on data to determine possible input errors.

reboot

To reload the operating system and restart the computer. See *boot*.

receiver

A device that accepts signals. Contrast with *transmitter*.

record

(1) A group of related fields that store data about a subject (master record) or activity (transaction record). A collection of records make up a file.

Master records contain permanent data, such as account number, and variable data, such as balance due. Transaction records contain only permanent data, such as quantity and product code. See *master file* and *transaction file* for examples of record contents.

(2) In certain disk organization methods, a record is a block of data read and written at one time without any relationship to records in a file.

record format, record layout

The structure of a data record, which includes the name, type and size of each field in the record.

record head

A device that writes a signal on tape. Some tape drives and all disk drives use a combination read/write head.

record locking

See *file and record locking.*

record mark

A symbol used to identify the end of a record.

record number

The sequential number assigned to each physical record in a file. Record numbers change when the file is sorted or records are added and deleted.

records management

The creation, retention and scheduled destruction of an organization's paper and film documents. Computer-generated reports and documents fall into the records management domain, but traditional data processing files do not.

recovery

See *backup & recovery, checkpoint/restart* and *tape backup.*

rectifier

An electrical circuit that converts AC into DC current with the use of diodes that act as one-way valves. Contrast with *inverter.*

recursion

In programming, the ability of a subroutine or program module to call itself. It is helpful for writing routines that solve problems by repeatedly processing the output of the same process.

redaction

The editing done to sensitive documents before release to the public.

Red Book

(1) The documentation for secure networks from the U.S. National Security Agency. See *NCSC.*

(2) The documentation for the technical specifications of audio CDs.

redirection

Diverting data from its normal destination to another; for example, to a disk file instead of the printer, or to a server's disk instead of the local disk.

redirector

In a LAN, software that routes workstation (client) requests for data to the server.

redundancy check

In communications, a method for detecting transmission errors by appending a calculated number onto the end of each segment of data. See *CRC.*

reengineering

Using information technology to improve performance and cut costs. Its main premise, as popularized by the book "Reengineering the Corporation" by Michael Hammer and James Champy, is to examine the goals of an organization and to redesign work and business processes from the ground up rather than simply automate existing tasks and functions. Reengineering is about radical improvement, not incremental changes.

reentrant code

A programming routine that can be used by multiple programs simultaneously. It is used in operating systems and other system software as well as in multithreading, where concurrent events are taking place. It is written so that none of its code is modifiable (no values are changed) and it does not keep track of anything. The calling programs keep track of their own progress (variables, flags, etc.), thus one copy of the reentrant routine can be shared by an any number of users or processes.

It is analogous to several people baking their own cake by looking at a single recipe on the wall. Everyone keeps track of their own progress on the master recipe by jotting down the step number they're at on their own sheet of paper so they can pick up where they left off.

referential integrity
A database management safeguard that ensures every foreign key matches a primary key. For example, customer numbers in a customer file are the primary keys, and customer numbers in the order file are the foreign keys. If a customer record is deleted, the order records must also be deleted otherwise they are left without a primary reference. If the DBMS doesn't test for this, it must be programmed into the applications.

referrer
The URL of the Web page you are viewing, which the browser sends along with the request for another page when you click on a hyperlink or when an image is called for on the same page. On a search site, in addition to the URL, the text you are searching for is often sent to an advertising agency that sends back a tailored banner ad or just simply collects demographics.

reflection mapping
A rendering method that simulates light reflecting on an object. It is a much faster method than ray tracing because it maps light over the image rather than actually computing the path the light takes. See *ray tracing* and *radiosity*.

reflective spot
A metallic foil placed on each end of a magnetic tape. It reflects light to a photosensor to signal the end of tape.

reformat
(1) To change the record layout of a file or database.

(2) To initialize a disk over again.

refraction
The bending of light, heat or sound as it passes through different materials.

refresh
To continously charge a device that cannot hold its content. CRTs must be refreshed, because the phosphors hold their glow for only a few milliseconds. Dynamic RAM chips require refreshing to maintain their charged bit patterns.

refresh rate
The number of times per second that a device is re-energized, such as a CRT or dynamic RAM chip. See *vertical scan frequency*.

regenerator
(1) In communications, the same as a *repeater*.

(2) In electronics, a circuit that repeatedly supplies current to a memory or display device that continuously loses its charges or content.

register
A small, high-speed computer circuit that holds values of internal operations, such as the address of the instruction being executed and the data being processed. When a program is debugged, register contents may be analyzed to determine the computer's status at the time of failure.

In microcomputer assembly language programming, programmers reference registers routinely. Assembly languages in larger computers are often at a higher level.

register level compatibility
A hardware component that is 100% compatible with another device. It implies that the same type, size and names of registers are used.

Registry
A Windows 95/98/NT/2000 database that holds configuration data about the hardware and environment of the PC it has been installed in. It is made up of the SYSTEM.DAT and USER.DAT files.

Many settings that were previously stored in WIN.INI and SYSTEM.INI in Windows 3.1 are in the Registry.

regression analysis

In statistics, a mathematical method of modeling the relationships among three or more variables. It is used to predict the value of one variable given the values of the others. For example, a model might estimate sales based on age and gender. A regression analysis yields an equation that expresses the relationship. See *correlation*.

regression testing

In software development, the complete and thorough testing of a program that has been modified in order to ensure that additional bugs have not been introduced. Adding source code to a program often introduces errors in other routines, and many of the old and stable functions must be retested along with the new ones.

related files

Two or more data files that can be matched on some common condition, such as account number.

relational algebra

(1) The branch of mathematics that deals with relations; for example, AND, OR, NOT, IS and CONTAINS.

(2) In relational database, a collection of rules for dealing with tables; for example, JOIN, UNION and INTERSECT.

relational calculus

The rules for combining and manipulating relations; for example De Morgan's law, "the complement of a union is equal to the union of the complements."

relational database

A database organization method that links files together as required. In non-relational systems (hierarchical, network), records in one file point to the locations of records in another, such as customers to orders and vendors to purchases. These are fixed links set up ahead of time to speed up daily processing.

In a relational database, relationships between files are created by comparing data, such as account numbers and names. A relational system has the flexibility to take any two or more files and generate a new file from the records that meet the matching criteria.

Routine queries often involve more than one data file. For example, a customer file and an order file can be linked in order to ask a question that relates to information in both files, such as the names of the customers that purchased a particular product.

In practice, a pure relational query can be very slow. In order to speed up the process, indexes are built and maintained on the key fields used for matching. Sometimes, indexes are created "on the fly" when the data is requested.

The term was coined in 1970 by Edgar Codd, whose objective was to easily accomodate a user's ad hoc request for selected data.

```
Relational terms      Common terms
table or relation     file
tuple                 record
attribute             field
```

relational operator

A symbol that specifies a comparison between two values.

```
Relational Operator      Symbol
EQ      Equal to               =
NE      Not equal to      <>  or  #  or !=
GT      Greater than      >
GE      Greater than or equal to      >=
LT      Less than                     <
LE      Less than or equal to  <=
```

relative address

A memory address that represents some distance from a starting point (base address), such as the first byte of a program or table. The absolute address is derived by adding it to the base address.

relative path

An implied path. When a command is expressed that references files, the current working directory is the implied, or relative, path if the full path is not explicitly stated. Contrast with *full path*.

relay

An electrical switch that allows a low power to control a higher one. A small current energizes the relay, which closes a gate, allowing a large current to flow through.

relocatable code

Machine language that can be run from any memory location. All modern computers run relocatable code. See *base/displacement*.

Rem

(**REM**arks) A programming language statement used for documentation. Rem statements are not executed by the compiler. To "rem the line out" means to place the letters REM in the beginning of the line.

remedial maintenance

A repair service that is required due to a malfunction of the product. Contrast with *preventive maintenance*.

remote access concentrator

A remote access server that supports one or more T1/E1 lines, allowing multiple analog and ISDN calls to come in over one port from the telephone company. Remote access concentrators can handle much higher call densities than remote access servers. They include the dial-up protocols, access control and provide the equivalent of a modem pool. See *remote access server*.

remote access server

A computer in a network that provides access to remote users via analog modem or ISDN connections. It includes the dial-up protocols and access control (authentication) and may be a regular file server with remote access software or a proprietary system such as Shiva's LANRover. The modems may be internal or external to the device. See *remote access concentrator*.

remote access software

See *remote control software*.

remote batch, remote job entry

See *RJE*.

remote communications

(1) Communicating via long distances.

(2) See *remote control software*.

remote console

A terminal or workstation in a remote location that is used to monitor and control a local computer.

remote control software

Software, installed in both machines, that allows a user at a local computer to have control of a remote computer via modem. Both users run the remote computer and see the same screen. Remote control operation is used to take control of an unattended desktop personal computer from a remote location as well as to provide instruction

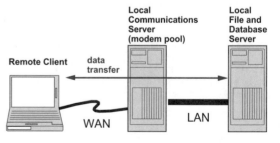

Remote Control
(remote user controls local client PC)

Local File and Database Server

Local Client

Remote PC — screen changes — keyboard

data transfer

WAN   LAN

Remote Node
(remote user logged directly onto server)

Local Communications Server (modem pool)

Local File and Database Server

Remote Client — data transfer

WAN   LAN

and technical support to remote users.

Remote control and remote node operations are not the same. In remote control, only keystrokes are transmitted to, and screen changes are received from, the remote user. In remode node, users access the LAN just as if they were connected to it locally, although with much slower data transfer.

remote node

A remote user or workstation. Access to the company LAN is made via POTS or ISDN modem to a connection at the remote access server. See *remote access server* and *remote control software*.

removable disk

A disk unit that is inserted into a disk drive for reading and writing and removed when not required; for example, floppy disks, disk cartridges and disk packs.

render

To draw a real-world object as it actually appears.

rendering

In computer graphics, creating a 3-D image that incorporates the simulation of lighting effects, such as shadows and reflection.

Renderman interface

A graphics format from Pixar, Point Richmond, CA, (www.pixar.com), that uses photorealistic image synthesis. Developer's Renderman (PCs and UNIX) and Mac Renderman (Macintosh) are Pixar programs that apply photorealistic looks and surfaces to 3-D objects.

repeater

A communications device that amplifies or regenerates the data signal in order to extend the transmission distance. Available for both analog and digital signals, it is used extensively in long distance transmission. It is also used to tie two LANs of the same type together. Repeaters work at layer 1 of the OSI model. See *bridge* and *router*.

replication

In database management, the ability to keep distributed databases synchronized by routinely copying the entire database or subsets of the database to other servers in the network.

report

A printed or microfilmed collection of facts and figures with page numbers and page headings. See *report writer* and *query*.

report file

A file that describes how a report is printed.

report format

The layout of a report showing page and column headers, page numbers and totals.

report generator

Same as *report writer*.

report writer

Software that prints a report based on a description of its layout. As a stand-alone program or part of a DBMS or file manager, it can sort selected records into a new sequence for printing. It may also print standard mailing labels.

Developed in the early 1970s, report writers (report generators) were the precursor to query languages and were the first programs to generate computer output without having to be programmed.

repository

A database of information about applications software that includes author, data elements, inputs, processes, outputs and interrelationships. It may be the central core of a CASE system; for example, Repository Manager in IBM's AD/Cycle is designed to integrate third-party CASE products.

reprographics

Duplicating printed materials using various kinds of printing presses and high-speed copiers.

reserved word

A verb or noun in a programming or command language that is part of the native language.

reset button

A computer button or key that reboots the computer. All current activities are stopped cold, and any data in memory is lost. On a printer, the reset button clears the printer's memory and readies it to accept new data.

resident module

The part of a program that must remain in memory at all times. Instructions and data that stay in memory can be accessed instantly.

resident program

A program that remains in memory at all times. See *TSR*.

resistor

An electronic component that resists the flow of current in an electronic circuit.

resolution

(1) The degree of sharpness of a displayed or printed character or image. On screen, resolution is expressed as a matrix of dots. VGA resolution of 640x480 means 640 dots across each of 480 lines. Sometimes the number of colors are added to the spec; for example, 640x480x16 or 640x480x256. The same resolution looks sharper on a small screen than a large one.

For printers, resolution is expressed as the number of dots per linear inch. 300 dpi means 90,000 dots per square inch (300x300). Laser printers and plotters have resolutions from 300 to 1000 dpi and more, whereas most display screens provide less than 100 dpi. That means jagged lines on screen may smooth out when they print.

(2) The number of bits used to record the value of a sample in a digitized signal. See *sampling rate*.

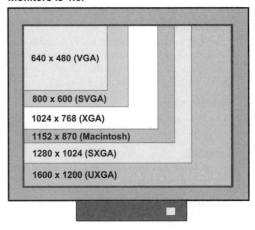

The aspect ratio of most computer monitors is 4:3.

640 x 480 (VGA)

800 x 600 (SVGA)

1024 x 768 (XGA)

1152 x 870 (Macintosh)

1280 x 1024 (SXGA)

1600 x 1200 (UXGA)

resolve

To change, transform or solve a problem. The phrase "external references are resolved" refers to determining the addresses that link modules together; that is, solving the unknown links.

resource compiler

In a graphical interface (GUI), software that converts and links a resource (menu, dialog box, icon, font, etc.) into the executable program.

resource fork

The resource part of a Macintosh file. For example, in a text document, it contains format codes with offsets into the text in the data fork. In a program, it contains executable code, menus, windows, dialog boxes, buttons, fonts and icons.

response time

The time it takes for the computer to comply with a user's request, such as looking up a customer record.

restart

To resume computer opertion after a planned or unplanned termination. See *boot, warm boot* and *checkpoint/restart*.

restricted function

A computer or operating system function that cannot be used by an application program.

retrieve

To call up data that has been stored in a computer system. When a user queries a database, the data is retrieved into the computer first and then transmitted to the screen.

reusability

The ability to use all or the greater part of the same programming code or system design in another application.

reverse DNS

(Reverse Domain Name System) Name resolution software that looks up an IP address to obtain a domain name. It performs the opposite function of the DNS server, which turns names into IP addresses.

reverse engineer

To isolate the components of a completed system. When a chip is reverse engineered, all the individual circuits that make up the chip are identified. Source code can be reverse engineered into design models or specifications. Machine language can be reversed into assembly langauge (see *disassembler*).

reverse polish notation

A mathematical expression in which the numbers precede the operation. For example, 2 + 2 would be expressed as 2 2 +, and 10 - 3 * 4 would be 10 3 4 * -. See *FORTH*.

reverse video

A display mode used to highlight characters on screen. For example, if the normal display mode is black on white, reverse video would be white on black.

revision level

See *version number*.

REXX

(REstructured EXtended eXecutor) An IBM mainframe structured programming language that runs under VM/CMS and MVS/TSO. It can be used as a general-purpose macro language that sends commands to application programs and to the operating systems. REXX is also included in OS/2 Version 2.0.

The following REXX example converts Fahrenheit to Celsius:

```
Say "Enter Fahrenheit "
Pull FAHR
Say "Celsius is "  (FAHR - 32) * (5 / 9)
```

RF

(Radio Frequency) The range of electromagnetic frequencies above the audio range and below visible light. All broadcast transmission, from AM radio to satellites, falls into this range, which is between 30KHz and 300GHz. See *RF modulation*.

RFI

(Radio Frequency Interference) High-frequency electromagnetic waves that eminate from electronic devices such as chips.

RF/ID

(Radio Frequency/IDentification) An identification system that uses tags that transmit a wireless message. The tag gets its power from a hand-held gun/reading unit.

RF modulation

The transmission of a signal through a carrier frequency. In order to connect to a TV's antenna input, some home computers and all VCRs provide RF modulation of a TV channel, usually Channel 3 or 4. See *FCC class*.

RFP

(Request For Proposal) A document that invites a vendor to submit a bid for hardware, software and/ or services. It may provide a general or very detailed specification of the system.

RFS

(Remote File System) A distributed file system for UNIX computers introduced by AT&T in 1986 with UNIX System V Release 3.0. It is similar to Sun's NFS, but only for UNIX systems.

RF shielding

A material that prohibits electromagnetic radiation from penetrating it. Personal computers and electronic devices used in the home must meet U.S. government standards for electromagnetic interference.

RFT

See *DCA*.

RGB

(Red Green Blue) A video color generation method that displays colors as varying intensities of red, green and blue dots. When all three are turned on high, white is produced. As intensities are equally lowered, shades of gray are derived. The base color of the screen appears when all dots are off.

RGB monitor

(1) A video display screen that requires separate red, green and blue signals from the computer. It generates a better image than composite signals (TV) which merge the three colors together. It comes in both analog and digital varieties.

(2) Sometimes refers to a CGA monitor that accepts digital RGB signals.

Rhapsody

Apple's next-generation operating system for the Macintosh. It is expected to be a blend of the NEXTSTEP OS from NeXT, which it acquired, and its internally-developed Copland, which was never released.

ribbon cable

A thin, flat, multiconductor cable that is widely used in electronic systems; for example, to interconnect peripheral devices to the computer internally.

Ribbon Cable

rich e-mail

E-mail annotated with voice messages.

rich media

Information that consists of any combination of graphics, audio, video and animation, which is more storage and bandwidth intensive than ordinary text. See *rich text*.

rich text

(1) Text that includes formatting commands for bold, italic, etc. It may also refer to the mixing of graphics with text. See *rich media*.

(2) Text in Microsoft's RTF format. See *RTF*.

RIFF

(Resource Interchange File Format) A multimedia data format jointly introduced by IBM and Microsoft. See *MCI*.

rightsizing

Selecting a computer system, whether micro, mini or mainframe, that best meets the needs of the application.

rigid disk

Same as *hard disk*.

ring

One stage or level in a set of prioritized stages or levels, typically involved with security and password protection.

ring network

A communications network that connects terminals and computers in a continuous loop.

RIP

(1) (Raster Image Processor) The hardware and/or software that rasterizes an image for display or printing. RIPs are designed to rasterize a specific type of data, such as PostScript or vector graphics images, as well as different kinds of raster data.

(2) (Routing Information Protocol) A router protocol that determines the best path for routing traffic over a network by analyzing hop counts. RIP protocols continuously announce themselves on the network and are known to waste bandwidth.

ripper

Software that extracts raw audio data from a music CD. See *digital audio extraction* and *MP3*.

RISC

(Reduced Instruction Set Computer) A computer architecture that reduces chip complexity by using simpler instructions. RISC compilers have to generate software routines to perform complex instructions that were previously done in hardware by CISC computers. In RISC, the microcode layer and associated overhead is eliminated.

RJ-11, RJ-45

RJ-11 is the four-wire connector used for telephone plugs and sockets. RJ-45 is an eight-wire connector widely used for Ethernet and Token Ring connections.

RJ-48

(Registered Jack-48) A telephone connector that holds up to eight wires. It uses the same plug and socket as RJ-45 but has different pinouts. RJ-48C is commonly used for T1 lines.

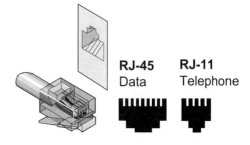

RJE

(Remote Job Entry) Transmitting batches of transactions from a remote terminal or computer. The receiving computer processes the data and may transmit the results back to the RJE site for printing. RJE hardware at remote sites can employ teleprinters with disk or tape storage or complete computer systems.

RLE

See *run length encoding*.

RLL

(Run Length Limited) An encoding method commonly used on magnetic disks. Extra bits are inserted to help in reading back the data. As technology improves, fewer extra bits are needed. The "run length" is the number of consecutive 0s before a 1 bit is recorded. For example, RLL 1,7 means there must be at least one 0 between every 1, and the 7 means a maximum of eight time periods between flux transitions.

RMI

(Remote Method Invocation) A standard from Sun for distributed objects written in Java. RMI is a remote procedure call (RPC), which allows Java objects (software components) stored in the network to be run remotely. Unlike CORBA and DCOM objects, which can be developed in different languages, RMI is designed for objects written only in Java.

RMON

(Remote MONitoring) Extensions to the Simple Network Management Protocol (SNMP) that provide comprehensive network monitoring capabilities. In standard SNMP, the device has to be queried to obtain information. RMON is proactive and can set alarms on a variety of traffic conditions, including specific types of errors. The full RMON capabilities are very comprehensive and generally only portions are used in routers and other network devices. See *SNMP*.

RMS

(1) (Record Management Services) A file management system used in VAXs.

(2) (Root Mean Square) A method used to measure electrical output in volts and watts.

RoboCAD

A CAD program from Robo Systems International, Inc., Newtown, PA, that runs under DOS and includes a wide variety of features and text functions. RoboCAD is noted for its performance and ease of use and is very popular in the education market.

robot

A stand-alone hybrid computer system that performs physical and computational activities. It is a multiple-motion device with one or more arms and joints that is capable of performing many different tasks like a human. It can be designed similar to human form, although most industrial robots don't resemble people at all.

It is used extensively in manufacturing for welding, riveting, scraping and painting. Office and consumer applications are also being developed. Robots, designed with AI, can respond to unstructured situations. For example, specialized robots can identify objects in a pile, select the objects in the appropriate sequence and assemble them into a unit.

Robots use analog sensors for recognizing real-world objects and digital computers for their direction. Analog to digital converters convert temperature, motion, pressure, sound and images into binary code for the robot's computer. The computer directs the physical actions of the arms and joints by pulsing their motors.

robotics

The art and science of the creation and use of robots.

robust

Refers to software without bugs that handles abnormal conditions well. It is often said that there is no software package totally bug free. Any program can exhibit odd behavior under certain conditions, but a robust program will not lock up the computer, cause damage to data or send the user through an endless chain of dialog boxes without purpose. Whether or not a program can be totally bug free will be debated forever. See *industrial strength*.

ROLAP

See *OLAP*.

rollback

A database management system feature that reverses the current transaction out of the database, returning the database to its former state. This is done when some failure interrupts a half-completed transaction.

roll in/roll out

A swapping technique for freeing up memory temporarily in order to perform another task. The current program or program segment is stored (rolled out) on disk, and another program is brought into (rolled in) that memory space.

ROM

(Read Only Memory) A memory chip that permanently stores instructions and data. Its contents are created at the time of manufacture and cannot be altered. ROM chips are used to store control routines in personal computers (ROM BIOS), peripheral controllers and other electronic equipment. They are also often the sole component inside a cartridge that plugs into printers, video games and other systems.

When computers are used in hand-held instruments, appliances, automobiles and any other such devices, the instructions for their routines are generally stored in ROM chips or some other non-volatile chip such as a PROM or EPROM. Instructions may also be stored in a ROM section within a general-purpose computer on a chip. See *PROM, EPROM* and *EEPROM*. Contrast with *RAM*.

ROMable

Machine language capable of being programmed into a ROM chip. Being "read only" the chip cannot be updated and ROMable programs must use RAM or disk for holding changing data.

ROM BIOS

A PC BIOS stored on a ROM chip. See *flash BIOS* and *BIOS*.

ROM card

A credit-card-sized module that contains permanent software or data. See *memory card*.

ROM emulator

A circuit that helps debug a ROM chip by simulating the ROM with RAM. The RAM circuit plugs into the ROM socket. Since RAM can be written over, whereas ROM cannot, programming changes can be made easily.

root directory

In hierarchical file systems, the starting point in the hierarchy. When the computer is first started, the root directory is the current directory. Access to directories in the hierarchy requires naming the directories that are in its path. In DOS, the command line symbol for the root directory is a backslash (\). In UNIX, it is a slash (/).

root server

A domain name server that is maintained by Network Solutions, Inc., Herndon, VA. It contains all the primary domain names that are registered, and it is updated daily. The data is replicated on several servers throughout the U.S. and abroad. See *DNS*.

rotational delay

The amount of time it takes for the disk to rotate until the required location on the disk reaches the read/write head.

RO terminal

(Receive Only terminal) A printing device only (no keyboard).

round robin

Continuously repeating sequence, such as the polling of a series of terminals, one after the other, over and over again.

routable protocol

A communications protocol that contains a network address as well as a device address, allowing data to be routed from one network to another. Examples of routable protocols are SNA, OSI, TCP/IP, XNS, IPX, AppleTalk and DECnet. Contrast with *non-routable protocol*.

router

A device that routes data packets from one local area network (LAN) or wide area network (WAN) to another. Routers see the network as network addresses and all the possible paths between them. They read the network address in each transmitted frame and make a decision on how to send it based on the most expedient route (traffic load, line costs, speed, bad lines, etc.). Routers work at the network layer (OSI layer 3), whereas bridges and switches work at the data link layer (layer 2).

router protocol

A protocol used by routers to report their status to other routers in the network and keep their internal tables up-to-date. See *RIP* and *OSPF*.

routine

A set of instructions that perform a task. Same as *subroutine, module, procedure* and *function*.

routing

See *intermediate node routing* and *router*.

routing protocol

A communications protocol used to update the routing table in a router.

RPC

(Remote Procedure Call) A programming interface that allows one program to use the services of another program in a remote machine. The calling programming sends a message and data to the remote program, which is executed, and results are passed back to the calling program.

RPG

(Report Program Generator) One of the first program generators designed for business reports, introduced in 1964 by IBM. In 1970, RPG II added enhancements that made it a mainstay programming language for business applications on IBM's System/3x midrange computers. RPG III, which added more programming structures, is widely used on the AS/400. RPG statements are written in columnar format.

rpm

(Revolutions Per Minute) The measurement of the rotational speed of a disk drive. Floppy disks rotate at 300 rpm, while hard disks rotate from 2,400 to 3,600 rpm and more.

RPN

See *reverse polish notation*.

RPQ

(Request for Price Quotation) A document that requests a price for hardware, software or services to solve a specific problem. It is created by the customer and delivered to the vendor.

RS-232

(Recommended Standard-232) A TIA/EIA standard for serial transmission between computers and peripheral devices (modem, mouse, etc.). It uses a 25-pin DB-25 or 9-pin DB-9 connector. Its normal cable limitation of 50 feet can be extended to several hundred feet with high-quality cable.

RS-422, 423

A TIA/EIA standards for serial interfaces that extend distances and speeds beyond RS-232. RS-422 is a balanced system requiring more wire pairs than RS-423 and is intended for use in multipoint lines. They use either a 37-pin connector defined by RS-449 or a 25-pin connector defined by RS-530.

RS-449 and RS-530 specify the pin definitions for RS-422 and RS-423. RS-422/423 specify electrical and timing characteristics.

RS-449

Defines a 37-pin connector for RS-422 and RS-423 circuits.

RS-485

A TIA/EIA standard for multipoint communications lines. It can be implemented with as little as a wire block with four screws or with DB-9 or DB-37 connectors. By using lower-impedance drivers and receivers, RS-485 allows more nodes per line than RS-422.

RS-530

Defines a 25-pin connector for RS-422 and RS-423 circuits. It allows for higher speed transmission up to 2Mbits/sec over the same DB-25 connector used in RS-232, but is not compatible with it.

RS/6000

(RISC System/6000) IBM family of RISC-based computer systems introduced in 1990. It comes in workstation (POWERstation) and server (POWERserver) models and uses the Micro Channel bus. It introduced Version 3 of AIX and two graphical user interfaces: AIXwindows Environment/6000 (enhanced X Window system) and AIX NeXTStep Environment/6000 from NeXT Computer.

RSA

(Rivest-Shamir-Adleman) A highly-secure cryptography method by RSA Data Security, Inc., Redwood City, CA. It uses a two-part key. The private key is kept by the owner; the public key is published. Data is encrypted by using the recipient's public key, which can only be decrypted by the recipient's private key.

RSA is very computation intensive, thus it is often used to create a digital envelope, which holds an RSA-encrypted DES key and DES-encrypted data. This method encrypts the secret DES key so that it can be transmitted over the network, but encrypts and decrypts the actual message using the much faster DES algorithm. RSA is also used for creating digital signatures. See *digital signature, cryptography* and *digital certificate*.

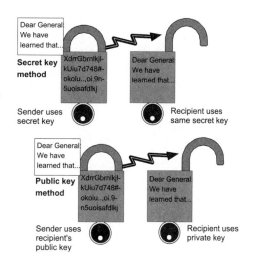

RSA

RSCS

(Remote Spooling Communications Subsystem) Software that provides batch communications for IBM's VM operating system. It accepts data from remote batch terminals, executes them on a priority basis and transmits the results back to the terminals. The RSCS counterpart in MVS is JES. Contrast with *CMS*, which provides interactive communications for VM.

RSI

(Repetitive Strain Injury) Ailments of the hands, neck, back and eyes due to computer use. The remedy for RSI is frequent breaks which should include stretching or yoga postures. See *carpal tunnel syndrome*.

RSVP

(ReSerVation Protocol) A communications protocol that signals a router to reserve bandwidth for realtime transmission. RSVP is designed to clear a path for audio and video traffic eliminating annoying skips and hesitations. It has been sanctioned by the IETF, because audio and video traffic is expected to increase dramatically on the Internet.

RTF

(Rich Text Format) A Microsoft standard for encoding formatted text and graphics. It was adapted from IBM's DCA format and supports ANSI, IBM PC and Macintosh character sets.

RTFM

(Read The Flaming Manual) The last resort when having a hardware or software problem!

RTOS

(RealTime Operating System) An operating system designed for use in a realtime computer system. See *realtime system, embedded system, process control* and *OS/9*.

RTP

(1) (Realtime Transport Protocol) An emerging protocol for the Internet that supports realtime transmission of voice and video. RTP communicates with the Resource Reservation Protocol (RSVP) dynamically to allocate appropriate bandwidth.

(2) (Rapid Transport Protocol) The protocol used in IBM's High Performance Routing (HPR).

RTS

(Request To Send) An RS-232 signal sent from the transmitting station to the receiving station requesting permission to transmit. Contrast with *CTS*.

rubber banding

In computer graphics, the moving of a line or object where one end stays fixed in position.

rubout key

A keyboard key on a terminal that deletes the last character that was entered.

rule-based expert system

An expert system based on a set of rules that a human expert would follow in diagnosing a problem. Contrast with *model-based expert system*.

ruler line

A graphic representation of a ruler on screen that is used for laying out text and graphics.

rules

(1) A set of conditions or standards which have been agreed upon.

(2) In printing, horizontal and vertical lines between columns or at the top and bottom of a page in order to enhance the appearance of the page.

rules based

Using "if-this, do that" rules to perform actions. Rules-based products implies flexibility in the software, enabling tasks and data to be easily changed by replacing one or more rules.

RUMBA

A family of PC-to-host connectivity programs from Wall Data Inc., Kirkland, WA, (www.walldata.com). On desktop computers connected to minis and mainframes, RUMBA provides a window that emulates a terminal session with these hosts. RUMBA supports Windows and OS/2 clients connected to IBM mainframes, AS/400s, VAXes and other hosts via coax adapters, twinax cards or the network.

run

(1) To execute a program.

(2) A single program or set of programs scheduled for execution.

run around

In desktop publishing, the flowing of text around a graphic image.

run length encoding

A simple data compression method that converts a run of identical symbols as a symbol followed by a count. A rough example might be []36* where [] is a code and 36* means 36 *'s follow.

run native

To "run native" is to execute software written for the native mode of the computer. Contrast with running a program under some type of emulation or simulation.

Running native has traditionally been the fastest way to execute instructions on a computer. However, if as expected in the future, machines are so fast they can run emulated programs without any noticeable delay to the user, this will no longer be the important issue it is today.

run on top of

To run as the control program to some other program, which is subordinate to it. Contrast with *run under*.

runtime

Refers to the actual execution of a program.

runtime version

Software that enables another program to execute on its own or with enhanced capabilities. For example, Visual Basic programs are interpreted, which means Visual Basic applications cannot be executed natively in the computer. They need the runtime module that interprets the Visual Basic code into the machine language of the computer. That actual module in a Windows PC is named VBRUN300.DLL, VBRUN400.DLL, etc.

run under

To run within the control of a higher-level program. Contrast with *run on top of.*

RUP

(Rational Unified Process) Software from Rational Software Corporation, Cupertino, CA, (www.rational.com), that provides guidelines, templates and examples for each team member in the system development process. It supports the Unified Modeling Language (UML).

S-100 bus

An IEEE 696, 100-pin bus standard used extensively in first-generation personal computers (8080, Z80, 6800, etc.). It is still used in various systems.

S3 chip

Refers to one of the chips from S3, Inc., San Jose, CA, (www.s3.com), used in a variety of graphics accelerator boards. After acquiring Diamond Multimedia, S3 has divested itself of most chip-making activities and is concentrating on Internet appliances.

S/3x

See *System/3x.*

S/360, S/370

See *System/360, System/370.*

S/390

Originally an abbreviation for IBM's System/390 machines. Today, IBM's CMOS-based System/390 systems are designated as S/390s.

SAA

(System Application Architecture) A set of interfaces designed to cross all IBM platforms from PC to mainframe. Introduced by IBM in 1987, SAA includes the Common User Access (CUA), the Common Programming Interface for Communications (CPI-C) and Common Communications Support (CCS). See *CUA, CPI-C* and *CCS.*

sag

A momentary drop in voltage from the power source. Contrast with *spike.*

sales force automation

Automating the sales activities within an organization. A comprehensive SFA package provides such functions as contact management, note and information sharing, quick proposal and presentation generation, product configurators, calendars and to-do lists. When sales functions are integrated with marketing and customer service, it is known as "enterprise relationship management" or ERM.

sampling

(1) In statistics, the analysis of a group by determining the characteristics of a significant percentage of its members chosen at random.

(2) In digitizing operations, the conversion of real-world signals or movements at regular intervals into digital code. See *sampling rate* and *oversampling.*

sampling rate

In digitizing operations, the frequency with which samples are taken and converted into digital form. The sampling frequency must be at least twice that of the analog frequency being captured. For example, the sampling rate for hi-fi playback is 44.1KHz, slightly more than double the 20KHz frequency a person can hear. The higher the sampling rate, the closer real-world objects are represented in digital form.

Another sampling attribute is quantizing, which creates a number for the sample. The larger the maximum number, also called "resolution" or "precision," the more granularity of the scale and the more accurate the digital sampling. An 8-bit sample provides 256 levels, while a 16-bit sample yields 65,535 levels. See *oversampling.*

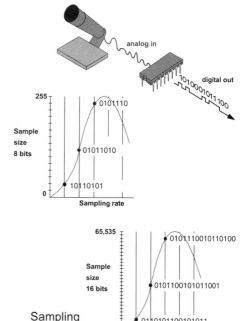

Sampling

SAN

(Storage Area Network) A back-end network connecting storage devices via peripheral channels such as SCSI, SSA, ESCON and Fibre Channel. There are two ways of implementing SANs: centralized and decentralized. A centralized SAN ties multiple hosts into a single storage system, which is a RAID device with large amounts of cache and redundant power supplies.

If a centralized storage system is not feasible, a SAN can connect multiple hosts with multiple storage systems. Considering the proliferation of file servers in an enterprise, SANs with distributed storage are expected to be widely employed.

sans-serif

A typeface style without serifs, which are the short horizontal lines added at the tops and bottoms of the vertical member of the letter. Helvetica is a common sans-serif font.

Santa Cruz Operation

See *SCO.*

SAP

(1) (Service Advertising Protocol) A NetWare protocol used to identify the services and addresses of servers attached to the network. The responses are used to update a table in the router known as the Server Information Table.

(2) (Secondary Audio Program) An NTSC audio channel used for auxiliary transmission, such as foreign language broadcasting or teletext.

(3) (SAP America, Inc., Wayne, PA, www.sap.com) The U.S. branch of the German software company, SAP AG. SAP's R/3 integrated suite of applications and its ABAP/4 Development Workbench became popular starting around 1993. See *R/3.*

SAS System

Originally Statistical Analysis System, SAS is an integrated set of data management tools from SAS Institute Inc., Cary, NC, (www.sas.com), that runs on PCs to mainframes. It includes a complete programming language as well as modules for spreadsheets, CBT, presentation graphics, project management, operations research, scheduling, linear programming, statistical quality control, econometric and time series analysis and mathematical, engineering and statistical applications.

satellite

See *communications satellite.*

satellite channel

A carrier frequency used for satellite transmission.

satellite computer

A computer located remotely from the host computer or under the control of the host. It can function as a slave to the master computer or perform offline tasks.

satellite link

A signal that travels from the earth to a communications satellite and back down again. Contrast with *terrestrial link.*

saturation

(1) On magnetic media, a condition in which the magnetizable particles are completely aligned and a more powerful writing signal will not improve the reading back.

(2) In a bipolar transistor, a condition in which the current on the gate (the trigger) is equal to or greater than what is necessary to close the switch.

(3) In a diode, a condition in which the diode is fully conducting.

save

To copy the document, record or image being worked on onto a storage medium. Saving updates the file by writing the data that currently resides in memory (RAM) onto disk or tape. Most applications prompt the user to save data upon exiting.

All processing is done in memory (RAM). When the processing is completed, the data must be placed onto a permanent storage medium such as disk or tape.

Save as

A command in the File menu of most applications that lets you make a copy of the current document or image you are working on. It differs from the regular Save command. Save stores your data back into the folder (directory) it originally came from. "Save as" lets you give it a different name and/or put it in a different folder on your hard disk or floppy disk.

Sbus

Originally a proprietary bus from Sun, the Sbus has been released into the public domain. The IEEE is standardizing on a 64-bit version in 1993.

SCAI

(Switch-to-Computer Applications Interface) A standard for integrating computers to a PBX. See *switch-to-computer.*

scalability

The ability to expand. See *scale.*

scalable

Capable of being changed in size and configuration.

scalable font

A font that is created in the required point size when needed for display or printing. The dot patterns (bitmaps) are generated from a set of outline fonts, or base fonts, which contain a mathematical representation of the typeface. The two major scalable fonts are Adobe's Type 1 PostScript and Apple/Microsoft's TrueType. Contrast with *bitmapped font*

scalar

A single item or value. Contrast with *vector* and *array*, which are made up of multiple values.

scalar processor

A computer that performs arithmetic computations on one number at a time. Contrast with *vector processor.*

scalar variable

In programming, a variable that contains only one value.

scale

(1) To resize a device, object or system, making it larger or smaller.

(2) To change the representation of a quantity in order to bring it into prescribed limits of another range. For example, values such as 1249, 876, 523, -101 and -234 might need to be scaled into a range from -5 to +5.

(3) To designate the position of the decimal point in a fixed or floating point number.

SCAM

(SCSI Configured AutoMatically) A subset of Plug and Play that allows SCSI IDs to be changed by software rather than by flipping switches or changing jumpers. Both the SCSI host adapter and peripheral must support SCAM.

scan

(1) In optical technologies, to view a printed form a line at a time in order to convert images into bitmapped representations, or to convert characters into ASCII text or some other data code.

(2) In video, to move across a picture frame a line at a time, either to detect the image in an analog or digital camera, or to refresh a CRT display.

(3) To sequentially search a file.

scan head

An optical sensing device in an scanner or fax machine that is moved across the image to be scanned.

scan line

One of many horizontal lines in a graphics frame.

scanner

A device that reads text, images and bar codes. Text and bar code scanners recognize printed fonts and bar codes and convert them into a digital code (ASCII or EBCDIC). Graphics scanners convert a printed image into a bitmap (raster graphics) without recognizing the actual content of the text or pictures.

scan rate

See *horizontal scan frequency*.

scatter diagram, scatter plot

A graph plotted with dots or some other symbol at each data point. Also called a "scatter plot" or "dot chart."

SCbus

See *SCSA*.

SC connector

A fiber-optic cable connector that uses a push-pull latching mechanism. It is used in FDDI, Fiber Channel and B/ISDN applications. See *SMA connector* and *ST connector*.

scheduler

The part of the operating system that initiates and terminates jobs (programs) in the computer. Also called a "dispatcher," it maintains a list of jobs to be run and allocates computer resources as required.

scheduling algorithm

A method used to schedule jobs for execution. Priority, length of time in the job queue and available resources are examples of criteria used.

schema

The definition of an entire database. See *subschema*.

Schottky

A category of bipolar transistor known for its fast switching speeds in the three-nanosecond range. Schottky II devices have switching speeds in the range of a single nanosecond.

scientific application

An application that simulates real-world activities using mathematics. Real-world objects are turned into mathematical models and their actions are simulated by executing the formulas.

For example, some of an airplane's flight characteristics can be simulated in the computer. Rivers, lakes and mountains can be simulated. Virtually any objects with known characteristics can be modeled and simulated.

Simulations use enormous calculations and often require supercomputer speed. As personal computers become more powerful, more laboratory experiments will be converted into computer models that can be interactively examined by students without the risk and cost of the actual experiments.

scientific computer

A computer specialized for high-speed mathematic processing. See *array processor* and *floating point processor*.

scientific language

A programming language designed for mathematical formulas and matrices, such as ALGOL, FORTRAN and APL. Although all programming languages allow for this kind of processing, statements in a scientific language make it easier to express these actions.

scientific notation

The display of numbers in floating point form. The number (mantissa) is always equal to or greater than one and less than 10, and the base is 10. For example, 2.345E6 is equivalent to 2,345,000. The number following E (exponent) represents the power to which the base should be raised (number of zeros following the decimal point).

scissoring

In computer graphics, the deleting of any parts of an image which fall outside of a window that has been sized and laid over the original image. Also called "clipping."

SCL

(Switch-to-Computer Link) Refers to applications that integrate the computer through the PBX. See *switch-to-computer*.

SCO

(The Santa Cruz Operation, Inc., Santa Cruz, CA, www.sco.com) The leading vendor of the UNIX operating system on the Intel x86 platform, which accounts for about one third of all UNIX servers worldwide. SCO has sold licenses for more than two million nodes of UNIX client and server products. Founded in 1979 as a custom programming house, its first operating system was SCO XENIX in 1984.

SCO OpenServer

A family of client and server operating systems for the Intel platform from SCO. SCO OpenServer Desktop is the client version. SCO OpenServer Enterprise is the server version with optional SMP support for up to 30 processors.

scope

(1) A CRT screen, such as used on an oscilloscope or common display terminal.

(2) In programming, the visibility of variables within a program; for example, whether one function can use a variable created in another function.

SCO UNIX

An enhanced version of UNIX System V Release 3.2 for Intel processors from SCO. In 1989, SCO UNIX was introduced as a major upgrade to SCO XENIX with more security, networking and standards conformance. SCO UNIX servers support dumb terminals, Windows, X terminal and SCO OpenServer clients. SCO OpenServer evolved from SCO UNIX.

SCO UnixWare

A family of client and server operating systems for the Intel platform from SCO. Server versions are available based on UNIX System V Release 4.2MP as well as an enhanced version known as SCO UnixWare System V Release 5, which combines UnixWare with SCO's OpenServer graphical front end. UnixWare Personal Edition is the client version which comes with the Mosaic Web browser.

UnixWare was originally developed by Univel, a joint venture of Novell and AT&T's UNIX System Labs (USL). In 1993, Novell purchased USL and UnixWare and sold it to SCO two years later.

SCO XENIX

A version of the UNIX System V operating system for Intel-based computers with dumb terminals. It was a fast multiuser system developed by Microsoft and licensed to SCO, which sold it to numerous vertical market developers. SCO OpenServer Host System currently provides the same capability.

scrambler

A device or software program that encodes data for encryption.

scrambling

Encoding data to make it indecipherable. See *cryptography*, *DES* and *RSA*.

Scrapbook

A Macintosh disk file that holds frequently-used text and graphics objects, such as a company letterhead. Contrast with *Clipboard*, which holds data only for the current session.

scratchpad

A register or reserved section of memory or disk used for temporary storage.

scratch tape

A magnetic tape that can be erased and reused.

screen

The display area of a video terminal or monitor. It is either a CRT or one of the flat panel technologies.

screen angle

The angle at which a halftone screen is placed over an image, typically 45ø.

screen capture

Transfering the current on-screen image to a text or graphics file.

screen dump

Printing the entire on-screen image. On DOS PCs, pressing Shift-PrintScreen prints the current text screen. For DOS graphics, third-party programs work best. For Windows, pressing PrintScreen copies the entire screen to the clipboard. Alt-PrintScreen copies the current window only. On the Mac, press Command-shift-3 to create a MacPaint file of the current screen.

screen font

A font used for on-screen display. For true WYSIWYG systems, screen fonts must be matched as close as possible to the printer fonts. Contrast with *printer font*.

screen frequency

The resolution of a halftone. It is the density of dots (how far they're spaced apart from each other) measured in lines per inch. In a digital system, the screen frequency is simulated by the placement of the dots within the halftone cells. See *halftone*.

screen overlay

(1) A clear, fine-mesh screen that reduces the glare on a video screen.

(2) A clear touch panel that allows the user to command the computer by touching displayed buttons on screen.

(3) A temporary data window displayed on screen. The part of the screen that was overlaid is saved and restored when the screen overlay is removed.

screen saver

A utility that prevents a CRT from being etched by an unchanging image. After a specified duration of time without keyboard or mouse input, it blanks the screen or displays moving objects. Pressing a key or moving the mouse restores the screen.

screen scraper

Also called "frontware," it is software that adds a graphical user interface to character-based mainframe and minicomputer applications. The screen scraper application runs in the personal computer which is used as a terminal to the mainframe or mini via 3270 or 5250 emulation.

script

(1) A typeface that looks like handwriting or calligraphy.

(2) A program written in a special-purpose programming language such as used in a communications program or word processor. Same as *macro*.

(3) A small program that is used to glue other programs together. It may be written in a full-blown programming language, but it is called a script in this instance.

ScriptX

A multimedia technology from Apple that includes data formats, a scripting language and runtime environment.

scroll

To continuously move forward, backward or sideways through the text and images on screen or within a window. Scrolling implies continuous and smooth movement, a line, character or pixel at a time, as if the data were on a paper scroll being rolled behind the screen.

scrollable field

A short line on screen that can be scrolled to allow editing or display of larger amounts of data in a small display space.

scroll arrow

On-screen arrow that is clicked in order to scroll the screen in the corresponding direction. The screen moves one line, or increment, with each mouse click.

scroll back buffer

Reserved memory that holds a block of transmitted data, allowing the user to browse back through it.

scroll bar

A horizontal or vertical bar that contains a box that ↕
to scroll the screen in the corresponding direction, or the
dragged to the desired direction.

Scroll Lock

On PC keyboards, a key used to toggle between a scrolling ↕
arrow keys scroll the screen regardless of the current cursor locati
intended purpose, if at all.

SCSA

(Signal Computing System Architecture) An open
architecture from Dialogic Corporation, Parsippany, NJ,
(www.dialogic.com), for transmitting signals, voice
and video. Its backbone is the SCbus, a
131Mbps data path that provides up to
2048 time slots, the equivalent of 1,024
two-way voice conversations at 64Kbps.

SCSI

(Small Computer System Interface)
Pronounced "scuzzy." SCSI is a hardware
interface that allows for the connection of
up to seven or 15 peripheral devices to a
single expansion board that plugs into the
computer called a "SCSI host adapter" or
"SCSI controller." Single boards are also
available with two controllers and support
up to 30 peripherals. SCSI is widely used
from personal computers to mainframes.

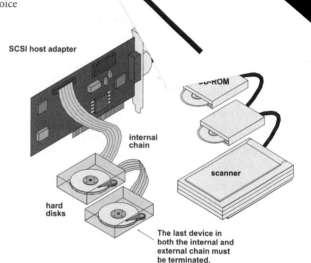

SCSI host adapter

internal chain

scanner

hard disks

The last device in both the internal and external chain must be terminated.

scuzzy

See *SCSI*.

SDF

(Standard Data Format) A simple file
format that uses fixed length fields. It is commonly used to transfer data between different programs.

```
SDF
Pat Smith      5 E. 12 St.      Rye        NY
Robert Jones   200 W. Main St.  Palo Alto  CA

Comma delimited
"Pat Smith","5 E. 12 St.","Rye","NY"
"Robert Jones","200 W. Main St.","Palo Alto","CA"
```

SDH

(Syncronous Digital Hierarchy) The European counterpart to SONET. Speeds supported include 155
and 622 Mbits/sec and 2.5 GBits/sec.

SDI

(1) (Switched Digital International) An AT&T dial-up service providing 56 and 64 Kbits/sec digital
transmission to international locations.

(2) (Single Document Interface) A Windows function that allows an application to display and lets
the user work with only one document at a time. SDI applications require that the user load the
application again for the second and each subsequent document to be worked on concurrently. Contrast
with *MDI*.

SDK

(Software Developer's Kit) See *developer's toolkit* and *Windows SDK*.

ol) The primary data link protocol used in IBM's SNA networks. It is
ocol that is a subset of the HDLC protocol.

sic Initiative) A secure digital format for distributing music over the Internet.
uary 1999, it is backed by the Recording Industry Association of America (RIAA) and
MG, EMI and Universal, the top five music production companies.

ynchronous **DRAM**) A type of dynamic RAM memory chip that has been widely used starting in
e latter part of the 1990s. SDRAMs are based on standard dynamic RAM chips, but have sophisticated
features that make them considerably faster.

SE

See *systems engineer* and *service engineer*.

seamless integration

An addition of a new application, routine or device that works smoothly with the existing system. It
implies that the new feature can be activated and used without problems. Contrast with *transparent*,
which implies that there is no discernible change after installation.

search and replace

To look for an occurrence of data or text and replace it with another set of data or text.

search engine

Software that searches for data based on some criterion. See *Web search sites*.

search key

In a search routine, the data entered and used to match other data in the database.

SEC

(Single Edge Contact) A CPU cartridge from Intel that contains the CPU and external L2 cache. It
plugs into a 242-pin Slot 1 receptacle on the motherboard that resembles an ISA bus slot.

SECAM

(Systeme Electronique Couleur Avec Memoire) A French and Eastern Europe TV standard. Contrast
with *NTSC*.

secondary channel

In communications, a subchannel that is derived from the main channel. It is used for diagnostic or
supervisory purposes, but does not carry data messages.

secondary index

An index that is maintained for a data file, but not used to control the current processing order of the
file. For example, a secondary index could be maintained for customer name, while the primary index is
set up for customer account number. See *primary index*.

secondary storage

External storage, such as disk and tape.

second-generation computer

A computer made of discrete electronic components. In the early 1960s, the IBM 1401 and
Honeywell 400 were examples.

second source

An alternative supplier of an identical or compatible product. A second source manufacturer is one
that holds a license to produce a copy of the original product from another manufacturer.

secret key cryptography

Using the same secret key to encrypt and decrypt messages. The problem with this method is
transmitting the secret key to a legitimate person that needs it. See *cryptography*.

sector

The smallest unit of storage read or written on a disk. See *magnetic disk*.

sector interleave

Sector numbering on a hard disk. A one to one interleave (1:1) is sequential: 0,1,2,3, etc. A 2:1 interleave staggers sectors every other one: 0,4,1,5,2,6,3,7.

In 1:1, after data in sector 1 is read, the disk controller must be fast enough to read sector 2, otherwise the beginning of sector 2 will pass the read/write head and must rotate around to come under the head again. The best interleave is based on the speed of the particular disk drive. Interleaves are created with the low-level format.

sector map

See *sector interleave*.

sector sparing

Maintaining a spare sector per track to be used if another sector becomes defective.

secure transaction

A transaction that has been encrypted for online transmission. See *secure Web server*.

secure Web server

A server on the World Wide Web that supports one or more of the major security protocols such as SSL, SHTTP and PCT. See *security protocol*.

security

The protection of data against unauthorized access. Programs and data can be secured by issuing identification numbers and passwords to authorized users of a computer. However, systems programmers, or other technically competent individuals, will ultimately have access to these codes.

Passwords can be checked by the operating system to prevent users from logging onto the system in the first place, or they can be checked in software, such as DBMSs, where each user can be assigned an individual view (subschema) of the database. Any application program running in the computer can also be designed to check for passwords.

Data transmitted over communications networks can be secured by encryption to prevent eavesdropping.

Although precautions can be taken to detect an unauthorized user, it is extremely difficult to determine if a valid user is performing unauthorized tasks. Effective security measures are a balance of technology and personnel management. See *NCSC*.

security kernel

The part of the operating system that grants access to users of the computer system.

security levels

See *NCSC*.

security protocol

A communications protocol that encrypts and decrypts a message for online transmission. Security protocols generally also provide authentication. SSL is widely used, and IPSec is expected to become popular.

sed

(Stream EDitor) A UNIX editing command that makes changes a line at a time and is used to edit large files that exceed buffer limitations of other editors.

seed

The starting value used by a random number generation routine to create random numbers.

seek

(1) To move the access arm to the requested track on a disk.
(2) An assembly language instruction that activates a seek operation on disk.
(3) A high-level programming language command used to select a record by key field.

seek time

The time it takes to move the read/write head to a particular track on a disk.

segment

(1) Any partition, reserved area, partial component or piece of a larger structure. See *overlay*.

(2) One of the bars that make up a single character in an LED or LCD display.

(3) For DOS segment addressing, see *paragraph*.

segmented address space

Memory addressing in which each byte is referenced by a segment, or base, number and an offset that is added to it. A PC running in 16-bit mode (Real Mode) uses a segmented address space. Memory is broken up into 64KB segments, and a segment register always points to the base of the segment that is currently being addressed. The PC's 32-bit mode is considered a flat address space, but it too uses segments. However, since one 32-bit segment addresses 4GB, one segment covers all of memory.

Sel

(SELect) A toggle switch on a printer that takes the printer alternately between online and offline.

selection sort

A search for specific data starting at the beginning of a file or list. It copies each matching item to a new file so that the selected items are in the same sequence as the original data.

selective calling

In communications, the ability of the transmitting station to indicate which station in the network is to receive the message.

selector channel

A high-speed computer channel that connects a peripheral device to the computer's memory.

self-booting

Refers to automatically loading the operating system upon startup.

self-clocking

Recording of digital data on a magnetic medium such that the clock pulses are intrinsically part of the recorded signal. A separate timer clock is not required. Phase encoding is a commonly-used self-clocking recording technique.

self-documenting code

Programming statements that can be easily understood by the author or another programmer. COBOL provides more self-documenting code than does C, for example.

self-extracting file

One or more compressed files that have been converted into an executable program which decompresses its contents when run.

semantic error

In programming, writing a valid programming structure with invalid logic.

semantic gap

The difference between a data or language structure and the real world. For example, in order processing, a company can be both customer and supplier. Since there is no way to model this in a hierarchical database, the semantic gap is said to be large. A network database could handle this condition, resulting in a smaller semantic gap.

semantics

The study of the meaning of words. Contrast with *syntax*, which governs the structure of a language.

semaphore

(1) A hardware or software flag used to indicate the status of some activity.

(2) A shared space for interprocess communications (IPC) controlled by "wake up" and "sleep"

commands. The source process fills a queue and goes to sleep until the destination process uses the data and tells the source process to wake up.

semiconductor

A solid state substance that can be electrically altered. Certain elements in nature, such as silicon, perform like semiconductors when chemically combined with other elements. A semiconductor is halfway between a conductor and an insulator. When charged with electricity or light, semiconductors change their state from nonconductive to conductive or vice versa.

The most significant semiconductor is the transistor, which is simply an on/off switch.

semiconductor device

An elementary component, such as a transistor, or a larger unit of electronic equipment comprised of chips.

sendmail

An SMTP-based mail transport program for UNIX developed at the University of California at Berkeley by Eric Allman in 1981. Sendmail is the MTA (message transfer agent) which stores and forwards the mail and is the most widely used MTA on the Internet. See *messaging system*.

sensor

A device that measures or detects a real world condition, such as motion, heat or light and converts the condition into an analog or digital representation. An optical sensor detects the intensity or brightness of light, or the intensity of red, green and blue for color systems.

sequence check

Testing a list of items or file of records for correct ascending or descending sequence based on the item or key fields in the records.

sequential

One after the other in some consecutive order such as by name or number.

sequential access method

Organizing data in a prescribed ascending or descending sequence. Searching sequential data requires reading and comparing each record, starting from the top or bottom of file.

serial

One after the other.

serial bus

A type of bus that transmits data serially. Ethernet is an example of a serial bus on a network. Serial buses are also expected to become popular for attaching multiple peripherals to computers.

Although both use serial transmission, a serial bus differs from a serial port. The serial port connects the computer to one peripheral device. A serial bus allows for the connection of multiple devices.

serial interface

A data channel that transfers digital data in a serial fashion: one bit after the other. Telephone lines use serial transmission for digital data, thus modems are connected to the computer via a serial port. So are mice and scanners. Serial interfaces have multiple lines, but only one is used for data.

For the difference between the serial and parallel ports, see *serial port*. Contrast with *parallel interface*. See *RS-232*

serialize

To convert a parallel signal made up of one or more bytes into a serial signal that transmits one bit after the other.

serial mouse

See *bus mouse*.

serial number

A unique number assigned by the vendor to each unit of hardware or software. See *signature*.

serial port

A socket on a computer used to connect a modem, mouse, scanner or other serial interface device to the computer. The Macintosh uses the serial port to attach a printer, whereas the PC uses the parallel port. Transferring files between two personal computers can be accomplished by cabling the serial ports of both machines together and using a file transfer program.

serial printer

(1) A printer that uses a serial port for connection to the computer.

(2) A printer that prints one character at a time, such as a dot matrix printer.

serial transmission

Transmitting data one bit at a time. Contrast with *parallel transmission*.

serif

Short horizontal lines added to the tops and bottoms of traditional typefaces, such as Times Roman. Contrast with *sans-serif*.

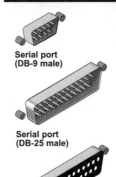

Serial & Parallel Ports on a PC

Serial port (DB-9 male)

Serial port (DB-25 male)

Parallel port (DB-25 female)

A PC comes with one or two serial ports (COM1, COM2) and one parallel port (LPT1).

On the back of the PC, the serial ports are either two male DB-9 connectors or one DB-9 and one DB-25. The parallel port is a DB-25 female connector.

serpentine recording

Tape recording format of parallel tracks in which the data "snakes" back and forth from track to track.

server

A computer in a network shared by multiple users. The term may refer to both the hardware and software or just the software that performs the service. See *file server, database server, application server, mail server, fax server, remote access server* and *Web server*.

server application

(1) An application designed to run in a server. See *client/server architecture*.

(2) Any program that is run in the server, whether designed as a client/server application or not.

(3) See *OLE*.

server farm

A group of network servers that are housed in one location. They might all run the same operating system and applications and use load balancing to distribute the workload between them. See *clustering*.

server-side include

An HTML command used to obtain changing data from the Web server. For example, it could obtain the latest sizes and dates of locally-stored files and insert that information into the page that describes them for the user to download.

server-side script

A small program run on the server that automates or controls certain functions or links one program to another. On the Web, a CGI script is an example of a server-side script.

service

Functionality derived from a particular software program. For example, network services may refer to programs that transmit data or provide conversion of data in a network. Database services provides for the storage and retrieval of data in a database.

service bureau

An organization that provides data processing and timesharing services. It may offer a variety of software packages, batch processing services (data entry, COLD, COM, etc.) as well as custom programming.

Customers pay for storage of data on the system and processing time used. Connection is made to a service bureau through dial-up terminals, private lines, or other networks, such as Telenet or Tymnet.

Service bureaus also exist that support desktop publishing and presentations and provide imagesetting, color proofing, slide creation and other related services on an hourly or per item basis.

service engineer

A technician that maintains and repairs computers.

servlet

A Java application that runs in a Web server or application server and provides server-side processing, typically to access a database or perform e-commerce processing. It is a Java-based replacement for CGI scripts, Active Server Pages (ASPs) and proprietary plug-ins written in C and C++ for specific Web servers (ISAPI, NSAPI).

servo

An electromechanical device that uses feedback to provide precise starts and stops for such functions as the motors on a tape drive or the moving of an access arm on a disk.

session

(1) In communications, the active connection between a user and a computer or between two computers.

(2) Using an application program (period between starting up and quitting).

SET

(Secure Electronic Transaction) A standard protocol from MasterCard and Visa for securing online credit card payments via the Internet.

set theory

The branch of mathematics or logic that is concerned with sets of objects and rules for their manipulation. UNION, INTERSECT and COMPLEMENT are its three primary operations and they are used in relational databases as follows.

Given a file of Americans and a file of Barbers, UNION would create a file of all Americans and Barbers. INTERSECT would create a file of American Barbers, and COMPLEMENT would create a file of Barbers who are not Americans, or of Americans who are not Barbers. See *fuzzy logic*.

set-top box

The cable TV box that "sits on top" of the TV set. A variety of new set-top boxes are emerging for Internet TV and other interactive services.

setup program

Software that configures a system for a particular environment. It is used to install a new application and modify it when the hardware changes. When used with expansion boards, it may change the hardware by altering on-board memory chips (flash memory, EEPROMs, etc.). See *install program*.

setup string

A group of commands that initialize a device, such as a printer. See *escape character*.

seven-segment display

A common display found on digital watches and readouts that looks like a series of 8s. Each digit or letter is formed by selective illumination of up to seven separately addressable bars.

sex changer

See *gender changer*.

SGI

(Silicon Graphics, Inc., Mountain View, CA, www.sgi.com) A manufacturer of graphics workstations and servers founded in 1982 by Jim Clark. SGI shipped its first graphics terminal in 1983 and first workstation in 1984. Computer models include the Indy desktop line, Indigo workstations, CHALLENGE servers and Onyx supercomputers, all running under the IRIX UNIX-based operating system.

The hardware is powered by MIPS 64-bit CPUs (MIPS Technologies, Inc., was acquired by SGI in 1992). In 1996, SGI acquired Cray Research, Inc., and turned it into a wholly-owned subsidiary of the company.

SGML

(Standard Generalized Markup Language) An ISO standard for defining the format in a text document. An SGML document uses a separate Document Type Definition (DTD) file that defines the format codes, or tags, embedded within it. Since SGML describes its own formatting, it is known as a meta-language. SGML is a very comprehensive language that includes hypertext links. The HTML format used on the Web is an SGML document that uses a fixed set of tags. See *HTML* and *XML*.

SGRAM

(Synchronous Graphics **RAM**) A type of dynamic RAM chip that is similar to the SDRAM technology, but includes enhanced graphics features for use with display adapters.

sh

(SHell) A UNIX command that invokes a different shell. It can be used like a batch file to execute a series of commands saved as a shell.

shadow batch

A data collection system that simulates a transaction processing environment. Instead of updating master files (customers, inventory, etc.) when orders or shipments are initiated, the transactions are stored in the computer. When a user makes a query, the master record from the previous update cycle is retrieved; but before it's displayed, it's updated in memory with any transactions that may affect it. The up-to-date master record is then displayed for the user. At the end of the day or period, the transactions are then actually batch processed against the master file.

shadow mask

A thin screen full of holes that adheres to the back of a color CRT's viewing glass. The electron beam is aimed through the holes onto the phosphor dots.

shadow RAM

In a PC, a copy of the operating system's BIOS routines in RAM to improve performance. RAM chips are faster than ROM chips.

shared logic

Using a single computer to provide processing for two or more terminals. Contrast with *shared resource*.

shared media LAN

A local area network that shares a common path (line, cable, etc.) between all nodes. The bandwidth of the line is the total transmission capacity of all transmitting stations at any given time. Contrast with a LAN that uses a *switching hub*, in which any two stations have the full bandwidth of the line.

shared resource

Sharing a peripheral device (disk, printer, etc.) among several users. For example, a file server and laser printer in a LAN are shared resources. Contrast with *shared logic*.

shareware

Software distributed on a trial basis through the Internet, online services, BBSs, mail-order vendors and user groups. Shareware is software on the honor system. If you use it regularly, you're required to register and pay for it, for which you will receive technical support and perhaps additional documentation or the next upgrade. Paid licenses are required for commercial distribution.

sheet feeder

A mechanical device that feeds stacks of cut forms (letterheads, legal paper, etc.) into a printer.

shelfware

Products that remain unsold on a dealer's shelf or unused by the customer.

shell

An outer layer of a program that provides the user interface, or way of commanding the computer. Shells are typically add-on programs created for command-driven operating systems, such as UNIX and DOS. It provides a menu-driven or graphical icon-oriented interface to the system in order to make it easier to use.

shell out

To temporarily exit an application, go back to the operating system, perform a function and then return to the application.

shell script

A file of executable UNIX commands created by a text editor and made executable with the Chmod command. It is the UNIX counterpart to a DOS batch file.

shift register

A high-speed circuit that holds some number of bits for the purpose of shifting them left or right. It is used internally within the processor for multiplication and division, serial/parallel conversion and various timing considerations.

Shlaer-Mellor

An object-oriented analysis and design method developed by Sally Shlaer and Stephen Mellor. The method is applied by partitioning the system into domains. Each domain is analyzed, and the analysis is verified by simulation. A translation method is specified, and the domain models are translated into the object-oriented architecture of the target system.

Shockwave

A browser plug-in that lets output from Macromedia's Director, Authorware and Freehand software be viewed on the Web. Shockwave is a popular plug-in for viewing animated sequences.

short card

In a PC, a plug-in printed circuit board that is half the length of a full-size board. Contrast with *long card*.

short-haul modem

In communications, a device that transmits signals up to about a mile. Similar to a line driver that can transmit up to several miles.

shrink-wrapped software

Refers to store-bought software, implying a standard platform that is widely supported.

SHTTP

(Secure HTTP) A protocol that provides secure transactions over the World Wide Web. It is endorsed by NCSA and a variety of organizations. See *security protocol*.

shunt

To divert, switch or bypass.

SI

See *systems integrator*.

sideband

In communications, the upper or lower half of a wave. Since both sidebands are normally mirror images of each other, one of the halves can be used for a second channel to increase the data-carrying capacity of the line or for diagnostic or control purposes.

Sidekick

The first desk accessory and personal information manager for DOS PCs. It was a very popular popup utility (TSR) from Borland that included a notepad and appointment calendar. Subsequent Windows versions were offered by Starfish Software, Scotts Valley, CA, (www.starfish.com).

SIG

(Special Interest Group) A group of people that meets and shares information about a particular topic of interest. It is usally a part of a larger group or association.

SIGGRAPH

(Special Interest Group on Computer Graphics, www.siggraph.org) The arm of the ACM that specializes in computer graphics. Providing publications, workshops and conferences, it serves technicians and researchers as well as the artist and business community.

sign

A symbol that identifies a positive or negative number. In digital code, it is either a separate character or part of the byte. In ASCII, the sign is kept in a separate character typically transmitted in front of the number it represents (+ and - is 2B and 2D in hex).

signal

Any electrical or light pulse or frequency.

signal converter

A device that changes the electrical or light characteristics of a signal.

signaling in/out of band

In communications, signaling "in band" refers to sending control signals within the same frequency range as the data signal. Signaling "out of band" refers to sending control signals outside of the frequency range of the data signal.

signal processing

See *DSP*.

signal to noise ratio

The ratio of the amplitude (power, volume) of a data signal to the amount of noise (interference) in the line. Usually measured in decibels, it measures the clarity or quality of a transmission channel or electronic device.

signature

A unique number built into hardware or software for identification. See *digital signature*.

significant digits

Those digits in a number that add value to the number. For example, in the number 00006508, 6508 are the significant digits.

silica

Same as *silicon dioxide*.

silica gel

A highly absorbent form of silicon dioxide often wrapped in small bags and packed with equipment to absorb moisture during shipping and storage.

silicon

(Si) The base material used in chips. Next to oxygen, it is the most abundant element in nature and is found in a natural state in rocks and sand. Its atomic structure and abundance make it an ideal semiconductor material. In chip making, it is mined from rocks and put through a chemical process at high temperatures to purify it. To alter its electrical properties, it is mixed (doped) with other chemicals in a molten state.

silicon compiler

Software that translates the electronic design of a chip into the actual layout of the components.

silicon dioxide

(SiO^2) A hard, glassy mineral found in such materials as rock, quartz, sand and opal. In MOS chip fabrication, it is used to create the insulation layer between the metal gates of the top layer and the silicon elements below.

silicon disk

A disk drive that is permanently simulated in memory. Typically used in laptops for weight reduction, it requires constant power from a battery to maintain its contents.

silicon foundry

An organization that makes chips for other companies that have only design, but not manufacturing facilities. It is typically a large chip maker that uses excess manufacturing capacity in this manner.

Silicon Graphics

See *SGI*.

silicon nitride

(Si^3N^4) A silicon compound capable of holding a static electric charge and used as a gate element on some MOS transistors.

silicon on sapphire

See *SOS*.

Silicon Valley

An area south of San Francisco, California that is noted for its huge number of computer companies. Tens of thousands of hardware, software and related firms have their headquarters in Silicon Valley, making it the largest confluence of high tech industries in the world.

SIM

(Society for Information Management, Chicago, IL, www.simnet.org) Founded in 1968 as the Society for MIS, it is a membership organization comprised of corporate and division heads of IT organizations. SIM provides a forum for exchange of technical information and offers educational and research programs, competitions and awards.

SIMD

(Single Instruction stream Multiple Data stream) A computer architecture that performs one operation on multiple sets of data, for example, an array processor. One computer or processor is used for the control logic and the remaining processors are used as slaves, each executing the same instruction. Contrast with *MIMD*.

SIMM

(Single In-line Memory Module) A narrow printed circuit board that holds memory chips. It plugs into a SIMM socket on the motherboard or memory board. The first SIMM format that became popular on personal computers was 3.5" long and used a 30-pin connector. A larger 4.25" format uses 72-pins and contains from one to 64 megabytes of RAM.

PCs use either nine-bit memory (eight bits and a parity bit) or eight-bit memory without parity. Macintoshes use eight-bit memory without parity.

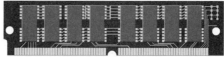

simplex

One way transmission. Contrast with *half-duplex* and *full-duplex*.

SIMSCRIPT

A programming language used for discrete simulations.

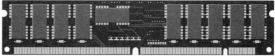

simulation

(1) The mathematical representation of the interaction of real-world objects. See *scientific application*.

(2) The execution of a machine language program designed to run in a foreign computer.

---

sine wave
A uniform wave that is generated by a single frequency.

single board computer
A printed circuit board that contains a complete computer, including processor, memory, I/O and clock.

single density disk
The first-generation floppy disk.

single-ended configuration
Electrical signal paths that use a common ground, which are more susceptible to noise than *differential configuration*.

single-mode fiber
An optical fiber with a core diameter of less than 10 microns, used for high-speed transmission and long distances. It provides greater bandwidth than multimode fiber, but its smaller core makes it more difficult to couple the light source. Contrast with *multimode fiber*.

single precision
The use of one computer word to hold a numeric value for calculation. Contrast with *double precision*.

single session
See *Photo CD*.

single sided disk
A floppy disk that stores data on only one side.

single-system image
An operational view of multiple networks, distributed databases or multiple computer systems as if they were one system.

single threading
Processing one transaction to completion before starting the next.

Single UNIX Specification
A common UNIX programming interface governed by X/Open. Formerly Spec 1170, it is the latest attempt to unify UNIX into one set of common programming calls. Products branded by X/Open with the UNIX 95 and UNIX 98 logos conform to Versions 1 and 2 of the specification respectively.

sink
A device or place that accepts something. See *heat sink* and *data sink*.

SIP
(Single In-line Package) A type of chip module that is similar to a SIMM, but uses pins rather than edge connectors. SIPs are sometimes SIPPs (Single In-Line Pin Package).

SIR
(Serial InfraRed) An infrared (IR) technology from HP that allows wireless data transmission between two devices up to one meter apart. Both devices must be lined up to each other. Future enhancements will allow greater distances and wider angles. SIR ports are very popular on laptops.

SISD
(Single Instruction stream Single Data stream) The architecture of a serial computer. Contrast with *SIMD* and *MIMD*.

site license
A license to use software within a facility. It provides authorization to make copies and distribute them within a specific jurisdiction.

skew
(1) The misalignment of a document or punched card in the feed tray or hopper that prohibits it from

being scanned or read properly.

(2) In facsimile, the difference in rectangularity between the received and transmitted page.

(3) In communications, a change of timing or phases in a transmission signal.

sky wave

A radio signal transmitted into the sky and reflected back down to earth from the ionosphere.

slave

A computer or peripheral device controlled by another computer. For example, a terminal or printer in a remote location that only receives data is a slave. When two personal computers are hooked up via their serial or parallel ports for file exchange, the file transfer program may make one computer the master and the other the slave.

SLDRAM

An enhanced version of the SDRAM memory technology that uses a multiplexed bus to transfer data to and from the chips rather than fixed pin settings.

sleep

(1) In programming, an inactive state due to an endless loop or programmed delay. A sleep statement in a programming language creates a delay for some specified amount of time.

(2) The inactive status of a terminal, device or program that is awakened by sending a code to it.

slew rate

(1) How fast paper moves through a printer (ips).

(2) The speed of changing voltage.

slice and dice

Refers to rearranging data so that it can be viewed from different perspectives. The term is typically used with OLAP databases that present information to the user in the form of multidimensional cubes similar to a 3-D spreadsheet. See *OLAP*.

sliding window

(1) A communications protocol that transmits multiple packets before acknowledgement. Both ends keep track of packets sent and acknowledged (left of window), those which have been sent and not acknowledged (in window) and those not yet sent (right of window).

(2) A view of memory that can be instantly shifted to another location.

SLIP

(Serial Line IP) A data link protocol for dial-up access to TCP/IP networks. It is commonly used to gain access to the Internet as well as to provide dial-up access between two LANs. SLIP transmits IP packets over any serial link (dial up or private lines). See *PPP*.

slipstream

To fix a bug or add enhancements to software without identifying such inclusions by creating a new version number.

slot

(1) A receptacle for additional printed circuit boards.

(2) A receptacle for inserting and removing a disk or tape cartridge.

(3) In communications, a narrow band of frequencies. See *time slot*.

(4) May refer to reserved space for temporary or permanent storage of instructions, data or codes.

Slot 1

A receptacle on the motherboard that holds an Intel SEC (Single Edge Contact) cartridge. The cartridge contains the CPU and cache, which plugs into the slot with a 242-pin edge connector. The Pentium II uses the SEC and Slot 1.

slot mask

A type of shadow mask used in CRTs. It refers to two different methods, which are (1) the vertical slots used in the aperture grille in Sony's Trinitron monitors, and (2) the elliptical slots used in NECT's CromaClear monitors. Both version use vertical phosphor stripes instead of round dots.

slot pitch

The distance between like-colored phosphor stripes in a CRT that uses a slot mask. This is slightly closer than the dot pitch in traditional shadow mask CRTs, which measures the diagonal distance between dots. See *slot mask*.

slug

A metal bar containing the carved image of a letter or digit that is used in a printing mechanism.

SMA

(1) (Software Maintenance Association) A membership organization from 1985 to 1996. With chapters worldwide, it was dedicated to advancements in software maintenance.

(2) (Systems Management Architecture) An IBM network management repository.

(3) (Spectrum Manufacturers Association) A DBMS standard for application compatibility.

SMA connector

A fiber-optic cable connector that uses a plug which is screwed into a threaded socket. It was the first connector for optical fibers to be standardized. See *ST connector* and *SC connector*.

Smalltalk

An operating system and object-oriented programming language that was developed at Xerox Corporation's Palo Alto Research Center. As an integrated environment, it eliminates the distinction between programming language and operating system. It also allows the programmer to customize the user interface and behavior of the system.

Smalltalk was the first object-oriented programming language and was used on Xerox's Alto computer, which was designed for it. It was originally used to create prototypes of simpler programming languages and the graphical interfaces that are so popular today.

smart cable

A cable with a built-in microprocessor used to connect two devices. It analyzes incoming signals and converts them from one protocol to another.

smart card

A credit card with a built-in microprocessor and memory used for identification or financial transactions. When inserted into a reader, it transfers data to and from a central computer. It is more secure than a magnetic stripe card and can be programmed to self-destruct if the wrong password is entered too many times. As a financial transaction card, it can store transactions and maintain a bank balance.

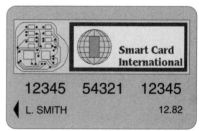

Smartdrive

A disk cache program that comes with DOS and Windows. In DOS 4.0 and Windows 3.0, the name of the driver file is SMARTDRV.SYS. Starting with DOS 5 and Windows 3.1, the name of the driver is SMARTDRV.EXE.

smart hub

See *intelligent hub*.

smart phone

A telephone with advanced information access features such as e-mail, text messaging, pager and Web access.

SmartSuite

A suite of applications for Windows and OS/2 from Lotus that includes the 1-2-3 spreadsheet, Ami Pro word processor, Freelance Graphics, Approach database, Organizer PIM and Adobe Type Manager. Also included is a common toolbar for launching the applications and selecting predefined macros that provide tighter integration between the applications.

smart terminal

A video terminal with built-in display characteristics (blinking, reverse video, underlines, etc.). It may also contain a communications protocol. The term is often used synonymously with intelligent terminal. See *intelligent terminal* and *dumb terminal*.

SMB

(Server Message Block) A file sharing protocol from Microsoft that is commonly used to retrieve files in DOS and Windows networks. SMB requests are carried within the NetBIOS network control block (NCB) and are also used within the server for internal operations. SMB provides services at the application layer (layer 7 of the OSI model).

SMD

(1) (Storage Module Device) A high-performance hard disk interface used with minis and mainframes that transfers data in the 1-4 MBytes/sec range (SMD-E provides highest rate). See *hard disk*.

(2) (Surface Mount Device) A surface mounted chip.

SMDS

(Switched Multimegabit Data Service) A high-speed, switched data communications service offered by the local telephone companies for interconnecting LANs in different locations. It was introduced in 1992 and became generally available nationwide by 1995.

SMF

(1) (Standard Messaging Format) An electronic mail format for Novell's MHS messaging system. The application puts the data into this format in order to send an e-mail message.

(2) (Standard MIDI file) The format of a MIDI file.

(3) See *single-mode fiber*.

SMI

(1) (Simple Mail Interface) A subset of functions within the VIM messaging protocol used by applications to send e-mail and attachments. Future versions of VIM will use the CMC API rather than SMI.

(2) (Structure of Management Information) A definition for creating MIBs in the SNMP protocol.

(3) (System Management Interrupt) A hardware interrupt in Intel SL Enhanced 486 and Pentium CPUs used for power management. This interrupt is also used for virus checking.

SMM

(System Management Mode) An energy conservation mode built into Intel SL Enhanced 486 and Pentium CPUs. During inactive periods, SMM initiates a sleep mode that turns off peripherals or the entire system.

smoke test

A test of new or repaired equipment by turning it on. If there's smoke, it doesn't work!

smoothed data

Statistical data that has been averaged or otherwise manipulated so that the curves on its graph are smooth and free of irregularities.

smoothing circuit

An electronic filtering circuit in a DC power supply that removes the ripples from AC power.

SMP

(Symmetric MultiProcessing) A multiprocessing architecture in which multiple CPUs, residing in one cabinet, share the same memory. SMP systems provide scalability. As business increases, additional CPUs can be added to absorb the higher transaction volume. System and application software that supports parallel operations (multithreading) takes most advantage of SMP. However, adding CPUs to an SMP system can increase performance for all tasks as there are more CPUs available, and each application can be run by a different processor. Contrast with *MPP*.

SMP

CPUs

RAM chips
(SIMMs)

OS

App

App

App

SMPTE

(Society for Motion Picture and TV Engineers, White Plains, NY, www.smpte.org) A professional society for motion picture and TV engineers with more than 9,000 members worldwide. It prepares standards and documentation for TV production. SMPTE time code records hours, minutes, seconds and frames on audio or videotape for synchronization purposes.

SMS

(1) (Storage Management System) Software used to routinely back up and archive files. See *HSM*.

(2) (Storage Management Services) Software from Novell that allows data to be stored and retrieved on NetWare servers independent of the file system the data is maintained in (DOS, OS/2, Mac, etc.). It is used to back up data from heterogeneous clients on the network.

(3) (Systems Management Server) Systems management software from Microsoft that runs on Windows NT Server. It requires a Microsoft SQL Server database and is used to distribute software, analyze network usage and perform various administration tasks.

SMT

(1) See *surface mount*.

(2) (Station ManagemenT) An FDDI network management protocol that provides direct management. Only one node requires the software.

SMTP

(Simple Mail Transfer Protocol) The standard e-mail protocol on the Internet. It is a TCP/IP protocol that defines the message format and the message transfer agent (MTA), which stores and forwards the mail. SMTP was originally designed for only ASCII text, but MIME and other encoding methods enable program and multimedia files to be attached to e-mail messages.

SMTP servers route SMTP messages throughout the Internet to a mail server, such as POP or IMAP, which provides a message store for incoming mail. See *POP, IMAP* and *messaging system*. See also *SNMP*.

SNA

(Systems Network Architecture) IBM's mainframe network standards introduced in 1974. Originally a centralized architecture with a host computer controlling many terminals, enhancements, such as APPN and APPC (LU 6.2), have adapted SNA to today's peer-to-peer communications and distributed computing environment.

SNADS

(SNA Distribution Services) An IBM messaging protocol used by IBM office automation products such as DISOSS and AS/400 Office. Various messaging gateways and messaging switches support SNADS.

snail mail

Mail sent via the postal system.

snapshot

The saved current state of memory including the contents of all memory bytes, hardware registers and status indicators. It is periodically taken in order to restore the system in the event of failure.

snapshot dump

A memory dump of selected portions of memory.

snapshot program
A trace program that provides selected dumps of memory when specific instructions are executed or when certain conditions are met.

snap to
A feature in a drawing program that moves a text or graphic element to the closest grid line.

snd
(SouND resource) A Macintosh resource fork that contains sound information, including compression ratios if used and sampling rate.

SND file
(SouND file) One of several digital audio file formats that were created by Apple, NeXT and others. It typically refers to an uncompressed sound file used on the Macintosh.

sneakernet
Carrying floppy disks from one machine to another to exchange information when you don't have a network.

sniffer
Software and/or hardware that analyzes traffic and detects bottlenecks and problems in a network.

SNMP
(Simple Network Management Protocol) A widely-used network monitoring and control protocol. Data about the network device (hub, router, etc.) is placed into a Management Information Base (MIB) format and passed by hardware and/or software agents to the workstation console.

snow
The flickering snow-like spots on a video screen caused by display electronics that are too slow to respond to changing data.

SNR
See *signal to noise ratio*.

socket
(1) A receptacle which receives a plug.

(2) See *UNIX socket*.

Socket 7, Socket 8
The receptacles on the motherboard that hold Pentium and Pentium Pro chips respectively. Socket 7 is also used for Pentium chip clones, such as the 5x86, 6x86, K5 and ~K6. See *Slot 1*.

soft
Flexible and changeable. Software can be reprogrammed for different results. The computer's soft nature is its greatest virtue; however, the reason it takes so long to get new systems developed has little to do with the concept. It is based on how systems are developed (file systems vs database management), the programming languages used (assembly vs high-level), combined with the skill level of the technical staff, compounded by the organization's bureaucracy.

Softbank
(Softbank Corporation, Tokyo, www.softbank.com) A computer conglomerate founded in 1981 by Masayoshi Son. The company has backed Yahoo! and more than 50 hardware, software, communications and Internet companies both in the U.S. and Japan.

soft boot
Same as *warm boot*.

soft copy
Refers to data displayed on a video screen. Contrast with *hard copy*.

soft error

A recoverable error, such as a garbled message that can be retransmitted. Contrast with *hard error*.

soft font

A set of characters for a particular typeface that is stored on the computer's hard disk, or in some cases the printer's hard disk, and downloaded to the printer before printing. Contrast with *internal font* and *font cartridge*.

soft hyphen

A hyphen that prints if it winds up at the end of the line, but does not print otherwise. Contrast with *hard hyphen*. See *discretionary hyphen*.

soft key

A keyboard key that is simulated by an icon on screen.

soft patch

A quick fix to machine language currently in memory that only lasts for the current session.

SoftPC

See *RealPC*.

soft return

A code inserted by the software into a text document to mark the end of the line. When the document is printed, the soft return is converted into the end-of-line code required by the printer. Soft returns are determined by the right margin and change when the margins are changed. Contrast with *hard return*.

soft sectored

A common method of identifying sectors on a disk by initially recording sector information on every track with a format program. Contrast with *hard sectored*.

software

Instructions for the computer. A series of instructions that performs a particular task is called a "program." The two major categories are "system software" and "application software." System software is made up of control programs, including the operating system, communications software and database manager.

Application software is any program that processes data for the user (inventory, payroll, spreadsheet, word processor, etc.). A common misconception is that software is also data. It is not. Software tells the hardware how to process the data. Software is "run." Data is "processed."

software architecture

The design of application or system software that incorporates protocols and interfaces for interacting with other programs and for future flexibility and expandability. A self-contained, stand-alone program would have program logic, but not a software architecture.

software bug

A problem that causes a program to abend (crash) or produce invalid output. Problems that cause a program to abend are invalid data, such as trying to divide by zero, or invalid instructions, which are caused by bad logic that misdirects the computer to the wrong place in the program.

A program with erroneous logic may produce bad output without crashing, which is the reason extensive testing is required for new programs. For example, if the program is supposed to add an amount, but instead, it subtracts it, bad output results. As long as the program performs valid machine instructions on data it knows how to deal with, the computer will run.

software codec

A compression/decompression routine that is implemented in software only without requiring specialized DSP hardware. See *codec*.

software engineering

The design, development and documentation of software. See *CASE, systems analysis & design, programming, object-oriented programming, software metrics* and *Systemantics*.

software failure

The inability of a program to continue processing due to erroneous logic. Same as *crash, bomb* and *abend.*

software house

An organization that develops customized software for a customer. Contrast with *software publisher,* which develops and markets software packages.

software interface

Same as *API.*

software interrupt

An interrupt caused by an instruction in the program. See *interrupt.*

software metrics

Software measurements. Using numerical ratings to measure the complexity and reliability of source code, the length and quality of the development process and the performance of the application when completed.

software package

An application program developed for sale to the general public.

software program

A computer program (computer application). All computer programs are software. Usage of the two words together is redundant, but common.

software programmer

Same as *systems programmer.*

software protection

See *copy protection.*

software publisher

An organization that develops and markets software. It does market research, production and distribution of software. It may develop its own software, contract for outside development or obtain software that has already been written.

software stack

A stack that is implemented in memory. See *stack.*

software tool

A program used to develop other software. Any program or utility that helps a programmer design, code, compile or debug sofware can be called a tool.

SoftWindows

A Windows emulator for the Macintosh from FWB Software, San Francisco, CA, (www.fwb.com). It was originally developed by Insignia Solutions. SoftWindows is used to run DOS and Windows applications on the Mac.

SOG

(Small Outline Gullwing) Same as *SOIC.*

SOHO

(Small Office/Home Office) Refers to the small business or business-at-home user. This market segment demands as much or more than the large corporation. The small business entrepreneur generally wants the latest, greatest and fastest equipment, and this market has always benefited from high technology, allowing it to compete on a level playing ground with the bigger companies.

SOIC

(Small Outline IC) A small-dimension, surface mount DIP that uses gullwing-shaped pins extending outward.

SOJ
(Small Outline J lead) A surface mount DIP that uses J-shaped pins extending inward.

Solaris
A multitasking, multiprocessing operating system and distributed computing environment for Sun's SPARC computers from Sun. It provides an enterprise-wide UNIX environment that can manage up to 40,000 nodes from one central station. Solaris is known for its robustness and scalability, which is expected in UNIX-based SMP systems. An x86 version of Solaris is available that can also run applications written for Sun's Interactive UNIX.

solder mask
An insulating pattern applied to a printed circuit board that exposes only the areas to be soldered.

solenoid
A magnetic switch that closes a circuit, often used as a relay.

solid ink printer
A laser-class printer that uses solid wax inks that are melted into a liquid before being used. Instead of jetting the ink onto the paper directly as ink jet printers do, solid ink printers jet the ink onto a drum. A better registration of color is obtained by transferring the ink to the drum first and then to the printer, because the drum can be more tightly controlled than moving paper.

solid logic
Same as *solid state*.

solid modeling
A mathematical technique for representing solid objects. It is the least abstract form of CAD. Unlike wireframe and surface modeling, solid modeling systems ensure that all surfaces meet properly and that the object is geometrically correct. A solid model can also be sectioned (cut open) to reveal its internal features. Solids allow interference checking, which tests to see if two or more objects occupy the same space.

solid state
An electronic component or circuit made of solid materials, such as transistors, chips and bubble memory. There is no mechanical action in a solid state device, although an unbelievable amount of electromagnetic action takes place within.

For data storage, solid state devices are much faster and more reliable than mechanical disks and tapes, but are more expensive. Although solid state costs continually drop, disks, tapes and optical disks also continue to improve their cost/performance ratio.

The first solid state device was the "cat's whisker" of the 1930s. A whisker-like wire was moved around on a solid crystal in order to detect a radio signal.

solid state disk
A disk drive made of memory chips used for high-speed data access or in hostile environments. Solid state disks are used in battery-powered, hand-held devices as well as in desktop units with hundreds of megabytes of storage that contain their own UPS systems.

solid state memory
Any transistorized, semiconductor or thin film memory that contains no mechanical parts.

solid state relay
A relay that contains no mechanical parts. All switching mechanisms are semiconductor or thin film components.

solver
Mathematical mechanisms that allow spreadsheets to perform goal seeking.

SOM
(1) (System Object Model) An object architecture from IBM that provides a full implementation of the CORBA standard. SOM is language independent and is supported by a variety of large compiler and

application development vendors. Distributed SOM (DSOM) allows objects to be run across the network.

(2) (Self Organizing Map) A two-dimensional map that shows relationships in a neural network.

SONET

(Synchronous Optical NETwork) A fiber optic transmission system for high-speed digital traffic. Employed by telephone companies and common carriers, SONET speeds range from 51 megabits to multiple gigabits per second. SONET is an intelligent system that provides advanced network management, a standard optical interface and more flexibility than the T1 and T3 lines now in common use. Although it is expected to eventually obsolete T-carrier lines, SONET can be used to carry existing T-carrier traffic in the meantime.

```
SONET CIRCUITS

Service              Speed (Mbps)
STS-1     OC-1        51.84 (28 DS1s or 1 DS3)
STS-3     OC-3       155.52 (3 STS-1s)
STS-3c    OC-3c      155.52 (concatenated)
STS-12    OC-12      622.08 (12 STS-1s, 4 STS-3s)
STS-12c   OC-12c     622.08 (12 STS-1s, 4 STS-3c's)
STS-48    OC-48     2488.32 (48 STS-1s, 16 STS-3s)
STS-192   OC-192    9953.28 (192 STS-1s, 64 STS-3s)
```

sort

To reorder data into a new sequence. The operating system can typically sort file names and text lists.

In word processors, sorting allows for all the text in the document or a marked block of text to be resequenced into either an ascending (normal) or descending sequence.

In database programs, sorting resequences all the records in the file by one or more fields and often generates an entirely new copy of the file.

sort algorithm

A formula used to reorder data into a new sequence. Like all complicated problems, there are many solutions that can achieve the same results. One sort algorithm can resequence data faster than another. In the early 1960s, when tape was "the" storage medium, the sale of a computer system may have hinged on the sort algorithm, since without direct access capability, every transaction had to be sorted into the sequence of the master file.

sorter

(1) A sort program.

(2) A person who manually puts data into a specific sequence.

(3) An early tabulating machine that routed punched cards into separate stackers based on the content of a card column. The complete operation required passing the cards through the machine once for each column sorted.

sort field

Same as *sort key*.

sort key

A field or fields in a record that dictate the sequence of the file. For example, the sort keys STATE and NAME arrange the file alphabetically by name within state. STATE is the major sort key, and NAME is the minor key.

SOS

(1) (Systems On Silicon) A complete system on a single chip. Increasingly, memory, logic and signal processing components are being combined in one integrated circuit.

(2) (Server Operating System) An operating system that resides on the server.

(3) (Silicon On Sapphire) An MOS chip-fabrication method that places a thin layer of silicon over a sapphire substrate (base).

sound bandwidth

A range of sound frequencies. The human ear can perceive approximately from 20 to 20,000Hz, but human voice is confined to within 3,000Hz.

Sound Blaster

A family of sound cards from Creative Labs, Inc., Milpitas, CA, (www.creativelabs.com). The Sound Blaster protocol has become a de facto audio standard for PCs.

sound board

Same as *sound card*.

sound card

Also called "sound board" and "audio adapter," it is a personal computer expansion board that records and plays back sound, providing outputs directly to speakers or an external amplifier. Many sound cards also include MIDI capability.

source

The source of current in a MOS transistor. Same as *emitter* in a bipolar transistor.

source code

A program in its original form as written by the programmer. It is not executable by the computer directly. It must be converted into machine language by compilers, assemblers and interpreters.

In some cases, source code can be converted into another dialect or a different language by a conversion program.

source code compatible

Able to run a program on a different platform by recompiling its source code into that machine code.

source data

The original data that is handwritten or printed on a source document or typed into the computer system from a keyboard or terminal.

source data acquisition, source data capture

Capturing data electronically when a transaction occurs; for example, at the time of sale.

source directory

The directory from which data is obtained.

source disk

The disk from which data is obtained. Contrast with *target disk*.

source document

The paper form onto which data is written. Order forms and employment applications are examples.

source drive

The disk or tape drive from which data is obtained. Contrast with *target drive*.

source language

The language used in a source program.

source program

A program in its original form, as written by the programmer.

source routing

A communications protocol in which stations are aware of bridges in the network and route messages via the bridges. Contrast with *transparent bridging*. See *SRT*.

source statement

An instructional phrase in a programming language (source language).

SPA

(Software Publishers Association, Washington, DC, www.spa.org) A trade organization of the personal

The Computer Glossary

computer software industry that supports legislation for copyright enforcement. It conducts raids on organizations suspected of illegal copying and files lawsuits against violators.

space

In digital electronics, a 0 bit. Contrast with *mark*.

space/time

The following units of measure are used to define storage and transmission capacities. See *binary values*.

```
SPACE - Bits/bytes    Power of 10
Kilo  (K)  Thousand       3
Mega  (M)  Million        6
Giga  (G)  Billion        9
Tera  (T)  Trillion      12
Peta  (P)  Quadrillion   15
Exa   (E)  Quintillion   18
Zetta (Z)  Sextillion    21
Yotta (Y)  Septillion    24
```

```
TIME - Fraction of second    Power of 10
Millisecond (ms)  Thousandth      -3
Microsecond (µs)  Millionth       -6
Nanosecond  (ns)  Billionth       -9
Picosecond  (ps)  Trillionth     -12
Femtosecond (fs)  Quadrillionth  -15
Attosecond  (as)  Quintillionth  -18
Zeposecond  (zs)  Sextillionth   -21
Yoctosecond (ys)  Septillionth   -24
```

```
Storage/channel capacity measured in:
CPU word size            bits
Bus size                 bits
Disk, tape               bytes
Overall memory capacity  bytes
SIMM and DIMM modules    bytes
Individual memory chip   bits
```

```
Transmission speed measured in:
Network line/channel   bits/sec
Disk transfer rate     bytes/sec
Disk access time       ms
Memory access time     ns
Machine cycle          µs, ns
Instruction execution  µs, ns
Transistor switching   ns, ps, fs
```

spaghetti code

Program code written without a coherent structure. The logic moves from routine to routine without returning to a base point, making it hard to follow. It implies excessive use of the GOTO instruction, which directs the computer to branch to another part of the program without a guarantee of returning.

In structured programming, functions are used, which are subroutines that guarantee a return to the instruction following the one that called it.

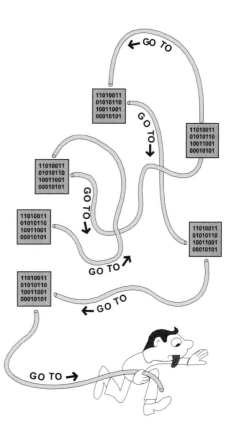

spamdexing

Techniques employed by some Web marketers and site designers in order to fool a search engine's spider and indexing programs. The objective is to ensure that their Web sites always appear at or near the top of the list of search engine results.

spamming

Sending copies of the same message to large numbers of newsgroups or users on the Internet. People spam the Internet to advertise products as well as to broadcast some political or social commentary.

SPARC

(Scalable Performance ARChitecture) A family of 32-bit RISC CPUs developed by Sun. The first chip was introduced on the SPARCstation 1 in 1989. The 64-bit UltraSPARC line was introduced in 1995.

spatial data

Data that is represented as 2-D or 3-D images. A geographic information system (GIS) is one of the primary applications of spatial data (land maps).

spawn

To launch another program from the current program. The child program is spawned from the parent program.

SPEC (SPECfp95, SPECint95, SPECmark)

(Standard Performance Evaluation Corporation, Manassas, VA, www.specbench.org) An organization founded in 1988 to establish standard benchmarks for computers. Its first benchmark was the SPECmark, in which one SPECmark was equivalent in performance to a VAX 11/780. Subsequent SPECint and SPECfp benchmarks measured integer and floating point performance respectively. In 1996, SPEC introduced SPEC CPU95 which includes SPECint95 and SPECfp95, replacing SPECint92 and SPECfp92.

Spec 1170

See *Single UNIX Specification*.

special character

Non-alphabetic or non-numeric character, such as @, #, $, %, &, * and +. special-purpose computer
A computer designed from scratch to perform a specific function. Contrast with *general-purpose computer*.

special-purpose language

A programming language designed to solve a specific problem or class of problems. For example, LISP and Prolog are designed for and used extensively in AI applications. Even more specific are languages such as COGO, for civil engineering problems, and APT for directing machine tools. Contrast with *general-purpose language*.

specification

A definition (layout, blueprint, design) of hardware or software. See *specs* and *functional specification*.

specs

(SPECificationS) The details of the components built into a device. See *specification*.

spec sheet

A detail listing of the components of a system.

spectral color

In computer graphics, the color of a single wavelength of light, starting with violet at the low end and proceeding through indigo, blue, green, yellow and orange and ending with red.

spectral response

The variable output of a light-sensitive device that is based on the color of the light it perceives.

spectrum

A range of electromagnetic frequencies.

speech codec

Also called a "voice codec" or "vocoder," it is a hardware circuit that converts the spoken word into digital code and vice versa. A speech codec is an audio codec specialized for human voice. The term may just refer to the speech compression method, which can be performed in software. See *audio codec*.

speech recognition

Same as *voice recognition*.

speech synthesis

Generating machine voice by arranging phonemes (k, ch, sh, etc.) into words. It is used to turn text input into spoken words for the blind. Speech synthesis performs realtime conversion without a pre-defined vocabulary, but does not create human-sounding speech. Although individual spoken words can be digitized into the computer, digitized voice takes a lot of storage, and resulting phrases still lack inflection.

Type	Frequency range (Hz)	Wavelength range	
Gamma rays	10^{20} - 10^{24}	<10^{-12} m	higher frequencies
X- rays	10^{17} - 10^{20}	1 nm - 1 pm	smaller wavelengths
Ultraviolet	10^{15} - 10^{17}	400 nm - 1 nm	
VISIBLE LIGHT	4 - 7.5 x 10^{14}	750 nm - 400 nm	
Near-infrared	1 x 10^{14} - 4 x 10^{14}	2.5 µm - 750 nm	
Infrared	10^{13} - 10^{14}	25 µm - 2.5 µm	
Microwaves	3 x 10^{11} - 10^{13}	1 mm - 25µm	larger wavelengths
Radio waves (amateur radio, aeronautical, cellular phone, taxis, aircraft, TV, FM, AM)	< 3 x 10^{11}	> 1 mm	lower frequencies

Spectrum

speed buffering

A technique that compensates for speed differences between input and output. Data is accepted into the buffer at high speed and transferred out at low speed, or vice versa.

speed of electricity/light

Electricity and light travel at approximately 186,000 miles per second, which is seven times around the equator per second. This inherent speed of Mother Nature is why computers are so fast. Within the tiny chip, electricity has to flow only a couple of millimeters, and, within an entire computer, only a few feet.

As fast as that is, it's never fast enough. There is resistance in the lines, and even though transistors switch in billionths of a second, CAD, image processing and scientific applications are always exhausting the fastest computers.

spelling checker

A separate program or word processing function that tests for correctly-spelled words. It can test the spelling of a marked block, an entire document or group of documents. Advanced systems check for spelling as the user types and can correct common typos and misspellings on the fly.

Spelling checkers simply compare words to a dictionary of words, and the wrong use of a correctly-spelled word cannot be detected. See *grammar checker*.

spherization

In computer graphics, turning an image into a sphere.

SPI

(Service Provider Interface) The programming interface for developing Windows drivers under WOSA. In order to provide common access to services, the application (query, word processor, e-mail program, etc.) is written to a particular WOSA-supported interface, such as ODBC or MAPI, and the developer of the service software (database manager, document manager, print spooler, etc.) writes to the SPI for that class of service.

SPICE

(Simulation Program with Integrated Circuit Emphasis) A program widely used to simulate the performance of analog electronic systems and mixed mode analog and digital systems.

spike

called a "transient," a spike is a burst of extra voltage in a power line that lasts only a fraction of a second. Contrast with *sag*. See *power surge*.

spindle

A rotating shaft in a disk drive. In a fixed disk, the platters are attached to the spindle. In a removable disk, the spindle remains in the drive.

SPL

(1) (Systems Programming Language) The assembly language for the HP 3000 series. See *assembly language* for an SPL program example.

(2) (Structured Programming Language) See *structured programming*.

spline

In computer graphics, a smooth curve that runs through a series of given points. The term is often used to refer to any curve. See *Bezier curve* and *B-spline*.

split screen

The display of two or more sets of data on screen at the same time. It implies that one set of data can be manipulated independently of the other. Split screens, or windows, are usually created by the operating system or application software, rather than the hardware.

spoofing

(1) In communications, creating fake responses or signals in order to keep a session active and prevent timeouts. For example, a mainframe or mini continuously polls its terminals. If the lines to remote terminals are temporarily suspended because there is no traffic, a local device spoofs the host with "I'm still here" reponses.

(2) Faking the sending address of a transmission in order to gain illegal entry into a secure system.

spooler

See *print spooler* and *spooling*.

spooling

(Simultaneous Peripheral Operations OnLine) The overlapping of low-speed operations with normal processing. It originated with mainframes in order to optimize slow operations such as reading cards and printing. Card input was read onto disk and printer output was stored on disk. In that way, the actual business data processing was done at high speed, since all I/O was on disk.

Today, spooling is used to buffer data for the printer as well as remote batch terminals. See *print spooler*.

spot color

A color that is printed from one printing plate which contains that particular ink. Contrast with *process color*.

spreadsheet

Software that simulates a paper spreadsheet, or worksheet, in which columns of numbers are summed for budgets and plans. It appears on screen as a matrix of rows and columns, the intersections of which are identified as cells. Spreadsheets can have thousands of cells and can be scrolled horizontally and vertically in order to view them.

The heart of the spreadsheet is the formula, which is used to add, subtract, mulitply or divide the contents of any cell or group of cells. The formula automatically recalculates whenever any cell that is referenced is changed.

spreadsheet compiler

Software that translates spreadsheets into stand-alone programs that can be run without the spreadsheet package that created them.

spread spectrum

A variety of radio transmission methods that continuously change frequencies or signal patterns. Direct sequence spread spectrum (DSSS), which is used in CDMA, multiplies the data bits by a very fast pseudo-random bit pattern (PN sequence) that "spreads" the data into a large coded stream that takes the full bandwidth of the channel (see *CDMA*).

Frequency hopping spread spectrum (FHSS) continuously changes the center frequency of a conventional carrier several times per second according to a pseudo-random set of channels, while chirp spread spectrum changes the carrier frequency.

sprite

An independent graphic object controlled by its own bit plane (area of memory). Commonly used in video games, sprites move freely across the screen, passing by, through and colliding with each other with much less programming.

SPS

(Standby Power System) A UPS system that switches to battery backup upon detection of power failure.

SPSS

A statistical package from SPSS, Inc., Chicago, IL, (www.spss.com), that runs on PCs, most mainframes and minis and is used extensively in marketing research. It provides over 50 statistical processes, including regression analysis, correlation and analysis of variance. Originally named Statistical Package for the Social Sciences, it was written by Norman Nie, a professor at Stanford. In 1976, he formed SPSS, Inc.

spt

(Sectors Per Track) The number of sectors in one track.

SPX

(Sequenced Packet EXchange) The NetWare communications protocol used to control the transport of messages across a network. SPX ensures that an entire message arrives intact and uses NetWare's IPX protocol as its delivery mechanism. Application programs use SPX to provide client/server and peer-to-peer interaction between network nodes. SPX provides services at layer 4 of the OSI model.

SQL

(Structured Query Language) Pronounced "SQL" or "see qwill," a language used to interrogate and process data in a relational database. Originally developed by IBM for its mainframes, there have been many implementations created for mini and micro database applications. SQL commands can be used to interactively work with a database or can be embedded within a programming language to interface to a database.

The following SQL query selects customers with credit limits of at least $5,000 and puts them into sequence from highest credit limit to lowest.

```
SELECT NAME, CITY, STATE, ZIPCODE
FROM CUSTOMER
WHERE CREDITLIMIT > 4999
ORDER BY CREDITLIMIT DESC
```

SQL/DS

(SQL/Data System) A full-featured relational DBMS from IBM for VSE and VM environments that has integrated query and report writing facilities.

SQL engine

A program that accepts SQL commands and accesses the database to obtain the requested data. Users' requests in a query language or database language must be translated into an SQL request before the SQL engine can process it.

SQL Server

A relational DBMS from Sybase, Emeryville, CA, (www.sybase.com), that runs on OS/2, Windows NT, NetWare, VAX and UNIX servers. It is designed for client/server use and is accessed by applications using SQL or via Sybase's own QBE and decision support utilities.

SQL Server was also available through Microsoft as Microsoft SQL Server for OS/2 and Microsoft SQL Server for Windows NT. In 1992, Microsoft started to modify the program and eventually rewrote its own version that it sells independently.

SQR

Query and reporting software from SQRIBE Technologies, Menlo Park, CA. SQR Workbench runs under Windows and provides a graphical front end for designing and viewing complex reports. SQR Server provides native drivers for all the major databases and runs under Windows and most versions of UNIX.

square wave

A graphic image of a digital pulse as visualized on an oscilloscope. It appears square because it rises quickly to a particular amplitude, stays constant for the duration of the pulse and drops fast at the end.

SRAM

See *static RAM*.

SRT

(Source Routing Transparent) An IEEE-standard technology that allows bridging between Ethernet and token ring networks (Token Ring, FDDI). Existing token ring bridges are not compatible with SRT bridges, but Proteon's (Westborough, MA) Adaptive SRT bridges are compatibile with the installed base. See *source routing*.

SS7

(Signaling System 7) The protocols used in the U.S. telephone system for setting up calls and providing modern transaction services such as caller ID, automatic recall and call forwarding.

SSA

(Serial Storage Architecture) A peripheral interface from IBM that transfers data up to 160 Mbps. SSA's ring configuration allows remaining devices to function if one fails. SCSI software can be mapped over SSA allowing existing SCSI devices to be used.

SSCP

(System Services Control Point) A controlling program in an SNA domain. It resides in the host and is a component within VTAM.

SSL

(Secure Sockets Layer) The leading security protocol on the Internet. When an SSL session is started, the browser sends its public key to the server so that the server can securely send a secret key to the browser. The browser and server exchange data via secret key encryption during that session.

SSP

(System Support Program) A multiuser, multitasking operating system from IBM that is the primary control program for System/34 and System/36.

ST

An early personal computer series from Atari that used a Motorola 680x0 CPU and included the GEM interface, ROM-based TOS operating system, MIDI interface and three-voice sound chip. The 520ST used 512K of RAM and subsequent 1040ST and STE models used 1MB. Its display was 640x200x16.

stack

A set of hardware registers or a reserved amount of memory used for arithmetic calculations or to keep track of internal operations. Stacks keep track of the sequence of routines called in a program. For example, one routine calls another, which calls another and so on. As each routine is completed, the computer returns control to the calling routine all the way back to the first one that started the sequence.

An "internal stack failure" is a fatal error which means that the operating system has lost track of its next operation. Restarting the computer usually corrects this, otherwise the operating system may have to be re-installed. See *protocol stack*.

stackable hub

A type of Ethernet hub that can be expanded by daisy chaining additional hubs together via dedicated ports for that purpose. They are designed to stack vertically and be treated as a single domain by the network management software.

stacker

(1) An output bin in a document feeding or punched card machine. Contrast with *hopper*.

(2) (Stacker) A realtime compression program from Stac Electronics, Carlsbad, CA, that doubles the disk capacity of a DOS, Windows, OS/2 or Mac computer.

stack overflow

An error condition that occurs when there is no room in the stack for a new item. This type of error occurs when the computer is not properly configured, or sometimes when a board isn't seated entirely in the slot. Contrast with *stack underflow*.

stack pointer

An address that identifies the location of the most recent item placed on the stack.

stack underflow

An error condition that occurs when an item is called for from the stack, but the stack is empty. Contrast with *stack overflow*.

STAIRS

(STorage And Information Retrieval System) An IBM text document management system for mainframes. It allows users to search for documents based on key words or word combinations.

standard

A specification for hardware or software that is either widely used and accepted (de facto) or is sanctioned by a standards organization (de jure).

standard cell

The finished design of an electronic function ready for chip fabrication. It can be as small as a clock circuit or as large as a microprocessor. It is used to make custom-designed chips.

standard deviation

In statistics, the average amount a number varies from the average number in a series of numbers.

Standard Mode

A mode of operation under Windows 3.x, but not Windows for Workgroups. Standard Mode Windows and applications would run in a 286.

Starlan

An early local area network from AT&T that uses twisted pair wire, the CSMA/CD access method, transmits at 1 Mbps and uses a star or bus topology. In 1988, Starlan was renamed Starlan 1, and Starlan 10 was introduced, a 10 Mbps Ethernet version that uses twisted pair or optical fibers.

star network

A communications network in which all terminals are connected to a central computer or central hub. PBXs are prime examples as well as IBM's Token Ring.

start bit

In asynchronous communications, the bit transmitted before each character.

start/stop transmission

Same as *asynchronous transmission*.

startup routine

A routine that is executed when the computer is booted or when an application is loaded. It is used to customize the environment for its associated software.

state

The current or last-known status, or condition, of a process, transaction or setting.

statement

In a high-level programming language, a descriptive phrase that generates one or more machine language instructions in the computer. In a low-level assembly language, programmers write instructions rather than statements, since each source language instruction is translated into one machine language instruction.

state-of-the-art
The most advanced technique or method used.

static binding
Same as *early binding*.

static column memory
A type of page mode memory that requires less electronic pulsing in order to access the memory bits.

static electricity
A stationary electrical charge that is the result of intentional charging or of friction in low-humidity environments.

static HTML
An HTML page that never changes. See *dynamic HTML*.

static RAM
A memory chip that requires power to hold its content. Static RAM chips have access times in the 10 to 30-nanosecond range. Dynamic RAMs are usually above 30, and Bipolar and ECL, under 10.

A static RAM bit is made up of a pretzel-like flip-flop circuit that lets current flow through one side or the other based on which one of two transistors is activated. Static RAMs do not require refresh circuitry as do dynamic RAMs, but they take up more space and use more power.

static SQL
See *embedded SQL*.

station
A computer, workstation or terminal in a network. Same as *node*.

statistical multiplexor
In communications, a device that combines several low-speed channels into a single high-speed channel and vice versa. A standard multiplexor is set to a fixed interleaving pattern, but the statistical multiplexor can analyze the traffic load and dynamically switch to different channel patterns to speed up transmission.

stat mux
(STATistical MUltipleXor) See *statistical multiplexor*.

status line
An information line displayed on screen that shows current activity.

ST connector
A fiber-optic cable connector that uses a bayonet plug and socket. It was the first de facto standard connector for most commercial wiring. Two ST connectors are used for each pair of cables.

STD bus
A bus architecture used in medical and industrial equipment due to its small size and rugged design. Originally an 8-bit bus, extensions have increased it to 16 and 32 bits.

stealth virus
A virus that is able to keep itself from being detected. See *polymorphic virus*.

steganography
Hiding one type of file within another. It is used as an alternate to encryption and takes advantages of unused areas within a file structure to enclose another.

step frame
To capture video images one frame at a time. If a computer is not fast enough to capture analog video in realtime, the video can be forwarded and processed one frame at a time.

stepper motor

A motor that rotates in small, fixed increments and is used to control the movement of the access arm on a disk drive. Contrast with *voice coil*.

stereophonic

Sound reproduction that uses two or more channels. Contrast with *monophonic*.

stick font

Same as *vector font*.

stick model

A picture made of lines, or vectors. For example, in biomedical applications, the limbs of a person or animal are converted into lines so that the motion can be visually observed and graphically plotted and analyzed.

sticky

Refers to an application or service that keeps you on a Web site. For example, stock quotes, glossaries, educational material, chat rooms and similar offerings give you reason to remain on the site, while it allows the company to show you more banner ads or more of its own messages.

stiction

(STatic frICTION) A type of hard disk failure in which the read/write heads stick to the platters. The lubricant used on certain drives heats up and liquifies. When the disk is turned off, it cools down and can become like a glue.

STN

(SuperTwisted Nematic) A passive matrix LCD technology that provides better contrast than twisted nematic (TN) by twisting the molecules from 180 to 270 degrees. See *DSTN*.

stop bit

In asynchronous communications, a bit transmitted after each character.

storage device

A hardware unit that holds data. In this Glossary, it refers only to external peripheral equipment, such as disk and tape, in contrast with memory (RAM).

storage hierarchy

The range of memory and storage devices within the computer system. The following list runs from lowest to highest speed. Items marked ** are obsolete.

```
Punched cards **
Punched paper tape **
Magnetic tape
Floppy disks
CD-ROM
Bubble memory
Optical disks
Magnetic disks (movable heads)
Magnetic disks (fixed heads) **
Low-speed bulk memory
Main memory
Cache memory
Microcode
Registers
```

storage management

Administration of a backup and archival program that moves less-timely information to more economical storage media; for example, from magnetic disk to optical disk to magnetic tape.

storage media

Refers to disks, tapes and bubble memory cartridges.

store and forward

The temporary storage of a message for transmission to its destination at a later time. Store and forward techniques allow for routing over networks that are not accessible at all times. For example, messages crossing time zones can be forwarded during daytime at the receiving side, or messages can be forwarded at night in order to obtain off-peak rates. See *messaging protocol*.

stored procedure

An SQL program stored in the database that is executed by calling it directly from the client or from a database trigger. When the SQL procedure is stored in the database, it does not have to be replicated in each client.

stored program concept

The fundamental computer architecture in which the computer acts upon (executes) internally-stored instructions.

STP

(Shielded Twisted Pair) Telephone wire that is wrapped in a metal sheath to eliminate external interference. See *twisted pair*.

stream

A contiguous group of data.

streaming audio

A one-way transmission of digital audio data to the listener. To compensate for momentary delays, the client side buffers a few seconds of data before sending it to the speakers. Audio conferencing requires two-way transmission in realtime.

streaming data

Data that is structured and processed in a continous flow, such as digital audio and video.

streaming tape

A high-speed magnetic tape drive that is frequently used to make a backup copy of an entire hard disk.

streaming video

A one-way transmission of digital video data to the viewer. To compensate for momentary delays, the client side buffers a few seconds of data before sending it to the screen. Videoconferencing requires two-way transmission in realtime.

stream-oriented file

A type of file, such as a text document or digital voice file, that is more openly structured than a data file. Text and voice are continuous streams of characters, whereas database records are repeating structures with a fixed or reasonably uniform format.

STREAMS

A feature of UNIX System V that provides a standard way of dynamically building and passing messages up and down a protocol stack. A STREAMS module would be a transport layer protocol such as TCP and SPX or a network layer protocol such as IP and IPX.

Streettalk

The directory service used in the VINES network operating system from Banyan Systems Inc., Westboro, MA, (www.banyan.com). Streettalk has always been highly regarded and versions are available for Windows NT.

string

(1) In programming, a contiguous set of alphanumeric characters that does not contain numbers used for calculations. Names, addresses, words and sentences are strings.

(2) Any connected set of structures, such as a string of bits, fields or records.

string handling

The abilty to manipulate alphanumeric data (names, addresses, text, etc.). Typical functions include the ability to handle arrays of strings, to left and right align and center strings and to search for an occurrence of text within a string.

striping

Interleaving or multiplexing data to increase speed. See *disk striping*.

stroke

(1) In printing, the weight, or thickness, of a character. For example, in the LaserJet, one of the specifications of the font description is the stroke weight from -3 to +3.

(2) In computer graphics, a pen or brush stroke or to a vector in a vector graphics image.

stroke font

Same as *vector font*.

stroke weight

The thickness of lines in a font character. The HP LaserJet defines stroke weights from Ultra Thin (-7) to Ultra Black (+7), with Medium, or Text, as normal (0).

StrongARM

A high-performance RISC-based microprocessor from Intel that was jointly developed by Digital and Advanced RISC Machines (ARM).

strong encryption

An encryption method that uses a very large number as its cryptographic key. The larger the key, the longer it takes to unlawfully break the code. Today, 128 bits is considered strong encryption. As computers become faster, the length of the key must be incresed.

structured analysis

Techniques developed in the late 1970s by Yourdon, DeMarco, Gane and Sarson for applying a systematic approach to systems analysis. It included the use of data flow diagrams and data modeling and fostered the use of implementation-independent graphical notation for documentation.

structured design

A systematic approach to program design developed in the mid 1970s by Constantine, Yourdon, et al, that included the use of graphical notation for effective documentation and communication, design guidelines and recipes to help programmers get started.

structured programming

Techniques that impose a logical structure on the writing of a program. Large routines are broken down into smaller, modular routines. The use of the GOTO statement is discouraged (see *spaghetti code*).

Certain programming statements are indented in order to make loops and other program logic easier to follow. Structured walkthroughs, which invite criticism from peer programmers, are also used.

Structured languages, such as Pascal, Ada and dBASE, force the programmer to write a structured program. However, unstructured languages such as FORTRAN, COBOL and BASIC require discipline on the part of the programmer.

stub

A small software routine placed into a program that provides a common function. Stubs are used for a variety of purposes. For example, a stub might be installed in a client machine, and a counterpart installed in a server, where both are required to resolve some protocol, remote procedure call (RPC) or other interoperability requirement.

Stuffit

A Macintosh shareware program from Aladdin Systems, Aptos, CA, (www.aladdinsys.com), that compresses files onto multiple floppies. A commercial version adds a scripting language, file viewing and supports multiple compression techniques. It was originally developed by Raymond Lau at age 16.

style sheet

In word processing and desktop publishing, a file that contains layout settings for a particular category of document. Style sheets include such settings as margins, tabs, headers and footers, columns and fonts.

stylus

A pen-shaped instrument that is used to "draw" images or point to menus. See *light pen* and *digitizer tablet*.

subarea node

In an SNA network, a system that contains network controlling functions. It refers to a host computer or a communications controller and its associated terminals.

subdirectory

A disk directory that is subordinate to (below) another directory. In order to gain access to a subdirectory, the path must include all directories above it.

submarining

The temporary visual loss of the moving cursor on a slow display screen such as found on a laptop computer. See *active matrix*.

submenu

An additional list of options within a menu selection. There can many levels of submenus.

subnet, subnetwork

A division of a network into an interconnected, but independent, subgroup, or domain, in order to improve performance and security.

subnet mask

The method used for splitting IP networks into a series of subgroups, or subnets. The mask is a binary pattern that is matched up with the IP address to turn part of the host ID address field into a field for subnets.

subnotebook

A laptop computer that weighs less than four pounds. Subnotebooks may use an external floppy disk to reduce weight.

subroutine

A group of instructions that perform a specific task. A large subroutine might be called a "module" or "procedure."

subschema

Pronounced "sub-skeema." In database management, an individual user's partial view of the database. The schema is the entire database.

subscript

(1) In word processing and mathematical notation, a digit or symbol that appears below the line. Contrast with *superscript*.

(2) In programming, a method for referencing data in a table. For example, in the table **PRICETABLE**, the statement to reference a specific price in the table might be **PRICETABLE (ITEM)**, ITEM being the subscript variable. In a two-dimensional table that includes price and discount, the statement **PRICETABLE (ITEM,DISCOUNT)** could reference a discounted price. The relative locations of the current ITEM and DISCOUNT are kept in two index registers.

subset

A group of commands or functions that do not include all the capabilities of the original specification. Software or hardware components designed for the subset will also work with the original. However, any component designed for the full original specification will not operate with the subset product. Contrast with *superset*.

substrate

The base material upon which integrated circuits are built. Silicon is the most widely used substrate for chips.

substring

A subset of an alphanumeric field or variable. The substring function in a programming language is used to extract the subset; for example, **substr(prodcode,4,3)** extracts characters 4, 5 and 6 out of a product code field or variable.

subtract

In relational database, an operation that generates a third file from all the records in one file that are not in a second file.

Sun

(Sun Microsystems, Inc., Mountain View, CA, www.sun.com) A major manufacturer of high-performance workstations and servers founded in 1982 by Stanford MBAs Andreas Bechtolsheim, Vinok Khosla and Scott McNeally. Sun's hardware is based on its SPARC architecture, and its Solaris operating system and networking are based on UNIX.

In 1994, Sun introduced the Java programming language and ushered in a new era for application development on the Internet. Sun is one of the major proponents behind network computers, which are leaner client workstations that download all their software from the server.

Sun-Netscape Alliance

A business association between Sun and Netscape to market Netscape's Web-based software products. The alliance was formed when AOL acquired Netscape in 1999. The alliance took advantage of the fact that the bulk of Netscape software was already running on Sun hardware. Netscape product names are replaced by the iPlanet brand name. For more information, visit www.iplanet.com.

Super7

A specification from AMD for PC motherboards or single board computers that allows non-Intel CPU chips to take advantage of faster bus speeds and newer peripheral technologies. It specifies the older Socket 7 CPU receptacle and adds support for AGP, USB, Ultra ATA and the 100MHz bus. See *Socket 7*.

Superbase

A relational database management (DBMS) and client/server application development system for Windows from Superbase Developers, Inc., Huntington, NY, (www.superbase.com). It includes a database that supports a variety of multimedia types, an object-based Super Basic Language similar to Visual Basic and a suite of visual programming tools. It supports the major SQL databases as well as ODBC-compliant databases.

SuperCalc

One of the first spreadsheets which followed in the footsteps of VisiCalc in the early 1980s. It was Computer Associates' first personal computer product.

supercomputer

The fastest computer available. It is typically used for simulations in petroleum exploration and production, structural analysis, computational fluid dynamics, physics and chemistry, electronic design, nuclear energy research and meteorology. It is also used for realtime animated graphics.

superconductor

A material that has little resistance to the flow of electricity. Traditional superconductors operate at -459 Fahrenheit (absolute zero).

Thus far, the major use for superconductors, made of alloys of niobium, is for high-powered magnets in medical imaging machines that use magnetic fields instead of x-rays. See *Josephson junction*.

SuperDisk

A floppy disk from Imation Enterprises Corporation, Oakdale, MN, that uses the LS-120 technology. SuperDisks hold 120MB, and SuperDisk drives also read and write standard 1.44MB floppies. See *LS-120*.

SuperDrive

The floppy disk drive used in the Macintosh. It stores 1.44MB of data and also reads and writes earlier Mac 400KB and 800KB disks, as well as Apple II ProDOS, DOS and OS/2 formats.

super floppy

(1) The "next" high-capacity floppy disk. The Zip and LS-120 disks are likely candidates. In the early 1990s, the Floptical was the super floppy drive for a while, but it did not catch on.

(2) An earlier 3.5" floppy disk introduced by IBM that held 2.88MB. The drives were compatible with standard floppies, but it was not widely used.

superframe

A T1 transmission format made up of 12 T1 frames (superframe) and 24 frames (extended superframe).

superscaler

A CPU architecture that allows more than one instruction to be executed in one clock cycle.

superscript

Any letter, digit or symbol that appears above the line. Contrast with *subscript*.

superserver

A high-speed network server with very large RAM and disk capacity. Superservers typically support multiprocessing.

superset

A group of commands or functions that exceed the capabilities of the original specification. Software or hardware components designed for the original specification will also operate with the superset product. However, components designed for the superset will not work with the original. Contrast with *subset*.

supertwist

An LCD technology that twists liquid molecules greater than 90ø in order to improve contrast and viewing angle. See *LCD*.

Super VGA

See *VGA*.

supervisor

Same as *operating system*.

supervisor call

The instruction in an application program that switches the computer to supervisor state.

supervisor control program

The part of the operation system that always resides in memory. Same as *kernel*.

supervisor state

Typically associated with mainframes, it is a hardware mode in which the operating system executes instructions unavailable to an application program; for example, I/O instructions. Contrast with *program state*.

supply chain management

The planning, scheduling and control of the supply chain, which is the sequence of organizations and functions that mine, make or assemble materials and products from manufacturer to wholesaler to retailer to consumer. The driving force behing supply chain management is to reduce inventory.

support

(1) The assistance provided by a hardware or software vendor in installing and maintaining its product.

(2) Software or hardware designed to include or work with some other software or hardware product. For example, if computer "supports multiprocessing," it can host more than one CPU internally. If a development system "supports Windows," it is used to create applications for Windows. If a system "supports the major databases," it provides interfaces to those databases.

SUPRA

A relational DBMS from Cincom Systems, Inc., Cincinnati, OH, (www.cincom.com), that runs on IBM mainframes and VAXs. It includes a query language and a program that automates the database design process.

surface

In CAD, the external geometry of an object. Surfaces are generally required for NC (numerical control) modeling rather than wireframe or solids.

surface modeling

In CAD, a mathematical technique for representing solid-appearing objects. Surface modeling is a more complex method for representing objects than wireframe modeling, but not as sophisticated as solid modeling.

Although surface and solid models can appear the same on screen, they are quite different. Surface models cannot be sliced open as can solid models. In addition, in surface modeling, the object can be geometrically incorrect; whereas, in solid modeling, it must be correct.

surface mount

A circuit board packaging technique in which the leads (pins) on the chips and components are soldered on top of the board, not through it. Boards can be smaller and built faster.

surfing

Scanning online material, such as databases, news clips and forums. The term originated from "channel surfing," the rapid changing of TV channels to find something of interest.

surge

See *power surge*.

surge protector

A device that protects a computer from excessive voltage (spikes and power surges) in the power line. See *voltage regulator* and *UPS*.

surge suppressor

Same as *surge protector*.

suspend and resume

To stop an operation and restart where you left off. In portable computers, the hard disk is turned off, and the CPU is made to idle at its slowest speed. All open applications are retained in memory.

SV

(Scientific Visualization) See *visualization*.

SVC

(Switched Virtual Circuit) A Network connection from sender to recipient that is established at the time the transmission is required. This is what occurs in a switched public network. Contrast with *PVC*.

SVD

(Simultaneous Voice and Data) The concurrent transmission of voice and data by modem over a single analog telephone line. The first SVD technologies on the market are MultiTech's MSP, Radish's VoiceView, AT&T's VoiceSpan and the all-digital DSVD, endorsed by Intel, Hayes and others.

SVG

(Scalable Vector Graphics) A vector graphics file format from the W3C that enables vector drawings to be included in XML pages on the Web. Vector drawings will scale to the size of the viewing window, whereas bitmaps remain constant. See *graphics* and *XML*.

SVGA

(Super VGA) Enhancements to the VGA standard that increased resolution to 800x600 and beyond (see *VGA*). The term may be used to refer to 800x600 resolution in general; for example:

```
VGA      640x480
SVGA     800x600
XGA      1024x768
```

S-VHS

(Super-VHS) A video recording and playback system that uses a higher-quality VHS cassette and the S-video technology. VCRs that support S-VHS can also record and play back normal VHS tapes.

SVID

(System V Interface Definition) An AT&T specification for the UNIX System V operating system. SVID Release 3 specifies the interface for UNIX System V Release 4.

S-video

(Super-video) A video technology, also called "Y/C video," that records and maintains luminance (Y) and color information (C) separately. S-video provide a better color image than standard VHS and 8mm formats. S-video hookups use a special 5-pin connector rather than the common RCA phono plug.

swap file

A disk file used to temporarily save a program or part of a program running in memory. See *Windows swap file*.

swapping

Replacing one segment of a program in memory with another and restoring it back to the original when required. In virtual memory systems, it is called "paging."

Swing

A Java toolkit for developing graphical user interfaces (GUIs). It includes elements such as menus, toolbars and dialog boxes. Swing is written in Java and is thus platform independent, unlike the Java Abstract Window Toolkit (AWT), which provides platform-specific code.

switch

(1) A mechanical or electronic device that directs the flow of electrical or optical signals from one side to the other. Switches with multiple input and output ports such as a PBX are able to route traffic. With regard to a simple on/off switch, remember... open is "off," closed is "on." See *data switch* and *transistor*.

(2) In programming, a bit or byte used to keep track of something. Sometimes refers to a branch in a program.

(3) A modifier of a command.

Switched 56

A dial-up digital service provided by local and long distance telephone companies. There is a monthly fee and per-minute charge like the analog voice network. For connection, a DSU/CSU is used instead of a modem. Switched 56 uses a 64 Kbps channel, but one bit per byte is used for in band signaling.

switched Ethernet

An Ethernet network that runs through a high-speed switch. Changing to switched Ethernet means replacing the Ethernet hub with a switch. Instead of sharing 10 Mbps for Ethernet or 100 Mbps for Fast Ethernet among all users on the network segment, the full bandwidth is made available to each sender and receiver pair.

If the switch and network adapters (NICs) provide full-duplex operation, the total bandwidth is 20 Mbps or 200 Mbps between nodes. A major advantage in migrating to switched Ethernet is that the existing NICs are still used.

switched line

In communications, a link that is established in a switched network, such as the international dial-up telephone system, a Switched 56 digital line or ISDN.

switched network

(1) The international dial-up telephone system.

(2) A network in which a temporary connection is established from one point to another for either the duration of the session (circuit switching) or for the transmission of one or more packets of data (packet switching).

switching hub

A device that acts as a central switch or PBX, connecting one line to another. In a local area network (LAN), a switching hub gives any two stations on the network the full bandwidth of the line. Contrast with *shared media LAN*, in which all stations share the bandwidth of a common transmission path. See *hub*.

switch-to-computer

To integrate voice telephone and database access. For example, in customer service applications, using telephone services, such as automatic number identification (ANI) and automatic call distribution (ACD), an incoming call can retrieve and route the customer's file to the next available human agent.

SYBASE System

A family of SQL development tools from Sybase, Inc., Emeryville, CA, (www.sybase.com), that includes SQL Server, SQL Toolset (design, development and control) and Client/Services Interfaces (distributed database architecture). See *SQL Server*.

symbol

In data compression, a unit of data (byte, floating point number, spoken word, etc.) that is treated independently.

symbol set

In printing, a group of symbols that are extensions to standard characters for use in a particular country or specific application. Symbol sets provide codes for the non-standard upper half of the ASCII character set.

symmetric multiprocessing

See *SMP*.

sync character

In synchronous communications systems, a special character transmitted to synchronize timing.

synchronous

(1) A sequence of fixed or concurrent events. See *synchronous transmission*.

(2) Completing the current I/O operation before the next one is started.

(3) In SCSI, the transfer of data without immediate acknowledgment of each byte.

(4) Contrast with *asynchronous*.

synchronous protocol

A communications protocol that controls a synchronous transmission, such as bisync, SDLC and HDLC. Contrast with *asynchronous protocol*.

synchronous transmission

The transmission of data in which both stations are synchronized. Codes are sent from the transmitting station to the receiving station to establish the synchronization, and data is then transmitted in continuous streams.

Modems that transmit at 1200 bps and higher often convert the asynchronous signals from a computer's serial port into synchronous transmission over the transmission line. Contrast with *asynchronous transmission*.

syntax

The rules governing the structure of a language statement. It specifies how words and symbols are put together to form a phrase.

syntax error

An error that occurs when a program cannot understand the command. See *parse*.

synthesizer

A device that generates sound by creating waveforms electronically (FM synthesis) or from stored samples of musical instruments (wave table synthesis). See *MIDI* and *speech synthesis*.

SyQuest disk

A family of removable hard drives from former SyQuest Technology, Inc., Fremont, CA. SyQuest's SCSI-based 5.25" drives use 44, 88 and 200MB cartridges, while the 3.5" format holds 105 and 270MB. The early generations of SyQuest disks were the first de facto standards used by commercial graphics companies and printers as a data transfer medium. SyQuest subsequently introduced a variety of new formats and went out of business in 1998.

sysgen

(**SYS**tem **GEN**eration) The installation of a new or revised operating system. It includes selecting the appropriate utility programs and identifying the peripheral devices and storage capacities of the system the operating system will be controlling.

sysop

(SYStem OPerator) Pronounced "siss-op." A person who runs an online communications system or bulletin board. The sysop may also act as mediator for system conferences.

Sysplex

See *Parallel Sysplex*.

SysReq key

(SYStem REQuest key) A keyboard key on a terminal keyboard that is used to get the attention of the central computer. The key exists on PC keyboards, but is rarely used by applications.

system

(1) A group of related components that interact to perform a task.

(2) A *computer system* is made up of the CPU, operating system and peripheral devices.

(3) An *information system* is made up of the database, all the data entry, update, query and report programs and manual and machine procedures.

(4) "The system" often refers to the operating system.

System 2000

An hierarchical, network and relational DBMS from the SAS Institute, Cary, NC, (www.sas.com), that runs on IBM, CDC and Unisys computers. It has been integrated into the SAS System.

System/3

A batch-oriented minicomputer from IBM. Introduced in 1969, it introduced a new punched card about half the size of previous ones. With the addition of the Communications Control Program (CCP), it could handle interactive terminals.

System/32

A batch-oriented minicomputer from IBM. Introduced in 1975, it provided a single terminal for operator use. It was superseded by the System/34, which could run System/32 applications.

System/34

A multiuser, multitasking minicomputer from IBM, introduced in 1977. The typical system had from a handful to a dozen terminals and could run System/32 programs in a special mode. Most large System/34 users migrated to the System/38, while small users migrated to the System/36.

System/36

A multiuser, multitasking minicomputer from IBM that was introduced in 1983. It superseded the System/34 and is mostly compatible with it. System/34 programs run in the System/36 after recompilation. The typical system supports from a handful to a couple of dozen terminals. It has been superseded by the AS/400.

System/360, System/370, System/390

In 1964, IBM introduced the System/360 family of computer systems. It was the first time in history that a complete line of computers was announced at one time. Much of the 360 architecture still exists in current-day IBM mainframes.

In 1970, the System/370 series was introduced, which added virtual memory and other enhancements. Subsequent lines included the 303x, 43xx, 308x, 309x and 9370 models, all based on the 370 architecture.

In 1990, IBM introduced the System/390 family that featured the ESA/390 architecture and operating systems, ES/9000 hardware, ESCON fiber optic channels and SystemView. In the mid-1990s, bipolar-based ES/9000s were superseded by the much smaller, microprocessor-based Parallel Enterprise Server and Multiprise series. See *Parallel/Sysplex*.

System/38

A minicomputer from IBM that includes an operating system and integrated relational database management system. It supports up to several dozen terminals. Introduced in 1978, it was an advanced departure from previous System/3x computers. It was superseded by the AS/400.

System/3x

Refers to IBM System/34, System/36 and System/38 midrange computers.

System 7

A major upgrade of the Macintosh operating system (1991). It included virtual memory, increased memory addressing, hot links (Publish & Subscribe), multitasking (MultiFinder was no longer optional), TrueType fonts and a variety of user interface enhancements.

System 8

The latest version of the Macintosh operating system introduced in 1997. Designed to take more advantage of the PowerPC chip, it includes an enhanced 3-D look and provides assistance for connecting to the Internet.

system administrator

A person who manages a multiuser computer system. Responsibilities are similar to that of a network administrator.

Systemantics

An insightful book on the systems process by John Gall (1977). The following is copied with permission from Random House.

A Concise Summary of the Field of General Systemantics

Systems are seductive. They promise to do a hard job faster, better, and more easily than you could do it by yourself. But if you set up a system, you are likely to find your time and effort now being consumed in the care and feeding of the system itself. New problems are created by its very presence. Once set up, it won't go away, it grows and encroaches. It begins to do strange and wonderful things. Breaks down in ways you never thought possible. It kicks back, gets in the way, and opposes its own proper function. Your own perspective becomes distorted by being in the system. You become anxious and push on it to make it work. Eventually you come to believe that the misbegotten product it so grudgingly delivers is what you really wanted all the time. At that point encroachment has become complete... you have become absorbed... you are now a systems person!

system board

A printed circuit board that contains the primary CPU. See *motherboard*.

system bus

See *local bus*.

system development cycle

The sequence of events in the development of an information system (application), which requires mutual effort on the part of user and technical staff.

1. SYSTEMS ANALYSIS & DESIGN
    feasibility study
    general design
    prototyping
    detail design
    functional specifications

2. USER SIGN OFF

3. PROGRAMMING
    design
    coding
    testing

4. IMPLEMENTATION
    training
    conversion
    installation

5. USER ACCEPTANCE

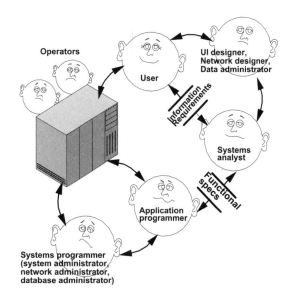

system development methodology
The formal documentation for the phases of the system development cycle. It defines the precise objectives for each phase and the results required from a phase before the next one can begin. It may include specialized forms for preparing the documentation describing each phase.

system disk
A hard or floppy disk that contains part or all of the operating system or other control program.

system failure
A hardware or operating system malfunction.

system file
A machine language file that is part of the operating system or other control program. It may also refer to a configuration file used by such programs.

system folder
The operating system folder in the Macintosh that contains the System, Finder and MultiFinder, printer drivers, fonts, desk accessories, INITs and cdevs.

system font
The primary font used by the operating system or other control program to display messages and menus unless otherwise directed.

system image
The current contents of memory, which includes the operating system and running programs.

SYSTEM.INI
(SYSTEMdows INItialization) The file read by Windows on startup that contains data about the hardware configuration and drivers. Information in SYSTEM.INI is updated by Windows when you change various defaults; however, the file can be manually edited. Although SYSTEM.INI was created in Windows 3.x, it is still used by Windows 95/98 and NT, although primarily for Windows 3.x compatibility. See *WIN.INI*.

system level
An operation that is performed by the operating system or some other control program.

system life cycle
The useful life of an information system. Its length depends on the nature and volatility of the business, as well as the software development tools used to generate the databases and applications. Eventually, an information system that is patched over and over no longer is structurally sound enough to be expanded.

Tools like DBMSs allow for changes more readily, but increased transaction volumes can negate the effectiveness of the original software later on.

system management
See *systems management*.

system memory
The memory used by the operating system.

system program
A component of system software.

System Resources
In Windows, fixed areas in memory used to keep track of icons, menus and other active components in open applications. In Windows 3.x, these areas can be easily filled up, and no more programs can be loaded. Windows 95/98 greatly expanded its room for these objects.

systems
A general term for the department, people or work involved in systems analysis & design activities.

systems analysis & design

The examination of a problem and the creation of its solution. Systems analysis is effective when all sides of the problem are reviewed. Systems design is most effective when more than one solution can be proposed. The plans for the care and feeding of a new system are as important as the problems they solve. See *system development cycle* and *Systemantics*.

systems analyst

The person responsible for the development of an information system. They design and modify systems by turning user requirements into a set of functional specifications, which are the blueprint of the system. They design the database or help design it if data administrators are available. They develop the manual and machine procedures and the detailed processing specs for each data entry, update, query and report program in the system.

Systems analysts are the architects, as well as the project leaders, of an information system. It is their job to develop solutions to user's problems, determine the technical and operational feasibility of their solutions, as well as estimate the costs to develop and implement them.

They develop prototypes of the system along with the users, so that the final specifications are examples of screens and reports that have been carefully reviewed. Experienced analysts leave no doubt in users' minds as to what is being developed, and they insist that all responsible users review and sign off on every detail.

Systems analysts require a balanced mix of business and technical knowledge, interviewing and analytical skills, as well as a good understanding of human behavior. See *Systemantics*.

systems disk

A disk pack or disk drive reserved only for system software, which includes the operating system, assemblers, compilers and other utility and control programs.

systems engineer

Often a vendor title for persons involved in consulting and pre-sales activities related to computers. See *systems analyst, systems programmer, programmer analyst* and *application programmer*.

systems house

An organization that develops customized software and/or turnkey systems for customers. Contrast with *software house*, which develops software packages for sale to the general public. Both terms are used synonymously.

systems integration

Making diverse components work together.

systems integrator

An individual or organization that builds systems from a variety of diverse components. With increasing complexity of technology, more customers want complete solutions to information problems, requiring hardware, software and networking expertise in a multivendor environment. See *OEM* and *VAR*.

systems management

(1) The management of systems development, which includes systems analysis & design, application development and implementation. See *system development cycle*.

(2) Software that manages computer systems in an enterprise, which may include any and all of the following functions: software distribution, version control, backup & recovery, printer spooling, job scheduling, virus protection and performance and capacity planning. Network management may be an integrated component of systems management.

system software

Programs used to control the computer and develop and run application programs. It includes operating systems, TP monitors, network operating systems and database managers. Contrast with *application program*.

systems program

See *system program* and *system software*.

systems programmer

(1) In the IS department of a large organization, a technical expert on some or all of the computer's system software (operating systems, networks, DBMSs, etc.). They are responsible for the efficient performance of the computer systems.

They usually don't write programs, but perform a lot of technical tasks that integrate vendors' software. They also act as technical advisors to systems analysts, application programmers and operations personnel. For example, they would know whether additional tasks could be added to the computer and would recommend conversion to a new operating or database system in order to optimize performance.

In mainframe environments, there is one systems programmer for about 10 or more application programmers, and systems programmers generally have considerably higher salaries than application programmers. In smaller environments, users rely on vendors or consultants for systems programming assistance. In fact, end users are actually performing systems programmer functions when they install new software or hardware on their own personal computers.

(2) In a computer hardware or software organization, a person who designs and writes system software. In this case, a systems programmer is a real programmer in the traditional sense.

system test

Running a complete system for testing purposes. See *unit test*.

system time/date

The on-going time of day in the computer, which is maintained by a battery when the computer is turned off. It is used to time stamp all newly-created files and activate time-dependent processes.

System Tray

An area on the right side of the taskbar on the Windows 95/98/NT/2000 interface used to display the status of various functions, such as speaker volume and modem transmission.

SystemView

An IBM architecture for computer systems management introduced with System/390 that provides an enterprise-wide approach for controlling multiple systems and networks. It will be implemented in stages through the 1990s. NetView is a major component.

systolic array

An array of processing elements (typically multiplier-accumulator chips) in a pipeline structure that is used for applications such as image and signal processing and fluid dynamics. The "systolic," coined by H. T. Kung of Carnegie-Mellon, refers to the rhythmic transfer of data through the pipeline like blood flowing through the vascular system.

T

See *tera*.

T1, T2, T3

A T1 is a 1.544 Mbps point-to-point dedicated line provided by the telephone companies. The monthly cost is typically based on distance. T1 lines are widely used for private networks and high-speed links to and from Internet service providers. A T1 line provides 24 64-Kbps voice or data channels. T2 provides 6.312 Mbps and 96 channels, and T3, 44.736 Mbps and 672 channels.

T9

(Text on 9 Keys) A text input system from Tegic Communications, Inc., Seattle, WA, (www.tegic.com), that enables text to be typed using a 9-key telephone keypad.

T.120

A series of ITU standards that define all aspects of data conferencing. It defines interfaces for whiteboards, application viewing and application sharing. The ITU standard for videoconferencing is H.320.

tab

(1) To move the cursor on screen or the print head on a printer to a specified column (tab stop). There are horizontal and vertical tab characters in the ASCII character set (horizontal ASCII 9, vertical ASCII 11).

(2) A small flap used for quick access that projects out from the end of a page of paper or file folder. Its electronic equivalent on screen can be clicked to gain access to a function.

tabbing

Moving the cursor on a video display screen or the print head on a printer to a specified column.

tab delimited

A text format that uses tab characters as separators between fields. Unlike comma delimited files, alphanumeric data is not surrounded by quotes.

tab key

A keyboard key that moves the cursor to the next tab stop.

table

(1) In programming, a collection of adjacent fields. Also called an "array," a table contains data that is either constant within the program or is called in when the program is run. See *decision table*.

(2) In a relational database, the same as a file; a collection of records.

table lookup

Searching for data in a table, commonly used in data entry validation and any operation that must match an item of data with a known set of values.

tablet

See *digitizer tablet*.

table view

A screen display of several items or records in rows and columns. Contrast with *form view*.

tabular form

Same as *table view* with respect to printed output.

tabulate

(1) To arrange data into a columnar format.

(2) To sum and print totals.

tabulating equipment

Punched card machines, including keypunches, sorters, collators, interpreters, reproducers, calculators and tabulators.

tabulator

A punched card accounting machine that prints and calculates totals.

TACACS

(Terminal Access Controller Access Control System) An access control protocol used to authenticate a user logging onto the network. TACACS is a simple username/password system. Extended TACACS (XTACACS) adds more intelligence in the server, and TACACS+ adds encryption and a challenge/response option. See *challenge/response*.

TACS

(Total Access Communication System) An analog cellular phone system deployed mostly in Europe. It was modelled after the AMPS system in the U.S.

tag

(1) A set of bits or characters that identifies various conditions about data in a file and is often found in the header records of such files.

(2) A name (label, mnemonic) assigned to a data structure, such as a field, file or paragraph.

(3) The key field in a record.

(4) A format code used in a document language such as HTML.

(5) A brass pin on a terminal block that is connected to a wire by soldering or wire wrapping.

tag sort

A sorting procedure in which the key fields are sorted first to create the correct order, and then the actual data records are placed into that order.

tag switching

A layer 3 switching technology from Cisco that uses tags (labels) containing forwarding information which is written into the data packets by routers and hosts. The tags use fixed positions within the packet header allowing for quick examination and transfer through routers and switches.

talk-off

An unintentional command activation when a human voice generates the same tone as a control signal.

Tandem

(Tandem Computers Inc., Cupertino, CA, www.tandem.com) A manufacturer of fault tolerant computers founded in 1974 by James Treybig to address the transaction processing market. Tandem introduced the first commercial computer based on a fault tolerant, multiprocessor architecture. In 1997, Tandem was acquired by Compaq.

tandem office

A telephone switching center (central office) that does not connect directly to the customer. It connects offices in the same network or between networks, but always deals with trunks rather than customer lines.

tandem processors

Two processors hooked together in a multiprocessor environment.

tandem switch

A central office switch (telco switch) that connects end offices together and does not deal directly with the customer.

tap

In communications, a connection onto the main transmission medium of a local area network. See *transceiver*.

tape

See *magnetic tape* and *paper tape*.

tape backup

The use of magnetic tape for storing duplicate copies of hard disk files. See *QIC, DAT, DLT, 3480* and *Exabyte*.

tape drive

A physical unit that holds, reads and writes the magnetic tape. See *magnetic tape*.

tape dump

A printout of tape contents without any report formatting.

tape mark

A control code used to indicate the end of a tape file.

tape transport

The mechanical part of a tape drive.

TAPI

(Telephony API) A programming interface from Microsoft and Intel. It allows Windows client applications to access voice services on a server. TAPI is designed to provide interoperability between PCs and telephone equipment, including phone systems and PBXs.

tar

(Tape ARchive) A UNIX utility that is used to archive files by combining several files into one. It is often used in conjunction with the "compress" or "gzip" commands to compress the data.

target

The destination. For example, a target disk is the disk onto which data is recorded. A target language is the resulting language from a translation process.

tariff

A schedule of rates for common carrier services.

task

An independent running program. See *multitasking*.

task management

The part of the operating system that controls the running of one or more programs (tasks) within the computer at the same time.

task swapping

Switching between two applications by copying the current running program to disk or other high-speed storage device (auxiliary memory, EMS, etc.) and loading another program into that program space.

task switching

Switching between active applications. See *context switching*.

TAWPI

(The Association for Work Process Improvement, Boston, MA, www.tawpi.org) A membership organization dedicated to the improvement of work processes in data capture, document and remittance processing. It was formerly the Recognition Technology Users Association (RTUA), founded in 1970. In 1993, RTUA merged with DEMA (Association for Input Technology and Management) and various OCR/Scanner/Fax associations and changed its name to TAWPI.

Tb, TB

(TeraBit, TeraByte) See *tera* and *space/time*.

Tbps, Tbits/sec

(TeraBits Per Second) Trillion bits per second. See *tera* and *space/time*.

TBps, Tbytes/sec

(TeraBytes Per Second) Trillion bytes per second. See *tera* and *space/time*.

TC

See *true color*.

...unications Access Method) IBM communications software widely used to transfer data ...mrames and 3270 terminals. See *access method*.

T-carrier

A digital transmission service from a common carrier. Introduced by AT&T in 1983 as a voice service, its use for data has grown steadily.

T-carrier service requires multiplexors at both ends that merge the various signals together for transmission and split them at the destination. Multiplexors analyze the traffic load and vary channel speeds for optimum transmission.

Tcl/Tk

(Tool Command Language/ToolKit) Pronounced "tickle" or "ticklet," it is an interpreted script language that is used to develop a variety of applications, including GUIs, prototypes and CGI scripts. Created for UNIX at the University of California at Berkeley, it now runs on PCs and Macs and is primarily supported by SunSoft.

TCM

(1) (Trellis-Coded Modulation/Viterbi Decoding) A technique that adds forward error correction to a modulation scheme by adding an additional bit to each baud. TCM is used with QAM modulation, for example.

(2) (Thermal Conduction Module) An IBM circuit packaging technique that seals chips, boards and components into a module that serves as a heat sink. TCMs are mostly water cooled, although some are air cooled.

TCO

(1) (Total Cost of Ownership) The cost of using a computer. It includes the cost of the hardware, software and upgrades as well as the cost of the inhouse staff and/or consultants that provide training and technical support.

(2) Refers to the Swedish Confederation of Professional Employees, which has set stringent standards for devices that emit radiation. See *MPR II*.

TCP/IP

(Transmission Control Protocol/Internet Protocol) A communications protocols developed under contract from the U.S. Department of Defense to internetwork dissimilar systems. It is a de facto UNIX standard, now supported on almost all platforms. TCP/IP is the protocol of the Internet.

File Transfer Protocol (FTP) and Simple Mail Transfer Protocol (SMTP) provide file transfer and e-mail. The Telnet protocol provides terminal emulation for all types of computers in the network. TCP controls data transfer. IP provides the routing. The combination of TCP/IP, NFS and NIS comprise the primary networking components of UNIX.

TCP/IP stack

An implementation of the TCP/IP protocol. Network architectures designed in layers, such as TCP/IP, OSI and SNA, are referred to as stacks.

TCU

(Transmission Control Unit) A communications control unit controlled by the computer that does not execute internally stored programs. Contrast with *front end processor*, which executes its own instructions.

TDM

(Time Division Multiplexing) A technique that interleaves several low-speed signals into one high-speed transmission. For example, if A, B & C are three digital signals of 1,000 bps each, they can be mixed into one 3,000 bps as follows: AABBCCAABBCCAABBCC. The receiving end divides the single stream back into its original signals.

TDM is the technology used in T-carrier service (DS0, DS1, etc.), which are the leased lines common in wide area networks (WANs). Contrast with *FDM*. See *baseband*.

TDMA

(Time Division Multiple Access) A cellular telephone technology that triples the capacity of the original analog method (FDMA). It divides each channel into three subchannels providing service to three users instead of one. See *FDMA, CDMA* and *CDPD*.

tear-off menu

An on-screen menu or palette that can be moved off of its primary position and relocated to any part of the screen.

technology transfer

(1) Sharing technical information by means of education and training.

(2) Using a technical concept or hardware or software product to solve a problem in an industry that is entirely different from the one the technology was developed for.

tech support

Technical assistance from the hardware manufacturer or software publisher. Unless you have a simple, straightforward question, in order to get help from a tech support representative, place your telephone call while you are at your computer. Intermittent problems are very difficult to resolve. If you cannot recreate the problem on screen, there may be very little a tech support person can do to help you.

tech writer

A person who is responsible for writing documentation for a hardware or software product.

telco

(TELephone COmpany) A company that provides telephone services. It generally refers to the local telephone companies rather than the long-distance suppliers.

Telcordia

(Telcordia Technologies, Morristown, NJ, www.telcordia.com, an SAIC company) A telecommunications software, engineering and consulting organization. Telcordia was originally founded as Bellcore in 1984 by the regional Bell telephone companies (RBOCs) after they were split apart from AT&T due to court order (Divestiture). Bellcore provided the research and development to the RBOCs that was originally within AT&T.

tele

Operations performed remotely or by telephone.

telecommunications (telecom)

Communicating information, including data, text, pictures, voice and video over long distance. See *communications*.

telecommunity

A society in which information can be transmitted or received freely between all members without technical incompatibilities.

telecommuting

Working at home and communicating with the office.

teleconferencing

("long distance" conferencing) An interactive communications session between three or more users that are geographically separated. See *audioconferencing, videoconferencing* and *data conferencing*.

telecopying

(long distance copying) The formal term for fax.

telefax

The european term for a fax machine.

telegraph

A low-speed communications device that transmits up to approximately 150 bps. Telegraph grade lines, stemming from the days of Morse code, can't transmit a voice conversation.

telemanagement
Management of an organization's telephone systems, which includes maintaining and ordering new equipment and monitoring the expenses for all telephone calls.

telemarketing
Selling over the telephone.

Telematics
The convergence of telecommunications and information processing.

telemetry
Transmitting data captured by instrumentation and measuring devices to a remote station where it is recorded and analyzed. For example, data from a weather satellite is telemetered to earth.

Telenet
One of the first value-added, packet switching networks that enabled terminals and computers to exchange data. Established in 1975, it was later acquired by Sprint and ultimately integrated into the SprintNet network. See also *Telnet*.

telephone channel
See *voice grade*.

telephone wiring
See *twisted pair*.

telephony
The science of converting sound into electrical signals, transmitting it within cables or via radio and reconverting it back into sound.

telephony server
A computer in a network that provides telephone integration. The term may refer to the entire system or to just the plug-in boards and software. An Internet telephony server links phone lines to the Internet.

telepresence surgery
A medical technology developed by SRI International that allows a surgeon to operate long distance. The surgeon actually performs the operation long distance using a robotic device that provides the sensory experience of hands-on surgery.

teleprinter
A typewriter-like terminal with a keyboard and built-in printer. Contrast with *video terminal*.

teleprocessing
An early IBM term for data communications. It means "long distance" processing.

teleprocessing monitor
See *TP monitor*.

teletext
A broadcasting service that transmits text to a TV set that has a teletext decoder. It uses the vertical blanking interval of the TV signal (black line between frames when vertical hold is not adjusted) to transmit about a hundred frames. See *videotex*.

Teletype
The trade name of Teletype Corporation, which refers to a variety of teleprinters used for communications. The Teletype was one of the first communications terminals in the U.S.

teletype interface
See *teletype mode*.

teletype mode
Line-at-a-time output like a typewriter. Contrast with *full-screen mode*.

teletypewriter

A low-speed teleprinter, often abbreviated "TTY."

televaulting

Continuous transmitting of data to vaults for backup purposes. The term was coined by TeleVault Technology Inc.

Telex

An international, dial-up data communications service administered in the U.S. by AT&T, MCI and other providers. In the 1960s, it was the first worldwide, realtime data communications service to use terminals for transmitting and receiving messages. Prior to Telex, telegrams and cablegrams were the primary method for delivering a text message. Although diminishing each year, Telex is still used for commerce in more than 200 countries.

Telnet

A terminal emulation protocol commonly used on the Internet and TCP/IP networks. It allows a user to log onto and run a program from a remote terminal or computer. Telnet was originally developed for ARPAnet and is part of the TCP/IP communications protocol. See also *Telenet*.

TEMPEST

Security against external radiation from data processing equipment. Equipment and cables that meet TEMPEST requirements have extra shielding in order to prevent data signals from escaping and being picked up by unauthorized listeners.

template

(1) A plastic or stiff paper form that is placed over the function keys on a keyboard to identify their use.

(2) The programmatic and descriptive part of a programmable application; for example, a spreadsheet that contains only descriptions and formulas or a HyperCard stack that contains only programming and backgrounds. When the template is filled with data, it becomes a working application.

temporary font

A soft font that remains in the printer's memory until the printer is reset manually or by software. Contrast with *permanent font*.

tera, terabit, terabyte

Trillion, trillion bits, trillion bytes. Also Tb, Tbit and T-bit, or TB, Tbyte and T-byte. See *space/time*.

teraflops

(tera FLoating point OPerations per Second) One trillion floating point operations per second.

terminal

(1) An I/O device for a computer that usually has a keyboard for input and a video screen or printer for output.

(2) An input device, such as a scanner, video camera or punched card reader.

(3) An output device in a network, such as a monitor, printer or card punch.

(4) A connector used to attach a wire.

terminal emulation

Using a computer to simulate the type of terminal required to gain access to another computer. See *virtual terminal*.

terminal mode

An operating mode that causes the computer to act like a terminal; ready to transmit typed-in keystrokes and ready to receive transmitted data.

terminal server

A computer or controller used to connect multiple terminals to a network or host computer.

terminal session
The time in which a user is working at a terminal.

terminal strip
An insulated bar that contains a set of screws to which wires are attached.

terminate and stay resident
See *TSR*.

terminator
(1) A character that ends a string of alphanumeric characters.

(2) A hardware component that is connected to the last peripheral device in a series or the last node in a network.

terrestrial link
A communications line that travels on, near or below ground. Contrast with *satellite link*.

test automation software
Software used to test new revisions of software by automatically entering a predefined set of commands and inputs.

test data
A set of data created for testing new or revised programs. It should be developed by the user as well as the programmer and must contain a sample of every category of valid data as well as many invalid conditions.

testing
Running new or revised programs to determine if they process all data properly. See *test data*.

TeX
A typesetting language used in a variety of typesetting environments. It uses embedded codes within the text of the document to initiate changes in layout including the ability to describe elaborate scientific formulas.

text
Words, sentences and paragraphs. Contrast with *data*, which are defined units, such as name and amount due. Text may also refer to alphanumeric data, such as name and address, to distinguish it from numeric data, such as quantity and dollar amounts. A page of text takes about 2,000 to 4,000 bytes. See *text field*.

text based
Also called "character based," the display of text and graphics as a fixed set of predefined characters. For example, 25 rows of 80 columns. Contrast with *graphics based*.

text box
An on-screen rectangular frame into which you type text. Text boxes are used to add text in a drawing or paint program. The flexibility of the text box is determined by the software. Sometimes you can keep on typing and the box expands to meet your input. Other times, you have to go into a different mode to widen the frame, then go back to typing in more text.

text editing
The ability to change text by adding, deleting and rearranging letters, words, sentences and paragraphs.

text editor
Software used to create and edit files that contain only text; for example, batch files, address lists and source language programs. Text editors produce raw ASCII or EBCDIC text files, and unlike word processors, do not usually provide word wrap or formatting (underline, boldface, fonts, etc.).

Editors designed for writing source code may provide automatic indention and multiple windows into the same file. They may also display the reserved words of a particular programming language in boldface or in a different font, but they do not embed format codes in the file.

text entry

Entering alphanumeric text characters into the computer. It implies typing the characters on a keyboard. See *data entry*.

text field

A data structure that holds alphanumeric data, such as name and address. If a text field holds large, or unlimited, amounts of text, it may be called a "memo" field. Contrast with *numeric field*.

text file

A file that contains only text characters. See *ASCII file*. Contrast with *graphics file* and *binary file*.

text management

The creation, storage and retrieval of text. It implies flexible retrieval capabilities that can search for text based on a variety of criteria. Although a word processor manages text, it usually has limited retrieval capabilities.

text messaging

Sending short messages to a smart phone, pager, PDA or other handheld device. Text messaging implies sending short messages generally no more than a couple of hundred characters in length. In Europe, text messaging was popularized by the GSM cellphone system's Short Messaging Service (SMS), which supports messages of up to 160 characters.

text mode

(1) A screen display mode that displays only text and not graphics.

(2) A program mode that allows text to be entered and edited.

text-to-speech

Converting text into voice output using speech synthesis techniques. Although initially used by the blind to listen to written material, it is now used extensively to convey financial data and other information via telephone for everyone.

texture mapping

In computer graphics, the creation of a special surface. With algorithms, all kinds of textures can be produced: the rough skin of an orange, the metallic surface of a can and the irregularity of a brick. It can also be done by electronically wrapping a secondary image around an object.

TFT

(Thin Film Transistor) The term typically refers to active matrix screens on laptop computers. Active matrix LCD provides a sharper screen display and broader viewing angle than does passive matrix. See *LCD* and *thin film*.

TFTP

(Trivial File Transfer Protocol) A version of the TCP/IP FTP protocol that has no directory or password capability.

thermal printer

A low-cost, low- to medium-resolution non-impact printer that uses heat-sensitive paper. Where the heated pins of the print head touch the paper, the paper darkens.

thermal recalibration

The periodic sensing of the temperature in hard disk drives in order to make minor adjustments to the alignment of the read/write heads.

thermal wax transfer

A printing process similar to dye sublimation, but uses a wax-based ink, not a transparent dye. Like other color printers, it puts down a solid dot of ink and produces shades of colors by placing color dots side by side (dithering). Wax transfer prints faster than dye sub and ribbon and paper are less expensive, but it does not produce photorealistic quality.

thick film

A layer of magnetic, semiconductor or metallic material that is thicker than the microscopic layers of the transistors on a chip. For example, metallic thick films are silk screened onto the ceramic base of hybrid microcircuits. Contrast with *thin film*.

ThickNet
See *Ethernet*.

thimble printer
A letter quality printer similar to a daisy wheel printer. Instead of a wheel, characters are formed facing out and around the rim of a thimble-shaped cup. For example, the NEC Spinwriters are thimble printers.

thin client
(1) A "thin processing" client in a client/server environment that performs very little data processing. X Windows terminals and Windows terminals are examples. Contrast with *fat client*.

(2) A "thin storage" client in a network computer environment. The client downloads the program from the server and performs processing just like a PC, but does not store anything locally. All programs and data are on the server.

thin film
A microscopically thin layer of semiconductor or magnetic material that is deposited onto a metal, ceramic or semiconductor base. For example, the layers that make up a chip and the surface coating on high-density magnetic disks are called thin films.

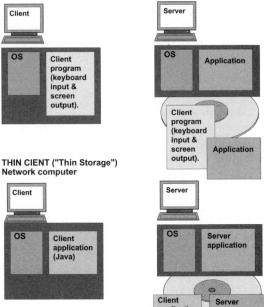

THIN CLIENT ("Thin Processing")
X Window terminal, Windows terminal

THIN CIENT ("Thin Storage")
Network computer

thin film head
A read/write head for high-density disks that is made from thin layers of a conducting film deposited onto a nickel-iron core.

thin server
A network-based computer specialized for some function such as a print server, ISDN router or network attached storage (NAS). Designed for ease of installation, it has little expandability and no keyboard or monitor.

third-generation computer
A computer that uses integrated circuits, disk storage and online terminals. The third generation started roughly in 1964 with the IBM System/360.

third-generation language
A traditional high-level programming language such as FORTRAN, COBOL, BASIC, Pascal and C.

third normal form
See *normalization*.

thrashing
Excessive paging in a virtual memory computer. If programs are not written to run in a virtual memory environment, the operating system may spend excessive amounts of time swapping program pages in and out of the disk.

thread
One transaction or message in a multithreaded system.

threading
See *multithreading*.

three-state logic element
An electronic component that provides three possible outputs: off, low voltage and high voltage.

throughput
The speed with which a computer processes data. It is a combination of internal processing speed, peripheral speeds (I/O) and the efficiency of the operating system and other system software all working together.

thumb
See *elevator*.

thumbnail
A miniature representation of a page or image. A thumbnail program may be stand-alone or part of a desktop publishing or graphics program. Thumbnails take considerable time to generate, but provide a convenient way to browse through multiple images before retrieving the one you need. Programs often let you click on the thumbnail to retrieve it.

thunk
In PCs, to execute the instructions required to switch between segmented addressing of memory and flat addressing.

THz
(TeraHertZ) One trillion cycles per second.

TI
(Texas Instruments, Inc., Dallas, TX, www.ti.com) A leading semiconductor manufacturer founded in 1930 as Geophysical Service, an independent contractor specializing in petroleum exploration using sound waves. In 1951, GSI was renamed Texas Instruments and soon after entered the semiconductor business. TI was the first to commercialize the silicon transistor, pocket radio, integrated circuit, hand-held calculator, single-chip computer and LISP chip.

TIA
(Telecommunications Industry Association, Arlington, VA, www.tiaonline.org) A membership organization founded in 1988 that sets telecommunications standards worldwide. It was originally an EIA working group that was spun off and merged with the U.S. Telecommunications Suppliers Association (USTSA), sponsors of the annual SUPERCOMM conferences.

TIA/EIA-232
See *RS-232*.

tickler
A manual or automatic system for reminding users of scheduled events or tasks. It is used in PIMs, contact management systems and scheduling and calendar systems.

TIFF (TIF file)
(Tagged Image File Format) A widely-used raster graphics file format developed by Aldus and Microsoft that handles monochrome, gray scale, 8-and 24-bit color. Since 1986, there have been six versions of TIFF. It uses several compression methods: LZW provides ratios of about 1.5:1 to 2:1. Ratios of 10:1 to 20:1 are possible for documents with lots of white space using ITU Group III & IV compression methods (fax). TIFF files use the .TIF extension. See *JPEG*.

tightly coupled
Refers to two or more computers linked together and dependent on each other. One computer may control the other, or both computers may monitor each other. For example, a database machine is tightly coupled to the main processor. Two computers tied together for multiprocessing are tightly coupled. Contrast with *loosely coupled*, such as personal computers in a LAN.

tiled
A display of objects side by side; for example, tiled windows cannot be overlapped on top of each other.

timbre

A quality of sound that distinguishes one voice or musical instrument from another. For example, MIDI synthesizers are multi-timbral, meaning that they can play multiple instruments simultaneously.

time base generator

An electronic clock that creates its own timing signals for synchronization and measurement purposes.

timer interrupt

An interrupt generated by an internal clock. See *interrupt*.

timesharing

A multiuser computer environment that lets users initiate their own sessions and access selected databases as required, such as when using online services. A system that serves many users, but for only one application, is technically not timesharing.

time slice

A fixed interval of time allotted to each user or program in a multitasking or timesharing system.

time slot

Continuously repeating interval of time or a time period in which two devices are able to interconnect.

timing clock

See *clock*.

timing signals

Electrical pulses generated in the processor or in external devices in order to synchronize computer operations. The main timing signal comes from the computer's clock, which provides a frequency that can be divided into many slower cycles. Other timing signals may come from a timesharing or realtime clock.

In disk drives, timing signals for reading and writing are generated by holes or marks on one of the platters, or by the way the digital data is actually recorded.

TIRIS

(Texas Instruments Registration and Identification System) An RF/ID system from TI that uses a 3.6x29mm cylindrical tag. Reading can be done from as far as 40 inches away.

TI-RPC

(Transport-Independent-Remote Procedure Call) A set of functions from Sun for executing procedures on remote computers. It is operating system and network independent and allows the development of distributed applications in multivendor environments.

Tivoli Enterprise Management

A comprehensive suite of applications from IBM subsidiary Tivoli Systems, Inc., Austin, TX, that provides enterprise-wide network and systems management across all platforms from IBM mainframes to desktop PCs.

TLA

(Three Letter Acronym) The epitome of acronyms!

TLI

(Transport Level Interface) A common interface for transport services (layer 4 of the OSI model) that is part of UNIX System V. It provides a common language to a transport protocol, allowing client/server applications to be used in different networking environments. See *STREAMS*.

TM1

(Tables Manager 1) A multidimensional analysis program for DOS and Windows from Applix, Inc., Westboro, MA, (www.applix.com), that allows data to be viewed in up to eight dimensions. The data is kept in a database, and the formulas are kept in a spreadsheet, which is used as a viewer into the database. TM1 makes it easy to display different slices of the data, and it is designed to import and cross tab large amounts of data. Originally developed by Sinper Corporation.

TMDS

(Transmission Minimized Differential Signalling) A transmission method for sending digital information to a flat panel display. TMDS is used in the VESA Plug and Display, DFP and DVI interfaces.

TME

See *Tivoli Enterprise Management.*

TN

(Twisted Nematic) The first LCD technology. It twists liquid crystal molecules 90 degrees between polarizers. TN displays require bright ambient light and are still used for low-cost applications. See *STN* and *LCD.*

TOF

(Top Of Form) The beginning of a physical paper form. To position paper in many printers, the printer is turned offline, the forms are aligned properly and the TOF button is pressed.

toggle

To alternate back and forth between two states.

token bus network

A LAN access method that uses the token passing technology in a logical ring over a physical bus. All tokens are broadcast to every station in the network, but only the station with the destination address can transmit. Tokens are passed to the next station by changing the destination address in the token. The MAP factory automation protocol uses the token bus method. See *token passing.*

token passing

A communications network access method that uses a continuously repeating frame (the token) that is transmitted onto the network by the controlling computer. When a terminal or computer wants to send a message, it waits for an empty token. When it finds one, it fills it with the address of the destination station and some or all of its message.

Every computer and terminal on the network constantly monitors the passing tokens to determine if it is a recipient of a message, in which case it "grabs" the message and resets the token status to empty. Token passing uses bus and ring topologies (see *token bus network* and *token ring network*).

token ring network

(1) A LAN access method that uses the token passing technology in a physical ring. Each station in the network passes the token on to the station next to it. Token Ring and FDDI LANs use the token ring access method. See *token passing.*

(2) (Token Ring Network) A LAN access method from IBM that conforms to the IEEE 802.5 token ring standard. It connects up to 255 nodes in a star topology at 4 or 16 Mbits/sec. All stations connect to a central wiring hub called the Multi-station Access Unit, or MAU, using special twisted wire cable. Faster Token Rings at 100 Mbps and 128 Mbps are also emerging.

Token Ring is a data link protocol and functions at the data link and physical levels of the OSI model (1 and 2). See *data link protocol* and *OSI.*

TokenTalk

Software for the Macintosh from Apple that accompanies its TokenTalk NB board and adapts the Mac to Token Ring Networks.

toll office

A telephone central office that generates toll call transactions. Toll accounting used to be performed in tandem offices, but today is mostly generated in the end offices. See *tandem office* and *central office.*

toner

An electrically charged ink used in copy machines and laser printers. It adheres to an invisible image that has been charged with the opposite polarity onto a plate or drum or onto the paper itself.

tool

(1) A program used for software development or system maintenance. Virtually any program or utility that helps programmers or users develop applications or maintain their computers can be called a tool. Examples of programming tools are compilers, interpreters, assemblers, 4GLs, editors, debuggers and application generators.

(2) A program that helps the user analyze or search for data. For example, query and report programs are often called query tools and report tools.

(3) An on-screen function in a graphics program; for example, a line draw, circle draw or brush tool.

toolbar

A row or column of on-screen buttons used to activate functions in the application. Some toolbars are customizable, letting you add and delete buttons as required. See *tool palette*.

ToolBook

A courseware development system for Windows from click2learn.com, Bellevue, WA, (www.click2learn.com), that uses a "page and book" metaphor analogous to HyperCard's "card and stack." Its OpenScript language is similar to HyperTalk.

toolbox, toolkit

A set of software routines that allow a program to be written for and work in a particular environment. The routines are called by the application program to perform various functions, for example, to display a menu or draw a graphic element.

tool palette

A collection of buttons grouped together on screen that provide a quick way to select the functions available in the program. A tool palette is typically found in graphics software such as a drawing program or image editor, but a tool palette can be used to provide functions for any kind of program.

TOP

(Technical Office Protocol) A communications protocol for office systems from Boeing Computer Services. It uses the Ethernet access method and is often used in conjunction with *MAP*, the factory automation protocol developed by GM. TOP is used in the front office, and MAP is used on the factory floor. TOP uses the CSMA/CD access method, while MAP uses token bus.

topdown design

A design technique that starts with the highest level of an idea and works its way down to the lowest level of detail.

topdown programming

A programming design and documentation technique that imposes a hierarchical structure on the design of the program. See *structured programming*.

top of file

The beginning of a file. In a word processing file, it is the first character in the document. In a data file, it is either the first record in the file or the first record in the index. For example, in a dBASE file that is indexed on name, **goto top** might go to physical record #608 if record #608 is AARDVARK.

topology

(1) In a communications network, the pattern of interconnection between nodes; for example, a bus, ring or star configuration.

(2) In a parallel processing architecture, the interconnection between processors; for example, a bus, grid, hypercube or Butterfly Switch configuration.

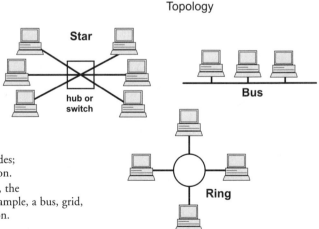

Topology

TOPS

(1) A multiuser, multitasking, timesharing, virtual memory operating system from Digital that runs on its PDP-6, DECsystem 10 and DECsystem 20 series.

(2) (Transparent OPerating System) A peer-to-peer LAN from Sitka Corporation, Alameda, CA, that uses the LocalTalk access method and connects Apple computers, PCs and Sun workstations. Its Flashcard plugs LocalTalk capability into PCs.

TOTAL

An early network DBMS from Cincom Systems that ran on a variety of minis and mainframes.

total bypass

Bypassing local and long distance telephone lines by using satellite communications.

touch screen

A touch-sensitive display screen that uses a clear panel over on the screen surface. The panel is a matrix of cells that transmit pressure information to the software.

tower

(1) A floor-standing cabinet taller than it is wide. Desktop computers can be made into towers by turning them on their side and inserting them into a floor-mounted base.

(2) (Tower) Series of UNIX-based single and multiprocessor computer systems from NCR that use the Motorola 68000 family of CPUs.

TP0-TP4

(Transport Protocol Class 0 to Class 4) The grades of OSI transport layers from least to most complete and specific. TP4 is a full connection-oriented transport protocol.

TPA

(Transient Program Area) See *transient area*.

TPC (TPC-A, TPC-B, TPC-C, TPC-D)

(Transaction Processing Performance Council, San Jose, CA, www.tpc.org) An organization devoted to benchmarking transaction processing systems. TPC benchmarks measure total system performance, including the computer, operating system, database management system and all related components.

Earlier TPC-A and TPC-B benchmarks produced tpsA and tpsB ratings, measured in transactions per second. Subsequent TPC-C benchmarks yield transactions per minutes (tpmC) ratings. TPC-D is designed for decision support and tests 17 complex queries. Its results are relative numbers based on the size of the database.

tpi

(Tracks Per Inch) The measurement of the density of tracks recorded on a disk or drum.

tpmC

See *TPC*.

TP monitor

(TeleProcessing monitor or Transaction Processing monitor) A control program that manages the transfer of data between multiple local and remote terminals and the application programs that serve them. It provides integrity in a distributed environment, ensuring that transactions do not get lost or damaged. It may also include programs that format the terminal screens and validate the data entered. CICS and BEA TUXEDO are examples of widely-used TP monitors.

TP-PMD

(Twisted Pair-Physical Medium Dependent) An ANSI standard for an FDDI network that uses UTP instead of optical fiber. See *CDDI*.

TPS

(1) (Transactions Per Second) The number of transactions processed within one second.

(2) (Transaction Processing System) Originally used as an acronym for such a system, it now refers to the measurement of the system (#1 above).

TQM

(Total Quality Management) An organizational undertaking to improve the quality of manufacturing and service. It focuses on obtaining continuous feedback for making improvements and refining existing processes over the long term. See *ISO 9000*.

track

A storage channel on disk or tape. On disks, tracks are concentric circles (hard and floppy disks) or spirals (CDs and videodiscs). On tapes, they are parallel lines. Their format is determined by the specific drive they are used in. On magnetic devices, bits are recorded as reversals of polarity in the magnetic surface. On CDs, bits are recorded as physical pits under a clear, protective layer. See *magnetic disk*.

trackball

An input device used in video games and as a mouse alternative. It is a stationary unit that contains a movable ball rotated with the fingers or palm and, correspondingly, moves the cursor on screen.

tractor feed

A mechanism that provides fast movement of paper forms through a printer. It contains pins on tractors that engage the paper through perforated holes in its left and right borders. Contrast with *sheet feeder*.

Tradacoms

A European EDI standard developed by the Article Numbering Association. See *X12* and *EDIFACT*.

traffic shaping

Limiting the amount of bandwidth an interface can accomodate. For example, an OC-3 port (155 Mbps) might be installed on a switch, but it can be limited to DS-3 (45 Mbps) traffic for an existing application.

trailer

In communications, a code or set of codes that make up the last part of a transmitted message. See *trailer label*.

trailer label

The last record in a tape file. May contain number of records, hash totals and other ID.

training

(1) In communications, the process by which two modems determine the correct protocols and transmission speeds to use.

(2) In voice recognition systems, the recording of the user's voice in order to provide samples and patterns for recognizing that voice.

transaction

An activity or request. Orders, purchases, changes, additions and deletions are typical business transactions stored in the computer. Queries and other requests are also transactions, but are usually just acted upon and not saved. Transaction volume is a major factor in figuring computer system size and speed.

transaction file

A collection of transaction records. The data in transaction files is used to update the master files, which contain the subjects of the organization. Transaction files also serve as audit trails and are usually transferred from online disks to the data library after some period of time. Contrast with *master file*.

transaction monitor

See *TP monitor*.

transaction processing

Processing transactions as they are received by the computer. Also called "online" or "realtime" systems, master files are updated as soon as transactions are entered at terminals or arrive over communications lines.

If you save receipts in a shoebox and add them up at the end of the year for taxes, that's batch processing. However, if you buy something and immediately add the amount to a running total, that's transaction processing.

transceiver

A transmitter and receiver of analog or digital signals. It comes in many forms; for example, a transponder or network adapter.

transcribe

To copy data from one medium to another; for example, from one source document to another, or from a source document to the computer. It often implies a change of format or codes.

transducer

A device that converts one energy into another; for example, a read/write head converts magnetic energy into electrical energy and vice versa. In process control applications, it is used to convert pressure into an electrical reading.

transfer

To send data over a computer channel or bus. "Transfer" generally applies to transmission within the computer system, and "transmit" refers to transmission outside the computer over a line or network.

Transfers are actually copies, since the data is in both locations at the end of the transfer. Input, output and move instructions activate data transfers in the computer.

transfer rate

Also called "data rate," the transmission speed of a communications or computer channel. Transfer rates are measured in bits or bytes per second.

transfer time

The time it takes to transmit or move data from one place to another. It is the time interval between starting the transfer and the completion of the transfer.

transformer

A device that changes AC voltage. Also called a "power adapter." It is made of steel laminations wrapped with two coils of wire. The coil ratio derives the voltage change. For example, if the input coil has 1,000 windings, and the output has 100, 120 volts is changed to 12. In order to create direct current (DC), the output is passed through a rectifier.

transient

A malfunction that occurs at random intervals; for example, a rapid fluctuation of voltage in a power line or a memory cell that intermittently fails.

transient area

An area in memory used to hold application programs for processing. The bulk of a computer's main memory is used as a transient area.

transient state

The exact point at which a device changes modes, for example, from transmit to receive or 0 to 1.

transistor

A semiconductor device used to amplify a signal or open and close a circuit. In a computer, it functions as an electronic switch. In its normal state, it is non-conductive. When voltage is applied at the gate, it becomes conductive and current flows from

The Transistor Concept

The transistor is an electronic switch. The switching element is made of semiconductor material which conducts electricity when it is pulsed.

If there is no pulse on the trigger line, the semiconductor element is in a non-conductive state. When it is pulsed, it becomes conductive and current flows from the input to the output.

Trigger line not pulsed. Switch is open.

| input line | trigger | output line |
| source / emitter | gate / base | drain / collector |

blue = FET transistor
red = bipolar transistor

semiconductor material

Trigger line pulsed. Switch closes.

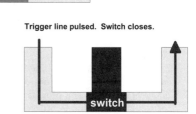

source to drain.

Transistors, resistors, capacitors and diodes, make up logic gates. Logic gates make up circuits, and circuits make up electronic systems.

translate

(1) To change one language into another; for example, assemblers, compilers and interpreters translate source language into machine language.

(2) In computer graphics, to move an image on screen without rotating it.

(3) In telecommunictions, to change the frequencies of a band of signals.

transmission

The transfer of data over a communications channel.

transmission channel

A path between two nodes in a network. It may refer to the physical cable, the signal transmitted within the cable or to a subchannel within a carrier frequency. In radio and TV, it refers to the assigned carrier frequency.

transmit

To send data over a communications line. See *transfer*.

transmitter

A device that generates signals. Contrast with *receiver*.

transparent

Refers to a change in hardware or software that, after installation, causes no noticeable change in operation.

transparent bridging

A communications protocol in which the stations are unaware of bridges in the network. Ethernet uses this method. Contrast with *source routing*.

transparent cache

A computer system or software within a computer system that determines if a requested page or file has already been stored in memory or on its hard disk. If it has not, the request is sent upstream to its normal destination.

transponder

A receiver/transmitter on a communications satellite. It receives a microwave signal from earth (uplink), amplifies it and retransmits it back to earth at a different frequency (downlink). A satellite has several transponders.

transport protocol (transport layer)

A communications protocol responsible for establishing a connection and ensuring that all data has arrived safely. It is defined in layer 4 of the OSI model. Often, the term transport protocol implies transport services, which includes the lower level data link protocol that moves packets from one node to another. See *OSI* and *transport services*.

transport services

The collective functions of layers 1 through 4 of the OSI model.

transputer

(TRANSistor comPUTER) A computer that contains a CPU, memory and communications capability on a single chip. Chips are strung together in hypercube or grid-like patterns to create large parallel processing machines, used in scientific, realtime control and AI applications.

trap

To test for a particular condition in a running program; for example, to "trap an interrupt" means to wait for a particular interrupt to occur and then execute a corresponding routine. An error trap tests for an error condition and provides a recovery routine. A debugging trap waits for the execution of a particular instruction in order to stop the program and analyze the status of the system at that moment.

trapdoor

A secret way of gaining access to a program or online service. Trapdoors are built into the software by the original programmer as a way of gaining special access to particular functions. For example, a trapdoor built into a BBS program would allow access to any BBS computer running that software.

trash can

An icon of a garbage can used for deleting files. The icon of a file is dragged to the trash can and released. In the Mac, the trash can is also used to eject the floppy disk.

trashware

Software that is so poorly designed that it winds up in the garbage can.

Travan

A backup tape technology from Imation Enterprises Corporation, Oakdale, MN, (www.imation.com). Travan has evolved from the QIC backup tapes, but uses wider tape, different tape guides and improved magnetic media to yield higher capacities.

tree

A hierarchical structure. See *directory tree*.

trichromatic

In computer graphics, the use of red, green and blue to create all the colors in the spectrum.

trigger

A mechanism that initiates an action when an event occurs such as reaching a certain time or date or upon receiving some type of input. A trigger generally causes a program routine to be executed.

In a database management system (DBMS), it is an SQL procedure that is executed when a record is added or deleted. It is used to maintain referential integrity in the database. A trigger may also execute a stored procedure. Triggers and stored procedures are built into DBMSs used in client/server environments. See *intelligent database*.

triple precision

The use of three computer words to hold a number used for calculation, providing an enormous amount of arithmetic precision.

troff

(Typesetting RunOFF) A UNIX utility that formats documents for typesetters and laser printers. Using a text editor, troff codes are embedded into the text and the troff command converts the document into the required output. See *nroff*.

Trojan horse

A program routine that invades a computer system by being secretly attached to a valid program that will be downloaded into the computer. It may be used to locate password information, or it may alter an existing program to make it easier to gain access to it. A virus is a Trojan horse that continues to infect programs over and over.

trolling

(1) Surfing, or browsing, the Web.

(2) Posting derogatory messages about sensitive subjects on newsgroups and chat rooms to bait users into responding.

(2) Hanging around in a chat room without saying anything, like a "peeping tom."

TRS-80

(Tandy Radio Shack 80) In 1977, the TRS-80 from Radio Shack was one of the three first personal computers on the market. TRS-DOS was its operating system. See *personal computer*. Also see *TSR*.

True BASIC

An ANSI-standard structured-programming version of BASIC for the PC, Mac and Amiga from True BASIC, Inc., West Lebanon, NH, (www.truebasic.com). Developed in 1984 by BASIC's creators, John Kemeny and Thomas Kurtz, it includes many enhancements over original BASIC. It comes in both interpreter and compiler form.

true color

(1) The ability to generate 16,777,216 colors (24-bit color). See *high color*.

(2) The ability to generate photo-realistic color images (requires 24-bit color minimum).

TrueType

A scalable font technology that renders fonts for both the printer and the screen. Originally developed by Apple, it was enhanced jointly by Apple and Microsoft. TrueType fonts are used in Windows, starting with Windows 3.1, as well as in the Mac System 7 operating system.

Unlike PostScript, in which the algorithms are maintained in the rasterizing engine, each TrueType font contains its own algorithms for converting the outline into bitmaps. The lower-level language embedded within the TrueType font allows unlimited flexibility in the design.

truncate

To cut off leading or trailing digits or characters from an item of data without regard to the accuracy of the remaining characters. Truncation occurs when data is converted into a new record with smaller field lengths than the original.

trunk

A communications channel between two points. It often refers to large-bandwidth telephone channels between major switching centers, capable of transmitting many simultaneous voice and data signals.

trusted computer system

A computer system that cannot be illegally accessed. See *NCSC*.

truth table

A chart of a logical operation's inputs and outputs. See *AND, OR and NOT*.

TSAPI

(Telephony Services **API**) A telephony programming interface from Novell and AT&T. Based on the international CSTA standard, TSAPI is designed to interface a telephone PBX with a NetWare server to provide interoperability between PCs and telephone equipment.

TSAT

See *VSAT*.

TSO

(Time Sharing Option) Software that provides interactive communications for IBM's MVS operating system. It allows a user or programmer to launch an application from a terminal and interactively work with it. The TSO counterpart in VM is CMS. Contrast with *JES*, which provides batch communications for MVS.

TSOP

(Thin Small Outline Package) One-millimeter-thick package used to house dynamic RAM chips.

TSR

(Terminate and Stay Resident) Refers to programs that remain in memory so they can be instantly popped up over the current application by pressing a hotkey. When the program is exited, previous screen contents are restored. TSRs are widely used in DOS-only environments. The term refers to loading a program, terminating its action but not removing it from memory.

TSS

See *ITU*.

TTL

(1) (Transistor Transistor Logic) A digital circuit composed of bipolar transistors wired in a certain manner. TTL logic has been widely used since the early days of digital circuitry. TTL designations may appear on input or output ports of various devices, which indicates a digital circuit in contrast to an analog circuit.

(2) (Time To Live) A set maximum amount of time a packet is allowed to propagate through the network before it is discarded.

TTY

(TeleTYpewriter) See *teletypewriter*.

TTY protocol

A low-speed asynchronous communications protocol with limited or no error checking.

tube

See *CRT* and *vacuum tube*.

tuner

An electronic part of a radio or TV that locks on to a selected carrier frequency (station, channel) and filters out the audio and video signals for amplification and display.

tuple

In relational database management, a record, or row. See *relational database*.

Turbo C

A C compiler from Inprise/Borland used to create a wide variety of commercial products. It is known for its well-designed debugger. Borland's object-oriented versions of C are Turbo C++ and Borland C++.

Turbo Pascal

A pascal compiler for DOS and Windows from Inprise/Borland. For a brief time, Borland moved Pascal from the academic halls to the commercial world.

turnaround document

A paper document or punched card prepared for re-entry into the computer system. Paper documents are printed with OCR fonts for scanning Invoices and inventory stock cards are examples.

turnaround time

(1) In batch processing, the time it takes to receive finished reports after submission of documents or files for processing. In an online environment, turnaround time is the same as *response time*.

(2) In half-duplex transmission, the time it takes to change from transmit to receive and vice versa.

turnkey system

A complete system of hardware and software delivered to the customer ready-to-run.

turnpike effect

In communications, a lock up due to increased traffic conditions and bottlenecks in the system.

turtle graphics

A method for creating graphic images in Logo. The turtle is an imaginary pen that is given drawing commands, such as go forward and turn right. On screen, the turtle is shaped like a triangle.

tutorial

An instructional book or program that takes the user through a prescribed sequence of steps in order to learn a product. Contrast with *documentation*, which, although instructional, tends to group features and functions by category.

TUV

(Technischer Uberwachungs-Verein) Literally "Technical Watch-Over Association." German certifying body involved with product safety for the European Community. The "TsV Rheinland" mark is placed on tested and approved electrical and electronic devices like our UL (Underwriters Laboratory) seal.

Tuxedo

See *BEA TUXEDO*.

TV board

An expansion board in a personal computer that contains a TV tuner. It derives its source from an antenna or cable TV just like any TV set.

TWAIN

A programming interface that lets a graphics application, such as a desktop publishing program, activate a scanner, frame grabber or other image-capturing device.

tweak

To make minor adjustments in an electronic system or in a software program in order to improve performance.

tweening

An animation technique that, based on starting and ending shapes, creates the necessary "in-between" frames. See *morphing*.

twinax, twinaxial

A type of cable similar to coax, but with two inner conductors instead of one. It is used in IBM midrange (AS/400, System/3x) communications environments.

twinax card

An expansion board in a personal computer that emulates a 5250 terminal, the common terminal on an IBM midrange system (AS/400, System/3x).

Twinaxial
Connector

twisted pair

A thin-diameter wire (22 to 26 guage) commonly used for telephone wiring. The wires are twisted around each other to minimize interference from other twisted pairs in the cable. Twisted pairs have less bandwidth than coaxial cable or optical fiber.

The two major types are unshielded twisted pair (UTP) and shielded twisted pair (STP). UTP is popular because it is very pliable and doesn't take up as much room in ductwork as does shielded twisted pair and other cables.

Shielded twisted pair is wrapped in a metal sheath for added protection against external interference. See *cable categories*.

two-out-of-five code

A numeric code that stores one decimal digit in five binary digits in which two of the bits are always 0 or 1 and the other three are always in the opposite state.

two-phase commit

A technique for ensuring that a transaction successfully updates all appropriate files in a distributed database environment. All DBMSs involved in the transaction first confirm that the transaction has been received and is recoverable (stored on disk). Then each DBMS is told to commit the transaction (do the actual updating).

two-wire lines

A transmission channel made up of only two wires, such as used in the common dial-up telephone network.

TWX

(TeletypeWriter eXchange Service) A U.S. and Canadian dial-up communications service that became part of Telex. See *Telex*.

TXD

(Transmitting Data) See *modem*.

TXT file

See *ASCII file*.

Tymnet

A value-added, packet switching network that enables many varieties of terminals and computers to exchange data. It is now part of Concert Communications Services, owned by MCI and British Telecom.

type

(1) In data or text entry, to press the keys on the keyboard.

(2) In programming, a category of variable that is determined by the kind of data stored in it. For example, integer, floating point, string, logical, date and binary are common data types.

(3) In DOS and OS/2, a command that displays the contents of a text file.

Type 1 font, Type 3 font

See *PostScript*.

typeahead buffer

See *keyboard buffer*.

type ball

A golf ball-sized element used in typewriters and low-speed teleprinters that contains all the print characters on its outside surface. It was introduced with IBM's Selectric typewriter.

typeface

The design of a set of printed characters, such as Courier, Helvetica and Times Roman.

typeface family

A group of typefaces that include the normal, bold, italic and bold-italic variations of the same design.

type family

See *typeface family*.

type font

A set of print characters of a particular design (typeface), size (point size) and weight (light, medium, heavy). See *font*.

typematic

A keyboard feature that continues to repeat a key as long as it is held down. The speed of the repeating key as well as the time interval before the repeat begins can be set by the DOS Mode command and control panels in Windows and the Mac.

typeover mode

In word processing and data entry, a state in which each character typed on the keyboard replaces the character at the current cursor location. Contrast with *insert mode*.

type scaler

See *font scaler*.

typesetter

See *imagesetter*.

U

UAE

(Uninterruptible Application Error) The Windows 3.0 equivalent of a GPF. See *GPF*.

UART

(Universal Asynchronous Receiver Transmitter) The electronic circuit for the serial port. It converts parallel bytes from the CPU into serial bits for transmission, and vice versa. It also generates and strips the start and stop bits appended to each character. A UART overrun is a condition in which a UART cannot process the byte that just came in fast enough before the next one arrives.

UCAID

(University Corporation for Advanced Internet Development, Washington, DC, www.ucaid.org) A non-profit consortium founded in 1997 dedicated to developing advanced networking technology. It started as the Internet2 project with 34 universities in late 1996. See *Internet2*.

UDF

(1) (Universal Disk Format) A file system for optical media developed by the Optical Storage Technology Association (OSTA). It was designed for read-write interoperability between all the major operating systems as well as compatibility between rewritable and write-once media.

(2) (User Defined Function) A routine that has been defined or programmed by the user of the system and has been included in a standard library of functions.

UDP

(User Datagram Protocol) A protocol within the TCP/IP protocol suite that is used in place of TCP when a reliable delivery is not required. For example, UDP is used for realtime audio and video traffic where lost packets are simply ignored, because there is no time to retransmit.

UHF

(Ultra High Frequency) The range of electromagnetic frequencies from 300MHz to 3GHz.

UI

See *user interface*.

UIDL

(Unique ID Listing) A POP3 mail server function that assigns a unique number to each incoming mail message. This allows mail to be left on the server after it has been downloaded to the user. Both the mail client and the POP server must support this feature.

u-Law

See *mu-Law*.

ULS server

(User Location Service server) A server on a TCP/IP network (intranet, Internet, etc.) that stores dynamically-assigned IP addresses for users that dial up to log on. When users log on, they notify the ULS server, and other parties can access the server and find out if you are currently online.

Ultra ATA, Ultra DMA, Ultra DMA/33

An enhanced version of the EIDE interface that allows data transfers up to 33 Mbytes/sec.

UltraSPARC

An enhanced series of SPARC chips introduced by Sun in 1995. The UltraSPARC chips are 64-bit CPUs that run all 32-bit SPARC applications.

ultraviolet

An invisible band of radiation at the high-frequency end of the light spectrum. It takes about 10 minutes of ultraviolet light to erase an EPROM chip.

Ultrium

See *LTO*.

UMA, UMB

(Upper Memory Area, Upper Memory Block) The UMA is memory in a PC between 640K and

1024K. UMBs are unused blocks in the UMA. A UMB provider, such as EMM386.EXE, is software that can load and manage drivers and TSRs in these unoccupied areas.

UML

(Unified Modeling Language) An object-oriented design language from the Object Management Group (OMG). Many design methodologies for describing object-oriented systems were developed in the late 1980s. UML "unifies" the popular methods into a single standard, including Grady Booch's work at Rational Software, Rumbaugh's Object Modeling Technique and Ivar Jacobson's work on use cases.

UMTS

(Universal Mobile Telecommunications System) The European implementation of the 3G wireless phone system. UMTS provides service in the 2GHz band and offers global roaming and personalized features. Designed as an evolutionary system for GSM network operators, multimedia data rates up to 2 Mbps are expected. See *IMT-2000*.

unary

Meaning one; a single entity or operation, or an expression that requires only one operand.

unbundle

To sell components in a system separately. Contrast with *bundle*.

UNC

(Universal Naming Convention) A standard for identifying servers, printers and other resources in a network, which originated in the UNIX community. A UNC path uses double slashes or backslashes to precede the name of the computer. The path (disk and directories) within the computer are separated with a single slash or backslash, as follows:

```
//servername/path      UNIX

\\servername\path      DOS/Windows
```

unconditional branch

In programming, a GOTO, BRANCH or JUMP instruction that passes control to a different part of the program. Constrast with *conditional branch*.

undelete

To restore the last delete operation that has taken place. There may be more than one level of undelete, allowing several or all previous deletions to be restored.

underflow

(1) An error condition that occurs when the result of a computation is smaller than the smallest quantity the computer can store.

(2) An error condition that occurs when an item is called from an empty stack.

underscan

Within the normal rectangular viewing area on a display screen. Contrast with *overscan*.

undo

To restore the last editing operation that has taken place. For example, if a segment of text has been deleted or changed, performing an undo will restore the original text. Programs may have several levels of undo.

Unibus

A bus architecture from Digital that was introduced in 1970 with its PDP-11 series. Unibus peripherals can be connected to a VAX through Unibus attachments on the VAXs.

Unicode

A superset of the ASCII character set that uses two bytes for each character rather than one. Able to handle 65,536 character combinations rather than just 256, it can house the alphabets of most of the world's languages. ISO defines a four-byte character set for world alphabets, but also uses Unicode as a subset.

unidirectional

The transfer or transmission of data in a channel in one direction only.

UNIFACE

An application development system for client/server environments from Compuware Corporation, Farmington Hills, MI, (www.compuware.com). It is a repository-driven system that imports a variety of CASE tools. It supports Windows, Mac and OS/2 clients and VMS and UNIX servers. UNIFACE is known for its scalability and deployment on large enterprise-wide applications.

Unify VISION

An application development system for client/server environments from Unify Corporation, Sacramento, CA, (www.unify.com). Introduced in 1993, it provides visual programming tools and supports a variety of UNIX platforms and databases. It provides automated application partitioning for developing three-tier client/server architectures.

uninstall

To remove hardware or software from a computer system. In order to remove a software application from a PC, an uninstall program, also called an "uninstaller," deletes all the files that were initially copied to the hard disk as well as all statements in the AUTOEXEC.BAT, CONFIG.SYS, WIN.INI and SYSTEM.INI files, if applicable. It may also remove the disk directory that was created for the application.

A generic uninstall program, which is used to uninstall any application, must also be running when a new application is initially installed. It records the names of the new directory and files and the changes to the various configuration files for use as reference if it needs to be uninstalled later.

union

In relational database, the joining of two files. See *set theory*.

UniSQL

An object-oriented DBMS from UniSQL, Austin, TX. UniSQL/X is a relational and object-oriented DBMS for UNIX servers that provides SQL and object access to the database. UniSQL/M adds object-oriented capability to SQL Server, ORACLE, Ingres and other relational DBMSs.

Unisys

(Unisys Corporation, Blue Bell, PA, www.unisys.com) An information technology company that was created in 1986 as a merger of the Burroughs and Sperry corporations. It was the largest merger of computer manufacturers in history. Today, Unisys offers a wide range of consulting and support services, as well as enterprise-class computer systems and software, for a variety of industries.

unit record equipment

See *tabulating equipment*.

unit test

Running one component of a system for testing purposes. See *system test*.

UNIVAC I

(UNIVersal Automatic Computer) The first commercially-successful computer, introduced in 1951 by Remington Rand. Over 40 systems were sold. In 1952, it predicted Eisenhower's victory over Stevenson, and UNIVAC became synonymous with computer (for a while).

universal client

A computer that can access a wide variety of applications on the network. The Web browser is hailed as a universal client because of its platform-independent ability to reach the Internet and corporate intranets. An e-mail client (mail program) that can access multiple messaging systems could be called a universal client.

universal server

(1) A database management system (DBMS) that stores all types of information including traditional data fields (relational database) as well as graphics and multimedia (object-oriented database). A universal server is called an "object-relational DBMS" (ORDBMS).

(2) (Universal Server) A universal server from Informix. It supports DataBlades, which are plug-ins designed to manage a particular type of complex data. For example, an image DataBlade might allow a user to search for matching images.

UNIX

A multiuser, multitasking operating system originally developed by AT&T. It is widely used on CAD and scientific workstations and network servers. The UNIX community also developed the protocols that have become the de facto standards on the Internet, such as TCP/IP and SMTP. Sun has been the biggest promoter of UNIX and has made significant contributions to it, but most every hardware vendor has a UNIX version, including IBM, HP and Digital.

UNIX 95, UNIX 98

An X/Open brand used on a product that is compliant with Version 1 and 2 respectively of the Single UNIX Specification.

UNIX socket

A UNIX communications interface that lets an application access a network protocol by "opening a socket" and declaring a destination. Sockets are very popular because they provide a simple way to direct an application onto the network (TCP/IP protocol). NetWare 3.x also supports sockets as one of the common transport interfaces.

UnixWare

See *SCO UnixWare*.

unload

To remove a program from memory or take a tape or disk out of its drive.

unmark

(1) In word processing, to deselect a block of text, which usually removes its highlight.
(2) To deselect an item that has been tagged for a particular purpose.

unpack

See *pack*.

unqualified address

An incomplete address. For example, a mail program may provide a default name for all recipient addressess that are given without a domain name.

unzip

To decompress a zipped archive with the PKUNZIP program.

up

Refers to a device that is working.

UP.Browser

(Unwired Planet.Browser) The trade name for Phone.com's microbrowsers that enable smart phones to interact with the Web. Version 3.x uses HDML, and Version 4.0 and up is WAP compliant. See *HDML* and *WAP*.

UPC

(Universal Product Code) The standard bar code printed on retail merchandise. It contains the vendor's identification number and the product number, which is read by passing the bar code over a scanner.

update

To change data in a file or database. The terms update and edit are often used synonymously.

uplink

A communications channel from an earth station to a satellite. Contrast with *downlink*.

upload

See *download*.

upper CASE

See *front-end CASE*.

UPS

(Uninterruptible Power Supply) Backup power used when the electrical power fails or drops to an unacceptable voltage level. Small UPS systems provide battery power for a few minutes; enough to power down the computer in an orderly manner. Sophisticated systems are tied to electrical generators that can provide power for days.

An online UPS provides a constant source of electrical power from the battery, while the batteries are being recharged from AC power. An offline UPS, also known as a standby power system (SPS), switches to battery within a few milliseconds after detecting a power failure.

uptime

The time during which a system is working without failure. Contrast with *downtime*.

upward compatible

Also called "forward compatible." Refers to hardware or software that is compatible with succeeding versions. Contrast with *downward compatible*.

URL

(Uniform Resource Locator) The address that defines the route to a file on the Web or any other Internet facility. URLs are typed into the browser to access Web pages, and URLs are embedded within the pages themselves to provide the hypertext links to other pages.

The URL contains the protocol prefix, port address, domain name, subdirectory names and file name. Port addresses are generally defaults and are rarely specified. To access a home page on a Web site, only the protocol and domain name are required. For example, **http://www.computerlanguage.com** retrieves the home page at The Computer Language Company's Web site. The **http://** is the Web protocol, and **www.computerlanguage.com** is the domain name.

If a required page is stored in a subdirectory, its name is separated by a slash. Like path names in DOS and Windows, subdirectories can be several levels deep. For example, the components of the following hypothetical URL are described below:

```
http://www.abc.com/clothes/shirts/formal.html
```

```
http://        protocol
www.abc.com/   domain name
clothes/       subdirectory name
shirts/        subdirectory name
formal.html    document name (Web page)
```

USB

(Universal Serial Bus) A personal computer bus endorsed by Intel and others that has a total bandwidth of 1.5MB per second. Up to 127 devices can be attached in a daisy chain fashion. For example, a USB keyboard or monitor could host several ports for additional devices. It is expected to be used for devices such as the mouse, keyboard, printer and scanner. USB ports began to appear on PCs in 1997.

used computers

There is so much computer equipment in the U.S. that a thriving used computer market has been created. There are several computer exchanges that match up buyers and sellers in the U.S., such as the American Computer Exchange, Atlanta, GA, (www.amcoex.com).

Usenet

(USEr NETwork) A public access network on the Internet that provides user news and e-mail. It is a giant, dispersed bulletin board that is maintained by volunteers willing to provide news and mail feeds to other nodes. It began in 1979 as a bulletin board between two universities in North Carolina. All the news that travels over the Internet is called "NetNews."

user

Any individual who interacts with the computer at an application level. Programmers, operators and other technical personnel are not considered users when working in a professional capacity on the computer.

user defined

Any format, layout, structure or language that is developed by the user.

user friendly

A system that is easy to learn and easy to use. This term has been so abused that many vendors are reluctant to use it.

user group

An organization of users of a particular hardware or software product. Members share experiences and ideas to improve their understanding and use of a particular product. User groups are often responsible for influencing vendors to change or enhance their products.

user interface

The combination of menus, screen design, keyboard commands, command language and help screens, which create the way a user interacts with a computer. Mice, touch screens and other input hardware is also included. A well-designed user interface is vital to the success of a software package. In time, interactive video, voice recognition and natural language understanding will be included.

USRT

(Universal Synchronous Receiver Transmitter) An electronic circuit that transmits and receives data on the serial port. It converts bytes into serial bits for transmission, and vice versa, and generates the necessary signals for synchronous transmission.

utility program (utilities)

A program that supports using the computer. Utility programs, or "utilities," provide file management capabilities, such as sorting, copying, comparing, listing and searching, as well as diagnostic and measurement routines that check the health and performance of the system.

UTP

See *twisted pair*.

UTF

(Universal Transformation Format) A method for converting 16-bit Unicode characters into 7- or 8-bit characters. UTF-7 converts to 7-bit ASCII for transmission over 7-bit mail systems, while UTF-8 converts Unicode to 8-bit bytes. See *Unicode* and *7-bit ASCII*.

UUCP

(UNIX to UNIX CoPy) A UNIX utility that copies a file from one computer to another. It is commonly used as a mail transfer. Unlike TCP/IP, which is a routable communications protocol, UUCP provides a point-to-point transmission where a user at one UNIX computer dials up and establishes a session with another UNIX computer.

UUencode (UUcoding)

A method for encoding binary files for tansmission via Internet e-mail, which was originally designed for ASCII text. UUencode and UUdecode were the first methods. Today, MIME is widely used. See *BinHex* and *MIME*.

UUNET

(UUNET Technologies, Inc., Fairfax, VA, www.uunet.net) Founded in 1987, UUNET was the first commercial Internet service provider. Originally offering e-mail and news, it is now a full Internet service organization providing dial-up and leased line accounts as well as archive space for files and Web pages. UUNET stands for UNIX to UNIX Network. In 1996, UUNET was acquired by MFS Communications, which itself was acquired by WorldCom, Inc., in that same year. Worldcom was later acquired by MCI.

V

V.17 - V.120 standards

Transmission standards originally developed by the CCITT, now known as the Telecommunications Standards Section of the International Telecommunications Union (ITU-TSS).

V.17 - (1991) A fax standard that uses TCM modulation at 12000 and 14400 bps for Group 3. Modulation use is a half-duplex version of V.32bis.

V.21 - (1964) Asynchronous 0-300 bps full-duplex modems for use on dial-up lines. It uses FSK modulation.

V.22 - (1980) Asynchronous and synchronous 600 and 1200 bps full-duplex modems for use on dial-up lines. It uses DPSK modulation.

V.22bis - (1984) Asynchronous and synchronous 2400 bps full-duplex modems for use on dial-up lines and two-wire leased lines, with fallback to V.22 1200 bps operation. It uses QAM modulation.

V.23 - (1964) Asynchronous and synchronous 0-600 and 0-1200 bps half-duplex modems for use on dial-up lines. It uses FSK modulation.

V.24 - (1964) Defines the functions of all circuits for the RS-232 interface.

V.25 - (1968) Automatic calling and/or answering equipment on dial-up lines.

V.25bis - (1968) Second standard for automatic calling and/or answering equipment on dial-up lines.

V.26 - (1968) Synchronous 2400 bps full-duplex modems for use on four-wire leased lines. It uses DPSK modulation and includes an optional 75 bps back channel.

V.26bis - (1972) Synchronous 1200 and 2400 bps full-duplex modems for use on dial-up lines. It uses DPSK modulation and includes an optional 75 bps back channel.

V.26ter - (1984) Asynchronous and synchronous 2400 bps full-duplex modems using DPSK modulation over dial-up and two-wire leased lines.

V.27 - (1972) Synchronous 4800 bps full-duplex modems for use on four-wire leased lines. It uses DPSK modulation.

V.27bis - (1976) Synchronous 2400 and 4800 bps full-duplex modems using DPSK modulation for use on four-wire leased lines. The primary difference between V.27 and V.27bis is the addition of an automatic adaptive equalizer.

V.27ter - (1976) Synchronous 2400 and 4800 bps half-duplex modems using DPSK modulation on dial-up lines. It includes an optional 75 bps back channel. V.27ter is used in Group 3 fax transmission without the back channel.

V.28 - (1972) Defines the functions of all circuits for the RS-232 interface. In the U.S., EIA-232 incorporates the electrical signal definitions of V.28, the control signals of V.25 and the connector and pin assignments defined in ISO 2110.

V.29 - (1976) Synchronous 4800, 7200 and 9600 bps full-duplex modems using QAM modulation on four-wire leased lines. It has been adapted for Group 3 fax transmission over dial-up lines at 9600 and 7200 bps.

V.32 - (1984) Asynchronous and synchronous 4800 and 9600 bps full-duplex modems using TCM modulation over dial-up or two-wire leased lines. TCM encoding may be optionally added. V.32 uses echo cancellation to achieve full-duplex transmission.

V.32bis - (1991) Asynchronous and synchronous 4800, 7200, 9600, 12000 and 14400 bps full-duplex modems using TCM and echo cancellation. Supports rate renegotiation, which allows modems to change speeds as required.

V.32terbo - This is an AT&T standard for 19200 bps modems adopted by some modem manufacturers.

V.33 - (1988) Synchronous 12000 and 14400 bps full-duplex modems for use on four-wire leased lines using QAM modulation. It includes an optional time-division multiplexor for sharing the transmission line among multiple terminals.

V.34 - (1994) A standard for 28800 bps modems. AT&T's V.32terbo and Rockwell International's V.FC are competing technologies that are faster than the V.32bis 14400 bps standard.

V.35 - (1968) Group band modems that combine the bandwidth of several telephone circuits to achieve high data rates. V.35 has become known as a high-speed RS-232 interface rather than a type of modem. The large, rectangular V.35 connector was never specified in V.35, but has become a de facto standard for a high-speed interface.

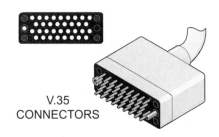

V.35
CONNECTORS

V.42 - (1989) Modem error checking that uses LAP-M as the primary protocol and provides MNP Classes 2 through 4 as an alternative protocol for compatibility.

V.42bis - (1989) Modem data compression. It uses the British Telecom Lempel Ziv technique to achieve up to a 4:1 ratio. V.42bis implies the V.42 error checking protocol.

V.54 - (1976) Various loopback tests that can be incorporated into modems for testing the telephone circuit and isolating transmission problems.

V.56 - (1972) Method of testing modems to compare their performance. Newer procedures are currently under study.

V.90 - (1998) A standard for 56 Kbps modems downstream and 33.6 Kbps upstream. It is intended for use only with ISPs and online services that are digitally attached to the telephone system. In practice, the downstream link isn't generally faster than 45 Kbps.

V.110 - (1984) Specifies how data terminal equipment (DTE) with asynchronous or synchronous serial interfaces can be supported on an ISDN network.

V.120 - (1988) Specifies how DTEs with asynchronous or synchronous serial interfaces can be supported on an ISDN network using a protocol (similar to LAP-D) to encapsulate the data to be transmitted.

VAC
(Volts Alternating Current) See *volt* and *AC*.

vacuum tube
An electronic device that controls the flow of electrons in a vacuum, used as a switch, amplifier or display screen. Used as on/off switches, they allowed the first computers to perform digital computations. Today, it is primarily the CRT in monitors and TVs.

VAD
(Value Added Dealer) Same as *VAR*.

validity checking
Routines in a data entry program that tests the input for correct and reasonable conditions, such as numbers falling within a range and correct spelling, if possible. See *check digit*.

value

(1) The content of a field or variable. It can refer to alphabetic as well as numeric data. For example, in the expression, **state** = "**PA**", PA is a value.

(2) In spreadsheets, the numeric data within the cell.

value-added network

A communications network that provides services beyond normal transmission, such as automatic error detection and correction, protocol conversion and message storing and forwarding. Telenet and Tymnet are examples of value-added networks.

VAN

See *value-added network.*

VAP

(Value Added Process) Software that enhances or provides additional server functions in a NetWare 286 server. Support for different kinds of workstations, database engines, fax and print servers are examples. The NetWare 386 counterpart is the NLM.

vaporware

Software that has been advertised but not delivered.

VAR

(Value Added Reseller) An organization that adds value to a system and resells it. For example, it could purchase a CPU and peripherals from different vendors and graphics software from another and package it together as a specialized CAD system. See *OEM.*

variable

A programming structure that holds data. It can contain numbers or alphanumeric characters and is given a unique named by the programmer. It holds the data until a new value is stored in it or the program is finished.

variable length field

A record structure that holds fields of varying lengths. For example, PAT SMITH takes nine bytes and GEORGINA WILSON BARTHOLOMEW takes 27. A couple of bytes of control information would also be added. If fixed length fields were used, 27 bytes would have to be reserved for both names.

variable length record

A data record that contains one or more variable length fields.

varname

(VARiable NAME) An abbreviation for specifying the name of a variable.

VAX

(Virtual Address eXtension) A family of 32-bit computers from Digital introduced in 1977 with the VAX-11/780 model. VAXes range from desktop personal computers to mainframes all running the same VMS operating system. Software compatibility between models caused the VAX family to achieve outstanding success during the 1980s.

VAXstation

A single-user VAX computer that runs under VMS introduced in 1988.

VB

See *Visual Basic.*

VBA

(Visual Basic for Applications) A subset of Visual Basic that provides a common macro language for Microsoft applications. VBA lets power users and programmers extend the functionality of programs such as Word, Excel and Access.

VBE

(VESA BIOS Extension) A VESA VGA standard for interrogating the capabilities of a graphics adapter. It allows the software developer to write a universal driver for all VBE-compliant VGA cards.

VBRUNxxx.DLL

(Visual Basic RUNtime version #.DLL) The Visual Basic runtime module. A Visual Basic application is made up of a series of calls to Visual Basic routines, which are contained in the DLL, and VBRUNxxx.DLL must be available to run them. The xxx represents the version of Visual Basic (VBRUN300, VBRUN400, etc.).

VB Script

(Visual Basic Script) A programming language for World Wide Web applications from Microsoft. It is an extension to Microsoft's Visual Basic language. See *Jscript*.

VBX

(Visual Basic EXtension) A component software technology from Microsoft that enables a Visual Basic (Windows) program to add funtionality by calling ready-made components (controls). Also called "Visual Basic Controls," they appear to the end user as just another part of the program. VBXs were Micrsofts's first component architecture, and 16-bit VBXs were superseded by 32-bit OCXs. See *OCX* and *ActiveX control*.

V-chip

A chip that blocks objectionable TV programs. The U.S. and Canada have mandated its implementation in new TVs, and other countries are considering it. When fully implemented, TV programs will transmit the program's rating in the vertical blanking interval, and the chip will decode it.

VCR

(Video Cassette Recorder) A videotape recording and playback machine. The most common format is VHS.

VDE

(Verband Deutscher Elektrotechniker) The German counterpart of the U.S. Underwriters Lab.

VDM

(Virtual DOS Machine) A DOS session created by OS/2 and Windows NT in order to run an individual DOS or 16-bit Windows applications.

VDT, VDU

(Video Display Terminal, Video Display Unit) A terminal with a keyboard and display screen.

vector

(1) In computer graphics, a line designated by its end points (x-y or x-y-z coordinates). When a circle is drawn, it is made up of many small vectors. See *vector graphics* and *graphics*.

(2) In matrix algebra, a one-row or one-column matrix.

vector display

A display terminal that draws vectors on the screen. Contrast with *raster display*.

vector font

A scalable font made of vectors (point-to-point line segments). It is easily scaled as are all vector-based images, but lacks the hints and mathematically-defined curves of outline fonts, such as Adobe Type 1 and TrueType.

vector graphics

In computer graphics, a technique for representing a picture as points, lines and other geometric entities. See *graphics*. Contrast with *raster graphics*.

vector processor

A computer with built-in instructions that perform multiple calculations on vectors (one-dimensional arrays) simultaneously. It is used to solve the same or similar problems as an array processor; however, a vector processor passes a vector to a functional unit, whereas an array processor passes each element of a vector to a different arithmetic unit. See *pipeline processing* and *array processor*.

Venn diagram

A graphic technique for visualizing set theory concepts using overlapping circles and shading to indicate intersection, union and complement.

verify

In data entry operations, to compare the keystrokes of a second operator with the files created by the first operator.

Verilog

A hardware description language (HDL) used to design electronic systems at the component, board and system level.

Veronica

A program that searches the Internet for specific resources. Using Boolean searches (this AND this, this OR this, etc.), users can search Gopher servers to retrieve a selected group of menus. See *Gopher*.

version control

The management of source code in a large software project. Version-control software provides a database that keeps track of the revisions made to a program by all the programmers involved in it.

version number

The identification of a release of software. The difference between Version 2.2 and 2.3 can be night and day, since new releases not only add features, but often correct bugs. What's been driving you crazy may have been fixed!

Numbers, such as 3.1a or 3.11, often indicate a follow-up release only to fix a bug in the previous version, whereas 3.1 and 3.2 usually mean routine enhancements. Version "1.0" drives terror into the hearts of experienced users. The program has just been released, and bugs are still to be uncovered.

vertical bandwidth

See *vertical scan frequency*.

VerticalNet

(VerticalNet Inc., Horsham, PA, www.verticalnet.com) An organization that develops, owns and operates business-to-business Web portals for scientific, industrial and manufacturing industries.

vertical portal

A vertical-market Web site that provides information and services to a particular industry.

vertical recording

A magnetic recording method that records the bits vertically instead of horizontally, taking up less space and providing greater storage capacity. The vertical recording method uses a specialized material for the construction of the disk.

vertical resolution

Number of lines (rows in a matrix). Contrast with *horizontal resolution*.

vertical scan frequency (vertical refresh)

Also called "refresh rate," it is the number of times an entire display screen is refreshed, or redrawn, per second. Measured in Hertz, display systems typically range from 56Hz to well over 100Hz. A minimum of 70Hz is recommended to help prevent eye strain. Contrast with *horizontal scan frequency*.

VESA

(Video Electronics Standards Association, San Jose, CA, www.vesa.org) A membership organization founded in 1989 that sets interface standards for the PC, workstation and computing environments. Note the following VESA standards following this entry.

VESA BIOS

A BIOS chip that conforms to a VESA standard. It typically refers to the BIOS on a VGA display adapter that is VESA compliant.

vesicular film

A film used to make copies of microforms. It contains its own developer and creates a pink negative or positive copy when exposed to a negative master through ultraviolet light.

VFAT

(Virtual File Allocation Table) The file system used in Windows for Workgroups and Windows 95/98. It provides 32-bit Protected Mode access for file manipulation. VFAT is faster than, but also compatible with, the DOS 16-bit File Allocation Table (FAT). In Windows for Workgroups, VFAT was called "32-bit file access." In Windows 95/98, it supports long file names up to 255 characters.

V.FC, V.Fast Class

A modem technology for 28800 bps from Rockwell International endorsed by many modem vendors before V.34 was finalized. V.FC is very similar to V.34, but V.FC modems require an upgraded chip for full compatibility.

VGA

(Video Graphics Array) The minimum standard for PC video display, which originated with IBM's PS/2 models in 1987. It supports earlier CGA and EGA modes and requires an analog monitor. VGA was initially 640x480 pixels with 16 colors, but non-IBM vendors quickly boosted resolution and colors to so-called "Super VGA," which was later standardized by VESA. All VGA display adapters today start at 256 colors.

VGA feature connector

A port on a VGA board that provides palette information and clock signals to another board that processes video. For example, a board that displays TV on screen requires synchronization from the VGA adapter. The feature connector uses a 26-pin male connector or a 26-pin (13 each side) edge connector at the top of the VGA board.

VGA pass through

A feature of a high-resolution display adapter that does not contain a standard VGA display. It couples internally to another VGA card inside the machine.

VHDL

(VHSIC Hardware Description Langauge) A language used to design electronic systems at the component, board and system level. It supports simulation for design verification and "what if" analysis.

VHF

(Very High Frequency) The range of electromagnetic frequencies from 30MHz to 300MHz.

VHS

A VCR format introduced by JVC in 1976 to compete with Sony's Beta format. VHS has become the standard for home and industry, and Beta is now obsolete. SVHS (Super VHS) is a subsequent format that improves resolution.

VHSIC

(Very High Speed Integrated Circuit) Pronounced "vizik." Ultra-high-speed chips employing LSI and VLSI technologies.

vi

(Visual Interface) A UNIX full-screen text editor that can be run from a terminal or the system console. It is a fast, programmer-oriented utility.

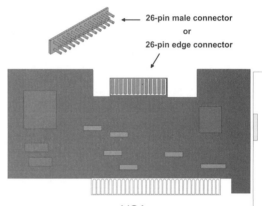

26-pin male connector
or
26-pin edge connector

VGA
FEATURE CONNECTOR

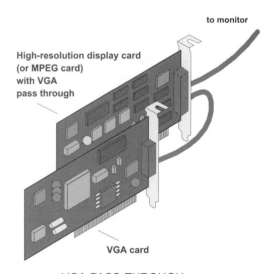

to monitor

High-resolution display card
(or MPEG card)
with VGA
pass through

VGA card

VGA PASS THROUGH

video

An audio/visual playback and recording technology used in TV. It also refers to computer screens and terminals. However, there is only one TV/video standard in the U.S., but there are dozens of computer/ video display standards.

video accelerator

A hardware component on a display adapter that speeds up full-motion video. The primary video accelerator functions are color space conversion, which converts YUV to RGB, hardware scaling, which is used to enlarge the image to full screen and double buffering which moves the frames into the frame buffer faster. See *graphics accelerator*.

video adapter

See *video capture board*, *video graphics board* and *display adapter*.

video bandwidth

The maximum display resolution of a video screen, measured in MHz, and calculated by horizontal x vertical resolution x refreshes/sec. For example, 800x600x60 = 28.8MHz. TV studio recording is limited to 5MHz; TV broadcasting is limited to 3.58Mhz.

video board

See *display adapter* and *video capture board*.

video camera

A camera that takes continuous pictures and generates a signal for display or recording. It captures images by breaking down the image into a series of lines. The U.S. and Canadian standard (NTSC) is 525 scan lines. Each line is scanned one at a time, and the continuously varying intensities of red, green and blue light across the line are filtered out and converted into a variable signal. Most video cameras are analog, but digital video cameras are also available. See *digital camera*.

video capture board

An expansion board that digitizes full-motion video from a VCR, camera or other NTSC video source. The board may also provide digital to analog conversion for recording onto a VCR.

video card

Same as *display adapter*.

Video CD

Video playback on a CD. Developed by Matsushita, Philips, Sony and JVC, Video CD holds 74 minutes of VHS-quality video, including CD-quality sound. Video CD movies are compressed using the MPEG I method and require an MPEG decoder.

video codec

A circuit that converts NTSC video into digital code and vice versa. It incorporates a compression technique to reduce the data and may or may not provide full-motion video.

videoconferencing

A video communications session among several people that are geographically separated. This form of conferencing started with room systems where groups of people meet in a room with a wide-angle camera and large monitors and conference with other groups at remote locations.

Desktop videoconferencing over LANs as well as over the plain old telephone system (POTS) is also available. Although many proprietary systems have been used, the H.323 and H.324 standards are expected to make interoperable systems mainstream.

video controller

(1) A device that controls some kind of video function.

(2) Same as *display adapter*.

video digitizer

Same as *frame grabber*.

videodisc

See *LaserDisc* and *Video CD*.

video display board, video display card

See *display adapter* and *video graphics board*.

video display terminal/unit

Same as *video terminal*.

video editing

See *nonlinear video editing*.

video editor

A dedicated computer that controls two or more videotape machines. It keeps track of frame numbers in its own database and switches the recording machine from playback to record. The video editor reads SMPTE time codes provided on professional tape formats.

Video for Windows

A video driver and utilities from Microsoft for Windows 3.1 and higher. It supports the AVI movie file format and three video compression methods (Microsoft Video 1, Microsoft RLE and Intel's Indeo).

videographer

A person involved in the production of video material.

video graphics board

A display adapter that generates text and graphics and accepts video from a camera or VCR. Truevision's Targa board and Vision Technologies Vision board are examples. The terms video graphics board and video display board sound alike, but video display board is another term for display adapter, which normally does not handle NTSC video.

video on demand

See *VOD*.

video overlay card

A graphics controller that allows NTSC video and computer images to be mixed.

video port

A socket on a computer used to connect a monitor. On a PC, the standard video port is a 15-pin VGA connector. See *VGA*.

video RAM

A specially-designed memory circuits on a video display board that are used to hold the image that appears on the video screen. Often uses dual-ported RAM, which allows simultaneous reads and writes.

video server

A computer that delivers streaming video for video on demand applications. Video servers may be computers that are specialized for this purpose. The term may just refer to the software that performs this service. See *streaming video*.

videotape

A magnetic tape used for recording full-animation video images. The most widely used videotape format is the 1/2" wide VHS cassette. VHS has all but obsoleted earlier videotape formats for home and commercial use.

video terminal

A data entry device that uses a keyboard for input and a display screen for output. Although the display screen resembles a TV, it usually does not accept TV/video signals.

videotex

The first attempts at interactive information delivery for shopping, banking, news, etc. Many trials were made, but it never caught on. It used a TV set-top box and keyboard. Data was delivered by phone line and stored in the box as predefined frames with limited graphics that were retrieved by a menu.

Video Toaster

A popular video production system for the Amiga computer from NewTek, Inc., San Antonio, TX. Considered the most affordable broadcast-quality system on the market, it includes hardware and software that provides digital effects, character generation and 3-D animation.

video window

The display of full-motion video (TV) in an independent window on a computer screen.

view

(1) To display and look at data on screen.

(2) In relational database management, a special display of data, created as needed. A view temporarily ties two or more files together so that the combined files can be displayed, printed or queried; for example, customers and orders or vendors and purchases. Fields to be included are specified by the user. The original files are not permanently linked or altered; however, if the system allows editing, the data in the original files will be changed.

viewer

See *file viewer*.

viewport

(1) In the Macintosh, the entire scrollable region of data that is viewed through a window.

(2) Same as *window*.

VIM

(Vendor Independent Messaging Interface) A programming interface developed by Lotus, Novell, IBM, Apple, Borland, MCI, WordPerfect and Oracle. In order to enable an application to send and receive mail over a VIM-compliant messaging system such as cc:Mail, programmers write to the VIM interface.

VINES

(VIrtual NEtworking System) A UNIX System V-based network operating system from Banyan Systems Inc., that runs on DOS and OS/2-based servers. VINES provides internetworking of PCs, minis, mainframes and other computer resources providing information sharing across organizations of unlimited size. Its Streettalk directory service provides access to all network users and resources.

viral marketing

A marketing approach that spreads like wildfire and has nothing to do with computer viruses. The term was coined by venture capital firm, Draper Fisher Jurvetson, Redwood City, CA, (www.venture-capital.com), after its investment in Hotmail grew dramatically. Hotmail automatically puts an advertisement at the end of everybody's e-mail message suggesting that they sign up for the free service. In a year and a half, more than 12 million people became Hotmail users.

viral programming

Developing programs that replicate themselves. Although known more as the means to write viruses, viral programming is used to develop software agents that replicate themselves throughout the network or Internet for the benefit of the user. Such programs can detect problems in a network or be used to find the best price for merchandise when replicated and snooping around multiple shopping sites.

virtual

An adjective applied to almost anything today that that expresses a condition without boundaries or constraints.

Virtual 8086 Mode

An operational mode in Intel x86 chips (starting with the 386) that allows it to perform as multiple 8086 CPUs. Under direction of a control program, each virtual machine runs as a stand-alone 8086 running its own operating system and applications, thus DOS, UNIX and other operating systems can be running simultaneously. All virtual machines are multitasked together.

This mode divides up the computer into multiple address spaces and maintains virtual registers for each virtual machine. This is not the same as the 386's virtual memory mode, which extends main memory to disk.

virtual circuit

The resulting pathway created between two devices communicating with each other in a switched communications system. A message from New York to Los Angeles may actually start in New York and go through Atlanta, St. Louis, Denver and Phoenix before it winds up in Los Angeles.

It can also be confined to smaller geography, say within a building or campus, in which case the virtual circuit traverses some number of switches, hubs and other network devices. See *PVC* and *SVC*.

virtual company, virtual office

An organization that uses computer and telecommunications technologies to extend its capabilities by working routinely with employees or contractors located throughout the country or the world.

virtual desktop

An infinitely-large desktop, which is provided either by a virtual screen capability or a shell program that enhances the user interface.

virtual desktop

An infinitely-large desktop, which is provided either by a virtual screen capability or a shell program that enhances the user interface. See *virtual screen*.

virtual device

See *virtual peripheral* and *VxD*.

virtual device driver

See *VxD*.

virtual disk

Same as *RAM disk*.

virtual image

In graphics, the complete graphic image stored in memory, not just the part of it that is displayed at the current time.

virtualize

(1) To activate a program in virtual memory.

(2) To create a virtual screen.

virtual LAN

Also called a "VLAN," it is a logical subgroup within a local area network that is created via software rather than manually moving cables in the wiring closet. It combines user stations and network devices into a single unit regardless of the physical LAN segment they are attached to and allows traffic to flow more efficiently within populations of mutual interest.

VLANs are implemented in port switching hubs and LAN switches and generally offer proprietary solutions. VLANs reduce the time it takes to implement moves, adds and changes.

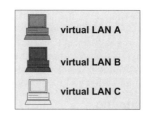

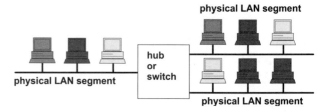

virtual machine

(1) A computer that runs an operating system that can host other operating systems or multiple copies of itself. Each operating system runs its own set of applications timeshared equally or in some priority with all the other operating systems. Computers can be built with hardware circuits that support a virtual machine environment; for example, the Virtual 8086 Mode in the 386. See *VM*.

(2) A computer that has built-in virtual memory capability.

The Computer Glossary

virtual memory

Simulating more memory than actually exists, allowing the computer to run larger programs or more programs concurrently. It breaks up the program into small segments, called "pages," and brings as many pages into memory that fit into a reserved area for that program. When additional pages are required, it makes room for them by swapping them to disk. It keeps track of pages that have been modified, so that they can be retrieved when needed again.

virtual monitor

In the Macintosh, the ability to dynamically configure to any monitor type and to use multiple monitors of different types including displaying the same object across two or more screens.

virtual network

An interconnected group of networks (an internet) that appear as one large network to the user. Optionally, or perhaps ideally, a virtual network can be centrally managed and controlled.

virtual operating system

An operating system that can host other operating systems. See *virtual machine*.

virtual peripheral

A peripheral device simulated by the operating system.

virtual printer

A simulated printer. If a program is ready to print, but all printers are busy, the operating system will transfer the printer output to disk and keep it there until a printer becomes available.

virtual private network

See *VPN*. Remember... look up the acronym first!

virtual processing

A parallel processing technique that simulates a processor for applications that require a processor for each data element. It creates processors for data elements above and beyond the number of processors available.

virtual processor

A simulated processor in a virtual processing system.

virtual reality

An artificial reality that projects the user into a 3-D space generated by computer. Implementations include the use of a data glove and head-mounted stereoscopic display, which allow users to point to and manipulate illusory objects in their view.

The term is also used for computer games and interactive environments on the Web that allow you to move from one room or area to another. They of course lack the 360 degree reality that comes from wearing the glove and goggles. See *HMD, CAVE, 6DOF, cyberspace* and *VRML*.

virtual route

Same as *virtual circuit*.

virtual screen

A viewing area that is larger than the physical borders of the screen. It allows the user to scroll very large documents or multiple documents side by side by moving the mouse pointer beyond the edge of the screen. For example, you might look through an 800x600 screen resolution into a 1600x1200 virtual screen.

virtual storage

Same as *virtual memory*.

virtual terminal

Terminal emulation that allows access to a foreign system. Often refers to a personal computer gaining access to a mini or mainframe.

virtual toolkit

Development software that creates programs for several computer environments. Its output may require additional conversions or translations to produce executable programs.

virus

Software used to infect a computer. After the virus code is written, it is buried within an existing program. Once that program is executed, the virus code is activated and attaches copies of itself to other programs in the system. Infected programs copy the virus to other programs.

The effect of the virus may be a simple prank that pops up a message on screen out of the blue or the actual destruction of programs and data. A virus cannot be attached to data. It must be attached to a runnable program that is downloaded into or installed in the computer. The virus-attached program must be executed in order to activate the virus. See *polymorphic virus, stealth virus* and *worm*.

Be Careful Out There!

Before you run any shareware, public domain or freeware program or any program from the Internet that was sent to you via e-mail without your request, be sure to check it with a virus detection program first! Antivirus programs can run in the background and automatically detect downloaded viruses.

virus signature

A binary pattern of the actual machine code of a particular virus. Antivirus programs use virus signatures for fast detection of known viruses.

VIS

(Voice Information Service) A variety of voice processing service applications.

ViSCA

(VIdeo System Control Architecture) A Sony protocol for synchronized control of multiple video peripherals. ViSCA is the software interface. Control-L is the hardware interface. A ViSCA-compatible VCR can be controlled directly by video capture software.

VisiCalc

The first electronic spreadsheet, introduced in 1978 for the Apple II. It was a command-driven program followed by SuperCalc, MultiPlan, Lotus 1-2-3 and others, each improving the user interface. Spreadsheets have also been implemented on minis and mainframes. It all started with VisiCalc.

VisualAge

A family of object-oriented development software from IBM that includes VisualAge for Basic, VisualAge for C++, VisualAge for COBOL, VisualAge for Java, VisualAge for PacBase and VisualAge for Smalltalk. For example, VisualAge for C++ is a multiplatform environment for writing C++ applications for OS/2, Windows, AS/400, MVS/ESA, AIX and Solaris. It is widely used to write an application on one platform that will be used on another.

Today, the skills of a VisualAge programmer are not implicit, as the term refers to several languages. In the past it implied one or two. The VisualAge name was first used in the late 1980s for Smalltalk, then in 1994 for C++ and later for all the others.

Visual Basic

A version of BASIC from Microsoft specialized for Windows applications that has become very popular. It is similar to Microsoft's QuickBASIC, but is not 100% compatible with it. User interfaces are developed by dragging objects from the Visual Basic Toolbox onto the application form.

Visual C++

A C and C++ development system for DOS and Windows applications from Microsoft. Introduced in 1993, the Standard Edition of Visual C++ replaces QuickC for Windows and the Professional Edition includes the Windows SDK and replaces Microsoft C/C++ 7.0.

Visual FoxPro

An Xbase development system for Windows from Microsoft. Originally known as FoxPro for Windows, FoxPro for DOS, etc., Visual FoxPro added object orientation and client/server support. Many applications have been written in this business-oriented language. Version 3.0 was the last Macintosh version and 2.6 was the last DOS version.

Visual InterDev

A Windows-based development system from Microsoft for building dynamic Web applications using Microsoft standards. It is used to write Active Server Pages that can interact with databases and ActiveX-based components in the server.

visualization

In computer graphics, the converting of numeric data into picture form to allow humans to recognize patterns that are difficult to identify in numeric form. It is used especially in research situations, both theoretical and practical.

Visual J++

A Windows-based Java development system from Microsoft. It is used to create Java applications that can run on any platform or to create Windows-specific applications that call ActiveX components or Windows directly. Visual J++ also includes a Java compiler.

visual programming

Developing programs with tools that allow menus, buttons and other graphics elements to be selected from a palette and drawn and built on screen. It may include developing source code by creating and/or interacting with flow charts that graphically display the logic paths and associated code.

Visual Studio

A suite of development tools from Microsoft that include its major programming languages and Web development package. The Enterprise Edition includes version control, a database, TP monitor and reference material.

VLAN

See *virtual LAN*.

VLB, VL-bus

(VESA Local-BUS) A peripheral bus from VESA that was primarily used in 486s. It provides a high-speed data path between the CPU and peripherals (video, disk, network, etc.). VL-bus is a 32-bit bus that supports bus mastering and runs at speeds up to 40MHz.

VLF

(Very Low Frequency) See *low radiation*.

VLIW

(Very Long Instruction Word) A CPU architecture that reads a group of instructions and executes them at the same time.

VLSI

(1) (Very Large Scale Integration) Between 100,000 and one million transistors on a chip.

(2) (VLSI Technology, Inc., Tempe, AZ, www.vlsi.com) A designer and manufacturer of custom chips that was acquired by Philips Semiconductor.

VM

(Virtual Machine) An IBM mainframe operating system, originally developed by its customers and eventually adopted as an IBM system product (VM/SP). It can run multiple operating systems within the computer at the same time, each one running its own programs. CMS (Conversational Monitor System) provides VM's interactive capability.

v-mail

(Video mail) The ability to send video clips along with e-mail messages. This is not the same as video conferencing, which requires realtime capabilities between sender and receiver, but it does require high-speed computers and networks.

VMEbus

(VersaModule Eurocard bus) A 32-bit bus developed by Motorola, Signetics, Mostek and Thompson CSF. It is widely used in industrial, commercial and military applications with over 300 manufacturers of VMEbus products worldwide. VME64 is an expanded version that provides 64-bit data transfer and addressing.

VMS

(1) (Virtual Memory System) A multiuser, multitasking, virtual memory operating system for the VAX series from Digital. VMS applications run on any VAX from the MicroVAX to the largest unit. See *OpenVMS*.

(2) (Voice Messaging System) See *voice mail*.

vocoder

(VOice CODER) Same as *speech codec*.

VOD

(Video On Demand) The ability to start delivering a movie or other video program to an individual Web browser or TV set whenever the user requests it. See *streaming video*.

voice channel

A transmission channel or subchannel that carries human voice.

voice coil

A type of motor used to move the access arm of a disk drive in very small increments. Like the voice coil of a speaker, the amount of current determines the amount of movement. Contrast with *stepper motor*, which works in fixed increments.

voice grade

Refers to the bandwidth required to transmit human voice, which is usually about 4,000Hz.

voice mail

A computerized telephone answering system that digitizes incoming voice messages and stores them on disk. It usually provides auto attendant capability, which uses prerecorded messages to route the caller to the appropriate person, department or mail box.

voice messaging

Using voice mail as an alternative to electronic mail, in which voice messages are intentionally recorded, not because the recipient was not available.

voice processing

The computerized handling of voice, which includes voice store and forward, voice response, voice recognition and text to speech technologies.

voice recognition

The conversion of spoken words into computer text. Speech is first digitized and then matched against a dictionary of coded waveforms. The matches are converted into text as if the words were typed on the keyboard.

voice response

The generation of voice output by computer. It provides pre-recorded information either with or without selection by the caller. Interactive voice response allows interactive manipulation of a database. See *audiotex*.

voice store and forward

The technology behind voice mail and messaging systems. Human voice is digitized, stored in the computer, routed to the recipient's mailbox and retrieved by the user when required.

volatile memory

A memory that does not hold its contents without power. A computer's main memory, made up of dynamic RAM or static RAM chips, loses its content immediately upon loss of power.

volt

A unit of measurement of force, or pressure, in an electrical circuit. The common voltage of an AC power line is 120 volts of alternating current (alternating directions). Common voltages within a computer are from 5 to 12 volts of direct current (one direction only).

voltage regulator

A device used to maintain a level amount of voltage in the electrical line. Contrast with *surge suppressor*, which filters out excessive amounts of current, and contrast with *UPS*, which provides backup power in the event of a power failure.

volt-amps

The measurement of electrical usage that is computed by multiplying volts times amps. See *watt*.

volume

(1) A physical storage unit, such as a hard disk, floppy disk, disk cartridge or reel of tape.

(2) A logical storage unit, which is a part of one physical drive or one that spans several physical drives.

volume label

(1) A name assigned to a disk (usually optional).

(2) An identifying stick-on label attached to the outside of a tape reel or disk cartridge.

(3) See *header label*.

voxel

(VOlume piXEL) A three-dimensional pixel. A voxel represents a quantity of 3-D data just as a pixel represents a point or cluster of points in 2-D data.

VPN

(Virtual Private Network) A wide area communications network provided by a common carrier that provides what seems like dedicated lines when used, but backbone trunks are shared among all customers as in a public network. It allows a private network to be configured within a public network. Today, VPNs are widely implemented via the Internet. See *PVC*.

VPS

(Vectors Per Second) The measurement of the speed of a vector or array processor.

VR

See *virtual reality*.

VRAM

See *video RAM*.

VRC

(Vertical Redundancy Check) An error checking method that generates and tests a parity bit for each byte of data that is moved or transmitted.

VRML

(Virtual Reality Modeling Language) A 3-D graphics language used on the Web. After downloading a VRML page, its contents can be viewed, rotated and manipulated. Simulated rooms can be "walked into." The VRML viewer is launched from within the Web browser.

VS

(1) (Virtual Storage) Same as *virtual memory*.

(2) (Virtual Storage) A family of minicomputers from Wang introduced in 1977.

VSAM

(Virtual Storage Access Method) An IBM access method for storing data, widely used in IBM mainframes. It uses the B+tree method for organizing data.

VSAT

(Very Small Aperture satellite Terminal) A small earth station for satellite transmission that handles up to 56 Kbits/sec of digital transmission. VSATs that handle the T1 data rate (up to 1.544 Mbits/sec) are called "TSATs."

VSE

(Disk Operating System/Virtual Storage Extended) An IBM multiuser, multitasking operating system that typically runs on IBM's 43xx series. It used to be known as simply "DOS," but after the abundance of DOS PCs came on the scene, it was later referred to as VSE.

VSX

(Verification Suite for X/Open) A testing procedure from X/Open that verifies compliance with their endorsed standards. VSX3 has over 5,500 tests for compliance with XPG3.

VT100, 200, 300

A series of asynchronous display terminals from Digital for its PDP and VAX computers. Available in text and graphics models in both monochrome and color.

VTAM

(Virtual Telecommunications Access Method) Formally known as ACF/VTAM (Advanced Communications Function/VTAM), software that controls communications in an IBM SNA environment. It usually resides in the mainframe under MVS or VM, but may be offloaded into a front end processor that is tightly coupled to the mainframe. It supports a wide variety of network protocols, including SDLC and Token Ring. VTAM can be thought of as the network operating system of SNA.

VTOC

(Volume Table Of Contents) A list of files on a disk. The VTOC is the mainframe counterpart to the FAT table on a PC.

VTR

(VideoTape Recorder) A video recording and playback machine that uses reels of magnetic tape. Contrast with *VCR*, which uses tape cassettes.

VUP

(VAX Unit of Performance) A unit of measurement equal to the performance of the VAX 11/780, the first VAX machine.

VxD

(Virtual Device Driver) A special type of Windows driver for 386 Enhanced Mode. VxDs run at the most priviledged CPU mode (ring 0) and allow low-level interaction with the hardware and internal Windows functions, such as memory management. WIN386.EXE, the 386 Enhanced Mode kernel of Windows, is itself made up of VxDs.

W

W3C

(World Wide Web Consortium, www.w3.org) An international industry consortium founded in 1994 to develop common standards for the World Wide Web. It is hosted in the U.S. by the Laboratory for Computer Science at MIT.

Wabi

(Windows **ABI**) Software from SunSoft that emulates Windows applications under UNIX by converting the calls made by Windows applications into X Window calls.

wafer

(1) The base material in chip making, which goes through a series of photomasking, etching and implantation steps. It is a slice approximately 1/30" thick from a salami-like silicon crystal up to 8" in diameter. Twelve-inch wafers are expected to become popular by the turn of the century.

(2) A small, thin continuous-loop magnetic tape cartridge that has been used from time to time for data storage and specialized applications.

wafer scale integration

A semiconductor technology that builds a complete computer on an entire wafer. It has been tried, but not yet successful.

WAIS

(Wide Area Information Server) A database on the Internet that contains indexes to documents that reside on the Internet. Using the Z39.50 query language, text files can be searched based on key words.

wait state

The time spent waiting for an operation to take place. It may refer to a variable length of time a program has to wait before it can be processed, or to a fixed duration of time, such as a machine cycle.

When memory is too slow to respond to the CPU's request for it, wait states are introduced until the memory can catch up.

wallpaper

A pattern or picture used to represent the desktop surface (screen background) in a graphical user interface. GUIs comes with several wallpaper choices, and third-party wallpaper files are available. You can also scan in your favorite picture and make it wallpaper.

If you wonder why you cover a desktop with wallpaper, don't. Very little makes sense in this industry, why should this?

WAN

(Wide Area Network) A communications network that covers a wide geographic area, such as state or country. It requires the network facilities of common carriers.

WAN analyzer

See *network analyzer*.

wand

A hand-held optical reader used to read typewritten fonts, printed fonts, OCR fonts and bar codes. The wand is waved over each line of characters or codes in a single pass.

Wang Labs

(Wang Laboratories, Inc., Lowell, MA, www.wang.com) A computer services and network integration company. Wang was one of the major early contributors to the computing industry from its founder's invention that made core memory possible, to leadership in desktop calculators and word processors. Founded in 1951 by Dr. An Wang and specializing in electronics, the company became world famous for its desktop calculators in the 1960s and its word processors in the 1970s.

WAP

(Wireless Application Protocol) A standard for providing cellular phones, pagers and other handheld devices with secure access to e-mail and text-based Web pages. Introduced in 1997 by Phone.com (formerly Unwired Planet), Ericsson, Motorola and Nokia, WAP provides a complete environment for wireless applications that includes a wireless counterpart of TCP/IP and a framework for telephony integration such as call control and phone book access. WAP features the Wireless Markup Language (WML), which was derived from Phone.com's HDML and is a streamlined version of HTML for small screen displays.

warm boot

Restarting the computer by performing a reset operation (pressing reset, Ctrl-Alt-Del, etc.). See *boot, cold boot* and *clean boot.*

Warnier-Orr diagram

A graphic charting technique used in software engineering for system analysis and design.

WARP

A parallel processor developed at Carnegie-Mellon University that was the predecessor of iWARP. See also *OS/2.*

watt

The measurement of electrical power. One watt is one ampere of current flowing at one volt. Watts are typically rated as AMPS x VOLTS; however, AMPS x VOLTS, or VOLT-AMP (V-A) ratings and watts are only equivalent when powering devices that absorb all the energy such as electric heating coils or incandescent light bulbs. With computer power supplies, the actual watt rating is only 60 to 70% of the VOLT-AMP rating.

WAV

The native digital audio format used in Windows. WAV files use the .WAV extension and allow different sound qualities to be recorded. Either 8-bit or 16-bit samples can be taken at rates of 11025 Hz, 22050 Hz and 44100 Hz. The highest quality (16-bit samples at 44100 Hz) uses 88KB of storage per second.

wave

The shape of radiated energy. All radio signals, light rays, x-rays, and cosmic rays radiate an energy that looks likes rippling waves. To visualize waves, take a piece of paper and start drawing an up and down line very fast while pulling the paper perpendicular to the line.

waveform

The pattern of a particular sound wave or other electronic signal in analog form.

waveguide

A rectangular, circular or elliptical tube through which radio waves are transmitted.

wavelength

The distance between crests of a wave, computed by speed divided by frequency (speed / Hz). Wavelength in meters of electromagnetic waves equals 300,000,000 / Hz. Wavelength in meters for sound travelling through the air equals 335 / Hz.

wavelet compression

A lossy compression method used for color images and video. Instead of compressing small blocks of 8x8 pixels (64 bits) as in JPEG and MPEG, the wavelet algorithms compress the entire image with ratios of up to 300:1 for color and 50:1 for gray scale.

wavetable synthesis

A MIDI technique for creating musical sounds by storing digitized samples of the actual instruments. It provides more realistic sound than the FM synthesis method, which generates the sound waves entirely via electronic circuits. The more notes sampled in the wave table method, the better the resulting sound recreation.

WBEM

(Web-Based Enterprise Management) An umbrella term for using Internet technologies to manage systems and networks throughout the enterprise. Both browsers and applications can be used to access the information that is made available in formats such as HTML and XML.

WDM

(Wavelength-Division Multiplexing) A high-speed optical fiber transmission technique that carries multiple signals, each within its own wavelength (color) of light. Vendors have announced WDM systems, or DWDM (dense WDM) systems, as they are also called, that can support more than 150 channels (wavelengths), each carrying up to 10 Gbps.

weak typing

Programming languages that allow different types of data to be moved freely among data structures, as is found in Smalltalk and other earlier object-oriented languages.

Web

See *World Wide Web*.

Web administrator

The Web equivalent of a system administrator. Web administrators are system architects responsible for the overall design and implementation of an Internet Web site or intranet. See *Webmaster*.

Web accelerator

Software that speeds up the retrieval of Web pages. Anticipating that you might click a link on the current page, it downloads the linked pages in the background. Most of these utilities require nothing more than your browser, while others require a counterpart component in the server.

Web appliance

See *Internet appliance*.

Web authoring software

A Web site development system that allows Web pages to be visually created like a desktop publishing program. The required HTML, JavaScript or Java code necessary within the pages is automatically generated by the software. It typically displays an entire Web site as a graphical hierarchy of pages and allows existing Web sites to be imported for on-going maintenance.

Web based

Any software that runs on or interacts with a Web site on the Internet or an intranet.

Web browser

The program that serves as your front end to the World Wide Web on the Internet. The two major browsers are Internet Explorer from Microsoft and Netscape Navigator from Netscape. See *URL*.

Web cache

Pronounced Web "cash." A computer system in a network that contains copies of the most-recently requested Web pages in memory and on the hard disk. Web caches may be dedicated caching servers or a component in a proxy server. See *browser cache, cache* and *proxy cache*.

WebCam

(WEB CAMera) A video camera that is used to send periodic images or continuous frames to a Web site for display. There are countless WebCam sites throughout the Internet that have cameras pointed at virtually anything, including animals and people doing their daily work. The images are refreshed every minute or so. Live video feeds for continuous action may also be provided.

Webcast

(1) To send live video programming to several Internet users simultaneously.

(2) To send selected information to Internet users based on individual requirements. See *push technology*.

Web clipping

(1) Extracting a smaller amount from a Web page in order to display effectively on a handheld Web appliance.

(2) An excerpt of information taken from the Web.

Web development software

Software used to develop Web sites. Although often synonymous with "Web authoring software," it implies a more programming-oriented set of tools for linking pages to databases and other software components.

Web enabled

Able to connect to or be used on the Web.

Web farm

A group of Web servers that are controlled locally, but centrally managed. Each Web site is administered by its own Webmaster; however, centralized monitoring provides load balancing and fault tolerance. See *server farm*.

Web filtering

Blocking the viewing of undesirable Internet content.

Web hosting

Placing a customer's Web page or Web site on a commercial Web server. Many ISPs host a personal Web page at no additional cost above the monthly service fee, while multi-page, commercial Web sites are hosted at a very wide range of prices.

Web hub

A business-to-business Web site for a particular industry. It provides a meeting ground for buyers and sellers in a specific field and rather than being advertising based, may charge a transaction fee for each purchase. Also known as a vertical portal, or "vortal." See *vertical portal*.

Web log

(1) A Web page that contains links to Web sites that cover a particular subject or that are based on some other criterion, such as interesting or entertaining sites.

(2) An analysis of traffic on a Web site. It would show the number of visitors, page views, etc.

Webmaster

A person responsible for the implementation of a Web site. Webmasters must be proficient in HTML as well as one or more scripting and interface languages such as JavaScript, Perl and CGI. They may also have experience with more than one type of Web server. See *Web administrator*.

Webpad

A handheld, wireless device designed for Web browsing which is expected to proliferate in the 2001-2003 timeframe. Using a touch screen, Webpads are expected to weigh no more than two pounds and be less than an inch thick.

Web page

A page in a World Wide Web document. See *World Wide Web* and *Webmaster*.

Web palette

See *Netscape color palette*.

Web payment service

A facility that manages the transfer of funds from a customer to a merchant of an e-commerce Web site. The money may come from a digital wallet inside the user's machine, from a credit card stored on a server of a digital wallet service or from a prepaid account stored in the payment service's server.

Web phone

See *Internet telephony*.

Webring

A navigation system that links related Web sites together. Each ring links sites that pertain to a particular topic.

Web search sites

There are various Web sites that maintain directory databases of other Web sites. Yahoo! was the first to gain worldwide attention. Some sites search other sites. Most sites are free and are paid for by advertising, while others charge for the service. Visit www.17.com/search.html for a list of search sites.

Web server

A computer that provides World Wide Web services on the Internet. The term may refer to just the software that provides this service or to the computer system and software.

Web switch

A network device that routes traffic to the appropriate Web server based on the URL of the request. The Web switch is designed to provide improved load balancing for a Web site, because different requests can be routed to the most efficient source for delivering their content.

Webtop

(1) Using a Web browser as the desktop interface in a client machine.

(2) A specification from Sun, IBM and Oracle for a common interface for Java-based network computers.

Webzine

A magazine published on the World Wide Web.

well behaved, well mannered

Refers to programs that do not deviate from a standard.

well-known port

A protocol port number that is widely used for a certain type of data on the network. For example, World Wide Web traffic (HTTP packets) is typically assigned port 80. See *protocol port*.

wetware

A biological system. It typically refers to the human brain and nervous system.

WFW

See *Windows for Workgroups*.

Whetstones

A benchmark program that tests floating point operations. Results are expressed in Whetstones per second. Whetstone I tests 32-bit, and Whetstone II tests 64-bit operations. See *Dhrystones*.

whiteboard

The electronic equivalent of chalk and blackboard. Whiteboards allow participants across a network to simultaneously view one or more users drawing on the computer.

White Book

The documentation for the technical specifications of Video CDs.

white box

Another term for a PC clone. It refers to the non-branded carton, which is typically white and is the original carton the metal case alone came in. White box marketing refers to the hundreds of small companies that assemble and sell PCs.

white noise

Same as *Gaussian noise*.

wide area network

See *WAN*.

widget set

A group of screen structures (menu, button, scroll bar, etc.) provided in a graphical interface.

wild cards

Symbols used to represent any letter or number when identifying groups of files for selection. In DOS and UNIX, the asterisk (*) represents any name, and the question mark (?) represents any single character. For example, *.exe means all files that have an .EXE extension.

ip interface
(Windows, Icons, Menus and a Pointing device) Same as *GUI*.

Win32
The programming interface (API) for 32-bit mode supported in Windows NT and Windows 95/98. When applications are written to Win32, they are activating the PCs native and most efficient internal functions.

Win95B
Same as *OSR2*.

Winbench
A benchmark from Ziff-Davis that tests the display, disk and CD-ROM performance of a PC running Windows. WinBench results are rated in WinMarks, which can change their rating scale with new releases of the software. WinBench is used to test raw system performance, but ZD's Winstone benchmark tests actual application performance. See *ZDBOp*.

Winchester disk
An early removable disk from IBM that put the heads and platters in a sealed unit for greater speed. Its dual 30MB modules, or 30-30 design, caught the "Winchester rifle" nickname. The term later referred to any fixed hard disk.

window
(1) A scrollable viewing area on screen. Windows are generally rectangular, although round and polygonal windows are used in specialized applications. See *GUI*.

(2) A reserved area of memory.

(3) A time period.

windowing software
Same as *windows program*.

window manager
Software incorporated into all popular GUIs, which displays a window with accompanying menus, buttons and scroll bars. It allows the windows to be relocated, overlapped, resized, minimized and maximized. See *desktop manager*.

Windows
The most widely used operating system. Developed by Microsoft, Windows provides a graphical user interface (GUI) and master control program for running applications in desktop and laptop PCs and servers.   Windows is also an environment. Microsoft has developed standard interfaces for interoperability that provide a complete software architecture for the enterprise. Microsoft also supplies the software for all stages of development and implementation, including application development, networking, databases and the Web. An organization could choose Microsoft-only software for everything. Following are the various versions of Windows that have been introduced.

Windows 1.0 and 2.0
The early versions of Windows were not appealing, and the hardware was too underpowered.

Windows 3.x
Introduced in 1990, Windows 3.0 became widely used very quickly even though it still required DOS to be loaded first. Windows 3.1 was a more stable version introduced in 1992, and Windows for Workgroups later added built-in networking.

Windows 3.1 is known as a 16-bit environment, because it uses the slower 16-bit mode of the computer as does DOS, and Windows 3.1 programs are known as 16-bit programs. Windows and DOS are designed to run in Intel x86-based PCs. Macs and UNIX machines can run Windows applications with varying degrees of success using emulators.

Although Windows 3.1 machines are still in use, software developers have long abandoned further development of 16-bit applications.

Windows 95/98

Introduced in 1995 as a major upgrade to Windows 3.1, it was the first time Windows booted directly after turning the computer on. Windows 95 includes built-in networking as well as DOS and 16-bit Windows for compatibility with existing applications.

Windows 95 includes a completely revised user interface that more closely resembles the Macintosh. All action takes place by pressing the Start button on the taskbar, which reveals a menu with installed applications and control panels. Windows 95 supports file names longer than eight characters and Plug and Play, which makes installing new peripherals much easier than in Windows 3.x.

Introduced in 1998, Windows 98 is a major upgrade. It includes numerous bug fixes, performance enhancements and support for more hardware, including the Universal Serial Bus (USB). It supports two monitors, which helps developers working in one resolution and testing in another. Microsoft's Internet Explorer Web browser is tightly integrated.

Windows NT and 2000

Introduced in 1993, NT (New Technology) is a 32-bit operating system that boots directly and includes built-in networking. Its first versions used the same interface as Windows 3.x, but NT 4.0, which came out in 1996, uses the same interface as Windows 95/98, although all functions are not identical.

Windows NT comes in versions for the desktop (NT Workstation) and the server (NT Server). It is an entirely different operating system than Windows 95 and is somewhat more stable. It too includes a version of DOS and 16-bit Windows for compatibility.

NT Server market share is growing rapidly, and Microsoft is working hard to make it as bulletproof as a mainframe. NT supports multiprocessing (SMP), provides more network administration functions than Windows 95/98 and comes with the Internet Explorer Web browser.

Windows 2000, introduced in 2000, is actually NT 5.0. It adds Plug and Play (not in 4.0) and Active Directory, which is an improved directory system. Windows 2000 Professional is the desktop version, and Windows 2000 Server is the server version, which supports two-way SMP.

Windows accelerator

A display adapter that provides 2-D functions in hardware. See *graphics accelerator*.

Windows CE

A version of Windows from Microsoft for handheld PCs (HPCs) and consumer electronics devices. It runs "Pocket" versions of popular applications such as Microsoft Word and Excel.

windows environment

(1) (lower case "w") Any software that provides multiple windows on screen such as Windows, OS/2, Mac, Motif and X Window, or any application that provides multiple windows for documents or pictures.

(2) (upper case "W") Refers to computers running under a Microsoft Windows operating system.

Windows for Workgroups

The later versions of Windows 3.1 which included built-in peer-to-peer networking. See *Windows*.

Windows Media Player

A media player utility from Windows that supports all the popular audio and video file formats including MP3. It also plays Microsoft's own streaming files (.asf, .asx) coming directly from the Web.

Windows Metafile

A vector graphics file format from Microsoft that also supports bitmaps and text. The Aldus Placeable Metafile is a PageMaker variation that contains a header indicating into what size rectangle the object will be rendered.

windows program

(1) Software that adds a windows capability to an existing operating system.

(2) An application program written to run under Windows.

Windows SDK

A set of development utilities for writing Windows applications in C and C++. It provides tools for creating custom cursors, fonts and icons, bitmaps, menus and online help.

Windows Second Edition

An upgrade to Windows 98 that includes bug fixes and enhancements. It includes the Windows 98 Service Pack 1 plus Internet Explorer 5, NetMeeting 3 and Media Player 6.1.

Windows shell

An add-on user interface for Windows. Numerous shells were created for Windows 3.x to streamline or replace Program Manager; for example, Norton Desktop for Windows was popular. Fewer products were made for Windows 95.

Windows swap file

A disk file used for virtual memory in Windows. The contents of memory are written to the swap file until they are needed again.

Windows terminal

An input/output terminal for a Windows NT server running multiuser software such as WinFrame or Windows Terminal Server. See *WinFrame* and *Windows Terminal Server*.

Windows Terminal Server

Microsoft's version of the Winframe multiuser architecture. Co-developed with Citrix, it turns an NT server into a centralized, timeshared computer.

WinFrame

Software from Citrix that turns a Windows NT server into a timeshared central computer. Windows applications are run in the server and only screen changes are sent to the attached PCs, NCs or Winterm terminals. Terminal input and output are governed by Citrix's Intelligent Console Architecture (ICA) protocol, which is also licensed to third parties.

WIN.INI

(WINdows INItialization) The file read by Windows on startup that contains data about the current environment (desktop, fonts, sounds, etc.) as well as individual applications. It is often updated by an install program to provide information for the application when it runs. Although WIN.INI was created in Windows 3.x, it is still used by Windows 95/98 and NT for Windows 3.x compatibility. See *SYSTEM.INI*.

Winmark

A unit of measurement of the WinBench benchmarks from Ziff-Davis. See *WinBench* and *ZDBOp*.

WINS

(Windows Internet Naming Service) Software from Microsoft that lets users locate computers on remote networks automatically. It runs under Windows NT Server and maintains a database of computer names and their physical IP address.

Winsock API

(WINdows SOCKets API) A common programming interface between a Windows application and the TCP/IP protocol. Most TCP/IP stacks designed to run under Windows and most Windows software that communicates via TCP/IP are Winsock compliant. The Winsock routines are implemented as a dynamic link library (DLL).

Wintel

(WINdows InTEL) Refers to the world's largest personal computer environment, which is Windows running on an Intel CPU.

Winterm

A family of Windows-based terminals from Wyse Technology, San Jose, CA, (www.wyse.com), designed to work with specialized versions of Windows NT. See *WinFrame*.

wireframe modeling

In CAD, a technique for representing 3-D objects, in which all surfaces are visibly outlined in lines, including the opposite sides and all internal components that are normally hidden from view. Compared to surface and solid modeling, wireframe is the least complex method for representing 3-D images.

wireless

Radio transmission via the airwaves. Various communications techniques are used to provide wireless transmission including infrared line of sight, cellular, microwave, satellite. packet radio and spread spectrum. See *FDMA, TDMA, CDMA* and *CDPD*.

wireless LAN

A local area network that transmits over the air typically in an unlicensed frequency such as the 2.4GHz band. A wireless LAN does not require lining up devices for line of sight transmission like IrDA. Wireless access points (base stations) are connected to an Ethernet hub or server and transmit a radio frequency over an area of several hundred to a thousand feet which can penetrate walls and other non-metal barriers.

wireless modem

A modem and antenna that transmits and receives over the air. Wireless modems come in several varieties, including units for CDPD, ARDIS, Mobitex, Ricochet, 802.11, OpenAir and other proprietary products.

wireless portal

A Web site that supports a user with a smart phone or alphanumeric pager. It may offer a variety of features, including providing a springboard to other (WAP based) wireless sites, the ability to select content to be pushed to the user's device as well as providing a point of entry for anyone to send the user a message. See *WAP*.

wire speed

The bandwidth of a particular transmission or networking system. For the example, the wire speed of 10BaseT Ethernet is 10 Mbps. When data is said to run at wire speed or at "wire rate," it implies there is little or no software overhead associated with the transmission and that the data travels at the maximum speed of the hardware.

wire wrap

An early method of wiring circuit boards. A tool strips the end of the wire and coils it. The coil is pressed onto a metal prong on the board.

wiring closet

The central distribution or servicing point for cables in a network.

wizard

Instructional help that guides the user through a series of steps to accomplish a task.

wizzy wig

See *WYSIWYG*.

WMF

See *Windows Metafile*.

WML

(Wireless Markup Language) A tag-based language used in the Wireless Application Protocol (WAP). WML is an XML document type allowing standard XML and HTML tools to be used to develop WML applications. It evolved from Phone.com's HDML, but WML is not a superset of HDML. Certain HDML features are not found in WML. See *WAP*.

word

(1) The computer's internal storage unit. Refers to the amount of data it can hold in its registers and process at one time. A word is often 16 bits, in which case 32 bits is called a "double word." Given the same clock rate, a 32-bit computer processes four bytes in the same time it takes a 16-bit machine to process two.

(2) The primary text element, separated by a blank space, comma or other word separator character.

(3) See *Microsoft Word*.

WordBASIC

A subset of Microsoft QuickBASIC with added word processing functions used to customize Microsoft Word word processors.

Word macro virus

A virus written into a macro that is stored in a Word document or template. When the document is opened, the macro is executed (providing macros have not been disabled in the program), and the virus does its damage.

WordPerfect

A full-featured word processing program for Windows from Corel. It is a sophisticated program that has been widely used on many platforms since its inception on the IBM PC in 1982. Under its original developer, WordPerfect became the leading word processor in the late 1980s. The company and product was acquired by Novell and later by Corel.

WordPerfect Office

A suite of office applications for Windows from Corel that includes WordPerfect, Quattro Pro, Corel Presentations, Paradox and CorelCENTRAL (PIM, scheduling, etc.). It is the successor to Corel WordPerfect Suite, which was the successor to Corel Office.

Word Pro

A full-featured Windows word processing program from Lotus. It provides groupware features that allow documents to be created and edited collaboratively and also includes version control for tracking document updates. Word Pro is the successor to Ami Pro.

word processing

The creation of text documents. Except for labels and envelopes, it has replaced the electric typewriter in most offices, because of the ease in which documents can be edited, searched and reprinted.

Advanced word processors function as elementary desktop publishing systems. Although there are still machines dedicated only to word processing, most word processing is performed on general-purpose computers using word processing software.

word processing machine

A computer that is specialized for only word processing functions.

word processor

(1) Software that provides word processing functions on a computer.

(2) A computer specialized for word processing. Until the late 1970s, word processors were always dedicated machines. Today, personal computers have replaced almost all dedicated word processors.

word separator

A character that separates a word, such as a blank space, comma, period, -, ? and !.

WordStar

A full-featured word processing program for CP/M and DOS from MicroPro International Corporation, later renamed WordStar International. Introduced in 1978 for the CP/M operating system, WordStar was the first program to give full word processing capabilities to personal computer users at far less cost than the dedicated word processors of the time. Many WordStar keyboard commands became de facto standards for text manipulation.

word wheel

A lookup method in which each character that is typed in moves the on-screen index to the closest match. By watching the index move character by character, you can easily tell if you have made a typo.

word wrap

A word processing feature that moves words to the next line automatically as you type based on the current right margin setting. Some word processing programs allow word wrap to be turned off for writing source code.

workflow, workflow automation

Automatically routing data and documents over the network to the users responsible for working with them. A workflow automation system keeps track of the processes a document goes through and alerts users when operations are overdue.

workgroup

Two or more individuals who share files and databases. LANs designed around workgroups provide electronic sharing of required data. See *groupware* and *workflow automation*.

workstation

(1) A high-performance, single-user microcomputer or minicomputer that has been specialized for graphics, CAD, CAE or scientific applications.

(2) A personal computer in a network. In this context, a workstation is the same as a client. Contrast with *server* and *host*.

(3) In the telecom industry, a combined telephone and computer.

(4) Any terminal or personal computer.

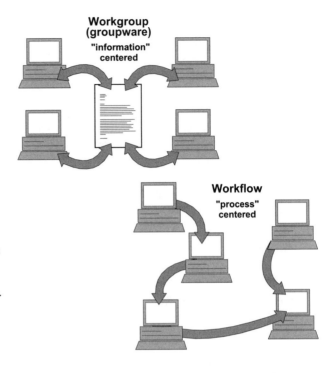

Workgroup (groupware)
"information" centered

Workflow
"process" centered

World Wide Web

The largest collection of online information in the World. The Web is an Internet facility that has become synonymous with the Interent. Its foundation is the HTML document, which contains links (URLs) to other documents on the same Web server or on servers anywhere in the world. The Web uses the HTTP protocol to download Web pages to a browser, such as Netscape Navigator or Internet Explorer.

Using a variety of new programming tools and architectures, such as Java, JavaScript, Jscript, VB Script and ActiveX, the Web is "the" worldwide information system for education, research, entertainment and commerce.

worm

(1) A destructive program that replicates itself throughout disk and memory, using up the computers resources and eventually putting the system down. See *virus* and *logic bomb*.

(2) A program that moves through a network and deposits information at each node for diagnostic purposes or causes idle computers to share some of the processing workload.

(3) (WORM) (Write Once Read Many) An optical disk that can be recorded only once. Updating requires destroying the existing data (all 0s made 1s), and writing new data to an unused part of the disk.

WOSA

(Windows Open System Architecture) Microsoft's umbrella term for its collection of programming interfaces that make Windows an enterprise-wide computing environment.

WP

See *word processing* and *WordPerfect*.

WPAN

(Wireless Personal Area Network) A wireless network that serves a single person or small workgroup. It has a limited range and is used to transfer data between a laptop or PDA and a desktop machine or server as well as to a printer.

wrapper

A data structure or software that contains ("wraps around") other data or software, so that the contained elements can exist in the newer system.

wrist rest, wrist support

A platform used to raise the wrist to keyboard level for typing. Well-designed wrist rests prevent and provide a therapy for carpal tunnel syndrome by keeping the hands in a neutral wrist position.

write

To store data in memory or record data onto a storage medium, such as disk and tape. Read and write is analogous to play and record on an audio tape recorder.

write back cache

A disk or memory cache that handles writing. Data written into the high-speed cache memory from the CPU is written onto disk or into real memory during idle machine cycles.

write cycle

The operation of writing data into a memory or storage device.

write error

The inability to store into memory or record onto disk or tape. Malfunctioning memory cells or damaged portions of the disk or tape's surface will cause those areas to be unusable.

write once-run anywhere

Refers to writing software that can run on multiple hardware platforms. Interpreted languages such as Java allow a program to be written once and run in any computer that supports the same version of the Java interpreter.

write precompensation

Using a stronger magnetic field to write data in sectors that are closer to the center of the disk. In CAV recording, in which the disk spins at a constant speed, the sectors closest to the spindle are packed tighter than the outer sectors.

One of the hard disk parameters stored in a PC's CMOS RAM is the WPcom number, which is the track where precompensation begins.

write protect

A mode that restricts erasing or editing a disk file. See *file protection*.

write protect notch

A small, square cutout on the side of a floppy disk used to prevent it from being written and erased. On 5.25" floppies, the notch must be covered for protection. To protect a 3.5" diskette, press the slide lever toward the edge of the disk uncovering a hole (upper left side viewed from the back).

WUGNET

(Windows Users Group Network, Media, PA, www.wugnet.com) Founded in 1988, it is the oldest and largest independent organization that supports the Windows environment. It provides technical information, software resources and tools, CompuServe forums and newsletters.

WWW

See *World Wide Web*.

WYSIWYG

(What You See Is What You Get) Pronounced "wizzy-wig." Refers to text and graphics appearing on screen the same as they print. To have WYSIWYG text, a screen font must be installed that matches each printer font. Otherwise, a 24-point font may display in correct size relationship to a 10-point font, but it won't look like the printed typeface.

It is almost impossible to get 100% identical representation, because screen and printer resolutions rarely match. Even a 300 dpi printer has a higher resolution than almost every monitor.

XYZ

x

(1) In programming, symbol used to identify a hexadecimal number. For example, 0x0A and \x0A specify the hex number 0A.

(2) See *X Window*.

X11

The current version of the X Window System. X11R5 (Version 11, Release 5, Sept. 1991) provides a stable and feature-rich environment.

X12

An ANSI standard protocol for EDI. See *Tradacoms* and *EDIFACT*.

X.21

An ITU standard protocol for a circuit switching network.

X.25

The first international standard packet switching network developed in the early 1970s and published in 1976 by the CCITT (now ITU). X.25 was designed to become a worldwide public data network similar to the global telephone system for voice, but it never came to pass due to incompatibilities and the lack of interest within the U.S. It has been used primarily outside the U.S. for low speed applications (up to 56 Kbps) such as credit card verifications and automatic teller machine (ATM) and other financial transactions.

X.28

An ITU standard (1977) for exchange of information between a DTE and a PAD; commonly known as PAD commands.

X.29

An ITU standard (1977) for exchange of information between a local PAD and a remote PAD; procedures for interworking between PADs.

X.3

An ITU standard (1977) for a PAD (packet assembler/disassembler), which divides a data message into packets for transmission over a packet-switched network and reassembles them at the receiving side.

X.32

An ITU standard (1984) for connecting to an X.25 network by dial up. It defines how the network identifies the terminal for billing and security purposes and how default parameters are negotiated for the connection.

X.400

An OSI and ITU standard messaging protocol. It is an application layer protocol (layer 7 in the OSI model). X.400 has been defined to run over various network transports including Ethernet, X.25, TCP/IP and dial-up lines. See *messaging protocol* and *CMC*.

X.500

An OSI protocol for maintaining online directories of users and resources. It is primarily designed to return information rather than update it. X.500 can be used to support X.400 and other messaging systems, but is not restricted to e-mail usage. It provides a hierarchical structure that fits the world's classification system: countries, states, cities, streets, houses, families, etc. The goal is to have a directory that can be used globally.

X.509

A widely-used specification for digital certificates that has been a recommendation of the ITU since 1988.

X.75

An ITU standard for connecting X.25 networks.

x86

Also 80x86. Refers to the Intel 8086 CPU family used in PCs, which includes the 8086, 8088, 80186, 80286, 386, 486, Pentium, Pentium Pro, Pentium II and Pentium III. This is the largest installed base of computers worldwide.

XAPIA

(X 4.00 API Association) A consortium dedicated to standardizing X.400 and other specifications, such as the CMC messaging API.

Xbase

Refers to dBASE-like languages such as Visual FoxPro and CA-Clipper, which are still supported. FoxBASE, QuickSilver, dBXL and Force were others.

X-based

See *X Window* and *Xbase*.

X Bitmap

A black and white bitmapped graphics format used in the UNIX environment. It uses the .XBM extension and is often used as a hypertext icon on a Web page.

XDR

(EXternal Data Representation) A data format developed by Sun that is part of its networking standards. It deals with integer size, byte ordering, data representation, etc. and is used as an interchange format. Different systems convert to XDR for sending and from XDR upon receipt.

xDSL

Refers to various DSL technologies. See *DSL*.

Xeon

A Pentium CPU chip designed for server and high-end workstation use. Xeon chips plug into Slot 2 on the motherboard and run the L2 cache at the same speed as the CPU. Xeon was introduced in the summer of 1998 using the Pentium II chip at 400MHz and in the spring of 1999 with the Pentium III at 500MHz.

XGA

(EXtended Graphics Array) An IBM video display standard introduced in 1990 that extended VGA to 132-column text and interlaced 1024x768x256 resolution. XGA-2 added non-interlaced 1024x768x64K. The term may be used to refer to 1024x768 resolution in general; for example:

```
XGA    1024x768
SVGA   800x600
VGA    640x480
```

Xlib

(X LIBrary) Functions in the X Window System. See *X Window*.

x86 PROCESSORS (from Intel)

	CPU	Clock Speed (MHz)	Bus Size (bits)	Max RAM MB	Floppy Disk	Typical Hard disk	Operating Systems
16-bit CPUs	8088	5	8	1	5.25" 360K	10-20MB	DOS DR DOS
	8086	5-10	16				
	286	6-12	16	16	5.25" 1.2MB	20-80MB	DOS DR DOS Windows 3.0 OS/2 1.x
32-bit CPUs	386DX	16-40		Max RAM GB		60-200MB	DOS DR DOS OS/2 1.x OS/2 2.x Win 3.x Win 95 Win 98
	386SX	16-33	32	4	5.25" 1.2MB		
	386SL	20-25			3.5" 1.44MB		
	486DX	25-100	32	4		200-500MB	Win NT Win 2000 UNIX (SCO) Solaris Linux
	486SX	20-40					
	Pentium	60-200		4			Misc. DOS multiuser
	Pentium MMX	150-233		4		500MB-40GB	
	Pentium Pro	150-200	64	64			
	Pentium II	233-450		4			
	Pentium III	450-1GHz		4			
	Celeron	266-500		4			
	Xeon	400-850		64			

The Computer Glossary

XML

(EXtensible Markup Language) An open standard for describing data from the W3C. It is used for defining data elements on a Web page and business-to-business documents. It uses a similar tag structure as HTML; however, whereas HTML defines how elements are displayed, XML defines what those elements contain. HTML uses predefined tags, but XML allows tags to be defined by the developer of the page. Thus, virtually any data items, such as product, sales rep and amount due, can be identified, allowing Web pages to function like database records.

Xmodem

The first widely-used file transfer protocol for personal computers

XMS

(eXtended Memory Specification) A programming interface that allows DOS programs to use extended memory in 286s and up. See *HIMEM.SYS*.

XNS

(Xerox Network Services) An early networking protocol suite developed at Xerox's Palo Alto Research Center (PARC). XNS has been the basis for many popular network architectures including Novell's NetWare, Banyan's VINES and 3Com's 3+.

xon-xoff

In communications, a simple asynchronous protocol that keeps the receiving device in synchronization with the sender.

X/Open

(X/Open, San Francisco, CA, division of The Open Group, www.opengroup.org) A consortium of international computer vendors founded in 1984 to resolve standards issues. In 1996, it merged with OSF into The Open Group. Its purpose is to integrate evolving standards in order to achieve an open environment. XPG are X/Open specifications, and VSK are X/Open testing and verification procedures.

XPG

(X/Open Portability Guide) Standards that specify compliance with X/Open's Common Application Environment (CAE). XPG3 (Release 3), introduced in early 1989, specifies standards for UNIX System V Release 4.0.

X Pixelmap

An 8-bit bitmapped graphics format used in the UNIX environment. It uses the .XPM extension and is similar to the X Bitmap format, but provides 256 colors. X Pixelmaps are often used for X Window icons and hypertext icons on Web pages.

X protocol

The message format of the X Window System. See *X Window*.

X server

The receiving computer in an X Window system. See *X Window*.

XT

(1) (EXtended Technology) The first IBM PC with a hard disk, introduced in 1983. See *PC*.
(2) (Xt) See *X toolkit*.

X terminal

A terminal with built-in X server capability. See *X Window*.

X toolkit

Development software for building X Window applications. Typically includes a widget set, X Toolkit Intrinsics (Xt) libraries for managing the widget set and the X Library (Xlib).

Xtrieve

A menu-driven query language and report writer from Novell that accesses Btrieve files.

X Window

Formally the X Window System, also called "X" and "X Windows," it is a windowing system developed at MIT, which runs under UNIX and all major operating systems. X lets users run applications on other computers in the network and view the output on their own screen.

X client software resides in the computer that performs the processing and X server software resides in the computer that displays it. Both components can also be in the same machine. This seems opposite to today's client/server terminology, but the concept is that the server is "serving up" the image.

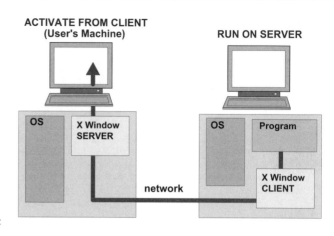

x-y matrix

A group of rows and columns. The x-axis is the horizontal row, and the y-axis is the vertical column. An x-y matrix is the reference framework for two-dimensional structures, such as mathematical tables, display screens, digitizer tablets, dot matrix printers and 2-D graphics images.

XyWrite

Pronounced "zy-write." A word processing program for Windows or DOS from The Technology Group, Baltimore, MD, (www.thetechnologygroup.com).

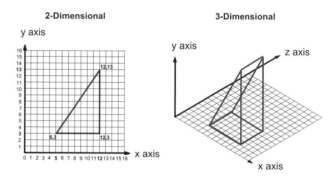

For many years, the DOS versions of XyWrite were used extensively by major newspapers and magazines throughout the country. XyWrite was noted for its typesetting orientation long before it was common to have the variety of fonts found in today's software. XyWrite differs from most word processors in that it generates a pure ASCII file like a text editor.

x-y-z matrix

A three-dimensional structure. The x and y axes represent the first two dimensions; the z axis, the third dimension. In a graphic image, the x and y denote width and height; the z denotes depth.

Y2K problem (Year 2000 problem)

Upgrading computer hardware and software to recognize four-digit years. More than $300 billion was spent upgrading systems in the late 1990s to prevent an information systems meltdown on January 1, 2000.

Yahoo!

(www.yahoo.com) The first search site on the Web to gain worldwide attention. Yahoo! indexes much of its material manually rather than from automated spiders that roam the Web indexing everything in sight. See *Web search sites*.

Yellow Pages

See *NIS* and *naming service*.

YIQ

The color model used for encoding NTSC video. Y is the luminosity of the original black and white TV signal. I and Q are subcarrier axes that are modulated with the color difference signals red minus Y and blue minus Y (R-Y and B-Y). YIQ refers specifically to NTSC video. See *YUV*.

YUV

The color model used for encoding video. Y is the luminosity of the black and white signal. U and V are color difference signals. U is red minus Y (R-Y), and V is blue minus Y (B-Y). In order to display YUV data on a computer screen, it must be converted into RGB through a process known as "color space conversion." YUV is used because it saves storage space and transmission bandwidth compared to RGB. YUV is not compressed RGB; rather, it is the mathematical equivalent of RGB. Also known as component video, the YUV elements are written in various ways: (1) Y, R-Y, B-Y, (2) Y, Cr, Cb and (3) Y, Pa, Pb.

Z

A mathematical language used for developing the functional specification of a software program. Developed in the late 1970s at Oxford University, IBM's CICS software is specified in Z.

Z80, Z8000

An 8-bit microprocessor from Zilog Corporation that was the successor to the Intel 8080. The Z80 was widely used in first-generation personal computers that used the CP/M operating system. The Z8000 was the 16-bit successor to the Z80.

ZAW

(Zero Administration for Windows) Features in Windows 98 and 2000 that provide improved administration of Windows client PCs.

z-axis

The third dimension in a graphics image. The width is the x-axis and the height is the y-axis.

ZDBOp

(Ziff-Davis Benchmark Operation, www.zdbop.com) A division of the Ziff-Davis Publishing Company that develops and supports the benchmark programs that all the Ziff-Davis magazines use to test computer products. The Winstone, WinBench, MacBench, NetBench, ServerBench, BatteryMark, BrowserComp and WebBench benchmarks are widely distributed and free at its Web site.

zero-slot LAN

Refers to transmitting between computers over a serial or parallel port, thus freeing up an expansion slot normally used by LAN cards (NICs).

zero wait state

Refers to a high-speed memory that transfers its data immediately upon being accessed without waiting one or more machine cycles to respond.

ZIF socket

(Zero Insertion Force socket) A chip socket that is easy to plug a chip into. Intel has popularized this type of socket with its OverDrive upgrades. The chip is dropped into the socket's holes and a small lever is turned to lock them in.

zinc air

A rechargeable battery technology that provides more charge per pound than nickel cadmium or nickel hydride and does not suffer from the memory effect. It uses a carbon membrane that absorbs oxygen, a zinc plate and potassium hydroxide as the electrolyte. AER Energy Systems, Smyrna, GA, is the pioneer in this emerging technology.

zine

See *Webzine* and *e-zine*.

zip

(1) To compress a file with PKZIP. See *PKZIP, PKUNZIP*.

(2) (ZIP) (**Z**ig-**Z**ag **I**nline **P**ackage) Similar to a DIP, but smaller and tilted on its side for mounting on boards with limited space.

Zip disk

A popular 3.5" removable disk drive from Iomega Corporation, Roy, UT, (www.iomega.com). It uses design concepts from Iomega's Bernoulli technology as well as hard disks to provide 100MB and 250MB removable cartridges.

Zoomed Video Port, ZV Port

An extension to the PC Card (PCMCIA) that allows full-screen playback of digital video. The ZV Port is built into the notebook computer and activated by plugging in an MPEG PC Card that is ZV Port-compliant. The ZV Port equivalent on a desktop computer is the pass through capability built into an MPEG board. The MPEG board is cabled directly to the monitor and provides a pass through for the VGA signals from the display adapter. See *VGA pass through*.

0-9

0.13 process, 0.18 process, 0.25 process
See *micron*.

10Base2, 10Base5, 10BaseT, 100BaseT
See *Ethernet*.

10/100 card
An Ethernet network adapter (NIC) that supports both 10BaseT (10 Mbps) and 100BaseT (100 Mbps) access methods. Most cards autonegotiate at startup, enabling them to run at the higher speed if supported by the device they are connected to (hub or switch).

1-2-3
See *Lotus 1-2-3*.

1284
See *IEEE 1284*.

16-bit color, 24-bit color
See *bit depth*.

2780, 3780
Standard communications protocols for transmitting batch data. The numbers originated with early IBM remote job entry (RJE) terminals that included a card reader and a printer.

286
Refers to the Intel 80286 CPU chip or to a PC that uses it (also known as an AT-class PC). It was introduced in 1982 as the successor to the 8086 and 8088 chips used in the first PCs. It is faster and not limited to the infamous one-megabyte memory barrier, but is very sluggish for Windows and other graphics-based applications. See *PC* and *x86*.

303x
A series of medium to large-scale IBM mainframes introduced in 1977, which includes the 3031, 3032 and 3033.

308x
A series of large-scale IBM mainframes introduced in 1980, which includes the 3081, 3083 and 3084.

3090
A series of large-scale IBM mainframes introduced in 1986. Before the ES/9000 models (System/390), 3090s were the largest mainframes in the System/370 line. Models 120, 150 and 180 are single CPUs. Models 200 through 600 are multiprocessor systems (first digit indicates the number of CPUs). The E, S and J models represent increased speed respectively.

3270
A family of IBM mainframe terminals and related protocols (includes 3278 mono and 3279 color terminal). See *3270 emulator*.

3270 emulator
A plug-in board that converts a personal computer or workstation into an interactive IBM mainframe terminal. The first 3270 emulator in widespread use was the IRMAboard.

32-bit color
See *bit depth*.

32-bit computer
A computer that uses a 32-bit word length. It processes four bytes (32 bits) at a time. See *32-bit processing*.

32-bit driver
A driver written for a 32-bit environment. It often refers to drivers written for Windows 95/98 or Windows NT in contrast to 16-bit drivers written for DOS and Windows 3.x.

32-bit processing

Refers to programs running in a 32-bit computer. A 32-bit computer processes four bytes at a time compared with two bytes in a 16-bit computer or one byte in an 8-bit computer. Starting with the 386 chip, Intel CPUs have been built with a split personality for compatibility with earlier models. They have both 16- and 32-bit modes of operation, the 32-bit mode being the native mode with more advanced capabilities.

32-bit version

A program that runs in a 32-bit environment. It typically refers to a program that was written for a Windows 95/98/NT or 2000 machine in contrast with a 16-bit version that was written for DOS or Windows 3.1.

32-bit Windows

Refers to Windows 95/98, NT or 2000, which use the 32-bit native mode of the Intel CPU. The 32-bit mode became available starting with the 386. The term explicitly excludes Windows 3.1 and previous versions of Windows. See *Win32*.

3480, 3490

Families of half-inch magnetic tape drives from IBM, typically used on mainframes and AS/400s. The 3480 drives use 18-track cartridges at 38000 bpi to yield 200MB. The 3490 uses built-in compression to obtain 400MB. The 3490e records 36 tracks and uses longer tape to hold 800MB. Tape libraries are available that hold from a handful to thousands of cartridges.

360, 370

See *System/360* and *System/370*.

370 architecture

Refers to a computer that will run IBM mainframe applications. See *System/370*.

370/XA

(370 EXtended Architecture) A major enhancement (1981) to System/370 architecture which improved multiprocessing, introduced a new I/O system and increased addressing from 24 to 31 bits (16MB to 2GB).

37xx

IBM communications controllers that includes the 3704, 3705, 3720, 3725 and 3745 models. The 3704 and 3705 are early units, and the 3745 models are newer and more versatile. The 3745 includes a cluster controller that can connect 512 terminals, eight token ring networks and 16 T1 lines.

386

The successor to the 286. Also known as the 386DX, it refers to the Intel 386 CPU chip or to a PC that uses it. The 386 was the first 32-bit CPU in the x86 line. It increased memory capacity to 4GB and provided more sophisticated memory management. It allowed both extended memory and expanded (EMS) memory to be allocated on demand. The 386 architecture has been followed in all of Intel's subsequent CPUs (486, Pentium, etc.).

The 387 was the math coprocessor for the 386. The 386SX was a slower-speed version of the 386 that addressed only 16MB of memory and supported only a 16-bit data bus. The 386SL was a version of the 386SX designed for laptops.

Although introduced in 1985, it took a decade before 32-bit applications began to flourish. The 386 is too slow for Windows and graphics-based applications.

386 Enhanced Mode

An operational mode in Windows 3.x that requires a 386 or higher CPU. Contrast with *Standard Mode*.

390

See *S/390*.

3Com

(3Com Corporation, Santa Clara, CA, www.3com.com) Founded in 1979 by Bob Metcalfe, 3Com is a leading communications hardware vendor, offering a wide variety of network adapters, hubs and related products. In 1997, 3Com and U.S. Robotics merged creating a $5 billion dollar company with more than 12,000 employees and the largest merger to date in the data networking industry.

3-D chat

A chat room environment that incorporates 3-D images. See *chat room, VRML* and *avatar*.

3GL

See *third-generation language*.

4004

The first microprocessor. Designed by Marcian E. "Ted" Hoff at Intel, it was a 4-bit, general-purpose CPU that was initially developed for the Japanese Busicom calculator.

43xx

A series of medium-scale IBM mainframes initially introduced in 1979, which include the 4300, 4321, 4331, 4341, 4361 and 4381.

486

Also known as the 486DX, it refers to the Intel 486 CPU chip or to a PC that uses it. It is the successor to the 386 and runs from two to five times as fast. Its built-in math coprocessor (the 487) is often required by CAD applications. Versions of the 486 were made that doubled (DX2) and tripled (DX4) the internal speed while maintaining the same external speeds and connections. The 486SL was a version designed for laptops, and the 486SX was a version without the math coprocessor. See *x86*.

4GL

See *fourth-generation language*.

4mm tape

See *DAT*.

5250

A family of terminals and related protocols for IBM midrange computers (System 3x, AS/400).

56 Kbps modem

A modem that communicates at 56 Kbps downstream and 33.6 Kbps upstream. It is intended for use only with ISPs and online services that are digitally attached to the telephone system, but in practice, the downstream link isn't generally faster than 45 Kbps. x2 from U.S. Robotics and K56Flex from Rockwell and Lucent were two incompatible technologies that competed until the V.90 standard was introduced.

640K

(640 Kilobytes) Typically refers to the first 640 kilobytes of memory in a PC, known as conventional memory. See *PC memory*.

6502

An 8-bit microprocessor from Rockwell International Corporation used in the Apple II and earlier Atari and Commodore computers.

6800

An 8-bit microprocessor from Motorola. The 6801 is a computer-on-a-chip version.

68000 (680x0, 68K)

A family of 32-bit microprocessors from Motorola that were the CPUs in Macintoshes and a variety of workstations.

```
68000 - 16MB of memory, 16-bit data bus.
68020 - 4GB of memory, 32-bit data bus.
68030 - 4GB of memory, 32-bit data bus, built-in cache.
68040 - Enhanced 68030.  Up to 3x faster.
```

6DOF

(6 Degrees Of Freedom) The amount of motion supported by a virtual reality system. Six degrees provides forward/back, up/down, left/right, up/down pitch, left/right yaw and left/right rotation movement. Three degrees of freedom, or 3DOF, provides the first three movements only.

7-bit ASCII

Refers to transferring ASCII text in which an 8-bit byte holds the ASCII character plus a parity bit. Some PBXs allow only 7-bit transmission.

7-track

Refers to older magnetic tape formats that record 6-bit characters plus a parity bit.

802.1, 802.2, etc.

See *IEEE 802*.

80286, 80386, 80386DX, 80386SX, 80387SL, 80486

See *286, 386* and *486*.

8080

An Intel 8-bit CPU chip introduced in 1974. It was the successor to the first commercial 8-bit microprocessor (8008) and precursor to the x86 family. It contained 4,500 transistors and other electronic components.

8086 (80x86), 8088

Introduced in 1978, the 8086 CPU chip defines the base architecture of Intel's x86 family (XT, AT, 386, 486, Pentium, etc.). The actual chip used in first-generation PCs was the 8088. Using an 8-bit data bus instead of 16, the 8088 eased migration from CP/M programs, the dominant operating environment at the time. See *x86*.

88000

A family of 32-bit RISC microprocessors from Motorola. The 88100 is the first processor in the 88000 family. Introduced in 1988, it incorporates four built-in execution units that allow up to five operations to be performed in parallel.

8mm tape

A tape format used in high-capacity tape drives for backup. See *Exabyte*.

9370

A series of 370-based entry-level mainframes from IBM, introduced in 1986. In 1990, the Enterprise System models (ES/9370) were introduced, which used the Micro Channel bus and a 386 for I/O processing.

9660

See *ISO 9660*.

9672

A family of CMOS-based mainframes from IBM introduced in 1994. The models were named Parallel Transaction Server and Parallel Enterprise Server, then G3 (Generation 3) and the latest, G4, introduced in June 1997. The G4s contain up to 10 CPUs and 32 clusters can be connected, providing a potential capacity well over 10,000 MIPS.

9-track

Refers to magnetic tape that records 8-bit bytes plus parity, or nine parallel tracks. This is the common format for 1/2" tape reels.